Productivity Tools

PC-DOS & MS-DOS®
WordPerfect® 5.0/5.1
Lotus® 1-2-3®
Release 2.01/2.2
dBASE III PLUS®

William S. Davis
Donald L. Byrkett
Paul W. Schreiner

Miami University, Oxford, Ohio

Craig A. Wood

Stephen F. Austin State University,
Nacogdoches, Texas

▲▼ Addison-Wesley Publishing Company

Reading, Massachusetts · Menlo Park, California · New York
Don Mills, Ontario · Wokingham, England · Amsterdam · Bonn
Sydney · Singapore · Tokyo · Madrid · San Juan

This book was produced by the Addison-Wesley Electronic Production Department on an Apple Macintosh II with PageMaker. The output was generated on an Apple LaserWriter II NTX.

This book is in the Addison-Wesley *Computing Fundamentals Series*.

Series Editor: William S. Davis

MS-DOS is a registered trademark of Microsoft Corporation.
WordPerfect is a registered trademark of WordPerfect Corporation.
Lotus and 1-2-3 are registered trademarks of Lotus Development Corporation. dBASE III Plus is a trademark of Ashton-Tate Corporation.

Library of Congress Cataloging-in-Publication Data

Computing Fundamentals: Productivity Tools / by William S. Davis...
[et al.].
    p. cm.
  ISBN 0-201-19820-7
  1. Electronic data processing. 2. Computer software. I. Davis,
William S., 1943– .
QA76.C584 1990   89–18180
004—dc20   CIP

ABCDEFGHIJ-HA-943210

Preface

This book was developed to support an introductory microcomputer applications course. If you are a typical student, this course may well be your first formal exposure to computers, so little or no computing experience is assumed. Some schools require this course; others offer it as an elective. However, few students view learning microcomputer applications as an end in itself. Instead, they see the computer as an important tool for future academic work or for a job.

Part One introduces basic computer concepts and terminology; you will need this background to fully understand the applications in Parts Two through Five. The first chapter is an overview of a microcomputer system. Chapter 2 discusses hardware, while Chapter 3 introduces software. A brief fourth chapter previews the tutorials.

MS-DOS/PC-DOS is the subject of Part Two. Chapter 5 introduces operating system concepts and sets the stage for the tutorials that follow. Chapters 6 and 7 teach you how to boot DOS and format a disk. This material is essential to all the tools, so start with these two tutorials. In Chapter 8 you will learn how to determine what files are stored on a disk. Chapter 9 shows you how to manipulate and copy files, while Chapter 10 teaches you how to back up disks and files. Finally, Chapter 11 explains directory structures and introduces the commands you will need to use a hard disk.

WordPerfect 5.0, the subject of Part Three, is a popular word processing program. Chapter 12 describes word processing and identifies the conventions used in this set of tutorials. In Chapter 13 you will create and print a document; in Chapter 14 you will retrieve and edit that document. Chapter 15 introduces form letters, boilerplate, and mail merge. Some techniques for controlling document format are introduced in Chapter 16. Columns and tables are the subject of Chapter 17. The last tutorial in this section, Chapter 18, shows you how to use some basic desktop publishing features. As this book went to press, WordPerfect version 5.1 had just been released. Appendix F covers the key differences between WordPerfect versions 5.0 and 5.1.

Lotus 1-2-3 is the best selling spreadsheet program. Chapter 19 discusses some spreadsheet concepts and previews the 1-2-3 tutorials that form the balance of Part Four. Chapter 20 teaches you how to create, save, and print a worksheet; in Chapter 21 you will retrieve and modify that worksheet; Chapter 22 shows you some shortcuts such as copying and moving data and formulas. Graphs are the subject of Chapter 23, and Chapter 24 introduces several other useful features. The sample screens were generated using Lotus 1-2-3 release 2.2, but the tutorials can be completed using release 2.01 or 2.2.

dBASE III Plus, the subject of Part Five, is a database management tool. Because the need for a database is not as obvious as the need for word processing or a spreadsheet, Chapter 25 introduces key data management concepts before previewing the tutorials. You will create a database in Chapter 26, maintain it in Chapter 27, and extract information from it in Chapter 28. Chapter 29 explains indexing, teaches you how to define filters and queries, and shows you how to print mailing labels. Finally, you will create and link two database files in Chapter 30.

It is likely that the computer you will use to complete these tutorials will be linked to a network. An understanding of basic network concepts is important, so those concepts are introduced in Part Six.

All the tutorials follow a common pedagogy. The first step in developing a tutorial was to list the tasks a typical beginner might want to perform. Next, the features needed to support those tasks were identified. The necessary features were then introduced *in the context* of the applications.

The process of learning a feature begins with a keystroke by keystroke description. Next, the principles underlying the feature are explained; in other words, you are told why each step is necessary. Finally, you are asked to use the feature on your own, with a sample screen showing the expected result. If you make a mistake, the "What Can Go Wrong?" feature identifies problems, tells you what happened, and suggests a solution.

The "What Can Go Wrong?" feature is particularly valuable. You *will* make mistakes, and software does not always perform as expected. Nothing is more intimidating or discouraging to a beginner than making a mistake and hitting a dead end. On the other hand, making a mistake, figuring out what happened, and getting back on track *by yourself* is tremendously reassuring.

Note that this book does not pretend to cover every feature of every tool; that is the job of a reference manual. Instead, these tutorials are designed to help you get started. Today, you may find the reference manual difficult to read, but then reference manuals are not written for beginners. However, when you finish these tutorials, the reference manuals *will* begin to make sense because you will no longer be a beginner.

The best way to learn how to use a computer is to use a computer. That, in a nutshell, is what these tutorials are designed to help you do. If you sit down at a computer and actually do the tutorials, you will learn to use these productivity tools. The rest is up to you.

Acknowledgements

Addison-Wesley's Computing Fundamentals series consists of brief, inexpensive books designed to teach beginners how to use specific software packages, operating systems, and programming languages. The individual titles that comprise the series are currently in use at hundreds of colleges and universities. *Computing Fundamentals: Productivity Tools* is derived from five series titles and offers comparable coverage at roughly half the cost.

Primary credit for this book goes to the authors of the individual titles. Much of Part One is taken from *Concepts, second edition*, by William S. Davis. Part Two, PC-DOS/MS-DOS, is based on Craig A. Wood's source text. The WordPerfect 5.0 chapters are from a text by William S. Davis. Don Byrkett wrote the Lotus 1-2-3 book. Part Five essentially duplicates the dBASE III Plus book by William S. Davis and Paul Schreiner. Part Six is derived in part from *Concepts*, but most of the material is new.

Key reviewers included: L. Anne Cole, SUNY at Plattsburg; Bill Petersen, Mount Hood Community College; Mary Rasley, Lehigh Community College; Dana Wyatt, University of North Texas; and Pat Williams from the National Education Center in Sacramento. Although there are too many names to mention here, the reviewers of the five source titles deserve additional thanks. To ensure the accuracy and effectiveness of this material, Addison-Wesley commissioned Ken Cantrell, Jean Cristoff, and Christine White, three Miami University students, to test the tutorials. They provided invaluable feedback. Finally, Addison-Wesley's production team, coordinated by Helen Wythe, did an excellent job on a complex project.

WSD
Oxford, Ohio

Contents

■ PART ONE

Computer Concepts

▪1

Getting Started

This chapter:

- discusses the importance of computer literacy
- summarizes the essential components of a modern computer
- introduces the stored program concept
- distinguishes between hardware and software

Computer Literacy

In the early 1950s the first commercial computer, the UNIVAC I, sold for over one million dollars. Today, an infinitely better computer can be purchased for a few *thousand* dollars. If the automobile industry had performed nearly as well, a luxury car would now cost less than $100, run thousands of miles on a single gallon of gasoline, and almost never break down.

In today's economy, **computer literacy** is almost as important as traditional literacy. Computers have become essential in virtually every discipline, and people who cannot (or will not) deal with them find it difficult to function effectively. Computer literacy implies an ability to *use* a computer. In this book you will learn how to use four popular computer programs. PC-DOS is an operating system; it serves as the base for the other applications. WordPerfect 5.0 is a word processing program, Lotus 1-2-3 is a spreadsheet program, and dBASE III Plus supports database management. They all run on IBM PC/XT/AT, PS-2, and compatible computers.

The book is organized as a series of tutorials. Don't just read them; you can't learn how to use these tools by reading about them. Instead, sit down at a computer and follow along, step by step. You'll be surprised at how quickly your confidence and skill develop.

There are some basic computer concepts that you should understand before you begin. They will be covered in the balance of this chapter and in Chapters 2 and 3.

What Is a Computer?

Data and Information

A medieval astronomer named Tycho Brahe spent his entire adult life observing and recording the positions of the planets. His successor, Johannes Kepler, sensed a pattern in those observations and spent much of his life processing them, performing tedious computations in an attempt to verify the pattern. He eventually succeeded, publishing his laws of planetary motion in 1621.

Tycho Brahe collected **data**, raw facts. Kepler's laws represent **information**. Using them, he could understand and predict the motions of the planets. Using them, modern scientists and engineers plan space flights. Information has meaning.

Clearly, Kepler's laws were derived from Brahe's data, but the raw data were useless without processing. Until they were organized and the necessary calculations performed, the data were just unstructured facts with no clear meaning. Knowing the exact position of Mars on April 1, 1599 might earn an extra move in Trivial Pursuit, but, by itself, that fact is not very useful. Processing data extracts their meaning.

Data Processing

A **computer** is a **data processing** machine. Data flow into the machine as **input** (Fig. 1.1). Information flows from the machine as

Figure 1.1

A computer is a machine that processes data into information. It accepts data, processes these data, and generates information as output.

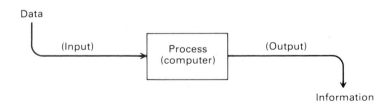

output. The computer processes the data. The computer's primary advantages are speed and accuracy. Johannes Kepler spent a lifetime performing the calculations that supported his laws of planetary motion. Today, a college student using a computer can verify those calculations in a few hours!

Iron ore is processed to make steel; wood pulp is processed to make paper. A computer processes data. The word "process" implies that a change takes place, that the raw materials are in some way restructured or manipulated. *Data* processing involves filtering and summarizing data so that underlying patterns can be perceived.

How does a computer process its data? What functions, what operations, can it perform? Generally, computers can add, subtract, multiply, divide, compare, copy, start input, and start output. So can most calculators. What makes a computer different?

The Stored Program Concept

To add two numbers on a calculator, you:

1. Enter the first number.

2. Press the add (+) button.

3. Enter the second number.

4. Press the result (=) button.

5. Record the sum for future reference.

The calculator finds the sum, but *you* provide control by deciding what button to push next. A calculator requires direct human intervention at each step.

A computer processes data automatically, with no need for human intervention. Computers are *not* intelligent, however. They cannot decide independently when to add, subtract, compare, or request input. If a computer is to function without direct human control, it must be given a set of instructions called a **program** to guide it. The program is physically stored inside the machine (Fig. 1.2). This **stored program** distinguishes a computer from a calculator and allows it to function without human intervention. Thus a computer

Figure 1.2

A computer processes data automatically under control of a stored program.

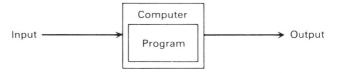

can be defined as *a machine that processes data into information under the control of a stored program*.

A Computer System

A computer system consists of several basic components (Fig. 1.3). An input device provides data. The data, along with a program, are stored in **memory**. Under control of the program the computer's **processor** manipulates the data, storing the results back into memory. The results then flow from the computer to an output device. Additionally, most modern computers use secondary storage to extend memory capacity.

Consider the computer system pictured in Fig. 1.4. The keyboard is an input device; the display screen is an output device. The image

Figure 1.3
A computer system consists of four basic components: an input device, an output device, main memory, and a processor. Secondary storage is often used to extend memory capacity.

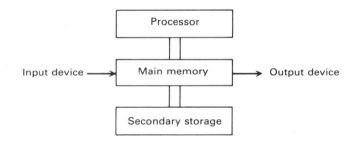

Figure 1.4
A typical computer system. Input is provided by a keyboard. Output goes to the screen or to the printer. The processor and main memory are located inside the cabinet. The disk drives provide secondary storage. (Courtesy of International Business Machines Corporation.)

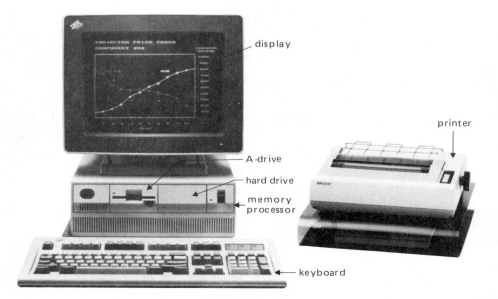

displayed on a screen is temporary; a more permanent copy of the output can be obtained by sending it to a printer. The computer's processor and main memory are located inside the cabinet. The diskette drives extend the computer's memory; programs often enter the system through such secondary storage devices.

A computer's physical components—the processor, memory, input devices, output devices, and secondary storage devices—are its **hardware**. You can see them, touch them, and feel them. Programs and data are different, existing only as electronic patterns stored in memory. **Software** is a general term for programs.

Hardware will be covered in a bit more detail in Chapter 2; software will be discussed in Chapter 3. The brief overview presented in this chapter will give you a sense of how all the components fit together.

Summary

In our modern information age, computer literacy is almost as important as the ability to read and write. In this book you will learn to use four popular computer programs.

A computer is a machine that processes data into information under the control of a stored program. A computer's hardware consists of a processor, memory, input and output devices, and secondary storage. Software is a general term for programs.

Key Words

computer	input
computer literacy	memory
data	output
data processing	processor
hardware	program
information	software
	stored program

Self-Test

At the end of each chapter, you will find a brief self-test; the answers are in Appendix E.

1. Unstructured facts are called _____.

2. Processing data yields _____, which has meaning.

3. A computer processes _____ into _____.

4. Data flow into the computer as _____.

5. Information flows from the computer as _____.

6. The _____ distinguishes a computer from a calculator.

7. Data and program instructions are stored in _____.

8. The computer component that actually manipulates the data is the _____.

9. The physical components of a computer are collectively called _____.

10. Programs are known collectively as _____.

Exercises

1. Briefly, what is computer literacy?

2. Distinguish between data and information.

3. Relate the terms "data" and "information" to the terms "input" and "output."

4. A stored program distinguishes a computer from a calculator. Explain.

5. What is a computer? Don't just reproduce the definition; explain the meaning of each term.

6. Draw a sketch showing the primary components of a typical computer system. Briefly explain what each component does.

7. Explain the difference between hardware and software.

▪2

Hardware

This chapter introduces a computer's primary hardware components, including

- memory
- the processor
- input and output devices
- secondary storage devices
- interfaces
- networks

Physical Storage Devices

A computer is a binary machine. It operates on precisely timed pulses of electric current that are conveniently represented as 0s and 1s. A computer's processor manipulates these binary patterns; its memory stores them.

For example, consider the bank of switches and light bulbs pictured in Fig. 2.1. Each switch can assume either of two states: on or off. If you supply an electric current, only those bulbs controlled by the switches set on will light. The switch is a primitive storage or memory device, with "on" representing a 1-bit and "off" representing a 0-bit.

Figure 2.1
A light switch is a simple example of a storage or memory device.

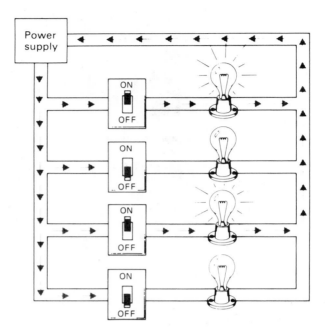

Carefully distinguish between the physical device (the switch) and its value (0 or 1). The *switch* is hardware; its *setting* represents software or data. The value is easy to change—just flip the switch. Hardware (the switch) is permanent; software or data (the switch setting) is not.

Any device that can assume and hold either of two states is a potential computer storage device. The **memory** of a modern computer is composed of a bank of **random access memory (RAM)** chips (Fig. 2.2). Each chip can store thousands of binary digits or **bits**.

Think of RAM as a scratch pad that holds current programs and current data; its contents can be changed in a tiny fraction of a second. In contrast, **read-only memory (ROM)** is permanent and cannot be easily changed. RAM is the computer's general-purpose memory. ROM is used for a few key program modules.

Bytes and Words

A single bit can hold either a 0 or a 1, which by itself is not very useful. That's why the contents of memory are generally envisioned as *groups* of bits. A **byte** contains eight bits, enough to represent a single character. Most computers can also work with a larger group of bits called a **word**; 16-bit- and 32-bit-word computers are common.

Figure 2.2

The memory of a modern computer is composed of random access memory (RAM) chips.

Typically, memory is organized as a hierarchy (Fig. 2.3). Bits are grouped to form bytes, which, in turn, are grouped to form words. In one application, a given word might be used to hold a binary number. In another, that word's bytes might hold individual characters or a program instruction.

A personal microcomputer contains 512K[1] or more bytes, while a large computer may have millions of bytes. To distinguish them, each is assigned a unique **address** by numbering the bytes sequentially — 0, 1, 2, and so on. The processor accesses a specific byte by referencing its address.

It is important to note that character data and numeric data are different. Characters are stored one per byte using a code. You cannot perform arithmetic on character data. Numbers are typically stored in a word as a series of digits. As you begin working with the computer, you will often be required to distinguish between numeric and character (or **string**) data because they are stored differently inside a computer.

[1] The suffix K, which stands for kilo, means 1024. Thus a computer with 512K bytes of memory contains 524,288 actual memory locations.

Figure 2.3

In a computer's memory, bits are combined to form bytes, and bytes in turn are combined to form words.

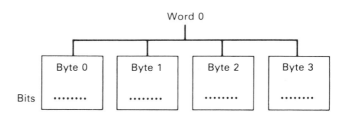

Figure 2.4
A processor contains three key components.

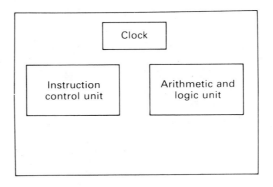

The Processor

The **processor** (Fig. 2.4), sometimes called the **central processing unit (CPU)**, manipulates the data, but it can do nothing without a program to provide control; whatever intelligence a computer has is derived from software, not hardware. The processor manipulates data stored in its memory under the control of a program stored in its memory. A program consists of a series of **instructions**. Each instruction tells the computer to perform one of its basic functions: add, subtract, multiply, divide, compare, copy, start input, or start output.

The processor executes one instruction during each **machine cycle** (Fig. 2.5). A cycle begins when the clock generates a pulse of current. During the first phase, called I-time, the instruction control unit fetches an instruction from memory. The arithmetic and logic unit then executes the instruction during E-time or execution time. This process is repeated over and over until the program is finished. The clock drives the process, generating pulses of current at precisely timed intervals. The rate at which the clock "ticks" is what determines the computer's operating speed.

Figure 2.5
The basic machine cycle is repeated over and over until all the instructions have been executed.

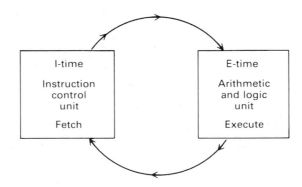

Input and Output

Input and output devices provide a means for people to access a computer. The basic input device on most small computers is a **keyboard**; you can see one in the foreground of Fig. 2.6. As characters are typed, they are stored in memory. From memory, they are copied to the basic output device, a **display screen**. In effect, the screen serves as a window on memory, allowing the user to view selected contents.

On most screens, a blinking bar or a shaded box called the **cursor** indicates where the next character will be displayed. Its position can be controlled by a set of cursor control keys on the keyboard or, on some computers, by a **mouse**. In many applications a user positions the cursor and either presses the ⏎ key or clicks the mouse to select a choice from a menu.

The image displayed on a screen is temporary. By routing the output to a **printer** (Fig. 2.7), a permanent copy (called a hard copy)

Figure 2.6
The basic output device on most small computer systems is a display screen. (Courtesy of International Business Machines Corporation)

Figure 2.7
A printer generates more permanent hard-copy output. (Courtesy of Hewlett-Packard Company.)

Figure 2.8

Increasingly, computers are being used to generate graphic output as well as character output. (Courtesy of Polaroid Corp. and 35mm Express by Business and Professional Products.)

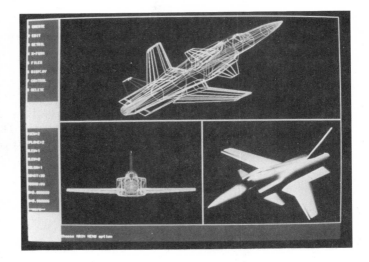

is obtained. Dot matrix printers form characters from patterns of dots; they are inexpensive, but the output can be difficult to read. Letter-quality printers type complete, solid characters. Laser printers are more expensive, but they produce very high quality output.

Computers are not limited to displaying characters; graphic output (Fig. 2.8) is possible, too. Because a computer outputs data from memory, if a graphic image is to be displayed, it must first be constructed in memory. Memory stores bits. How can a caricature, a bar chart, or a schematic drawing be defined as a pattern of bits? The secret is to divide the screen into a grid of picture elements, or pixels (Fig. 2.9). Each pixel represents a dot or a point; by selectively turning the points on or off, a picture is formed. That on/off pattern is binary.

Figure 2.9

To display graphic output, the screen is divided into a grid of picture elements, or pixels. Each pixel represents one point. Pictures are formed by turning selected pixels on and off.

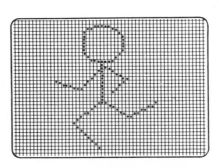

Figure 2.10
The most popular microcomputer secondary storage medium is the diskette.

Secondary Storage

Physical Storage Devices

Data and programs are stored in memory. Unfortunately, memory is relatively expensive, and the supply of memory on most machines, though substantial, is still limited. Volatility is another problem; memory loses its contents when the power is cut. **Secondary storage** is a fast, accurate, inexpensive, high-capacity, nonvolatile extension of memory.

The most common microcomputer secondary storage medium is the **diskette** (Fig. 2.10). Until recently, flexible 5.25-inch disks were the accepted standard, but newer micros use rigid, higher-capacity 3.50-inch disks. To save data, you copy them from memory to **disk**. Then, if you should lose power or decide to quit working, you can later pick up where you left off simply by telling the computer to copy the data back into memory.

A diskette drive works much like a record turntable. The hole in the center of a disk allows the drive mechanism to engage and spin the disk; an access mechanism, analogous to the tone arm, reads and writes the surface through a window near the bottom of the jacket. The drive hole is on the back of a 3.50-inch disk; the metal shield near the top moves aside to reveal the recording surface when the disk is inserted into the drive.

Data are recorded on a series of concentric circles called tracks (Fig. 2.11). The outer track is numbered 0; moving inward, subsequent tracks are numbered 1, 2, 3, and so on. Most disks record data on both sides, so one position of the access mechanism represents two tracks, one on the top and one on the bottom. This single access mechanism position is sometimes called a cylinder.

The tracks are subdivided into sectors. To distinguish the sectors, they are also numbered sequentially. A track number, a side, and a sector number together define a unique disk address. The access mechanism steps from track to track, stopping on the desired track. Then it reads or writes the desired sector. It is the contents of a sector that move between the disk's surface and memory.

Figure 2.11
Data are recorded on a series of concentric circles called tracks. The tracks are subdivided into sectors. Data move between the disk surface and memory one sector at a time.

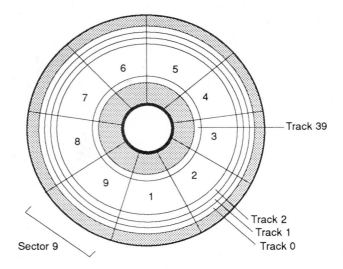

Track 39

Track 2
Track 1
Track 0

Sector 9

Data on **hard disk** (Fig. 2.12) can be accessed far more quickly than data on diskette. Another advantage of hard disk is its storage capacity. A typical 5.25-inch diskette can store 360,000 characters; most 3.50-inch disks hold 1.4 million characters. A hard disk can store 40 million or more characters.

Given the tremendous capacity of a hard disk, losing one through human error, fire, flood, or similar disaster can destroy a great deal of important data. That's why the data are regularly backed up by copying them to another disk or to magnetic tape. Should a hard disk be damaged, the backup copy is used to restore the data.

Secondary storage is an extension of main memory, not a replacement for it. A computer cannot execute a program stored on disk

Figure 2.12
Hard disk is faster than diskette and has a greater storage capacity.

unless it is first copied into memory. A computer cannot manipulate the data stored on a secondary medium until they have been copied into memory. Memory holds the current program and the current data; secondary storage is long-term storage.

Input and output devices provide human access to the computer. Secondary storage does not. Data are stored on disk in a form convenient to the computer and can be read and written only by the machine. The only way people can access the data stored on a disk is by instructing the computer to read them into memory and then output them to a display screen or a printer.

Accessing Secondary Storage

Because of its storage capacity, a single disk can hold numerous programs, the data for dozens of different applications, or both. If you are a computer user, however, you want a particular program or a particular set of data. How does the computer find the right program or the right data?

The location of each program or data file stored on a disk is recorded in the disk's **directory** (Fig. 2.13). When the file is first

Figure 2.13
A directory is maintained to keep track of the programs and data files stored on disk.

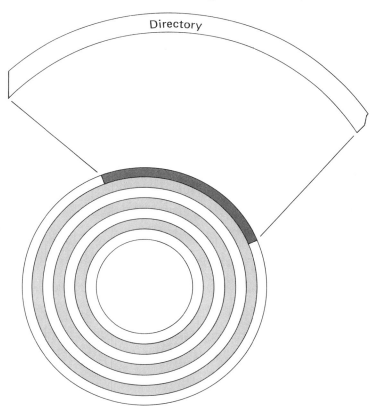

created, it is assigned a name, and that name, along with the file's disk location, is recorded in the directory. Later, to retrieve the program, a user enters the program's name. The computer then reads the directory, searches it for the name, finds the file, and accesses the data.

Linking the Components

Data are stored in a computer as patterns of bits. Within a given machine, the patterns are consistent; for example, if the code for the letter A is 01000001, that pattern, and only that pattern, will be used to represent an A inside the computer. Peripheral devices are not so consistent, however. On a keyboard, each key generates one character. With graphics, pixels are displayed, while a dot matrix printer represents characters as patterns of dots. Each input or output device represents or interprets data in its own unique way, and the signals used by a peripheral device might or might not match the signals stored inside the computer. If these dissimilar devices are to communicate, translation is necessary. This is the function of the **interface** board.

Consider, for example, a keyboard. When a key is pressed, an electronic signal is sent to the keyboard's interface. In response, the interface generates the code used to represent that character inside the computer and transfers the coded data into memory (Fig. 2.14a). Change the device to a printer (Fig. 2.14b). As output begins, the data are stored inside the computer as binary-coded characters. The printer requires a dot pattern, so translation is necessary. The coded

Figure 2.14
The functions of an interface board.
(a) Input from the keyboard enters the interface and is converted to the computer's internal form. (b) Data stored in main memory are sent to the printer interface, converted to printer form, and output.

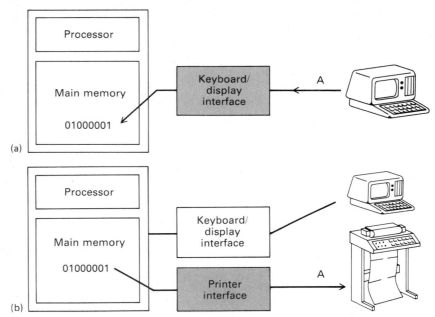

Figure 2.15
On a small computer, secondary storage devices are linked to the system through interface boards.

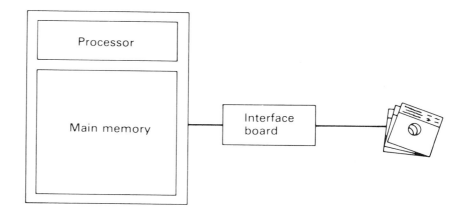

characters are sent to the printer's interface, which translates the computer's binary codes to printer form.

Secondary storage devices are also linked to the computer through an interface (Fig. 2.15). The binary patterns stored on disk are the same patterns stored in memory, so no code translation is necessary. Instead, a disk interface physically controls the disk drive, positioning the access mechanism, selecting the proper sector, and transferring that sector's contents between the disk's surface and memory.

Networks

There is a good chance that the computer you will use to complete the tutorials in this book will be part of a **network**. A network is a group of computers linked by communication lines. On a local area network or LAN, all the computers are located in the same building or complex. In a wide area network the telephone system or some other long-distance communication medium is used to link widely separated computers. A computer is often linked to a network through a modem.

The most common microcomputer network configuration is built around a relatively powerful network server, often a minicomputer (Fig. 2.16). The server controls a high-capacity hard disk that holds all the software supported by the network. To access a particular program, you sit down at one of the microcomputers and, by entering a few commands, ask the server to supply the software. The server then reads the software from its disk and downloads it over the communication line to your computer's memory. The centralized control afforded by such a network greatly simplifies the task of managing the software.

Figure 2.16
A typical
microcomputer
network
configuration.

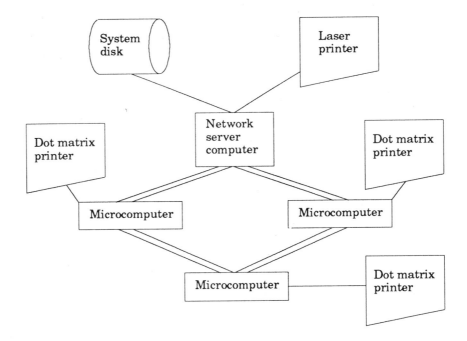

Many networks perform other functions, too. For example, an expensive, high-quality laser printer is often attached to the network server. Draft output is sent to inexpensive dot matrix printers attached to each computer; finished documents are sent over the network to the laser printer. On some systems, user data are stored on the central hard disk, although most schools expect students to use diskettes. Electronic mail is another popular application; it allows users to send messages between computers.

Summary

A computer is a binary machine. Its memory is divided into bytes and words. Typically, each byte is assigned a unique address; using these addresses, the processor can access selected bytes. The processor manipulates data. During I-time the instruction control unit fetches an instruction from memory; during E-time the arithmetic and logic unit executes it. Precisely timed pulses generated by a clock drive this machine cycle.

People access a computer through its input and output devices. The basic input device on most small computers is a keyboard; the basic output device is a display screen. If a permanent copy of the output is required, it can be sent to a printer. Many systems support graphics.

Because of memory's cost, limited capacity, and volatility, secondary storage is necessary. Diskette is the most popular medium. Data are stored on a series of concentric circles called tracks, which are subdivided into sectors; the contents of a sector move between memory and the disk's surface. Hard disk is faster and has more storage capacity than diskette. A single disk can contain numerous programs and data files. A directory identifies the programs and files and indicates where on the disk each one is stored.

Because each input and output device is electronically different, interface boards are used to link peripherals to the computer. On input, the interface converts the data from the external device's form to the computer's internal form and stores them in memory. On output, information moves from memory to the interface, where it is converted to the external device's form and then output. Secondary storage is linked to the computer through interface boards, too.

A network is a group of computers linked by communication lines. Many local area networks are built around a central server that downloads software to the other computers. A network might also control access to a high-quality printer, manage user data on a central disk, and support electronic mail.

Key Words

address	keyboard
bit	machine cycle
byte	memory
central processing unit (CPU)	mouse
cursor	network
directory	printer
disk	processor
diskette	random access memory (RAM)
display screen	read-only memory (ROM)
hard disk	secondary storage
instruction	string
interface	word

Self-Test

1. A _____ holds enough bits to store a single character. A _____ is a larger group of bits that often holds a number.

2. A location in memory is accessed by its _____.

3. During I-time the processor's _____ fetches an instruction from memory. During E-time the processor's _____ executes that instruction.

4. The basic input device on a small computer is a _____. The basic output device is a _____.

5. Main memory is _____; it loses its contents when power is cut.

6. Data on disk are recorded on a series of concentric circles called _____. Data are transferred between memory and the disk surface a _____ at a time.

7. The combination of a sector number, a side, and a track number forms a unique disk _____.

8. The location of each program or data file stored on a disk is found in the disk's _____.

9. External devices are linked to a computer system through _____.

10. A _____ is a group of computers linked by communication lines.

Exercises

1. Distinguish between bits, bytes, and words. How is a computer's main memory addressed?

2. Briefly explain what happens during a single machine cycle.

3. What is the purpose of a computer's input and output devices?

4. What is the cursor? How is the cursor's position controlled?

5. Why is secondary storage necessary?

6. What advantages are gained by using a hard disk instead of a diskette?

7. Distinguish between a track and a sector.

8. What is an interface? Why are interfaces necessary?

9. What is a network? What functions are performed by a network?

10. In Chapter 1 you sketched a simple computer system. Modify your sketch, adding the internal components and peripheral devices you studied in this chapter.

▪3
Software

This chapter introduces several key software concepts, including

- programming languages
- commercial software
- the user interface
- the software environment

Writing Programs

Machine and Assembler Language

A **program** is a series of **instructions** that guides a computer through a process. Each instruction tells the machine to perform one of its basic functions: add, subtract, multiply, divide, compare, copy, start input, or start output. The program must be stored in the computer's memory, so **machine language** programs are binary. For example, Fig. 3.1 shows the machine language code needed to add two

Figure 3.1
The machine-language instructions needed to add two numbers on a typical computer.

```
0101100000110000110000000000000000

0101100001000000110000000000000100

0001101000110100

0101000000110000110000000000001000
```

Figure 3.2

An assembler programmer writes one mnemonic instruction for each machine-level instruction.

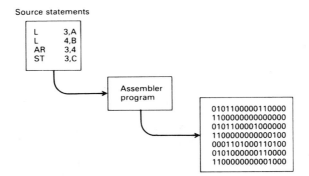

numbers. First-generation computer programs were actually written in machine language.

Second-generation **assembler** languages were a significant improvement. An assembler programmer writes one mnemonic (memory-aiding) source statement for each machine-level instruction (Fig. 3.2). Unfortunately, assembler language programs are difficult to write, debug, and maintain, so assemblers are rarely used today.

Compilers and Interpreters

A computer needs all those instructions to add two numbers because that's the way a computer works. Human beings shouldn't have to think like computers. For example, one way to view addition is as an algebraic expression

    C = A + B

Why not allow a programmer to write something like algebraic expressions, read those source statements into a program, and have the program generate the necessary machine-level code?

That's exactly what happens with a **compiler**, a special program that reads a programmer's source statements and translates them into machine language (Fig. 3.3). Many compiler languages, including FORTRAN, BASIC, Pascal, and PL/1, are algebraically based. Statements in the most popular business-oriented language, COBOL, resemble English sentences (Fig. 3.4). Compilers represent software's third generation; most professional programmers use compiler languages.

The difference between an assembler and a compiler is subtle. Each assembler language statement is translated into a *single* machine language instruction. Each compiler language statement is translated into one or more (usually more) machine language instructions. Thus the compiler programmer writes fewer instructions to accomplish the same task. On the other hand, because the assembler

Figure 3.3
A compiler translates each source statement into one or more (usually more) machine-language instructions.

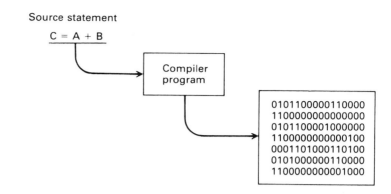

programmer works one-to-one with machine language, he or she can eliminate all unnecessary instructions and produce a highly efficient program.

An assembler or compiler reads a complete source program and generates a complete machine language routine called an object module. An **interpreter** accepts a *single* source statement, translates it into one or more machine-level instructions, executes those instructions, and then accepts the next source statement. Interpreters are very useful during program development, but because each line of code must be translated before it can be executed, interpreters tend to be quite slow. With a compiler the complete machine language program can be created, captured on disk, and then executed over and over without further translation.

Nonprocedural Languages

With traditional assemblers, compilers, and interpreters the programmer defines a procedure to tell the computer how to solve a problem. However, with a modern, **nonprocedural language**

Figure 3.4
COBOL source statements resemble sentences.

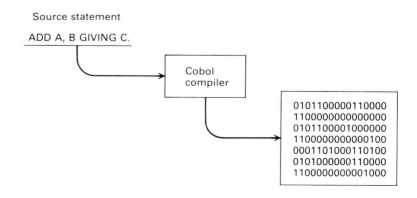

(sometimes called a fourth-generation or declarative language) the programmer simply defines the logical structure of the problem and lets the language translator figure out how to solve it. Examples of commercially available nonprocedural languages include Prolog, Focus, and many others. Nonprocedural languages are becoming increasingly popular.

Commercial Software

Relatively few people actually write original programs. Instead, most access the computer through such **commercial software** packages as spreadsheets, word processors, database managers, accounting programs, and so on. These ready-to-use programs are sold much like sound recordings; a consumer purchases a copy on disk, loads it onto his or her computer, and uses the software.

Word processing software simplifies the task of writing text (Fig. 3.5). On a superficial level the computer becomes a replacement for a typewriter, but there is more to writing than just mechanics. The secret to quality writing is to revise and rewrite material several times. A word processor supports document revision by making it easy to delete, insert, and move words, sentences, paragraphs, and even large blocks of text. Most word processors include a spelling checker and a thesaurus, and some can even identify style problems. Efficient mail merge routines are another common feature.

Much of this book was written using WordPerfect, a popular word processing program and the subject of Part Three. Major competitors include DisplayWrite, Microsoft Word, Multimate, Wordstar, and many others. **Desktop publishing** is a step beyond word processing. Programs such as PageMaker and Ventura Publisher allow a user to lay out the contents of a page, integrate text and graphics, and generate a document that resembles set type (Fig. 3.6). Some advanced word processors incorporate desktop publishing features.

Figure 3.5
A word processing program simplifies the task of writing text.

```
                        Howard and Johnson, Ltd.
                        "Creativity is Our Thing!"
                              P.O. Box Z
                           Oxford, Ohio 01056

                                                      March 3, 1989

      Ms. Charlie Angel
      Program Director
      CBS Television
      New York, New York   10001

      Dear Ms. Angel:

      Mary Howard and Hector Johnson, two of the most creative minds in
      television today, have been responsible for such hits as "Bleep
      the Boss" and "Humiliate Your Spouse." Graduates of the South
      Dakota School of Broadcasting, this incredible team has been a
      gold mine of original ideas since 1988.

      Today, Howard and Johnson are proud to announce the development
      of their newest mega-hit, The Betagosa Hillbillies." Please see
      the attached press release for details.

                                     Doc 1 Pg 1 Ln 1" Pos 1"
```

Figure 3.6
Desktop publishing
software generates
output that resembles
set type.

A Philodendron That's Smarter Than Einstein

They can do math, but can he photosynthesize?

British scientists last week revealed the results of an amazing three-year study that proves that plants can do simple arithmetic and algebra. Some can even solve trigonometric problems!

"My daughter's in the tenth grade and she could learn a thing or two from some of the ferns in my lab!" exclaimed a triumphant Dr. Wisebaum. "These plants really know their numbers."

Researchers have found that plants can actually subtract and add numbers as high as 1,000. Incredible!

"We've known for a long time that plants respond well when they are talked to, but we had no idea how much they understood!"

What next? Will plants ring up our groceries, collect tolls on the highway, read our electric meters? "I'm not sure of the application of these experiments," says Doctor Wisebaum. "But it sure is neat!"

An **electronic spreadsheet** program called Visicalc was the first commercially significant microcomputer application. An accountant's spreadsheet is a piece of paper with horizontal and vertical lines dividing it into rows and columns; the software allows a user to simulate a spreadsheet on the screen (Fig. 3.7). Lotus 1-2-3, the subject of Part Four, is today's biggest selling electronic spreadsheet; key competitors include Javelin, Quattro, and Supercalc.

Database management is another significant microcomputer application; dBASE III Plus, widely accepted as a standard, is the subject of Part Five. Database software is concerned with the efficient

Figure 3.7
Spreadsheet software
simulates an
accountant's
spreadsheet on the
screen.

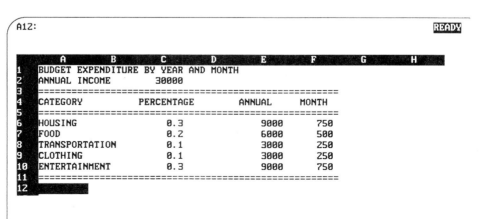

```
A12:                                                            READY

        A        B         C          D        E        F        G        H
1  BUDGET EXPENDITURE BY YEAR AND MONTH
2  ANNUAL INCOME        30000
3  =================================================================
4  CATEGORY          PERCENTAGE        ANNUAL     MONTH
5  =================================================================
6  HOUSING              0.3             9000       750
7  FOOD                 0.2             6000       500
8  TRANSPORTATION       0.1             3000       250
9  CLOTHING             0.1             3000       250
10 ENTERTAINMENT        0.3             9000       750
11 =================================================================
12
```

Figure 3.8
Most database
management systems
can generate
sophisticated reports.

```
Page No.      1
10/02/89
                               CAMPUS THREADS
                            MONTH END REPORT OF
                           DEPOSITS BY DORMITORY

  FIRST NAME      LAST NAME            ROOM  DORMITORY           DEPOSIT


** DORMITORY BAG END HALL
   FRODO           BAGGINS             105   BAG END HALL          40.00
   BILBO           BAGGINS             105   BAG END HALL          30.00
** Subtotal **
                                                                  70.00


** DORMITORY BRANDYWINE HALL
   ARAGORN         STRIDER             400   BRANDYWINE HALL       50.00
** Subtotal **
                                                                  50.00


** DORMITORY ELROND HOUSE
   THORIN          OAKENSHIELD         113   ELROND HOUSE          90.00
** Subtotal **
                                                                  90.00


** DORMITORY EMERISON HALL
   LISA            KALO                108   EMERISON HALL         50.00
```

storage and retrieval of data, and most packages include facilities to quickly assemble reports (Fig. 3.8). Key competitors include dBase IV, R Base, Reflex, and many others.

Accounting software is a big seller in the business world. Programs to perform such tasks as payroll, accounts receivable, accounts payable, general ledger, inventory, and many others are commercially available. Some packages are generic; payroll is, after all, payroll. Others are more specialized, providing the programs needed to run a dental practice, a construction firm, or some other organization.

The User Interface

As the user of an application routine, your link to the computer will be through the software's **user interface**. Some programs are designed to respond to **commands**; others display a **menu** of commands or options and invite the user to select one. Sometimes the menu choices are presented as pictures or icons.

Menu-driven software (Fig. 3.9) is relatively easy to learn because all possible choices are displayed on the screen. The menu supports a "point and select" mode of operation that is particularly convenient when the system is equipped with a mouse. The problem with menus is that they sometimes get in the way. As you begin to learn how to use a program, the sequence of steps required to perform a common function eventually becomes almost second nature, and working through a series of menus can become annoying.

Figure 3.9
A typical menu

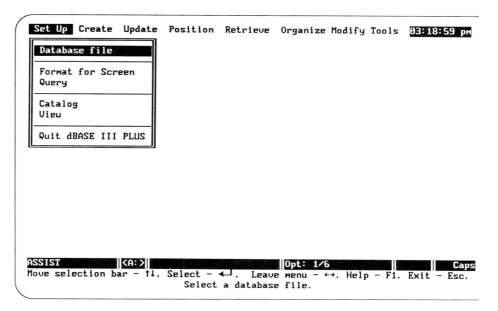

Experienced users tend to favor command-driven software (Fig. 3.10) because all the steps required to perform even a complex function can often be typed on a single line or quickly issued by pressing a series of function keys. Unfortunately, beginners sometimes struggle with command-driven programs because several commands might be required to perform even the most elementary task.

Recognizing the limitations of both approaches, the designers of many software packages give you a choice. For example, Lotus 1-2-3 is menu driven (Fig. 3.11), but you can select a command from the menu by typing the first letter of the command name. dBASE III Plus allows the user to work through a series of menus or to issue commands in "dot prompt" mode. WordPerfect is command driven, but the commands are all issued by pressing function keys, and a color-coded template serves as a convenient, menulike reference.

Another common feature of many popular application programs is the use of **windows** to display error messages and secondary menus

Figure 3.10
Some programs are driven by user commands.

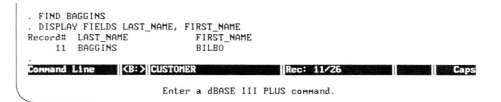

Figure 3.11
Lotus 1-2-3 is menu driven, but you can select a choice from the menu by typing the first letter of the command name.

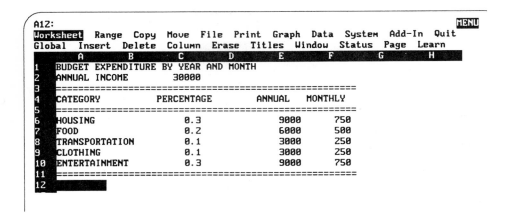

Figure 3.12
Error messages and menus are sometimes displayed in a window.

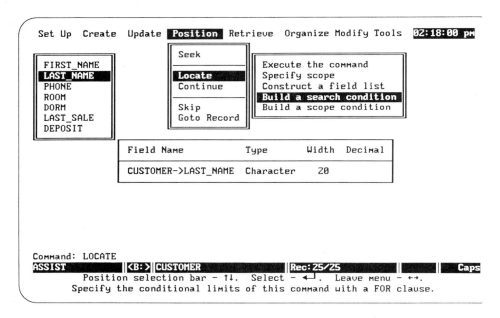

(Fig. 3.12). A window is a small box that displays a message on a portion of the screen, leaving much of the original screen visible in the background. Windows allow the program to communicate with the user without breaking the link to the primary task.

The Software Environment

WordPerfect, Lotus 1-2-3, and dBASE III Plus are examples of **application programs**. They perform end-user tasks. Another type of software, called **system software**, performs its assigned support

Figure 3.13
The operating system serves as an interface between hardware and application software.

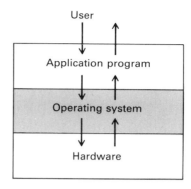

tasks behind the scenes. An excellent example is the **operating system** found on most computers. An operating system serves as an interface (Fig. 3.13), bridging the gap between hardware and application software.

An operating system performs a number of support functions. For example, picture an application program stored on disk. Before the program can be executed, it must first be loaded into memory; the operating system contains the program logic that controls the loading process. Other key operating system functions include communicating with peripheral devices, maintaining disk directories, and responding to user commands. The operating system is a collection of software modules that insulate the user from the hardware and thus make the system easier to use.

At the hardware level, computers distributed by different manufacturers are often incompatible, so a program written for one computer won't work on another. Remember, however, that the operating system sits between the hardware and the application program. With

Figure 3.14
The operating system presents the application program with a smooth, consistent interface.

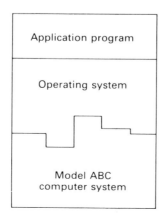 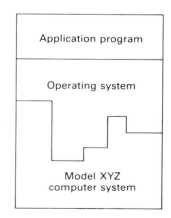

a common operating system in the middle it is possible for the same program to run on two quite different machines (Fig. 3.14). Of course, the portions of the operating system that communicate with the hardware might be very different, but software would see a smooth, common interface. Consequently, a standard operating system promotes software compatibility between computers from different suppliers.

In Part Two of this book you will study an operating system called PC-DOS. It is a standard operating system for IBM PC/XT/AT and PS/2 computers. A functionally identical operating system called MS-DOS is marketed by Microsoft Corporation for use on IBM-compatible microcomputers distributed by such firms as Compaq, Tandy, Dell, Zenith, and many others. Because the operating system provides a common interface, most programs designed for IBM computers will run on the compatible machines. The operating system, DOS, can be viewed as a standard **platform** on which application programs are constructed.

There are other types of system software, too. For example, if your computer is linked to a network, its memory will hold a data communication routine to handle the details of interacting with the other computers on the network (Fig. 3.15). In Part Five of this book you will learn to use a database management system called dBASE III Plus. Sometimes, database routines are used as system software, and an application program (payroll, general ledger) communicates with the database through the DBMS.

Figure 3.15 illustrates a typical software environment. The application routine provides a user interface. Communication with the hardware is handled by the operating system. The database manage-

Figure 3.15

An operating system, a database management system, and a data communication routine define the software environment.

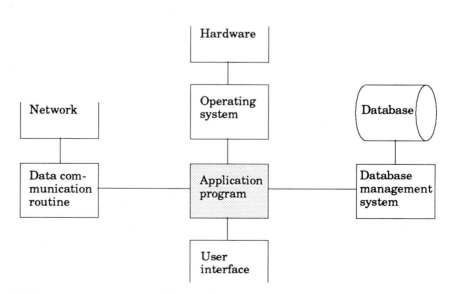

ment system is responsible for accessing the database, while the data communication routine serves as an interface to the network. Such modular design is typical of modern software.

Summary

A computer executes binary, machine-level instructions. An assembler language programmer writes one mnemonic instruction for each machine-level instruction. A compiler reads source statements, translates each one into one or more machine-level instructions, and combines them to form an object module. An interpreter works with one source statement at a time, translating it and executing the resulting machine-level code before moving on to the next instruction. A programmer using a nonprocedural, fourth-generation language defines the problem's logical structure and lets the translator program figure out how to solve it.

Few computer users write original programs. Numerous software packages are commercially available. A word processor simplifies the task of writing text. An electronic spreadsheet simulates an accountant's spreadsheet on the computer. Database management software is concerned with data storage and retrieval. Accounting packages are available to perform many common business tasks.

Some programs have a command-based user interface; others use menus. Many popular programs give the user a choice between commands and menus. Often, windows are used to display secondary menus or error messages.

Application programs perform end-user tasks; system software performs support tasks. An operating system serves as an interface between hardware and software. A common operating system can allow the same application routine to run on two dissimilar computers. Data communication software is often placed between the application program and the network, and a database management system might be used as an interface between an application program and a database. System software defines the operating environment of an application routine.

Key Words

accounting software	machine language
application program	menu
assembler	nonprocedural language
command	operating system
commercial software	platform
compiler	program
database management	system software
desktop publishing	user interface
electronic spreadsheet	window
instruction	word processing
interpreter	

Self-Test

1. An _____ programmer writes one source instruction for each machine-level instruction. A _____ translates each source statement into one or more machine-level instructions.

2. An _____ reads a single source statement, immediately translates it into one or more machine-level instructions, and then executes it before reading the next source statement.

3. With a _____ the programmer simply defines the logical structure of a problem.

4. A _____ program simplifies the task of writing text.

5. A _____ program allows you to lay out the contents of a page and integrate text and graphics.

6. The first commercially successful spreadsheet program was _____. Today's best selling spreadsheet program is _____.

7. _____ is concerned with the efficient storage and retrieval of data.

8. Typically, a software user communicates with the program by issuing _____ or by selecting choices from a _____.

9. Application programs perform _____ tasks; system software performs _____ tasks.

10. The _____ serves as a hardware/software interface.

Exercises

1. Relate machine-level instructions to a computer's basic machine cycle.

2. Distinguish between an assembler and a compiler. Distinguish between a compiler and an interpreter.

3. Text can be prepared on a typewriter. What is the advantage of using a computer and a word processor?

4. Spreadsheets can be done by hand. What is the advantage of using a computer?

5. A menu interface is best for beginners, while a command interface is best for experienced users. Why?

6. Compile a list of the commercial software packages used in your organization.

7. Distinguish between application programs and system software.

8. An operating system serves as an interface between application programs and hardware. Explain.

9. A standard operating system promotes software compatibility. Why is this important?

10. Briefly explain how system software defines an application program's operating environment.

▪4

The Tools

This chapter

- previews the upcoming tutorials
- describes the IBM PC keyboard
- explains several conventions used throughout this book

A Plan of Attack

The first three chapters barely scratched the surface of hardware and software; in the future you should consider studying computer concepts in more depth. However, you do know enough to start using some productivity tools. Most people learn best by doing, and that is the underlying assumption of the upcoming tutorials. Additional concepts will be introduced in context and in Part Six.

An operating system called **PC-DOS** (or **MS-DOS**) is the subject of Part Two. The other tools all run under PC-DOS. WordPerfect 5.0, a popular word processing program, is introduced in Part Three. Part Four covers the best-selling spreadsheet program, Lotus 1-2-3, while dBASE III Plus, a standard-setting microcomputer database management system, is the subject of Part Five.

Start with Part Two, PC-DOS. Chapter 5 presents several operating system concepts and explains key PC-DOS terminology; read it first. Chapters 6 and 7 present material that is common to all the tools; complete these two tutorials next. After you finish Chapter 7, you can continue with PC-DOS or start one of the other tools. You can study WordPerfect 5.0, Lotus 1-2-3, and dBASE III Plus in any order.

Figure 4.1
This diagram shows how the PC-DOS tutorials are related. Consult it if you plan to skip one or more chapters.

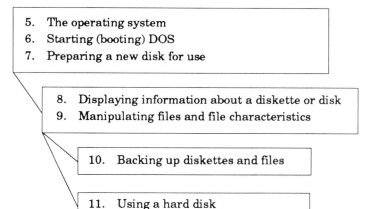

5. The operating system
6. Starting (booting) DOS
7. Preparing a new disk for use

8. Displaying information about a diskette or disk
9. Manipulating files and file characteristics

10. Backing up diskettes and files

11. Using a hard disk

Once you start a tool, your best bet is to work through all its tutorials in order, but that is not always possible. If you choose to skip one or more topics, you should know how the tutorials are related. For example, Fig. 4.1 shows the links between the PC-DOS tutorials. Chapters 5, 6, and 7 are essential. Once you have completed them, you can move to a different tool or turn to the tutorials in Chapters 8 and 9. Chapters 10 and 11 depend on Chapters 8 and 9 but not on each other; they can be read in any order.

The WordPerfect 5.0 tutorials are pictured in Fig. 4.2. Chapters 12, 13, and 14 are tightly linked; complete them as a unit. However, Chapters 15 through 18 are independent. (One lesson in Chapter 16 uses files created in Chapter 15, but it involves only a few pages.)

Figure 4.2
This diagram shows how the WordPerfect 5.0 tutorials are related.

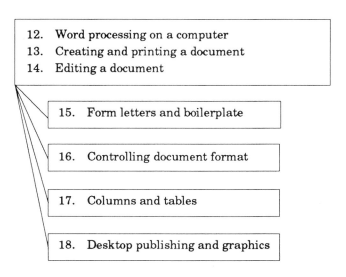

12. Word processing on a computer
13. Creating and printing a document
14. Editing a document

15. Form letters and boilerplate

16. Controlling document format

17. Columns and tables

18. Desktop publishing and graphics

Figure 4.3
This diagram shows
how the Lotus 1-2-3
tutorials are related.

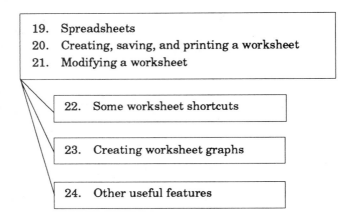

Figure 4.3 summarizes the Lotus 1-2-3 material. Chapters 19, 20, and 21 should be completed as a unit. The other three chapters are independent.

Database management is a somewhat more complex application that requires at least four chapters for a basic understanding (Fig. 4.4). Chapter 29 builds on that base, while Chapter 30 depends on Chapter 29.

The relationships between the tutorials do not suggest their relative importance; only you or your instructor can make that determination. If there is a specific topic that you want to cover, check the diagrams in Figs. 4.1 through 4.4 to identify the appropriate path. It is frustrating to start a tutorial and then be unable to complete it because key data are missing.

This book does not pretend to cover every feature of these four productivity tools; its intent is to help you get started. Sit down at a computer, complete the tutorials, and you'll be surprised how quickly your confidence and skill develop. When you finish, you'll be able to

Figure 4.4
This diagram shows
how the dBASE III
Plus tutorials are
related.

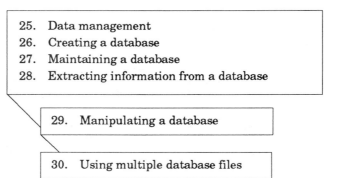

use the appropriate reference manual to learn additional features on your own.

Getting Ready

The Keyboard

Before you turn to the first tutorial, briefly preview the equipment and the software you'll be using. Start with the keyboard (Fig. 4.5). To the left on a standard IBM PC keyboard is a set of ten **function keys** labeled F1 through F10. To the keyboard's right is a **numeric keypad**; the words and arrows on the bottoms of those keys are for **cursor** control.

The center section resembles a typewriter keyboard. A few keys are particularly important. On the top row, just to the left of the digit 1, is the Esc, or escape key. Directly under it is the ⇄, or tab key. Continue moving down to the Ctrl, or control key, a ⇧, or shift key, and the Alt, or alternate key.

Just to the right of the space bar, still in the bottom row, is the Caps Lock, or caps lock key. To its right are the Ins, or insert key and the Del, or delete key. Directly above Caps Lock is another ⇧ key. To its right is a key marked Prt Sc; if you simultaneously press ⇧ *and* Prt Sc, a copy of whatever appears on the screen will be printed. Just above Prt Sc is the ↵ key, often called return or enter. Above ↵ is the ←, or backspace key. Moving to the right are the Num Lock, or numeric lock key and the Break, or scroll-lock/break key. Below Break are the − and + keys.

Figure 4.5
The standard IBM PC style keyboard.

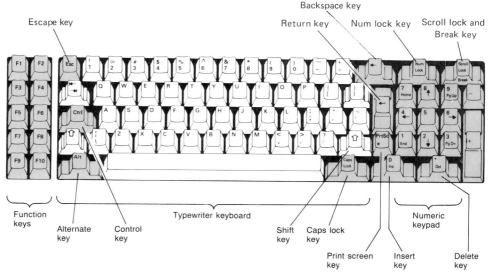

Figure 4.6
The enhanced IBM
style (101 style)
keyboard. (Courtesy
of International
Business Machines
Corporation).

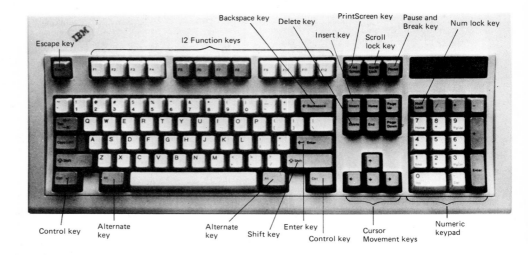

The PS/2 keyboard is a bit different (Fig. 4.6). Its 12 function keys are arrayed across the top along with the Esc, *scroll*, and *pause* keys. The typewriter keyboard is at the left; the numeric keypad is at the right; except for the positions of a few keys they resemble their PC equivalents. The big difference is a bank of cursor control keys located just to the right center of the keyboard.

If you are using an IBM-compatible computer, the layout might be slightly different. Review your keyboard and find the equivalent keys.

Disks and Disk Drives

Many microcomputers are equipped with two diskette drives. To distinguish them, the left or top one is usually known as drive A, and the right or bottom one is called drive B. If only one diskette drive is present, it is almost always called drive A.

There are two types of 5.25-inch diskette drives. A 360KB (kilobyte) drive can store approximately 360,000 bytes of information on a 360KB double-sided double-density diskette. A 1.2MB (megabyte) diskette drive can store approximately 1,200,000 bytes on a 1.2MB high density diskette.

Many newer microcomputer systems use 3.50-inch diskettes. A 720KB drive can store approximately 720,000 bytes on a 720MB diskette, while a 1.44MB drive can store roughly 1,440,000 bytes on a 1.44MB diskette. Although technically not correct, the smaller-capacity 3.50-inch diskettes are commonly called 1MB diskettes, while the higher-capacity 1.44MB diskettes are commonly called 2MB diskettes.

The hard disk, if you have one, is normally located inside the computer cabinet and identified as drive C. If your computer is linked to a network, check with your instructor or your system manager for the appropriate drive or drives.

The tutorials assume that you have a working copy of the appropriate software, at least one formatted data disk, and an operating system disk (PC-DOS or MS-DOS).

Conventions

By convention you will generally be instructed to *press* control keys (for example, press ⏎) and to *type* character keys (for example, type the letter Y). If a task requires you to press two keys simultaneously, the key symbols will be separated by the word *and* (in these tutorials), for example,

Ctrl *and* End

Press the keys in three distinct steps. Hold down the first key (Ctrl). Next, tap and release the second key (End) as though you were typing a single character. Finally, release the first key. That sequence will quickly become second nature.

Wherever possible, commands and features will appear in the tutorials much as they do on your screen. If necessary, references to specific commands will be italicized to distinguish them from the narrative. Because of page width limitations, a few messages that are displayed on a single screen line will be spread over two lines in the text.

Finally, depending on your system, the disk drives that hold your program and your data could be almost anything. Rather than trying to show every possible permutation, the illustrations in this book will generally assume that the program disk is accessed through drive A and the data are sent to diskette drive B. Substitute your own disk drives where appropriate.

∎ *What Can Go Wrong?*

Many tutorials assume that the reader will follow the instructions to the letter and nothing will go wrong. That's not always true. Instructions can be misinterpreted. A user may decide to experiment. Hardware (or software) may fail. Throughout this book, you'll find a series of boxes labeled "What Can Go Wrong?." They anticipate common problems, explain what probably happened, and suggest how you might recover. Of course, not every error can be anticipated, and some problems (a disk failure, for example) require expert attention. If you can't find a solution to your problem, ask for help. ∎

Summary

This chapter previewed the upcoming tutorials. Figures 4.1 through 4.4 showed how specific tutorials are linked. The IBM PC keyboard was reviewed, and several conventions used throughout this book were explained. A key feature, "What Can Go Wrong?," was briefly previewed.

Given the nature of this chapter, a self-test is not appropriate.

Key Words

cursor   numeric keypad
function keys   PC-DOS (MS-DOS)

Exercises

1. List the four software tools covered in this book.

2. Imagine that you want to learn about using a hard disk under PC-DOS. Identify the minimum sequence of chapters you must complete.

3. Imagine that you want to learn about columns and tables under WordPerfect 5.0. Identify the minimum sequence of chapters you must complete.

4. Imagine that you want to learn about creating graphs under Lotus 1-2-3. Identify the minimum sequence of chapters you must complete.

5. Imagine that you want to learn about using multiple database files under dBASE III Plus. Identify the minimum sequence of chapters you must complete.

6. If you have not already done so, review your computer's keyboard.

7. Explain what it means when a tutorial tells you to press [Ctrl] *and* [Home].

8. Identify the program and data disk drives you'll be using on your computer. If necessary, check with your instructor or your system manager.

■ PART TWO

PC-DOS & MS-DOS

▪5

The Operating System

This chapter

- explains basic operating system functions
- introduces DOS commands and terminology

Operating System Functions

As you discovered in Chapter 3, a computer's **operating system** serves as an interface (Fig. 5.1), bridging the gap between hardware and application software. In the next several chapters you will learn how to use a popular microcomputer operating system called **DOS**, an acronym for **disk operating system**. DOS is a collection of special

Figure 5.1
The operating system serves as an interface between hardware and application software.

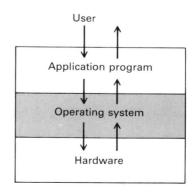

programs that supervise and control the operation of your personal computer. These programs allow you to create and manage files, execute programs, and use the peripheral devices attached to your computer.

DOS was developed for IBM Corporation by Microsoft, a leading microcomputer software company. A version called **PC-DOS** is designed to run on IBM personal computers. Microsoft also sells versions of DOS (called **MS-DOS**) for computers marketed by other companies. The differences between PC-DOS and MS-DOS are minor, so only the term DOS will be used in this book.

The Command Processor

An operating system is a collection of software modules that perform support functions. Computers are not intelligent. Before the operating system can perform one of its support functions, the person using the computer must tell it what to do. The user, much like a military officer, issues orders. The operating system responds like a sergeant, gathering the necessary resources and carrying out each command. The operating system module that accepts, interprets, and carries out commands is called the **command processor** (Fig. 5.2). The DOS command processor is called **COMMAND.COM**.

Figure 5.2
The structure of DOS.

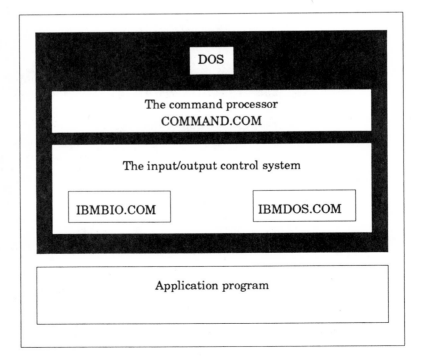

COMMAND.COM displays a **prompt** on the screen. The user responds by typing a DOS **command** and then pressing ⏎ to issue the command. COMMAND.COM then interprets the command and activates the operating system module that performs the requested function. Finally, COMMAND.COM displays a new prompt and waits for the next command. In the next several chapters you will learn how to write DOS commands.

The Input/Output Control System

One of the most difficult tasks facing a computer is accessing an input or output device. Because the computer and its peripherals are physically separate, there are numerous hardware details associated with establishing communication. Most users (and most programmers) are concerned with reading or writing selected data and have little or no interest in those details. Fortunately, an operating system contains a module called the **input/output control system (IOCS)** that communicates directly with the peripheral devices. A program or a user issues a *logical* request for I/O to the input/output control system. The IOCS then interprets the request and issues the necessary *physical* input or output commands.

Managing a disk's directory is another input/output control system task. When you first create a file, the IOCS assigns disk space and records the file's name and address in the directory. When you access a file, the IOCS reads the directory and locates the file. When you add data to or delete data from a file, the IOCS makes the necessary changes to the directory entry. When you delete a file, the IOCS removes its entry from the directory.

Under PC-DOS the input/output control system functions are performed by two modules (Fig. 5.2). The **IBMBIO.COM** (basic input/output) program handles communications between the computer and its peripheral devices; its MS-DOS equivalent is called IO.SYS. The **IBMDOS.COM** program receives all requests for DOS services, interprets them, and sends the appropriate physical commands to IBMBIO.COM. Its MS-DOS equivalent is MSDOS.SYS.

Loading the Operating System

An operating system function is initiated by a command that the operating system reads and interprets. Clearly, the operating system must be in memory before the command is issued. How does it get there? On a few systems the operating system is stored in read-only memory. ROM is permanent; it keeps its contents even when power is lost. A ROM-based operating system is always there.

However, most computers use random access memory. RAM is volatile; it loses its contents when power is cut. Thus each time the computer is activated, the operating system must be loaded. Unfortunately, you cannot simply type a command, such as LOAD OS, and let the operating system take care of loading itself. When the computer is first turned on, memory is empty. If the operating system is not yet in memory, it can't possibly read, interpret, and carry out the command.

The Boot

Typically, the operating system is stored on disk. The idea is to copy it into memory. This objective is achieved by a special program called a **boot** (Fig. 5.3). The boot routine is stored on the first sector of a disk. Hardware is designed to read this sector automatically whenever the power is turned on (Fig. 5.3a). The boot consists of only a few instructions, but they are sufficient to read the rest of the operating system into memory (Fig. 5.3b). Note how the boot is seemingly "pulled in by its own bootstraps." Now a user can type commands.

Figure 5.3
The operating system is loaded into main memory by a special program called the boot. (a) When the computer is first turned on, hardware automatically reads the boot program from the first sector of a disk. (b) The boot routine contains the instructions that read the rest of the operating system from disk into memory.

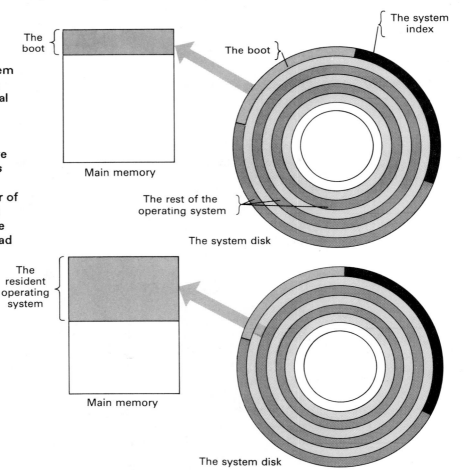

DOS System Files

Normally, the term DOS is used to refer to the three **DOS system files**: COMMAND.COM, IBMBIO.COM, and IBMDOS.COM. When you boot DOS, the three system files are loaded from disk into the computer's memory. Your personal computer is considered to be at **command level** if all three system programs are resident in memory and a system prompt is displayed on the screen.

DOS Commands

Each of the special programs that is included in DOS has a unique name. A **DOS command** is a character string specification that references the name of a DOS program. Often the terms DOS command and DOS program are used interchangeably. More accurately, when you issue a DOS command, you specify the execution of a DOS program. Appendix A is a quick reference for the DOS commands introduced in this section.

DOS commands (programs) that reside in memory as part of DOS are called **internal DOS commands**. The command processor COMMAND.COM contains the programs that are associated with each of the internal DOS commands.

DOS commands (programs) that are contained on disks as program files are called **external DOS commands**. These files have the extension .COM or .EXE as part of their name. When an external DOS command is used, the command processor COMMAND.COM loads the appropriate program file from disk into memory and then initiates its execution.

Several programs that come on the DOS diskettes are not considered to be DOS commands. These special programs are called **DOS utility programs**. They may be helpful in editing files, linking programs together, or performing other specialized tasks.

DOS allows you to build a file of DOS commands and then execute these commands as a group. Such a file is called a **batch file** and has the extension .BAT as part of its name. When a batch file name is used as a command, it is referred to as a **batch command**.

The term **DOS System diskette** or **DOS diskette** is used to denote a diskette that contains the three DOS system files and most, if not all, of the DOS external commands (programs). You will need the DOS System diskette and a few blank diskettes to perform the procedures outlined in each of the chapters in this section.

If a personal computer system is at command level, the **normal DOS prompt** consists of a disk drive letter followed by the > (greater than) character. The drive letter identifies the **default disk drive** or **default drive**. For example, the DOS prompt A > implies that the system is at command level and diskette drive A is the default disk drive.

Entering DOS Commands

To enter a DOS command, perform the following steps:

1. Your personal computer must be at command level.

2. Type a command name and its parameters using proper syntax (punctuation and grammar). This sequence of characters is called a **command line**. For example, a typical command line may look like

   ```
   DISKCOPY A: B:
   ```

   where DISKCOPY is a command name and A: and B: are parameters.

3. Press the ⏎ key to end the command and send the command line to the DOS command processor for processing.

If you enter an invalid command, a command with improper syntax, or a command that DOS cannot locate in memory or on a disk, then DOS displays the following message:

```
Bad command or file name
```

DOS command syntax involves the proper use of delimiters. A command line **delimiter** is a special character, such as a space, comma (,), or slash (/), that is used to separate items in a list or sequence. In general, spaces are used as delimiters in DOS command lines; that is, spaces are used to separate a DOS command name from its parameter list and to separate individual parameter fields. A **parameter** is any item appearing on a command line after the DOS command name. Parameters reside in fields that are separated by command line delimiters. Spaces are required between the different parts of a DOS command line that do not already contain delimiters. If a delimiter is already present, a space may also be included before the delimiter to make the command line more readable.

Disk Files and Naming

Information on a disk is organized into files. In particular, a **disk file** or **file** is a collection of related information that is treated as a basic unit of storage. In order for DOS to identify a file on a disk, the file must be assigned a file name.

Naming a Disk File

A **file name** has two parts. The first part, **filename**, consists of at least one and up to eight of the following characters:

```
A-Z  a-z  0-9  $  &  #  @  !  %  -  _  '  (  )  {  }
```

Some versions of DOS allow the use of additional characters in a filename. The second part of a file name is called the extension of the filename, filename extension, file extension, or just **extension**. It consists of a period followed by one to three valid filename characters. The notation .ext is normally used to denote a filename extension. Filename extensions are optional. The notation **filename[.ext]** denotes that the extension is optional.

A file name may be preceded by a disk drive designator (A:, B:, or C:) and/or information about where to locate the file on a disk (path name). The term **file specification** is used to denote a sequence of characters that completely identifies a file and where to find it. The abbreviation **filespec** is sometimes used to denote file specification.

A file name should give you a general idea of what information is in the file. Proper naming of files can save you a great deal of time in searching for a particular file. You should note that DOS makes no distinction between uppercase and lowercase alphabetical characters in a file name.

Wildcard (Global) Filename Characters

DOS allows you to specify groups of file names through the use of two special characters, * and ?, called **wildcard (global)** file name characters. The asterisk (*) can be used to represent zero or more characters at the end of a filename or filename extension, while the question mark (?) can be used to represent a single character in a filename or filename extension.

User (Visible) Files and Hidden Files

A **user** or **visible file** is a file that you as a user can access through normal DOS commands. File names for user files are listed on the screen when DOS displays directory information. A **hidden file** is a file that you as a user cannot access through normal DOS commands. File names for hidden files are not listed when DOS displays directory information. In this book the term "files" is used to denote user files. The term "user files" may be used to emphasize that hidden files are not included in the discussion.

Earlier, you learned about the three DOS System files. COMMAND.COM is a visible file, while IBMDOS.COM and IBMBIO.COM are hidden files.

Types of User (Visible) Files

Text files are data files that contain alphanumeric (both alphabetic and numeric) and special symbol characters in an ASCII format. ASCII is an acronym for American Standard Code for Information Interchange and refers to a code scheme that computers use to represent characters of information. Text files are sometimes referred to as ASCII files or ASCII format files.

COM files contain executable (binary, machine language) programs that can be loaded directly into memory and executed without modification. The name COM file comes from the .COM filename extension. **EXE files** contain executable programs that require some address modification before they can be executed. The name EXE file comes from the .EXE filename extension.

Files containing programs written in a programming language such as BASIC are called programming language files. These files contain information that a corresponding language processor can read and translate into executable programs. For example, BASIC language files have .BAS as a filename extension.

Application programs create application data files in a format that can be read and understood by that application. Application data files have filename extensions associated with the application. For example, a word processing application might use .DOC as a filename extension, and a spreadsheet (worksheet) application might use .WKS as a filename extension.

DOS Device Names

DOS assigns special DOS **device names** to input/output (I/O) devices such as the keyboard, the display screen, and the printer. These device names have a special meaning when used in a DOS command and are reserved for use only with the assigned devices.

CON is an abbreviation for console. CON is assigned to the keyboard for input and the display screen for output. PRN is an abbreviation for printer. It refers to the parallel printer that DOS uses unless you specify otherwise. LPT1 is another abbreviation for printer and is equivalent to PRN.

Equipment Utilized

The material presented in this section covers all versions of IBM PC-DOS and MS-DOS. While research was done on a variety of personal computers, including IBM, Texas Instruments, Compaq, and Zenith personal computers, the procedures were performed on an IBM PC AT using IBM PC-DOS Version 3.30. The IBM PC AT contained one megabyte of memory, a 1.2MB diskette drive (drive A), a 360KB diskette drive (drive B), and a 30MB hard disk drive (drive C).

Summary

An operating system is a collection of special modules or programs that perform support functions. Users communicate with the operating system through a command language. The command processor accepts, interprets, and carries out user commands. The input/output control system communicates with a computer's peripheral devices and maintains disk directories.

This section teaches you how to write commands for a popular microcomputer operating system called DOS. The DOS command processor is called COMMAND.COM. Two DOS programs,

IBMBIO.COM and IBMDOS.COM, perform the functions associated with the input/output control system.

The balance of the chapter introduced DOS commands and terminology. The key word list provides an excellent summary.

Key Words

batch command	file
batch file	file name
boot	filename
COM file	filename[.ext]
command	file specification (filespec)
command level	hidden file
command line	IBMBIO.COM
command processor	IBMDOS.COM
COMMAND.COM	input/output control system (IOCS)
default disk drive	
delimiter	internal DOS command
device name	MS-DOS
disk file	normal DOS prompt
DOS (disk operating system)	operating system
DOS command	parameter
DOS system file	PC-DOS
DOS System diskette	prompt
DOS utility program	text file
EXE file	user file
extension	visible file
external DOS command	wildcard (global) character

Self-Test

1. The version of DOS written for IBM computers is called _____. The versions of DOS written for other manufacturers' computers are called _____.

2. The operating system module that accepts, interprets, and carries out commands is called the _____.

3. The operating system module that communicates directly with peripheral devices and manages disk directories is called the _____.

4. The DOS command processor is called _____. The two modules that comprise the DOS input/output control system are called _____ and _____. These three programs represent the DOS _____.

5. The operating system is loaded into memory from disk by a _____ routine.

6. DOS programs that reside in memory are called _____ DOS commands. DOS programs that reside on disk and are read into memory only when needed are called _____ DOS commands.

7. A file of DOS commands that are executed as a group is called a _____ file.

8. The normal DOS prompt identifies the _____ disk drive.

9. A DOS file name contains a maximum of _____ characters. The optional extension contains a maximum of _____ characters.

10. DOS files with the extensions _____ or _____ contain executable machine-language programs.

Exercises

1. What functions are performed by an operating system's command processor?

2. What functions are performed by an operating system's input/output control system?

3. Explain how an operating system is booted. Why is booting necessary?

4. Sketch the component parts of PC-DOS.

5. Briefly characterize the different types of disk drives used on a personal computer. Identify the type of drive(s) on the computer you will use.

6. Briefly outline the steps needed to enter a DOS command.

7. State the rules for naming a disk file.

8. Briefly explain the difference between user and hidden files.

∎6

Starting (Booting) DOS

The material in this chapter introduces the DOS features and commands that allow you to:

- start DOS running (boot the system)
- check and change the DOS system date (DATE)
- check and change the DOS system time (TIME)
- change the current (default) disk drive
- clear the screen (CLS)
- display the active version of DOS (VER)
- obtain a hard copy listing of the information displayed on the screen using the ⬆ *and* PrtSc key combination
- turn the printer echo mode on or off using the Ctrl *and* PrtSc or Ctrl *and* P key combination
- log off DOS

Booting the Operating System

The term DOS System diskette is used to denote a diskette that contains the DOS system files and most, if not all, of the disk operating system programs. All of the internal DOS commands and most of the external DOS commands can be loaded and executed from this diskette.

Before you can use your computer to perform any useful tasks, the operating system (DOS) must be loaded (copied) from the DOS System diskette into the computer's memory. The process of starting a computer is referred to as the boot process, **booting** the system, booting DOS, or starting DOS.

Booting the System from a Diskette

To begin the boot (start) process on a personal computer containing only diskette drives, you need a working copy of the DOS System diskette. Insert the DOS System diskette in drive A.

1. If the power to your computer is off, turn the power switch from OFF to ON (or from 0 to 1). If necessary, turn on the monitor's power, too. Initiating the boot process by turning the power on is called a **cold start** or **cold boot**.

2. If your computer is already on, hold the Ctrl and Alt keys down and press Del (denoted by Ctrl *and* Alt *and* Del). Using the Ctrl *and* Alt *and* Del key combination to initiate the boot process is called a **warm start, warm boot, system reset,** or **system restart**.

Once the boot process has been initiated, several tasks are performed automatically by your computer system. Your computer contains two special programs that permanently reside in its read-only memory. If the boot process begins with a cold start, your computer's central processing unit automatically executes both of these special programs. If the boot process begins with a warm start, only the second program is executed by your CPU. The first program performs a short self-test on some of the computer's component parts, checking for certain types of hardware (equipment) failures. The execution of this program is the reason your computer appears to be doing nothing for several seconds after the boot process is initiated. The second program is called the **bootstrap loader** because it "pulls DOS up by the bootstrap." It begins the process of loading DOS into the computer's memory by first loading and then executing a program called the **bootstrap program** from the initial part of the DOS disk. The execution of this program causes DOS's two hidden files (IBMBIO.COM and IBMDOS.COM) and the file COMMAND.COM to be loaded into your computer's memory.

Once the DOS system files have been loaded into memory, DOS displays its current date followed by a message to enter a new date. Respond to the message

```
Enter new date (mm-dd-yy):
```

by pressing ↵ to accept the displayed date as the current system date or by typing the current date in the displayed format (Fig. 6.1) and then pressing ↵. For example, if today's date is August 8, 1989, type

Figure 6.1

The current date should be entered in this format.

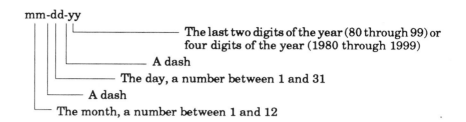

mm-dd-yy

The last two digits of the year (80 through 99) or four digits of the year (1980 through 1999)

A dash

The day, a number between 1 and 31

A dash

The month, a number between 1 and 12

8-8-89 and press ⏎. Next DOS displays its current time followed by a message to enter a new time. Respond to the message

```
Enter new time:
```

by pressing ⏎ to accept the displayed time as the current system time or by typing the current time in the displayed format using a twenty-four hour clock (Fig. 6.2) and then pressing ⏎. Since DOS uses a twenty-four hour clock, 10:15 A.M. is entered as 10:15, and 3:45 P.M. is entered as 15:45. Thus if the present time of day is 4:25 P.M., type 16:25 and press ⏎.

After the above preliminaries have been completed, DOS sends a multiline message (Fig. 6.3) to the screen identifying the version of DOS and copyright information, followed by the normal DOS prompt A> from the DOS command processor. This prompt indicates that the system is at command level, waiting for a command from you, and that the current (default) disk drive is drive A.

You should always be careful to enter the correct date and time during the boot process. In addition to DOS, many application programs, such as word processors and spreadsheet applications, use the DOS system date and time. If the date and time are not entered correctly when you boot the system, this information will not be correct when applications use functions that reference the DOS system date and time. Also, if the current date and time are not correctly entered into the computer, then the date and time associated with any file that is created or modified during this session will not be correct. This might cause problems in the future when you try to determine the creation date or the last modification date of a particular file.

You might notice that some personal computers never display the correct date and time when you boot the system, while other comput-

Figure 6.2

The current time should be entered in this format.

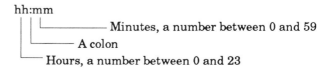

hh:mm

Minutes, a number between 0 and 59

A colon

Hours, a number between 0 and 23

Figure 6.3
After the system is booted, information similar to this is displayed. The DOS prompt is A>, which indicates that the system is at command level and diskette drive A is the default disk drive.

Current date is Tue 8-08-1988

Enter new date (mm-dd-yy): 1-31-89

Current time is 0:00:15.47

Enter new time: 15:45

The IBM Personal Computer DOS

Version 3.30 (C)Copyright International Business Machines Corp 1981, 1987

     (C)Copyright Microsoft Corp 1981, 1986

A>

ers always appear to display the correct date and time. If a personal computer contains a real-time clock/calendar (permanent clock) with battery backup, then the system date and time should be correct when they are displayed during the boot process, since this device automatically keeps track of the date and time. If a personal computer does not contain a permanent clock, you will have to enter the correct date and time each time you boot the system.

■ *Keystroke Summary*

Booting the system from a diskette

    Insert: DOS System diskette in drive A

    Perform: cold boot (turn computer's power switch on) or warm boot ([Ctrl] *and* [Alt] *and* [Del])

    Check: displayed system date

        Press: [↵] to accept the displayed system date or

        Type: *mm-dd-yy* and Press: [↵]

        See Fig. 6.1 for the date format.

    Check: displayed system time

        Press: [↵] to accept the displayed system time or

        Type: *hh:mm* and Press: [↵]

        See Fig. 6.2 for the time format.

Booting the System from a Hard Disk

DOS must be installed on a hard disk before a hard disk can be used to boot the system. Unless you are using a new personal computer with a hard disk that has not been prepared for use by DOS, DOS is more than likely installed on the hard disk. If for some reason DOS is not installed on the hard disk, you should consult your instructor. The material covered in this section assumes that your hard disk is prepared for use by DOS and that all DOS programs are on the hard disk.

Before you begin the boot process on a personal computer containing a hard disk, make sure that there is no diskette in drive A. Next perform one of the following steps:

1. If the power to your computer is off, perform a cold boot (cold start); that is, turn the power switch from OFF to ON (or from 0 to 1). If necessary, turn on the monitor's power, too.

2. If the power to your computer is on, perform a warm boot (warm start); that is, hold the [Ctrl] and [Alt] keys down and press [Del] (denoted by [Ctrl] *and* [Alt] *and* [Del]).

The steps performed when booting the system from a hard disk are essentially the same as those performed when booting the system from a diskette.

After the boot process has been completed, the DOS command processor displays the normal DOS prompt C> on the screen. This prompt indicates that the system is at command level waiting for a command from you and that the current (default) disk drive is drive C.

If your personal computer contains a hard disk, then it should automatically boot from the hard disk when drive A contains no formatted diskette. If a formatted diskette is in drive A, most personal computers will attempt to boot the system from that diskette. A comprehensive discussion on using a hard disk is given in Chapter 11.

Booting the system from a hard disk

■ *Keystroke Summary*

Remove: any diskette from drive A

Perform: cold boot (turn computer's power switch on) or warm boot ([Ctrl] *and* [Alt] *and* [Del])

Check: displayed system date

Press: [↵] to accept the displayed system date or

Type: *mm-dd-yy* and Press: [↵]

See Fig. 6.1 for the date format.

Check: displayed system time

Press: [↵] to accept the displayed system time or

Type: *hh:mm* and Press: [↵]

See Fig. 6.2 for the time format.

■ What Can Go Wrong?

1. A message similar to the following is displayed when you attempt to boot the system:

```
Non-System disk or disk error
Replace and strike any key when ready
```

Cause: The diskette in drive A does not contain the three DOS system files that are necessary to boot the system.

Solution: Remove the diskette from drive A and check to be sure that it is the DOS System diskette. If it is, center the diskette in the diskette jacket, insert it back in drive A, and press any key to reinitiate the boot process. If the same message appears again, you have a bad DOS System diskette and it must be replaced.

2. One of the following messages is displayed after you enter the date or the time:

```
Invalid date              or    Invalid time
Enter new date (mm-dd-yy):      Enter new time:
```

Cause: You probably typed the date or the time in the wrong format.

Solution: Check the proper format for typing the date (Fig. 6.1) or the time (Fig. 6.2), and retype your entry.

3. You realize that you typed the wrong date or time but DOS accepted it.

Cause: You typed an incorrect date or time but it was accepted by DOS because it was typed in a valid format.

Solution: DOS cannot determine whether a date or time that you enter is correct. DOS can only determine whether the format of the date or time is valid. For example, 5-6-81 is a valid date to DOS, but it is not today's date. The next two lessons show how to correct an invalid date and an invalid time.

4. The boot process does not have steps that prompt you for the date and time, or the sequence and type of tasks are different from the steps described above.

Cause: The DOS System diskette contains a special file named AUTOEXEC.BAT, which may alter the tasks that DOS performs after the DOS system files have been loaded into memory.

Solution: You should follow any prompt messages that appear on the screen. If you are not prompted for the current date and time, you can use the DATE and TIME commands to verify and change (if necessary) the system date and time. The next two lessons cover these commands.

5. You initiate a cold boot, but no information is displayed on the screen.

Cause: The power to the monitor is off or the brightness/contrast setting for the screen is too low.

Solution: Check the power switch to the monitor and make sure that it is turned on. Check the brightness/contrast controls for the screen to see whether it needs to be adjusted to a brighter setting. ■

Checking and Changing the System Date (DATE)

Note: If you booted your system from drive C, substitute C for A as the default drive in the discussions that follow.

The **DATE** command is an internal DOS command that allows you to check and change (if necessary) the DOS system date. With the cursor positioned after the A> prompt, type

    DATE

and press ⏎. A message followed by the current DOS system date is displayed (Fig. 6.4). If the date is correct, press ⏎. If the date is not correct, type the correct date (Fig. 6.1) and press ⏎.

▪ *Keystroke Summary*

Checking and changing the system date

Type: DATE

Press: ⏎

Check: displayed system date

Press: ⏎ to accept the displayed system date   or

Type: *mm-dd-yy* and Press: ⏎

See Fig. 6.1 for the date format.

▪ *What Can Go Wrong?*

1. DOS displays the following message:

    Bad command or file name

Cause: You probably mistyped the DOS command name.

Solution: Check the characters you typed for the DOS command name and retype your entry. ▪

Figure 6.4
When the DATE command is used to check and/or change the system date, information similar to this is displayed. 5-06-1989 is May 6, 1989.

    A>DATE
    Current date is Sat 5-06-1989
    Enter new date (mm-dd-yy):

Checking and Changing the System Time (TIME)

The **TIME** command is an internal DOS command that allows you to check and change (if necessary) the DOS system time. With the cursor positioned after the A> prompt, type

    TIME

and press ⏎. A message followed by the current DOS system time is displayed in a twenty-four hour clock format (Fig. 6.5). Check the time displayed on the screen. If the time is correct, press ⏎. If the time is not correct, type the correct time (Fig. 6.2) and press ⏎.

■ *Keystroke Summary*

Checking and changing the system time

Type: TIME

Press: ⏎

Check: displayed system time

Press: ⏎   to accept the displayed system time   or

Type: *hh:mm* and Press: ⏎

See Fig. 6.2 for the time format.

Changing the Current (Default) Disk Drive (d:)

When the system is at command level and drive A is the current (default) disk drive, DOS displays the A> prompt. If you want to change the default drive to a different drive, enter the letter identifying the drive followed by a colon (:).

With the cursor positioned after the A> prompt, type B: and press ⏎. This entry instructs DOS to change the current drive to drive B and to display the B> prompt. If your computer contains a hard disk, type C: and press ⏎. The current disk drive is changed to drive C (the hard disk drive), and DOS displays the C> prompt. To change the current disk drive back to drive A, type A: and press ⏎.

Figure 6.5
When the TIME command is used to check and/or change the system time, information similar to this is displayed. 19:37:45.76 is approximately 7:37 P.M.

```
A>TIME
Current time is 19:37:45.76
Enter new time:
```

■ *Keystroke*
Summary

Changing the current (default) disk drive

Type: d: where d: denotes the designated drive

Press: ⏎

■ *What Can*
Go Wrong?

1. DOS displays the following message:

    Invalid drive specification

Cause: You did not specify a valid disk drive.

Solution: If you entered C: and your computer does not contain a hard disk, the above message will be displayed on your screen. Check the drive specification and correct it by entering a valid drive specification for your computer. ■

**Clearing the
Screen (CLS)**

The **CLS** (CLear Screen) command is an internal DOS command that allows you to clear all displayed information from the screen. With the cursor positioned after the A> prompt, type

    CLS

and press ⏎. All information that was displayed on your screen is cleared, and the A> prompt is displayed in the upper left-hand corner of the screen.

■ *Keystroke*
Summary

Clearing the screen

Type: CLS

Press: ⏎

**Different
Versions of DOS**

DOS has been revised several times since the introduction of the first version of DOS, Version 1.00. The **DOS version number** is displayed in the format X.xx where X denotes a major revision number and xx denotes a minor revision number. A change in xx, the number following the decimal point, indicates a minor change that leaves DOS virtually the same. A change from DOS Version 3.10 to Version 3.20 is an example of such a change. A change in X, the number preceding the decimal point, indicates a major change in DOS. A change from Version 2.10 to Version 3.10 is an example of a major change in DOS.

WARNING: **Since all parts of DOS work very closely together, you should be careful not to mix parts of DOS from two different versions. Unpredictable things can happen as a** result of mixing different versions of DOS, such as losing an entire data disk.

Determining the DOS Version (VER)

Since some applications run only under certain versions of DOS, you need a way to determine which version of DOS is active in your computer system. The **VER** (VERsion) command is an internal DOS command that allows you to display the active version of DOS. With the cursor positioned after the A> prompt, type

```
VER
```

and press ↵. A message similar to the following is displayed:

```
IBM Personal Computer DOS Version 3.30
```

▪ *Keystroke Summary*

Determining the DOS version

Type: VER

Press: ↵

Printing Information Displayed on the Screen

Many times you encounter a situation in which you want a hard copy (printed) listing of information that is displayed on the screen. DOS has no command that allows you to print a screen image. However, most personal computers support a hardware **print screen** function that allows you to obtain a hard copy listing of the information that is displayed on the screen. The print screen function is initiated by holding the ⑨ key down and pressing PrtSc (denoted by ⑨ *and* PrtSc).

Insert the DOS system diskette in drive A and reboot the system. After you respond to the date and time prompts, information similar to that given in Fig. 6.3 is displayed on the screen. To obtain a hard copy listing of this information, first make sure the printer is on. Then hold the ⑨ key down and press PrtSc. After the cursor scans each row on the screen and sends the displayed information to the printer, it returns to its original position following the A> prompt.

Turning the Printer Echo Mode On and Off

When you are working on a personal computer, the information that you type on the keyboard and the information and messages generated from DOS commands are displayed on the screen. When the screen becomes full, the information scrolls from the bottom toward the top and then disappears. Sometimes you may want a hard copy listing of what is being displayed. DOS supports a printer echo mode that can be turned on and off with a special key combination. To turn the **printer echo mode** from off to on or from on to off, hold the Ctrl key down and press [PrtSc] or hold the [Ctrl] key down and type P (denoted by [Ctrl] *and* [PrtSc] or [Ctrl] *and* P). When the printer echo mode is turned on, everything that DOS sends to be displayed on the screen is also sent (echoed) to the computer's printer. This feature allows you to automatically get a printed copy of what appears on the screen. Normally, the printer echo mode is turned off.

Try it. Turn the printer echo mode on by holding the [Ctrl] key down and pressing [PrtSc] or by holding the [Ctrl] key down and typing P. With the cursor positioned after the A> prompt, type DATE and press [↵]. Notice that once the printer echo mode is turned on, everything that is displayed on the screen is also printed on the printer. Respond to the date prompt. With the cursor positioned after the A> prompt, type VER and press [↵]. Again notice that the DOS version information is displayed on the screen and echoed to the printer. Now turn the printer echo mode off using the same [Ctrl] *and* [PrtSc] or [Ctrl] *and* P key combination. With the cursor positioned after the A> prompt, type VER and press [↵]. With the printer echo mode turned off, the DOS version information is displayed only on the screen.

Logging Off DOS

When you are finished using a personal computer, you log off DOS. This is a very simple but important task. The process of **logging off DOS** consists of first removing your diskette(s) from the appropriate diskette drive(s) and then turning the computer's power switch off. In many computer labs the standard procedure is to clear the screen, remove your diskette(s), and leave the computer on for the next user.

Summary

Topic or Feature	Command or Reference	Page
Boot DOS from a diskette	Insert DOS System diskette in drive A; turn power switch on or press [Ctrl] *and* [Alt] *and* [Del]	56
Boot DOS from a hard disk	Remove any diskette from drive A; turn power switch on or press [Ctrl] *and* [Alt] *and* [Del]	59
Check and/or change system date	DATE Figs. 6.1, 6.4	61
Check and/or change system time	TIME Figs. 6.2, 6.5	62
Change the current (default) disk drive	*d:* where *d* denotes the designated drive	62
Clear the screen	CLS	63
Display active version of DOS	VER	64

Topic or Feature	Command or Reference	Page
Print screen information	⇧ *and* Prt Sc	64
Printer echo mode on and off	Ctrl *and* Prt Sc or Ctrl *and* P	64
Log off DOS	Remove diskettes and turn power switch off	65

Self-Test

1. The process of starting a personal computer is known as _____. A cold boot or cold start is initiated by _____. A warm boot or system restart is initiated by _____.

2. The three DOS system files that must be on a disk before it can be used to successfully boot the system are _____ , _____ , and_____.

3. During the boot process, you normally enter the system _____and_____.

4. The_____ command is used to check and/or change the system date. The_____ command is used to check and/or change the system time.

5. To change the current disk drive from drive A to drive B, type _____.

6. The_____ command is used to clear all displayed information from the screen.

7. The_____ command is used to determine the version of DOS that is running in a personal computer.

8. To obtain a hard copy (printed) listing of the information displayed on the screen, press _____.

9. To turn the printer echo mode on and off, press _____.

10. To log off DOS, _____ and _____.

Exercises

1. Perform the appropriate function and/or use an appropriate DOS command to perform each of the assigned tasks.

   a. Boot the system.

   b. Make sure the correct date and time are entered.

   c. Display but do not change the system date.

   d. Display and change the system time to 7:53 P.M.

    e. Display the active version of DOS.

    f. Change the default drive to a different drive.

    g. Obtain a hard copy listing of the information displayed on the screen.

    h. Clear the screen.

    i. Log off DOS.

2. Perform the appropriate function and/or use an appropriate DOS command to perform each of the assigned tasks.

    a. Boot the system.

    b. Make sure the correct date and time are entered.

    c. Turn the printer echo mode on so that you will obtain a hard copy listing of parts (d) through (g).

    d. Display but do not change the system date.

    e. Display and change the system time to 3:29 P.M.

    f. Display the active version of DOS.

    g. Change the default drive to a different drive.

    h. Turn the printer echo mode off.

    i. Clear the screen.

    j. Log off DOS.

∎7

Preparing a New Disk for Use

The material in this chapter introduces the DOS commands that allow you to:

- prepare a data diskette (FORMAT)
- prepare a bootable diskette (FORMAT /S)
- transfer the three DOS system files to a formatted diskette with an empty directory (SYS)
- prepare a diskette with a volume label (FORMAT / V)

Formatting a Disk

Suppose you are in charge of a new post office building that has 5000 post office boxes. How will you manage the use of these boxes? First, you realize that the boxes must be systematically numbered so that your employees can distribute the mail correctly and so that your customers can locate their mail. If you simply rent (allocate) the boxes in sequential order, you might encounter a few problems. You might have a very short person assigned a top box that he or she cannot reach; you might have customers who want a large box or more than one box; you might have a box that was rented but is now free because the renter moved out of town; you might have several boxes with broken locks that should not be rented (allocated) until they are repaired. You soon realize that if you are going to be successful at managing this facility (space), you must have ways

- for your employees to place (store) mail (information) in the correct boxes,

- for your customers to get (retrieve) their mail (information), and

- for you to determine what boxes are being used, what boxes are bad and should not be used, what boxes can be rented (allocated), and in what order you will rent (allocate) the free boxes.

DOS encounters some of the same problems in managing the finite storage space on the surface of a disk. Consequently, DOS must prepare (format) a disk so that it knows how the surface of the disk is subdivided and numbered (addressed), whether one or two sides of the disk are being used, where to find (read) information previously stored on the disk, where bad spots are on the disk, where to store (write) new information on the disk, and how to free space for information that you want to delete from the disk. In the next two sections you will see how the surface of a disk is subdivided and addressed for use by DOS and what tasks are actually performed during the formatting process.

Characteristics of Unformatted and Formatted Disks

Figure 7.1 illustrates a 5.25-inch diskette that has not been formatted. Notice that the surface of the diskette is not subdivided and no addressing (numbering) scheme is present on the diskette. Figure 7.2 illustrates the top and bottom view of a 3.50-inch diskette that has not been formatted. Figure 7.3 illustrates a 5.25-inch 360KB diskette that has been formatted by DOS. Similar characteristics hold for all types of disks, including hard disks, so the remarks in the remainder of this section refer to disks in general.

Figure 7.1
Unformatted 5.25-inch diskette

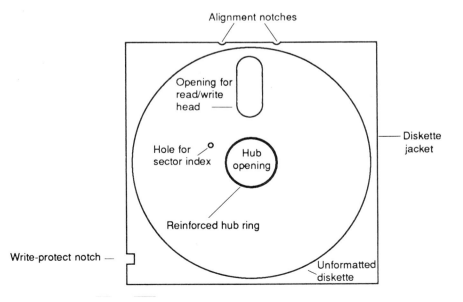

Figure 7.2
Unformatted 3.50-inch
diskette

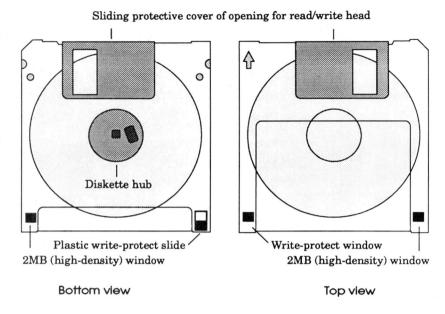

Sliding protective cover of opening for read/write head

Diskette hub

Plastic write-protect slide
2MB (high-density) window

Write-protect window
2MB (high-density) window

Bottom view

Top view

A formatted disk is divided into narrow concentric circles called **tracks**. Each track is subdivided into smaller areas called **sectors**; each sector can hold 512 bytes (characters) of information. DOS uses the disk side (bottom is side 0, top is side 1), track, and sector numbers to save and retrieve information; that is, usable areas of a disk's surface are addressed by using the side, track, and sector numbers. Even though a formatted disk is electronically divided into tracks and

Figure 7.3
Formatted 5.25-inch
360KB diskette

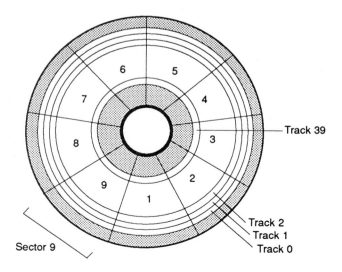

Track 39

Track 2
Track 1
Track 0

Sector 9

sectors as illustrated in Fig. 7.3, the format structure on the surface of a disk is not visible. The number of tracks and sectors that are created on a formatted disk is determined by the version of DOS that you use, the type of disk drive that is used in the formatting process, and the parameters that are specified in the formatting process.

Once a diskette has been formatted, a diskette drive can write information on the diskette and read information from the diskette. If a **write-protect tab** (sticker) is placed over the write-protect notch on the diskette jacket of a 5.25-inch diskette (Fig. 7.1), a diskette drive can read information from the diskette but cannot write information to the diskette. The diskette is said to be **write protected**. If the write-protect window on a 3.50-inch diskette (Fig. 7.2) is closed, a diskette drive can read and write information on the diskette. If the write-protect window on a 3.50-inch diskette is open, the diskette is write protected; that is, a diskette drive can read information from the diskette but cannot write information to the diskette. Normally, a diskette is write protected to protect important information from being changed or deleted and to prevent a diskette drive from writing additional information on the diskette.

Results of the FORMAT Command

The **FORMAT** command is an external DOS command that prepares (formats) a disk so that it can be used by DOS to save (store) and retrieve (read) information. The FORMAT command does five things to a disk.

1. FORMAT addresses the usable area of the disk by writing electronic guidelines on the surface of the disk as outlined in Fig. 7.3. These guidelines allow DOS to locate a particular area of the disk by using the side, track, and sector numbers (addresses).

2. FORMAT writes on each sector of the disk to determine whether it is free of defects. Bad or defective sectors are marked as write protected so that DOS cannot use the bad parts of the disk to store data.

3. FORMAT creates a **directory** (main or root directory) for the disk, which contains information about files stored on the disk. The directory of a disk serves as a table of contents for the information stored on the disk.

4. FORMAT creates a **file allocation table (FAT)** for the disk. This table contains the information to keep track of bad tracks on the disk, to identify which sectors belong to which files, and to identify which sectors are not being used (free sectors). The file allocation table may be thought of as an index to the usable area of a disk.

5. FORMAT places a copy of the **boot record** on the first sector of the disk (side 0, track 0, sector 1). The boot record contains information about the format structure of the disk along with the bootstrap program.

Note that the FORMAT command identifies five types of sectors on a formatted disk: boot record sector, directory sectors, file allocation table sectors, bad or defective sectors, and data sectors (where file data are stored). The boot record sector, the directory sectors, and the file allocation table sectors are considered to be disk overhead.

Preparing Data Diskettes (FORMAT)

Now that you know why a disk must be formatted and what the formatting process actually does to a disk, you are ready to learn how to format a disk using the FORMAT command. Plan to format several diskettes so that you always have extra formatted diskettes available for immediate use. The first time you lose data because your data diskette is full and will accept no more information, and you do not have a formatted diskette available for use, you will understand the true value of having formatted diskettes readily available. You will need at least two blank diskettes to perform the procedures outlined in the remaining sections of this chapter. In preparation for subsequent tutorials, it might be wise to format five or six diskettes.

WARNING: **The FORMAT command is one of the most dangerous DOS commands and should be used with great caution. Any data residing on a diskette will be destroyed by the formatting process. Before you format a diskette, you should be sure that there are no valuable data on the diskette.**

Boot DOS. Because FORMAT is an external command, leave the DOS System diskette in drive A. With the cursor positioned after the A> prompt, type

```
FORMAT B:
```

and press ⏎. The FORMAT program must be loaded into memory from the DOS System diskette. Once the loading process is complete, DOS initiates the execution of the FORMAT program, which displays the following message:

```
Insert new diskette for drive B:
and strike ENTER when ready
```

After you insert a blank (target) diskette in drive B, press ⏎. As the diskette in drive B is being formatted, the head number (indicating bottom [0] or top [1] of the diskette) and cylinder number (indicating the track number) are displayed. When the formatting process is complete, FORMAT displays summary information indicating the

Figure 7.4
When the FORMAT command is used to format a 360KB diskette, messages similar to these are displayed. Note that once the formatting process is complete, the head number and cylinder number are no longer displayed.

```
A>FORMAT B:
Insert new diskette for drive B:
and strike ENTER when ready

Format complete

    362496 bytes total disk space
    362496 bytes available on disk

Format another (Y/N)?
```

number of bytes available on the target diskette followed by a prompt message that asks if you want to format another diskette (Fig. 7.4). With the cursor positioned after the prompt message, type Y and press ⏎ to format another diskette. Remove your formatted diskette from drive B, insert another blank diskette, and press ⏎ to begin the formatting process. After formatting several diskettes, type N and press ⏎ to terminate the formatting process. System control returns to command level, and DOS displays the A > prompt.

When the FORMAT command is used without any special formatting parameters, the diskette drive type dictates the diskette format; a 360KB diskette drive formats a 360KB diskette, a 1.2MB diskette drive formats a 1.2MB diskette, a 720KB diskette drive formats a 720KB diskette, and a 1.44MB diskette drive formats a 1.44MB diskette. There are FORMAT parameters that allow you to specify different capacities. For example, you can format a diskette on only one side (single-sided) or eight sectors per track. See the DOS reference manual for details.

If you are using a computer system with a 1.2MB (high-density) diskette drive and a 360KB (double-density) diskette drive, you need to be careful how you use these two types of drives. A 360KB diskette drive cannot read from or write to a formatted 1.2MB diskette. A 1.2MB diskette drive can read from and write to a formatted 360KB diskette. However, while 360KB diskettes written on by a 1.2MB drive can be reliably read in another 1.2MB drive, they may not be reliably read in a 360KB diskette drive. For this reason you should never format a 360KB diskette in a 1.2MB diskette drive. Similarly, a 720KB diskette drive cannot read from or write to a formatted 1.44MB diskette, but a 1.44MB diskette drive can read from and write to a formatted 720KB diskette. Also, 720KB diskettes written on by a 1.44MB drive can be reliably read by both 720KB and 1.44MB diskette drives.

Formatting a diskette

Insert:	DOS System diskette in drive A
Set:	default drive to drive A
Type:	FORMAT B:
Press:	⏎
Insert:	blank (target) diskette in drive B
Press:	⏎
Type:	Y to format another diskette or
	N to terminate the FORMAT command
Press:	⏎

■ *What Can Go Wrong?*

1. The FORMAT command displays information that includes a message about bad sectors:

```
Format complete

362496 bytes total disk space
  5120 bytes in bad sectors
357376 bytes available on disk
```

Cause: When the FORMAT program finds sectors that cannot be written to and read from in a reliable manner, it marks these sectors as write protected so that they cannot be used by DOS to store information.

Solution: When the FORMAT command displays bad sector information for a diskette, you should format the diskette again to verify that the diskette does have bad sectors. As a general rule, do not use diskettes that contain bad or defective sectors. Not only do bad sectors decrease the space available to store information, they also raise a question about the quality and reliability of the diskette's surface. A diskette that contains bad sectors should be discarded.

2. The FORMAT command displays the following message after it attempts to format a diskette:

```
Attempted write-protect violation
Format failure
Format another (Y/N)?
```

Cause: The FORMAT command cannot format the target diskette because the diskette drive latch is not closed or the disk is write protected.

Solution: Check to be sure that the target diskette is inserted in the target drive with the drive latch closed. If it is, remove the target diskette from the diskette drive and check to see whether the diskette is write protected. If you determine that the diskette is write protected and is an important diskette that should not be formatted, replace this diskette with a blank diskette to be formatted. Otherwise, remove the write-protect tab from a 5.25-inch diskette or close the write-protect window on a 3.50-inch diskette.

3. The FORMAT command displays the following message after it attempts to format a diskette:

```
Invalid media or Track 0 bad - disk unusable
Format failure
Format another (Y/N)?
```

Cause: The FORMAT command cannot format the target diskette because it has a bad track 0 on side 0 (bottom side).

Solution: Remember that one of the tasks performed by the FORMAT command is to place the boot record on the initial track of the diskette. Consequently, when the first track (track 0) of the bottom side (side 0) of the diskette is bad, the diskette cannot be formatted. A diskette that causes this message to be displayed should be discarded.

4. After the disk is formatted, a message similar to the following is displayed:

```
Volume label (11 characters, ENTER for none)?
```

Cause: You are probably using MS-DOS. Some versions automatically prompt you for a volume label.

Solution: Press ↵ to indicate no volume label. Volume labels will be discussed later in this chapter. ■

Preparing Bootable Diskettes (FORMAT /S)

The previous section showed you how to format a diskette. A *bootable* diskette must contain the two hidden system files IBMBIO.COM and IBMDOS.COM and the visible system file COMMAND.COM. The /S (system) parameter can be used with the FORMAT command to prepare a bootable diskette.

Insert the DOS System diskette in drive A. With the cursor positioned after the A> prompt, type

```
FORMAT B: /S
```

and press ↵. After the FORMAT program is loaded into memory, it displays a message that asks you to insert a new diskette in drive B (Fig. 7.5). Insert a blank (target) diskette in drive B and press ↵. As soon as the target diskette is formatted, the /S parameter instructs the FORMAT program to transfer the three DOS system files from the diskette in drive A to the target diskette in drive B. When the transfer

Figure 7.5
When the FORMAT command is used with the /S (system) parameter to format a 360KB diskette, messages similar to these are displayed. Note that the three DOS system files occupy 78,848 bytes on the target diskette.

```
A>FORMAT B:/S
Insert new diskette for drive B:
and strike ENTER when ready

Format complete
System transferred

    362496 bytes total disk space
     78848 bytes used by system
    283648 bytes available on disk

Format another (Y/N)?
```

of the DOS system files is complete, FORMAT displays summary information indicating the number of bytes available on the target diskette followed by a prompt message that asks whether you want to format another diskette (Fig. 7.5). Type Y and press ↵ to repeat the above process, or type N and press ↵ to terminate the FORMAT command.

The space before the slash (/) in the above FORMAT command is optional. Since a slash is interpreted by DOS as a delimiter (separator), the space before the /S parameter is used only to help make the command more readable.

Any diskette that is formatted by the FORMAT command with the /S parameter can be used to boot the system, since it contains the three DOS system files. The disadvantage of having the three DOS system files on a diskette is that they occupy some of the diskette's usable space. As a general rule, you might want to put the DOS system files on your program diskettes but not on your data diskettes.

■ Keystroke Summary

Preparing a bootable diskette

Insert: DOS System diskette in drive A

Set: default drive to drive A

Type: FORMAT B: /S

Press: ↵

Insert: blank (target) diskette in drive B

Press: ↵

Type: Y to prepare another bootable diskette or

N to terminate the FORMAT command

Press: ↵

Transferring DOS to a Formatted Diskette (SYS)

The /S option on the FORMAT command is not the only method for creating a bootable diskette. The **SYS** (SYStem) command is an external DOS command that is used to copy the two DOS hidden files (IBMBIO.COM and IBMDOS.COM) to a formatted diskette. For this process to work, the formatted diskette must have an empty directory or the diskette must have been originally formatted with the /S or /B parameter. (See the DOS reference manual for information about the / B parameter.)

Insert the DOS System diskette in drive A and insert a formatted diskette with an empty directory in drive B. With the cursor positioned after the A > prompt, type

```
SYS B:
```

and press ⏎. After the SYS program is loaded into memory, it checks the directory of the diskette in drive B. If the directory is empty, SYS instructs DOS to copy the two DOS hidden files IBMBIO.COM and IBMDOS.COM from the DOS System diskette in drive A to the formatted diskette in drive B. When this process is complete, SYS displays the message

```
System transferred
```

before returning to command level.

At this point, two-thirds of the DOS system files have been transferred to the formatted diskette. The third DOS system file (COMMAND.COM) must now be copied to the formatted diskette. With the cursor positioned after the A > prompt, type

```
COPY COMMAND.COM B:
```

and press ⏎. This command copies the DOS file COMMAND.COM from the DOS System diskette in drive A to the diskette in drive B. When this process is complete, the COPY command displays the message

```
1 File(s) copied
```

before returning to command level. (A comprehensive discussion of the COPY command is given in Chapter 9.) Since the diskette in drive B now contains the three DOS system files, it can be used to boot the system.

■ *Keystroke Summary*

Transferring DOS to a formatted diskette

Insert: DOS System diskette in drive A

Set: default drive to drive A

Insert: formatted diskette with an empty directory in drive B

Type: SYS B:

Press: ⏎

Type: COPY COMMAND.COM B:

Press: ⏎

▪ What Can Go Wrong?

1. The SYS command displays the following message and returns to command level after it attempts to transfer the two DOS hidden files to a formatted diskette:

```
No room for system on destination disk
```

Cause: The SYS command cannot copy the two DOS hidden files to the formatted diskette because the directory of the formatted diskette is not empty.

Solution: In Chapters 8 and 9 you will learn about DOS commands that might be used to help correct this situation. At this point, however, the DOS hidden files cannot be transferred to this diskette. Consequently, you cannot make this diskette bootable. Try a different diskette.

2. The SYS command displays the following message after it attempts to transfer the two DOS hidden files to a diskette:

```
Insert destination disk in drive B
and strike any key when ready
```

Cause: The SYS command cannot copy the two DOS hidden files to the target diskette because it is not a formatted diskette.

Solution: Remove the unformatted target diskette from the diskette drive, insert a formatted diskette with an empty directory in the diskette drive, and press ⏎. If a formatted diskette with an empty directory is not available for your use, you need to terminate the SYS command. This can be accomplished by holding the Ctrl key down and typing C (denoted by Ctrl and C). This process is called **breaking out of a command** and may also be accomplished by holding the Ctrl key down and pressing Break (denoted by Ctrl and Break). Notice that DOS displays the characters ^C on the screen and returns you to command level. The Ctrl and C and Ctrl and Break key combinations give you a way to abort a DOS command. ▪

Formatting a Diskette with a Volume Label (FORMAT /V)

When you are working with several diskettes, you might want to assign a name to each of your diskettes to assist you with diskette identification. There are two ways that you can label a diskette. One is by writing information on a paper label and attaching it to the diskette jacket. This is an external label that can be read by you when the diskette is not in a drive. The second way is to have DOS place an identifying name (label) in the directory of the diskette. When this is done, you can direct DOS to display the diskette name on the screen (Chapter 8). This allows you to identify a diskette without having to remove it to read the paper label. This also allows you to identify a diskette that has lost its paper label. A name assigned to a disk by DOS is commonly referred to as a **volume label**. A volume label consists of one to eleven filename characters. You can also include one or more space characters in a volume label. The / **V** (volume label) parameter can be used with the FORMAT command to allow you to format a diskette and assign a volume label to the diskette. Additional DOS commands that allow you to display, assign, change, and remove a volume label will be introduced in Chapter 8.

Insert the DOS System diskette in drive A. With the cursor positioned after the A > prompt, type

```
FORMAT B: /V
```

and press ⏎. After the FORMAT program is loaded into memory, it displays a message that asks you to insert a new diskette in drive B. Insert a blank (target) diskette in drive B and press ⏎. As soon as the target diskette has been formatted, the / V parameter instructs the FORMAT program to display the following prompt message for a volume label:

```
Volume label (11 characters, ENTER for none)?
```

With the cursor positioned after the question mark (?), type the volume label SAMPLE-DISK (or a name of your choice) and press ⏎. If you press ⏎ without typing any characters, no volume label will be placed on the diskette. When a volume label is entered, the FORMAT command places the volume label in the diskette's directory and then displays summary information indicating the number of bytes available on the target diskette followed by a prompt message that asks if you want to format another diskette (Fig. 7.6). Type Y and press ⏎

Figure 7.6
When the FORMAT command is used with the /V (volume label) parameter to format a 360KB diskette, messages similar to these are displayed.

```
A>FORMAT B:/V
Insert new diskette for drive B:
and strike ENTER when ready

Format complete

Volume label (11 characters, ENTER for none)? SAMPLE-DISK

     362496 bytes total disk space
     362496 bytes available on disk

Format another (Y/N)?
```

to repeat the above process, or type N and press ⏎ to terminate the FORMAT command.

The space before the slash (/) in the above FORMAT command is optional. Since a slash is interpreted by DOS as a parameter field delimiter (separator), the space before the / V parameter is used only to help make the command more readable.

If you want to prepare a bootable diskette with a volume label, you can use both the /S and the /V parameters. Insert the DOS System diskette in drive A. With the cursor positioned after the A > prompt, type

```
FORMAT B:/S /V
```

and press ⏎. The prompts and messages generated by this FORMAT command are the same as those described above (Fig. 7.7).

■ *Keystroke Summary*

Formatting a diskette with a volume label

Insert:	DOS System diskette in drive A
Set:	default drive to drive A
Type:	FORMAT B: /V **or** FORMAT B: /S /V
Press:	⏎
Insert:	blank (target) diskette in drive B
Press:	⏎
Type:	*volume-label*
Press:	⏎

Figure 7.7
When the FORMAT command is used with the /S (system) and /V (volume label) parameters to format a 360KB diskette, messages similar to these are displayed.

```
A>FORMAT B:/S/V
Insert new diskette for drive B:
and strike ENTER when ready

Format complete
System transferred

Volume label (11 characters, ENTER for none)? SAMPLE-DISK

     362496 bytes total disk space
      78848 bytes used by system
     283648 bytes available on disk

Format another (Y/N)?
```

Type: Y   to prepare another diskette with a volume label
        or

        N   to terminate the FORMAT command

Press: ⏎

Summary

Topic or Feature	Command or Reference	Page
Format a diskette	FORMAT *d:* where *d:* denotes the specified drive Fig. 7.4	72
Format a bootable diskette	FORMAT *d:* /S where *d:* denotes the specified drive Figs. 7.5, 7.7	75
Format a diskette with a volume label	FORMAT *d:* /V where *d:* denotes the specified drive Figs. 7.6, 7.7	79
Format a bootable diskette with a volume label	FORMAT *d:* /S /V where *d:* denotes the specified drive Fig. 7.7	80
Transfer DOS to a formatted diskette	SYS *d:* and COPY COMMAND.COM *d:* where *d:* denotes the specified drive	77

Self-Test

1. Before a disk can be used by DOS, it must be _____. This process is accomplished by using the _____ command.

2. Addressing a disk for use by DOS is accomplished by subdividing the disk into concentric circles called _____ and into pie-shaped areas called _____.

3. The FORMAT command_____ the usable area of the disk by writing guidelines on the surface. It also marks_____ sectors so they are not subsequently used to store data.

4. The FORMAT command creates a_____ and a_____ for the disk and places a copy of the_____on the first sector.

5. The FORMAT command is potentially dangerous because it_____ any data that might exist on the target disk.

6. A bootable diskette must contain the three DOS system files _____ ,_____, and_____.

7. The _____ parameter is used with a FORMAT command to add the three system files to the disk.

8. The _____ parameter is used with a FORMAT command to add a volume label to the disk.

9. To use both the /S and /V parameters, type the FORMAT command_____.

10. The_____ command is used to transfer the two DOS hidden files to a formatted diskette with an empty directory.

Exercises

1. Use an appropriate DOS command to perform each of the assigned tasks.

   a. Format a data diskette with volume label *namef*#7-1a, where *name* denotes the first five characters of your last name or your entire last name (whichever is shorter) and *f* denotes the first character of your first name.

   b. Format a data diskette with volume label *namef*#7-1b, where *namef* is defined above.

2. Use the FORMAT command to format a bootable diskette with volume label BOOT-DISK. Use this diskette to boot the system.

3. Use an appropriate DOS command to perform each of the assigned tasks.

   a. Format a diskette without a volume label.

   b. Use the diskette prepared in part (a) to attempt to boot the system. (Remember that this diskette must be inserted in drive A.) Note the message displayed on the screen.

   c. Use the DOS System diskette to boot the system.

   d. Transfer the two DOS hidden files from the DOS System diskette to the formatted diskette.

   e. Use this modified diskette to attempt to boot the system. Note the message displayed on the screen.

   f. Use the DOS System diskette to boot the system.

   g. Copy the file COMMAND.COM from the DOS System diskette to the modified diskette.

   h. Use this modified diskette to boot the system.

   (This exercise shows that the three DOS System files must be on a diskette before it can be used to boot the system.)

■8

Displaying Information about a Diskette or Disk

The material in this chapter introduces the DOS commands that allow you to:

- display the contents of a disk's directory (DIR)
- display directory information for selected files using the wildcard file name characters * and ?
- send directory information to the printer using the output redirection operator >
- sort (SORT) directory information by using the piping operator
- display directory information one screen at a time (MORE)
- check a disk and memory for important information (CHKDSK)
- display and modify the volume label of a disk (VOL and LABEL)

Displaying the Table of Contents (Directory Information) of a Disk

In Chapter 7 you learned that a disk directory is created by the FORMAT command during the formatting process and serves as a table of contents for the information stored on a disk. Since information is stored as a file, DOS keeps track of this information through file entries in a directory. Each file entry contains a name for the file, an address (side, track, and sector numbers) specifying where the file is placed on the disk, the size of the file in bytes, and a date and time when the file was created or last modified. The **DIR** (DIRectory) command is an internal DOS command that allows you to display the contents of a disk's directory on the screen.

Displaying Complete Directory Information (DIR)

Boot DOS. Then insert any usable diskette in drive A; it need not be the DOS System diskette. With the cursor positioned after the A > prompt, type

```
DIR A:
```

and press ⏎. Since the DIR command is an internal DOS command, the DOS System diskette need not be available to execute this command. The DIR command instructs DOS to display the complete directory information from the diskette in drive A, the specified drive. When the DIR command completes its task, control returns to command level. The information displayed on the screen will be similar to Fig. 8.1. SAMPLE-DISK is the volume label of the diskette. If a disk contains no volume label, heading information similar to the following will be displayed:

```
Volume in drive A has no label
Directory of  A:\
```

Figure 8.1

When the DIR command is used to display the directory contents of a 360KB diskette in drive A, information similar to this is displayed.

```
A>DIR A:

 Volume in drive A is SAMPLE-DISK
 Directory of  A:\

COMMAND   COM     25307    3-17-87   12:00p
TREE      COM      3571    3-17-87   12:00p
FIND      EXE      6434    3-17-87   12:00p
FORMAT    COM     11616    3-18-87   12:00p
APPNDA    DOC     11776    7-15-87   10:49p
WSFORM    WKS     17024    9-16-88   10:43p
APPNDC    DOC      4096    1-31-89   10:52p
BUDGET88  WKS      9216   12-03-88   11:34p
BUDGFORM  WKS      5888    8-29-87   12:41a
APPNDA    ASC     10752    8-08-88   11:03p
APPNDC             2816    1-31-89   11:31p
FONT2     DOC      1536    5-06-88    1:35a
FONT11    DOC      1536    8-04-88   12:21a
APPNDA           73216   10-26-88   11:12p
APPND             7936    3-05-89   11:22p
        15 File(s)      110592 bytes free

A>
```

Notice that the heading information displayed by the DIR command also includes a message identifying the path to the directory. In this case the path includes the disk drive specification A: followed by a backslash (\). A:\ specifies the root (main) directory of the diskette in drive A. You will learn in Chapter 11 that a disk can contain subdirectories and that directory paths are used to access these subdirectories.

Immediately following the heading information is a list of file names for all visible (user) files that are contained in the disk's directory. Notice from the example in Fig. 8.1 that each line contains a filename followed by the filename extension (if any), the number of bytes in the file, and a date and time indicating when the file was created or last modified. At the conclusion of the list of files, the DIR command displays a summary line similar to the following:

```
27 File(s)      79872 bytes free
```

This line shows the number of files listed from the directory and the number of free bytes available for use on the disk. When the DIR command is finished listing the directory information, control returns to command level, and the A > prompt is displayed.

Remove the diskette from drive A and insert it in drive B. With the cursor positioned after the A > prompt, type

```
DIR B:
```

and press ⏎. The DIR command instructs DOS to display the complete directory information from the diskette in drive B, the specified drive.

Remove the diskette from drive B and insert it into drive A. With the cursor positioned after the A > prompt, type

```
DIR
```

and press ⏎. Notice that the DIR command instructs DOS to display the complete directory information from the disk in the default drive—in this case, drive A. If you want to display the directory contents of a disk in the default drive, you need not specify a disk drive after the DIR command.

■ *Keystroke Summary*

Displaying complete directory information

Insert: any usable diskette in drive A

Set: default drive to drive A

Type: DIR A: or DIR

Press: ⏎

Pausing after Each Screen Image (DIR /P)

Insert the DOS System diskette in drive A. With the cursor positioned after the A > prompt, type

```
DIR
```

and press ⏎. Notice that the entries from the directory of the DOS System diskette cannot all be displayed in one screen image. Some of the directory information scrolls off of the top of the screen before it can be read. There are two ways to pause the output to the screen so that you have an opportunity to read it. One method involves sending an interrupt signal to DOS instructing it to suspend output to the screen until it receives a second command telling it to continue. An **interrupt signal** is a signal that causes a break in the normal sequence of executing instructions. Interrupting the flow of information to the screen is accomplished by holding the Ctrl key down and typing S (denoted by Ctrl *and* S).

With the DOS System diskette inserted in drive A and the cursor positioned after the A > prompt, type

```
DIR
```

and press ⏎. As the directory information begins to appear on the screen, hold the Ctrl key down and type S. Notice that the output to the screen immediately stops. Type S again, and the output will resume. You instruct DOS to suspend output to the screen by holding the Ctrl key down and typing S; you instruct DOS to resume sending output to the screen by typing any character key on the keyboard. Note that holding the Ctrl key down and then pressing the NumLock key (denoted by Ctrl *and* NumLock) has a similar effect to the Ctrl *and* S key combination. If a personal computer has an enhanced IBM PC AT keyboard (a 101 style keyboard), then pressing the *Pause* key has a similar effect.

The second way to pause output from the DIR command to the screen is to use the /P (pause) parameter in the DIR command. With the DOS System diskette inserted in drive A and with the cursor positioned after the A > prompt, type

```
DIR /P
```

and press ⏎. Note that you need not specify A: in the DIR command (DIR A: /P), since drive A is the default drive. The /P parameter instructs the DIR command to pause the directory output listing after a full screen of directory entries is displayed. When the directory output pauses, the DIR command displays a message similar to the following:

```
Strike a key when ready . . .
```

Type any character key or press ⏎, and the display continues, pausing each time the screen is filled with new information. This process might be repeated several times for directories with a large number of entries.

▪ *Keystroke Summary*

Displaying directory information one screen at a time

Insert: a diskette in drive A that contains a directory with a large number of entries (for example, the DOS System diskette)

Set: the default drive to drive A

Type: DIR /P

Press: ⏎

Displaying Abbreviated Directory Information (DIR /W)

The DIR command can also be used to display the directory entries of a disk in an abbreviated format by using the /**W** (wide-line) parameter in the DIR command. The /W parameter instructs the DIR command to display only the filenames and filename extensions in a wide-line format.

Insert any usable diskette in drive A. With the cursor positioned after the A > prompt, type

DIR /W

and press ⏎. Again note that you need not specify A: in the DIR command (DIR A: /W), since drive A is the default drive. The /W parameter instructs the DIR command to display only the filenames and extensions from the directory of the diskette in drive A in a wide-line format. The format of the displayed information resembles Fig. 8.2.

Figure 8.2
When the DIR command is used with the /W (wide-line) parameter to display the file names from the directory of a diskette in drive A, information similar to this is displayed.

```
A>DIR /W

 Volume in drive A is SAMPLE-DISK
 Directory of  A:\

COMMAND COM    TREE    COM    FIND     EXE    FORMAT    COM    APPNDA  DOC
WSFORM  WKS    APPNDC  DOC    BUDGET88 WKS    BUDGFORM  WKS    APPNDA  ASC
APPNDC         FONT2   DOC    FONT11   DOC    APPNDA           APPND
        15 File(s)    110592 bytes free

A>
```

Displaying directory information in a wide-line format

Insert: any usable diskette in drive A

Set: default drive to drive A

Type: DIR /W

Press: ⏎

Displaying Directory Information for Selected Files

The DIR command can be used to display directory information about a single file or about groups of files having similar filenames and/or extensions. The wildcard file name characters * and ?, introduced in Chapter 5, are used extensively to specify groups of files in the DIR command.

Insert the DOS System diskette in drive A. With the cursor positioned after the A > prompt, type

```
DIR FORMAT.COM
```

and press ⏎. This DIR command displays one file name:

```
Volume in drive A has no label
Directory of  A:\

FORMAT   COM    11616    3-18-87   12:00p
        1 File(s)       79872 bytes free
```

You can also request a list of all file names that begin with the same letter. For example, with the cursor positioned after the A > prompt, type

```
DIR C*
```

and press ⏎. The C* specification instructs the DIR command to display all file names in the default drive (drive A) diskette's directory that begin with the character C and have any extension. Directory information similar to the following is displayed:

```
Volume in drive A has no label
Directory of  A:\

COMMAND   COM    25307    3-17-87   12:00p
CHKDSK    COM     9850    3-18-87   12:00p
COMP      COM     4214    3-17-87   12:00p
         3 File(s)       79872 bytes free
```

A list of all file names that have the same extensions might prove useful. For example, with the cursor positioned after the A > prompt, type

```
DIR *.EXE
```

and press ⏎. The *.EXE specification instructs the DIR command to display all file names that have .EXE as an extension. Directory information similar to the following is displayed:

```
Volume in drive A has no label
Directory of  A:\

FASTOPEN EXE     3919    3-17-87   12:00p
REPLACE  EXE    11775    3-17-87   12:00p
APPEND   EXE     5825    3-17-87   12:00p
ATTRIB   EXE     9529    3-17-87   12:00p
FIND     EXE     6434    3-17-87   12:00p
JOIN     EXE     8969    3-17-87   12:00p
SHARE    EXE     8608    3-17-87   12:00p
SORT     EXE     1977    3-17-87   12:00p
SUBST    EXE     9909    3-17-87   12:00p
XCOPY    EXE    11247    3-17-87   12:00p
       10 File(s)     79872 bytes free
```

Remove the DOS System diskette from drive A and insert it in drive B. With the cursor positioned after the A > prompt, type

```
DIR B:F*.COM
```

and press ⏎. The B:F*.COM specification instructs the DIR command to display all file names in the directory of the diskette in the specified drive (drive B) that begin with the character F and have .COM as an extension. Directory information similar to the following is displayed:

```
Volume in drive B has no label
Directory of  B:\

FORMAT   COM    11616    3-18-87   12:00p
        1 File(s)     79872 bytes free
```

Assume that SAMPLE-DISK denotes the diskette used to generate the information in Fig. 8.1 and that SAMPLE-DISK has been inserted in drive A. The next few examples illustrate the effect of the wildcard file name characters (* and ?) when they are used in the DIR command to access the directory of SAMPLE-DISK.

With the cursor positioned after the A > prompt, type

```
DIR BUDG*.*
```

and press ⏎. The BUDG*.* specification instructs the DIR command to display all file names in the directory of SAMPLE-DISK that begin with BUDG and have any extension. This DIR command would display the following directory information from SAMPLE-DISK:

```
Volume in drive A is SAMPLE-DISK
Directory of  A:\

BUDGET88 WKS     9216  12-03-88  11:34p
BUDGFORM WKS     5888   8-29-87  12:41a
         2 File(s)    110592 bytes free
```

With the cursor positioned after the A > prompt, type

```
DIR *.
```

and press ⏎. The *. specification instructs the DIR command to display all file names in the directory of SAMPLE-DISK that have no extension. This DIR command would display the following directory information from SAMPLE-DISK:

```
Volume in drive A is SAMPLE-DISK
Directory of  A:\

APPNDC         2816   1-31-89  11:13p
APPNDA        73216  10-26-88  11:12p
APPND          7936   3-05-89  11:22p
         3 File(s)    110592 bytes free
```

With the cursor positioned after the A > prompt, type

```
DIR APPNDA.*
```

and press ⏎. The APPNDA.* specification instructs the DIR command to display all file names in the directory of SAMPLE-DISK that have the same filename—in this case, APPNDA—and any extension. This DIR command would display the following directory information from SAMPLE-DISK:

```
Volume in drive A is SAMPLE-DISK
Directory of  A:\

APPNDA   DOC  11776   7-15-87  10:49p
APPNDA   ASC  10752   8-08-88  11:03p
APPNDA        73216  10-26-88  11:12p
         3 File(s)    110592 bytes free
```

With the cursor positioned after the A > prompt, type

```
DIR APPND?
```

and press ⏎. The APPND? specification instructs the DIR command to display all file names in the directory of SAMPLE-DISK that begin with the same first five characters—in this case, APPND—, have at most six characters in the filename, and have any extension. This DIR command would display the following directory information from SAMPLE-DISK:

```
Volume in drive A is SAMPLE-DISK
Directory of  A:\

APPNDA    DOC    11776   7-15-87   10:49p
APPNDC    DOC     4096   1-31-89   10:52p
APPNDA    ASC    10752   8-08-88   11:03p
APPNDC           2816   1-31-89   11:13p
APPNDA          73216  10-26-88   11:12p
APPND            7936   3-05-89   11:22p
        6 File(s)      110592 bytes free
```

■ *What Can Go Wrong?*

1. The DIR command displays the following message:

```
File not found
```

Cause: The directory of the disk contains no user files or it contains no file names as specified in the DIR command.

Solution: Check the DIR command line to see whether it contains any errors in the file specification. For example, you might have typed V* instead of C* in the command. If the DIR command that you entered is correct, then either the disk's directory contains no user files or it contains no file names that satisfy the file specification in the DIR command.

2. The DIR command displays the following message:

```
General Failure error reading drive A
Abort, Retry, Fail?
```

Cause: The diskette is not formatted, or its format is incompatible with the diskette drive that is attempting to read it.

Solution: If the diskette is not formatted, then the diskette cannot be accessed by any DOS command. If the diskette is formatted, it might have a format that is not compatible with the diskette drive trying to read it. For example, a 1.2MB (high-density) diskette cannot be read by a 360KB diskette drive. If you want the DIR command to attempt to read the directory again, type R. If you want to abort the DIR command, type A, and the system returns to command level. ■

Sending Directory Information to the Printer (DIR > PRN)

In the previous sections the output of the DIR command was displayed on the screen. DOS gives you the capability to **redirect** (send) the output from the DIR command to the printer to get a **hard copy** (printed copy) of the directory information. This is accomplished by using the **output redirection operator** > in the DOS command sequence.

Insert the DOS System diskette in drive A. Make sure that your printer is turned on and ready to print. With the cursor positioned after the A> prompt, type

```
DIR > PRN
```

and press ⏎. The output redirection operator > instructs DOS to send the output from the DIR command to the printer that is specified by PRN. Notice that the directory information is not displayed on the screen. When the printing is completed, DOS returns to command level.

■ *Keystroke Summary*

Sending directory information to the printer

Insert:	any usable diskette in drive A
Ready:	printer
Set:	default drive to drive A
Type:	DIR > PRN
Press:	⏎

■ *What Can Go Wrong?*

1. After you enter the command DIR > PRN, your computer system appears to stop and will not respond to anything that you type. After approximately one minute the following message is displayed:

```
Not ready error writing device PRN
Abort, Retry, Ignore, Fail?
```

Cause: Either your personal computer has no printer or the printer is not ready to print.

Solution: If your personal computer has no printer, type A after the question mark (?) to abort the DOS command, and the system will return to command level. If your personal computer has a printer attached to it, make sure that the printer is turned on and that it is ready to print. After you have readied the printer, type R to instruct DOS to retry sending the information to the printer. ■

Displaying Directory Information in Alphabetical Order (DIR | SORT)

Directory entries can be displayed in alphabetical order by **piping** (sending) the output from the DIR command to the SORT command. The **SORT** command is an external DOS command that sorts each line it receives into alphabetical order. The symbol | is used to specify piping. On a standard IBM PC keyboard it is located just to the left of the space bar; press ⇧ and the backslash key.

Insert the DOS System diskette in drive A. With the cursor positioned after the A> prompt, type

```
DIR | SORT
```

and press ⏎. The list of file names will be displayed in alphabetical order. The piping operator causes the output from the DIR command to be held in a temporary file on the diskette in the default drive instead of being sent to the screen. That ouput is subsequently used as input to the SORT command. Piping will not work if the diskette in the default drive is write protected because DOS will not be able to write the temporary files to the diskette.

▪ *Keystroke Summary*

Displaying directory information in alphabetical order

Insert: DOS System diskette in drive A

Insert: target diskette in drive B

Set: default drive to drive A

Type: DIR B: I SORT

Press: ⏎

▪ *What Can Go Wrong?*

1. The following message is displayed:

```
Bad command or file name
```

Cause: Either you misspelled a command name or the SORT command is not on the diskette in drive A. (SORT is an external command.)

Solution: Make sure the DOS system disk is in drive A. Issue a DIR command with no piping and make sure the SORT command is present. Then reissue the command. ▪

Displaying DIrectory Information One Screen at a Time (DIR I MORE)

The piping operator has many uses. For example, you can display the output from any command one screen at a time by piping it to the MORE command (another external command). Try it. With the DOS System diskette in drive A, type the command

```
DIR | More
```

and press ⏎. The first screen of directory entries will appear, and then the display will pause. Press any key (for example, the space bar) to view the next screen of entries. After all the directory entries have been displayed, the system will return to command mode.

▪ *Keystroke Summary*

Displaying directory information one screen at a time

Insert: DOS System diskette in drive A

Insert: target diskette in drive B

Set: default drive to drive A

Type: DIR B: I MORE

Press: ⏎

Checking a Diskette/Disk (CHKDSK)

Even though the DIR command displays a great deal of information about the contents of a disk, it does not give you a complete picture. The **CHKDSK** (CHecK DiSK) command is an external DOS command that can be used to display certain important characteristics of a disk and memory that are not displayed by the DIR command. More specifically,

1. CHKDSK analyzes the directory of the specified disk, comparing the directory entries with the locations and lengths of the files. It reports any errors that it finds.

2. CHKDSK displays information about how the disk space is being utilized. Information about bad sectors (if they exist) is also reported to you.

3. CHKDSK displays a report on the amount of memory in your personal computer that DOS recognizes and the amount of memory that is free for use. The maximum amount of memory that DOS Version 3.30 and previous versions of DOS recognize in an IBM Personal Computer is 640KB. Your personal computer may have additional memory installed that is not recognized by DOS.

4. CHKDSK can be used to display the file names from the directory of a disk for both user and hidden files.

Using CHKDSK to Display Summary Information about a Disk and Memory

Insert the DOS System diskette in drive A. With the cursor positioned after the A > prompt, type

    CHKDSK A:

and press ⏎. Since CHKDSK is an external DOS command, it must be loaded into memory. Once the loading process is complete, DOS initiates the execution of the CHKDSK program, which analyzes the disk in the specified or default drive—in this case, drive A. When the CHKDSK program completes the check disk process, it displays a summary of the total disk space and a summary of total memory in your personal computer (Fig. 8.3) before the system returns to command level. Note that the drive specifier A: in the above command is not necessary, since drive A is the default drive.

The CHKDSK status report in Fig. 8.3 contains two parts. The first part of the status report tells you that the DOS System diskette contains 27 user files occupying 229,376 bytes of disk space, two hidden files occupying 53,248 bytes of disk space, and 79,872 bytes of free space on the disk. If the checked disk had contained any bad sectors, the first part of the status report would also have included a statement specifying the number of bytes in bad sectors.

Figure 8.3
When the CHKDSK command is used to check the contents of a disk—in this case, the DOS System diskette—information similar to this is displayed.

```
A>CHKDSK A:

   362496 bytes total disk space
    53248 bytes in 2 hidden files
   229376 bytes in 27 user files
    79872 bytes available on disk

   655360 bytes total memory
   600160 bytes free

A>
```

The second part of the CHKDSK status report states the number of bytes of total memory recognized by DOS and the number of bytes of free memory in your personal computer. The memory information in Fig. 8.3 tells you that the personal computer contains 655,360 bytes of total memory recognized by DOS and that 600,160 bytes of this memory are free. The difference between the bytes of total memory and the bytes of free memory is the amount of memory being used by DOS to house the three DOS system files and certain DOS support programs.

If you want to check the contents of a diskette other than the DOS System diskette, you should perform the following steps. Insert the DOS System diskette in drive A and the diskette you want to check in drive B. With the cursor positioned after the A > prompt, type

```
CHKDSK B:
```

and press ⏎. After the CHKDSK program is loaded into memory from the DOS System diskette in drive A, it does a disk check of the disk in the specified drive—in this case, drive B—and displays a summary similar to the one given in Fig. 8.3.

▪ *Keystroke Summary*

Checking a diskette and memory for summary information

Insert: DOS System diskette in drive A

Insert: diskette to be checked in drive B

Set: default drive to drive A

Type: CHKDSK B:

Press: ⏎

Using CHKDSK to Display Hidden and User File Names

The DIR command lists all the user files in a disk's directory but gives you no information about any hidden files. The CHKDSK command gives you the number of hidden files and the number of user files in a disk's directory but not the names of those files. To obtain a complete list of the file names for both user and hidden files, use the / **V** (view) parameter with the CHKDSK command.

Insert the DOS System diskette in drive A. With the cursor positioned after the A > prompt, type

    CHKDSK /V

and press ⏎. After the CHKDSK program is loaded into memory, it does a disk check of the DOS System diskette in drive A and displays the names of all files, hidden and user, from the diskette's directory before it displays the CHKDSK status report. Recall that holding the Ctrl key down while typing S allows you to control the flow of output to the screen. Note that the two DOS hidden files, IBMBIO.COM and IBMDOS.COM, are the first two entries in the displayed directory list.

If you want to display the names of all files in the directory of a diskette other than the DOS System diskette, you should perform the following steps. Insert the DOS System diskette in drive A and the diskette you want to check in drive B. With the cursor positioned after the A > prompt, type

    CHKDSK B: /V

and press ⏎. After the CHKDSK program is loaded into memory from the DOS System diskette in drive A, it does a disk check of the disk in the specified drive—in this case, drive B—and displays a summary similar to the one given in the second half of Fig. 8.4. Notice the difference between the information generated by the DIR command and the CHKDSK command in Fig. 8.4. The DIR command displays only directory information about user files. The CHKDSK command with the / V parameter displays the names of all files, both hidden and user, in a disk's directory. Note that the two DOS hidden files, IBMBIO.COM and IBMDOS.COM, are listed and that the volume label of the diskette, SAMP-DISK, is displayed as a hidden file name.

■ *Keystroke Summary*

Displaying hidden and user file names

Insert:	DOS System diskette in drive A
Insert:	diskette to be checked in drive B
Set:	default drive to drive A
Type:	CHKDSK B: /V
Press:	⏎

Figure 8.4

When the DIR command and the CHKDSK command with the /V (view) option are used to display directory information about the same diskette, information similar to this is displayed.

```
A>DIR B:

 Volume in drive B is SAMP-DISK
 Directory of  B:\

COMMAND   COM    25307    3-17-87   12:00p
FIND      EXE     6434    3-17-87   12:00p
FORMAT    COM    11616    3-18-87   12:00p
WSFORM    WKS    17024    9-16-88   10:43p
         4 File(s)     246784 bytes free


A>CHKDSK B:/V
Volume SAMP-DISK    created Aug 8, 1988 6:52p
Directory B:\
        B:\IBMBIO.COM
        B:\IBMDOS.COM
        B:\COMMAND.COM
        B:\SAMP-DIS.K
        B:\FIND.EXE
        B:\FORMAT.COM
        B:\WSFORM.WKS

   362496 bytes total disk space
    53248 bytes in 3 hidden files
    62464 bytes in 4 user files
   246784 bytes available on disk

   655360 bytes total memory
   600160 bytes free

A>
```

■ *What Can Go Wrong?*

1. After you enter the CHKDSK command, the following message is displayed:

```
Bad command or file name
```

Cause: Either you made an error in typing CHKDSK or the CHKDSK program is not available on the disk in the default or specified drive.

Solution: Check the characters you typed for CHKDSK and retype the command if you made an error. If there is no error in what you typed, then the CHKDSK program is not on the disk in the default or specified drive. If the CHKDSK program is not on the diskette being accessed, replace that diskette with the DOS System diskette and retype the command. ■

Diskette/Disk Volume Label

In Chapter 7 you learned that names can be assigned to diskettes to assist you with diskette identification. The / V option was used with the FORMAT command to assign a **volume label** (name) to a diskette at the completion of the formatting process. DOS supports a separate command that allows you to assign a volume label to any diskette or hard disk.

Displaying a Volume Label (VOL)

The **VOL** (VOLume) command is an internal DOS command that allows you to display the volume identification label of the disk in the specified or default drive.

Insert the DOS System diskette in drive A. With the cursor positioned after the A > prompt, type

        VOL A:

and press ⏎. The VOL command looks for a volume label in the directory of the diskette in the specified drive—in this case, drive A. If the diskette contains no volume label, the VOL command displays a message similar to

        Volume in drive A has no label

If the diskette in drive A had contained the volume label SYSTEM-DISK, then the VOL command would have displayed

        Volume in drive A is SYSTEM-DISK

Note that the drive specifier A: in the above command is not necessary, since drive A is the default drive. To display the volume label of a disk in a different drive, you should perform the following steps. Insert the diskette to be checked in drive B. With the cursor positioned after the A > prompt, type

        VOL B:

and press ⏎. The VOL command displays one of the above two messages, depending upon whether or not the diskette contains a volume label.

■ *Keystroke Summary*

Displaying the volume label of a disk

  Insert: diskette to be checked for a volume label in drive A

     Set: default drive to drive A

    Type: VOL

   Press: ⏎

Assigning, Changing, and Removing a Volume Label (LABEL)

The **LABEL** command is an external DOS command that allows you to assign a volume label to a disk that has been formatted without one, change a volume label that was previously assigned to a disk, and remove a volume label from a disk.

Insert the DOS System diskette in drive A. With the cursor positioned after the A > prompt, type

```
LABEL A:
```

and press ⏎. After the LABEL program is loaded into memory, it displays a message about the disk in the specified or default drive; for example:

```
Volume in drive A has no label
Volume label (11 characters, ENTER for none)?
```

Recall from Chapter 7 that the volume label can be up to eleven characters long. With the cursor positioned after the question mark (?), type SYSTEM-DISK (or a label of your choice) and press ⏎. The DOS System diskette is assigned the volume label you typed, and then the system returns to command level. To verify that SYSTEM-DISK is the volume label for the diskette in drive A, type

```
VOL
```

and press ⏎. The VOL command will display a message similar to the following:

```
Volume in drive A is SYSTEM-DISK
```

The LABEL command can also be used to change or delete the volume label. To change or delete the volume label on the DOS System diskette in drive A, type

```
LABEL
```

after the A> prompt and press ⏎. Notice that the drive specification A: is optional, since drive A is the default drive. After the LABEL program is loaded into memory, it displays a message similar to the following:

```
Volume in drive A is SYSTEM-DISK
Volume Label (11 characters, ENTER for none)?
```

To change the volume label, simply enter a different volume label after the question mark (?); for example, type DOS-SYS-DSK and press ⏎ to change the volume label of the DOS System diskette in drive A to DOS-SYS-DSK. If you wish to delete the SYSTEM-DISK volume label, just press ⏎, and the LABEL command displays a message similar to the following:

```
Delete current volume label (Y/N)?
```

With the cursor positioned after this prompt message, type Y and press ⏎, and the volume label will be removed from the DOS System diskette.

Similar steps can be used to assign a volume label to a diskette other than the DOS System diskette. Insert the DOS System diskette in drive A and the diskette you want to relabel in drive B. With the cursor positioned after the A > prompt, type

```
LABEL B:
```

and press ⏎. The remaining steps match those already described.

When you assign a volume label to a disk, you can use the CHKDSK command with the / V option to observe that the volume label has been entered into the directory of the disk as a hidden file entry.

■ *Keystroke Summary*

Assigning a volume label to a diskette

Insert:	DOS System diskette in drive A
Set:	default drive to drive A
Insert:	diskette to be assigned a volume label in drive B
Type:	LABEL B:
Press:	⏎
Type:	*volume-label*
Press:	⏎

Summary

Topic or Feature	Command or Reference	Page
Display complete directory information	DIR Fig. 8.1	84
Control the flow of directory information to the screen	DIR /P Ctrl *and* S	86
Display directory entries in wide-line format	DIR /W Fig. 8.2	87
Display directory information for selected files	use of the wildcard characters * and ? in the file specification of the DIR command	88

Topic or Feature	Command or Reference	Page
Send directory informa- tion to the printer	DIR > PRN	91
Display information in alphabetical order	DIR | SORT	92
Display information one screen at a time	DIR | MORE	93
Check a disk and memory	CHKDSK Fig. 8.2	94
Check a disk and display hidden and user file names	CHKDSK /V Fig. 8.3	96
Display a disk volume label	VOL	98
Assign, change, and delete a disk volume label	LABEL	99

Self-Test

1. The _____ command is used to display information from a disk's directory.

2. To pause a directory listing, press_____ or add a _____ parameter to the DIR command.

3. To display directory entries in wide line format, add a _____ parameter to the DIR command.

4. To display all file names in the directory of the disk in drive A that begin with T and have any extension, type the command _____ . To display all the file names in the directory of the diskette in drive B that have extension .WK, type the command _____ .

5. The _____ operator can be used to redirect DIR command output to the printer.

6. The piping operator, _____ ,can be used to send the output from the DIR command to another command.

7. The _____ command outputs data in alphabetical order. The _____ command can be used to display data one screen at a time.

8. The _____ command is used to display utilization information about a disk and memory.

9. The _____ command can be used to display a disk's volume label.

10. The _____ command can be used to assign, change, and delete a disk's volume label.

Exercises

1. Use an appropriate DOS command to display the following groups of file names from the directory of the DOS System diskette.

   a. File names for all user files.

   b. File names for all user files that have .COM as an extension.

   c. File names for all user files that have .EXE as an extension.

   d. File names for all user files that begin with the character F and have .COM as an extension.

   e. File names for all user files that begin with the character S.

   f. File names for all files both user and hidden.

2. Use the output redirection operator to obtain a hard copy listing for each of the sets of file names generated in Exercise 1.

3. Turn the printer echo mode on so that you can obtain a hard copy listing for each of the sets of file names generated in Exercise 1. Then turn the printer echo mode off.

4. a. Use a DOS command to display the amount of memory that DOS recognizes in your personal computer and the amount of memory that is free for use by an application program.

   b. Use the output redirection operator to obtain a hard copy listing of the information generated from the command in part (a).

5. Use an appropriate DOS command to perform each of the assigned tasks.

   a. Format a bootable diskette with volume label BOOT-DISK.

   b. Display all file names for both user and hidden files on the diskette prepared in part (a).

   c. Use the output redirection operator to obtain a hard copy listing of the output from the command in part (b).

   d. Delete the volume label from the diskette.

   e. Show that the diskette has no volume label.

   f. Assign the volume label *namef*#8-5 to the diskette, where name denotes the first six characters of your last name or your entire last name (whichever is shorter) and *f* denotes the first character of your first name.

g. Display the volume label on the screen.

6. The CHKDSK command can also be used to determine whether a file is stored in contiguous or adjacent sectors or stored in disjoint (separated) blocks (sectors). A file is **fragmented** if it is stored on a disk in nonadjacent sectors. Disks that have a lot of file creation and deletion activity become fragmented, since disk space is not allocated sequentially. A computer user is interested in file fragmentation because a disk drive uses more time to read and write fragmented files than it does to access files stored on contiguous sectors. Assume that the DOS System diskette is in drive A and that drive A is the default drive.

   a. Use the command CHKDSK *.* to determine whether the DOS System diskette has any fragmented files.

   b. Use the output redirection operator to obtain a hard copy listing of the output from the command in part (a).

   c. Insert a diskette in drive B and use the command CHKDSK B:*.* to determine whether this diskette has any fragmented files.

7. Insert the DOS System diskette (or a diskette supplied by your instructor) in drive A. Assume that drive A is the default drive.

   a. Use the DOS command sequence DIR | SORT to display the directory information for the DOS System diskette in alphabetical order.

   b. Insert a usable diskette in drive B, set the default drive to drive B, and use the DOS command sequence DIR A: | A:SORT to display the directory information for the DOS System diskette in alphabetical order.

   c. Use the output redirection operator to obtain a hard copy listing of the output from the commands in parts (a) and (b).

■9

Manipulating Files and File Characteristics

The material in this chapter introduces the DOS commands that allow you to:

- copy a specified file to the same disk or to another disk (COPY)
- copy groups of files from one disk to another disk using the wildcard file name character *
- remove file names from the directory of a disk (DEL or ERASE)
- change a file name (RENAME)
- create a text file by copying data from the keyboard (COPY CON)
- display the contents of a text file (TYPE)

Copying One User File (COPY)

To make a copy of a single user file, you must know the name of the file to be copied, the disk drive that contains the disk on which the file is stored, and the location of the file on that disk. This information is referred to as the **file specification**. Normally, a file specification consists of a filename and an optional filename extension. Sometimes a file specification includes a disk drive specifier and/or information about where to locate the file on a disk (path name). The **COPY** command is an internal DOS command that allows you to copy a specified file to the same disk using a different filename and/or extension or to a second disk using the same filename and extension or a different filename and/or extension.

Since the COPY command is an internal DOS command, the DOS System diskette need not be available to use the COPY command. However, the DOS System diskette will be used in the next two sections as a source of user files to help illustrate the COPY command. Refer to Fig. 9.1 for a directory listing.

Figure 9.1
When the DIR command is used to display the directory contents of a 360KB DOS System diskette for Version 3.30, information similar to this is displayed.

```
A>DIR

 Volume in drive A has no label
 Directory of  A:\

COMMAND  COM    25307    3-17-87   12:00p
FASTOPEN EXE     3919    3-17-87   12:00p
REPLACE  EXE    11775    3-17-87   12:00p
SYS      COM     4766    3-17-87   12:00p
ASSIGN   COM     1561    3-17-87   12:00p
BACKUP   COM    31913    3-18-87   12:00p
APPEND   EXE     5825    3-17-87   12:00p
ATTRIB   EXE     9529    3-17-87   12:00p
CHKDSK   COM     9850    3-18-87   12:00p
COMP     COM     4214    3-17-87   12:00p
FIND     EXE     6434    3-17-87   12:00p
DISKCOMP COM     5879    3-17-87   12:00p
DISKCOPY COM     6295    3-17-87   12:00p
EDLIN    COM     7526    3-17-87   12:00p
FORMAT   COM    11616    3-18-87   12:00p
GRAFTABL COM     6128    3-17-87   12:00p
GRAPHICS COM     3300    3-17-87   12:00p
LABEL    COM     2377    3-17-87   12:00p
MORE     COM      313    3-17-87   12:00p
PRINT    COM     9026    3-17-87   12:00p
RECOVER  COM     4299    3-18-87   12:00p
JOIN     EXE     8969    3-17-87   12:00p
TREE     COM     3571    3-17-87   12:00p
SHARE    EXE     8608    3-17-87   12:00p
SORT     EXE     1977    3-17-87   12:00p
SUBST    EXE     9909    3-17-87   12:00p
XCOPY    EXE    11247    3-17-87   12:00p
        27 File(s)     79872 bytes free

A>
```

Copying One User File to the Same Disk, Different Filename and/or Extension

Boot DOS and leave the DOS System diskette in drive A. With the cursor positioned after the A > prompt, type:

```
COPY A:FORMAT.COM A:FORMAT.BAK
```

and press ⏎. This COPY command instructs DOS to copy a single file—in this case, FORMAT.COM—from the diskette in drive A to the diskette in drive A, giving it the same filename but a different extension. The first parameter in the COPY command identifies the file to be copied and is called the **source file specification**. The second parameter identifies the destination of the copied file and is called the **target file specification**. The term file specification is sometimes denoted by the abbreviation **filespec**. In this example, A:FORMAT.COM is the source file specification, and A:FORMAT.BAK is the target file specification (Fig. 9.2). When the COPY command finishes copying the specified file, a message similar to the following is displayed:

```
1 File(s) copied
```

The DOS System diskette in drive A now contains two copies of the FORMAT program, the original copy and the newly created FORMAT.BAK. The DIR command can be used to verify that there are two copies of the FORMAT program. With the cursor positioned after the A > prompt, type

```
DIR FORMAT.*
```

and press ⏎. Directory information similar to the following is dis-

Figure 9.2
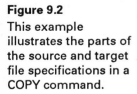
This example illustrates the parts of the source and target file specifications in a COPY command.

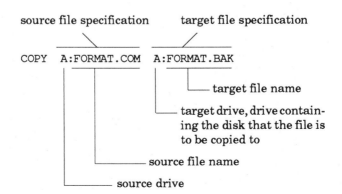

played:

```
Volume in drive A has no label
Directory of  A:\

FORMAT    COM    11616    3-18-87   12:00p
FORMAT    BAK    11616    3-18-87   12:00p
         2 File(s)      67584 bytes free
```

With the DOS System diskette in drive A and the cursor positioned after the A > prompt, type

```
COPY FORMAT.COM FORMT.*
```

and press ⏎. This COPY command instructs DOS to copy FORMAT.COM from the diskette in the default drive (drive A) to the diskette in the default drive (drive A), giving the new copy a different filename (FORMT) but the same extension (.COM). This example illustrates two things. First, when the default drive is the disk drive for the source file specification (or the target file specification), the drive letter need not be specified in that COPY command parameter. Consequently, the command COPY FORMAT.COM FORMAT.BAK could have been typed in place of the first COPY command in this section. Second, when the wildcard file name character * is used in place of a filename (or an extension) in the target file specification of a COPY command, the corresponding filename (or file extension) in the source file specification is substituted for the * character. The command COPY FORMAT.COM *.BAK could have been typed in place of the first COPY command in this section.

With the cursor positioned after the A > prompt, type

```
DIR FOR*
```

and press ⏎. Directory information similar to the following is displayed:

```
Volume in drive A has no label
Directory of  A:\

FORMAT    COM    11616    3-18-87   12:00p
FORMAT    BAK    11616    3-18-87   12:00p
FORMT     COM    11616    3-18-87   12:00p
         3 File(s)      55296 bytes free
```

This directory information indicates that the DOS System diskette now contains three copies of the FORMAT program: FORMAT.COM, FORMAT.BAK, and FORMT.COM. You will learn how to remove the extra files from the directory before the end of this chapter.

Copying one user file to the same disk

Insert: diskette in drive A that contains a file to be copied

Set: default drive to drive A

Type: COPY *source-file-name target-file-name*

Press: ⏎

Copying One User File to a Second Disk

The COPY command is normally used to copy named files from a disk in one drive (source disk) to a disk in a second drive (target disk) using either the same or different filenames and extensions. Insert the DOS System diskette in drive A and a formatted diskette with an empty directory in drive B. With the cursor positioned after the A > prompt, type

```
COPY FORMAT.COM B:FORMAT.COM
```

and press ⏎. This COPY command instructs DOS to copy FORMAT.COM from the diskette in the default (source) drive (drive A) to the diskette in the specified (target) drive (drive B) using the same file name. Each of the following commands produces the same result:

```
COPY FORMAT.COM B:FORMAT.*
COPY FORMAT.COM B:*.COM
COPY FORMAT.COM B:*.*
COPY FORMAT.COM B:
```

The last COPY command illustrates that when you want the target filename and extension to be the same as the source filename and extension, only the target drive must be specified in the COPY command.

With the cursor positioned after the A > prompt, type B: and press ⏎ to change the default drive to drive B. With the cursor positioned after the B> prompt, type

```
COPY A:CHKDSK.COM
```

and press ⏎. Since drive B is the default drive, this COPY command copies CHKDSK.COM from the diskette in the specified drive (drive A) to the diskette in the default drive (drive B). When no target file specification is given in the COPY command, the default drive is assumed, and the source filename and extension are used for the target file.

With the cursor positioned after the B> prompt, type

```
DIR
```

and press ⏎. Directory information similar to the following is displayed:

```
Volume in drive B has no label
Directory of  B:\

FORMAT    COM     11616    3-18-87   12:00p
CHKDSK    COM      9850    3-18-87   12:00p
          2 File(s)     339968 bytes free
```

This directory information indicates that the diskette in drive B contains the two files you copied to it.

With the cursor positioned after the B> prompt, type

```
COPY A:FORMAT.COM FRMT.BAK
```

and press ⏎. Since drive B is the default drive, this COPY command copies the specified file, FORMAT.COM, from the diskette in the specified drive (drive A) to the diskette in the default drive (drive B) using a different filename and extension, FRMT.BAK.

With the cursor positioned after the B> prompt, type

```
DIR
```

and press ⏎. Directory information similar to the following is displayed:

```
Volume in drive B has no label
Directory of  B:\

FORMAT    COM     11616    3-18-87   12:00p
CHKDSK    COM      9850    3-18-87   12:00p
FRMT      BAK     11616    3-18-87   12:00p
          3 File(s)     327680 bytes free
```

This directory information indicates that the diskette in drive B now contains three files.

■ Keystroke Summary

Copying one user file to a second disk

Insert: source diskette in drive A

Insert: target diskette in drive B

Set: default drive to drive A

Type: COPY *source-file-name* B: **or**

COPY *source-file-name* B:*target-file-name*

Press: ⏎

■ *What Can Go Wrong?*

1. After you enter a COPY command, information similar to the following is displayed:

```
File cannot be copied onto itself
       0 File(s) copied
```

Cause: The source and target file specifications in a COPY command cannot specify the same file. For example, a COPY command like COPY FORMAT.COM attempts to copy the specified file—in this case, FORMAT.COM—from the default drive to the default drive using the same file name.

Solution: There are two possible solutions to this problem. If you want to copy a file onto the same disk, you must specify a target file name that is different from the source file name. If you want to copy a file to a different disk using the same file name, then the source file drive and the target file drive must be different. ■

Copying Selected User Files (COPY)

Recall from Chapter 8 that the wildcard file name characters * and ? are used to identify groups of files having similar filenames and/or extensions. Insert the DOS System diskette in drive A and a formatted diskette with an empty directory in drive B. Reset the default drive to A by typing A: and pressing ⏎. Then, with the cursor positioned after the A > prompt, type

```
COPY A:F*.COM B:
```

and press ⏎. This COPY command instructs DOS to copy from the diskette in the specified drive (drive A) all files having the same first character in the filename (F) and the extension .COM to the diskette in the specified drive (drive B) using the same filenames and extensions. Note that DOS displays the specification of each file being copied when a wildcard character is used in the source file specification (Fig. 9.3).

With the cursor positioned after the A > prompt, type

```
DIR B:
```

Figure 9.3
When a wildcard file name character is used in the source file specification of the COPY command, the specification of each file being copied is displayed.

```
A>COPY A:F*.COM B:
A:FORMAT.COM
        1 File(s) copied

A>
```

and press ⏎. Directory information similar to the following is displayed:

```
Volume in drive B has no label
Directory of  B:\

FORMAT    COM    11616   3-18-87  12:00p
          1 File(s)     350208 bytes free
```

This directory information indicates that the diskette in drive B contains the file copied to it by the above COPY command.

With the cursor positioned after the A > prompt, type

```
COPY F*.* B:
```

and press ⏎. This COPY command copies from the diskette in the default drive (drive A) all files having the same first character in the filename (F) and any extension to the diskette in the specified drive (drive B) using the same filenames and extensions. Again, note that DOS displays the specification of each file being copied (Fig. 9.4).

With the cursor positioned after the A > prompt, type

```
DIR B:
```

and press ⏎. Directory information similar to the following is displayed:

```
Volume in drive B has no label
Directory of  B:\

FORMAT    COM    11616   3-18-87  12:00p
FASTOPEN  EXE     3919   3-17-87  12:00p
FIND      EXE     6434   3-17-87  12:00p
          3 File(s)     338944 bytes free
```

Figure 9.4
When the wildcard file name characters are used in the source file specification of the COPY command, the specification of each file being copied is displayed.

```
A>COPY F*.* B:
FASTOPEN.EXE
FIND.EXE
FORMAT.COM
        3 File(s) copied
A>
```

This directory information indicates that the diskette in drive B now contains three files. Note that the information in Fig. 9.4 shows that the command, COPY F*.* B:, copied three files from the DOS System diskette in drive A to the diskette in drive B. The command copied the file FORMAT.COM from the diskette in drive A over the file with the same name in drive B; it also copied two new files, FASTOPEN.EXE and FIND.EXE, to the diskette in drive B. Even though DOS will not copy a file over itself on the same disk, this example illustrates that DOS will copy a file from one disk over a file on another disk having exactly the same file name. For this reason you should use the DIR command to carefully check file dates before copying files between disks.

With the cursor positioned after the A > prompt, type B: and press ⏎ to change the default drive to drive B. With the cursor positioned after the B> prompt, type

```
COPY A:F*.*
```

and press ⏎. This COPY command copies from the diskette in the specified drive (drive A) all files having the same first character in the filename (F) and any extension to the diskette in the default drive (drive B) using the same filenames and extensions. In other words, this COPY command duplicates the previous COPY command. The only difference is that the default drive for this command is drive B, while the default drive for the previous COPY command was drive A. This example illustrates that when the target file specification parameter in a COPY command is omitted, the default drive is assumed to be the target drive, and the target file names are assumed to be the same as the corresponding source file names.

With the cursor positioned after the B> prompt, type

```
COPY A:*.COM
```

and press ⏎. This COPY command copies from the diskette in the specified drive (drive A) all files having the extension .COM to the default drive (drive B) using the same filenames and extensions.

With the cursor positioned after the B> prompt, type

```
DIR *.COM
```

and press ⏎. This DIR command displays from the directory of the diskette in the default drive (drive B) all file names having the specified extension. Directory information similar to the following is displayed:

```
Volume in drive B has no label
Directory of  B:\

FORMAT   COM   11616   3-18-87   12:00p
COMMAND  COM   25307   3-17-87   12:00p
SYS      COM    4766   3-17-87   12:00p
ASSIGN   COM    1561   3-17-87   12:00p
BACKUP   COM   31913   3-18-87   12:00p
CHKDSK   COM    9850   3-18-87   12:00p
COMP     COM    4214   3-17-87   12:00p
DISKCOMP COM    5879   3-17-87   12:00p
DISKCOPY COM    6295   3-17-87   12:00p
EDLIN    COM    7526   3-17-87   12:00p
GRAFTABL COM    6128   3-17-87   12:00p
GRAPHICS COM    3300   3-17-87   12:00p
LABEL    COM    2377   3-17-87   12:00p
MORE     COM     313   3-17-87   12:00p
PRINT    COM    9026   3-17-87   12:00p
RECOVER  COM    4299   3-18-87   12:00p
TREE     COM    3571   3-17-87   12:00p
        17 File(s)    203776 bytes free
```

With the cursor positioned after the B> prompt, type

```
COPY A:MO*.COM *.BAK /V
```

and press ⏎. This COPY command copies from the diskette in the specified drive (drive A) all files having the same first two characters in the filename (MO) and the same extension (.COM) to the diskette in the default drive (drive B) using the same filenames but the new specified extension .BAK. The / **V** (verify) parameter at the end of this COPY command instructs DOS to verify that the source and target files are identical after copying. When you want to be certain that the copied file(s) is identical to the source file(s), you should use the / V parameter at the end of the COPY command. The disadvantage of using the / V parameter is that file verification slows down the file copying process.

With the cursor positioned after the B> prompt, type A: and press ⏎ to change the default drive back to drive A. With the cursor positioned after the A > prompt, type

```
COPY *.* B:
```

and press ⏎. This COPY command copies all user files from the diskette in the default drive (drive A) to the diskette in the specified drive (drive B) using the same file names. Note that this command copied all *user* files from the DOS System diskette in drive A to the diskette in drive B but not the two hidden system files IBMBIO.COM and IBMDOS.COM. The above COPY command is a good command to use when you want to make duplicate copies of all user files on a diskette. The topic of backing up disks will be covered in Chapter 10.

■ *Keystroke*
Summary

Copying selected user files

Insert:	source diskette in drive A
Insert:	target diskette in drive B
Set:	default drive to drive A
Type:	COPY *source-filespec* B: **or**
	COPY *source-filespec* B:*target-filespec*
Press:	⏎

Removing (Deleting, Erasing) File Names from a Disk's Directory (DEL, ERASE)

The **DEL** (DELete) and **ERASE** commands are internal DOS commands that allow you to remove specified files from the directory of a disk. Only the DEL command will be used in this section, since the DEL and the ERASE commands perform exactly the same operations.

Removing One User File Name from a Disk's Directory

The DEL command can be used to delete a single file name from a disk's directory by specifying the file name in the DEL command. Recall from the first part of this chapter that you created two new files on the DOS System diskette. Insert the DOS System diskette in drive A. With the cursor positioned after the A > prompt, type

```
DIR FOR*
```

and press ⏎. Directory information similar to the following is displayed:

```
Volume in drive A has no label
Directory of  A:\

FORMAT    COM    11616    3-18-87   12:00p
FORMAT    BAK    11616    3-18-87   12:00p
FORMT     COM    11616    3-18-87   12:00p
        3 File(s)      55296 bytes free
```

The two extra files have the names FORMAT.BAK and FORMT.COM.
    With the DOS System diskette in drive A and the cursor positioned after the A> prompt, type

```
DEL A:FORMAT.BAK
```

and press ⏎. This DEL command instructs DOS to remove FORMAT.BAK from the directory of the DOS System diskette in drive

A. After the DEL command is finished, control returns to command level.

With the cursor positioned after the A > prompt, type

```
DEL FORMT.COM
```

and press ⏎. This DEL command instructs DOS to remove FORMT.COM from the directory of the diskette in the default drive. With the cursor positioned after the A > prompt, type

```
DIR FOR*
```

and press ⏎. Directory information similar to the following is displayed:

```
Volume in drive A has no label
Directory of  A:\

FORMAT    COM    11616   3-18-88  12:00p
          1 File(s)      79872 bytes free
```

Notice that the two extra file names have been deleted from the directory of the DOS System diskette. This diskette is now back to its original form.

▪ *Keystroke Summary*

Removing one user file name from a disk's directory

Insert: diskette in drive A that contains a file to be deleted from the disk's directory

Set: default drive to drive A

Type: `DEL file-name`

Press: ⏎

Removing Selected User File Names from a Disk's Directory

The examples in this section illustrate the use of the wildcard file name character * with the DEL command to delete groups of files having similar file names from the directory of a disk. To avoid accidentally deleting an important file from the DOS System diskette, a scratch copy of the DOS System diskette will be used as a source of user files to help illustrate the use of the DEL command.

To prepare a scratch copy, insert the DOS System diskette in drive A and a scratch diskette in drive B. Use the command FORMAT B: /S to prepare a bootable diskette from the scratch diskette in drive B. Finally, use the command COPY A:*.* B: to copy all user files from the DOS System diskette to the scratch diskette.

Note that in each of the following examples the DIR command is used with the file specification from the DEL command before the

DEL command is entered and executed. This practice should be followed regularly when you are using wildcard file name characters in the DEL command. It gives you an opportunity to review the file names to be deleted before they are actually deleted from a disk's directory. A second DIR command is used after the DEL command to verify that the file names were deleted from the disk's directory.

Insert the scratch DOS System diskette in drive B. To avoid accidentally deleting files, remove the DOS System diskette from drive A and leave drive A empty. With the cursor positioned after the A > prompt, type

```
DIR B:F*.COM
```

and press ⏎. Directory information similar to the following is displayed:

```
Volume in drive B has no label
Directory of  B:\

FORMAT    COM     11616    3-18-87  12:00p
         1 File(s)       79872 bytes free
```

The directory of the diskette in drive B contains one file name that has F as the first character in the filename and .COM as an extension.

With the cursor positioned after the A > prompt, type

```
DEL B:F*.COM
```

and press ⏎. This DEL command instructs DOS to delete from the directory of the diskette in the specified drive (drive B) each file having the same first character in the filename (F) and the same extension (.COM).

With the cursor positioned after the A > prompt, type

```
DIR B:F*.COM
```

and press ⏎. Directory information similar to the following is displayed:

```
Volume in drive B has no label
Directory of  B:\

File not found
```

The directory of the diskette in drive B does not contain any file names that satisfy the specification F*.COM because the command DEL B:F*.COM deleted the appropriate file name from the directory.

With the cursor positioned after the A > prompt, type

```
DIR B:S*.*
```

and press ⏎. Directory information similar to the following is dis-

played:

```
Volume in drive B has no label
Directory of  B:\

SYS       COM    4766    3-17-87   12:00p
SHARE     EXE    8608    3-17-87   12:00p
SORT      EXE    1977    3-17-87   12:00p
SUBST     EXE    9909    3-17-87   12:00p
        4 File(s)      92160 bytes free
```

The directory of the diskette in drive B contains four file names that have S as the first character in the filename and any extension.

With the cursor positioned after the A > prompt, type

```
DEL B:S*.*
```

and press ⏎. This DEL command instructs DOS to delete from the diskette's directory in the specified drive (drive B) all file names that start with S and have any extension.

With the cursor positioned after the A> prompt, type

```
DIR B:S*.*
```

and press ⏎. Directory information similar to the following is displayed:

```
Volume in drive B: has no label
Directory of  B:\


File not found
```

The directory of the diskette in drive B does not contain any file names that satisfy the S*.* specification because the command DEL B:S*.* deleted the four file names that originally satisfied this specification.

With the cursor positioned after the A > prompt, type B: and press ⏎ to change the default drive to drive B. With the cursor positioned after the B> prompt, type

```
DIR *.EXE
```

and press ⏎. Directory information similar to the following is displayed:

```
Volume in drive B has no label
Directory of  B:\

FASTOPEN EXE     3919    3-17-87   12:00p
REPLACE  EXE    11775    3-17-87   12:00p
APPEND   EXE     5825    3-17-87   12:00p
ATTRIB   EXE     9529    3-17-87   12:00p
FIND     EXE     6434    3-17-87   12:00p
JOIN     EXE     8969    3-17-87   12:00p
XCOPY    EXE    11247    3-17-87   12:00p
        7 File(s)     118784 bytes free
```

The directory of the diskette in drive B contains seven file names that have .EXE as an extension. Note that there are now 118,784 bytes free on the diskette. Each time a file name is deleted from the directory, the disk space occupied by the named file is freed for future use by DOS.

With the cursor positioned after the B> prompt, type

```
DEL *.EXE
```

and press ⏎. This DEL command instructs DOS to delete from the directory of the diskette in the default drive (drive B) all file names having the specified extension—in this case, .EXE.

With the cursor positioned after the B> prompt, type

```
DIR *.EXE
```

and press ⏎. Directory information similar to the following is displayed:

```
Volume in drive B has no label
Directory of  B:\


File not found
```

The directory of the diskette in drive B does not contain any file names that satisfy the *.EXE specification because the command DEL *.EXE deleted the seven file names that originally satisfied this specification.

With the cursor positioned after the B> prompt, type

```
DIR *.*
```

and press ⏎. Directory information similar to the following is displayed:

```
Volume in drive B has no label
Directory of  B:\

COMMAND  COM    25307    3-17-87   12:00p
ASSIGN   COM     1561    3-17-87   12:00p
BACKUP   COM    31913    3-18-87   12:00p
CHKDSK   COM     9850    3-18-87   12:00p
COMP     COM     4214    3-17-87   12:00p
DISKCOMP COM     5879    3-17-87   12:00p
DISKCOPY COM     6295    3-17-87   12:00p
EDLIN    COM     7526    3-17-87   12:00p
GRAFTABL COM     6128    3-17-87   12:00p
GRAPHICS COM     3300    3-17-87   12:00p
LABEL    COM     2377    3-17-87   12:00p
MORE     COM      313    3-17-87   12:00p
PRINT    COM     9026    3-17-87   12:00p
RECOVER  COM     4299    3-18-87   12:00p
TREE     COM     3571    3-17-87   12:00p
       15 File(s)    179200 bytes free
```

The parameter *.* specifies every user file name in the directory. The command DIR *.* is equivalent to the command DIR. The directory of the diskette in drive B contains fifteen file names, and there are 179,200 bytes free on the diskette.

With the cursor positioned after the B> prompt, type

```
DEL *.*
```

and press ⏎. This DEL command instructs DOS to delete every user file name from the directory of the diskette in the default drive (drive B). Before the DEL command carries out its assigned task, it gives you a chance to reconsider the execution of this command by displaying the following message:

```
Are you sure (Y/N)?
```

With the cursor positioned after the question mark (?), type Y and press ⏎. This response deletes all user file names from the directory of the diskette in drive B. If you had typed N and pressed ⏎, execution of the above DEL command would have terminated, no file names would have been deleted, and control would have returned to command level.

With the cursor positioned after the B> prompt, type

```
DIR
```

and press ⏎. Directory information similar to the following is displayed:

```
Volume in drive B has no label
Directory of  B:\

File not found
```

The directory of the diskette in drive B contains no user file names. You should be careful to properly interpret the above information. It does not state that the directory is empty; it states only that there are no user file names in the directory. Recall that the DEL command is used to delete *user* file names from the directory of a disk.

The CHKDSK command (see Chapter 8) will be used to determine the status of the diskette in drive B. Insert the DOS System diskette in drive A. With the cursor positioned after the B> prompt, type

```
A:CHKDSK B: /V
```

and press ⏎. Since CHKDSK is an external DOS command, it must be loaded into memory from the DOS System diskette. The specification A:CHKDSK instructs DOS to locate the CHKDSK command on the disk in the specified drive (drive A) and load it into memory. Once the loading process is complete, DOS initiates the execution of the CHKDSK program, which analyzes the disk in the specified drive (drive B). The / V (view) parameter is used to display a list of the file names for both user and hidden files. The above CHKDSK command displays information similar to the following:

```
Directory B:\
      B:\IBMBIO.COM
      B:\IBMDOS.COM

   362496 bytes total disk space
    53248 bytes in 2 hidden files
   309248 bytes available on disk

   655360 bytes total memory
   600160 bytes free
```

This information indicates that the diskette in drive B contains no user files but does contain two hidden files, IBMBIO.COM and IBMDOS.COM. Since the directory of the diskette in drive B contains the names for these two hidden files, it is not an empty directory.

▪ *Keystroke Summary*

Removing selected user file names from a disk's directory

Insert:	diskette in drive A that contains selected files to be deleted from the disk's directory
Set:	default drive to drive A
Type:	DEL *filespec*
Press:	⏎

▪ *What Can Go Wrong?*

The DOS System diskette will be used as a source of user files to help illustrate different interpretations of a file specification when used with different DOS commands.

1. When you enter the command DIR D*, information similar to the following is displayed:

```
Volume in drive A has no label
Directory of  A:\

DISKCOMP COM      5879   3-17-87  12:00p
DISKCOPY COM      6295   3-17-87  12:00p
       2 File(s)      30720 bytes free
```

When you enter the command DEL D*, the following message is displayed:

```
File not found
```

Cause: The file specification D* is interpreted differently in the DIR command than it is in other DOS commands such as the DEL, COPY, and CHKDSK commands.

Solution: When the file specification D* is used with the DIR command, it specifies each file name in the disk's directory that starts with D and has any extension. When the file specification D* is used in the DEL command, it specifies each file name in the disk's directory that starts with D and has *no* extension. If you want to delete all file names from the directory of a disk that have D as the first character in the filename and any extension, you should use the specification D*.* in the DEL command. If you want to display all file names in the directory of a disk that have D as the first character in the filename and no extension, you should use the specification D*. in the DIR command. Consequently, D*. in a DIR command acts like D* and D*. in a DEL command. Note that when a file specification such as D* is used in COPY and CHKDSK commands, its interpretation is the same for these commands as it is for the DEL command. ■

Changing File Names (RENAME)

The **RENAME** command is an internal DOS command that allows you to change a file name or a selected group of file names within the same disk directory. Since the RENAME command is an internal DOS command, the DOS System diskette need not be available to use the RENAME command.

The DOS System diskette contains numerous user files, so a scratch copy of the DOS System diskette will be used as a source of user files to help illustrate the use of the RENAME command. Type A: and press ⏎ to set the default drive to A. Insert the DOS System diskette in drive A and a scratch diskette in drive B. Format the scratch diskette using a \S parameter. Then copy all the files from the DOS System diskette to the scratch diskette.

Before you proceed, remove the DOS System diskette from drive A. This will prevent you from accidentally renaming files on the DOS System diskette.

In the following examples the DIR command is used to display the results of the RENAME command. With the cursor positioned after the A > prompt, type

```
DIR B:F*
```

and press ⏎. Directory information similar to the following is displayed:

```
Volume in drive B has no label
Directory of  B:\

FASTOPEN EXE      3919    3-17-87   12:00p
FIND     EXE      6434    3-17-87   12:00p
FORMAT   COM     11616    3-18-87   12:00p
        3 File(s)      79872 bytes free
```

With the cursor positioned after the A > prompt, type

```
RENAME B:FORMAT.COM FRMT.COM
```

and press ⏎. Two file specifications appear in the RENAME command. The first specification identifies the file name that is going to be changed—in this case, FORMAT.COM. The second parameter specifies the new name for the file—in this case, FRMT.COM. Thus the above RENAME command changes the file name FORMAT.COM to FRMT.COM before returning to command level. Notice that the disk drive specifier is not included as part of the new file specification (second parameter).

With the cursor positioned after the A > prompt, type

```
DIR B:F*
```

and press ⏎. Directory information similar to the following is displayed:

```
Volume in drive B has no label
Directory of  B:\

FASTOPEN EXE      3919    3-17-87   12:00p
FIND     EXE      6434    3-17-87   12:00p
FRMT     COM     11616    3-18-87   12:00p
         3 File(s)     79872 bytes free
```

The file name FORMAT.COM has been changed to FRMT.COM in the directory of the diskette in drive B.

With the cursor positioned after the A > prompt, type B: and press ⏎ to change the default drive to drive B. With the cursor positioned after the B> prompt, type

```
RENAME FIND.EXE FIND.OLD
```

and press ⏎. This RENAME command changes the file name FIND.EXE to FIND.OLD.

With the cursor positioned after the B> prompt, type

```
RENAME FASTOPEN.EXE FSTOPN.BAK
```

and press ⏎. This RENAME command changes file name FASTOPEN.EXE to FSTOPN.BAK.

With the cursor positioned after the B> prompt, type

```
DIR F*
```

and press ⏎. Directory information similar to the following is dis-

played:

```
Volume in drive B has no label
Directory of  B:\

FSTOPN    BAK      3919    3-17-87   12:00p
FIND      OLD      6434    3-17-87   12:00p
FRMT      COM     11616    3-18-87   12:00p
          3 File(s)      79872 bytes free
```

The names of the three files have been changed in the directory of the diskette in drive B. Note that the RENAME command can be used to change the filename part of a file name, the extension of a file name, or both the filename and extension.

■ *Keystroke Summary*

Changing the name of a file

Insert: in drive A a diskette that contains a file name to be changed

Set: default drive to drive A

Type: RENAME *current-file-name new-file-name*

Press: [↵]

■ *What Can Go Wrong?*

1. After you enter a RENAME command, a message similar to the following is displayed:

```
Invalid Parameter
```

Cause: This message refers to an error in the second parameter of the RENAME command. The second parameter of the RENAME command can specify only a file name; it cannot include a disk drive specification.

Solution: Check the second parameter of the RENAME command. If it contains a disk drive specification, the drive specification must be removed. Note that if the disk in the default drive contains the file name to be changed, no disk drive specification is necessary in the first parameter. If the file name to be changed is on a disk in a drive different from the default drive, then the first parameter of the RENAME command must contain the appropriate drive specification. ■

Text Files

Text (character, ASCII) files contain character information, that is, information similar to what is found on this page or in this book. ASCII refers to a code scheme that computers use to represent character information and to facilitate the interchange of data (character information) among various types of computing equipment.

Creating a Text File with the COPY CON Command

The source information for the COPY command need not come from a file. It can come directly from the keyboard. Consequently, the COPY command can be used to create text files by copying information entered directly from the keyboard (CON) to the file specified in the command. This process is a convenient way to generate short text files.

Insert a formatted diskette in drive A. Then type A: and press ↵ to reset the default drive to drive A. With the cursor positioned after the A> prompt, type

```
COPY CON A:INFO.TXT
```

and press ↵. After ↵ is pressed, the COPY command instructs DOS to position the cursor at the beginning of the next line and wait to capture information that is entered from the keyboard (CON). Type the following information:

```
This example creates a file called INFO.TXT on the
diskette in drive A and then copies the information
entered from the keyboard console (CON) into that file.
```

At the end of each line you should press ↵. All information that you type is temporarily saved in the computer's memory. When you finish, enter an **end-of-file marker** by holding the Ctrl key down and typing Z (denoted by Ctrl *and* Z); then release the Ctrl key and press ↵. At this point, the COPY command copies the information entered from the keyboard and temporarily saved in memory to the target file specified in the COPY CON command—in this case, the file INFO.TXT on the diskette in drive A. When the copying process is completed, the message

```
1 File(s) copied
```

is displayed on the screen before control returns to command level with the A> prompt. The information displayed on the screen is similar to Fig. 9.5.

Figure 9.5
When the COPY CON command is used to create a text file, you can enter information from the keyboard.

```
A>COPY CON INFO.TXT
This example creates a file called INFO.TXT on the
diskette in drive A and then copies the information
entered from the keyboard console (CON) into that file.
^Z
        1 File(s) copied

A>
```

Creating a text file with the COPY CON command

Insert: formatted diskette in drive A

Set: default drive to drive A

Type: COPY CON *filespec*

Press: ⏎

Type: information you want copied to the specified file

Press: ⏎ at the end of each line

Enter: end-of-file marker by holding the Ctrl key down and typing Z (Ctrl *and* Z)

Press: ⏎

Displaying Information in a Text FIle (TYPE)

The **TYPE** command is an internal DOS command that allows you to display the contents of a specified file on the standard output device (normally the screen). Although the TYPE command can be used to display the contents of any file, only text files are displayed in a legible format. Using the TYPE command to display information in a nontext file usually produces unreadable information because of the presence of special character codes, control characters, and escape sequences (nondisplayable characters) in the file. It might also cause strange things to happen to your personal computer. Your system might crash, your keyboard might lock up, or your screen might change characteristics. If this happens, you might have to restart (boot) your system.

Insert the diskette containing the text file INFO.TXT in drive A. With the cursor positioned after the A> prompt, type

```
TYPE INFO.TXT
```

and press ⏎. The TYPE command instructs DOS to display the contents of the specified file. After the information is displayed, control returns to command level.

Displaying information in a text file

Insert: diskette containing a text file in drive A

Set: default drive to drive A

Type: TYPE *text-filespec*

Press: ⏎

Summary

Topic or Feature	Command or Reference	Page
Copy one user file to the same disk	COPY *source-file-name* *target-file-name* Fig. 9.2	106
Copy one user file to a second disk	COPY *source-file-name* B:	108
Copy selected user files	COPY *source-filespec* B: COPY *source-filespec* B:*target-filespec* Figs. 9.3, 9.4	110
Remove one user file name from a disk's directory	DEL *file-name*	114
Remove selected user file names from a disk's directory	DEL *filespec*	115
Change the name of a file	RENAME *current-file-name* *new-file-name*	121
Create a text file from the keyboard	COPY CON *filespec*	124
Display the contents of a text file	TYPE *text-filespec*	125

Self-Test

1. The _____ command is used to copy a user file to the same disk or to a second disk.

2. If the default drive is A, write a COPY command to copy a file named MYFILE from the disk in drive A to the disk in drive A using extension .BAK for the target file. _____

3. If the default drive is A, write a COPY command to copy a file named MYFILE.WPF from drive A to drive B using the same filename and extension. _____

4. Write a COPY command to copy all the user files on the disk in drive A to the disk in drive B. _____

5. The _____ command is used to remove specified user file names from a disk directory.

6. If the default drive is A, write a command to delete all user file names having the extension .WKS from the directory of the disk in drive B. _____

7. The _____ command is used to change a file name in a disk directory.

8. Character information is stored in a _____ file.

9. The DOS device name _____ is used to designate the keyboard.

10. The _____ command displays the contents of a text file.

Exercises

1. The DOS System diskette (or a diskette supplied by your instructor) should be used as the source diskette for this exercise. Use an appropriate DOS command to perform each of the assigned tasks.

    a. Format a data diskette with volume label *namef*#9-1, where *name* denotes the first six characters of your last name or your entire last name (whichever is shorter) and *f* denotes the first character of your first name.

    b. Copy all user files having file names that begin with the character F and have any extension from the source diskette to the data diskette using the same file names.

    c. Use the output redirection operator to obtain a hard copy listing of the directory information for the data diskette.

    d. Copy all user files having file names that begin with the character S and have .COM as an extension from the source diskette to the data diskette using the same filename but changing the extension to .EX.

    e. Use the output redirection operator to obtain a hard copy listing of the directory information for the data diskette.

    f. Copy all user files having file names that have .COM as an extension from the source diskette to the data diskette using the same filename but changing the extension to .BAK.

    g. Use the output redirection operator to obtain a hard copy listing of the directory information for the data diskette.

    h. Remove all user file names from the directory of the data diskette.

    i. Use the output redirection operator to obtain a hard copy listing of the directory information for the data diskette.

2. The DOS System diskette (or a diskette supplied by your instructor) should be used as the source diskette for this exercise. Use an appropriate DOS command to perform each of the assigned tasks.

    a. Format a data diskette with volume label *namef*#9-2, where *name* denotes the first six characters of your last name or your entire last name (whichever is shorter) and *f* denotes the first character of your first name.

b. Copy all user files from the source diskette to the data diskette using the same file names.

c. Turn the printer echo mode on so that you can obtain a hard copy listing of your work in parts (d) through (l).

d. Display the directory information for the data diskette.

e. Display all user file names that have .EXE as an extension from the directory of the data diskette.

f. Remove from the directory of the data diskette all user file names that have .EXE as an extension.

g. Display the directory information for the data diskette.

h. Display all user file names that begin with the character C and have .COM as an extension from the directory of the data diskette.

i. Remove from the directory of the data diskette all user file names that begin with the character C and have .COM as an extension.

j. Display the directory information for the data diskette.

k. Remove all user file names from the directory of the data diskette.

l. Display the directory information for the data diskette.

m. Turn the printer echo mode off.

·10

Backing Up Diskettes and Files

The material in this chapter introduces the DOS commands that allow you to:

- back up an entire diskette by making an identical copy of a diskette (DISKCOPY)
- back up individual and selected files (COPY)
- interactively select files to back up (XCOPY)
- back up files based on a specified date (XCOPY)
- compare the contents of two files (COMP)

Backup Copies of Files and Diskettes

Making backup copies of important files and complete diskettes minimizes the amount of time and information you might lose if something goes wrong with a file or an entire diskette. Even though you are very careful with your diskettes, they can be misplaced or damaged by accident, and files can be inadvertently modified or deleted. The amount of time and effort it takes to make these backup copies is small in comparison to the time and effort it would take to recreate lost information. Making backup copies of files and diskettes is a very wise investment of your time.

Making Identical Diskette Copies (DISKCOPY)

The **DISKCOPY** command is an external DOS command that allows you to copy the entire contents of one diskette (source diskette) onto another diskette (target diskette) of the same format. If the target diskette is not formatted, the DISKCOPY command will automatically format the target diskette to the source diskette format. The DISKCOPY command reproduces the contents of the source diskette sector by sector on the target diskette.

Boot DOS and leave the DOS System diskette in drive A. With the cursor positioned after the A > prompt, type

```
DISKCOPY A: B:
```

and press ⏎. Since DISKCOPY is an external DOS command, it must be loaded into memory from the DOS System diskette in drive A. Once the loading process is complete, DOS initiates the execution of the DISKCOPY program, which displays the following messages:

```
Insert SOURCE diskette in drive A:

Insert TARGET diskette in drive B:

Press any key when ready . . .
```

Following the above messages, remove the DOS System diskette from drive A and insert the diskette to be copied (duplicated). Insert a blank (target) diskette in drive B, and press any key to begin the copying process. The DISKCOPY program determines the format of the source diskette by reading information from its boot record. Once the format type of the source diskette is determined, a message similar to the following is displayed:

```
Copying 40 tracks
9 Sectors/Track, 2 Side(s)
```

The DISKCOPY program now begins to read the source diskette sector by sector, temporarily storing the information in memory. After all of the information has been read from the source diskette (or no more memory is available to store information), the DISKCOPY program tests the format of the target diskette in drive B. If the target diskette has the same format type as the source diskette, the DISKCOPY program begins copying the information from memory onto the target diskette. If the target diskette is not formatted or if the target diskette has a different format type than the source diskette, a message similar to the following is displayed:

```
Formatting while copying
```

This message indicates that the DISKCOPY program is formatting the target diskette to agree with the format type of the source diskette. After the target diskette is formatted, the DISKCOPY program begins copying the information from memory onto the target diskette. The information is copied onto the target diskette sector by sector in exactly the same order that it was read from the source diskette. In other words, the target diskette is an identical copy of the source diskette. After the copying process is completed, the DISKCOPY program displays the following message:

```
Copy another diskette (Y/N)?
```

If you want to make a duplicate copy of another diskette, type Y and the above process will be repeated. If you want to terminate the DISKCOPY program, type N and control returns to command level.

■ Keystroke Summary

Making identical diskette copies

Insert:	DOS System diskette in drive A
Set:	default drive to drive A
Type:	DISKCOPY A: B:
Press:	⏎
Remove:	DOS System diskette from drive A after the prompt messages are displayed
Insert:	diskette to be copied (source diskette) in drive A
Insert:	blank diskette (target diskette) in drive B
Press:	⏎ or any key to begin the copying process
Type:	Y to copy another diskette or
	N to terminate the DISKCOPY program.

Disadvantages of Using the DISKCOPY Command

The DISKCOPY command is easy to use when making backup copies of diskettes. If you want an identical copy of a source diskette or if the source diskette has any hidden files that you want copied, then you should use the DISKCOPY command. There are, however, some disadvantages.

■ If the source diskette has any bad sectors, the same sectors on the target diskette will be marked as bad. When the source diskette contains bad sectors, the DISKCOPY command will display messages similar to the following:

```
Unrecoverable read error on drive A:
Side 1, track 37
Target diskette may be unusable
```

The DISKCOPY command is informing you through these messages that the target diskette may not be usable.

■ If the target diskette contains bad sectors, the information written to these sectors may not be usable. The DISKCOPY command does not check the target diskette for bad sectors; it copies the source diskette sector by sector to the target diskette. Consequently, no message about this possible problem is ever displayed. This problem can be alleviated by first formatting the target diskette with the FORMAT command and then checking it for bad sectors with the CHKDSK command. If a diskette contains bad sectors, do not use it as the target diskette for the DISKCOPY command.

■ A **fragmented file** is stored on a disk in nonadjacent sectors. If the source diskette contains fragmented files, the file fragmentation is duplicated on the target diskette by the DISKCOPY program. Regular use of fragmented files will slow DOS's reading speed.

Backing Up Files

Backing Up Files with the COPY Command

The COPY command, introduced in Chapter 9, is an internal DOS command that can be used to back up individual files, groups of files, or all the files in the directory of a disk. The files to be backed up are defined in the source file specification part of the COPY command.

Insert the diskette to be backed up (source diskette) in drive A. Insert a blank formatted diskette (target diskette) in drive B. With the cursor positioned after the A > prompt, type

```
COPY *.* B:
```

and press ↵. The COPY command copies all user files from the diskette in the default drive (drive A) to the diskette in the specified drive (drive B) using the same file names. If the directory of the diskette inserted in drive B is empty, the files are copied onto this diskette using contiguous sectors. This means that file fragmentation on the source diskette will be eliminated on the target diskette.

Backing Up Files with the XCOPY Command (Interactive Selection)

The **XCOPY** command is an external DOS command that allows you to selectively copy files from a disk in one drive to a disk in another drive. Although the XCOPY command functions very much like the COPY command, it supports different ways to identify the files to be copied. One of the most commonly used options allows you to interactively select or reject the name of each file to be copied from the group of specified files.

Insert the DOS System diskette in drive A and a formatted target diskette in drive B. With the cursor positioned after the A > prompt, type

```
XCOPY A: B: /W /P
```

and press ⏎. Since XCOPY is an external DOS command, it must be loaded into memory from the DOS System diskette in drive A. Once the loading process is complete, DOS initiates the execution of the XCOPY program. The / **W** (wait) parameter instructs the XCOPY command to display the following message and then wait before it starts to copy any files:

```
Press any key to begin copying files
```

Remove the DOS System diskette from drive A, and insert the source diskette that contains files to be backed up. Now that the source diskette is in drive A and the target diskette is in drive B, press any key. The / **P** (prompt) parameter instructs XCOPY to prompt you with (Y/N)? after each file name in the directory of the source diskette in drive A before it copies that file to the diskette in drive B.

The XCOPY command does not have to specify all file names in the directory of the source diskette. You can restrict the file specifications displayed by the XCOPY command to certain groups of files by using wildcard file name characters. The use of wildcard file name characters in the XCOPY command is analogous to their use in the COPY command.

∎ *Keystroke Summary*

Copying files with the XCOPY command (interactive selection)

Insert: DOS System diskette in drive A

Insert: formatted target diskette in drive B

Set: default drive to drive A

Type: XCOPY *source-filespec* B: /W /P

Press: ⏎

Remove: DOS System diskette from drive A

Insert: source diskette in drive A

Press: ⏎ or any key to begin the copying process

Type: Y to copy the specified file or

N to not copy the specified file

Backing Up Files with the XCOPY Command (Dated Selection)

The XCOPY command can also be used to selectively copy files on the basis of a specified date. If a date parameter is included in the XCOPY command, the command will copy all specified files that have creation or modification dates on or after the stated date. The general format of the date parameter is **/D:mm-dd-yy**, where mm denotes the month

(01 through 12), dd denotes the day (01 through 31), and yy denotes the year (80 through 99, or 1980 through 1999). The /W (wait) and /P (prompt) parameters can also be used with the date parameter.

■ *Keystroke Summary*

Copying files with the XCOPY command (dated selection)

Insert: DOS System diskette in drive A

Insert: formatted target diskette in drive B

Set: default drive to drive A

Type: XCOPY *source-filespec* B: /W /D:*mm-dd-yy*

Press: ⏎

Remove: DOS System diskette from drive A

Insert: source diskette in drive A

Press: ⏎ or any key to begin the copying process

Comparing the Contents of Files (COMP)

The **COMP** (COMPare) command is an external DOS command that allows you to compare the contents of two files or two sets of files and display any differences about the files on the screen. The DISKCOMP command compares two *disks*. See the DOS reference manual for more information.

Summary

Topic or Feature	Command or Reference	Page
Make an identical copy of a diskette	DISKCOPY A: B:	130
Back up individual or selected files	COPY *source-filespec* B:	132
Back up files interactively	XCOPY *source-filespec* B: /W /P	132
Back up files by dated selection	XCOPY *source-filespec* B: /W /D:mm-dd-yy	133
Compare two files	COMP	134

Self-Test

1. The _____ command is used to make an identical copy of a diskette.

2. The _____ command can be used to back up individual files, groups of files, or all files specified in the directory of a disk.

3. The _____ command can be used to interactively select or reject files to be copied.

4. The _____ command can be used to selectively copy files on the basis of a specified date.

5. The _____ command is used to compare the contents of two files.

Exercises

1. Use an appropriate DOS command to perform each of the assigned tasks.

   a. Format a blank diskette.

   b. Verify that the diskette has no bad sectors. If the diskette has bad sectors, repeat part (a) using a different diskette.

   c. Using the formatted diskette as the target diskette, make a duplicate (identical) copy of the DOS System diskette.

   d. Verify that the two DOS hidden files are on the duplicate copy of the DOS System diskette. Display their names.

   e. Assign the volume label SYSTEM-DISK to the duplicate copy of the DOS System diskette.

2. Use an appropriate DOS command to perform each of the assigned tasks.

   a. Format a bootable diskette with volume label DOS-DISK.

   b. Verify that the formatted diskette has no bad sectors and show that it contains the three DOS system files by displaying their names.

   c. Complete the duplication process of the DOS System diskette by copying all user files from the DOS System diskette to the diskette prepared in part (a).

·11

Using a Hard Disk

The material in this chapter introduces the DOS commands that allow you to:

- manage files on a hard disk
- create subdirectories on a disk (MKDIR or MD)
- change the current directory of a disk (CHDIR or CD)
- display the current directory of a drive (CD and DIR)
- automatically display the current directory name (PROMPT)
- copy files between different directories on a disk
- display information about the directory structure of a disk (TREE and CHKDSK)
- set an extended search path for DOS to locate commands (PATH)
- delete (remove) subdirectories from a disk (RMDIR or RD)

Background Information

This chapter is devoted primarily to DOS commands that are used to help manage information on a hard disk. You should note that each command presented in this chapter can also be applied to a diskette drive. Therefore, even if you do not have a personal computer with a hard disk, you can perform the commands presented in this chapter.

If your personal computer contains a hard disk, the material presented in this chapter assumes the following:

1. the hard disk is formatted,

2. DOS is installed on the hard disk,

3. all files from the DOS Startup diskette and the DOS Operating diskette are in the main directory of the hard disk, and

4. the hard disk drive is referenced as drive C.

If any of these assumptions is not correct, consult your instructor.

Managing Disk Files

When you first begin to use a personal computer, you probably have three or four diskettes that you regularly use: a DOS System diskette, one or two diskettes containing application programs such as word processing programs, and a data diskette. Initially, you have one diskette to hold all of your data files. As the number of files grows, you realize that managing a large number of unrelated files on one data diskette is not a good idea. At this point you decide to separate your data files into similar categories and put each category of files onto a separate diskette containing an appropriate label. The same thing occurs with application programs. You separate different application programs by putting them on different diskettes. Through the use of multiple diskettes you are better able to manage your computer application programs and their associated data files.

Managing information on a hard disk is similar to managing information in an office file cabinet. Suppose you store letters, memorandums, reports, and other items in a file cabinet without using any labeled file folders and without using any topical organization of the information in the file cabinet. The lack of any file cabinet organization is fine until you try to locate a particular piece of information. The more information you have in an unorganized file cabinet, the more trouble you will have in trying to locate any particular item in the cabinet. Consequently, you put labels on file folders and separate groups of file folders according to certain common characteristics so that information can be retrieved in a timely manner. These same ideas carry over to storing files of information on a hard disk. You must organize your computer files in a manner that allows you to use a hard disk effectively. This is accomplished through the use of directories.

Types of Directories

A directory is a table of contents that DOS maintains for information that is stored on a disk. The directory of a disk contains, for each file on the disk, an entry that consists of the filename, the filename extension, the file size in bytes, the date and time the file was created or last updated, and the location of the beginning of the file data on the disk.

Root Directory

A directory is created by DOS each time the FORMAT command is used to format a disk. This directory is called the **root (main) directory** because a multilevel directory structure, called a tree structure, can grow from it.

Subdirectories

To make your computer filing system more flexible, DOS allows you to create additional directories called **subdirectories**. Subdirectories allow you to divide a disk into separate storage areas that can be used like separate disks. A subdirectory is a special file that contains directory entries. These entries have the same form as the entries in the root directory. Since a subdirectory is a directory, the terms subdirectory and directory may be used interchangeably.

Subdirectory names follow the same format as file names. They contain one to eight characters followed by an optional extension that consists of a period and one to three characters. All valid characters for file names are also valid for subdirectory names. Normally subdirectory names are short and do not include extensions; this makes them convenient to use.

Current Directory

The **current directory** associated with a disk is the directory that you are currently working in or the directory that you were working in on another drive. DOS keeps track of the current directory in the same way that it keeps track of the current (default) disk drive. When the system is booted, the current drive is the drive containing the disk from which the DOS system programs were loaded into memory, and the current directory is the root directory of the disk in this drive. The terminology **current directory** is used to denote the current directory of the disk in the default drive. The terminology **current directory of a drive** is used to denote the current directory of the disk in that drive.

Directory Path

When DOS is attempting to locate a file and no particular directory is specified, DOS looks for the file only in the current directory. If the file is in another directory, DOS must be given directions on how to access that directory. A **directory path** or **path** is the route you must follow to trace your way from the disk's main or root directory to a particular

Figure 11.1
Multilevel directory
structure.

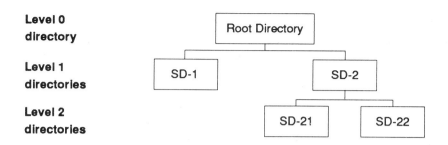

Level 0
directory

Level 1
directories

Level 2
directories

place in the directory structure. The description of a path is called the **directory path name, path name,** or **path specification.**

Consider the multilevel directory structure in Fig. 11.1. Note that this tree structure grows out of the root directory. The root directory contains two subdirectories, SD-1 and SD-2. Directory SD-1 contains no subdirectories, and directory SD-2 contains two subdirectories (SD-21 and SD-22).

Suppose that you want to access a file in subdirectory SD-21. You get to this directory by following the path: root directory to subdirectory SD-2 to subdirectory SD-21. The path name (specification) for this path is \SD-2\SD-21. In this specification the initial backslash (\) instructs DOS to start the path at the root directory, while the second backslash is used as a directory name delimiter.

Suppose that the file name EXAMPLE.DOC is contained in subdirectory SD-21. The following specification contains the directory path name and the file name and denotes the complete specification for the file EXAMPLE.DOC:

```
\SD-2\SD-21\EXAMPLE.DOC
```

Note that the specification begins with the root directory and gets to EXAMPLE.DOC in subdirectory SD-21 via subdirectory SD-2.

Path Name Notation

A path consisting of only the **backslash (\)** specifies the root directory. A path name beginning with a backslash (\) specifies that the path starts in the root directory. The backslash (\) is also used as a delimiter between two directory names or between a directory name and a file name. Recall that a space is not a valid character for a file specification or path specification, since it is interpreted by DOS as a parameter field delimiter (separator). Thus spaces should never be used in a file or path specification. Figure 11.2 illustrates how the backslash is used in a file specification that contains a directory path.

Directory Structure Terminology

If U and V are subdirectories of a directory T, then U and V are **offspring directories** of T, and T is called the **parent directory** for

Figure 11.2
This example illustrates how a backslash (\) is used in a file specification that contains a directory path.

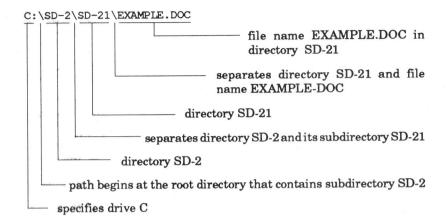

```
C:\SD-2\SD-21\EXAMPLE.DOC
```

file name EXAMPLE.DOC in directory SD-21

separates directory SD-21 and file name EXAMPLE-DOC

directory SD-21

separates directory SD-2 and its subdirectory SD-21

directory SD-2

path begins at the root directory that contains subdirectory SD-2

specifies drive C

U and V. U and V are called **sibling directories**. Using the notation of Fig. 11.1, subdirectories SD-21 and SD-22 are sibling directories and have directory SD-2 as their parent directory. Subdirectory SD-21 is an offspring directory of SD-2.

Creating (Making) Subdirectories (MKDIR, MD)

The **MKDIR** (MaKe DIRectory) command is an internal DOS command that instructs DOS to create a subdirectory with the directory path and name specified in the command. **MD** is an abbreviation for MKDIR. The MD command is used in the next two sections to create the directory structure of Fig. 11.1.

Creating Subdirectories in the Root Directory (First Level)

A **level 1 directory** in a directory structure is defined as a subdirectory of the root directory. If you have not already done so, boot DOS. Assume that the current directory of the hard disk in drive C is the root directory. With the cursor positioned after the C> prompt, type

```
MD SD-1
```

and press ⏎. With the cursor positioned after the C> prompt, type

```
MD SD-2
```

and press ⏎. The MD commands instruct DOS to create the specified subdirectories—SD-1 and SD-2—in the root directory of the hard disk in drive C. After DOS creates each subdirectory, control returns to command level.

The DIR command can be used to verify that the two subdirectories were created in the root directory of the hard disk in drive C. With the cursor positioned after the C> prompt, type

```
DIR SD-*
```

and press ⏎. The DIR command instructs DOS to display all entries in the current directory of the default drive (drive C) having SD- as their first three characters. DOS displays information similar to the following:

```
Volume in drive C is HARD-DISK
Directory of  C:\

SD-1          <DIR>       1-31-89   10:46p
SD-2          <DIR>       1-31-89   10:46p
         2 File(s)   31139840 bytes free
```

Note that C:\ in the second line indicates that the two listed directories are subdirectories of the root directory in drive C. Also note that <DIR> specifies that the listed names are directory names.

The DIR command can also be used to display the contents of a subdirectory. With the cursor positioned after the C> prompt, type

```
DIR SD-1
```

and press ⏎. The DIR command instructs DOS to display the contents of the specified directory on the disk in the default drive (drive C). DOS displays information similar to the following:

```
Volume in drive C is HARD-DISK
Directory of  C:\SD-1

.             <DIR>       1-31-89   10:46p
..            <DIR>       1-31-89   10:46p
         2 File(s)   31139840 bytes free
```

Note that the newly created directory SD-1 contains two special directory entries. The **single-period entry (.)** represents the current directory. The **double-period entry (..)** represents its parent directory. All directories except the root directory contain these two entries.

■ *Keystroke Summary*

Creating subdirectories in the root directory (first level)

Set: default drive to drive C with the current directory set to the root directory

Type: MD *subdirname*

Press: ⏎

■ *What Can Go Wrong?*

1. When you attempt to boot the system, a message similar to the following is displayed:

```
Non-System disk or disk error
Replace and strike any key when ready
```

Cause: There is a non-system disk in drive A.

Solution: Remove the disk from drive A, leave the drive door open, and reboot the system. ■

Creating Second-Level Subdirectories from the Root Directory

A **level 2 directory** in a directory structure is defined as a subdirectory of a level 1 directory. Note in Fig. 11.1 that directories SD-21 and SD-22 are subdirectories of directory SD-2, a level 1 directory. Assume that the current directory of the hard disk in drive C is the root directory. With the cursor positioned after the C> prompt, type

```
MD \SD-2\SD-21
```

and press ⏎. The MD command instructs DOS to create the specified subdirectory. Note that \SD-2 in the above command specifies a directory path that begins with the root directory. Also note that the leading backslash in the path specification of the above command is not necessary, since the current directory is the root directory and SD-2 is a subdirectory of the root directory.

With the cursor positioned after the C> prompt, type

```
MD SD-2\SD-22
```

and press ⏎. The MD command instructs DOS to create the specified subdirectory on the disk in the default drive (drive C). Note that the path specification SD-2 in the above MD command does not begin with a backslash, since the current directory is the root directory and SD-2 is a subdirectory of the root directory. The creation of the multilevel directory structure given in Fig. 11.1 is now complete.

The DIR command can be used to verify that directories SD-21 and SD-22 were created in directory SD-2. With the cursor positioned after the C> prompt, type

```
DIR SD-2
```

and press ⏎. The DIR command instructs DOS to display the contents of the specified directory. The DIR command knows that SD-2 is a directory name because of the <DIR> designator for SD-2 in the root directory. Thus, DOS displays information similar to the following:

```
Volume in drive C is HARD-DISK
Directory of  C:\SD-2

.                <DIR>       1-31-89   10:46p
..               <DIR>       1-31-89   10:46p
SD-21            <DIR>       1-31-89   10:50p
SD-22            <DIR>       1-31-89   10:50p
        4 File(s)   31135744 bytes free
```

Note that directory SD-2 contains four subdirectory entries, the two special directory entries and the two newly created directories SD-21 and SD-22.

Once you have created several directories on a disk, you can use the CHKDSK command to give you information about the amount of disk space that is occupied by files and directories. With the cursor positioned after the C> prompt, type

```
CHKDSK
```

Figure 11.3
When the CHKDSK command is used to generate a status report for the hard disk in drive C, information similar to this is displayed.

```
C>CHKDSK
Volume HARD-DISK   created Aug 8, 1988 10:18a
 31768576 bytes total disk space
    53248 bytes in 3 hidden files
     8192 bytes in 4 directories
   571392 bytes in 64 user files
 31135744 bytes available on disk

   655360 bytes total memory
   600080 bytes free

C>
```

and press ⏎. After the CHKDSK program is loaded into memory, it displays a status report for the disk similar to the information in Fig. 11.3. Note that 8192 bytes are used by four directory entries, so 2048 bytes of disk space were allocated for each directory. The type of disk determines the number of bytes that DOS allocates for each subdirectory.

Note that all the subdirectories have unique names. DOS allows you to create two or more subdirectories with the same name as long as they have different path specifications. For example, the three commands

    MD \SD-1\DATA

    MD \SD-2\DATA

    MD \SD-2\SD-21\DATA

create three different subdirectories with the name DATA. The first is a subdirectory of SD-1 with path specification \SD-1\DATA; the second is a subdirectory of SD-2 with path specification \SD-2\DATA; and the third is a subdirectory of SD-21 with path specification \SD-2\SD-21\DATA.

■ *Keystroke Summary*

Creating second-level subdirectories from the root directory

Set: default drive to drive C with the current directory set to the root directory

Type: MD *Level-1-subdirname\Level-2-subdirname*

Press: ⏎

■ *What Can Go Wrong?*

1. Following a MD command, an error message indicates that the path is invalid.

Cause: The path name contains one or more nonexistent subdirectory names. You probably mistyped SD-2 either in this command or in the MD command.

Solution: Use a DIR command to verify the subdirectoy name. Then retype the command. ■

Changing the Current Directory (CHDIR, CD)

The **CHDIR** (CHange DIRectory) command is an internal DOS command that instructs DOS to change the current directory of a disk to the directory specified in the command. This command can also be used to display the current directory. **CD** is an abbreviation for CHDIR.

Changing the Current Directory to a Subdirectory of the Current Directory

Assume that the directory structure in Fig. 11.1 is on the hard disk in drive C and that the current directory of the hard disk is the root directory. With the cursor positioned after the C> prompt, type

```
CD SD-2
```

and press ↵. The CD command instructs DOS to change the current directory of the disk in the default drive—in this case, the root directory of the hard disk in drive C—to the specified directory, subdirectory SD-2. After the current directory of drive C is changed to SD-2, control returns to command level. With the cursor positioned after the C> prompt, type

```
CD SD-21
```

and press ↵. The CD command instructs DOS to change the current directory of the disk in the default drive—in this case, directory SD-2 of the hard disk in drive C—to subdirectory SD-21, a subdirectory of SD-2.

■ *Keystroke Summary*

Changing the current directory to a subdirectory of the current directory

Set: default drive to drive C with *subdirname* a subdirectory of the current directory

Type: CD *subdirname*

Press: ↵

Changing the Current Directory to the Root Directory

With the cursor positioned after the C> prompt, type

```
CD \
```

and press ↵. The command instructs DOS to change the current directory of the disk in the default drive (drive C) to the root directory.

Changing the current directory to the root directory

Set: default drive to drive C

Type: CD \

Press: ⏎

Displaying the Current Directory of a Drive

When the root directory of the hard disk in drive C is the current directory, C> is the DOS command prompt. When subdirectory SD-2 of the hard disk in drive C is the current directory, C> is still the DOS command prompt. The CHDIR (CD) command can be used without any parameters to display the path specification for the current directory of the disk in the default drive. In addition to displaying entries in a directory, the DIR command can also be used to display the current directory.

With the cursor positioned after the C> prompt, type

```
CD
```

and press ⏎. The CD command instructs DOS to display the path specification for the current directory of the default drive (drive C). The following directory path specification is displayed before control returns to command level:

```
C:\
```

The current directory of the default drive (drive C) is the root directory.

With the cursor positioned after the C> prompt, type

```
CD SD-2
```

and press ⏎. This command instructs DOS to change the current directory of the default drive (drive C) to subdirectory SD-2. With the cursor positioned after the C> prompt, type

```
CD
```

and press ⏎. The following directory path specification is displayed:

```
C:\SD-2
```

This specification indicates that the current directory of the default drive (drive C) is directory SD-2, a subdirectory of the root directory.

With the cursor positioned after the C> prompt, type

```
DIR
```

and press ⏎. When the DIR command is used without any parameters, it instructs DOS to display the contents of the current directory for the default drive—in this case, the contents of directory SD-2 on the hard disk in drive C. The DIR command displays directory information similar to the following:

```
Volume in drive C is HARD-DISK
Directory of  C:\SD-2

    .              <DIR>       1-31-89   10:46p
    ..             <DIR>       1-31-89   10:46p
SD-21              <DIR>       1-31-89   10:50p
SD-22              <DIR>       1-31-89   10:50p
        4 File(s)   31135744 bytes free
```

Note that the second line of the directory information states that \SD-2 is the path specification for the current directory on the hard disk in drive C.

With the cursor positioned after the C> prompt, type

```
CD SD-21
```

and press ⏎. This command instructs DOS to change the current directory of the default drive (drive C) to subdirectory SD-21. With the cursor positioned after the C> prompt, type

```
CD
```

and press ⏎. The CD command instructs DOS to display the path specification for the current directory of the default drive. The following directory path specification is displayed:

```
C:\SD-2\SD-21
```

This specification indicates that the current directory of the default drive (drive C) is directory SD-21, a subdirectory of directory SD-2, which is a subdirectory of the root directory.

■ *Keystroke Summary*

Displaying the current directory of a drive

Set: default drive to drive C

Type: CD

Press: ⏎

Changing the Current Directory with a Path from the Root Directory

In each of the following examples, notice that the path specified in each CD command begins with the root directory of the hard disk, since the first character of the directory path specification is a backslash. With the cursor positioned after the C> prompt, type

```
CD \SD-2\SD-22
```

and press ↵. The CD command instructs DOS to change the current directory of the disk in the default drive (drive C) directory SD-22, a subdirectory of directory SD-2, which is a subdirectory of the root directory.

With the cursor positioned after the C> prompt, type

```
CD \SD-1
```

and press ↵. The CD command instructs DOS to change the current directory of the disk in the default drive (drive C) to directory SD-1, a subdirectory of the root directory.

Note that every directory on a disk can be specified by a path that begins with the root directory. Thus you do not need to know the current directory to use the CD command to change the current directory to another directory. To change the current directory of the default drive to a new directory using the CD command, just specify the path of the new directory that begins with the root directory.

■ *Keystroke Summary*

Changing the current directory with a path from the root directory

Set: default drive to drive C

Type: CD *pathname*   where *pathname* is a valid directory path name that begins with a backslash (\)

Press: ↵

Creating Subdirectories of the Current Directory

You need not type a complete path starting with the root directory to create a subdirectory. Type the command

```
CD \
```

and press ↵ to make the root directory the current directory. Then, with the cursor positioned after the C> prompt, type

```
CD SD-2
```

and press ↵. The CD command instructs DOS to change the current directory of the default drive (drive C) to subdirectory SD-2. With the cursor positioned after the C> prompt, type

```
MD SD-23
```

and press ↵. With the cursor positioned after the C> prompt, type

```
MD SD-24
```

and press ⏎. The two MD commands instruct DOS to create directories SD-23 and SD-24, respectively, as subdirectories of the current directory (SD-2) of the default drive (drive C).

This example illustrates the normal way in which the MD command is used to create subdirectories of a directory. First use the CD command to change the current directory of the default drive to the appropriate directory. Then use the MD command to create subdirectories of the current directory.

Automatically Displaying the Current Directory Name with PROMPT

When you use a disk that has several subdirectories, you need a convenient way to keep track of the current directory. The **PROMPT** command is an internal DOS command that allows you to change the normal DOS prompt to a customized DOS prompt that includes the default drive and the path specification for the current directory. The PROMPT command instructs DOS to automatically display the customized prompt in place of the normal DOS prompt.

Type the command

```
CD \
```

and press ⏎ to make the root directory the current directory. With the cursor positioned after the C> prompt, type

```
PROMPT $P$G
```

and press ⏎. The PROMPT command instructs DOS to change the DOS prompt to the character string specified by PG. $P defines the first part of the new prompt to be the current directory specification. $G indicates that the > symbol is to be the last character in the new prompt. When control returns to command level, the following prompt is displayed:

```
C:\>
```

The new prompt indicates that drive C is the default drive and that the current directory is the root directory. With the cursor positioned after the C:\> prompt, change the current directory by typing

```
CD SD-2\SD-21
```

and pressing ⏎. When control returns to command level, the following prompt is displayed:

```
C:\SD-2\SD-21>
```

The new prompt indicates that drive C is the default drive and that the current directory is subdirectory SD-21.

With the cursor positioned after the C:\SD-2\SD-21> prompt, type

```
PROMPT
```

and press ⏎. When the PROMPT command is used without any parameters, it instructs DOS to reset its prompt to the normal DOS prompt. Notice that the normal DOS prompt C> is displayed after control returns to command level.

∎ *Keystroke Summary*

Changing the normal DOS prompt with the PROMPT command

Set: default drive to any drive

Type: PROMPT PG

Press: ⏎

Copying Files between Different Directories

Now that you know how to specify paths to different directories, you can use the COPY and XCOPY commands to copy files from one directory to another in the same way that you copy files between diskettes.

Copying Files from the Root Directory to a Subdirectory

If necessary, issue a CD command to change the current directory of the hard disk to the root directory. With the cursor positioned after the C> prompt, type

```
COPY CHKDSK.COM SD-1
```

and press ⏎. The COPY command instructs DOS to copy the specified file CHKDSK.COM from the current directory (root directory) of the default drive (drive C) to the specified subdirectory SD-1 (target directory) of the default drive using the same file name. Note that when the target parameter of the COPY command specifies a directory, the file name specified in the source parameter is used as the target file name. The complete specification for the copied file is C:\SD-1\CHKDSK.COM. With the cursor positioned after the C> prompt, type

```
COPY FORMAT.COM SD-1\FRMT.*
```

and press ⏎. The COPY command instructs DOS to copy the specified file FORMAT.COM from the current directory (root directory) of the default drive (drive C) to the specified subdirectory SD-1 of the default drive (drive C) using FRMT.COM as the target file name.

With the cursor positioned after the C> prompt, type

```
DIR SD-1
```

and press ⏎. The DIR command instructs DOS to display the contents of directory SD-1 for the default drive (drive C). Information similar to the following is displayed:

```
Volume in drive C is HARD-DISK
Directory of  C:\SD-1

.               <DIR>      1-31-89   10:46p
..              <DIR>      1-31-89   10:46p
CHKDSK  COM     9850       3-18-87   12:00p
FRMT    COM     11616      3-18-87   12:00p
        4 File(s)   31113216 bytes free
```

Note that subdirectory SD-1 now contains four entries. Two are directories, and two are the names of files that were just copied to directory SD-1.

With the cursor positioned after the C> prompt, type

```
COPY F*.COM SD-2\SD-22\*.BAK
```

and press ⏎. The COPY command instructs DOS to copy from the current directory (root directory) of the default drive (drive C) each file having F as the the first character of its filename and the extension .COM to the specified subdirectory SD-22 of the default drive (drive C) using the same filename and the extension .BAK.

With the cursor positioned after the C> prompt, type

```
DIR SD-2\SD-22
```

and press ⏎. The DIR command instructs DOS to display the contents of directory SD-22 for the default drive (drive C). Information similar to the following is displayed:

```
Volume in drive C is HARD-DISK
Directory of  C:\SD-2\SD-22

.               <DIR>      1-31-89   10:50p
..              <DIR>      1-31-89   10:50p
FDISK   BAK     48216      3-18-87   12:00p
FORMAT  BAK     11616      3-18-87   12:00p
        4 File(s)   31051776 bytes free
```

Note that subdirectory SD-22 now contains the two files copied to it.

Copying Files from One Subdirectory to Another Subdirectory

With the cursor positioned after the C> prompt, type

```
CD SD-1
```

and press ⏎. The CD command instructs DOS to change the current directory of the default drive (drive C) to the specified directory SD-1. With the cursor positioned after the C> prompt, type

```
COPY CHKDSK.COM \SD-2\SD-21
```

and press ⏎. The COPY command instructs DOS to copy the specified file CHKDSK.COM from the current directory of the default drive—in this case, subdirectory SD-1 of drive C—to the specified subdirectory SD-21 of the default drive (drive C) using the same file name. Note that the target directory specification begins with a backslash (\). The leading backslash is necessary because directory SD-2 is not a subdirectory of the current directory SD-1 on the default drive (drive C). Consequently, the target directory specification must begin with the root directory to define a valid directory path to subdirectory SD-21.

Displaying Information in a Directory Structure

In several of the previous sections the DIR command was used to display the contents of a particular directory. The DIR command, however, does not give you a complete picture of the directory structure of a disk. The **TREE** command is an external DOS command that allows you to display information describing the directory structure of a disk. See the DOS reference manual for more information about the TREE command.

The CHKDSK command can be used with the /V (view) parameter to display the path specification for each directory and the file specifications for all entries in each directory on a disk. Refer to Chapter 8 for more information about the CHKDSK /V command.

Setting an Extended Search Path for DOS to Locate Commands (PATH)

Recall that an external DOS command must be loaded into memory from a disk before it can be executed. If such a command is entered and if no path specification precedes the command name, DOS searches only the current directory of the disk in the default drive to find the command. If the command is not in the current directory, DOS displays the following message:

```
Bad command or file name
```

When you boot the system on your personal computer, the default search path is set to null (no path). This means that DOS searches only the current directory for an external DOS command. The **PATH** command is an internal DOS command that allows you to extend the **search path** that DOS uses to locate an external DOS command. When an extended search path is set by the PATH command, DOS uses the extended search path to search for external commands and batch files (files having an extension of .COM, .EXE, or .BAT) that were not found while searching the current directory.

Change the current directory back to the root directory. With the cursor positioned after the C> prompt, type

    PATH

and press ⏎. The PATH command instructs DOS to display the following message:

    No Path

With the cursor positioned after the C> prompt, type

    CHKDSK

and press ⏎. Since there is no extended search path, DOS searches for the CHKDSK program in the current directory—in this case, the root directory of the disk in the default drive (drive C). Since the CHKDSK program is located in the current directory, it is loaded into memory and executed.

With the cursor positioned after the C> prompt, type

    CD SD-2

and press ⏎. The CD command changes the current directory of the disk in the default drive (drive C) to subdirectory SD-2. With the cursor positioned after the C> prompt, type

    CHKDSK

and press ⏎. DOS searches the current directory of the disk in the default drive—in this case, subdirectory SD-2 on the hard disk in drive C—to find the CHKDSK program. Since the CHKDSK program is not in subdirectory SD-2, DOS displays the following message:

    Bad command or file name

With the cursor positioned after the C> prompt, type

    \CHKDSK

and press ⏎. The leading backslash (\) specifies a path to the root directory of the default drive (drive C). Consequently, the path specification (\) before the command name instructs DOS to look in the specified directory—in this case, the root directory of drive C—for the CHKDSK program. You should see the normal CHKDSK output.

The PATH command can be used to automatically tell DOS to search a particular directory (or directories) if the specified command is not found in the current directory. With the cursor positioned after the C> prompt, type

    PATH \

and press ⏎. The PATH command instructs DOS to set the extended search path to the root directory of the default drive. With the cursor positioned after the C> prompt, type

    PATH

and press ⏎. This PATH command instructs DOS to display the extended search path that was set in the first PATH command. The following information is displayed:

```
PATH=\
```

With the cursor positioned after the C> prompt, type

```
CHKDSK
```

and press ⏎. DOS searches for the CHKDSK program in the current directory of the disk in the default drive—in this case, subdirectory SD-2 on the hard disk in drive C. When DOS does not find the CHKDSK program in the current directory, it checks to see whether an extended search path is defined. DOS determines that the root directory of the disk in the default drive (drive C) is specified as an extended search path, and this is where DOS finds the CHKDSK program.

Insert a blank formatted diskette in drive A. With the cursor positioned after the C> prompt, type A: and press ⏎ to change the default disk drive to drive A. With the cursor positioned after the A > prompt, type

```
CHKDSK
```

and press ⏎. DOS searches the current directory of the disk in the default drive (drive A) and then the root directory (extended search path) of the disk in the default drive for the CHKDSK program. DOS cannot find the CHKDSK program on the diskette in drive A, so it displays the following message:

```
Bad command or file name
```

Since the DOS commands are in the root directory of the hard disk in drive C, the search path must specify more than the root directory of the disk in the default drive. It needs to specify the root directory of the hard disk in drive C.

With the cursor positioned after the A > prompt, type

```
PATH C:\
```

and press ⏎. This PATH command instructs DOS to set the extended search path to the root directory of the hard disk in drive C. With the cursor positioned after the A > prompt, type

```
CHKDSK
```

and press ⏎. DOS uses the extended search path—in this case, the root directory of the hard disk in drive C—to locate and execute the CHKDSK program.

Just as the PATH command can be used to set an extended search path, it can also be used to remove an extended search path, that is, to set the extended search path to null (no path). With the cursor positioned after the A > prompt, type

```
PATH;
```

and press ⏎. When the PATH command is followed by only a semicolon (;), it instructs DOS to reset the search path to no path.

■ *Keystroke Summary*

Displaying the extended search path

Type: PATH

Press: ⏎

■ *Keystroke Summary*

Setting the extended search path

Type: PATH *pathspec*   where *pathspec* specifies a valid path specification

Press: ⏎

■ *Keystroke Summary*

Resetting the extended search path to no path

Type: PATH;

Press: ⏎

Deleting (Removing) Subdirectories (RMDIR, RD)

The **RMDIR** (ReMove DIRectory) command is an internal DOS command that instructs DOS to remove (delete) a subdirectory entry from its parent directory. Note that a subdirectory must be empty (except for the period (.) and double-period (..) entries) before it can be removed from its parent directory. Also note that you cannot remove the current directory or the root directory of a disk. **RD** is an abbreviation for RMDIR.

Change the current directory back to the root directory of the hard disk in drive C. With the cursor positioned after the C> prompt, type

```
DEL SD-1\*.*
```

and press ⏎. The DEL command instructs DOS to delete all file entries from subdirectory SD-1 on the disk in the default drive (drive C). After the files are deleted, subdirectory SD-1 contains only the period (.) and double-period (..) entries. Thus subdirectory SD-1 can now be removed from its parent directory. With the cursor positioned after the C> prompt, type

```
RD SD-1
```

and press ⏎. The RD command instructs DOS to remove subdirectory SD-1 from its parent directory—in this case, the root directory of the hard disk in drive C.

With the cursor positioned after the C> prompt, type

```
CD SD-2
```

and press ⏎. The CD command changes the current directory of the disk in the default drive (drive C) to subdirectory SD-2. With the cursor positioned after the C> prompt, type

```
DEL SD-21
```

and press ⏎. This DEL command is equivalent to DEL SD-21*.* and instructs DOS to delete all file entries from subdirectory SD-21 on the disk in the default drive (drive C). With the cursor positioned after the C> prompt, type

```
RD SD-21
```

and press ⏎. The RD command instructs DOS to remove subdirectory SD-21 from its parent directory—in this case, subdirectory SD-2 on the hard disk in drive C.

With the cursor positioned after the C> prompt, type

```
DEL SD-22
```

and press ⏎. The DEL command instructs DOS to delete all file entries from subdirectory SD-22 on the disk in the default drive (drive C). With the cursor positioned after the C> prompt, type

```
RD SD-22
```

and press ⏎. The RD command instructs DOS to remove subdirectory SD-22 from its parent directory—in this case, subdirectory SD-2 on the hard disk in drive C.

Issue two more RD commands to delete subdirectories SD-23 and SD-24. Then, with the cursor positioned after the C> prompt, type

```
DEL *.*
```

and press ⏎. The DEL command instructs DOS to delete all file entries from the current directory of the default drive—in this case, subdirectory SD-2 on the hard disk in drive C. Subdirectory SD-2 is now ready to be removed from the directory structure.

The current directory needs to be changed to its parent directory—in this case, the root directory—since the current directory cannot be removed from the directory structure of a disk. With the cursor positioned after the C> prompt, type

```
CD ..
```

and press ⏎. The CD command changes the current directory of the default drive to SD-2's parent, the root directory of the hard disk in drive C. With the cursor positioned after the C> prompt, type

```
RD SD-2
```

and press ⏎. The RD command instructs DOS to remove subdirectory SD-2 from its parent directory.

Removing a subdirectory from the current directory

Set: default drive to drive C with *subdirname* a subdirectory of the current directory

Type: `DEL` *subdirname*

Press: ⏎

Type: `RD` *subdirname*

Press: ⏎

■ *What Can
Go Wrong?*

1. After you enter a RD command, the following message is displayed:

```
Invalid path, not directory,
or directory not empty
```

Cause: There are four possible causes: (1) the path specification is invalid, (2) the specified subdirectory is the current directory, (3) the specified subdirectory is invalid, or (4) the specified subdirectory is not empty.

Solution: Check the RD command line for errors. If you specified the current directory, change directories to its parent and reissue the command. If there is no obvious error, issue a DIR command to display the contents of the specified subdirectory, delete everything but the period (.) and double period (..) entries, and then repeat the RD command. ■

Summary

Topic or Feature	Command or Reference	Page
Create (make) a subdirectory	MKDIR *subdirspec* MD *subdirspec*	140
Change the current directory	CHDIR *pathspec* CD *pathspec*	144
Display the current directory	CD	145
Change the current directory to the parent directory	CD ..	155
Change the current directory to the root directory	CD \	144
Change the normal DOS prompt to a customized DOS prompt	PROMPT PG	148
Reset the DOS prompt to the normal DOS prompt	PROMPT	149

Topic or Feature	Command or Reference	Page
Display the directory structure of a disk	TREE	151
Display the directory structure of a disk along with file and directory names	CHKDSK /V	151
Display the extended search path	PATH	151
Set the extended search path	PATH *pathspec*	152
Reset the extended search path to no path	PATH;	154
Remove (delete) a subdirectory	RMDIR *subdirspec* RD *subdirspec*	154

Self-Test

1. The _____ directory is created by DOS each time the FORMAT command is used to format a disk. _____ are used to divide a disk into separate storage areas that can be used like separate disks.

2. The _____ of a disk is the directory that you are currently working in or the directory that you were working in on another drive.

3. A _____ is the route you must follow to trace your way from the disk's root directory to a particular place in the directory structure.

4. The backslash (\) is used in a path name to indicate the _____ directory or to act as a _____ to separate directory names.

5. The _____ command is used to create subdirectories on a disk.

6. The _____ command is used to change the current directory.

7. The _____ command can be used to change the normal DOS prompt to a customized DOS prompt.

8. The _____ command can be used to display information describing the directory structure of a disk.

9. The _____ command can be used to extend the search path that DOS uses to locate an external DOS command.

10. The _____ command is used to delete a subdirectory entry from its parent directory.

Exercises

In each exercise, choose the environment that exists on your personal computer: (1) your personal computer has a hard disk (drive C) that contains the DOS programs and a diskette drive (drive A) that contains a target diskette, or (2) your personal computer contains two diskette drives, drive A that contains the DOS System diskette and drive B that contains a target diskette.

1. Insert a blank diskette in the target diskette drive. Use an appropriate DOS command to perform each of the assigned tasks.

   a. Format the target diskette as a bootable diskette with volume label *namef*#8-1, where *name* denotes the first six characters of your last name or your entire last name (whichever is shorter) and *f* denotes the first character of your first name.

   b. Create the directory structure given in the following diagram on the target diskette:

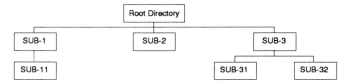

   c. Display the directory structure for the target diskette on the screen.

   d. Use the output redirection operator to obtain a hard copy listing of the directory structure for the target diskette.

   e. Make the current directory of the target diskette the root directory.

   f. Copy all DOS files that have file names beginning with the character F into subdirectory SUB-2 on the target diskette.

   g. Make subdirectory SUB-32 the current directory of the target diskette.

   h. Change the DOS prompt to a customized DOS prompt that contains the current directory specification followed by the > symbol.

   i. Copy all DOS files that have file names beginning with the character C into subdirectory SUB-32 of the target diskette.

   j. Copy COMMAND.COM from the current directory (SUB-32) of the target diskette into subdirectory SUB-1.

   k. Make subdirectory SUB-11 the current directory of the target diskette.

l. Copy CHKDSK.COM from subdirectory SUB-32 into the current directory (SUB-11) of the target diskette.

m. Display the directory structure for the target diskette along with all file names and directory names on the screen.

n. Use the output redirection operator to obtain a hard copy listing of the directory structure for the target diskette along with all file names and directory names.

o. Delete subdirectories SUB-1, SUB-11, and SUB-31 from the directory structure of the target diskette.

p. Repeat parts (m) and (n).

■ PART THREE

WordPerfect 5.0

·12

Word Processing on a Computer

This chapter

- describes the functions of a word processor
- previews WordPerfect 5.0

Word Processing

Perhaps the most obvious reason for learning to use a word processing program is that, compared with a typewriter, a word processor simplifies the mechanics of typing. Most word processors include a **word wrap** feature that senses when you have gone beyond the right margin and automatically moves the last word to the next line, so you don't have to count characters after the bell rings. With a typewriter, all but the most trivial errors mean retyping a page. With a word processor you can add or delete material on the screen and let the software adjust the text.

Beyond supporting document creation, most word processors can check your spelling and help you make corrections. (The bad news is that there is no longer any excuse for spelling errors.) You can even purchase programs that check document *style* and suggest improvements.

There is more to writing than just mechanics, however. The secret to quality writing is revising material again and again. A word processor helps by making it easy to insert, delete, and move text. With a typewriter, you might prepare a first draft, mark corrections, and then type the final version. With a word processor you can prepare *several* drafts before printing the document. The result is often better quality in less time.

Word processing programs also support efficient document storage and retrieval. To a college student, electronic filing may seem insignificant, but to business people it is crucial. The problem is volume; as the number of documents grows, finding the one you need becomes increasingly difficult. Most word processors work with the operating system to create and manage directories and files. (See Chapter 11.) Some allow a user to search through several documents on disk for a key word or phrase. For example, you might be able to locate "the Crosby memo" by searching a set of files for the name "Crosby." Additionally, most include a mail merge routine and other features to support mass mailings.

Many word processors allow you to improve the physical appearance of a document by changing type fonts, varying the pitch (characters per inch), or drawing lines to box or offset portions of the text. A few allow you to insert graphics into the text. There is a fine line between a sophisticated word processor and a desktop publishing program.

WordPerfect 5.0 is a word processing program that runs on IBM PC, PS-2, and compatible computers. (A Macintosh version is available but will not be discussed here.) WordPerfect incorporates most of the features described above, although not all of them will be introduced in these tutorials.

As this book went to press, WordPerfect version 5.1 had just been released. See Appendix F for a summary of how the new version affects the tutorials in this text.

Conventions

Program and Data Disks

Before you start the first tutorial (Chapter 13), you should have a working copy of WordPerfect 5.0 and a formatted data diskette; see Chapter 7 for instructions on formatting a disk. You will need an operating system disk (PC-DOS or MS-DOS), too. The tutorials assume that your program disk is accessed through drive A and your data disk is accessed through drive B; substitute your own disk drives as appropriate.

Entering WordPerfect Commands

WordPerfect is **command-driven**; to tell the program to perform a task, the user issues a command by pressing a **function key**, either by itself or in combination with another key. The various key combinations are summarized on a template that fits around a PC's function keys (Fig. 12.1) or just above a PS/2's function keys. The template is color coded: red for Ctrl, green for ⇧, blue for Alt, and black for no

Figure 12.1
The template summarizes the keystrokes needed to activate the various WordPerfect commands. Courtesy of WordPerfect Corporation.

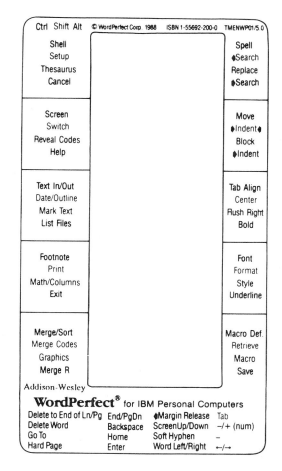

companion key. Note the sequence; match the order of the features on the template with the relative positions of the Ctrl, ⬆, and Alt keys.

For example, consider function key F7. The word *Footnote* is printed in red. Red means Ctrl, so press

Ctrl *and* F7

to add a footnote to a document. On the next line, *Print* appears in green. Green means ⬆, so pressing

⬆ *and* F7

generates a print command. On the third line, *Math / Columns* is blue, which corresponds to Alt. Press

Alt *and* F7

to use WordPerfect's math and columns features. Finally, the word *Exit* is printed in black, which means "no companion key." Press

F7

by itself to exit WordPerfect.

To many people, simultaneously pressing two keys feels unnatural. Release one key too soon, and you get the wrong function. Hold both keys for too long, and the computer might "beep" at you or activate the wrong function. Timing is the key. For example, imagine that you want to print a document. The command is indicated by simultaneously pressing

⬆ and F7

Do it in three distinct steps. First, hold down the ⬆ key. Next, tap F7 as though you were typing a single character, and then release it. (Note that pressing the function key is always the second step.) Finally, release ⬆. Soon that sequence will become second nature.

WordPerfect responds to many commands by displaying a menu. Some occupy a full screen; others, a single line. These menus will be reproduced here as accurately as possible, but typesetting limitations will occasionally make it necessary to spread a one-line menu over two lines.

Defaults

WordPerfect is incredibly rich, with features to support almost anything you can imagine doing with text. For an experienced user, that's great, but too much complexity can get in the way of learning. Thus WordPerfect assumes **default** values for many key parameters. When you first begin using the program, the defaults are fine. As you'll discover in Chapter 13, it is very easy to enter, save, and print a standard, "plain vanilla" document. Later, you will learn how to override the defaults to produce more sophisticated documents.

A Look Ahead

This book does not pretend to cover every WordPerfect feature; its intent is to help you learn this powerful word processing tool. It is organized as a series of tutorials. In Chapter 13 you'll learn how to create a document, print a copy, and save the text on disk. Chapter 14 introduces more sophisticated document editing. In subsequent chapters you'll learn how to store and retrieve documents, merge previously written material to create new, customized documents, control document format, type columns of data, and add graphic images to a document. When you finish, you will be able to use the WordPerfect reference manual to learn additional features on your own.

Don't just read the tutorials; you can't learn WordPerfect by reading about it. Sit down at a computer and follow along, step by step. If you commit a reasonable amount of time, you'll be surprised at how quickly your confidence and skill develop.

Summary

You'll find a summary of new WordPerfect features at the end of each chapter. No features were introduced in Chapter 12.

Self-Test

1. A word processing program's _____ feature automatically moves the last word to the beginning of the next line when you type beyond the right margin.

2. The secret to quality writing is _____.

3. Most WordPerfect commands are issued by pressing a _____, often in combination with another key.

4. The WordPerfect commands are summarized on a _____ that fits around (or just above) the computer's function keys.

5. To simplify producing a "plain vanilla" document, WordPerfect assumes _____ values for many key parameters.

Exercises

1. Briefly explain how a word processing program helps to simplify the mechanics of typing.

2. "The secret to quality writing is revising material again and again." Do you agree? Why or why not?

3. Why are efficient document storage and retrieval important?

4. WordPerfect is a command-driven operating system. What does that mean?

5. What is a default? Why are defaults useful?

∎13
Creating and Printing a Document

This chapter introduces the WordPerfect features and commands that allow you to:

- start WordPerfect
- exit WordPerfect
- type a document
- save a document
- replace a document on disk
- control the cursor
- correct typing errors
- print a document

Starting WordPerfect

This first tutorial shows you how to enter, save, and print a document. Don't just read it. You'll learn to use WordPerfect much more quickly if you actually sit down at a computer and follow along, step by step.

Necessary Equipment

You'll need an IBM PC, PS/2, or compatible computer equipped with a keyboard, a screen, a printer, and at least 384K bytes of memory. It should have either two diskette drives or one diskette and a hard disk.

If you have a two-diskette system, you will also need a formatted data disk and a working copy of WordPerfect 5.0 consisting of two disks labeled WordPerfect 1 and WordPerfect 2. You will also need a copy of the operating system, PC-DOS or MS-DOS. Place a WordPerfect template around or above your keyboard's function keys before you begin.

Booting the Operating System

Boot the operating system and enter the current date and time. (See Chapter 6 for details.) If your system has two diskette drives, insert the WordPerfect 1 disk into drive A and your data disk into drive B, and make sure that both drive doors are closed.

Loading WordPerfect on a Two-Disk System

Skip this section if you are using a hard disk. If you have correctly booted DOS, your screen will resemble the top several lines of Fig. 13.1, with the cursor following the A> prompt. Type B: and then press ⏎; the last screen line will read

    A>B:

A new prompt, B>, will appear (Fig. 13.1). Drive B, the new default drive, holds your data disk.

The next step is to load WordPerfect. Immediately following the B> prompt, type A:WP; the last line on the screen will read

    B>A:WP

(Fig. 13.1). The B> prompt identifies the default drive as B, but the WordPerfect program is on the disk in drive A. The A: prefix tells the operating system to access drive A for this operation. WP is the WordPerfect program's name. Thus A:WP means "access drive A and load the program named WP."

Figure 13.1

Type two commands to load WordPerfect. The B: command tells the operating system to use the disk in drive B to save and retrieve documents. The A:WP command tells the operating system to get the WordPerfect program from the disk in drive A.

```
Current date is Tue  8-02-1988
Enter new date (mm-dd-yy): 3-1-89
Current time is 11:21:09.23
Enter new time: 10:15

The IBM Personal Computer DOS
Version 3.30 (C)Copyright International Business Machines Corp 1981, 1987
              (C)Copyright Microsoft Corp 1981, 1986

A>B:

B>A:WP_
```

Press ⏎ to enter the command. The disk drive will activate, and a logo and some messages will appear on the screen. At this point the system will pause, and you might see the message

```
Insert diskette labeled "WordPerfect 2" and press any key
```

just below the copyright statement. Remove the WordPerfect 1 disk from drive A, insert the WordPerfect 2 disk, and close the drive door. Then press any key (the space bar is a good choice). The drive will activate, and the WordPerfect work screen will appear.

Loading WordPerfect on a Hard Disk System

Skip this section if you are using two diskettes. If you have properly booted your hard disk system, the last line will contain a C> prompt followed by the cursor. Type CD, a space, and \WP50, and then press ⏎ (Fig. 13.2); the line should read

```
C>CD  \WP50
```

CD is a DOS change directory command. The space is optional. Following it is a backslash and then the name of a directory, WP50, that keeps track of the files and documents stored on a portion of the hard disk. See Chapter 11 for more on directories. The backslash (\) key is just to the left of the space bar on an IBM PC keyboard and between the ⬅ and ⏎ keys on a PS/2 keyboard.

After you press ⏎, the hard disk will activate, and a fraction of a second later a new C> or C:\WP50> prompt will appear on the screen. Type WP; your screen will resemble Fig. 13.2, with the last line reading

```
C>WP
```

or

```
C:\WP50>WP
```

Figure 13.2

Type two commands to load WordPerfect. The CD \WP50 command tells the operating system to use the directory named WP50 to save and retrieve documents. The WP command tells the operating system to load the WordPerfect program.

```
Current date is Tue  1-01-1980
Enter new date: 3-1-89
Current time is  0:00:38.33
Enter new time: 11:45


The IBM Personal Computer DOS
Version 3.30 (C) Copyright International Business Machines Corp 1981, 1987
              (C) Copyright Microsoft Corp 1981, 1986

C>CD  \WP50
C>WP
```

Then press ⏎. You'll see a logo and some messages. A few seconds later the WordPerfect work screen will appear.

■ *Keystroke Summary*

Loading WordPerfect

Diskette:		**Hard Disk:**	
Type:	**B:**	Type:	**CD \WP50**
Press:	⏎	Press:	⏎
Type:	**A:WP**	Type:	**WP**
Press:	⏎	Press:	⏎
Remove:	WordPerfect 1		
Insert:	WordPerfect 2		
Press:	any key		

■ *What Can Go Wrong?*

1. Following the CD \WP50 command, a message indicates that the directory does not exist or could not be found.

Cause: When WordPerfect was installed, the WP50 directory was not created or the directory was subsequently deleted.

Solution: For now, enter the following DOS commands:

```
Type:   MD C:\WP50
Press:  ⏎
Type:   CD C:\WP50
Press:  ⏎
```

Then insert the WordPerfect 1 disk in the diskette drive, type A:WP, and press ⏎. When the logo screen appears, remove WordPerfect 1 from the diskette drive and insert the disk marked WordPerfect 2. See Chapter 11 for more on directories.

2. After you type WP, a "File not found" message appears.

Cause: You might have misspelled the program name. The disk in drive A might not contain WordPerfect. On a hard disk system the program might not be stored on the disk.

Solution: Make sure the WordPerfect 1 disk is in drive A, retype WP, and press ⏎. On a hard disk system, retype the program name, WP, and press ⏎. If that doesn't work, insert the WordPerfect 1 disk in the diskette drive, type A:WP, press ⏎, and follow the instructions for loading WordPerfect from a diskette drive.

3. A message indicates that the WordPerfect 2 disk could not be found. A B> prompt is displayed on the last screen line.

Cause: Unable to find WordPerfect 2, the operating system quit trying. Perhaps you pressed a key *before* you inserted the WordPerfect 2 disk.

Solution: Make sure you have both the WordPerfect 1 and WordPerfect 2 disks. Insert WordPerfect 1 into drive A, type WP, and press ⏎. After the logo appears, when the system stops reading drive A, remove WordPerfect 1 and insert WordPerfect 2. Do *not* press a key until *after* the WordPerfect 2 disk is in the drive and the drive door is closed.

4. A message reading "Are other copies of WordPerfect currently running?" appears near the bottom of the logo screen.

Cause: The person who last used your copy of WordPerfect did not exit the system properly.

Solution: Type the letter N (for no), and WordPerfect will reset the system for you. *Caution:* If you and another person are trying to use WordPerfect at the same time on the same computer (a rare event), postpone your session or get help. ■

The WordPerfect Work Screen

The WordPerfect **work screen** (Fig. 13.3) simulates a blank sheet of paper. The last line on the screen is called the **status line**. It indicates the document number (in a later chapter you'll learn how to switch between two documents) and the cursor's page, line, and character position. As you begin, the cursor is located at the top left of the screen on page 1. The line position, 1", is measured in inches from the top of

Figure 13.3
The WordPerfect work screen simulates a clean sheet of paper. The status line indicates the document number, the cursor's current page, line, and character position, and other information.

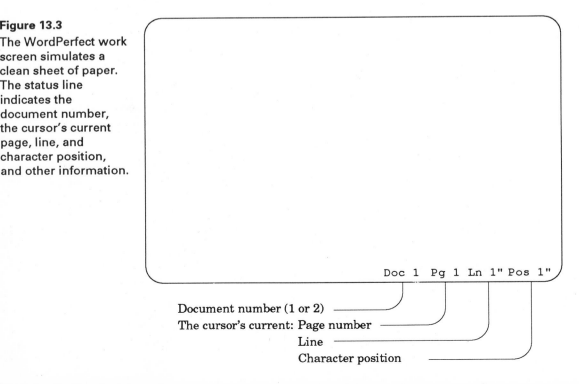

Doc 1 Pg 1 Ln 1" Pos 1"

Document number (1 or 2)
The cursor's current: Page number
Line
Character position

the page; by default, six lines are displayed per vertical inch. The character position, 1", is measured in inches from the left edge of the simulated sheet of paper; by default, ten characters are displayed per horizontal inch. The balance of the status line is blank; later, however, important information will appear there.

Most screens display twenty-five 80-character lines; because the last line is reserved for status information, at most 24 lines of text can be seen. A typical document contains more than 24 lines, so each screen shows only part of the document. Later in this chapter you'll learn how to move from screen to screen.

When you do print a document, WordPerfect assumes an 8.5 x 11-inch sheet of paper with one-inch margins at the top, the bottom, and both sides. The equivalent typewriter settings are side margins of 10 and 75, ten characters per inch, and 54 single-spaced lines per page. The tab stops are initially set every half-inch. In Chapter 16 you'll learn how to change the page defaults, but for now they are quite reasonable.

▪ *What Can Go Wrong?*

1. Your status line indicates line 1 (instead of 1") and character position 10 (instead of 1").

Cause: Your copy of WordPerfect is set to display the line count and the character count instead of inches.

Solution: If you prefer lines and characters, there is no need to change the unit of measure. Several position references in this book will require mental translation, but all WordPerfect 5.0 features will work as indicated. To change to inches, perform the following steps:

```
Press:  ⇧ and F1 to issue a Setup command
Type:   8 to select Units of measure
Type:   2 to control the Status Line Display
Type:   " (a double quote mark) to select inches
Press:  F7 to return to the work screen ▪
```

Exiting WordPerfect

Ideally, these tutorials should be completed in a single session, but that's not always possible. Note that on the template the word *Exit* is printed in black near F7. Black means no companion key, so

```
Press:    F7
```

by itself to exit WordPerfect. Try it. A message will appear on the status line:

```
Save document? (Y/N) Yes
```

Because no document exists, there is no point in saving one; type N for no. The process of saving a document will be discussed later in this chapter.

Almost immediately, another message will be displayed:

```
Exit WP? (Y/N) No   (Cancel to return to document)
```

Type Y. The work screen will disappear, and if you are using a two-diskette system, a message

```
Insert disk with  \COMMAND.COM in drive A and strike any key
when ready
```

will be displayed. Remove WordPerfect 2 from drive A and insert WordPerfect 1; then press any key (for example, the space bar), and a B> prompt will appear. If you are using a hard disk system, a C> prompt will be displayed as soon as the work screen clears. At this point, assuming that you really are finished, you can remove your disks and quit.

To continue with the tutorial, reload WordPerfect; go back to the beginning of the chapter if you don't remember how. When the work screen appears, move on to the next section. If you had started a document and saved it to disk, you could retrieve it and continue working. The retrieve command will be covered in Chapter 14.

■ *Keystroke Summary*

Exit WordPerfect

Press:	F7
Type:	**Y** or **N**
Type:	**Y**
Remove:	WordPerfect 2
Insert:	WordPerfect 1
Press:	any key

Typing a Document

The First Two Paragraphs

You are now ready to begin the tutorial. The first step is to type a sample document; Fig. 13.4 shows how the screen should look when you are finished.

As you begin, the cursor should be at the top left of the screen (line 1", position 1"); if it isn't, press ⬅ until it is. Type the first line, PROGRAM PROPOSAL, in capital letters. Hold down ⬆ and type each character in turn, or use the CapsLock key. This key works like a toggle switch. Press CapsLock once, and the alphabetic keys generate capital letters. (Press ⬆ and a key for lowercase.) Press CapsLock again, and the keyboard returns to normal. Note that only the alphabetic keys are affected; for example, if you press 1, you will enter the digit 1 no matter how CapsLock is set.

How can you tell if CapsLock has been pressed? Look to the right of the status line and find the abbreviation Pos (for position). If the

Figure 13.4

After you type the first two paragraphs, your screen will resemble this one.

```
PROGRAM PROPOSAL

THE BETAGOSA HILLBILLIES

This proposed new show combines the best of Star Treck, The
Beverly Hillbillies, and Gilligan's Island. The main characters
include:

        Captain Jed, the expedition leader
        Granny Sock, his crusty old assistant
        Professor Gallagher, the off-beat science officer

Professor Gallagher will be the focus of humor. He is a cross
between Star Trek's Scotty and Gilligan (from Gilligan's Island).
An early episode will establish that he was named after the 20th
century conedian Gallagher. This part could be a star vehicle for
a young commedian with a Gallagher-like style.

_




                                        Doc 1 Pg 1 Ln 3.83" Pos 1"
```

Caps Lock key has been pressed, POS will appear in all capital letters. Press Caps Lock again, and the o and the s will change to lowercase.

Type the first line from Fig. 13.4 and press ↵. As you type, note the cursor's changing position. After you finish, the status line will indicate line 1.16", position 1".

Press ↵ to insert a blank line; note that the cursor moves to line 1.33". Type the title, THE BETAGOSA HILLBILLIES, in capital letters and press ↵. Press ↵ again to insert another blank line.

Make sure the Caps Lock feature is off before you start typing the first paragraph; use Fig. 13.4 as a guide. Press ⇧ and an alphabetic key to type a capital letter. Like most word processors, WordPerfect has a **word wrap** feature, so press ↵ only at the end of a paragraph or a short line.

Type as quickly as you can. The document in Fig. 13.4 contains intentional errors; do not correct them yet. If you make unintentional errors, the ← key moves the cursor one position to the left and erases the character at that position; after you have erased the bad character or characters, simply resume typing. If you notice other mistakes, correct them later.

The first paragraph's third line is an example of a **short line**. Because you don't want anything else on that line, type the word *include*, type a colon, and then press ↵. After you do, the status line will indicate line 2.16"; press ↵ once more to add another blank line.

The next three lines list the main characters. Note that the list is indented. You could use the space bar and count spaces before typing each entry, but it's easier to use the ⇥ key. Press ⇥ once, and the cursor will move five positions to the right. Now type Captain Jed's description and press ↵. Use the same procedure for the other two characters.

Skip a line after Professor Gallagher and type the second paragraph. Once again use the ⬅ key to erase obvious typing errors. Note that there are spelling errors in the last two lines; do not correct them. Press ↵ when you reach the end of the paragraph.

■ *What Can
Go Wrong?*

1. A message appears on the status line or a new screen replaces the work screen.

Cause: You might have pressed a function key. When you press a function key, even accidentally, WordPerfect assumes that you want the associated service performed.

Solution: Press ⒡. If that doesn't work, read the message. Many WordPerfect features display a menu; often, typing 0 or pressing ⒡ will return you to your document. ■

Saving the Document

A computer's memory is volatile. You have typed two paragraphs. If power should suddenly fail, everything you have typed would be lost. To be safe, it's a good idea to save your document to disk at regular intervals. The examples in these tutorials assume that files are saved to a diskette in drive B or on hard disk directory WP50. Your instructor might want you to use different procedures.

Check the WordPerfect template. The word *Save* is printed in black near ⒡. When you press ⒡ by itself, you generate a save command. Try it.

Press: ⒡

A message will appear on the status line:

Document to be saved:

The cursor follows the message. WordPerfect is asking you to name the file. It is possible to save many different documents (or files) on a single disk. To distinguish them, each file is assigned a unique name. It is your responsibility to name your files.

A **file name** (see Chapter 9) consists of from one to eight characters. Select a name that suggests the file's contents. BETAHILL is a good choice for this document. Type BETAHILL; the status line will read

Document to be saved: BETAHILL

Then press ↵. A message will tell you that the file is being saved. Do be careful, however. If you should accidentally select a name that matches the name of a file already stored on disk, you could destroy that other file. See "What Can Go Wrong?".

After the file has been saved, the cursor will return to its last position in the document (Fig. 13.5). Note that the file name appears

Figure 13.5

Note that once you have saved the file, its name appears on the status line.

```
      Professor Gallagher, the off-beat science officer

Professor Gallagher will be the focus of humor. He is a cross
between Star Trek's Scotty and Gilligan (from Gilligan's Island).
An early episode will establish that he was named after the 20th
century conedian Gallagher. This part could be a star vehicle for
a young commedian with a Gallagher-like style.
_




B:\BETAHILL                                    Doc 1 Pg 1 Ln 3.83" Pos 1"
```

on the status line. The B:\ or C:\WP50 preceding the file name is a path name that shows where the document is stored.

■ *Keystroke Summary*

Save document

Press: [F10]

Type: *file name*

Press: [↵]

■ *What Can Go Wrong?*

1. After you type the file name and press [↵], a message reading "Replace B:\BETAHILL? (Y/N)" appears on the status line.

Cause: The name you chose matches the name of another file on the disk. If your file is saved, it will replace—and thus destroy—the old file.

Solution: If the old file is yours and you no longer need it, type Y (for yes). Your new file will replace (and thus erase) the old one. If you are not sure what the old file is, type N (for no). The next screen will ask you to enter a file name; this time, pick a different one. Try BETAHILL.xyz, where x, y, and z are your initials.

2. A cryptic message on the status line (for example, "Disk error") indicates that the system was unable to access your disk.

Cause: Fortunately, this is rare. There are many possible causes, including a defective disk drive, a bad disk, and an unformatted disk.

Solution: First, make sure that you have a data disk in drive B. If you do, try replacing it with a different data disk and follow the instructions on the status line. You will be presented with two choices: (1) retry or (2) cancel. After you have verified that drive B holds a formatted data disk, type 1. On a hard disk system, just type 1. If the error message reappears, get help.

3. The status line message indicates that your data disk is full.

Cause: As the message states, all available space on your data disk has been assigned to other files.

Solution: Replace the data disk with a blank, formatted data disk and then save the file. ■

Typing More Material

Figure 13.6 shows how the screen should look after the third paragraph has been entered; skip a line and type the paragraph. Note that, as you begin typing the 25th line, the first line **scrolls** out of sight. Don't worry, it's still in memory. There is simply no room on the screen to display it.

Saving the Document (Again)

Now that the entire document has been typed, it's a good idea to save it to disk. Once again, check the template. The word *Save* is printed in black near F10. Black means no companion key, so

    Press: F10

to issue a save command. This time, the previously assigned file name appears on the status line:

    Document to be saved: B:\BETAHILL

Remember that the prefix indicates a path name; the file name is BETAHILL. There is no reason to change the name; you're still working on the same document. Because the suggested name is acceptable, press ⏎.

A second message will appear:

    Replace B:\BETAHILL? (Y/N) No

The data disk already holds a file named BETAHILL. If the new version of the document is saved, it will replace the old one. Before WordPerfect carries out such potentially destructive operations, it

Figure 13.6

After all three paragraphs have been typed, your screen will resemble this one.

```
include:

     Captain Jed, the expedition leader
     Granny Sock, his crusty old assistant
     Professor Gallagher, the off-beat science officer

Professor Gallagher will be the focus of humor. He is a cross
between Star Trek's Scotty and Gilligan (from Gilligan's Island).
An early episode will establish that he was named after the 20th
century conedian Gallagher. This part could be a star vehicle for
a young commedian with a Gallagher-like style.

The story is set on the planet Betagosa, where the crew of the
starship Hindenberg find themselves marooned after Professor
Gallagher miscalculates E from Einstein's famous equation. The
planet is occupied by an advanced race called Betas. Many
humorous incidents are based on the crew's reaction to the
manners and customs of there new planet. Their problems are
complicated by the fact that the Betas have three arms, and
certain common human arm gestures are considered obscene. Another
source of embarassment is the way crew members keep disappearing
in the middle of important discussions because Professor
Gallagher accidentally beams them home.

B:\BETAHILL                                    Doc 1 Pg 1 Ln 5.83" Pos 1"
```

always asks the user's permission. Note that the cursor is blinking on the letter N. If you did not want to replace the old file, you could simply press ⏎; WordPerfect always suggests the least destructive option. If you want to replace the file, you must say so.

Some time ago, you saved the first two paragraphs of this document. What you've typed since then is in the computer's memory, but it has not yet been transferred to disk because nothing goes to disk unless you, the user, specifically order it. Thus the contents of disk and the contents of memory are different. Memory currently holds everything on the disk copy of BETAHILL plus the new paragraph, so if you copy memory to disk, you lose nothing. To replace the old version of your file, type Y. The word "Yes" will appear momentarily, and the file will be saved.

Correcting Typing Errors

Controlling the Cursor

After the completed document has been saved, your screen should once again resemble Fig. 13.6. You probably noticed a few errors in the sample text, and you might have made several more as you typed. The first step in correcting errors is learning to control the cursor. See Fig. 13.7 for a summary of the cursor control keys.

The cursor should be located just below the last line of the text. (If it isn't, don't worry.) Find the cursor control keys on your keyboard. When you press ↑, the cursor moves up one line. Press ↑ several times to move the cursor near the center of the screen. Press → to move

Figure 13.7

This table summarizes the keys that control the cursor.

Press	to move the cursor:
↑	one line up
↓	one line down
→	one character to the right
←	one character to the left
Ctrl *and* ←	one word to the left
Ctrl *and* →	one word to the right
End	to the end of the line
−	to the top of the screen
+	to the bottom of the screen
Home *then* ←	to the left margin
Home *then* →	to the end of the line
Home *then* ↑	to the top of the screen
Home *then* ↓	to the bottom of the screen
Home, *then* Home, *then* ↑	to the beginning of the document
Home, *then* Home, *then* ↓	to the end of the document
PgUp	to the prior page
PgDn	to the next page
⇥	right, to the next tab stop
⇧ *and* ⇥	left, to the next tab stop

it one character to the right; press ⬇ to move it down one line; press ⬅ to move it one character to the left. Hold down ➡, and the cursor moves rapidly to the right. (Release the key after a dozen characters or so.) If you hold a key, its action is repeated until you release it. (⇧, Alt, and Ctrl are the only keys that do not repeat.)

It is sometimes more convenient to move word by word than character by character. With the cursor anywhere on the screen, hold down Ctrl and tap ➡. The cursor should move to the first character in the next word. Press Ctrl *and* ⬅ to move the cursor one word to the left. If you hold down both Ctrl *and* ➡, the cursor moves rapidly from word to word until you release at least one of the keys. The same is true for Ctrl *and* ⬅.

The screen's top, bottom, left margin, and right margin are key points, and it is often useful to move to them quickly. With the cursor near the middle of the screen, press End. The cursor should move to the right margin. Next, look to the right of the numeric keypad and find the ⊟ and ⊞ keys. When you press ⊟, the cursor moves to the top of the screen. Press ⊞ to move the cursor to the bottom of the screen. Then press ⬆ several times to move it back near the middle of the screen.

Reaching the left margin involves two keys. Find Home. Press it, and release it. Then press ⬅ and the cursor will move to the left margin. Press Home, release it, and then press ⬆ to move the cursor to the top of the screen. Home *then* ➡ moves the cursor to the right margin, while Home *then* ⬇ moves it to the bottom of the screen. Home tells WordPerfect to move to a margin, and the arrow key indicates which margin.

Note that this key sequence is a bit different from those described earlier. For example, to move one word to the right, you *simultaneously* press Ctrl *and* ➡. To move to the left margin, you press the keys *sequentially*; in other words, press Home, release it, and *then* press ⬅.

The control keys discussed so far move the cursor around the screen, but the screen displays only a portion of the document. Press ⊟ to move to the top of the screen. Now, press ⬆, and a new line will appear. Do it again, and another new line appears. For each new line at the top of the screen, one line scrolls out of sight at the bottom. To get the now-hidden bottom lines back, press ⊞ to go to the bottom of the screen and then press ⬇.

Scrolling line by line is not very efficient. Press ⊟ to move the cursor back to the top of the screen. Now press ⊟ again. The cursor will move to the top of the *prior* screen, and you'll see a complete new screen. By pressing ⊟ again and again, you can scroll backward, screen by screen, through an entire document. The ⊞ key works the same way. Press it once, and the cursor moves to the bottom of the current screen. Press it again to get to the bottom of the next screen.

Later, when you begin writing longer documents, you will find the PgUp and PgDn keys useful. They move the cursor a page at a time. A

Figure 13.8

The Go To command, Ctrl *and* Home, can be used to move the cursor.

Press Go To and then:	to move the cursor to:
any alphabetic character	next occurrence of the character
a number	top of that page
↑	top of current page or column
↓	bottom of current page or column
Alt *and* F4	beginning of block
←	prior column
→	next column
Home *then* ←	first column
Home *then* →	last column

screen is limited to 24 lines of text, but a page holds, by default, 54 lines.

The beginning and end of the document are important reference points. To move the cursor to the beginning, press Home, release it, press Home again, and then press ↑. To move to the end of the document, press Home, then Home again, and then ↓. Press Home and an arrow key to move to one of the *screen's* margins. Press Home, Home again, and then an arrow key to move to one of the *document's* margins.

The key combination Ctrl *and* Home is known as the **Go To** key. Use it to quickly move the cursor. For example, press Home, *then* Home, *then* ↑ to return to the top of the document. Then press Ctrl *and* Home, and the message

```
Go to
```

will appear on the status line. Type K, and the cursor will stop just after the first letter K in the document. Other Go To options are summarized in Fig. 13.8.

Experiment with the cursor control keys until you feel comfortable with them.

■ *What Can Go Wrong?*

1. When you press a cursor control key, a number is displayed.

Cause: You probably pressed the NumLock key. Check the status line; if "Pos" is blinking, that's the problem.

Solution: Like CapsLock, NumLock is a toggle switch. Press it once, and the numeric keypad enters digits; press it again, and those same keys control the cursor. Press NumLock and then try the cursor keys. ■

Making Corrections

The cursor should be on the first line in the body of the text (line 1.66), just after the word *Treck*. (If it isn't, move it there.) *Treck* is spelled incorrectly. Move the cursor to the letter c in *Treck*, press Del, and the c will disappear. Pressing Del deletes a single character.

Next, replace the fourth word on that line, *show*, with the phrase *half-hour comedy*. The first step is to delete *show*. One option is to use [Del] to delete one character at a time, but there is an easier way. With the cursor on any character in the word *show*, press [Ctrl] and simultaneously press [←]. The word will disappear, and the cursor will mark the first letter in the next word, *combines*. (Don't hold down [←] or you will delete several consecutive words.)

Now type

```
half-hour comedy
```

The line will shift to the right to accommodate the new phrase. Initially, the line will extend beyond the right margin; after you finish typing, press any cursor control key, and WordPerfect will reformat the screen. Don't forget to insert a blank space between the words.

Figure 13.9 summarizes the rules for deleting text. Another common editing function is inserting text. For example, the program titles in the first paragraph should be enclosed in quotation marks. Move the cursor to the S in *Star* and type a quotation mark; it will be inserted just in front of the word. Now move the cursor to the blank space following the comma after *Trek* and type another quotation mark; it will appear just after the comma. Use the same procedure to enclose the other two titles in quotation marks.

Sometimes, instead of inserting a character, you want to replace one. For example, locate the word *conedian* in line 3.5". It's spelled incorrectly; it should be *comedian*. Position the cursor on the letter n. One option is to delete it and then insert the letter m. Another is to switch to **typeover mode**.

```
Press: [Ins]
```

The word *Typeover* will appear at the left of the status line. Type m, and it will replace n.

In typeover mode, each character you type replaces the one marked by the cursor. In **insert mode**, each character you type is inserted just to the left of the cursor. Like [Caps Lock], [Ins] is a toggle switch. Change back to insert mode by pressing [Ins] again; the file name will reappear on the status line.

There are two additional errors in the document. Drop down a line (to line 3.66"). Comedian is properly spelled with a single m, so delete

Figure 13.9

These keys and key combinations can be used to delete selected portions of the text.

To delete:	Press:
a character	[Del]
a character after moving the cursor one position to the left	[←]
a word	[Ctrl] *and* [←]
from cursor to end of line	[Ctrl] *and* [End]
from cursor to end of page	[Ctrl] *and* [PgDn]

one of them. Next, look at the list of characters. The second character's name is spelled incorrectly; it should be Socks, not Sock. Make sure you are in insert mode, position the cursor just after the k, and type s. If you spot more errors, correct them, too.

Saving the Corrections

Some time ago, you saved a copy of the document. Since then, you have made several changes that have not been saved to disk. If power were to fail now, the changes would be lost; so, before you move to the next step, save the revised document. Press [F10]. The file's name has not changed, so press [↵]. The contents of memory are more current than the contents of disk, so type Y to replace the file.

■ *What Can Go Wrong?*

1. When characters are typed, they replace existing characters.

Cause: If the word Typeover appears on the status line, you pressed [Ins].

Solution: Press [Ins]. Typeover will disappear from the status line, indicating insert mode.

2. You accidentally deleted the wrong material.

Cause: You made a common mistake.

Solution: If you deleted only a few characters, retype them. If you deleted a lengthy word or several words, press [F1]. The word *Undelete* and a menu will appear on the status line; the text to be undeleted will be highlighted. Type 1 to restore what you deleted.

3. After you finish a correction, the line is split just after the change.

Cause: You probably pressed [↵] after you made the correction. In some other software packages, such as Lotus, that's how you finish a correction.

Solution: Move the cursor to the end of the short line and press [Del]. If necessary, insert a blank space to separate the words. ■

Printing the Document

Read the document one more time and correct any remaining errors. When you're satisfied, make sure the printer is on and the paper is correctly loaded, and then print the document.

Once again, check the template. Find the word *Print* in green near function key [F7]. Green means [⇧], so to get the print menu, simultaneously

Press: [⇧] *and* [F7]

A new screen will appear (Fig. 13.10). It summarizes the features that control the printer. Note that the cursor marks the digit 0 near the bottom of the screen; by default, option 0 returns you to the prior screen. To print the complete document, type 1. After a brief delay, the document will start printing. Type 0 or press [↵] to return to the work screen.

Figure 13.10

The print menu lists the features that control the printer.

```
  Print

        1 - Full Document
        2 - Page
        3 - Document on Disk
        4 - Control Printer
        5 - Type Through
        6 - View Document
        7 - Initialize Printer

  Options

        S - Select Printer          Panasonic KX-P1091i
        B - Binding                 0"
        N - Number of Copies        1
        G - Graphics Quality        Medium
        T - Text Quality            High




  Selection: 0
```

By default, WordPerfect right-justifies printed text, inserting blank spaces between the words to force the last letter in each line to the right margin. The result is an attractive document with straight left and right margins. You'll learn how to change the defaults in Chapter 16.

It is possible to vary the print quality on some printers. By default, WordPerfect normally selects the best quality level. To conserve ribbons, you might prefer draft quality. If so, before you start the printer, type the letter T to select *Text Quality* from the print menu. Then type 2 to select *Draft* quality. Finally, print the document.

■ *Keystroke Summary*

Print document

Press: ⬆ *and* F7

Type: **1**

■ *What Can Go Wrong?*

1. Nothing prints.

Cause: You might have forgotten to turn on the printer. The printer might be out of paper. The ribbon might be out of ink or improperly installed. You might have a system problem.

Solution: Check to be sure the printer is on and the paper is properly loaded. Check the ribbon to be sure it is properly installed. In some computer centers, a single printer may be shared by two or more computers; look for a device called a T-switch and make sure it's set to your machine.

If the printer still does not start, press ⬆ *and* F7 and select option 4, printer control. Look for a message just below the center of the new screen. If it indicates that the system is "Waiting for a go," type the letter g, and the printer should start. Press ↵ twice to return to the work screen. If the printer *still* won't work, save the file, exit WordPerfect, reboot DOS, reload WordPerfect, retrieve the file (see Chapter 14), and try printing it again.

2. The printer works, but it prints garbage.

Cause: Something is wrong either with the printer or with the way the printer is defined to WordPerfect.

Solution: For now, skip the print step and try it later. Ask your instructor or the system manager to check the WordPerfect printer definition. ■

Exiting WordPerfect

That brings you to the end of the first tutorial. To exit WordPerfect,

    Press: F7

A message will appear on the status line:

    Save document? (Y/N) Yes

You saved the document just before you printed it, so there is nothing to be gained from saving it again. Type N (for no).

    Almost immediately, another message will appear:

    Exit WP? (Y/N) No   (Cancel to return to document)

Type Y. The work screen will disappear and, if you are using a two-diskette system, a message

    Insert disk with \COMMAND.COM in drive A and strike any key when ready

will be displayed. At this point, assuming that you really are finished, you can remove your disks and quit or start another application. If you are working in a lab, follow laboratory procedures.

    Do be careful when you respond to the exit WP prompt. If you type Y, you will return to the operating system, and everything in memory will be lost. If you type N, WordPerfect will remain active, but the screen will clear, and everything in memory will be lost. (Material stored on disk is safe, of course.) What do you do if you suddenly realize you forgot to save your document? Just press F1 (the cancel key) and cancel the command. Then press F7 to exit again. This time, save the file.

Summary

Topic or Feature	Command or Reference	Option	Page
Cancel a command	F1	—	176
Cursor control	Fig. 13.7	—	179
Delete text	Fig. 13.9	—	182
Exit WordPerfect	F7	—	173
Go To	Fig. 13.8	—	181
Load WordPerfect (diskette)	—	—	169
Load WordPerfect (hard disk)	—	—	170
Print a document	⇧ *and* F7	1	183

Topic or Feature	Command or Reference	Option	Page
Replace a document on disk	F10	—	178
Save a document	F10	—	176

Self-Test

1. How would you report today's date to DOS? _____ The current time? _____

2. The last line on the WordPerfect work screen is called the _____.

3. Because of WordPerfect's _____ feature, it is not necessary to press ⏎ at the end of each line.

4. Press _____ to save a document.

5. WordPerfect documents are saved and retrieved by a _____ assigned by the user.

6. Indicate the key (or keys) that move the cursor:
   a. one character to the right. _____
   b. one line up. _____
   c. one word to the right. _____
   d. to the top of the screen. _____
   e. to the screen's left margin. _____
   f. to the end of the document. _____
   g. to the end of the current line. _____
   h. to the top of the prior screen. _____

7. In _____ mode, WordPerfect inserts characters to the left of the cursor. In _____ mode, WordPerfect replaces the character marked by the cursor with the typed character.

8. To print a document, press _____ and then select from the menu.

9. Press _____ to exit WordPerfect.

10. Press _____ to cancel a WordPerfect command.

Exercises

1. If you press ⇧ *and* PrtSc, a copy of whatever is currently displayed on the screen is sent to the printer. Use this feature to give your instructor a step-by-step record of your progress through the tutorial. As a minimum, submit copies of a blank work screen, the

document before you begin editing, and the chapter tutorial's final document.

2. Use WordPerfect to write a letter to your spouse, your parents, your brother or sister, a relative, or a friend.

3. Use WordPerfect to type and print a class paper.

4. Type the following paragraph and save it using file name MAJORS. The paragraph contains several intentional typing errors; you will correct them in Exercise 5. The line numbers are for reference only; do not type them.

```
 1  ENROLLMENT IN COMPUTING MAJORS
 2
 3  Data processing, computer programming, and computer
 4  science are relatively new disciplines. At most
 5  schools, these programs started in the early 1970s.
 6  Given industrys demand for entry-level computer
 7  professionals, enrolment in these disciplines boomed,
 8  reaching a peak in the early 1980s. Since then, the
 9  number of students majoring in computer-related fields
10  has declined, sharply. Today there is a a shortage of
11  trained entry-level people.
```

5. Make the following corrections to the paragraph you typed in Exercise 4:

Line Change

```
 1  Replace COMPUTING with COMPUTER-RELATED.
 6  Change industrys to industry's.
 7  Change enrolment to enrollment.
10  Insert the word serious between a and shortage.
```

When you finish, replace the document on disk with the new version. Then print the document.

·14

Editing a Document

This chapter introduces the WordPerfect features and commands that allow you to:

- retrieve a file from disk
- add material to a document
- set tab stops
- indent a block of text
- move, copy, and delete blocks of text
- reveal and delete hidden codes
- restore deletions
- check spelling
- use the HELP feature

The Second Tutorial

In Chapter 13 you learned the basics of WordPerfect, essentially using the computer as a replacement for a typewriter. In this chapter you'll learn how to use a word processor to edit and improve your writing. This second tutorial is organized as a series of modules, each introducing a single feature. Boot DOS and load WordPerfect. When you see the initial work screen, you're ready to begin.

Retrieving a Document from Disk

At the end of the first tutorial you saved the new program proposal document on disk using the file name BETAHILL. A computer can display and manipulate only what is stored in its memory. Thus the first step in this tutorial is to copy the document back into memory.

Check the template and note the word *Retrieve* printed in green near F10. Green means ⬆. Assuming that you know the document's file name,

    Press: ⬆ *and* F10

to **retrieve** it from disk. A message

    Document to be retrieved:

will appear on the status line. Type the file name; the status line should read:

    Document to be retrieved: BETAHILL

Then press ⏎. The disk drive will activate, and the document will appear on the screen (Fig. 14.1). Note the file name on the status line.

If you don't know the file name, retrieve it through the **list files** screen. Check the template. *List files* is printed in black near function key F5, so

    Press: F5

by itself. Try it. A new message

    Dir B:*.*   (Type = to change default Dir)

Figure 14.1

After you retrieve a document, its first 24 lines are displayed on the screen. Note the file name on the status line.

```
PROGRAM PROPOSAL

THE BETAGOSA HILLBILLIES

This proposed new half-hour comedy combines the best of "Star
Trek," "The Beverly Hillbillies," and "Gilligan's Island." The
main characters include:

        Captain Jed, the expedition leader
        Granny Socks, his crusty old assistant
        Professor Gallagher, the off-beat science officer

Professor Gallagher will be the focus of humor. He is a cross
between Star Trek's Scotty and Gilligan (from Gilligan's Island).
An early episode will establish that he was named after the 20th
century comedian Gallagher. This part could be a star vehicle for
a young comedian with a Gallagher-like style.

The story is set on the planet Betagosa, where the crew of the
starship Hindenberg find themselves marooned after Professor
Gallagher miscalculates E from Einstein's famous equation. The
planet is occupied by an advanced race called Betas. Many
humorous incidents are based on the crew's reaction to the
manners and customs of there new planet. Their problems are
B:\BETAHILL                                Doc 1 Pg 1 Ln 1" Pos 1"
```

Figure 14.2

The list files screen shows the names of all the files you can access. Move the cursor to mark the desired file, and type 1 to retrieve the file.

```
03/02/89  11:51              Directory B:\*.*
Document size:    1859   Free:   360448   Used:      1616      Files:   1

. <CURRENT>    <DIR>                 |  .. <PARENT>     <DIR>
BETAHILL.          1616  03/01/89 10:51




1 Retrieve; 2 Delete; 3 Move/Rename; 4 Print; 5 Text In;
6 Look; 7 Other Directory; 8 Copy; 9 Word Search; N Name Search: 6
```

or, on a hard disk system,

        Dir C:\WP50*.*   (Type = to change default Dir)

will appear on the status line. Respond by pressing ⏎.

After a brief delay, the list files screen (Fig. 14.2) will replace the work screen. It shows the names of all the files you can access. At this point, you should have already retrieved the program proposal, so type 0 to return to the work screen. If you hadn't retrieved the proposal, you could press the arrow keys to move the cursor (a reverse video bar) to the desired file's name and then type 1 to retrieve it.

Most people assume that the document just retrieved from disk replaces the one already in memory, but that's *not* how WordPerfect works. Replacing a document destroys the old version. WordPerfect destroys *nothing* unless the user authorizes it. Thus if you already have a document in memory and you retrieve a new one, *both* documents will be stored. It's easier to delete an extra copy than to recover accidentally destroyed text.

If you did retrieve two copies of BETAHILL, don't worry. Later in this chapter, you'll learn how to mark and delete a block of text.

■ *Keystroke Summary*

Retrieve document

File Name Known:		File Name Not Known:	
Press:	⇧ *and* F10	Press:	F5
Type:	*file name*	Press:	⏎
Press:	⏎	Move:	cursor to mark file
		Type:	1

■ *What Can Go Wrong?*

1. The message on the status line reads ERROR: file not found.

Cause: You might have misspelled the file name. You might have inserted the wrong data diskette or specified the wrong hard disk directory when you loaded WordPerfect. Your file might have been deleted.

Solution: Retype the file name and press ⏎. If that doesn't work, check the disk in drive B to be sure that you inserted the correct one; if not, replace it and try again. On a hard disk system, type the path name \WP50\BETAHILL rather than just the file name. To learn more about directories, path names, and file names, read Chapter 11.

2. File name BETAHILL does not appear in the list of files.

Cause: You might have inserted the wrong data disk or specified the wrong hard disk directory when you loaded WordPerfect. Someone might have deleted your file. You might have assigned a different file name in Chapter 13.

Solution: See problem 1.

3. While viewing the list files screen, you pressed ⏎, but nothing happened.

Cause: Look to the right of the status line in Fig. 14.2. The default option is 6; with the cursor marking <CURRENT>, that option generates a list of file names. You might have (reasonably) assumed that the default is to retrieve a document or return to the work screen, but it isn't.

Solution: Type 1 to retrieve a document or 0 to return to the work screen.

4. After you have moved the cursor to mark a file name on the list files screen, the desired document appears on something other than the work screen. The message on the status line tells you to "Press EXIT when done."

Cause: You probably pressed ⏎, thus accepting the default option, 6. With the cursor marking a file name, option 6 lets you view the file's contents.

Solution: Press F7 to return to the list files screen. Type 1 to retrieve a document or 0 to return to the work screen. ■

Adding Material to a Document

The document as typed is not yet complete. For one thing, two names were omitted from the list of characters. Also, the list is difficult to read. It might be better to type it in two columns; for example,

Captain Jed	the expedition leader
Granny Socks	his crusty old assistant
Professor Gallagher	the off-beat science officer
Lt. Salt	the male hunk
Pepper	the female hunk

Setting Tabs

If you were using a typewriter to prepare such a list, you would start by first setting the **tab stops**. By default, WordPerfect's tabs are set every half inch (or every five characters). The first step in resetting them is determining the proper settings.

Look at the list in Fig. 14.1. Professor Gallagher is the longest name. It begins in position 1.5. Move the cursor to the last letter in his name and check the status line; the name ends in position 3.3. The character names will occupy positions 1.5 through 3.3. You'll need some blank spaces to separate the columns, so start the second column in position 4.0. Your tab stops are 1.5 and 4.0.

When you reset WordPerfect's tabs, text preceding the cursor is controlled by the old tab settings. You want to format the entire list, so move the cursor to the blank line just above Captain Jed (line 2.16"). Then check the WordPerfect template. This is a formatting function. The word *Format* is printed in green near F8. Green means ⬆, so

Press: ⬆ *and* F8

The **format menu** (Fig. 14.3) will replace the work screen; it lists options for formatting a line, a page, or the entire document. Type 1, and the line format menu (Fig. 14.4) will appear. Type 8 to select the tab set option. The work screen will reappear with the current tab settings displayed near the bottom (Fig. 14.5).

Press Ctrl *and* End to clear the tabs. (This key combination is called delete EOL, or delete to end of line.) To enter the new tab settings, type 1.5 and press ↵; then type 4.0 and press ↵; the screen will resemble Fig. 14.6. Press F7, the **exit** key, to return to the line format menu. Then press F7 again to get back to the work screen.

Figure 14.3

The format menu lists options for formatting a line, a page, or an entire document.

```
Format

    1 - Line
            Hyphenation                 Line Spacing
            Justification               Margins Left/Right
            Line Height                 Tab Set
            Line Numbering              Widow/Orphan Protection

    2 - Page
            Center Page (top to bottom) New Page Number
            Force Odd/Even Page         Page Numbering
            Headers and Footers         Paper Size/Type
            Margins Top/Bottom          Suppress

    3 - Document
            Display Pitch               Redline Method
            Initial Codes/Font          Summary

    4 - Other
            Advance                     Overstrike
            Conditional End of Page     Printer Functions
            Decimal Characters          Underline Spaces/Tabs
            Language

Selection: 0
```

Figure 14.4
The line format menu lists options for controlling the format of a line.

```
Format: Line
      1 - Hyphenation                       Off
      2 - Hyphenation Zone - Left           10%
                            Right           4%
      3 - Justification                     Yes
      4 - Line Height                       Auto
      5 - Line Numbering                    No
      6 - Line Spacing                      1
      7 - Margins - Left                    1"
                    Right                   1"
      8 - Tab Set                           0", every 0.5"
      9 - Widow/Orphan Protection           No


      Selection: 0
```

Figure 14.5
When you reset the tabs, the current tab settings are displayed at the bottom of the screen.

```
The story is set on the planet Betagosa, where the crew of the
starship Hindenberg find themselves marooned after Professor
L....L....L....L....L....L....L....L....L....L....L....L....L....L....L...
|         |         |         |         |         |         |         |
1"        2"        3"        4"        5"        6"        7"        8"
Delete EOL (clear tabs); Enter Number (set tab); Del (clear tab);
Left; Center; Right; Decimal; .= Dot Leader
```

Figure 14.6
After you have reset the tabs, the tab ruler reflects the new settings.

```
The story is set on the planet Betagosa, where the crew of the
starship Hindenberg find themselves marooned after Professor
.....L..............................L.................................
|         |         |         |         |         |         |         |
1"        2"        3"        4"        5"        6"        7"        8"
Delete EOL (clear tabs); Enter Number (set tab); Del (clear tab);
Left; Center; Right; Decimal; .= Dot Leader
```

The tabs are now set. Captain Jed's name begins at position 1.5" (as it should), so there is no need to move it. Move the cursor to the comma following his name (line 2.33", position 2.6"). (Because your typing might differ slightly from the author's, view these suggested positions as approximate.) Delete the comma and the blank space; the cursor should be on the letter t. Press ⊟, and the description will move to position 4". Use the same technique to align Granny Socks and Professor Gallagher.

Once the three existing character descriptions have been reformatted, type the new ones. Start with the cursor in position 1" on the blank line following Professor Gallagher (line 2.83"). Press ⬄, and the cursor will move to position 1.5". Type

```
Lt. Salt
```

Press ⬄ again, and the cursor will move to position 4". Type

```
the male hunk
```

and press ↵. Use the same technique to type an entry for Pepper, the female hunk. When you finish, your screen should resemble Fig. 14.7.

The new tab settings make sense for the list of characters, but not for the rest of the document. To reset the tabs to their original positions, make sure the cursor is on the blank line following the list (line 3.16"). Just as a reminder, find the word *Format* on the template; then

Press: ⬆ *and* F8

The format menu will reappear. Select option 1 to get the line format menu; then type 8 to set the tabs. Clear the tabs by pressing Ctrl *and* End. Then type

```
1.0,0.5
```

and press ↵. The value 1.0 is the initial tab setting; the number following the comma, 0.5, is an interval; together, they indicate that tabs should be set at positions 1", 1.5", 2", 2.5", and so on. The new tab stops will affect the rest of the document. The custom settings control only the list. Press F7 twice to return to the work screen.

Figure 14.7
When you have completed the character list, your screen should resemble this one.

```
PROGRAM PROPOSAL

THE BETAGOSA HILLBILLIES

This proposed new half-hour comedy combines the best of "Star
Trek," "The Beverly Hillbillies," and "Gilligan's Island." The
main characters include:

        Captain Jed            the expedition leader
        Granny Socks           his crusty old assistant
        Professor Gallagher    the off-beat science officer
        Lt. Salt               the male hunk
        Pepper                 the female hunk

Professor Gallagher will be the focus of humor. He is a cross
between Star Trek's Scotty and Gilligan (from Gilligan's Island).
An early episode will establish that he was named after the 20th
century comedian Gallagher. This part could be a star vehicle for
a young comedian with a Gallagher-like style.

The story is set on the planet Betagosa, where the crew of the
starship Hindenberg find themselves marooned after Professor
Gallagher miscalculates E from Einstein's famous equation. The
planet is occupied by an advanced race called Betas. Many
B:\BETAHILL                              Doc 1 Pg 1 Ln 3.16" Pos 1"
```

Incidentally, there are tab settings to the left of the default margin at 0" and 0.5". Because they were not deleted, it is not necessary to reset them.

If you made a mistake or feel that you missed something in this module, see "What Can Go Wrong?" for instructions on repeating the lesson. If you're satisfied with what you have done, save the new version of the document to disk. Press F10. The file name will appear on the status line; press ⏎. Type Y in response to the system's replace message.

▪ **Keystroke Summary**

Set tabs

Press: ⇧ *and* F8

Type: **1**

Type: **8**

Press: Ctrl *and* End to delete existing tabs

For each tab stop,

Type: *new tab position*

Press: ⏎

Press: F7 to return to format menu

Press: F7 to return to work screen

▪ *What Can Go Wrong?*

To repeat the module:

```
Press:   F7
Type:    N (Do not save the file.)
Type:    N (Do not exit WordPerfect.)
```

The work screen will clear. Press ⇧ *and* F10 to retrieve an unchanged copy of the document and start over. If you save the document at the end of each module, you can follow this procedure to repeat the next module. ▪

Indenting Material

The other new material to be added is a quotation from a critic. Move the cursor to the end of the document (line 6.16"). Press ⏎ to insert a blank line and type the lead-in sentence that identifies the critic; use Fig. 14.8 as a guide. Then press ⏎ to insert another blank line and get ready to type the quotation.

Such lengthy quotations are generally set off from the body of the text by indenting them. One option is to tab line by line, but that's

Figure 14.8
WordPerfect makes it
easy to indent a block
of text.

```
source of embarassment is the way crew members keep disappearing
in the middle of important discussions because Professor
Gallagher accidentally beams them home.
┌──────────────────────────────────────────────────────────────────┐
│When Jean Rogers, nationally syndicated TV critic, was shown this│
│program proposal, she said:                                         │
│                                                                    │
│     Last week I had an opportunity to review the latest program│
│     proposal by Howard and Johnson. That madcap pair has done it│
│     again! "The Betagosa Hillbillies" incorporates virtually│
│     every hackneyed cliche ever seen in a situation comedy.│
│     Brilliant!                                                     │
└──────────────────────────────────────────────────────────────────┘
B:\BETAHILL                                    Doc 1 Pg 1 Ln 7.66" Pos 1"
```

inefficient. Check the template and find the word *Indent* printed in black near F4. Then

Press: F4

The cursor will move to the next tab stop, position 1.5". Type the quotation; once again, use Fig. 14.8 as a guide. When you reach the end of a line, the next word will automatically shift to the left and align with the tab stop. Press ↵ when the entire quotation has been typed, and the cursor will return to the left margin. In other words, pressing ↵ ends indenting.

To summarize, press F4 once to indent to the first tab stop; press F4 twice to indent to the second tab stop, and so on. Indented alignment continues until you press ↵.

Should you wish to repeat this lesson, press F7, respond to both prompts by typing N, retrieve the document, and start over. When you're ready to move on, press F10 and save the document.

■ *Keystroke Summary*

Indent

Press: F4

Type: *text*

Press: ↵ to end indent

■ *What Can Go Wrong?*

1. The quotation is indented too far to the right.

Cause: You might have pressed F4 more than once; perhaps you held the key down too long.

Solution: Move the cursor to the first character in the indented block and press ← until alignment is correct. ■

Editing

Marking a Block

The document is typed, but it could be better. Its purpose is to convince someone to buy (or watch) the show. The critic's comment is perhaps the single most important point, and placing it at the end tends to lessen its impact. Move the quotation to the beginning of the document.

The first step in moving a **block** of text is to **mark** it. Start by positioning the cursor at the beginning of the block, in this case on the blank line just above the sentence that identifies Jean Rogers (line 6.16"). The word *Block* is printed in blue near [F4]. Blue means [Alt], so

Press: [Alt] *and* [F4]

The words

```
Block on
```

blinking on the status line indicate that the block feature has been activated. Move the cursor to the end of the quotation. Your screen should resemble Fig. 14.9, with the block highlighted.

To cancel the block feature, press [Alt] *and* [F4] again. Try it. The highlighting will disappear, and the file name will reappear on the status line. The next step in the tutorial assumes that the quotation is marked, so move the cursor back to the top of the block (line 6.16") and mark it again.

▪ *Keystroke Summary*

Mark block

Move:	cursor to start of block
Press:	[Alt] *and* [F4]
Move:	cursor to mark block

Figure 14.9

A marked block is highlighted in reverse video.

```
certain common human arm gestures are considered obscene. Another
source of embarassment is the way crew members keep disappearing
in the middle of important discussions because Professor
Gallagher accidentally beams them home.

When Jean Rogers, nationally syndicated TV critic, was shown this
program proposal, she said:

     Last week I had an opportunity to review the latest program
     proposal by Howard and Johnson. That madcap pair has done it
     again! "The Betagosa Hillbillies" incorporates virtually
     every hackneyed cliche ever seen in a situation comedy.
     Brilliant!

Block on                                    Doc 1 Pg 1 Ln 7.66" Pos 1"
```

Moving a Block

Once a block has been marked, you can move it, copy it, delete it, change it to all capital letters, or perform other operations on it. The word *Move* is printed in red near F4, so to move the block,

        Press: Ctrl *and* F4

The menu

        Move: 1 Block; 2 Tabular Column; 3 Rectangle: 0

will appear on the status line. It presents three choices; to choose one, type the appropriate number. The suggested or default option is 0; typing 0 or pressing ↵ returns you to the prior screen. To move a block of text, type 1.

Another menu will appear:

        1 Move; 2 Copy; 3 Delete; 4 Append: 0

When you **move** a block, you cut it from its present position and then shift it somewhere else. When you **copy** a block, you duplicate it. In this case you want to move the block, so type 1. The status line will read

        Move cursor; press Enter to retrieve.

Move the cursor to the target location, in this case to the blank line right after the title (line 1.5"). Then

        Press: ↵

and the block will appear in its new position (Fig. 14.10).

Figure 14.10
When a block is moved, the text is shifted, without change, to another place in the document.

```
PROGRAM PROPOSAL

THE BETAGOSA HILLBILLIES

When Jean Rogers, nationally syndicated TV critic, was shown this
program proposal, she said:

        Last week I had an opportunity to review the latest program
        proposal by Howard and Johnson. That madcap pair has done it
        again! "The Betagosa Hillbillies" incorporates virtually
        every hackneyed cliche ever seen in a situation comedy.
        Brilliant!

This proposed new half-hour comedy combines the best of "Star
Trek," "The Beverly Hillbillies," and "Gilligan's Island." The
main characters include:

        Captain Jed              the expedition leader
        Granny Socks             his crusty old assistant
        Professor Gallagher      the off-beat science officer
        Lt. Salt                 the male hunk
        Pepper                   the female hunk

Professor Gallagher will be the focus of humor. He is a cross
B:\BETAHILL                                   Doc 1 Pg 1 Ln 1.5" Pos 1"
```

It is interesting to note what really happens when a block is moved. Remember that the document is stored in the computer's memory. Another portion of memory is set aside as a **buffer**. When a block is moved or copied, its contents are recorded in the buffer. Later, the buffer's contents can be moved to another memory location and thus to another place in the document.

Note, on both move menus, that a single letter is boldfaced or highlighted on each choice. If you wish, instead of typing the number associated with your choice, you can type the key letter. This feature is particularly valuable to touch typists who prefer not to look at the keyboard.

Should you wish to repeat this lesson, press F7, respond to both prompts by typing N, retrieve the document, and start over. When you're ready to move on, press F10 and save the document.

▪ *Keystroke Summary*

Move block

Mark:	block
Press:	Ctrl *and* F4
Type:	1
Type:	1
Move:	cursor to target position
Press:	↵

▪ *What Can Go Wrong?*

1. You do not seem to be marking any text.

Cause: You might have held F4 down. When you hold a key, its function is repeated, and a second block command cancels the first one.

Solution: Press Alt, hold it, and then quickly tap F4 once, as though you were typing a single character.

2. After you move the quotation, it is no longer indented.

Cause: You probably marked the block starting on the first character in the quotation, *after* the indent code (see the next section).

Solution: Move the cursor to the first character in the quotation and press F4. Then press ↓. After you read about hidden codes, move to the end of the document and delete the indent code if it's still there. ▪

Hidden Codes

How exactly does the system "remember" that the quotation is to be indented? Some word processors insert blank characters and maintain in memory an image of what appears on the screen, but WordPerfect inserts **hidden codes** into the text.

Figure 14.11

Many WordPerfect features insert hidden codes in the text. You can view and edit codes on the reveal codes screen.

```
PROGRAM PROPOSAL

THE BETAGOSA HILLBILLIES

When Jean Rogers, nationally syndicated TV critic, was shown this
program proposal, she said:

     Last week I had an opportunity to review the latest program
     proposal by Howard and Johnson. That madcap pair has done it
     again! "The Betagosa Hillbillies" incorporates virtually
     every hackneyed cliche ever seen in a situation comedy.
B:\BETAHILL                                   Doc 1 Pg 1 Ln 2.16" Pos 1"
[                                             ]
program proposal, she said:[HRt]
[HRt]
[Indent]Last week I had an opportunity to review the latest program[SRt]
proposal by Howard and Johnson. That madcap pair has done it[SRt]
again! "The Betagosa Hillbillies" incorporates virtually[SRt]
every hackneyed cliche ever seen in a situation comedy.[SRt]
Brilliant![HRt]
[HRt]
This proposed new half[-]hour comedy combines the best of "Star[SRt]
Trek," "The Beverly Hillbillies," and "Gilligan's Island." The[SRt]

Press Reveal Codes to restore screen
```

Normally, the codes are of little interest, but there are times when you might want to see and perhaps even modify them. Move the cursor to the beginning of the quotation (line 2.16"). The words *Reveal codes* are printed in blue near F3. If you

Press: Alt *and* F3

the **reveal codes** window will appear on the bottom half of the screen (Fig. 14.11). Note that the cursor and the hidden codes are highlighted.

Find the **[Indent]** code near the left margin. Then look to the right margin. The **[SRt]** code marks a soft return, while **[HRt]** indicates a hard return. A soft return means that the word wrap feature automatically shifted the next word to the left margin. A hard return means that you pressed ↵. Most codes are self-explanatory; check the WordPerfect reference manual for a complete list.

While the reveal codes screen is visible, you can move the cursor, edit and delete codes and text, and issue WordPerfect commands, although in most cases it's easier to manipulate the text on the work screen. Try an experiment. Move the cursor to mark the indent code and press Del. The code will disappear, and the quotation will shift to the left margin as though it had never been indented. Then

Press: Alt *and* F3

to return to the work screen (Fig. 14.12). Note the alignment of the quotation.

Figure 14.12
If you delete a code, the text on the screen will be reformatted as though the code had never been there.

```
PROGRAM PROPOSAL

THE BETAGOSA HILLBILLIES

When Jean Rogers, nationally syndicated TV critic, was shown this
program proposal, she said:

Last week I had an opportunity to review the latest program
proposal by Howard and Johnson. That madcap pair has done it
again! "The Betagosa Hillbillies" incorporates virtually every
hackneyed cliche ever seen in a situation comedy. Brilliant!

This proposed new half-hour comedy combines the best of "Star
Trek," "The Beverly Hillbillies," and "Gilligan's Island." The
main characters include:
```

■ *Keystroke Summary*

Reveal codes

Press: [Alt] *and* [F3]

Press: [Alt] *and* [F3] to exit

Double Indenting

One problem with the last experiment is that the quotation really should be indented. Put the indent code back in, only this time do it differently. The proper format for a lengthy quotation is to indent it from both the left and the right. Start with the cursor on the first character in the quotation (line 2.16", position 1"). Check the template. *Indent* with one arrow is printed in black near [F4]; *Indent* with two arrows appears in green. To double indent,

Press: [↑] *and* [F4]

When you move the cursor down, the screen will be reformatted, and the block will be indented from both margins (Fig. 14.13). Press [Alt] *and* [F3], and look at the codes. Find the double indent code,

Figure 14.13
Lengthy quotations are often indented equally from both margins.

```
PROGRAM PROPOSAL

THE BETAGOSA HILLBILLIES

When Jean Rogers, nationally syndicated TV critic, was shown this
program proposal, she said:

        Last week I had an opportunity to review the latest
        program proposal by Howard and Johnson. That madcap
        pair has done it again! "The Betagosa Hillbillies"
        incorporates virtually every hackneyed cliche ever seen
        in a situation comedy. Brilliant!

This proposed new half-hour comedy combines the best of "Star
Trek," "The Beverly Hillbillies," and "Gilligan's Island." The
main characters include:
```

[->Indent<-]. Now find the end of the quotation and note the hard return, [HRt]. Every line between the indent code and the next hard return is indented. Press (Alt) *and* (F3) to return to the work screen.

Should you wish to repeat this lesson, press (F7), respond to both prompts by typing N, retrieve the document, and start over. When you're ready to move on, press (F10) and save the document.

■ *Keystroke Summary*

Double indent

Press: (↑) *and* (F4)

Type: *text*

Press: (↵) to end indent

Block Copy

Earlier you moved a block of text; in this lesson you'll *copy* one. Consider the list of characters. At present it appears near the beginning of the document, but it might be better near the end. Both locations are reasonable, so copy the list, duplicate it, read the document, and decide where you like it better.

First, mark the block. Move the cursor to the first letter in the sentence that introduces the list (line 3.33", position 6.9"). To activate the block feature,

```
Press:   (Alt) and (F4)
```

Mark the block by moving the cursor to the blank line following Pepper (line 4.66") and

```
Press:   (Ctrl) and (F4)
```

The move menu will appear on the status line:

```
Move: 1 Block; 2 Tabular Column; 3 Rectangle: 0
```

Type 1, for block, and the second move menu

```
1 Move; 2 Copy; 3 Delete; 4 Append: 0
```

will appear. This time, type 2. The status line will read

```
Move cursor; press Enter to retrieve.
```

Move the cursor to the end of the document and press (↵). A new copy of the list will appear. Press (↵) to insert a blank line to separate the list from the rest of the text (Fig. 14.14).

Use the cursor control keys to move back and forth between the two copies. Read the material both ways. Mentally delete the list, first in one place and then in the other. Decide which version you like better, and then delete the unwanted block.

Figure 14.14

When you copy a block, it is not deleted from its original position. This screen shows that the list of characters now appears in two places.

```
      Lt. Salt                    the male hunk
      Pepper                      the female hunk

Professor Gallagher will be the focus of humor. He is a cross
between Star Trek's Scotty and Gilligan (from Gilligan's Island).
An early episode will establish that he was named after the 20th
century comedian Gallagher. This part could be a star vehicle for
a young comedian with a Gallagher-like style.

The story is set on the planet Betagosa, where the crew of the
starship Hindenberg find themselves marooned after Professor
Gallagher miscalculates E from Einstein's famous equation. The
planet is occupied by an advanced race called Betas. Many
humorous incidents are based on the crew's reaction to the
manners and customs of there new planet. Their problems are
complicated by the fact that the Betas have three arms, and
certain common human arm gestures are considered obscene. Another
source of embarassment is the way crew members keep disappearing
in the middle of important discussions because Professor
Gallagher accidentally beams them home.

The main characters include:

      Captain Jed                 the expedition leader
B:\BETAHILL                                  Doc 1 Pg 1 Ln 8.16" Pos 1"
```

■ *Keystroke Summary*

Copy block

Mark: block

Press: Ctrl *and* F4

Type: **1**

Type: **2**

Move: cursor to target position

Press: ↵

Deleting a Block

Deleting a block is easy; just mark it and press Del. For example, assume that you prefer the list of characters at the end of the document. Move the cursor to the second *The* (position 6.9") in line 3.33" and

Press: Alt *and* F4

Then move the cursor to the blank line after *Pepper* (line 4.66"), thus marking the first character list. Press Del. A message

```
Delete Block? (Y/N) No
```

will appear on the status line. To delete the block, type Y; your screen should then resemble Fig. 14.15.

Figure 14.15

To delete a block, mark it and press (Del). Note that the list of characters that was near the beginning of the document is gone.

```
PROGRAM PROPOSAL

THE BETAGOSA HILLBILLIES

When Jean Rogers, nationally syndicated TV critic, was shown this
program proposal, she said:

        Last week I had an opportunity to review the latest
        program proposal by Howard and Johnson. That madcap
        pair has done it again! "The Betagosa Hillbillies"
        incorporates virtually every hackneyed cliche ever seen
        in a situation comedy. Brilliant!

This proposed new half-hour comedy combines the best of "Star
Trek," "The Beverly Hillbillies," and "Gilligan's Island."
Professor Gallagher will be the focus of humor. He is a cross
between Star Trek's Scotty and Gilligan (from Gilligan's Island).
An early episode will establish that he was named after the 20th
century comedian Gallagher. This part could be a star vehicle for
a young comedian with a Gallagher-like style.

The story is set on the planet Betagosa, where the crew of the
starship Hindenberg find themselves marooned after Professor
Gallagher miscalculates E from Einstein's famous equation. The
B:\BETAHILL                            Doc 1 Pg 1 Ln 3.33" Pos 6.9"
```

■ *Keystroke Summary*

Delete block

Mark: block

Press: (Del)

Type: **Y**

Undelete

What if you make a mistake and accidentally delete the wrong block? Fortunately, there is a way to get the deleted text back. Remember the buffer introduced earlier in the chapter? In addition to cut or copied material, it also holds deleted characters, words, lines, or blocks. Check the template and note the word *Cancel* printed in black near (F1). That's the cancel key. Use it to cancel a command or to **undelete** material.

Press: (F1)

The most recent deletion will be highlighted just after the cursor, and a message

    Undelete: 1 Restore; 2 Previous Deletion: 0

will appear on the status line. Option 2 allows you to back up one deletion. To restore the highlighted material, type 1. Try it. Then remark the block and delete it again.

Before you move on, check the codes. Start with the cursor near the end of line 3.33" (where the deleted block used to be) and press (Alt) and F3. You might see a hard return [HRt] code. If you do, delete it; a hard return marks the end of a paragraph, and there should be no paragraph break. If necessary, insert a blank space between the quotation mark and the word "Professor." Because the codes are hidden, they are easy to overlook, and extraneous codes can cause problems when you print the document. Press Alt *and* F3 to return to the work screen.

Should you wish to repeat this lesson, press F7, respond to both prompts by typing N, retrieve the document, and start over. When you're ready to move on, press F10 and save the document.

■ *Keystroke Summary*

Undelete

Press: F1

Type: **1**

Finishing Touches

Checking Your Spelling

Spelling errors are easy to make and often difficult to spot, even with careful proofreading. With a modern word processor it is so easy to check spelling that there is no reason to release a document that contains spelling errors.

If your hard disk system was properly installed, the **spelling dictionary** should be on the disk. If you are using a two-diskette system, remove the data disk from drive B and insert the spelling disk. Like many WordPerfect features, the spelling checker proceeds from the cursor to the end of the document, so to check the entire document, move the cursor to line 1", position 1".

Check the template and find the word *Spell* printed in red near F2. To activate the spelling checker,

Press: Ctrl *and* F2

After WordPerfect locates the spelling dictionary, a menu will appear on the status line:

```
Check: 1 Word; 2 Page; 3 Document; 4 New Sup. Dictionary;
5 Look Up; 6 Count: 0
```

(The menu will be displayed on a single line.) Type 3 to check the entire document.

WordPerfect checks spelling by looking up words in its dictionary; if what you typed matches a dictionary entry, the word is assumed to be correct. When an unknown word is encountered, the program stops, highlights the word, offers some suggestions, and waits for your response. After you respond, WordPerfect moves on to the next error.

BETAGOSA should be the first word marked. It is spelled correctly, but it's not in WordPerfect's dictionary. Look for the menu at the bottom of the screen:

```
Not Found: 1 Skip Once; 2 Skip; 3 Add Word; 4 Edit;
5 Look Up: 0
```

(The menu will be displayed on a single line.) The first option, 1, tells the system to skip the word once but to flag it if it appears again. The second option means to skip the word for the rest of the document. The third option adds the word to the dictionary. Type 2. Many formal names and place names (for example, Howard) will be flagged. Read them carefully to make sure they are spelled correctly. If they are, tell WordPerfect to skip them.

Near the end of the document is a real error (Fig. 14.16); embarrassment is properly spelled with two r's. WordPerfect has suggested the correct spelling. Look near the center of the screen and find the word *embarrassment*. Preceding it is the letter A. Often, several options will be presented, each identified by a letter: A, B, C, and so on. To replace the incorrect word, type the letter that identifies your choice; in this case, type A.

What if none of the suggestions is correct? Look at the options near the bottom of the screen. 1, 2, and 3 have already been discussed. To edit a word manually, type 4. The cursor will move to the highlighted word; make your corrections, and press ⏎ when you're finished. WordPerfect will recheck your spelling before moving on to the next word.

Correct any remaining misspelled words. After the document has been checked, WordPerfect displays the word count and a message on

Figure 14.16

To select one of WordPerfect's suggested corrections, type the letter that precedes your choice. Select other options from the menu at the bottom of the screen.

```
planet is occupied by an advanced race called Betas. Many
humorous incidents are based on the crew's reaction to the
manners and customs of there new planet. Their problems are
complicated by the fact that the Betas have three arms, and
certain common human arm gestures are considered obscene. Another
source of embarassment is the way crew members keep disappearing
in the middle of important discussions because Professor
Gallagher accidentally beams them home.

The main characters include:

===============================================================================

  A. embarrassment




Not Found: 1 Skip Once; 2 Skip; 3 Add Word; 4 Edit; 5 Look Up:  0
```

Figure 14.17

The spelling checker does not flag grammatical errors.

```
humorous incidents are based on the crew's reaction to the
manners and customs of there new planet. Their problems are
complicated by the fact that the Betas have three arms, and
certain common human arm gestures are considered obscene. Another
source of embarrassment is the way crew members keep disappearing
in the middle of important discussions because Professor
Gallagher accidentally beams them home.

The main characters include:

        Captain Jed              the expedition leader
        Granny Socks             his crusty old assistant
        Professor Gallagher      the off-beat science officer
```

the status line; for example,

```
Word count: 259  Press any key to continue
```

If you are ever asked to write a 500-word paper, you'll find the word count useful. Press any key to return to the work screen.

Note that the spelling checker will *not* flag grammatical errors. For example, the word *there* on line 5.33", position 3.3" is incorrect (Fig. 14.17); it should be *their*. Change it. Don't forget to proofread your document.

It is possible to obtain a word count without checking spelling. Simply select option 6 on the spelling menu.

Remove the spelling disk from drive B and reinsert the data disk. If you wish to repeat this lesson, press [F7], respond to both prompts by typing N, retrieve the document, and start over. When you're ready to move on, press [F10] and save the document.

■ *Keystroke Summary*

Check spelling

If you are using a two-diskette system,

Remove:	the data disk from drive B
Insert:	the spelling disk in drive B
Press:	[Ctrl] *and* [F2]
Type:	**3**
Respond:	to prompts
Press:	any key to return to the work screen

■ *What Can Go Wrong?*

1. You accidentally saved your document on the spelling disk.

Cause: You made a common mistake. Saving the document immediately after making a correction gets to be a habit.

Solution: Remove the spelling disk from drive B, insert your data disk, and save the file again. See Chapter 9 for information on deleting a file from disk. ■

Printing the Document

Press ⧆ *and* F7, and print the document. Study the output and explain, to your own satisfaction, how WordPerfect defined each line.

The HELP Feature

Before you end this tutorial, briefly explore WordPerfect's **HELP feature**. If you're using a two-diskette system, remove your working copy of WordPerfect from drive A and insert the original WordPerfect 1 disk. The word *Help* appears in black near F3, so

    Press: F3

to activate HELP. Type a letter of the alphabet (A–Z) for a list of all the features beginning with that letter. Press the key or keys associated with any WordPerfect feature to get information about that feature; for example, press ⧆ and F7 for a description of the print feature. In effect, HELP is an on-line reference manual. Press ⏎ or the space bar to return to the work screen.

■ *Keystroke Summary*

HELP

If you are using a two-diskette system,

Remove:	data disk from drive B
Insert:	original WordPerfect 1 disk in drive B
Press:	F3
Press:	key(s) for any WordPerfect feature
Press:	space bar or ⏎ to return to work screen

Exiting WordPerfect

This ends the second tutorial. Press F7 to exit WordPerfect. Because you saved BETAHILL after checking the spelling, there is no need to save it again. Type Y in response to the exit WordPerfect prompt.

Summary

Topic or Feature	Command or Reference	Option	Page
Copy a block	Ctrl *and* F4	1	202
Delete a block	Alt *and* F4	Del	203
HELP feature	F3	—	208
Hidden codes, reveal	Alt *and* F3	—	200
Indent a block	F4	—	195
Indent from left and right	⧆ *and* F4	—	201

Topic or Feature	Command or Reference	Option	Page
Mark a block	Alt *and* F4	—	197
Move a block	Ctrl *and* F4	1	198
Reveal hidden codes	Alt *and* F3	—	200
Retrieve document, list files	F5	1	189
Retrieve document, work	⇧ *and* F10	—	189
Spell check a document	Ctrl *and* F2	3	205
Tab stops, set	⇧ *and* F8	1	192
Undelete	F1	1	204

Self-Test

1. Files on disk are stored and retrieved by _____.

2. If you know a document's file name, you can retrieve it from disk by pressing _____ and then typing the file name.

3. Press _____ to obtain a list of the files.

4. WordPerfect's format menu lists options that control the format of a line, a page, or the entire document. To access that menu, press _____.

5. To indent a block of text, press _____. To indent from both the left and the right, press _____. To terminate indenting, press _____.

6. Press _____ to mark a block. Press _____ to move or copy that block.

7. When you cut or copy a block, the text is temporarily saved in a _____.

8. WordPerfect "remembers" certain functions by inserting _____ into the text.

9. When you _____ a block, the text is deleted from its original position. When you _____ a block, the original version is not deleted.

10. Press _____ to check your spelling.

Exercises

1. Type a first draft of a personal or business letter. Save it to disk and print it. Read through the letter and improve it. Save and print the improved version. Compare the two versions.

2. Type a first draft of a class paper. Save it and print it. Read the paper and improve it. Save and print the improved version. Compare the two versions.

3. Retrieve the file you created in Exercises 4 and 5 of Chapter 13. Move the cursor to the end of the document. Then skip a line and add the following material:

```
Today, the following programs are common:

Computer Science                Arts and Science
Computer Engineering            Engineering
Management Information Systems  Business
Computer Technology             Technical Schools

Other programs are known by a variety of names.
```

4. If necessary, refer to the line numbers in Exercise 4 of Chapter 13 as you peform the following tasks. Note that the references might not match the line numbers on your screen.

   a. Move the cursor to the end of line 5 (just after *1970s*) and press ⏎ twice to end the paragraph and insert a blank line. Line 6 (*Given* ...) will now start a new paragraph.

   b. Mark the material you added in Exercise 3 and move it between the first two paragraphs.

   c. Move the cursor to the end of line 5 (just after *1970s*). Activate the reveal codes screen. Delete the [HRt] code that marks the end of the first paragraph. The material you added in Exercise 3 will become part of the first paragraph. Return to the work screen.

   d. Move the cursor to the last line in the newly added material. Replace the phrase *a variety of* with *several*.

   e. Undelete *a variety of* and delete *several*.

   f. Check your spelling.

   g. Replace the document on disk and then print it.

■15

Form Letters and Boilerplate

After briefly explaining boilerplate, form letters, and mail merge, this chapter introduces the WordPerfect features and commands that allow you to:

- create several files
- access the list files screen
- combine existing files
- create a template
- insert the date flush right
- search and replace
- switch screens
- create form letters using mail merge

Business Communications

Boilerplate

When a student writes a paper, originality is rewarded. In a business environment, by contrast, the objective of most memos, reports, and letters is accuracy, not originality. For example, when a firm's public relations department responds to letters from outside the organization, the individual department members' ideas are irrelevant. Employees are expected to accurately convey the organization's viewpoint, not their own.

Often, business correspondence is prepared, at least in part, from **boilerplate**. (The term *boilerplate* is derived from an old engineering practice of building custom boilers from standard metal plates.) Perhaps the best way to understand this concept is through an example. Imagine working in public relations. You have at your disposal several press releases and corporate policy statements. These documents have been carefully checked for style, grammar, and spelling and have been approved by management.

When a letter arrives on your desk, you read it, search through the press releases and policy statements, select those that are relevant, and arrange them in a logical order. Then you write the transitional phrases needed to produce a smooth document, add the date and a closing, and print your "customized" response. If an acceptable response cannot be prepared from the boilerplate, an original letter is written and submitted to management for approval.

Form Letters

Form letters are commonly used when the same information must be communicated to large numbers of people. Most of us react negatively to obvious form letters, and halfhearted attempts at personalization are almost as bad; generally, the more personal the letter, the more effective it is. However, consistency is just as important, and typing the same material over and over again is not very efficient.

By using a word processor it is possible to achieve a reasonable balance between personalization and consistency. The first step is to prepare a **template** consisting of the common text. (Boilerplate might be used here.) Given a template, the variable data (name, address, and so on) can be typed for the first recipient, and the finished letter saved and printed. Then, after clearing the screen, a fresh copy of the template can be retrieved, the second recipient's variable data typed, and the second letter saved and printed. This process continues until all the letters have been prepared.

If the number of documents needed is small, variable data can be entered from the keyboard or inserted through the replace feature. For larger volumes you might consider using **mail merge**. Both techniques will be discussed in this chapter's tutorial.

Creating Some Boilerplate Files

In Chapters 13 and 14 you wrote a program proposal for "The Betagosa Hillbillies." The next step is to send the proposal to several producers and network executives in an effort to sell the concept. Given the audience, form letters are unacceptable; professional people expect customized correspondence. Consistency is also necessary, however; you want to convey the same basic message to everyone. A common solution to such conflicting objectives is to prepare several approved "press releases" and then combine them to create original, personalized letters.

The first step is to create several boilerplate files. For example, type this brief biographical sketch:

```
Mary Howard and Hector Johnson, two of the most creative minds
in television today, have been responsible for such hits as
"Bleep the Boss" and "Humiliate Your Spouse." Graduates of the
South Dakota School of Broadcasting, this incredible team has
been a gold mine of original ideas since 1988.
```

(Spacing on the screen will differ from what is shown above.) Press ⏎ at the end of the paragraph. Then press F7. The message

```
Save document? (Y/N) Yes
```

will appear on the status line. Type Y, or press ⏎. In response to the file name prompt, type BIO, and then press ⏎. After the file is saved, the next prompt,

```
Exit WP? (Y/N) No   (Cancel to return to document)
```

will ask whether you want to exit WordPerfect. Type N, and the work screen will clear.

Technically, of course, it's not the screen that is cleared, but memory; the screen displays a small portion of memory's contents. However, it is convenient to think of using the exit key, F7, to clear the screen.

Incidentally, many instructors prefer that you not save a file as part of the exit process. Instead, they suggest that you first save the file by pressing F10, and *then* press F7. Their concern is safety; typing the wrong response during exit can destroy a document.

Figure 15.1 shows four additional files. Type document TBH, press ⏎ at the end of the paragraph, save the file, and clear the screen. Follow the same procedure for NETHEAD, INDEPEN, and TOP. Don't forget to center the lines in TOP.

■ *What Can Go Wrong?*

1. You saved a file under file name Y.

Cause: In Chapters 13 and 14 you learned to save your document each time you changed it. To update a file on disk, you pressed ⏎ to accept the suggested file name and then typed Y to replace it. That pattern can become a habit. This time, you pressed ⏎ to save the file. You were then prompted to type a file name; if you typed Y, the system assumed that Y was a file name.

Solution: Access the list files screen (next section). Mark file Y and then type 3 to select *Rename*. Follow the sreen prompts to rename the file.

Figure 15.1
Type and save these
documents.

File name	File contents
TBH	Howard and Johnson are proud to announce the development of their newest mega-hit, "The Betagosa Hillbillies." Please see the attached press release for details.
NETHEAD	As program director for our favorite net-work, XXX, we wanted you to see it first. As usual, all things being equal, our dream is to see our new show on good old XXX.
INDEPEN	Of course, our first thought was to send this proposal to you, our very favorite independent producer. With your help, we're sure this new proposal will set the standard for the next decade.
TOP	Howard and Johnson, Ltd. "Creativity is Our Thing!" P.O. Box Z Oxford, Ohio 01056

Note: Center all lines in file TOP.

The List Files Screen

Your work disk now contains several files. To obtain a list, access the **list files** screen. Find *List files* on the template; it's printed in black near F5. To display the screen,

    Press: F5

The current directory's path name

    Dir B:*.*   (Type = to change default Dir)

or, on a hard disk system,

    Dir C:\WP50*.*   (Type = to change default Dir)

will appear on the status line. The message requests a list of every file in the specified directory. Press ⏎. The work screen will be replaced by a list files screen (Fig. 15.2). If you are using a hard disk system, several other file names will appear, too. Entries <CURRENT> and <PARENT> are directories; see Chapter 11. Below the directories you should see BETAHILL and the names of the new files you just created.

Near the bottom of the screen is a menu that lists the following options:

1. *Retrieve* a file from disk.

2. *Delete* a file.

3. *Move* or *Rename* a file.

Figure 15.2

The list files screen shows a list of all the files in the current directory.

```
10/02/89  11:02                    Directory B:\*.*
Document size:            0   Free:    354304   Used:       6446        Files:  6

. <CURRENT>      <DIR>                        °  .. <PARENT>     <DIR>
BETAHILL.        2780   10/02/89 10:55        °  BIO       .              841  10/02/89 11:02
INDEPEN  .        737   10/02/89 10:58        °  NETHEAD  .              712  10/02/89 10:57
TBH      .        708   10/02/89 10:56        °  TOP       .             668  10/02/89 10:59



















1 Retrieve; 2 Delete; 3 Move/Rename; 4 Print; 5 Text In;
6 Look; 7 Other Directory; 8 Copy; 9 Word Search; N Name Search: 6
```

4. *Print* a file directly from disk without first retrieving it. One suboption allows you to print selected pages.

5. *Text In* retrieves an ASCII file.

6. *Look* allows you to check the contents of a file without retrieving it.

7. *Other Directory* allows you to change DOS directories. See Chapter 11.

8. *Copy* a file. This option is often used to back up a file by copying it to another disk.

9. *Word Search* searches through several files and identifies those that contain a search string.

N. *Name Search* allows you to select a file by typing its name rather than by moving the cursor.

See the WordPerfect reference manual for additional details. Note that option 6, *Look*, is the default option.

To select an option, first use the cursor control keys to mark the target file's name. (The cursor appears as a reverse video bar on this screen.) Then type the number associated with your option. Typing the digit 0 sends you back to the work screen.

■ *Keystroke Summary*

List files

Press: F5

Press: ↵

Type: 0 to exit

Figure 15.3

When you retrieve a file, its contents are copied into memory. If memory already contains other text, the file's contents are placed just after the cursor's current position and thus are merged with the existing text.

```
                    Howard and Johnson, Ltd.
                   "Creativity is Our Thing!"
                            P.O. Box Z
                        Oxford, Ohio 01056
Mary Howard and Hector Johnson, two of the most creative minds in
television today, have been responsible for such hits as "Bleep
the Boss" and "Humiliate Your Spouse." Graduates of the South
Dakota School of Broadcasting, this incredible team has been a
gold mine of original ideas since 1988.
```

Retrieving Files

To retrieve a file from disk and copy it into memory, move the cursor to mark the desired file's name and then choose option 1. For example, move the cursor to TOP and type 1. After a brief delay, the contents of TOP will appear on the work screen.

Next, move the cursor to the end of the document and press F5. Then press ⏎, and the list files screen will reappear. Move the cursor to BIO and type 1. A message will appear on the status line:

```
Retrieve into current document? (Y/N) No
```

It tells you that memory already holds a document. Type Y, for yes. Once again, you'll be back to the work screen, but this time the contents of *both* TOP and BIO will appear (Fig. 15.3).

Why didn't BIO *replace* TOP? Because replacing a file implies deleting it from memory, and WordPerfect *never* deletes anything unless you explicitly tell it to. You can delete a character, a word, a line, or a block. You can clear memory. But WordPerfect will not delete anything on its own.

Move the cursor to the top of the screen. Press F5 and then press ⏎ to return to the list files screen. Retrieve file TBH and type Y in response to the "Retrieve into current document" prompt. When you go back to the work screen, the contents of TBH will appear *first*, before the header. A newly retrieved file is *inserted* into the document immediately after the cursor.

Before you continue, clear the screen by pressing F7 and typing N in response to both questions.

■ *Keystroke Summary*

Retrieve file

Press: F5

Press: ⏎

Move: cursor to mark file

Type: **1**

■ *What Can Go Wrong?*

1. An empty work screen reappears.

Cause: You probably typed 0, the menu's exit code.

Solution: Press F5 and then ⏎ to return to the list files screen.

2. The list files screen briefly goes blank, and then the same information reappears.

Cause: You probably typed 6 (*Look*) or pressed ⏎.

Solution: Continue as though nothing happened.

3. Text appears, and a note tells you to "Press Exit when done."

Cause: After moving the cursor to mark a file, you probably typed 6 (*Look*) or pressed ⏎.

Solution: Press F7, the exit key, to return to the list files screen.

4. An unexpected message appears on the status line.

Cause: You probably typed some other digit.

Solution: Press F1, the cancel key, to return to the list files screen. ■

Creating Templates

The First Template

The program proposal will be sent to both network executives and independent producers, so you'll need two different cover letters. Start with the independent producers. Press F5 and then press ⏎ to access the list files screen. Move the cursor to mark TOP and type 1. The work screen will appear with the contents of TOP at the top (Fig. 15.4).

Figure 15.4

Once all the boilerplate has been retrieved, the template is almost finished. Note that the file name on the status line is still TOP, the name of the first file retrieved.

```
                    Howard and Johnson, Ltd.
                    "Creativity is Our Thing!"
                          P.O. Box Z
                        Oxford, Ohio 01056

Mary Howard and Hector Johnson, two of the most creative minds in
television today, have been responsible for such hits as "Bleep
the Boss" and "Humiliate Your Spouse." Graduates of the South
Dakota School of Broadcasting, this incredible team has been a
gold mine of original ideas since 1988.

Howard and Johnson are proud to announce the development of their
newest mega-hit, "The Betagosa Hillbillies." Please see the
attached press release for details.

Of course, our first thought was to send this proposal to you,
our very favorite independent producer. With your help, we're
sure this new proposal will set the standard for the next decade.



B:\TOP                                        Doc 1 Pg 1 Ln 3.5" Pos 1"
```

Move the cursor to the end of the document and press ⏎ to insert a blank line. Retrieve a second file, BIO; the work screen should show both files. Move the cursor to the end of the document, insert a blank line, and retrieve TBH. Finally, insert another blank line at the end of the document and retrieve INDEPEN. When you finish, your screen should resemble Fig. 15.4. Note that the name on the status line is still TOP. When subsequent documents are merged with a file already in memory, the first file name prevails.

With a few changes this collection of boilerplate can be converted to a reasonable letter. To add a hint of timeliness, insert the word *today*, followed by a comma, just before Howard and Johnson at the beginning of the second paragraph (line 2.83"). Finally, move the cursor to the end of the document, insert a blank line, and add a closing; the changes are highlighted in Fig. 15.5.

Adding the Date, Flush Right

Before you save the template, add the current date just after the header, near the right margin. Move the cursor to the blank line below the header (line 1.66"), and press ⏎ to insert another blank line. Then check the template. *Flush right* is printed in blue near ⑥. Blue means Alt, so

Press: Alt *and* F6

to activate WordPerfect's **flush right** feature. The cursor will move to the right margin.

Figure 15.5
The template for independent producers.

```
                        Oxford, Ohio 01056

Mary Howard and Hector Johnson, two of the most creative minds in
television today, have been responsible for such hits as "Bleep
the Boss" and "Humiliate Your Spouse." Graduates of the South
Dakota School of Broadcasting, this incredible team has been a
gold mine of original ideas since 1988.

Today, Howard and Johnson are proud to announce the development
of their newest mega-hit, "The Betagosa Hillbillies." Please see
the attached press release for details.

Of course, our first thought was to send this proposal to you,
our very favorite independent producer. With your help, we're
sure this new proposal will set the standard for the next decade.

Contact us for additional details.


Sincerely,
Mary Howard
Hector Johnson

B:\TOP                                    Doc 1 Pg 1 Ln 5.33" Pos 1"
```

```
                        Oxford, Ohio 01056

                                          March 3, 1989
Mary Howard and Hector Johnson, two of the most creative minds in
television today, have been responsible for such hits as "Bleep
the Boss" and "Humiliate Your Spouse." Graduates of the South
Dakota School of Broadcasting, this incredible team has been a
gold mine of original ideas since 1988.
```

Once again, check the template. The word *Date* appears in green near F5. To insert the date,

Press: ⬆ *and* F5

A message will appear on the status line:

```
1 Date Text; 2 Date Code; 3 Date Format; 4 Outline;
5 Para Num; 6 Define: 0
```

(The menu will be displayed as a single line.) Option 1 inserts a text version of the current date into the document immediately after the cursor. Type 1. The status line message will disappear, and because the flush right feature is on, the current date will scroll in from the right margin. Press ⏎ to insert a blank line, and the template is ready to save (Fig. 15.6). Press F10 and save the template under file name INDPRO.

∎ *Keystroke Summary*

Insert date, flush right

Press: Alt *and* F6

Press: ⬆ *and* F5

Type: 1

The Second Template

The letter currently displayed on your screen is for independent producers. You need a different template for the network people. The return address, the first two paragraphs, and the closing are fine, but the third paragraph refers to independent producers, so move the cursor to the beginning of that third paragraph (line 3.83"), mark it as a block, and delete it.

Leave the cursor where it is and retrieve NETHEAD. The paragraph referencing a network executive should appear on your screen just above the closing (Fig. 15.7). Read through the new template and make sure it's correct. Then save it using file name NETWORK.

Figure 15.7

The third paragraph refers to independent producers. Delete it and replace it with NETHEAD.

```
Today, Howard and Johnson are proud to announce the development
of their newest mega-hit, "The Betagosa Hillbillies." Please see
the attached press release for details.

As program director for our favorite network, XXX, we wanted you
to see it first. As usual, all things being equal, our dream is
to see our new show on good old XXX.

Contact us for additional details.

B:\NETWORK                                      Doc 1 Pg 1 Ln 3.83" Pos 1"
```

Adding Custom Data

Adding the First Name and Address

Imagine that you have the names and addresses of both network and independent producers written on a set of index cards (Fig. 15.8). The first one identifies Ms. Charlie Angel, the Program Director for CBS. The network template is already in memory, so you're ready to begin.

Move the cursor to the blank line just after the date (line 2.0"), insert another blank line, and type

    Ms. Charlie Angel

Then press ⏎. Now type the rest of the address, pressing ⏎ at the end of each line; when you finish, the cursor should be on line 2.83". Insert one more blank line, type the salutation

    Dear Ms. Angel:

and press ⏎ again. Your screen should resemble Fig. 15.9.

Figure 15.8

The names and addresses of both network and independent producers are written on a set of index cards.

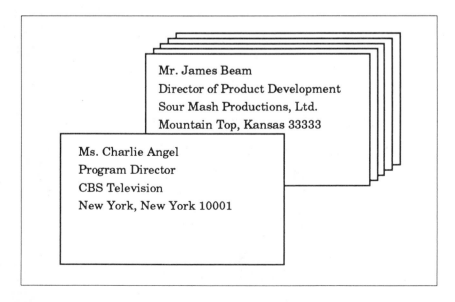

Mr. James Beam
Director of Product Development
Sour Mash Productions, Ltd.
Mountain Top, Kansas 33333

Ms. Charlie Angel
Program Director
CBS Television
New York, New York 10001

Figure 15.9
This screen shows the first letter with the recipient's name and address and the salutation in place.

```
                     Howard and Johnson, Ltd.
                    "Creativity is Our Thing!"
                           P.O. Box Z
                       Oxford, Ohio 01056

                                             March 3, 1989

Ms. Charlie Angel
Program Director
CBS Television
New York, New York  10001

Dear Ms. Angel:

Mary Howard and Hector Johnson, two of the most creative minds in
television today, have been responsible for such hits as "Bleep
the Boss" and "Humiliate Your Spouse." Graduates of the South
Dakota School of Broadcasting, this incredible team has been a
gold mine of original ideas since 1988.
```

The Replace Feature

One more change remains before this letter is ready to go. Move the cursor to the end of the document. The last full paragraph begins on line 5". It contains two references to a dummy network; XXX must be replaced by Ms. Angel's network, CBS. You could, of course, move the cursor, replace the first XXX, move the cursor again, and replace the second one, but it's easier to use the replace feature. If you give WordPerfect a search string of characters and/or codes and a replacement string, the program will search the document, find every occurrence of the search string, and, subject to your veto, substitute the replacement string.

Move the cursor to the top of the document. (The replace feature searches from the cursor to the end of the document.) *Replace* is printed in blue near F2, so

> Press: Alt *and* F2

The status line will read

> w/Confirm? (Y/N) No

You have two choices. If you type Y, each time WordPerfect finds the search string you'll be given the option of replacing or not replacing it. If you type N, replacement is automatic. There is no need to confirm this operation, so type N.

The next status line message,

> -> Srch:

asks you to enter the search string. WordPerfect can search for any combination of characters and/or hidden codes. For example, pressing

Figure 15.10

Use the replace feature to substitute CBS for XXX.

> Today, Howard and Johnson are proud to announce the development of their newest mega-hit, The Betagosa Hillbillies." Please see the attached press release for details.
>
> As program director for our very favorite network, CBS, we wanted you to see it first. As usual, all things being equal, our dream is to see our new show on good old CBS.

⏎ generates a hard return code, so do not press ⏎ unless you want to search for a hard return. Type XXX; the status line should read

        -> Srch: XXX

Do *not* press ⏎. Instead, press F2, and a new status line message

        Replace with:

will appear. Type CBS; the status line should then read

        Replace with: CBS

Press F2, and the letters CBS will replace XXX in the document (Fig. 15.10).

Do be careful when specifying search strings. To choose an extreme example, imagine that you are searching for the word a. If, following the search prompt, you simply type a and then press F2, WordPerfect will look for every occurrence of the *letter* a. If, on the other hand, you type a space, the letter a, and then another space before pressing F2, WordPerfect will search for the three-character string space/a/space.

■ *Keystroke Summary*

Replace

Press:	Alt *and* F2
Type:	**Y** (to confirm) or **N** (to skip confirm)
Type:	*search string*
Press:	F2
Type:	*replacement string*
Press:	F2
Respond:	to prompts

■ *What Can Go Wrong?*

1. You pressed ⏎ after typing a search or replace string.

Cause: This is a common error. Pressing ⏎ when you finish typing almost anything just seems like the natural thing to do.

Solution: Press ← to erase the hard return code. Then press F2.

2. The replace operation ended, but nothing was replaced.

Cause: You might have started the search with the cursor located after the target strings. You might have pressed ⏎ or some other key that inserts a hidden code before pressing F2 to end the search string.

Solution: Move the cursor to the top of the document and try again. This time, type *only* the search string, and then press F2.

3. After replace runs, changed lines end with the replace string followed by a hard return code.

Cause: You pressed ⏎ and then F2 after typing the replace string.

Solution: Move the cursor to the top of the document and repeat the replace operation. This time, type the search string, press ⏎, and then press F2. Type the replace string, do *not* press ⏎, and press F2. ■

Printing and Saving the Letter

The first letter is finished. Print it. Then press F7 and save it; use the file name CBS. Do *not* exit WordPerfect, but do clear the screen. Retrieve a new copy of the template, NETWORK, and you're ready to start the next letter.

Switching Screens

The next index card in Fig. 15.8 identifies an independent producer named James Beam. The template in memory is intended for someone affiliated with a network; it's the wrong template. One option is to clear memory and retrieve the independent producer template. Another is to use WordPerfect's switch screen feature to keep *both* templates in memory.

·*Switch* is printed in green near F3. To switch screens,

Press: ⇧ *and* F3

After a brief pause, a new blank work screen will appear (Fig. 15.11). Note the reference to document 2 on the status line. To return to document 1, press ⇧ *and* F3 again. Try it; the network template will reappear, and the status line will once again reference document 1. Think of ⇧ *and* F3 as a toggle switch that moves you back and forth between the two screens.

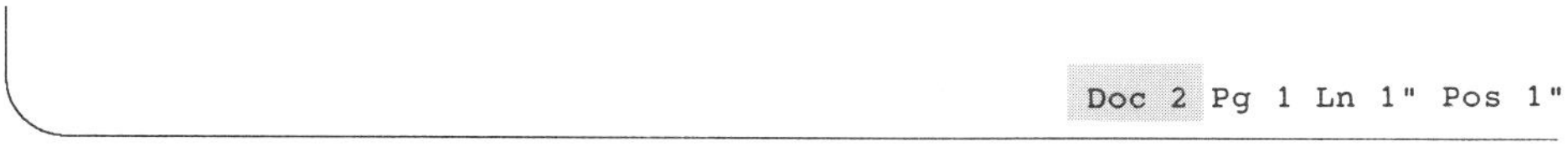

Figure 15.11

When you first switch screens, you get a blank work screen. Note the reference to document 2 on the status line.

Doc 2 Pg 1 Ln 1" Pos 1"

Figure 15.12

Retrieve the independent producer template and display it as document 2.

```
              Howard and Johnson, Ltd.
              "Creativity is Our Thing!"
                    P.O. Box Z
                 Oxford, Ohio 01056

                                        March 3, 1989

Mary Howard and Hector Johnson, two of the most creative minds in
television today, have been responsible for such hits as "Bleep
the Boss" and "Humiliate Your Spouse." Graduates of the South
Dakota School of Broadcasting, this incredible team has been a
gold mine of original ideas since 1988.

Today, Howard and Johnson are proud to announce the development
of their newest mega-hit, "The Betagosa Hillbillies." Please see
the attached press release for details.

Of course, our first thought was to send this proposal to you,
our very favorite independent producer. With your help, we're
sure this new proposal will set the standard for the next decade.

Contact us for additional details.

 B:\INDPRO                              Doc 2 Pg 1 Ln 1" Pos 1"
```

Go back to screen 2 (the blank screen), press F5, and go to the list files screen. Move the cursor to mark INDPRO and then type 1. The second template will appear on the document 2 work screen (Fig. 15.12).

■ *Keystroke Summary*

Switch screens

Press: ⬆ *and* F3

Completing the Remaining Letters

Now you're ready for the second letter. Insert a blank line after the date and type

Mr. James Beam

Then press ↵. Type the rest of the address, insert a blank line, type the salutation, and insert another blank line; use Fig. 15.13 as a guide.

Figure 15.13

The second letter.

```
              Howard and Johnson, Ltd.
              "Creativity is Our Thing!"
                    P.O. Box Z
                 Oxford, Ohio 01056

                                        March 3, 1989

Mr. James Beam
Director of Product Development
Sour Mash Productions, Ltd.
Mountain Top, Kansas  33333

Dear Mr. Beam:

Mary Howard and Hector Johnson, two of the most creative minds in
television today, have been responsible for such hits as "Bleep
the Boss" and "Humiliate Your Spouse." Graduates of the South
Dakota School of Broadcasting, this incredible team has been a
gold mine of original ideas since 1988.
```

Figure 15.14
Prepare finished
letters for these three
people.

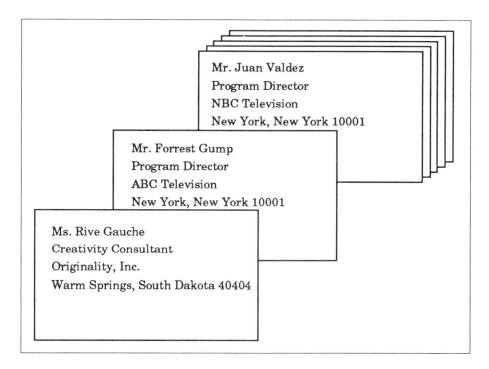

Mr. Juan Valdez
Program Director
NBC Television
New York, New York 10001

Mr. Forrest Gump
Program Director
ABC Television
New York, New York 10001

Ms. Rive Gauche
Creativity Consultant
Originality, Inc.
Warm Springs, South Dakota 40404

The second letter is complete. Print it. Then press F7, save the document using file name SOURMASH, clear the screen, and retrieve a fresh copy of INDPRO.

Three more names and addresses are listed in Fig. 15.14; prepare, print, and save letters for them. Another independent producer, Rive Gauche, is next, so use the template on screen 2. The last two names are network executives; switch to screen 1 to type their letters. Use file names ORIGINAL, ABC, and NBC. Don't forget to retrieve a copy of NETWORK or INDPRO after you clear the screen.

Exiting Document 2

When you finish, switch back to document 2 and press F7. A message on the status line will ask whether you want to save the document; respond by typing N. (You have already saved it.) The next status line message will read

```
Exit doc 2? (Y/N) No
```

It asks whether you are ready to exit document 2. You are, so type Y. The document 1 screen will reappear. Because document 1 still exists, WordPerfect will not send you back to the operating system.

Press F7 again. Do not save the document (type N). The status line will read

```
Exit WP? (Y/N) No
```

Note the difference between this message and the last one. Earlier, you were asked whether you wanted to exit *document 2*. This time, you're asked whether you want to exit *WordPerfect*. If you type Y, you will end the session and go back to the operating system. Do *not* exit WordPerfect; instead, type N to clear the screen.

■ *What Can Go Wrong?*

1. The status line disappears, and the DOS prompt is displayed near the bottom of the screen.

Cause: You told WordPerfect to exit to DOS, probably by typing Y in response to an exit WP prompt. As you begin to feel more comfortable with WordPerfect, certain responses, such as typing Y, become almost automatic.

Solution: Because all files were saved, no harm was done. Reload WordPerfect and continue with the tutorial.

2. When you exit from screen 2, you exit to DOS.

Cause: Screen 1 is probably empty. Perhaps you failed to retrieve a copy of NETWORK after you saved the last letter.

Solution: Reload WordPerfect and continue with the tutorial. ■

Mail Merge

Manually adding custom data to a template is reasonable for preparing a few letters, but it simply will not do for large numbers of documents. WordPerfect's mail merge feature is an excellent solution for all but the largest mass mailings. To run mail merge, two files must be created. The **primary file** holds a template with codes marking the positions of variable data. The **secondary file** holds such data as names and addresses. The two files are combined when the mail merge routine is executed.

Planning the Primary File

The first step in preparing a mail merge application is planning the primary file. Earlier in the chapter, you defined a template for network executives (NETHEAD); that letter will serve as a base.

Look back at Fig. 15.9. Note that the recipient's mailing address consists of a name, a title, a company name, and the city, state, and zip code. Those four lines will be different on each letter. Next, consider the salutation. Its format differs from the name, and it, too, will change on each letter. Finally, the company name appears in two places in the body of the letter (Fig. 15.10).

Data Structures

The variable data represent the minimum content of the secondary file. The smallest unit of data is called a **field**; in this application, five

Figure 15.15

The data in the secondary file are organized to form a data structure.

	Field	Contents
	1	Ms. Charlie Angel
	2	Program Director
Record	3	CBS Television
	4	New York, New York 10001
	5	Ms. Angel

fields—a recipient's name, title, company name, address, and a salutation—will be printed on each letter (Fig. 15.15). To distinguish the fields, they are assigned numbers; Ms. Angel's name is field 1, her title is field 2, and so on. All five fields, taken together, comprise a **record**, and a similar record will be created for *each* person on the mailing list. A different application might call for a different data structure, but the relationship between fields and records will still hold.

The mail merge routine starts by retrieving the primary file. Next, it reads a single record from the secondary file and uses the fields in that record to customize the template. Then it reads the *next* secondary record and repeats the process, continuing until there are no more records in the secondary file.

Every record in the file must contain the *same* fields entered in the same order; in other words, every record in *this* secondary file must have a name, a title, a company name, a city/state/zip code, and a salutation. You are not limited to five fields, of course; that number is a function of the application. For example, Ms. Angel's record could have been defined as containing a title (Ms.), a first name, a last name, a business title, a company name, a city, a state, a zip code, and a salutation for a total of nine fields, and more fields containing additional personal data could have been added.

Creating a Secondary File

The commands associated with mail merge are all controlled by function key F9. Make sure the screen is clear, and type the first record's first field

```
Ms. Charlie Angel
```

Check the WordPerfect template and note that *Merge R* is printed in black near F9. To end a field,

```
Press:  F9
```

by itself. A code, ^R, will appear on the screen following the name, and the cursor will advance to the next line. The code marks the end of the

Figure 15.16

The first secondary file record with field codes in place.

```
Ms. Charlie Angel^R
Program Director^R
CBS Television^R
New York, New York   10001^R
Ms. Angel^R
```

field. Type the rest of the address using Fig. 15.16 as a guide; press F9 at the end of each line. Finally, type the salutation, Ms. Angel, and press F9.

You must insert another code to mark the end of the record. Check the template. *Merge codes* is printed in green, so

Press: ⬆ *and* F9

The message

^C; ^D; ^E; ^F; ^G; ^N; ^O; ^P; ^Q; ^S; ^T; ^U; ^V:

will appear on the status line. The letters identify the various merge codes; they are summarized in Fig. 15.17. Type E (for end of record), and an ^E code will appear just below the salutation (Fig. 15.18). Note that the record is followed by a double horizontal line.

Use the same procedure to type the two additional name and address records shown on Fig. 15.18. Do not type the codes; ^R will be inserted when you press F9, and ^E will be inserted when you press ⬆ *and* F9 and select code E.

Figure 15.17

WordPerfect merge codes.

Code	Meaning
^C	Pause to accept text from the keyboard.
^D	Insert current date.
^E	End of a secondary file record.
^Fn^	Insert text from field n.
^G	Start a macro at the end of a merge.
^N	Get next secondary record.
^O	Display a message on the status line.
^P	Insert contents of a file.
^Q	Stop the merge.
^R	End of a secondary file field.
^S	Change to a new secondary file.
^T	Send text to the printer.
^U	Update the screen.
^V	Transfer merge codes.

Figure 15.18
Type the next two secondary records. Note the ^E code that ends each record.

```
Ms. Charlie Angel^R
Program Director^R
CBS Television^R
New York, New York   10001^R
Ms. Angel^R
^E
==================================================================================
Mr. Forrest Gump^R
Program Director^R
ABC Television^R
New York, New York   10001^R
Mr. Gump^R
^E
==================================================================================
Mr. Juan Valdez^R
Program Director^R
NBC Television^R
New York, New York   10001^R
Mr. Valdez^R
^E
==================================================================================


                                          Doc 1 Pg 4 Ln 1" Pos 1"
```

When you finish typing the names and addresses, press F7 and save the file. Use file name N&A. Do not exit WordPerfect, but do clear the screen.

∎ *Keystroke Summary*

Create secondary file

For each record:

Type:	*contents of field*	⎤ for each field
Press:	F9	⎦
Press:	⇧ *and* F9	⎤ to end record
Type:	**E**	⎦

Creating the Primary File

Earlier in the chapter, you created a template for a letter to a network executive. Use that template as a basis for the primary file. Retrieve NETWORK. To convert the template to a primary file, you must add codes to indicate where the variable data from the secondary file should be inserted.

Before you start, briefly review the contents of the secondary file. Each record consists of five fields; to distinguish them, WordPerfect numbers them. Keep the field numbers in mind as you complete the primary file.

The recipient's name, the first field, should be printed just below the date. Move the cursor to the blank line after the date (line 2"), press

Figure 15.19

This screen shows the merge codes for a name, address, and salutation inserted in the template text.

```
                    Howard and Johnson, Ltd.
                   "Creativity is Our Thing!"
                         P.O. Box Z
                      Oxford, Ohio 01056

                                              March 3, 1989
^F1^
^F2^
^F3^
^F4^

Dear ^F5^:

Mary Howard and Hector Johnson, two of the most creative minds in
television today, have been responsible for such hits as "Bleep
the Boss" and "Humiliate Your Spouse." Graduates of the South
Dakota School of Broadcasting, this incredible team has been a
gold mine of original ideas since 1988.
```

⏎ to insert a blank line, and then

    Press: ⬆ *and* F9

The list of merge codes will appear on the status line. To select a field, type the letter F. The message

    Field:

will be displayed. The recipient's name is field 1, so type 1 and press ⏎. The code ^F1^ will be inserted into the text. (You can see it in Fig. 15.19.)

Press ⏎ to move the cursor to the beginning of the next line. Then press ⬆ *and* F9 again, and the merge codes will reappear. Type F to insert a field. The title (field 2) goes on this line, so type 2 and press ⏎. Move the cursor to the next line and insert the company name, which is field 3. Then drop down one more line and insert field 4, the city, state, and zip code.

The salutation comes next. Press ⏎ to insert a blank line, type the word Dear, and press the space bar to insert a blank character. Then press ⬆ *and* F9. Type F to insert a field. The salutation is field 5, so type 5 and press ⏎. Type a colon to end the salutation, press ⏎, and the top portion of the encoded template is finished (Fig. 15.19).

Move the cursor to the end of the document and look at the last full paragraph. It contains two references to network XXX. Replace them with field 3, the actual network name.

Move the cursor to the first XXX (line 5") and delete it. Then press ⬆ *and* F9, type F, type 3 to indicate the third field, and press ⏎. The code ^F3^ will appear in the document (Fig. 15.20). Move the cursor to the second XXX (line 5.33") and replace it with the code for field 3.

That completes the primary file. Press F7 and save the file under file name PRIME. Do *not* exit WordPerfect, but do clear the screen.

Figure 15.20
Merge codes can be
inserted into the body
of the primary
document, too.

```
Today, Howard and Johnson are proud to announce the development
of their newest mega-hit, The Betagosa Hillbillies." Please see
the attached press release for details.

As program director for our very favorite network, ^F3^, we
wanted you to see it first. As usual, all things being equal, our
dream is to see our new show on good old ^F3^.
```

■ *Keystroke Summary*

Create primary file

Retrieve:	template	
Move:	cursor to target position	
Press:	Alt *and* F9	
Type:	**F**	for each field
Type:	*field number*	
Press:	↵	

Running the Merge Routine

Note that *Merge/Sort* is printed in red on the WordPerfect template. To start the merge routine,

Press: Ctrl *and* F9

The message

```
1 Merge; 2 Sort; 3 Sort Order: 0
```

will appear on the status line. Type 1. The next message

```
Primary file:
```

is self-explanatory. Type the name of the primary file; the status line should read

```
Primary file: PRIME
```

Press ↵, and a new message

```
Secondary file:
```

appears. Type the secondary file's name

```
Secondary file: N&A
```

and press ↵. The merge operation will begin.

When it ends, the cursor will be at the end of the merged file. Move it to the beginning of the document, where you will see the first several lines of the first letter (Fig. 15.21). Note the name, address, and salutation.

Figure 15.21

After the merge routine runs, the completed letters are all stored in memory. This screen shows the beginning of the first letter.

```
                          Howard and Johnson, Ltd.
                         "Creativity is Our Thing!"
                                P.O. Box Z
                          Oxford, Ohio  01056

                                                    March 3, 1989

Ms. Charlie Angel
Program Director
CBS Television
New York, New York  10001

Dear Ms. Angel:

Mary Howard and Hector Johnson, two of the most creative minds in
television today, have been responsible for such hits as "Bleep
the Boss" and Humiliate Yous Spouse." Graduates of the South
Dakota School of Broadcasting, this incredible team has been a
gold mine of original ideas since 1988.

Today, Howard and Johnson are proud to announce the development
of their newest mega-hit, "The Betagosa Hillbillies." Please see
the attached press release for details.

                                        Doc 1 Pg 1 Ln 1" Pos 1"
```

Press ⊞ to move the cursor to the bottom of the screen, and then press ⊞ again. The second screen shows the end of the first letter; note the references to CBS Television near the top of the screen. Just below the closing, a double horizontal line marks a hard page break. The beginning of the second letter comes just after the page break.

Use ⊞ to scroll through the rest of the document. You should find one letter for each record in the secondary file. If additional customizing is necessary, you can change selected letters on the screen.

At this point you have several options. One is to send the complete "document" to the printer. Since each letter is followed by a hard page break, each will be printed on a separate page. You might also want to save the letters for future reference. Because they are all in memory, the complete set can be saved under a single file name.

■ *Keystroke Summary*

Run merge

Press: Ctrl *and* F9

Type: **1**

Type: *primary file name*

Press: ↵

Type: *secondary file name*

Press: ↵

Exiting WordPerfect

This ends the third tutorial. Exit WordPerfect or move on to Chapter 16.

Summary

Topic or Feature	Command or Reference	Option	Page
Date, insert	⬆ *and* F5	1	219
Flush right	Alt *and* F6	—	218
List files screen, exit	F5	0	215
List files screen, go to	F5	—	214
Merge code, insert	⬆ *and* F9	—	230
Merge, start	Ctrl *and* F9	—	231
Replace (search and)	Alt *and* F2	—	221
Secondary file field, end	F9	—	227
Secondary file record, end	⬆ *and* F9	E	228
Switch screens	⬆ *and* F3	—	223

Self-Test

1. The term _____ is sometimes applied to previously written paragraphs and phrases that are later combined to form a document.

2. Personalized form letters are often prepared by adding variable data to a _____.

3. WordPerfect's _____ feature combines data from two files to produce a set of personalized form letters.

4. Choose option _____ to exit the list files screen. Choose option _____ to retrieve a file.

5. To clear the work screen, press _____, optionally save the file, and then type _____ when asked whether you want to exit WordPerfect.

6. In WordPerfect you can concurrently work on _____ different documents.

7. The template for a mail merge is stored in the _____ file.

8. The name and address file for a mail merge is stored in the _____ file.

9. The most elementary unit of data in a mail merge secondary file is called a _____. On a secondary file, a set of these elementary units forms a _____.

10. Press _____ to start the mail merge routine.

Exercises

1. To catch up on your personal correspondence, type and save descriptions of incidents that have occurred recently in your life. Use them as boilerplate and build several personal letters around them.

2. Create your own name and address file. Write a single-page template announcing your impending marriage, graduation, promotion, or some other significant event. Use mail merge to prepare copies for all your relatives and friends.

3. Create and save each of the following files:

File Name	Contents
MATH	Most computer-related programs require a great deal of mathematics, and students tend to avoid mathematics.
INDUSTRY	The computer industry is not growing as fast as it was in the 1970s. To many people, that suggests reduced opportunity.
TOUGH	Many students consider the computer-related degree programs to be among the most difficult on campus.
JOBS	Many students pick a major based on the expected availability of a postgraduation job. In the 1970s and the early 1980s the computer field seemed to have limitless growth potential.

4. Start this exercise with a clear screen. Retrieve file MAJORS. (You created it in Exercises 4 and 5 of Chapter 13.) Move the cursor to the end of the file and press ⏎ to insert a blank line. Then perform the following tasks:

   a. Type the sentence: *There are many possible explanations*. End the sentence with a period and skip a space.

   b. Retrieve file TOUGH.

   c. Move the cursor to the end of the document. Type *For example,*, skip a space and retrieve file MATH. Change the *M* in *Most* from uppercase to lowercase.

   d. Move the cursor to the end of the document. Press ⏎ to end the paragraph, and then press ⏎ again to skip a line. Retrieve file JOBS.

   e. Move the cursor to the end of the document. Skip a space and then retrieve file INDUSTRY.

   f. Print the document. Then save it using file name ENROLL.

5. Start with file ENROLL. (You created it in Exercise 4.) With the cursor at the top of the document, press ⏎ to insert a blank line. Then create a primary file for mail merge.

   a. On the top line, enter today's date, flush right.

   b. Skip a line. Then type *TO:* followed by a blank space. One the same line, insert a code for secondary file field 1.

   c. Skip another line. Then type *FROM:* followed by your own name, and press ⏎.

Save the primary file using file name ENROLL.PF. Next create a secondary file. Each record will hold an individual's name and title as a single field. Use the following names (or substitute names from your own school).

```
President Barr
Provost Gonzalez
Dean Martin
Professor Fuji
Professor Bon Jovi
```

Save the file using file name PEOPLE.SF. Then run the merge routine and print the letters.

·16

Controlling Document Format

This chapter introduces the WordPerfect features and commands that allow you to:

- change the default page size
- add headers and page numbers
- double-space a document
- center a line
- boldface and underline
- add footnotes
- write a macro

   Several other features will be discussed briefly.

Preparing a Document for Printing

The tutorials in Chapters 13 through 15 required only the most basic printing. WordPerfect can create much more sophisticated documents. For example, imagine that Howard and Johnson use custom 8 x 10-inch paper for their correspondence. By typing a single command, you can easily redefine the page size to fit this new format. (*Note:* Use standard 8.5 x 11 inch forms to simulate the custom paper size.)

Figure 16.1

"The Betagosa Hillbillies" program proposal before the page format is changed.

```
PROGRAM PROPOSAL

THE BETAGOSA HILLBILLIES

When Jean Rogers, nationally syndicated TV critic, was shown this
program proposal, she said:

        Last week I had an opportunity to review the latest
        program proposal by Howard and Johnson. That madcap
        pair has done it again! "The Betagosa Hillbillies"
        incorporates virtually every hackneyed cliche ever seen
        in a situation comedy. Brilliant!

This proposed new half-hour comedy combines the best of "Star
Trek," "The Beverly Hillbillies," and "Gilligan's Island."
Professor Gallagher will be the focus of humor. He is a cross
between Star Trek's Scotty and Gilligan (from Gilligan's Island).
An early episode will establish that he was named after the 20th
century comedian Gallagher. This part could be a star vehicle for
a young comedian with a Gallagher-like style.

The story is set on the planet Betagosa, where the crew of the
starship Hindenberg find themselves marooned after Professor
Gallagher miscalculates E from Einstein's famous equation. The
B:\BETAHILL                                    Doc 1 Pg 1 Ln 1" Pos 1"
```

Changing the Page Size

Boot the operating system and load WordPerfect. Retrieve the program proposal, BETAHILL (Fig. 16.1). The cursor should be at the top of the screen. (Like most codes, the one that sets page size takes effect from the cursor location to the end of the document.) Check the WordPerfect template. The word *Format* appears in green near F8, so

Press: ⇧ *and* F8

to get the **format** screen (Fig. 16.2).

Figure 16.2

The format screen summarizes options for setting line, page, or document format.

```
Format

    1 - Line
            Hyphenation                    Line Spacing
            Justification                  Margins Left/Right
            Line Height                    Tab Set
            Line Numbering                 Widow/Orphan Protection

    2 - Page
            Center Page (top to bottom)    New Page Number
            Force Odd/Even Page            Page Numbering
            Headers and Footers            Paper Size/Type
            Margins Top/Bottom             Suppress

    3 - Document
            Display Pitch                  Redline Method
            Initial Codes/Font             Summary

    4 - Other
            Advance                        Overstrike
            Conditional End of Page        Printer Functions
            Decimal Characters             Underline Spaces/Tabs
            Language

Selection: 0
```

Figure 16.3
The page format
menu.

```
Format: Page

       1 - Center Page (top to bottom)    No

       2 - Force Odd/Even Page

       3 - Headers

       4 - Footers

       5 - Margins - Top                  1"
                     Bottom               1"

       6 - New Page Number                1
           (example: 3 or iii)

       7 - Page Numbering                 No page numbering

       8 - Paper Size                     8.5" x 11"
                Type                       Standard

       9 - Suppress (this page only)

Selection: 0
```

Type 2 to access the **page format** menu (Fig. 16.3). Note that option 8 sets the page size. Type 8, and a list of page sizes will appear (Fig. 16.4). If your page format is on that list, just type the number; for example, a government employee desiring 8 x 11 paper would type 7. Since Howard and Johnson's 8 x 10 paper is not listed, type the letter O, for other.

Figure 16.4

The paper size menu.
Option O, for other,
allows you to define
unusual paper sizes.

```
Format: Paper Size

       1 - Standard              (8.5" x 11")

       2 - Standard Landscape    (11" x 8.5")

       3 - Legal                 (8.5" x 14")

       4 - Legal Landscape       (14" x 8.5")

       5 - Envelope              (9.5" x 4")

       6 - Half Sheet            (5.5" x 8.5")

       7 - US Government         (8" x 11")

       8 - A4                    (210mm x 297mm)

       9 - A4 Landscape          (297mm x 210mm)

       O - Other

Selection: 1
```

A message listing the current default paper width will appear on the status line

```
Width: 8.5
```

Type the desired width; the status line should read

```
Width: 8
```

Press ⏎, and the default page height will appear:

```
Height: 11
```

Once again, type the desired value:

```
Height: 10
```

and press ⏎. A new menu will allow you to select the paper type; type 1 for standard paper. The page format menu will reappear; note the new paper size.

Because the standard 1-inch top and bottom margins have not been changed, a 10-inch sheet of paper has 8 inches available for text. At six lines per inch, that's 48 (instead of the default 54) lines per page. On 8-inch-wide paper, 1-inch side margins leave only 6 inches for text; at 10 characters per inch, that's 60 per line. WordPerfect automatically recomputes these values for you. Other commands allow you to change line height, line spacing, top, bottom, and side margins, and characters per inch, but space does not permit detailed coverage here.

■ *Keystroke Summary*

Change paper size

Press:	⇧ *and* F8
Type:	**2**
Type:	**8**
Type:	*choices from menus*
Press:	F7 to return to the work screen

■ *What Can Go Wrong?*

1. When you attempt to change the page size, the page format menu reappears.

Cause: You probably typed the digit zero instead of the letter O. Typing zero sends you back one screen.

Solution: Type 8 to select the paper size menu; then type the letter O, for other. ■

Page Headers

On a lengthy document it often helps to identify each page. Check the page format menu. **Headers**, option 3, are printed at the top of a page; **footers**, option 4, appear at the bottom.

Type 3, and the message

```
1 Header A; 2 Header B: 0
```

will appear on the status line. You can define two different headers. This time, since only one header is called for, type 1, and a new status line message

```
1 Discontinue; 2 Every Page; 3 Odd Pages; 4 Even Pages;
5 Edit: 0
```

will appear. (The menu will be displayed as a single line.) Type 2 to print the header on every page.

The page format screen will be replaced by a blank work screen. Type the header (Fig. 16.5); use the figure as a guide. Press ⏎ at the end of both lines. Press F7 when you're finished, and the page format screen will reappear.

Headers and footers are printed within the text area of the document, not in the margins. One blank line is inserted between the header and the start of the text. In this example you typed two lines and pressed ⏎, yielding a three-line header. Including WordPerfect's blank line, the header consumes four lines. Thus of the 48 text lines per page, only 44 are still available.

■ *Keystroke Summary*

Headers

Press:	⇧ *and* F8
Type:	**2**
Type:	**3**
Type:	*code for header type*
Type:	*code for header frequency*
Type:	*(or edit) header text*
Press:	F7 to return to the page format screen
Press:	F7 to return to the work screen

Figure 16.5

Type your header or footer on the header/footer work screen. Press F7 to return to the page format screen.

```
The Betagosa Hillbillies
March 1, 1989
```

Figure 16.6
The page number position screen allows you to specify where page numbers will be printed.

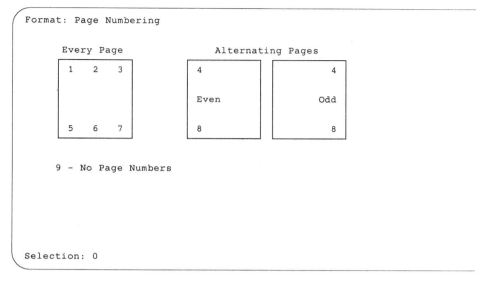

Page Numbers

Page numbers are set through page format menu option 7. Type 7, and a new screen will appear (Fig. 16.6). The rectangles represent pages. The digit 1 appears at the top left, so choosing option 1 will print page numbers at the top left of each page. Option 2 specifies the top center of each page; option 3 is top right. Option 4 is a bit different; it prints even page numbers at the top left and odd page numbers at the top right. Options 5 through 8 define equivalent bottom-of-page positions.

Type 3 to position numbers at the top right of each page. The page format menu will reappear (Fig. 16.7). Note the reference to header A

Figure 16.7
The page format screen shows the new settings.

```
Format: Page

    1 - Center Page (top to bottom)      No

    2 - Force Odd/Even Page

    3 - Headers                          HA Every page

    4 - Footers

    5 - Margins - Top                    1"
                  Bottom                 1"

    6 - New Page Number                  1
         (example: 3 or iii)

    7 - Page Numbering                   Top Right

    8 - Paper Size                       8" x 10"
            Type                         Standard

    9 - Suppress (this page only)

Selection: 0
```

following option 3. Note also that page numbers are to be printed and that the paper size is 8 x 10. The page format menu reflects the changes you made.

Page numbers

Press:	⬆ *and* F8
Type:	**2**
Type:	**7**
Select:	page number position from menu
Press:	F7 to return to the work screen

Double-Spacing

One more formatting task remains. The program proposal will be much easier to read if it is double-spaced. Line spacing is not set through the page format menu, so type 0 to return to the general format menu. Then type 1 to access the **line format menu** (Fig. 16.8).

Line spacing is controlled by option 6. Type 6, and the cursor will move to the digit 1 following the option. To double-space, type 2 and press ⏎. For future reference, type 3 to triple-space, type 4 to skip four lines, and so on.

Figure 16.8
The line format menu.

```
Format: Line

    1 - Hyphenation                    Off

    2 - Hyphenation Zone - Left        10%
                          Right         4%

    3 - Justification                  Yes

    4 - Line Height                    Auto

    5 - Line Numbering                 No

    6 - Line Spacing                   1

    7 - Margins - Left                 1"
                  Right                1"

    8 - Tab Set                        0", every 0.5"

    9 - Widow/Orphan Protection        No


Selection: 0
```

▪ *Keystroke*
Summary

Line spacing

Press:	⬆ *and* F8
Type:	**1**
Type:	**6**
Type:	*desired spacing*
Press:	↵
Press:	F7 to return to the work screen

▪ *What Can*
Go Wrong?

1. After you double-space the document, the top part is still single-spaced.

Cause: You probably moved the cursor from the top of the document.

Solution: Go to the reveal codes screen and delete the line spacing code. Then move the cursor to the top of the document and change the line spacing to 2. ▪

Checking the Codes

The document is now reformatted. Type 0 to return to the format screen; then type 0 again to get to the work screen (Fig. 16.9). (Typing 0 always sends you back one screen.) An alternative is to press the exit key, F7; it returns you directly to the work screen from any of the secondary format screens.

Figure 16.9
The work screen after reformatting.

```
PROGRAM PROPOSAL


THE BETAGOSA HILLBILLIES


When Jean Rogers, nationally syndicated TV critic, was shown
this program proposal, she said:


     Last week I had an opportunity to review the
     latest program proposal by Howard and Johnson.
     That madcap pair has done it again! "The Betagosa
     Hillbillies" incorporates virtually every
     hackneyed cliche ever seen in a situation comedy.

B:\BETAHILL                                Doc 1 Pg 1 Ln 1.66" Pos 1"
```

Figure 16.10

This reveal codes screen shows that all the document control codes precede the first text character.

```
PROGRAM PROPOSAL


THE BETAGOSA HILLBILLIES


When Jean Rogers, nationally syndicated TV critic, was shown

this program proposal, she said:
B:\BETAHILL                                        Doc 1 Pg 1 Ln 1.66" Pos 1"
(                                    )
[Paper Sz/Typ:8" x 10",Standard][Header A:2;The Betagosa Hillbillies[HRt]
March 1, 1989[HRt]
][Pg Numbering:Top Right][Ln Spacing:2]PROGRAM PROPOSAL[HRt]
[HRt]
THE BETAGOSA HILLBILLIES[HRt]
[HRt]
When Jean Rogers, nationally syndicated TV critic, was shown[SRt]
this program proposal, she said:[HRt]
[HRt]
[IndentLast week I had an opportunity to review the[SRt]
Press Reveal Codes to restore screen
```

Clearly, the document is double-spaced. Although it's less obvious, moving the cursor to the right margin and then down to the second page should convince you that the page size has changed. The header and the page numbers are not visible on the screen, but they will appear when the document is printed.

WordPerfect implements such features as page format, headers, page numbers, and line spacing by inserting hidden codes into the text. Move the cursor to the top of the document and press Alt *and* F3 to access the reveal codes screen (Fig. 16.10). The page size, header, page number, and line spacing codes should precede the first text character. Press Alt *and* F3 to return to the work screen.

■ *What Can Go Wrong?*

1. The reveal codes screen shows that one or more text characters precede at least one of the hidden codes added in this chapter.

Cause: You moved the cursor from the top of the screen.

Solution: Note that the codes themselves can be in any order as long as they all precede the first text character. If only one code is in the wrong position, delete it, move the cursor to the correct position, and reinsert the code. If several codes are wrong, clear the screen, retrieve BETAHILL, and start over. ■

Saving the Document

Several document formatting tasks have been performed. You could have returned to the work screen after each one, but that would have been inefficient. Still, given the number of features covered, you might have missed something. If you did, repeat the tutorial by pressing [F7] and typing N in response to both prompts. Then retrieve BETAHILL and start over. When you're ready to move on, press [F10] and save the new version of the document.

Other Line Format Options

Although space does not allow detailed coverage of all formatting options, there are several that you might find useful.

For example, by default, documents are printed right-justified, with straight left and right margins. To achieve justification, blanks are added between words to force the last letter on a line to the right margin. For most documents, that's fine, but not always. The alternative, called ragged right, is a straight left margin with a right margin that moves in and out with the length of the line. Use line format option 3 to turn justification on or off.

Block protection is a useful way to avoid having a table split by a page break. Start by marking the table as a block. Then press [↑] *and* [F8] to activate the format feature, and type Y in response to the prompt.

Finally, top and bottom margins are reset from the page format menu, while left and right margins are controlled by the line format menu.

Special Effects

Centering the Titles

Move the cursor to the top of the document and position it on the letter P in PROGRAM. Then check the template. *Center* is printed in green near [F6], so

    Press: [↑] *and* [F6]

Move the cursor down, and the first title will be centered; this procedure works for any line that ends with a hard return. Repeat the steps to center THE BETAGOSA HILLBILLIES.

Next, add the creators' names just under the program title. With the cursor on line 2.66" (a blank line),

    Press: [↑] *and* [F6]

The cursor will move to the center of the line. Now type

    by: Howard and Johnson

and press [↵]. Your screen should resemble Fig. 16.11.

■ *Keystroke Summary*

Center text

    Press: [↑] *and* [F6]

    Type: *text*

    Press: [↵]

Figure 16.11
After the headers
have been centered,
your screen should
resemble this one.

```
                    PROGRAM PROPOSAL


              THE BETAGOSA HILLBILLIES
                by: Howard and Johnson


When Jean Rogers, nationally syndicated TV critic, was shown

this program proposal, she said:
```

■ *What Can Go Wrong?*

1. Although you issued a center command, the target line is not centered.

Cause: The line might not end with a hard return. You might not have moved the cursor to rewrite the screen.

Solution: First, try moving the cursor; when the screen is rewritten, the line might center. If that doesn't work, move the cursor to the end of the target line and press ⏎. ■

Boldface and Underline

One way to emphasize selected portions of a document is to boldface them. For example, move the cursor to the first character in the program title, press Alt *and* F4, and mark THE BETAGOSA HILL-BILLIES as a block. Check the template and find the word *Bold* printed in black near F6.

```
Press:  F6
```

and the title will be boldfaced. Press Alt *and* F3, and look at the reveal codes screen. A [**BOLD**] code should precede the title; a [**bold**] code should follow it.

Press Alt *and* F3 to get back to the work screen. Depending on your screen, the bold material might appear dark or in a contrasting color. On printouts from most printers, the bold characters will be darker than normal text.

To illustrate the process of underlining as you type, add some column identifiers to the list of characters. Move the cursor to the end of the document, and then move it to the blank line preceding the list (page 2, line 7"). Press ⏎ to insert another blank line. Then use ⊟ to align the cursor with the list of characters. *Underline* appears in black near F8, so

```
Press:  F8
```

to start underlining. Type the word

```
Character
```

and then

```
Press: F8
```

again to end underlining. Use the tab key to align the cursor with the character descriptions, press F8, type the word

```
Description
```

and press F8 again. Depending on your screen, the column identifiers might be highlighted or displayed in a contrasting color. When the document is printed, they will be underlined.

To underline a block, mark it and press F8. To boldface text as you type, press F6, type the text, and then press F6 to end boldfacing.

■ *Keystroke Summary*

Boldface and underline

A Block:		As You Type:	
Mark:	block	Press:	F6 for bold
Press:	F6 to bold		and/or
	or		F8 for underline
	F8 to underline	Type:	*text*
		Press:	F6 to end bold
			and/or
			F8 to end underline

Footnotes

When you quote someone directly, you generally identify the source in a footnote. Move the cursor to the end of the quotation (line 6", position 2.5"), just after *Brilliant!*. The word *Footnote* is printed in red near F7, so

```
Press: Ctrl and F7
```

A new menu

```
1 Footnote; 2 Endnote; 3 Endnote Placement:0
```

will appear on the status line. **Footnotes** are printed at the bottom of the page on which they are referenced. **Endnotes** are printed at the end of the document or at some other place specified by the user; they are particularly useful when you want to collect a set of references to prepare a bibliography.

To create or edit a footnote, type 1. The footnote menu

```
Footnote: 1 Create; 2 Edit; 3 New number; 4 Options: 0
```

```
    1Rogers, Jean, "Howard and Johnson Do It Again!", THE
WEEKLY INTRUDER, February 29, 1989, page 48.
```

will appear on the status line. Type 1. The work screen will be replaced by a new screen with the footnote number (in this case, 1) near the upper left. Type the footnote (Fig. 16.12); do *not* press ⌷ when you're done. Press the exit key, ⌷F7⌷, to end the footnote and return to the work screen (Fig. 16.13). Note that the footnote is *not* displayed; it will appear when the document is printed. The footnote number is highlighted, however.

WordPerfect inserts a blank line between the last line of text and the first footnote. Note that the footnotes are printed in the text area, not in the bottom margin. Pressing ⌷ inserts an extra blank line after the footnote, so do not press ⌷ unless you encounter a paragraph break. The software automatically keeps track of footnote numbers and positions them on the proper page even if you later modify the text or add more footnotes. On most printers the footnote number will appear as a superscript. (If your printer will not print superscripts, enclose the footnote reference in parentheses.)

Later, when you want to edit an existing footnote, press ⌷Ctrl⌷ *and* ⌷F7⌋, choose option 1, and then choose option 2 (edit) from the second menu. Type the footnote number, and the footnote will be displayed; make your corrections and press ⌷F7⌷ when you're finished. To delete a footnote, move the cursor to the footnote number in the document and press ⌷Del⌷. WordPerfect will ask whether you want to delete the footnote; respond by typing Y, for yes.

```
    That madcap pair has done it again! "The Betagosa

    Hillbillies" incorporates virtually every

    hackneyed cliche ever seen in a situation comedy.

    Brilliant!1
B:\BETAHILL                              Doc 1 Pg 1 Ln 5.66" Pos 2.55"
```

∎ *Keystroke*
Summary

Footnotes

Move: cursor to target position

Press: Ctrl *and* F7

Type: **1**

Type: **1**

Type: *footnote*

Press: F7 to exit

A Final Proofreading

Before you declare the program proposal finished, proofread it one more time. For example, there is a mistake in the reference to Professor Gallagher. The character's name is Gallagher, and he was named after a well-known comedian, but the model for the character is a different comedian, Eddie Murphy. The name Gallagher appears several times in the narrative, and some, but not all, of those references must be changed.

One option is reading through the text line by line, finding each reference, and either verifying or changing it. That process is both time consuming and error prone, particularly on a lengthy document. Instead, use the replace feature.

Start with the cursor at the top of the document. The word *Replace* appears on the template in blue near F2, so

Press: Alt *and* F2

A message will appear on the status line:

```
w/Confirm? (Y/N) No
```

In this case you want to replace some but not all occurrences, so type Y.

The next status line message,

```
-> Srch:
```

asks you to enter the search string; the arrow indicates that the search will proceed from the cursor's current position to the end of the document. Type the string; the status line should read

```
-> Srch: Gallagher
```

Do *not* press ↵. Press F2.

The next status line message reads

```
Replace with:
```

Type the replacement string; the status line should read

```
Replace with: Eddie Murphy
```

Press F2, and the search begins.

Watch the screen. When WordPerfect finds an occurrence of the search string, the cursor marks the string and a message,

```
Confirm? (Y/N) No
```

appears on the status line. If you want to replace this string, type Y. If not, type N. Once you have indicated your choice, WordPerfect will make the appropriate change and then continue the search, stopping at the next occurrence and displaying another confirmation message.

The string Gallagher occurs several times in this document. In line 7.33" and again on page 2, line 1.66" the reference is to the character, so do not replace the string. Page 2, line 2.33" refers to a potential real-life comedian. Replace it; *Gallagher-like* will change to *Eddie Murphy-like*. Note that the hyphen and the suffix do not confuse WordPerfect. Continue with the search. None of the remaining occurrences should be changed.

Continue reviewing the document. Note the word *a* just before Eddie Murphy's name (page 2, line 2"); it should be *an*, so change it. There is no way for WordPerfect, or any other word processor, to catch such errors; there is simply no substitute for careful proofreading. If you spot any other errors, correct them before you move on.

Saving and Printing the Document

You have made several changes to the document since you last saved it. If you think you might have missed something, press F7, type N in response to both prompts, retrieve BETAHILL, and repeat the centering, boldface, underlining, and footnote exercises. When you're ready to move on, press F10 and save the document.

Now that the document is formatted, it's ready to print. Press ⇧ *and* F7 to get the print menu; then type 1 to print the entire document. The output might overlap the perforations because the document size is defined as 8 x 10, while your printer almost certainly contains 8.5 x 11 paper. Type 0 to return to the work screen.

Printing the Letters

Changing Page Format

Now that the program proposal has been printed, clear the screen and retrieve file ABC. Make sure the cursor is at the top of the document. Then change the page size to match Howard and Johnson's custom stationary by

1. pressing ⇧ an*d* F8 to access the format menu,

2. selecting option 2 to get the page format menu,

3. selecting option 8 and defining 8 x 10 paper,

4. pressing F7 to return to the work screen.

Save ABC and then print a copy. Clear the screen, retrieve CBS, change its page size, save it, and print it. Then do the same thing for NBC, ORIGINAL, and SOURMASH.

Creating a Macro

Changing the page format for each of five letters is no problem, but as the number of documents increases, the task quickly becomes tedious. It would have made sense to insert the codes into file TOP when you created it. Then, when you retrieved it to start a letter, the codes would already be in place. Unfortunately, introducing features before they are needed is incompatible with the tutorial approach of this book. In real life, always add common codes to a template before creating custom documents.

An option is to create a **macro**. To avoid cluttering the example, start by clearing the screen. The words *Macro Def* appear on the template in red near F10, so

    Press: Ctrl *and* F10

to define a macro. A message

    Define macro:

will appear on the status line.

Respond by typing the macro's name. You can assign a one- to eight-character name (like a file name) and then press ↵. Optionally, you can press ↵ and let WordPerfect name the macro for you, but only one such macro can be active at any given time. The most popular option is to hold down Alt and press a single alphabetic key. In this case, because the macro will generate a letterhead, simultaneously press Alt *and* L.

A second message will appear:

    Description:

Type a brief description (up to 39 characters) of the macro; the status line should read

    Description: Letterhead for 8 x 10 paper.

Then press ↵. The screen will clear and the message

    Macro Def

will begin blinking on the status line.

Define the macro by going through the keystrokes. Start by pressing ⇧ and F8 to access the format menu. Choose option 2 for the page menu; then select option 8 and set the paper size to 8 x 10 (choose paper type 1, standard). Press F7 to get back to the work screen. Then center each line of the following letterhead:

```
Howard and Johnson, Ltd.
"Creativity is Our Thing!"
P.O. Box Z
Oxford, Ohio 01056
```

Press ⏎ at the end of the last line, and the macro is done.

Move the cursor to the top of the screen and then press [Alt] *and* [F3] to reveal the hidden codes (Fig. 16.14). Note the words *Macro Def* near the bottom of the top window. Note also the paper size code, the center codes, and the letterhead text. Press [Alt] *and* [F3] to get back to the macro definition screen. When you are satisfied with the macro,

Press: [Ctrl] *and* [F10]

The macro will be saved to disk under the name you assigned.

■ *Keystroke Summary*

Macro creation

Press: [Ctrl] *and* [F8]

Type: *macro name*

Press: ⏎

Type: *macro description*

Press: ⏎

Type: *sequence of keystrokes*

Press: [Ctrl] *and* [F8]

Figure 16.14
Macros are defined on a macro work screen. The reveal codes window allows you to see the hidden codes.

```
                    Howard and Johnson, Ltd.
                    "Creativity is Our Thing!"
                          P.O. Box Z
                       Oxford, Ohio 01056




Macro Def                                          Doc 1 Pg 1 Ln 1" Pos 1"
{                                               }
[Paper Sz/Typ:8" x 10",Standard][Cntr]Howard and Johnson, Ltd.[C/A/Flrt][HRt]
[Cntr]"Creativity is Our Thing!"[C/A/Flrt][HRt]
[Cntr]P.O. Box Z[C/A/Flrt][HRt]
[Cntr]Oxford, Ohio 01056[C/A/Flrt][HRt]




Press Reveal Codes to restore screen
```

Executing a Macro

Once a macro has been defined, you can execute it by issuing a command and typing its name. Try the letterhead macro. First, clear the screen. Then check the template and find the word *Macro* printed in blue near F10.

    Press: [Alt] *and* [F10]

A message will appear on the status line:

    Macro:

Respond by typing the macro's name; in this case, press [Alt] *and* L. After a brief delay, the macro's contents will appear on the screen.

    Generally, any time you find yourself repeating the same keystrokes over and over again, consider defining a macro. See the WordPerfect reference manual for additional details.

■ *Keystroke Summary*

Macro execution

    Press: [Alt] *and* [F10]

    Type: *macro name*

    Press: [↵]

    Type: **0** to return to print screen

    Type: **0** to return to work screen

Other Print Options

When you press [⇧] *and* [F7], the print menu is displayed. Option 1 prints the full document; option 2 prints a single page. Option 3 allows you to print a document from disk without retrieving it. Option 4 accesses a printer control screen that shows the status of active jobs. Although space does not permit detailed coverage, you should be at least familiar with the other print options. Option 5, type-through, allows you to use the computer like a typewriter, sending individual characters or lines directly to the printer. It is useful for filling out preprinted forms or typing envelopes. Option 6, view document, displays the document on the screen with headers, page numbers, footnotes, and other normally hidden features in place. Use it to preview a lengthy document. Option 7 downloads fonts to printers that can accept them.

    Many computer systems are equipped with more than one printer; for example, a dot matrix printer might produce draft documents, while a laser printer outputs finished work. Option S allows you to select a printer. Some printers can be switched between fast draft-quality and slower high-quality output. To select the desired quality level, choose print menu option T; option G performs the same function for a graphics printer. Use B to shift text on the page to allow room for binding a document.

Exiting WordPerfect

This ends the fourth tutorial. Exit WordPerfect after all jobs have printed or move on to Chapter 17.

Summary

Topic or Feature	Command or Reference	Option	Page
Boldface text	F6	—	246
Center line	⇧ *and* F6	—	245
Double-space text	⇧ *and* F8	1	242
Footnote, create	Ctrl *and* F7	1	247
Footnote, edit	Ctrl *and* F7	1	248
Headers and footers	⇧ *and* F8	2	240
Macro, define	Ctrl *and* F10	—	251
Macro, execute	Alt *and* F10	—	253
Page numbering	⇧ *and* F8	2	241
Paper size, select	⇧ *and* F8	2	237
Underline text	F8	—	246

Self-Test

1. Parameters that affect an entire page are set through the _____ screen.

2. Parameters that affect individual lines are set through the _____ screen.

3. _____ are printed at the top of a page; _____ are printed at the bottom of a page.

4. On a _____ document, both the left and right margins are straight.

5. Press _____ to center a line.

6. To boldface selected text, press _____.

7. To underline selected text, press _____.

8. _____ are printed on the page where they are referenced; _____ are grouped at the end of a document.

9. To add a footnote to a document, position the cursor and press
_____.

10. Press _____ to create a macro. Press _____ to execute a macro.

Exercises

1. Retrieve the file TOP. Add codes to change the page length and the line width to the beginning of TOP and replace the file. Generate letters to network and independent producers, this time using the new version of TOP.

2. Create the macro defined in the text. Generate letters to the network and independent producers using the macro instead of retrieving file TOP.

3. Retrieve file ENROLL from Exercise 4 of Chapter 15. Change to legal size paper. Center the titles. Then locate and underline each occurrence of the word *students*. Print the modified document; use standard printer paper to simulate legal size.

4. Start with the document you prepared in Exercise 3. Activate the reveal codes screen and delete the code that changed the paper size. Then return to the work screen and reset the paper size to 5 inches by 7 inches. Print the modified document; once again use standard printer paper to simulate the new size.

·17
Columns and Tables

This chapter introduces the WordPerfect features and commands that allow you to:

- type a table by setting tabs
- move a tabular column
- define and type parallel columns
- edit columns

Creating a Table

A table presents data in a gridlike pattern, with **columns** going across and **rows** going down a page. Often, leaders at the top of each column identify the table's contents. Examples include student grade reports, statistical data, and the list of characters from "The Betagosa Hillbillies" program proposal.

Planning a Table

The first step in creating a table is planning its format. There is no limit to the table's length; it can contain any number of rows spread over as many pages as necessary. However, the table's width is limited by the page width, so it is necessary to carefully plan how the columns will fit on the page.

For example, imagine that Howard and Johnson want to track the status of the letters prepared in Chapter 15. For each letter, they plan

Figure 17.1
The first step in planning a table is defining its contents.

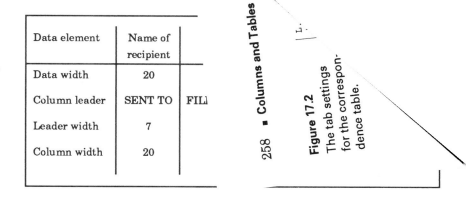

Data element	Name of recipient	
Data width	20	
Column leader	SENT TO	FILE
Leader width	7	
Column width	20	

Figure 17.2
The tab settings for the correspondence table.

to record the recipient's name, a file name, the date the letter was mailed, the date the response was received, and the respondent's reaction. Thus the table will need one row for each letter, and, moving across the page, five columns, one for each data element.

To determine the column widths, start by recording each data element's *maximum* width (Fig. 17.1). The number of characters in a person's name can vary, but 20 seems a reasonable upper limit. A file name contains up to eight characters. Dates are typed as a two-digit month, a slash, a two-digit day, a slash, and a two-digit year, for a total of eight characters. Possible responses include yes, no, and maybe, so you'll need five characters in the last column.

Next, turn your attention to the column leaders. Choose brief but meaningful words, phrases, or abbreviations (Fig. 17.1); for example, SENT TO clearly identifies the first column's meaning, while FILE-NAME is an excellent choice for a list of file names. After you've selected the column leaders, count the characters in each one.

Now that you know the data and the leader widths, look through the table, compare the two widths, select the larger value, and record it for each column (Fig. 17.1). In this example, assign 20 characters to the first column and 8 to each of the others for a total of 52.

To make the table easy to read, blank spaces are inserted between the columns. At ten characters per inch, WordPerfect's default margins allow for 65 characters per line. You need 52 for the data, leaving 13 for spacing. To separate five columns, you need four sets of spaces. Divide 13 by 4; the quotient is 3 with a remainder of 1. Use 3 spaces between columns and shift the extra space to the right margin.

Given column widths and spacing, the last step in the planning process is to lay out the table on paper. Print the column leaders. Then skip a line and use dummy characters (Xs for letters and 9s for digits) to position the data. You'll discover that the columns start at character positions 10, 33, 44, 55, and 66. At ten characters per inch, those values suggest tab settings of 1", 3.3", 4.4", 5.5", and 6.6".

```
.. . . . . . . . . . . . . . . . . . . .L. . . . . . . . . .L. . . . . . . . . .L. . . . . . . . . .L. . . . . . . . . . . . . . . . . . . .
   ^        ^        ^        ^        ^        ^        ^        ^
   |        |        |        |        |        |        |        |
  1"       2"       3"       4"       5"       6"       7"       8"
Delete EOL (clear tabs); Enter Number (set tab); Del (clear tab);
Left; Center; Right; Decimal; .= Dot Leader
```

Typing the Table

Now that the groundwork has been done, boot DOS and load WordPerfect. Then center both lines of the following title:

```
THE BETAGOSA HILLBILLIES
Correspondence Record
```

Boldface the first line. Insert a blank line between the title and the table.

Before you begin typing the table's contents, set the tabs. The cursor should be on the fourth line. To get the line format menu,

Press: ⬆ *and* F8

and select option 1. When the menu appears, type 8. The planning process suggested tabs at 1", 3.3", 4.4", 5.5", and 6.6". Press Ctrl *and* End to clear the existing tabs. To enter the new tab settings, type 1 and press ⏎, then type 3.3 and press ⏎, and so on. When you have finished, the bottom of the screen will resemble Fig. 17.2. Press F7 twice to return to the work screen.

Start with the column leaders. Type SENT TO (in capital letters) and press ⇥. Then type FILENAME and press ⇥, and so on; use Fig. 17.3 as a guide. When you finish the leader line, press ⏎. Insert a blank line and then type the data; once again, use Fig. 17.3 as a guide. When you have finished, save the table using file name RESPONSE.

Normally, data typed in a column are aligned with the column's left margin, and that is WordPerfect's default. Options include centering the data in the column or aligning them with the right margin or a decimal point. See the WordPerfect reference manual for details.

Figure 17.3

The completed correspondence table

```
                  THE BETAGOSA HILLBILLIES
                    Correspondence Record

SENT TO             FILENAME    DATE      RESPONSE   REACTION

Charlie Angel       CBS         3/1/89
James Beam          SOURMASH    3/1/89
Rive Gauche         ORIGINAL    3/1/89
Forrest Gump        ABC         3/1/89
Juan Valdez         NBC         3/1/89
```

Moving Tabular Columns

The purpose of a table is to present data in an easy-to-read, visually pleasing format. There is a touch of art involved. Often, in spite of careful planning, when you first see the table in typed form, you won't like it. Of course, leaders can be changed simply by retyping them, but reordering the columns presents more of a challenge.

Study the table pictured in Fig. 17.3. Two character fields, the recipient's name and the file name, are listed side by side. The table *might* look better if the order of the second and third columns were reversed, thus placing a date between them. Switch those two columns.

Move the cursor to the second column's first line. Position it anywhere on the column leader, FILENAME, and

Press: [Alt] *and* [F4]

The message

Block on

will begin blinking on the status line. Move the cursor to the last line in the column and position it anywhere on NBC. Note that all the intermediate text (not just the target column) will be marked (Fig. 17.4).

Once the block is marked,

Press: [Ctrl] *and* [F4]

The menu

Move 1 Block; 2 Tabular Column; 3 Rectangle: 0

will appear on the status line. Type 2. The target column will be highlighted, and a new message:

1 Move; 2 Copy; 3 Delete; 4 Append: 0

Figure 17.4

To mark a column as a block, position the cursor anywhere on the column's first line, press [Alt] *and* [F4], and then move the cursor to any character in the column's last line. Note that all intermediate text is marked.

```
                        THE BETAGOSA HILLBILLIES
                          Correspondence Record

SENT TO                 FILENAME   DATE       RESPONSE     REACTION

Charlie Angel           CBS        3/1/89
James Beam              SOURMASH   3/1/89
Rive Gauche             ORIGINAL   3/1/89
Forrest Gump            ABC        3/1/89
Juan Valdez             NBC        3/1/89
```

Figure 17.5

When you move a column, it disappears from the screen.

```
                    THE BETAGOSA HILLBILLIES
                      Correspondence Record

SENT TO              DATE      RESPONSE   REACTION

Charlie Angel        3/1/89
James Beam           3/1/89
Rive Gauche          3/1/89
Forrest Gump         3/1/89
Juan Valdez          3/1/89
```

will be displayed. Type 1. The target column will disappear (Fig. 17.5), and yet another message:

```
Move cursor; press Enter to retrieve.
```

will be displayed. Note that the file names are gone and the remaining columns have been shifted to fill the free space.

The file names should go between the columns headed DATE and RESPONSE, so move the cursor to the R in RESPONSE. Then press ⏎, and the column will be inserted back into the table (Fig. 17.6). Note that WordPerfect automatically adjusts spacing.

Look at the new version of the table and compare it with the old one (Fig. 17.3). If you like the new version better, save it; if you prefer the old one, do not replace it. For this example, save the new version.

■ *Keystroke Summary*

Move tabular column

Move:	cursor to top of target column
Press:	Alt *and* F4
Move:	cursor to bottom of target column
Press:	Ctrl *and* F4
Type:	**2**
Type:	**1**
Move:	cursor to target position
Press:	⏎

Figure 17.6

When you insert a column into a table, WordPerfect automatically adjusts spacing.

```
                    THE BETAGOSA HILLBILLIES
                      Correspondence Record
SENT TO              DATE      FILENAME   RESPONSE   REACTION

Charlie Angel        3/1/89    CBS
James Beam           3/1/89    SOURMASH
Rive Gauche          3/1/89    ORIGINAL
Forrest Gump         3/1/89    ABC
Juan Valdez          3/1/89    NBC
```

Parallel Columns

Character Sketches

As the creators of "The Betagosa Hillbillies," Howard and Johnson plan to develop brief sketches similar to the one pictured in Fig. 17.7 for each of the program's main characters. The first column lists the character's name. The second column contains adjectives and phrases that describe the character's personality, appearance, physical attributes, and so on. The last column lists well-known personalities who might be used as models for developing the character.

Note that both the second and third columns contain more than one line. That complicates the table. It could, of course, be typed using tabs, but not conveniently. Fortunately, the math/columns feature allows you to create such parallel columns with a minimum of effort.

Planning the Table

Start by planning the table. The first column holds character names. Professor Gallagher's name, the longest, contains 19 characters, so allocate at least 20 positions, or 2 inches, for the first column. The last column holds names, too; once again, 2 inches seems a reasonable width. Put 2 spaces, or 0.2 inch, between columns; with three columns you will need 0.4 inch total. That accounts for 4.4 inches. A line is 6.5 inches wide, leaving 2.1 inches for the second column. Figure 17.8 shows the table structure.

The Table Title

Clear the screen, and then center the following two lines:

```
THE BETAGOSA HILLBILLIES
Character Sketches
```

Boldface the program title. Press ⏎ to insert a blank line, and you're ready to start the table.

Figure 17.7
The planned character sketches will resemble this one.

Professor Gallagher	Mature man, 30–45.	Eddie Murphy
	Loud, Obnoxious.	Robin Williams
	Impulsive. Boorish.	
	Inquisitive. Shows extreme annoyance when interrupted.	

Figure 17.8
A plan for the character sketches table.

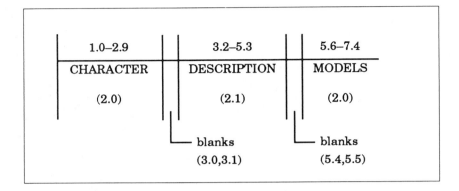

Defining Parallel Columns

To define parallel columns,

    Press: Alt and F7

The math/columns menu

    1 Math On; 2 Math Def; 3 Column On/Off; 4 Column Def: 0

will appear. Type 4, and the column definition screen will replace the work screen (Fig. 17.9).

The screen shows the defaults; to change a setting, type its number and enter the new value. For example, consider column type.

Figure 17.9
The column definition screen.

```
Text Column Definition

   1 - Type                          Newspaper

   2 - Number of Columns             2

   3 - Distance Between Columns

   4 - Margins

   Column     Left      Right     Column    Left      Right
     1:       1"        4"         13:
     2:       4.5"      7.5"       14:
     3:                            15:
     4:                            16:
     5:                            17:
     6:                            18:
     7:                            19:
     8:                            20:
     9:                            21:
    10:                            22:
    11:                            23:
    12:                            24:

Selection: 0
```

With **newspaper columns** the text moves down the first column to the bottom of the page, wraps back to the top of the page, and then moves down the second column. That's not what you want. With **parallel columns** a relationship is assumed between the columns, and each set is treated as a block; for example, a given character's name is linked with his or her description and one or more model personalities. To change the default, type 1. A new menu will appear on the status line:

```
Column Type: 1 Newspaper; 2 Parallel; 3 Parallel with Block
Protect: 0
```

Type 2, and *Parallel* will replace *Newspaper* on the column definition screen.

The default number of columns is 2. To change it, type 2, and the cursor will move to the value following *Number of Columns*. Type 3, for three columns, and press ⏎. To define the space between columns, type 3, and the cursor will move to the default value. Type 0.2 and press ⏎; see Fig. 17.10.

Given the number of columns and the spacing between them, WordPerfect will compute a set of suggested margins. Type 4 to redefine them. The cursor will move to the first column's left margin. The suggested value (1") agrees with the plan, so just press ⏎. The cursor will move to column 1's right margin. The planned value, 2.9", differs from WordPerfect's suggestion, so type 2.9 and press ⏎. Continue until all the margins are set (Fig. 17.10); refer to the figure if you don't remember the planned settings.

Note that the new values for column type, number of columns, distance between columns, and margins are all listed on the column definition screen. Check them to make sure they're correct. Then type 0 or press ⏎ to return to the work screen. The math/columns menu will once again appear on the status line; type 3 to activate the column feature.

Figure 17.10

The column definition screen after parallel columns have been defined.

```
Text Column Definition

   1 - Type                             Parallel

   2 - Number of Columns                3

   3 - Distance Between Columns         0.2"

   4 - Margins

   Column    Left      Right      Column    Left       Right
     1:       1"        2.9"       13:
```

Define parallel columns

Press:	Alt *and* F7
Type:	**4**
Type:	**1**
Type:	**2** (for parallel)
Type:	**2**
Type:	*number of columns*
Press:	↵
Type:	**3**
Type:	*space between columns*
Press:	↵
Type:	**4**
Type:	*column limits*
Press:	↵ after each limit
Type:	**0** to return to menu
Type:	**3** to activate columns

Typing Column Leaders

Type the first column leader, CHARACTER. As you type, note that the column number is displayed on the status line just to the left of the document number, indicating that the columns feature is active. To end a column,

    Press: Ctrl *and* ↵

(hard return). The cursor will move to the beginning of the second column, and the column indicator will change to 2. Type DESCRIP-TION and press Ctrl *and* ↵. The cursor will advance to the third column, and the indicator will read 3. Type MODELS and press Ctrl *and* ↵ again. The screen should resemble Fig. 17.11, with the cursor back on column 1.

Figure 17.11
The screen after the column leaders have been typed.

```
                    THE BETAGOSA HILLBILLIES
                       Character Sketches

CHARACTER                DESCRIPTION              MODELS
```

Figure 17.12
The reveal codes
screen shows that
WordPerfect turns the
column feature on at
the beginning and off
at the end of a set of
parallel columns.

```
                        THE BETAGOSA HILLBILLIES
                           Character Sketches

   CHARACTER                   DESCRIPTION              MODELS




                                               Col 1 Doc 1 Pg 1 Ln 1.5" Pos 1"
   [              ] [              ] [              ]
   [Cntr]Character Sketches[C/A/Flrt][HRt]
   [HRt]
   [Col Def:3,1",2.9",3.2",5.3",5.6",7.4"][Col On]CHARACTER[HPg]
   DESCRIPTION[HPg]
   MODELS[Col Off]
   [HRt]
   [Col On]



   Press Reveal Codes to restore screen
```

To help you understand how WordPerfect implements columns, move the cursor to the first column leader, CHARACTER (line 1.5", position 1"), press Alt *and* F3, and look at the hidden codes (Fig. 17.12). The column definition should be easy to spot; it consists of a series of numbers. It is followed by a **[Col On]** code, which activates the column feature. Then comes the first leader and a hard page **[HPg]** code; you generated it when you pressed Ctrl *and* ⏎.

The next line shows DESCRIPTION followed by a **[HPg]** code. MODELS, comes next. Look just to its right, and note the **[Col Off]** code. It marks the end of the first set of columns. Locate the **[HRt]** code just below MODELS. It moves the cursor back to the right margin. On the next line, the **[Col On]** code reactivates columns. The column feature is turned on at the beginning of a set of columns and then turned off when the set ends. In effect, each set of columns is treated as an independent entity; that's how WordPerfect keeps them together.

Press Alt *and* F3 to get back to the work screen.

Typing the Data

The first set of data is shown near the top of Fig. 17.13. Press Home *then* Home *then* ⬇ to get back to the end of the document. Then type

```
Captain Jed
```

and press Ctrl *and* ⏎. The cursor will move to the top of column two. Type the description using the figure as a guide; note that the word

Figure 17.13
The data for the first three characters.

```
                    THE BETAGOSA HILLBILLIES
                       Character Sketches

    CHARACTER              DESCRIPTION            MODELS

    Captain Jed            Older man, 55-65.      James Earl Jones
                           Deep, rich voice.
                           Credible man of
                           action.

    Granny Socks           Older woman, 55 and    Dr. Ruth
                           up. Small. High        Gilda Radner
                           pitched, funny voice.  Whoopi Goldberg
                           Will provide some
                           comic relief.

    Professor Gallagher    Mature man, 30-45.     Eddie Murphy
                           Loud. Obnoxious.       Robin Williams
                           Impulsive. Boorish.
                           Inquisitive. Shows
                           extreme annoyance
                           when interrupted.


                                          Col 1 Doc 1 Pg 1 Ln 4.83" Pos 1"
```

wrap feature operates within a column. Press Ctrl *and* ↵ when you're done, and the cursor will move to the top of the third column. Type

        James Earl Jones

and press Ctrl *and* ↵ to end the first block.

Follow the same procedure to type the rest of the data; remember to press Ctrl *and* ↵ at the end of each column. The list of models in column 3 is potentially confusing. Press ↵ after each individual's name, and the cursor will advance to the column's next line. Press Ctrl *and* ↵ after all entries associated with a single character have been typed. The results for the first three characters are shown in Fig. 17.13; use it as a typing guide. The last two characters appear in Fig. 17.14.

When you finish typing Pepper's entry,

        Press: Alt *and* F7

and the math/columns menu will reappear. Type 3 to turn off the columns feature. Save the document under file name CHARS.

■ *Keystroke Summary*

Typing parallel columns

        Press: Ctrl *and* ↵ to end each column

        Press: Alt *and* F7 when all data are entered

        Type: **3** to turn off the columns feature

Figure 17.14
The data for the last two characters.

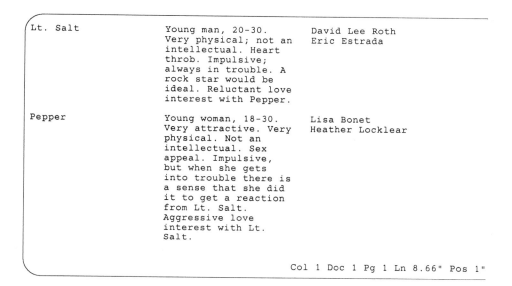

```
Lt. Salt              Young man, 20-30.        David Lee Roth
                      Very physical; not an    Eric Estrada
                      intellectual. Heart
                      throb. Impulsive;
                      always in trouble. A
                      rock star would be
                      ideal. Reluctant love
                      interest with Pepper.

Pepper                Young woman, 18-30.      Lisa Bonet
                      Very attractive. Very    Heather Locklear
                      physical. Not an
                      intellectual. Sex
                      appeal. Impulsive,
                      but when she gets
                      into trouble there is
                      a sense that she did
                      it to get a reaction
                      from Lt. Salt.
                      Aggressive love
                      interest with Lt.
                      Salt.

                                    Col 1 Doc 1 Pg 1 Ln 8.66" Pos 1"
```

■ *What Can Go Wrong?*

1. As you enter the data, you discover that the cursor is in the wrong column.

Cause: You might have inadvertently pressed Ctrl *and* ↵ or pressed that key combination with the cursor in the wrong place.

Solution: Press ← repetitively until the cursor enters the target column, and then resume typing. ■

Editing Columns

It's unusual to type data without making at least a few mistakes, and editing columns presents some unique problems. The key to correcting errors is understanding how the cursor moves through the columns.

The cursor should be located at the end of the document. Press ↑ several times, and watch it move along the left margin, from Pepper, to Lt. Salt, to Professor Gallagher, and so on. Press ↓. Once again, the cursor will move along the left margin. Stop it on Professor Gallagher's name and then press → several times. Predictably, the cursor will move to the right. Press ← to move it to the left. Within a column, the cursor control keys work the same way they do on a normal page.

Press End to move the cursor to the end of Professor Gallagher's name. Earlier in the chapter, you pressed Ctrl *and* ↵ after you typed the name. That key combination inserts a hard page break into the text; you saw the code when you accessed the reveal codes screen. Normally, a hard page break marks the end of a page, and when you move the cursor past the end of a page it jumps to the beginning of the

Press	to move to
Ctrl *and* Home, *then* —	prior column
Ctrl *and* Home, *then* —	next column
Ctrl *and* Home, *then* Home, *then* —	first column
Ctrl *and* Home, *then* Home, *then* —	last column

next page. Similarly, when the cursor hits the hard page code at the end of a column, it jumps to the start of the next column. Try it. Press —, and the cursor will move to column two.

Press End to move the cursor to the end of the first line in Gallagher's description. Then press —, and the cursor will wrap to the second line. Move the cursor to the last line in Gallagher's description, and then press — to move it through the very last word. When you pass the period at the end of the sentence, the cursor will jump to the first name in column three. The cursor can move between columns *only* at the columns' terminal points. Use the Go To feature to move quickly between columns (Fig. 17.15).

Add Sean Connery to the list of model personalities for Captain Jed. Move the cursor to the third column and then up to the first letter in James Earl Jones. Press End to move to the end of the line. Then go to the reveal codes screen and make sure the cursor lies just after the s in Jones and on the [**Col Off**] code that marks the end of the column; if it doesn't, move it there. (Improperly positioned codes can cause alignment problems.) Press Alt *and* F3 to return to the work screen, press ↵ to move to the next line, and type Mr. Connery's name (Fig. 17.16). (*Note:* Do *not* press Ctrl *and* ↵; you already did that.)

There is one other error in the character descriptions. Pepper is described as "not an intellectual." That's not exactly right. The creators' intent is that Pepper be a bright young woman who hides her

Figure 17.16
Data can be added to a column by positioning the cursor and inserting characters.

```
Captain Jed        Older man, 55-65.    James Earl Jones
                   Deep, rich voice.    Sean Connery
                   Credible man of
                   action.

Granny Socks       Older woman, 55 and  Dr. Ruth
                   up. Small. High      Gilda Radner
                   pitched, funny voice. Whoopi Goldberg
                   Will provide some
                   comic relief.
```

intelligence in an attempt to appeal to Lt. Salt. Move the cursor to Pepper's description. Delete the phrase

    Not an intellectual.

and replace it with

    Bright, but acts with calculated dizziness.

Note how the second column changes to accommodate the new phrase.

Read through the table of character sketches, correct any remaining errors, and then save the document.

Next, try one more experiment. Move the cursor to the top of the document. Press ⬆ and F8, select option 1 (line format), and double-space the text. Press F7 to return to the work screen. The character list will occupy two pages; press ⊞ two or three times until you can see the page break (Fig. 17.17). Note how column continuity is maintained across the break.

One final note: The procedure for moving a tabular column described earlier in the chapter does *not* work for parallel columns.

∎ *What Can Go Wrong?*

1. You can't get the cursor to the target column.

Cause: You might be visualizing the screen as a normal page. Remember, the column limits are barriers that the cursor can cross only at the beginning or the end of a column.

Solution: Move the cursor to the beginning of the column and press ⊟ to get to the prior column. Move the cursor to the end of a column and press ⊟ to get to the next column. Think of each *column* as a separate page.

Figure 17.17
A column's continuity is maintained across a page break.

```
                          Very physical; not an    Eric Estrada
                          intellectual. Heart
                          throb. Impulsive;
------------------------------------------------
                          always in trouble. A
                          rock star would be
                          ideal. Reluctant love
                          interest with Pepper.


Pepper                    Young woman, 18-30.      Lisa Bonet
                          Very attractive. Very    Heather Locklear
                          physical. Bright, but
B:\CHARS                           Col 2 Doc 1 Pg 2 Ln 3.66" Pos 3.2"
```

2. After you insert some text into a column, subsequent data shift to the wrong column.

Cause: You might have inserted the data *after* the hidden codes that mark the end of a column.

Solution: First, *always* save a copy of your table before you edit the columns; that way, if anything goes wrong, you can delete the table, retrieve a clean copy, and start over. To correct a mistake, delete the new data. Then check the hidden codes, locate the column boundaries, move the cursor inside the proper column, and retype the data.

3. After you move a set of parallel columns, subsequent columns are no longer aligned.

Cause: As a result of moving the columns, one or more hidden codes were shifted to the wrong position.

Solution: Be very careful when you move parallel columns. Move only a complete set of columns. Make sure the hidden codes that begin and end the set are included in the block. When you move or copy the block, make sure it is placed *after* the column definition code.

4. After inserting data into a column, you accidentally press (Ctrl) *and* (↵).

Cause: Habit.

Solution: Press (←) until you have deleted the last character you typed. Then type that last character again. Any unnecessary codes you might have inserted will be deleted. ■

Newspaper Columns

With newspaper columns, text flows from the top to the bottom of the first column, wraps back to the top of the second column, flows down the page, and so on. When the text reaches the bottom of the last column, it jumps to the top of the next page's first column. Think of each column as a page, and you'll have a good mental picture of how the cursor flows from column to column. Newspapers, magazines, and some textbooks are set in this style.

Newspaper columns are useful for typing newsletters, articles, and similar materials. Should you need them, you will have little difficulty in learning to use them; check the WordPerfect reference manual for details.

Exiting WordPerfect

That completes the fifth tutorial. Exit WordPerfect or move on to Chapter 18.

Summary

Feature	Command or Reference	Option	Page
End column	Ctrl *and* ⏎	—	264
Mark column	Alt *and* F4	—	259
Move marked column	Ctrl *and* F4	2	259
Parallel columns, define	Alt *and* F7	4	262

Self-Test

1. A table can contain any number of _____, but the number of _____ is limited by the page width.

2. Simple tables can be typed by first setting the _____.

3. To determine a column's width, define the data width and the leader width and use the _____ of those two values.

4. The tab setting window suggests that you press "delete EOL," or _____, to clear the tabs.

5. To access the column definition screen, press _____ .

6. With _____ columns, the text moves down a column to the bottom of the page and then wraps back to the top of the next column.

7. With _____ columns, a relationship is assumed between the columns, and each set of columns is treated as a block.

8. When typing parallel columns, press _____ to mark the end of each column.

9. To make sure a set of parallel columns is not interrupted by a page break, _____ it.

10. To visualize how the cursor moves through a column, think of each column as a separate _____.

Exercises

1. Edit the second table by converting the list of personalities in the third column to the characters they played in a movie or a television show.

2. Define a set of parallel columns to record an inventory of your personal belongings. Include columns to hold, as a minimum, the item name, a brief description, the date you purchased it, and the purchase price.

3. Type the following table after setting your tab stops.

Enrollment in Computing Majors

Year	Percentage of Freshmen Choosing:		
	Computer Science	Data Processing	Both
1979	1.8	1.8	3.6
1980	2.5	2.4	4.9
1981	3.5	3.0	6.5
1982	4.4	4.0	8.4
1983	4.5	3.8	8.3
1984	3.4	2.4	5.8
1985	2.3	2.1	4.4
1986	1.9	1.6	3.5
1987	1.6	1.1	2.7
1988	1.7	1.1	2.8

The data are taken from *The American Freshman*, an annual survey of incoming freshmen published by the Cooperative Institutional Research Program, U.C.L.A. Add a footnote to the table's title to identify the source.

4. Exercise 3 of Chapter 15 presented the contents of four small files in the form of a table. As an exercise in creating parallel columns, type that table.

▪18

Desktop Publishing and Graphics

This chapter explains basic desktop publishing concepts and then introduces the WordPerfect features and commands that allow you to:

- check the graphics capability of your printer
- change print size and appearance
- draw lines and borders
- add clip art to a document

Desktop Publishing

Word processing simplifies the task of writing text. **Desktop publishing**, a step beyond word processing, is concerned with the *appearance* of that text. The most obvious feature of a desktop publishing system is the integration of text and graphics on the same page. Most also support multiple type fonts and allow the user to vary type size and style.

There is more to desktop publishing than just graphics and type styles, however. Page design is an art. On a well-designed page the borders, lines, columns, graphics, white space, and a variety of carefully selected type styles combine to produce an attractive appearance that actually enhances the clarity of the material.

The key to desktop publishing was the development of the laser printer. The first commercially successful systems ran on Apple Macintosh computers, and even IBM-based systems simulate the Mac's graphic interface. PageMaker and Ventura Publisher are two popular desktop publishing programs; both are available for Macintosh and IBM computers. This book was designed using PageMaker, and a book about PageMaker by Jacqueline Davies is part of Addison-Wesley's *Computing Fundamentals* series.

Generally, text and images are created separately and stored as independent files. A word processor, such as WordPerfect, is used to prepare the text. Original images can be created using a screen painter or some other graphics program, electronic **clip art** can be purchased from a variety of sources, and scanners are available to convert existing images to electronic form. The desktop publishing program integrates the graphics and the text just before the page is printed.

Introducing a program such as PageMaker is beyond the scope of this book, but WordPerfect 5.0 incorporates enough graphics features to give you sense of desktop publishing. In the balance of this chapter you'll learn how to change type size and appearance, draw lines, and insert clip art into a document.

Checking Your System

Before you begin, check your system to be sure your printer supports the features described in this chapter; you won't learn much from these lessons if you can't see the printed output. Boot DOS and load WordPerfect. If you are using diskettes, insert the Conversion disk in drive B and then retrieve a printer test document named PRINTER.TST. (If you are using a hard disk, the test file should be stored under the default directory, WP50, so retrieve file C:\WP50\PRINTER.TST.) Remove the Conversion disk and insert your work disk in drive B after you retrieve the file.

Print the document. (Your printer might behave strangely.) Then read the output. You should see a bar separating the header from the first paragraph. The third, fourth, and fifth lines of the first paragraph should show several different print sizes and styles. On line 5 the word *italics* should appear in italics or, on some printers, underlined. You should also see a graphic image of a jet airplane near the center of page 2.

■ What Can Go Wrong?

1. Your printer does not support one or more of the referenced features.

Cause: A daisy wheel printer cannot reproduce graphics. Some dot matrix printers support graphics; others do not. Some laser printers require that fonts be downloaded.

Solution: If at all possible, use another printer. Try a dot matrix printer with graphics capability, an ink jet printer, or a laser printer. (For best results, use a laser printer with a Postscript interface.) If your laser printer doesn't work, ask your instructor whether fonts must be downloaded. If you can't change printers, note features that do work and substitute them in the lessons that follow; for example, use fine instead of extra large print or shadow instead of italic type.

2. On a laser printer, only the first page prints.

Cause: Different printers use different algorithms for counting lines. Because of the complexity of this document, your printer might not "think" it has reached the end of the second page, so it holds the "partial" page in its memory and waits for more data.

Solution: Reprint the first page. When the printer receives a new page, it should clear its memory and output the first page.

3. The output is spread over three pages.

Cause: Similar to number 2 above.

Solution: Continue with the tutorial. ■

Changing Print Size and Appearance

Clear the screen. Then retrieve file BETAHILL (Fig. 18.1).

To emphasize the program title, it might be useful to print it in large type. Move the cursor to the first character in the title and mark THE BETAGOSA HILLBILLIES as a block. Check the template and note the word *Font* printed in red near function key [F8]. Press [Ctrl] *and* [F8], and a menu

```
Attribute: 1 Size; 2 Appearance: 0
```

will appear at the bottom of the screen. Type 1 to select *Size*, and a new menu will appear (on a single line):

```
1 Suprscpt; 2 Subscpt; 3 Fine; 4 Small; 5 Large; 6 Vry Large;
7 Ext Large: 0
```

Figure 18.1
The document before changes are made.

```
                       PROGRAM PROPOSAL

                   THE  BETAGOSA  HILLBILLIES
                      by: Howard and Johnson

When Jean Rogers, nationally syndicated TV critic, was shown this
program proposal, she said:

        Last week I had an opportunity to review the latest
        program proposal by Howard and Johnson. That madcap
        pair has done it again! "The Betagosa Hillbillies"
        incorporates virtually every hackneyed cliche ever seen
        in a situation comedy. Brilliant!1

This proposed new half-hour comedy combines the best of "Star
Trek," "The Beverly Hillbillies," and "Gilligan's Island."
Professor Gallagher will be the focus of humor. He is a cross
between Star Trek's Scotty and Gilligan (from Gilligan's Island).
An early episode will establish that he was named after the 20th
century comedian Gallagher. This part could be a star vehicle for
a young comedian with an Eddie Murphy-like style.

The story is set on the planet Betagosa, where the crew of the
starship Hindenberg find themselves marooned after Professor
B:\BETAHILL                                 Doc 1 Pg 1 Ln 1" Pos 1"
```

Figure 18.2

The font codes can be seen on the reveal codes screen.

```
                        PROGRAM PROPOSAL

                     THE BETAGOSA HILLBILLIES
                       by: Howard and Johnson
When Jean Rogers, nationally syndicated TV critic, was shown this
program proposal, she said:

       Last week I had an opportunity to review the latest
       program proposal by Howard and Johnson. That madcap
       pair has done it again! "The Betagosa Hillbillies"
B:\BETAHILL                                 Doc 1 Pg 1 Ln 1.33" Pos 6.65"

[Cntr]PROGRAM PROPOSAL[C/A/Flrt][HRt]
[HRt]
[Cntr][EXT LARGE][BOLD]THE BETAGOSA HILLBILLIES[bold][C/A/Flrt][ext large][HRt]
[Cntr]by: Howard and Johnson[C/A/Flrt][HRt]
[HRt]
When Jean Rogers, nationally syndicated TV critic, was shown this[SRt]
program proposal, she said:[HRt]
[HRt]
[IndentLast week I had an opportunity to review the latest[SRt]
program proposal by Howard and Johnson. That madcap[SRt]

Press Reveal Codes to restore screen
```

Type 7 to select *Extra Large*. The menu will disappear, and you'll be back on the work screen. Although the color or background of the title might change, the characters will still be the same size; you won't see the extra large letters until you print the document. Press ⌥Alt *and* F3 to reveal the codes (Fig. 18.2) and note the **[EXT LARGE]** code. Then press ⌥Alt *and* F3 to return to the work screen.

Next, move the cursor to the first letter in the indented quotation (line 2.33") and mark Jean Roger's comments as a block. Then press Ctrl *and* F8 to issue another *Font* command. This time when the *Attribute* menu appears, type 2 to select *Appearance*. A new menu will appear (on a single line):

```
1 Bold 2 Undrln 3 Dbl Und 4 Italc 5 Outln 6 Shadw 7 Sm Cap 8
Redln 9 Stkout: 0
```

See the PRINTER.TST output for samples of each of these type styles. Type 4 to select *Italic*, and the menu will disappear. Once again the color or background might change on the work screen, but you won't see the new type style until you print the document. You can see the **[ITALC]** code on the reveal codes screen.

Now print the document; it should resemble Fig. 18.3. Save the file as BETAHILL.DTP to distinguish it from the old BETAHILL file.

In these two examples you changed the font for a block of text. For future reference, you can also change fonts as you type. Press Ctrl *and* F8 to issue the *Font* command and select the character size and/or appearance. Then type the affected material. When you finish, press Ctrl *and* F8 again and select option 3, *Normal*, to return to normal type.

Figure 18.3
Oversized and italicized characters can be seen when you print the document.

PROGRAM PROPOSAL

THE BETAGOSA HILLBILLIES

by: Howard and Johnson

When Jean Rogers, nationally syndicated TV critic, was shown this program proposal, she said:

Last week I had an opportunity to review the latest program proposal by Howard and Johnson. That madcap pair has done it again! "The Betagosa Hillbillies" incorporates virtually every hackneyed cliche ever seen in a situation comedy. Brilliant![1]

This proposed new half-hour comedy combines the best of "Star Trek," "The Beverly Hillbillies," and "Gilligan's Island." Professor Gallagher will be the focus of humor. He is a cross between Star Trek's Scotty and Gilligan (from Gilligan's Island). An early episode will establish that he was named after the 20th century comedian Gallagher. This part could be a star vehicle for a young comedian with an Eddie Murphy-like style.

■ *Keystroke Summary*

Change print size or appearance

Mark: block to be changed

Press: Ctrl *and* F8

Select: *Size* or *Appearance*

Select: option

Press: ↵

■ *What Can Go Wrong?*

1. The indented quotation is underlined, not italicized.

Cause: Some printers simulate italics by underlining the characters.

Solution: Underlining is fine, given the objectives of this chapter. If you really want to see italics, switch to another printer. ■

Drawing Lines

Professional publishers have long recognized that simple lines and rules can greatly enhance the appearance of text. In this exercise you will draw a horizontal bar to separate the headers from the body of the material.

Move the cursor to the blank line following the creators' names (line 1.66"). Press ↵ to skip a line. Then press Alt *and* F9 to select the *Graphics* feature. A menu will appear on a single line:

1 Figure; 2 Table; 3 Text Box; 4 User-defined Box; 5 Line: 0

Figure 18.4
The line definition
menu.

```
Graphics: Horizontal Line

     1 - Horizontal Position              Left & Right

     2 - Length of Line

     3 - Width of Line                    0.01"

     4 - Gray Shading (% of black)        100%




Selection: 0
```

Type 5 to select Line, and another menu will appear:

```
1 Horizontal Line; 2 Vertical line: 0
```

You want to draw a horizontal line, so type 1.

A new menu will appear (Fig. 18.4). It shows a set of default values. Following *Horizontal Position* is the entry *Left & Right*. It means that the line will stretch from the left margin to the right margin, which is what you want. You can also define lines that start at the left or right margin or that are centered on the page. *Length of Line* is assumed for *Left & Right*; had you specified a different option, you would have had to define the line's length.

Width of Line is set, by default, at 0.01". To change the line width, type 3. The cursor will move to the default value 0.01. Type 0.10 to define a line 1/10 of an inch wide; then press ⏎, and the cursor will return to the bottom of the menu.

The percentage *Gray Shading* defines the darkness of the line, with 100% representing solid black. Type 4, and the cursor will move to the default value. Type 60 and press ⏎ to define a 60% (medium grey) line. The cursor will return to the bottom of the menu.

Press ⏎ or type 0 to return to the work screen. Then press ⏎ again to insert a blank line between the horizontal line and the text. The line will not appear on the screen, but the reveal codes screen will show the hidden codes. Print the document; you should see a line separating the headers from the body of the text (Fig. 18.5). Save the file (BETAHILL.DTP) before you move on.

You can use horizontal lines to separate major sections of a document, to separate a table's headers from its content, or, using a

Figure 18.5
Lines appear when the document is printed.

PROGRAM PROPOSAL

THE BETAGOSA HILLBILLIES

by: Howard and Johnson

When Jean Rogers, nationally syndicated TV critic, was shown this program proposal, she said:

> *Last week I had an opportunity to review the latest program proposal by Howard and Johnson. That madcap pair has done it again! "The Betagosa Hillbillies" incorporates virtually every hackneyed cliche ever seen in a situation comedy. Brilliant!*[1]

This proposed new half-hour comedy combines the best of "Star Trek," "The Beverly Hillbillies," and "Gilligan's Island." Professor Gallagher will be the focus of humor. He is a cross between Star Trek's Scotty and Gilligan (from Gilligan's Island). An early episode will establish that he was named after the 20th century comedian Gallagher. This part could be a star vehicle for a young comedian with an Eddie Murphy-like style.

light grey bar, to overprint or highlight selected text. Vertical lines can be used to separate columns or to mark lengthy passages.

■ *Keystroke Summary*

Draw a line

Position:	cursor
Press:	Alt *and* F9
Type:	5
Select:	line type
Define:	line parameters
Press:	↵

■ *What Can Go Wrong?*

1. The default line width reads 0.08, not 0.01".

Cause: Your version of WordPerfect was set to display a line count rather than a vertical measure from the top of the page. A line width of 1.00 represents a full line (the size of an uppercase letter).

Solution: Use a line width of 0.8. ■

Graphics

Clip Art

Several clip art images are found on the WordPerfect 5.0 Fonts/ Graphics disk; they can be seen in the appendix to the WordPerfect

Figure 18.6

A clip art image of a
quill pen in an inkwell.

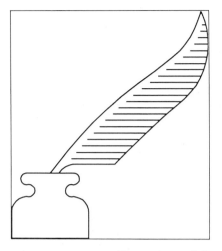

reference manual. One shows a quill pen in an inkwell (Fig. 18.6); it
is stored under file name QUILL.WPG. Assume that Howard and
Johnson have adopted it as their logo. (If you have access to a clip art
library, feel free to substitute your favorite image for QUILL.WPG.)

Defining the Box

Like most desktop publishing programs, WordPerfect treats each
graphic image as an *object* to be manipulated independently from the
text. Picture the image as an empty rectangular box. The basic idea
is to define the box's size and position on the page. The text then flows
around the box; in effect, WordPerfect leaves space for the box's
contents to be added later. A box can hold a graphic image, a table,
additional text, or anything else you can store as a file. Just before the
document is printed, WordPerfect retrieves the files that hold the
contents of the various boxes and prepares a finished document.

Assume that Howard and Johnson have developed a standard
design for their documents. Header material goes on top, with a
horizontal line separating it from the text; you did that in the previous
two exercises. A one-inch-wide logo is then placed near the left margin
and aligned with the top line of the first paragraph. The text flows
around the logo, with the first several lines indented. Below the logo,
subsequent lines begin at the left margin.

You want a one-inch-wide box aligned with the top of the first
paragraph. Move the cursor to the first letter, W, in the first word in
the first paragraph. Then press Alt *and* F9 to select *Graphics*, and a
menu will appear on a single line:

```
1 Figure; 2 Table; 3 Text Box; 4 User-defined Box; 5 Lines: 0
```

Figure 18.7
The figure definition
menu.

```
Definition: Figure

     1 - Filename

     2 - Caption

     3 - Type                        Paragraph

     4 - Vertical Position           0"

     5 - Horizontal Position         Right

     6 - Size                        3.25" wide x 3.25" (high)

     7 - Wrap Text Around Box        Yes

     8 - Edit




Selection: 0
```

Type 1 to select *Figure*, and yet another menu will appear:

```
Figure: 1 Create; 2 Edit; 3 New Number; 4 Options: 0
```

Select 1 for *Create*.

A new menu will appear (Fig. 18.7). Type 1 to define the file name of the image that will eventually fill the box. A prompt

```
Enter filename:
```

will appear near the bottom of the screen. If you plan to access the image from the Fonts/Graphics diskette, insert the disk in drive B, close the drive door, and type QUILL.WPG. If the clip art is stored on hard disk, type C:\WP50\QUILL.WPG. Then press ⏎. WordPerfect will verify the file and place its name after the first menu choice.

The second option, *Caption*, allows you to specify a caption for the figure. No caption is needed for the logo.

Option 3, *Type*, specifies how the box is related to the text. The default, *Paragraph*, links the box to the contents of a paragraph. In this case you want the logo aligned with the first line in the first paragraph, so accept the default. For future reference, *Page* specifies a specific location on the page (top, bottom, 3.5 inches from the top). In contrast, *Character* treats the box like a character; you might use it to define a special symbol such as the key symbols that appear throughout this text.

The box's *Vertical Position* represents an offset from a reference position. Because you selected *Paragraph*, the offset is measured from the top of the paragraph. You want the image aligned with the first line, so accept the default offset, 0.

The logo should be aligned with the left margin, but *Right* is the default *Horizontal Position*. Type 5. When the new menu appears, type 1 to select *Left*.

The default *Size* is 3.25 inches wide by 3.88 inches high. You want a one-inch-wide logo, so select option 6. A new menu will appear:

```
1 Width (auto height); 2 Height (auto width);
3 Both Width and Height: 0
```

Select 1 for *Width (auto height)*. As the name suggests, when you specify the width, WordPerfect will automatically compute the appropriate height for the selected image. Type 1.0 and press ⏎. You can see the figure's parameters in Fig. 18.8.

Press ⏎ or type 0 to return to the work screen (Fig. 18.9). The empty box shows where the graphic image will appear when you print the document. The entry *Fig 1* on the top line identifies the figure; it will not be printed. The figure number is useful if you have multiple boxes in a document and want to edit the contents of one of them.

If you're using diskettes, make sure the Fonts/Graphics disk is in drive B. Then print the document. When you issue the print command, WordPerfect reads QUILL.WPG from disk, changes its scale to match the specified size, and inserts the image into the box. Then the document is sent to the printer. If your printer supports graphics, you'll see the quill pen logo just to the left of the first paragraph (Fig. 18.10). Note how the text wraps around the image.

Figure 18.8

The parameters for the quill pen image.

```
Definition: Figure

     1 - Filename                  QUILL.WPG (Graphic)

     2 - Caption

     3 - Type                      Paragraph

     4 - Vertical Position         0"

     5 - Horizontal Position       Left

     6 - Size                      1" wide x 1.19" (high)

     7 - Wrap Text Around Box      Yes

     8 - Edit




Selection: 0
```

Figure 18.9

The empty box shows where the graphic image will appear when you print the document.

```
                        PROGRAM PROPOSAL

                    THE BETAGOSA HILLBILLIES
                      by: Howard and Johnson

 ┌FIG 1──────┐  When Jean Rogers, nationally syndicated TV critic,
 │           │  was shown this program proposal, she said:
 │           │
 │           │      Last week I had an opportunity to review the
 │           │      latest program proposal by Howard and Johnson.
 │           │      That madcap pair has done it again! "The
 │           │      Betagosa Hillbillies" incorporates virtually
 │           │      every hackneyed cliche ever seen in a
 └───────────┘      situation comedy. Brilliant!1

 This proposed new half-hour comedy combines the best of "Star
 Trek," "The Beverly Hillbillies," and "Gilligan's Island."
 Professor Gallagher will be the focus of humor. He is a cross
 between Star Trek's Scotty and Gilligan (from Gilligan's Island).
 An early episode will establish that he was named after the 20th
 century comedian Gallagher. This part could be a star vehicle for
                                     Doc 1 Pg 1 Ln 1.16" Pos 1"
```

▪ *Keystroke Summary*

Define box for clip art

Position:	cursor
Press:	[Alt] *and* [F9]
Type:	1
Define:	box parameters
Press:	[↵]

Figure 18.10

The graphic image can be seen when you print the document.

PROGRAM PROPOSAL

THE BETAGOSA HILLBILLIES

by: Howard and Johnson

When Jean Rogers, nationally syndicated TV critic, was shown this program proposal, she said:

Last week I had an opportunity to review the latest program proposal by Howard and Johnson. That madcap pair has done it again! "The Betagosa Hillbillies" incorporates virtually every hackneyed cliche ever seen in a situation comedy. Brilliant![1]

This proposed new half-hour comedy combines the best of "Star Trek," "The Beverly Hillbillies," and "Gilligan's Island." Professor Gallagher will be the focus of humor. He is a cross between Star Trek's Scotty and Gilligan (from Gilligan's Island). An early episode will establish that he was named after the 20th century comedian Gallagher. This part could be

■ *What Can Go Wrong?*

1. WordPerfect cannot find file QUILL.WPG.

Cause: You might have forgotten to type the extension WPG after the file name. Perhaps you failed to insert the Fonts/Graphics diskette into drive B. The clip art files might be stored under a different directory on the hard disk.

Solution: The file name is QUILL.WPG; you must type the extension. Insert the Fonts/Graphics diskette into drive B and try again. If you are using a hard disk, display the files in the current directory. If QUILL.WPG is not listed, check with your instructor or the system manager for the proper path name. ■

Exiting WordPerfect

That completes the last tutorial. Save file BETAHILL.DTP and exit WordPerfect.

By now you should have a solid working knowledge of WordPerfect 5.0. Even more important, now that you know the basics, the reference manual should begin to make sense. It's not that the manual is badly written; WordPerfect's is pretty good. But reference manuals are written for experienced users, not beginners. The reason the reference manual will seem more accessible is that you are no longer a beginner.

Summary

Feature	Command or Reference	Option	Page
Change print size/appearance	Ctrl *and* F8	1 or 2	275
Define box for clip art	Alt *and* F9	1	280
Draw a line	Alt *and* F9	5	277

Self-Test

1. Word processing simplifies writing text. Desktop publishing is concerned with the _____ of that text.

2. The key to desktop publishing was the development of the _____.

3. A desktop publishing program integrates _____ and _____ just before a page is printed.

4. Use test file _____ to check your printer's graphic capability.

5. Press _____ to issue a *Font* command.

6. To define character size, select option _____ from the *Font* menu. To define character appearance, select _____.

7. Press _____ to insert a horizontal or vertical line in a document.

8. WordPerfect's sample clip art is found on the _____ disk.

9. When you add a graphic image to a manuscript, you first define a _____ to hold space for it.

10. To align a box with the first line in a paragraph, choose figure type _____ .

Exercises

1. Retrieve document BETAHILL from disk.
   a. Reset PROGRAM PROPOSAL in large type.
   b. Reset THE BETAGOSA HILLBILLIES in extra large type.
   c. Reset the creators' names in small type.
   d. Skip a line after the creators' names.
   e. Insert a 75% line, 0.15 inches wide.
   f. Skip another line.
   g. Insert clip art file APPLAUSE.WPG to the right of the first paragraph. Make it 1.5 inches wide.
   h. Print the document.

2. Retrieve the file you created in Exercise 3 of Chapter 17. Add horizontal and vertical lines to complete the table; experiment with line widths and positions. Print the finished table.

3. Retrieve file MAJORS. (You created it in Exercises 4 and 5 of Chapter 13.) Center the title and reset it using large text. The last sentence reads "Today there is a shortage of trained entry-level people."; change the type font to italics. Add the clip art image stored as NEWSPAPR.WPG to the upper left of the page; make the figure 1.0 inches wide. Then center the clip art image stored as CONFIDEN.WPG at the bottom of the page; make it 2.0 inches wide.

■ PART FOUR

Lotus 1-2-3

·19

Electronic Spreadsheets

This chapter:

- introduces the functions performed by an electronic spreadsheet
- previews Lotus 1-2-3

Electronic Spreadsheets

Electronic spreadsheet software was one of the first major types of programs to become available for microcomputers. VISICALC, the first electronic spreadsheet program, was released in 1979 and initially ran only on Apple microcomputers. There is a strong correlation between the advent of VISICALC and the initial growth of Apple computer sales. When the IBM PC was introduced in 1981, VISICALC was converted for use on IBM equipment. In 1983, Lotus Development Corporation introduced 1-2-3 for use on the PC. Many people credit the growth of microcomputer usage in business to the availability of these and other early spreadsheet packages.

Manual Spreadsheets

Before the introduction of electronic spreadsheets, accountants and other business analysts used manual spreadsheets to organize information and perform calculations. For example, an analyst might wish to perform a sales projection over the next four years with an annual

Figure 19.1
A typical manually created spreadsheet.

Sales Projection
Annual growth rate = 10 %

Product line	Sales (1000's)			
	Year 1 (Current)	Year 2	Year 3	Year 4
Trucks	$ 750	$ 825	$ 908	$ 998
Cars	3,580	3,938	4,332	4,765
Vans	2,120	2,332	2,565	2,822
Four wheel drive	250	275	303	333
Exports	1,120	1,232	1,355	1,491
Total annual sales	$ 7,820	$ 8,602	$ 9,462	$ 10,408

growth rate of 10 percent (Fig. 19.1). The analyst would take a sheet of paper (or a columnar tablet) and list the major product lines down the left edge of the paper, forming a row for each product. Four columns would be used to display the sales figures for each year. Sales for the current year would be listed in column 1 for each product. Using a calculator and the 10 percent growth rate, the analyst would calculate the sales figures for each product in each successive year. Column totals would also be calculated to provide total annual sales figures.

However, developing these tables manually presents some problems. They are subject to calculation errors, since the calculations are performed manually by entering the numbers in a calculator. Data entry errors are also easy to make. The tables often require revision or updating. In the above example, new products might be added or new projections might be required as each year passes. These updates require developing the spreadsheet all over again. Finally, analysts often wish to calculate the same spreadsheet under different sets of assumptions. In the above example the analyst might wish to perform the same projection with a 5 percent growth rate. This would require recalculating the entire spreadsheet.

Electronic Spreadsheets

Electronic spreadsheets duplicate the functions of manual spreadsheets but overcome many of their shortcomings. Electronic spreadsheets provide increased calculation accuracy, easy updating, and the ability to recalculate column and row totals quickly under different sets of assumptions. With electronic spreadsheets, formulas are used that, once verified, may be used over and over with a high degree of accuracy. Electronic spreadsheets may be modified and updated easily as situations change. Columns and rows may be added, deleted, or rearranged. Data elements and formulas may be changed. Finally, electronic spreadsheets are recalculated automatically when any numbers are modified. This allows the analyst to evaluate a series of business scenarios or growth rates by simply reentering certain numbers in the spreadsheet.

Today, most electronic spreadsheet programs provide enhanced capabilities such as graphing, data management and retrieval, and custom programming. **Graphing capability** allows a user to select certain columns or rows of the spreadsheet to be displayed visually as a bar chart, pie chart, or plot. **Data management and retrieval capability** allows the user to treat the spreadsheet as a database in which the rows represent records and the columns represent fields. This allows the spreadsheet user to search for records containing certain types of information and to reorder or sort the records in the spreadsheet. Many spreadsheet programs allow **custom programming or macro capability**, which allows many functions to be performed by writing a sequence of steps that may be executed by giving a single command. In addition, many other capabilities are provided, including the possibility of combining several spreadsheets, enhancing the appearance of a printed spreadsheet, the creation of spreadsheets with three or more dimensions, and the use of functions to perform mathematical and statistical operations.

Lotus 1-2-3 (generally referred to simply as **1-2-3**) is the most popular electronic spreadsheet on the market. Since its initial release (version 1A), it has been enhanced several times. The current version of 1-2-3 includes most of the enhanced capabilities mentioned above.

Applications

The applications of electronic spreadsheets are countless. Basically, any situation that can be summarized in a table with rows and columns representing different categories can be organized as an electronic spreadsheet. Calculations are easily implemented at each row and column intersection. The more experience you have with spreadsheets, the more creative you'll be in developing applications. Listed below are some possible applications to stimulate your thinking. Potential row and column categories are indicated.

1. Budget (*rows*: budget categories; *columns*: time periods)

2. Economic analysis (*rows*: revenue and cost categories; *columns*: time periods)

3. Inventory (*rows*: stock items; *columns*: characteristics of each item such as stock level, unit cost, target, units on order, and so on)

4. Grade sheet (*rows*: students; *columns*: test and homework results)

5. Batting average calculation (*rows*: possible batting results such as singles, doubles, and so on; *columns*: frequency of each result)

6. Personnel records (*rows*: employees; *columns*: wage and salary information)

7. Income tax calculation (*rows*: line items on tax schedule; *columns*: dollar amount)

8. Mortgage amortization table (*rows*: payment number; *columns*: accumulated interest paid, unpaid principal after each payment, and so on)

9. Experiment results (*rows*: subjects; *columns*: response variable measurements)

10. Mathematics tables (*rows*: argument to function; *columns*: value of function)

Lotus 1-2-3

Program and Data Disks

The tutorial will assume that you have access to the Lotus 1-2-3 program, version 2.2, via one of three media: (1) the system disk, a floppy disk that came when you purchased 1-2-3, (2) a subdirectory of a hard disk that contains copies of the 1-2-3 program files, or (3) a network menu system that allows downloading of 1-2-3 program files to your computer. Most of the features will work with Lotus 1-2-3, version 2.01, although some screens may look a bit different. It is also assumed that you will store the worksheets you create on a formatted data disk (floppy) or a data subdirectory of the hard disk. You might also need an operating system disk (PC-DOS or MS-DOS) if you need to boot your computer when you start.

Entering 1-2-3 Commands

The majority of 1-2-3 functions are accessed by pressing a *sequence* of keystrokes (press the first, release it, then press the second, release it, and so on). 1-2-3 is a **menu-driven** software product; to perform a task, the user selects an item from a list of choices called a menu. The process begins by pressing the slash (/) key (located on the same key as the question mark). This causes a list of one-word menu items to be displayed horizontally across the top of the screen. One of these items is selected by pressing the first letter of the menu choice you desire. Depending on the letter selected, a new menu will appear, and another selection is made by pressing the first letter of the next menu choice. This process might continue for five or more levels before a task is complete. The sequential keystrokes required to select a series of menu items will be indicated by listing the keys to be pressed horizontally. The corresponding menu items selected will be spelled out below the keystrokes. For example, to exit 1-2-3, you will be asked to press

This indicates that the keys /, Q, and Y are to be pressed sequentially.

The Tutorials

This part of the book does not pretend to cover every 1-2-3 feature; the intent is to help you learn to use this powerful electronic spreadsheet program. It is organized as a series of tutorials. In Chapter 20 you will learn how to create a spreadsheet, experiment with the spreadsheet, print a copy, and save the spreadsheet on disk. Chapter 21 introduces more sophisticated ways to format the spreadsheet. In subsequent chapters you will learn how to develop spreadsheets more efficiently, produce graphs, and create macro programs. When you finish the tutorials, you will be able to use the 1-2-3 Reference Manual to learn additional features on your own.

Don't just read the tutorials; you can't learn 1-2-3 by simply reading about it. Sit down at a computer and follow along, step by step. Look at the 1-2-3 menus as you press the required keys to see what's happening. If you commit a reasonable amount of time, you'll be surprised at how quickly your confidence and skill develop.

Summary

You'll find a summary of new 1-2-3 features at the end of each chapter and a complete summary of all features is found in Appendix C. No features were introduced in Chapter 19.

Self-Test

The answers to self-tests are in Appendix E.

1. The first electronic spreadsheet program was _____.

2. A spreadsheet is a sheet of paper divided into horizontal _____ and vertical _____.

3. An electronic spreadsheet provides increased _____ and the ability to _____ totals using different assumptions.

4. Today's most popular electronic spreadsheet is _____ .

5. Lotus 1-2-3 is a _____ driven software product.

Exercises

1. Briefly discuss the advantages of electronic spreadsheets over manual spreadsheets.

2. Develop a manual spreadsheet for each of the following applications mentioned in the chapter:

   a. Budget

   b. Economic analysis

   c. Batting average calculation

■20

Creating, Saving, and Printing a Worksheet

This chapter introduces the 1-2-3 features and commands that allow you to:

- start 1-2-3
- create a worksheet
- move the cursor around the worksheet
- enter labels, numbers, and formulas
- select menu options
- save a worksheet
- make changes to a worksheet
- print a worksheet
- exit 1-2-3

Starting 1-2-3

This first tutorial will show you how to enter, save, and print a spreadsheet (hereafter called a "worksheet" to be consistent with the 1-2-3 Reference Manual). Don't just read through the tutorials. You will learn to use 1-2-3 much more quickly if you actually sit down at a computer and follow along, step by step.

Necessary Equipment

You will need an IBM PC, PS/2, or compatible computer equipped with a keyboard, a screen, a printer, and either two floppy disk drives or a hard disk. If you have a two-floppy-disk system, you'll also need the 1-2-3 System Disk, a formatted data disk, and a disk containing the operating system (DOS). If your computer has a hard disk, you probably won't need anything else. The 1-2-3 program files, the operating system, and your worksheet files should all be contained on the hard disk.

If you are using the facilities of a microcomputer laboratory, your starting procedures will likely be different from those described below. In this case, all you will probably need is a formatted data disk to store your worksheet files. Check with the manager of the laboratory to determine the proper starting procedures.

Loading 1-2-3 on a Two-Floppy-Disk System

Skip this section if you are using a hard disk system. Boot DOS; the cursor should follow the A> prompt. Replace the DOS disk in drive A with the 1-2-3 System Disk. Insert the formatted data disk in drive B. Type

    123

and then press

    ⏎

This loads the 1-2-3 program from the disk in drive A into memory and begins execution of the program. A 1-2-3 logo and some messages will appear briefly on the screen; then you will see an empty worksheet as illustrated in Fig. 20.1.

Loading 1-2-3 on a Hard Disk System

Skip this section if you are using a two-floppy-disk system. Boot your hard disk system; the last line will show a C> (or C:\>) prompt followed by the cursor. Type

    CD \123

and then press

    ⏎

CD is a DOS command that changes the default directory of the hard disk. Following it is a slash and then the name of a directory, 123, that stores all of your 1-2-3 program files.

After you press ⏎, the hard disk should activate, and a short time later, a new C> or C:\123> prompt should appear on the screen. Type

123

Figure 20.1

The 1-2-3 work screen simulates a worksheet of columns and rows. The cell pointer highlights the cell indicated by the cell address. Valuable information is displayed in the control panel and the status line.

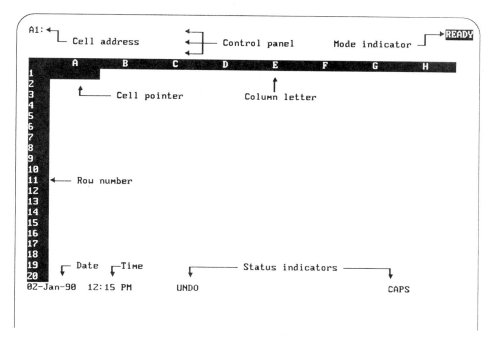

and press

⏎

This loads the 1-2-3 program from the 123 directory of the hard disk into memory and begins executing the program. A 1-2-3 logo and some messages will appear briefly on the screen; then you will see an empty worksheet as illustrated in Fig. 20.1.

■ *Keystroke Summary*

Load 1-2-3

Two-floppy-disk system:

Insert: System Disk in drive A and data disk in drive B

Type: **123**

Press: ⏎

Hard disk system:

Type: **CD \123**

Press: ⏎

Type: **123**

Press: ⏎

■ *What Can Go Wrong?*

1. Following the CD\123 command (on hard disk), a message indicates that the directory does not exist or could not be found.

Cause: The 1-2-3 program files are not on your hard disk or they are stored in a directory with a different name than 123.

Solution: If the 1-2-3 program files are not on your hard disk, get help. Otherwise, ask the person who installed 1-2-3 on your hard disk for the name of the directory containing the 1-2-3 program files. Replace 123 in the command CD\123 with the directory name containing the program files.

2. After you type 123, a "File not found" message appears.

Cause: You might have misspelled the program name. The disk in drive A might not contain 1-2-3. On a hard disk system the program might not be stored on the disk. You might be using an earlier version of 1-2-3.

Solution: First, be sure you typed the program name, 123, correctly by typing it again. If the same message reappears, make sure you are using the 1-2-3 system disk in drive A or that 1-2-3 is available in the 123 directory of your hard disk. Finally, if you are using version 1A of 1-2-3, enter the following commands to load 1-2-3 into memory and obtain the initial worksheet screen.

Type:	**lotus**
Press:	⏎
Press:	⏎ after the initial screen appears
Press:	⏎ after the next screen appears ■

The 1-2-3 Work Screen

Study the empty work screen illustrated in Fig. 20.1. The center of the screen simulates a worksheet composed of rows and columns. The columns are labeled with letters, and the rows are labeled with numbers. An individual element of the worksheet where a column intersects a row is called a **cell**. A cell is designated by a column letter followed by a row number (for example, A1, B14, E4). The current cell is highlighted by the **cell pointer** and indicated by the **cell address** at the upper left corner of the screen.

The top three lines of the screen are called the **control panel**. Keep an eye on these lines as you follow the tutorial; they often provide useful information or instructions. For example, the cell address indicates the current position of the cell pointer. The **mode indicator** displays keywords such as READY, WAIT, or MENU. READY indicates that 1-2-3 is ready for you to enter information in the worksheet. WAIT indicates that 1-2-3 is performing computations and is not ready. MENU is displayed when 1-2-3 is accepting menu selections. At times, other information appears on lines 2 and 3 to give you feedback on what 1-2-3 is doing and to prompt you for input data.

The last line of the screen contains an optional date and time display and several status indicators. For example, CAPS, at the lower right side of the screen, is an indicator that the [Caps Lock] key is toggled on. Try pressing the [Caps Lock] key and notice how the status indicator for CAPS toggles on and off with each press. There is a similar indicator for the [Num Lock] key. The UNDO indicator tells you that you can press a certain key combination to cancel the last operation.

Creating a Worksheet

You are now ready to begin the tutorial. In this chapter you will create the worksheet shown in Fig. 20.2. This worksheet represents a personal budget. A title appears in row 1, and a person's annual income appears in row 2. The worksheet is used to break the annual income figure into five budget categories: housing, food, transportation, clothing, and entertainment. The percentages of annual income allocated to each category are multiplied by the annual income to calculate the amount to be spent annually in each category. The monthly budgeted expenditure is computed by dividing the annual amount by 12. This personal budget worksheet will be used in several chapters to illustrate how worksheets are created and manipulated with 1-2-3.

As with manual worksheets, electronic worksheets are created by organizing the worksheet information into a set of rows and columns. This information is then entered into the worksheet one cell at a time. 1-2-3 classifies the data in a cell as a **label**, **number**, or **formula**. Worksheet titles, column headings, and row descriptions are examples of labels. Numeric constants (such as the annual income figure and the percentages for each budget category in Fig. 20.2) are called numbers. Numeric values that are calculated (such as the annual housing budget of 0.3 times 30,000) are created by entering formulas.

Figure 20.2

This is the finished worksheet that you will be creating in the tutorial presented in this chapter.

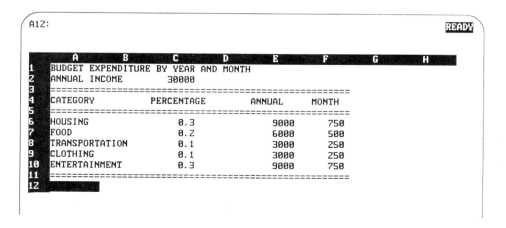

Figure 20.3
Use these keys to
position the cell
pointer.

Press	To Move the Cell Pointer
↑	one cell up
↓	one cell down
→	one cell to the right
←	one cell to the left
Home	to the upper left corner
PgDn	one screen down
PgUp	one screen up
Ctrl *and* →	one screen to the right
Ctrl *and* ←	one screen to the left
F5	to a particular cell address

In general, worksheets are created by positioning the cell pointer on a particular cell and entering a label, a number, or a formula into that cell position. You'll begin by learning to position the cell pointer.

Positioning the Cell Pointer

The cell pointer is positioned by using the cursor control keys; see Fig. 20.3 for a summary of the keys you'll be using. When you are beginning to create a worksheet, the cell pointer is positioned at cell A1. Locate the cursor control keys on your keyboard.

Press →. The cell pointer moves one cell to the right, and the cell address in the upper left corner of the screen changes to B1 to indicate the current position of the cell pointer. Press ↓, and the cell pointer moves one cell down; press ← to move one cell to the left and ↑ to move one cell up. Each time you move the cell pointer, notice that the cell address changes to indicate the current position of the cell pointer.

Hold down →, and the cell pointer moves rapidly to the right. (Release the key after several cells.) If you hold a key down, its action is repeated until you release the key.

Frequently, a worksheet contains more rows and/or columns than can be shown on the screen. To see additional columns, position the cell pointer on the right edge of the screen and press →. Repeat this several times, and the columns will scroll left across the screen. To see additional rows, position the cell pointer at the bottom of the screen and press ↓. Continue to press ↓ several more times and watch the rows scroll up the screen.

Figure 20.4

The display screen is capable of displaying only a portion of the worksheet at a time.

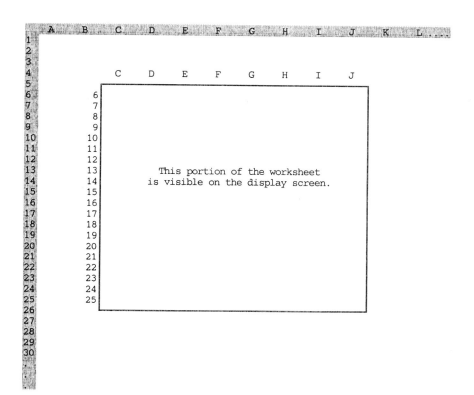

This portion of the worksheet
is visible on the display screen.

Look at Fig. 20.4 to see what is happening. The worksheet may be several hundred rows in length by several hundred columns in width, yet the screen shows only 8 columns and 20 rows of the worksheet at a time. When you position the cell pointer on the right edge and press ⊡, the screen moves to the right one column to display an additional column of the worksheet. It appears to you that the columns have moved left across the screen. Likewise, when you position the cell pointer at the bottom of the screen and press ⊡, the screen moves down one row to include a new row on the screen; the top row scrolls off. Though most of the worksheets in these tutorials fit within the bounds of the display screen, most real applications require worksheets with more rows and columns than will fit on the display screen at one time. To return the cell pointer to the upper left corner of the worksheet, press [Home].

When working with large worksheets, it is often convenient to move the cell pointer an entire screen at a time rather than a single cell at a time. Horizontal movement requires a combination of keys. To move the cell pointer one screen to the right, press [Ctrl] *and* ⊡; to move the cell pointer one screen to the left, press [Ctrl] *and* ⊡. Begin by pressing [Ctrl] *and* ⊡. Notice that the cell pointer is now positioned eight columns to the right. Press [Ctrl] *and* ⊡, and the cell pointer is positioned eight columns to the left.

Vertical movement is accomplished with a single key. To move the cell pointer one screen (20 rows) down, press `PgDn`; to move the cell pointer one screen up, press `PgUp`. Go ahead and try it. When you are finished experimenting, press `Home` to return the cell pointer to cell A1.

Finally, the cell pointer may be moved directly to a particular cell by using the function key `F5`. To illustrate, press

`F5`

The prompt

```
Enter address to go to: A1
```

appears on line 2 of the control panel. At this point, you may type the cell address to which you wish to move the cell pointer. Suppose you want cell Q38. Type

```
Q38
```

and this value will replace A1. Press

`⏎`

The cell pointer is moved directly to cell Q38.

Practice positioning the cell pointer using all the keys listed in Fig. 20.3. Before you go on, you should be able to move the cell pointer quickly to any cell on the worksheet using these keys.

■ *Keystroke Summary*

Move cell pointer to a particular cell

Press: `F5`

Type: *cell address*

Press: `⏎`

■ *What Can Go Wrong?*

1. You accidentally pressed a key other than a cursor control key, causing characters to appear on the second line of the control panel.

Cause: 1-2-3 thinks you are entering a label, number, or formula into the current cell position.

Solution: Press `Esc`. The escape key cancels the current action.

2. You pressed a cursor control key on the numeric keypad, but the cursor did not move. A numeric value appears on the second line of the control panel.

Cause: The ⌷Num Lock⌷ key is toggled on so that the numeric keypad is in use rather than the cursor control keys.

Solution: Press ⌷Esc⌷ to cancel the current action. Then press ⌷Num Lock⌷ to switch from the numeric keypad to the cursor control keys. ▪

Entering Labels and Numbers

This section begins the creation of the budget example by entering labels and numbers into the appropriate cells. Recall that descriptive information such as titles, column headings, and row labels is entered as labels and numeric constants are entered as numbers. Both labels and numbers are used to represent information that does not change. They are entered by positioning the cell pointer over the desired cell and typing the label or number to be placed in that cell. On the other hand, formulas that represent calculated numeric values do change; they are discussed in the next section.

Begin by entering the title of the worksheet (a label) into cell A1. Position the cell pointer to cell A1 (press ⌷Home⌷).

Type the first entry (Fig. 20.5):

BUDGET EXPENDITURE BY YEAR AND MONTH

Hold down ⌷↑⌷ and press each character in turn. Better yet, use the ⌷Caps Lock⌷ key. The ⌷Caps Lock⌷ key works like a toggle switch. Press ⌷Caps Lock⌷ once, and the alphabetic keys generate uppercase letters. Press it again, and the keyboard returns to lowercase letters. Note that only the alphabetic keys are affected; for example, if you press a 1, you will enter the digit 1 no matter how the ⌷Caps Lock⌷ key is set. The state of the ⌷Caps Lock⌷ key is indicated by a status indicator on line 25.

As soon as you begin typing, the mode indicator switches from READY to LABEL, indicating that a label is being prepared for entry into the current cell. A label is simply a string of characters that will appear exactly as entered on the worksheet. As each character is

Figure 20.5

For entering a label, the mode indicator changes from READY to LABEL. The information entered appears on line 2 of the control panel until the ⌷↵⌷ key is pressed.

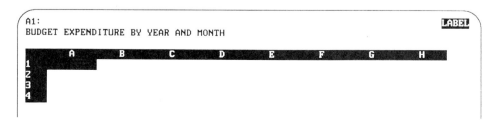

Figure 20.6

When the ⏎ key is pressed, the label is moved to the worksheet and displayed on line 1 of the control panel. Whenever the cell pointer is pointing to a given cell, its contents will be displayed on line 1. Notice also the label-prefix character preceding the label definition.

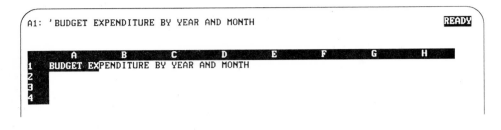

typed, it will appear on line 2 of the control panel. If you make any typing errors, press ⬅ (*not* ⬅) to erase the previous character; then retype it. Make sure your screen looks like Fig. 20.5 before continuing. If it doesn't, press Esc and try again.

Now press

⏎

This moves the label from the second line of the control panel to the highlighted position on the worksheet (Fig. 20.6). All cell entries, labels, numbers, and formulas are initially displayed on line 2 of the control panel and moved onto the worksheet when you press ⏎ or any of the cell pointer positioning keys listed in Fig. 20.3. Once the ⏎ key is pressed, the label is moved to the worksheet, line 2 of the control panel is cleared, and the mode indicator is reset to READY.

Notice that line 1 of the control panel displays the current contents of the highlighted cell. If the cell pointer is moved, the cell address and the cell contents on line 1 will change to indicate the address and contents of the highlighted cell.

The control panel entry in cell A1 is preceded by an apostrophe (') character. This is called a **label-prefix character**. One of these characters (see Fig. 20.7 for a list of label-prefix characters) precedes each label entry and indicates how the label is to be positioned in the cell. The ' character indicates that the label in this cell is to be aligned at the left edge of the cell. Other characters are used to position a label in the center of the cell (^), to align the label with the right edge of the cell ("), and to repeat the label across the width of the cell (\). The label-prefix character may be typed as the label is entered, or, as in this case, the default label-prefix will be entered automatically by 1-2-3.

Figure 20.7
Use these label-prefix characters to position labels in the worksheet cell.

Prefix Character	Label Position
'	aligns label with left edge of cell
"	aligns label with right edge of cell
^	centers label between left and right edges of cell
\	repeats label across width of cell

Finally, notice that the label entry in cell A1 extends into cells B1, C1, and D1. Labels that are too long to fit in a single column are permitted to extend over columns to the right *provided that the following cells are empty*. If an entry is made in one of the following cells, the label is truncated to fit in the space available. However, the entire label is stored so that if the following cells are later empty, the entire label may be displayed again.

Now continue the example by positioning the cell pointer to cell A2 and typing

'ANNUAL INCOME

Press . This time, you are typing the label-prefix character ' as part of the label.

Next, enter the annual income figure by positioning the cell pointer to cell C2 (Fig. 20.8) and typing

30000

As soon as you begin typing, the mode indicator changes to VALUE. This indicates that the current cell will contain numeric information, either the direct entry of a number, as in this case, or the implied entry

Figure 20.8
When a number is entered, the mode indicator changes from READY to VALUE. The number entered appears on line 2 of the control panel until the ⏎ key is pressed, as with labels.

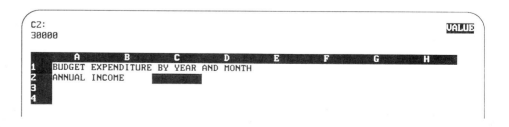

Figure 20.9
When the ↵ key is pressed, the number is moved to the worksheet and displayed on line 1 of the control panel. Numbers do not use label-prefix characters; they are aligned with the right edge of the cell.

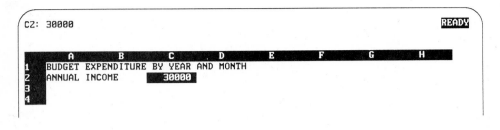

of a number via a formula, as described in the next section. 1-2-3 classifies both numbers and formulas as values.

As before, the cell entry is initially displayed on line 2 of the control panel. ← may be used to erase and correct the previously typed character, and Esc may be used to abandon the cell entry and start over again.

Press

↵

The number 30000 is entered in worksheet cell C2 and displayed on line 1 of the control panel (Fig. 20.9). The mode indicator returns to READY mode. There is no label-prefix character because numeric information is always aligned with the right edge of the cell. (In the next chapter you will learn how to control the position of the decimal point.)

You may be curious to know how 1-2-3 determines whether the entry you are making in a cell is a label or a value. It all depends on the first key pressed. The entry is considered a value if it begins with any of the following characters: 0 1 2 3 4 5 6 7 8 9 . + − $ (@ #. Otherwise, it is considered a label.

This raises the question of how you create a label composed of numbers. For example, suppose you wish to create a label called 123. You can enter 123 as a label by preceding it with a label-prefix character such as ^ (located on number key 6). Entering ^123 will cause the 1-2-3 program to treat the digits 123 as a label that is centered in the cell.

Since pressing any key begins the creation of a label or value in the highlighted cell, accidentally pressing a key will also begin this process. To stop a cell entry process that is begun accidentally, press Esc.

Return to the example in Fig. 20.2. Notice that rows 3, 5, and 7 contain a series of equals signs (=) to highlight the column headings and boundaries of the table. Creating table boundary characters can

Figure 20.10

The backslash (\) character is a label-prefix character designed to repeat the label entered across the entire width of the cell. Entering \= will produce a cell full of equals signs for a worksheet divider.

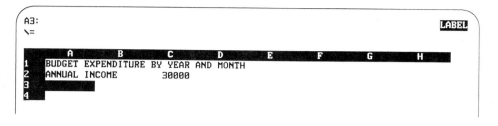

```
A3:                                                              LABEL
\=

        A       B       C       D       E       F       G       H
1  BUDGET EXPENDITURE BY YEAR AND MONTH
2  ANNUAL INCOME           30000
3
4
```

be accomplished by creating a label composed of an appropriate number of equal signs (or other characters) in each cell position. However, it is more convenient and flexible to use the repeating label-prefix character as illustrated in Fig. 20.10. Try it. Position the cell pointer to cell A3 and type

  \=

Press

  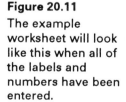

Cell A3 will be filled with equals signs. The backslash (\) is a label-prefix character to indicate that the equals sign (or other symbol you may choose) is to be repeated across the entire cell width.

  Practice your skills at entering labels and numbers, creating a copy of the example up to the point illustrated in Fig. 20.11. Use the following steps:

1. Complete row 3 by entering repeating equals signs in cells B3, C3, D3, E3, and F3 as you did in cell A3.

Figure 20.11

The example worksheet will look like this when all of the labels and numbers have been entered.

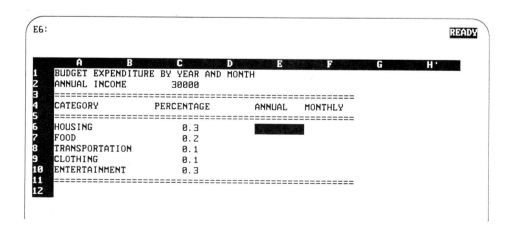

```
E6:                                                             READY

        A       B       C       D       E       F       G       H'
1  BUDGET EXPENDITURE BY YEAR AND MONTH
2  ANNUAL INCOME           30000
3  =================================================
4  CATEGORY            PERCENTAGE       ANNUAL   MONTHLY
5  =================================================
6  HOUSING                 0.3
7  FOOD                    0.2
8  TRANSPORTATION          0.1
9  CLOTHING                0.1
10 ENTERTAINMENT           0.3
11 =================================================
12
```

2. Enter the column headings CATEGORY, PERCENTAGE, AN-NUAL, and MONTHLY as labels in cells A4, C4, E4, and F4 in the same way you did the labels in A1 and A2.

3. Enter repeating equals signs in row 5, cells A5, B5, C5, D5, E5, and F5, as in step 1.

4. Enter the row labels HOUSING, FOOD, TRANSPORTATION, CLOTHING, and ENTERTAINMENT in cells A6, A7, A8, A9, and A10, as in step 2.

5. Enter repeating equals signs in row 11, cells A11, B11, C11, D11, E11, and F11, as in step 1.

6. Enter the percentages to be used for each budget category as numbers in cells C6, C7, C8, C9, and C10 in the same way you entered the annual income in cell C2.

In general, you may enter information into the cells in any order. Numbers may begin with a zero or a decimal point. The process of entering equals signs (the boundary character in the example) in 18 cells may seem a little tedious, but you will learn some shortcuts for doing this in Chapter 22.

■ *What Can Go Wrong?*

1. You made a mistake entering a label or number in a cell and pressed a cursor control key to go back and correct your mistake. The incorrect information is now entered in your worksheet.

Cause: A label or number is entered in the worksheet by pressing ⏎ as described above *or* by moving the cell pointer to another cell using the cursor movement keys. Thus when you pressed the cursor movement key to correct your cell entry, the cell pointer was moved, and the entry in the cell was completed.

Solution: Reposition the cell pointer on the incorrect cell. Type in the correct label or number and press ⏎. This entry will then replace the incorrect entry. Later in this chapter you will learn a better method of correcting or editing the contents of a cell. Until then, use ← to correct typing mistakes.

2. You entered a label or number in the wrong cell position.

Cause: The cell pointer was not positioned over the correct cell when you typed the label or number.

Solution: Position the cell pointer over the contents of the incorrect cell location. Erase the contents of the cell using the following sequence of keystrokes. You are using the 1-2-3 menus, which are explained later in this chapter.

Press: / R E

Press: ⏎

3. You typed the backslash label-prefix character, and the mode indicator changed to MENU rather than LABEL.

Cause: Instead of pressing the slash key (\) as intended, you pressed the (/) key. The (/) key activates the menu system.

Solution: Press (Esc) to exit the menu system and try again using the backslash key (\). ■

Undoing the Last Operation

Beginning with releases 2.2 and 3.0, Lotus 1-2-3 provides an *Undo* feature to cancel the last cell entry of the results of the last operation. *Undo* is a convenient way to correct mistakes. To illustrate, move the cell pointer to cell A1 and type the label

    THIS IS A MISTAKE

Then press ⏎ to enter the erroneous label in cell A1 (Fig. 20.12).
    To correct the error, simultaneously press

    (Alt) *and* (F4)

and the last operation is canceled. The worksheet will once again resemble Fig. 20.11.
    Press (Alt) *and* (F4) again. Note that the erroneous label reappears. This key combination acts as a toggle switch, allowing you to do and undo the last operation as many times as you wish. Press (Alt) *and* (F4) one more time to restore the worksheet to the correct title. As you continue the tutorial, use this feature as necessary to cancel the most recent cell entry or the most recent menu operation.

Figure 20.12
An erroneous label is entered in cell A1.

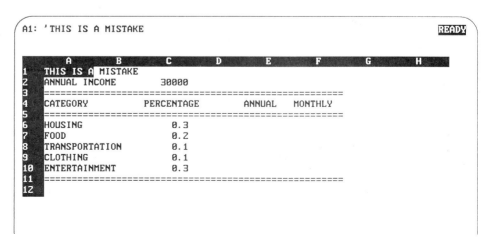

Entering Formulas

If you think this seems like a lot of work without much advantage, you are right! The real power of electronic spreadsheet programs is obtained by using formulas. Formulas are used to define cell values that are calculated from other numeric values in a worksheet. In the budget example the annual and monthly amounts budgeted in each category can be calculated via formulas from values in other cells of the worksheet.

Position the cell pointer over cell E6. In this cell you wish to display the annual amount available for housing. This number is 0.3 of the 30,000 dollar annual income, which equals 9000 dollars. You could enter 9000 as a number in this cell, but if you later wished to change the annual income or the percentage allowance for housing, you would also have to change the contents of this cell.

A better way to express the contents of this cell is as a formula. Type

    +C2*C6

as illustrated in Fig. 20.13. This formula tells 1-2-3 to calculate the value of the current cell by multiplying the value in cell C2 by the value in cell C6. The initial plus sign is necessary to inform 1-2-3 that the entry is a numeric value. (If you typed C2*C6, this entry would be treated as a label.) The asterisk is an operator used to indicate that a multiplication operation is to take place. (Other common operators are + for addition, − for subtraction, and / for division.) Complete the cell entry by pressing

↵

Figure 20.13
The amount in cell E6 is computed by a formula that multiplies the contents of cell C2 times the contents of cell C6. The formula is preceded by a plus sign to make sure 1-2-3 will not treat this entry as a label. The result will be a number, and so the mode indicator is set to VALUE.

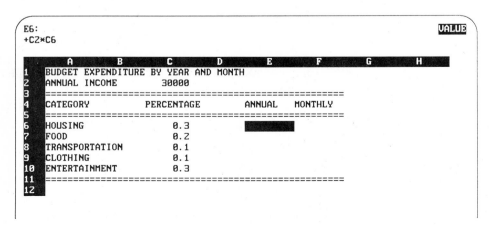

The value 9000 appears on the worksheet in cell E6. The contents of cell E6 on line 1 of the control panel are recorded as a formula rather than a number. This way, if the value of cell C2 or C6 changes, the value of cell E6 will change automatically.

Now consider cell E7. Its value may be calculated by multiplying the annual income (30000 in cell C2) by the food percentage (0.2 in cell C7). An appropriate formula is +C2*C7. Position the cell pointer over cell E7 and type

    +C2*C7

Press ⏎, and the value 6000 will appear in cell E7. Practice by entering similar formulas in cells E8, E9, and E10 to calculate the annual budget amount for each of the remaining categories (+C2*C8, +C2*C9, and +C2*C10, respectively).

The monthly allocation for housing can be calculated by dividing the annual budget allocation for housing (cell E6) by 12. Position the cell pointer to cell F6. Type the formula

    +E6/12

as illustrated Fig. 20.14. In a formula you can refer to another cell whose value is the result of a formula because 1-2-3 automatically makes sure that all formulas are calculated in the proper order. Press

    ⏎

and the value 750 appears on the worksheet in cell F6.

The remaining monthly budget allocations may be calculated by using formulas that divide the annual budget allocations by 12. Complete the sample worksheet by entering similar formulas in cells F7, F8, F9, and F10 (+E7/12, +E8/12, +E9/12, and +E10/12, respectively).

Figure 20.14

The content of cell F6 is computed by a formula that divides the values in cell E6 by 12. 1-2-3 automatically makes sure that the formula for cell E6 is computed before the formula for cell F6.

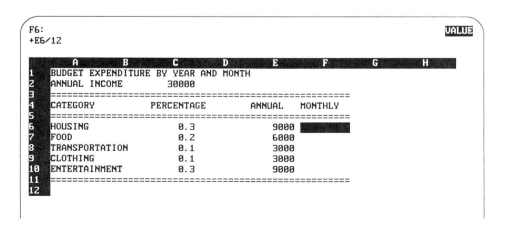

■ *What Can Go Wrong?*

1. The formula appeared in the worksheet cell

Cause: The formula was treated as a label.

Solution: Position the cell pointer on the problem worksheet cell. Retype the formula beginning with a +, and press ⏎. The initial plus sign is a signal that this cell contains a value. If the formula starts with a cell address, such as C2, the initial letter C signals 1-2-3 that this cell contains a label. ■

1-2-3 Menus

Congratulations, you have now completed your first worksheet. You know how to position the cell pointer and enter labels, numbers, and formulas into worksheet cells. Please do not stop the tutorial here. At this point the worksheet is stored in the computer's memory and will be lost when you turn the machine off. You need to save the worksheet from memory to disk. To do this, you need to learn about the 1-2-3 **menu** system.

Press the slash character,

/

to access the 1-2-3 menu system. A menu, as the name suggests, provides a list of items, and you will be called upon to select one of these items. Often, when you select one item, another menu or list of items is provided. The process of selecting menu items might continue for several levels before a task is complete.

Fig. 20.15 displays the first level of menu options obtained by pressing the / key. The mode indicator is changed to MENU, and a series of one-word menu options is displayed horizontally across the second line of the control panel. A brief description of each of the main menu options is given in Fig. 20.16.

Figure 20.15

Line 2 of the control panel displays a list of one-word menu items. These are the main menu choices. Line 2 displays the second-level list of menu items available if the highlighted option (*Worksheet*) is selected. The mode indicator is set to MENU.

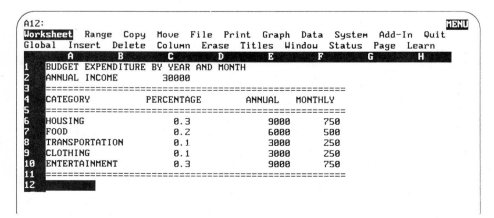

Figure 20.16
The main menu in
1-2-3 is organized as
follows.

Menu Choice	Provides Options for
Worksheet	modifying the entire worksheet
Range	modifying a portion of the worksheet
Copy	copying the contents of a specific set of worksheet cells to another location
Move	moving the contents of a specific set of worksheet cells to another location
File	saving or retrieving worksheets to or from disk storage
Print	printing a worksheet or portion of a worksheet on your printer
Graph	creating graphs using the data obtained from the worksheet
Data	sorting and searching the data in your worksheet
System	temporarily returning to the operating system, leaving 1-2-3 and your worksheet in memory
Add-In	for using add-in programs created by Lotus and other software developers
Quit	returning to the operating system and removing 1-2-3 and your worksheet from memory

Line 3 of the control panel either describes the function performed by the highlighted menu item or lists the menu items at the next level below it. In Fig. 20.15, *Worksheet* is highlighted, and the list of menu items at the next level under *Worksheet* is displayed on line 3. If the *Worksheet* option is selected, the list on the third line moves to the second line and becomes available for selection.

In MENU selection mode, the ⊡ and ⊡ keys no longer move the cell pointer but allow you to highlight different menu items. Press ⊡. This highlights the *Range* option and displays on line 3 of the control panel the menu items at the next level under *Range*. Press ⊡ again and review the description under the *Copy* option. Move the cursor to highlight each menu option. Read line 3 for each menu option so that you begin to get familiar with the options under each main menu choice.

Figure 20.17

In this case, *File* is highlighted, so line 3 displays the second-level list of menu items if *File* is selected. These include retrieving files, saving files, combining files, and so forth.

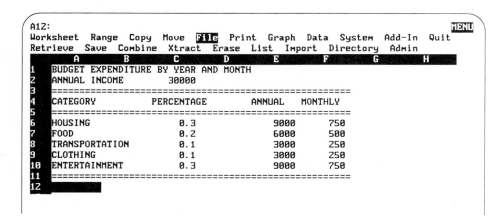

There are two ways to select a menu option. One is to use the ⊡ and ⊡ keys to highlight the desired option and then press ⊡ to perform the selection. To illustrate, use

⊡

to highlight the *File* menu option (Fig. 20.17). Notice that the menu choices under the *File* option are displayed on line 3 of the control panel. Press ⊡ to select the *File* option. The menu choices under the *File* option are now displayed on line 2 of the control panel. Use ⊡ to highlight the *Directory* menu option (Fig. 20.18). Line 3 indicates that this option is used to "Display and/or change the current directory". Press ⊡ and line 2 will prompt you to enter the name of the directory where worksheet files are to be stored (Fig. 20.19). You may either type in a new directory name or press ⊡ to accept the given directory name (probably B:\, or C:\123DATA on a hard disk system). Press ⊡

Figure 20.18

Menu option *File* has been selected. The second-level list of menu items is moved from line 3 to line 2 of the control panel. The second-level option *Directory* is highlighted, and line 3 describes the function of this menu item.

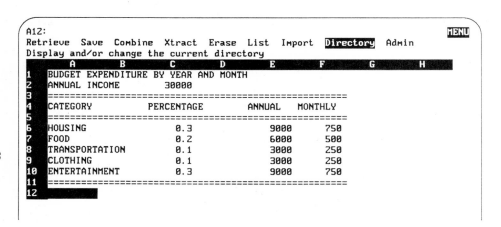

Figure 20.19
Menu option *Directory*
has been selected.
You are being
prompted either to
accept the current
directory by pressing
⏎ or to type the name
of the directory in
which you would like
to store files. The
mode indicator has
changed to EDIT,
since you are to type a
response. Line 3 of
the control panel is
blank, since there are
no further menu
choices.

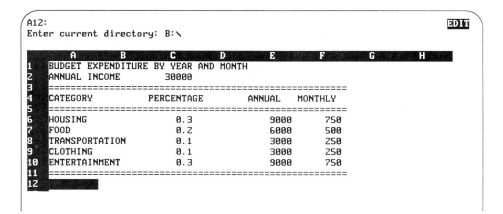

to accept the default directory and return to READY mode. If you have any difficulty following these steps, press Esc until you return to READY mode and try again.

An alternative procedure for selecting menu options is to press the key corresponding to the first letter of the menu choice. Repeat the menu selections made above using this procedure. Make sure you are in READY mode and press

/

to activate the menu system and to display the main menu choices (Fig. 20.15). Press

F
└── File

to select the *File* menu option and display the *File* menu choices (Fig. 20.18). Press

D
└── Directory

to select the *Directory* menu option (Fig. 20.19). Press ⏎ to accept the directory name and return to READY mode.

You may use either procedure to select menu choices in the tutorials. The first method (highlighting the menu choice and pressing ⏎) is slower but gives you the opportunity to look at the other menu options and read about them on line 3 of the control panel. It's a useful method for exploring the menu system and learning new menu features. You are encouraged to use this method, especially during the early tutorials.

The second method (pressing the first letter of a menu choice) requires fewer keystrokes to select an option and thus is faster. Experienced 1-2-3 users tend to use this method because they are already familiar with the menu system. Use this method after you become more experienced.

In the tutorials you will be directed to select menu options using the second method. For the example illustrated above, the tutorial would instruct you to press

```
/ F D
    |  |_____ Directory
    |_____ File
```

This is a convenient form for expository purposes and for reference purposes. However, when you encounter these instructions, please feel free to select the menu choices by highlighting the desired menu choices and pressing ↵, especially until you become comfortable with the menu system.

Take some time now to explore some of the menu options (except *Quit*). Use → or ← to highlight various menu choices and read the descriptions on line 3 of the control panel.

Press ↵ to select some options and study the next set of menu choices. Work your way down through several levels of menus as desired. If you get confused, you can work your way back up through the menu levels by pressing

Esc

Each time Esc is pressed, you move up one menu level until you are out of the menu system completely and in READY mode. You can reenter the menu system by pressing the / key. Practice moving around in the menu system.

■ *Keystroke Summary*

Select menu option

Method 1:

Press: /

Press: → or ← to highlight menu option choice

Press: ↵

Method 2:

Press: /

Press: first letter of menu option

Saving a Worksheet

You are now ready to copy the worksheet you created from the computer's memory to a disk file. This is accomplished by accessing the menu system and choosing the *File* option. The secondary menu under *File* has an option called *Save*, which is used to save a worksheet in a disk file. Press

Remember that you can select these menu options by highlighting the desired choices and pressing ⏎. A message will appear on line 2 of the control panel:

```
Enter name of file to save: B:\*.wk1
```

The cursor follows the message. 1-2-3 is telling you that the worksheet will be stored on the diskette in drive B with any file name that you specify (*), and with the extension *wk1*. If you are using a hard disk system, the message will be slightly different:

```
Enter name of file to save: C:\123DATA\*.wk1
```

Carefully read the suggested file name because it tells you *where* your file will be stored. If you are using two diskettes, you will normally want to save your data to drive B. If you are using a hard disk, you may want to use diskette drive A or a subdirectory on drive C. (If you aren't sure, check with your instructor.)

If the suggested (default) drive and/or directory are correct, skip to the next paragraph. Otherwise, press [Esc] to cancel the current operation. Then press

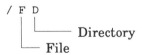

Type the correct drive identifier (for example, B:) or drive and directory (for example, C:\dirname) and press ⏎. When 1-2-3 returns to READY mode, press / F S again, and you're ready to save the file.

It is possible to store many different worksheets (more generally, **files**) on a single disk. To distinguish them, each must be assigned a unique name. It is your responsibility to name your files. A **file name** consists of one to eight characters. Although some punctuation marks are legal, others aren't, so restrict your name to combinations of letters and digits. Type either uppercase or lowercase letters. Following the file name, you can (optionally) type a period and add a one- to three-character **extension**. If you choose not to give an extension, then 1-2-3 will automatically add the extension *wk1* (or *wks* for earlier versions of 1-2-3). Normally, you will choose a file name that suggests

Figure 20.20

After choosing the menu options to save a file, you are prompted to enter the name to be given to your worksheet file. Type BUDGET, and the screen will appear as above. The file will be named BUDGET.wk1 and will be stored on the diskette in drive B.

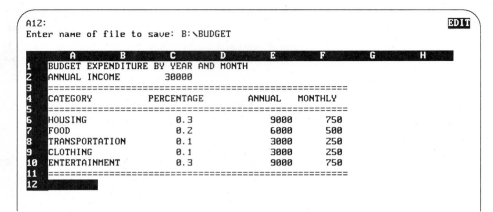

```
A12:                                                              EDIT
Enter name of file to save: B:\BUDGET

        A        B        C        D        E        F        G        H
1   BUDGET EXPENDITURE BY YEAR AND MONTH
2   ANNUAL INCOME          30000
3   ========================================================
4   CATEGORY          PERCENTAGE          ANNUAL    MONTHLY
5   ========================================================
6   HOUSING                 0.3            9000       750
7   FOOD                    0.2            6000       500
8   TRANSPORTATION          0.1            3000       250
9   CLOTHING                0.1            3000       250
10  ENTERTAINMENT           0.3            9000       750
11  ========================================================
12
```

the worksheet contents and omit the extension. BUDGET might be a good choice. Type

    BUDGET

Your screen will look like Fig. 20.20. Press

    ↵

The mode indicator will switch briefly to WAIT while the worksheet is copied to a disk file and then will return to READY mode. Your worksheet is now stored on a floppy disk or a hard disk under the file name BUDGET.wk1. This is a convenient place to stop the tutorial if necessary.

■ **Keystroke Summary**

Save a worksheet

Press: / F S

                    └── Save
              └── File

Type: *file name*

Press: ↵

■ **What Can Go Wrong?**

1. When the message "Enter save file name" appears on line 2 of the control panel, line 3 contains a list of file names and directory names with the first one highlighted.

Cause: There is really nothing wrong with this. 1-2-3 is providing you with a list of existing worksheet files and directory names (those names ending with a \ character). This allows you to select an existing file name or directory by pressing ⊡ or ⊡ until your choice is highlighted. Then press ↵.

Solution: No solution is required. Simply type the file name and ignore the choices provided.

2. When you type the file name and press ⏎, another menu appears, giving you the options *Cancel*, *Replace*, and *Backup*.

Cause: There is already a file on the disk with the name you chose.

Solution: Press C to choose the *Cancel* option. This will return you to READY mode, and nothing will have been saved. Save the worksheet again, but choose a different file name. If you press R to choose the *Replace* option, your worksheet will be saved by replacing the existing file with your worksheet. You will choose this option when updating a worksheet. ■

Modifying a Worksheet

One of the most beneficial aspects of working with spreadsheets electronically is the ability to easily make modifications. You might wish to change the labels, numbers, formulas, layout, spacing, or formatting. You might also wish to add, delete, or relocate certain rows or columns, or you might wish to recalculate the formulas in the worksheet using different numeric values. You will now see how to **edit** the contents of a cell, using the budget worksheet example. You have already learned that you can change a label, number, or formula in a cell by retyping it, but in this section you'll learn to change the contents of a cell by modifying (or editing) the previous contents. If the cell content contains only a few keystrokes, it is usually easier to retype, but if the cell contains many keystrokes and you wish to make only a small change, it is easier to edit.

To illustrate editing, suppose you wish to modify the column label MONTHLY so that it reads MONTH and is centered in the cell. To edit the contents of this cell, you need to change the label-prefix character from ' to ^ and to delete the last two letters, LY, from the label MONTHLY.

Begin by positioning the cell pointer to F4, which contains the label MONTHLY. Function key F2 is used to edit a cell. Press

F2

and you will obtain the screen shown in Fig. 20.21. You are in EDIT mode, and the contents of this cell have been copied to line 2 of the

Figure 20.21

Highlighting cell F4 and pressing F2 copies the contents of this cell onto line 2 of the control panel and allows you to modify or edit the contents of this cell. The mode indicator changes to EDIT.

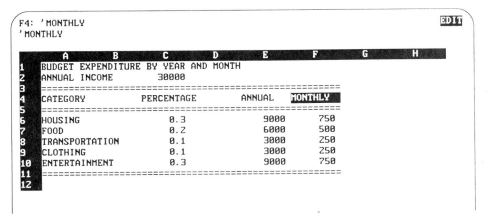

```
F4: 'MONTHLY                                                    EDIT
    'MONTHLY

        A         B          C          D        E       F        G       H
1   BUDGET EXPENDITURE BY YEAR AND MONTH
2   ANNUAL INCOME          30000
3   ============================================================
4   CATEGORY            PERCENTAGE            ANNUAL    MONTHLY
5   ============================================================
6   HOUSING                 0.3                9000      750
7   FOOD                    0.2                6000      500
8   TRANSPORTATION          0.1                3000      250
9   CLOTHING                0.1                3000      250
10  ENTERTAINMENT           0.3                9000      750
11  ============================================================
12
```

Figure 20.22
Use these keys to edit
the contents of a cell.

Press	To Do the Following
→	move the edit cursor one position right
←	move the edit cursor one position left
Home	move the edit cursor to beginning of line
End	move the edit cursor to end of line
Del	delete the character at the edit cursor
Ins	insert or replace characters beginning at the edit cursor
↵	complete the entry and return to READY

control panel for editing. The edit cursor is initially positioned at the end of the line. Once in EDIT mode, you may use the keys listed in Fig. 20.22 to perform the editing functions indicated.

To change the label-prefix character from ' to ^, first press Home. Notice that the edit cursor is positioned under the ' character at the beginning of the line. Press Del, and the character ' is deleted. Press ⊙ *and* ^ (key 6 above the alphabetic keys), and the ^ character is inserted in the first character position of the cell.

Delete the LY as follows. Use → to position the edit cursor under the L. Press Del twice, and both the L and Y will be deleted. Finally, press ↵ to complete the editing of this entry and return to READY mode.

Your worksheet should now contain the label MONTH centered in cell position F4 (Fig. 20.23). For practice, edit another label such as the

Figure 20.23
The label MONTHLY
has been edited to
MONTH and is
centered in the cell
rather than aligned
with the left edge of
the cell.

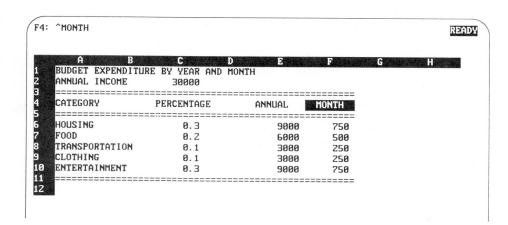

report heading in cell A1. Position the cell pointer on A1 and press F2. Try all the keys in Fig. 20.22 so that you're sure what they do. If you want to leave EDIT mode without saving the changes, press

Esc

to return to READY mode. You may have noticed by now that the Esc key allows you to return to a previous state without taking any action, while ↵ is generally used to complete an action.

Next, edit a numeric value. Suppose you wish to change the annual income figure from 30000 to 45000. Return to READY mode and position the cell pointer at C2, the cell containing the numeric value 30000. Press F2 to enter EDIT mode. Change this numeric value to 45000 by pressing Home to position the edit cursor at the beginning of the line. Press Ins to change from insert to replacement mode, and type 45.

Now press ↵ and watch the worksheet closely. Amazing! You changed one number, and all of the formulas based on annual income were automatically recalculated (Fig. 20.24). *The ability to change a number and have the worksheet automatically recalculated is a major reason for using an electronic spreadsheet program.*

Many people like to use worksheets as an experimental tool to help them study the impact of varying certain numerical values in the worksheet. For example, you could experiment with annual income to find out how much you would need to handle $900 per month in housing costs. Experiment by changing the annual income figure again. If the number you enter does not produce an even result when multiplied by the percentage, 1-2-3 will display as many decimal places as possible. Don't worry about this right now. You'll learn how to make the worksheet neater in the next chapter.

If you wish to save the new worksheet you have created in this section, follow the procedure for saving the worksheet described in the

Figure 20.24
When you change the numeric entry in cell C3 from 30000 to 45000, all the formulas that depend on this value are updated automatically. The annual and monthly budget amounts change as indicated.

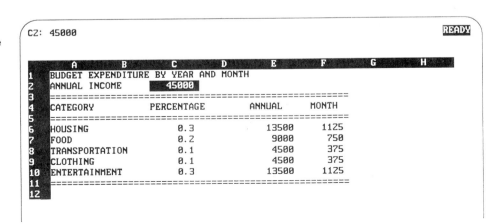

previous section. Press

```
/ F S
    |   |
    |   |_____ Save
    |
    |_____ File
```

Line 2 of the control panel will display the prompt

```
Enter name of file to be saved: B:\BUDGET.wk1
```

Since the worksheet was assigned a file name the last time you saved it, 1-2-3 inserts the current name of the file for you. If you wish to change that name, type in a new name; if you wish to accept the current name, press ⏎. It is important to note that if you save the current worksheet under the previous file name, the old worksheet will be lost. But if you save the current worksheet under a new file name, both the current worksheet and the previous worksheet will be available.

Since you will be using the original budget worksheet in the tutorial in Chapter 21, save this worksheet under a different file name (for example, BUDGETA). Type

```
BUDGETA
```

As soon as you begin typing, the previous file name is removed, and the new file name is inserted. Press ⏎, and this worksheet is saved under the file name BUDGETA.wk1.

For future reference, if you press ⏎ to accept the previous name, line 2 of the control panel will display the menu options

```
Cancel Replace Backup
```

Selecting *Cancel* will return you to READY mode without saving the file. Selecting *Replace* will save the current worksheet in the disk file BUDGET, replacing the previously saved worksheet. Selecting *Backup* will rename the file containing the previously saved worksheet to BUDGET.bak and save the current worksheet in the file named BUDGET.wk1.

■ *Keystroke Summary*

Edit cell contents

Locate:	Cell pointer on cell to be modified
Press:	F2
Edit:	Change cell contents using the editing keys in Fig. 20.22
Press:	⏎

Printing a Worksheet

In this section you'll print a copy of the worksheet shown in Fig. 20.24, using your printer. Before printing, you need to understand worksheet ranges.

Worksheet Ranges

Often, it is necessary to work with a portion of the worksheet at a time. A rectangular block of cells in a worksheet is called a **range**. For example, the middle of the table in Fig. 20.24 that includes rows 6 through 10 and columns A through F forms a range.

Earlier, you learned that cells are addressed by typing a column letter and row number such as B3. Ranges are addressed by typing the address of two cells on diagonally opposite corners of the range, separated by one or two periods. For example, the range referred to above is referenced as

```
A6.F10 or A10.F6 or F10.A6 or F6.A10
```

Generally, the first form, specifying the cell in upper left corner and the cell in lower right corner, is the most convenient to use. When typing a **range address**, use either one or two periods between the corner cell addresses, and do not leave any spaces. Either way, 1-2-3 displays range addresses with two periods between the corner cell addresses.

See whether you understand the idea of worksheet ranges by writing a range address that contains all the cells in Fig. 20.24. One possible answer is A1.F11. A1 is the cell in the upper left corner, and F11 is the cell in the lower right corner of the desired range. Verify that the range addresses given below are correct.

Desired Range	Range Address
Column headings	A4.F4
Row headings	A6.A10
Cells containing formulas	E6.F10
Cells containing percentages	C6.C10
Cell C4	C4.C4

The concept of a range is extremely important. You will be required to enter a range address many times in future tutorials.

Figure 20.25

After selecting the menu options to print a worksheet range on the printer, line 2 will display the print menu options, and (on release 2.2) the worksheet will be replaced by a table indicating the current print settings. First choose option *Range* to specify the range address to be printed. Then choose option *Go* to commence printing. When finished, choose option *Quit* to return to READY mode.

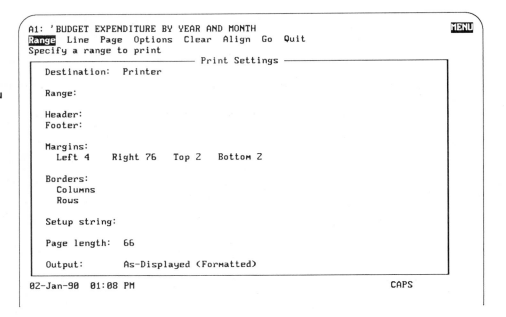

```
A1: 'BUDGET EXPENDITURE BY YEAR AND MONTH                    MENU
Range Line Page Options Clear Align Go Quit
Specify a range to print
                         ┌──────── Print Settings ────────┐
   Destination:  Printer

   Range:

   Header:
   Footer:

   Margins:
     Left 4      Right 76    Top 2    Bottom 2

   Borders:
     Columns
     Rows

   Setup string:

   Page length:  66

   Output:        As-Displayed (Formatted)

02-Jan-90  01:08 PM                                    CAPS
```

Printing

Printing a worksheet is accomplished by using the 1-2-3 menu system. Press

/ P
└── Print

to enter the menu system and select the *Print* option. Respond to the menu

    Printer File

by pressing P to choose the menu option of printing the worksheet on the *Printer* rather than on a disk *File*. You are now at the third level of menu options having to do with printing a worksheet (see line 2 of the control panel in Fig. 20.25). The worksheet is replaced by a table indicating the current print settings.

Press

R
└── Range

to define the range of cells to be printed. Respond to the prompt on line 2 of the control panel,

    Enter print range: A1

by typing

    A1.F11

This range address specifies that all of the cells in the worksheet are to be printed. When you have correctly typed the range address, press

Rather than returning to READY mode, you will return to the third-level menu containing the printing options (Fig. 20.25). The print setting for *Range* will specify A1..F11.

Check your printer. It should be turned on and set to on-line mode. Once the printer is set correctly, press

G
└──── Go

to commence printing the selected range of the worksheet. After the printing is completed, you will again return to the third level of menu options. Press

Q
└──── Quit

to return to READY mode.

If you would like some additional practice, try following the procedure again, but define a different print range. For example, try the range A1.E11 and notice that the last column will be missing. Also, feel free to experiment with the *Options* menu choice to specify other print settings.

■ *Keystroke Summary*

Print a worksheet range

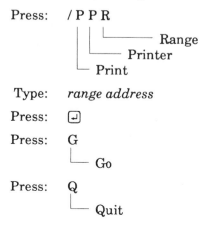

Press: / P P R
                │ │ └──── Range
                │ └──── Printer
                └── Print

Type: *range address*

Press: ⏎

Press: G
             └── Go

Press: Q
             └── Quit

■ *What Can Go Wrong?*

1. You pressed G to begin printing, but the mode indicator says ERROR and the message "No print range specified" appears.

Cause: A range address must be specified before attempting to print a worksheet.

Solution: Press (Esc) to return to the third-level print menu. Press R and define a range address for printing followed by (↵). Now press G.

2. You pressed G to begin printing, but after some delay the mode indicator says ERROR and the message "Printer error" appears.

Cause: You may have forgotten to turn the printer on. The printer may be out of paper or in off-line mode. If you are using a T-switch, it may not be set to your computer.

Solution: Determine the cause from the above list and take the appropriate action; turn the printer on, replace the paper, set the printer to on-line mode, or set the T-switch to your machine. Then press (Esc). This will return you to READY mode. Start over by selecting the print menu option. ■

Exiting 1-2-3

This concludes the first tutorial. Be sure to save your current worksheet to disk whenever exiting 1-2-3; otherwise, your worksheet will be lost.

To exit, use the menu system. Press

```
/ Q
  └── Quit
```

Line 2 of the control panel will display the menu options

```
No Yes
```

If you select *Yes*, you are confirming that you are ready to exit. The 1-2-3 program and your worksheet will be removed from memory. If you select *No*, you will not exit 1-2-3; instead, you'll return to your worksheet. This additional menu layer is designed to protect you from exiting 1-2-3 accidentally or before your worksheet has been saved. Press

```
Y
 └── Yes
```

to exit 1-2-3 and return to the operating system.

■ *Keystroke Summary*

Exit 1-2-3

Press: / Q Y

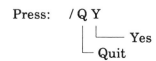

```
        │   └── Yes
        └── Quit
```

■ *What Can Go Wrong?*

1. After pressing / Q Y, you did not return to the operating system but returned to another 1-2-3 menu system called the access system.

Cause: You initially loaded 1-2-3 by using the command "lotus," which loaded 1-2-3 into memory through the access system.

Solution: Press E for menu option *Exit* followed by Y to confirm, *Yes*, that you wish to exit. ■

Summary

Function	Reference or Keystrokes	Page
Cell entry, formula	Formula, ⏎	310
Cell entry, label	Label, ⏎	303
Cell entry, number	Number, ⏎	305
Cell pointer, move cursor	Fig. 20.3	300
Cell pointer, move direct	F5, cell address, ⏎	302
Edit cell contents	F2, Fig. 20.22	319
Exit 1-2-3	/ Q Y	326
File names	—	317
Label-prefix characters	Fig. 20.7	305
Load 1-2-3, floppy disk	—	296
Load 1-2-3, hard disk	—	296
Menu, access	/	312
Menu, back out	Esc	316
Menu, select method 1	→ or ←, ⏎	313
Menu, select method 2	First letter of menu option	315
Print a worksheet	/ P P R, range address, ⏎, G, Q	324
Range, definition	—	323
Save a worksheet	/ F S, file name, ⏎	317
Undo last operation	Alt *and* F4	309

Self-Test

1. The cell address of the upper left corner of the worksheet is _____ , and the cell address of the third row and fifth column is _____ .

2. A worksheet cell may contain a _____ , a _____ , or a _____ .

3. Labels are preceded by a _____ to indicate how the label is to be positioned in the cell.

4. The following formula entry will add the values in cells A1 and A2: _____ .

5. Press _____ to bring up the 1-2-3 menu system. Then press _____ to select the *File* option from the main menu.

6. Press _____ to save a worksheet.

7. Press _____ to edit the contents of the highlighted cell.

8. In general, the _____ key is used to return to a previous state without taking any action, and the _____ key is used to complete an action.

9. Press _____ to define the range for printing. Then press _____ to print the defined range.

10. Press _____ to exit 1-2-3.

Exercises

1. Print two worksheets that you created by following the tutorial in this chapter, and submit them to your instructor. One worksheet should be based on an annual income figure of 30000, and the other should be based on 45000.

2. Use 1-2-3 to create a worksheet representing a college student budget. Use a format similar to the one given below. Treat the annual expenditure, annual tuition, annual housing, and annual book figures as numbers. The annual entertainment is a formula that computes the amount left over after expenses in the other categories. Use a formula for all the monthly expenditures. Save and print the completed worksheet.

```
COLLEGE BUDGET
ANNUAL EXPENDITURE      9600
====================================
CATEGORY            ANNUAL   MONTH
====================================
TUITION               4800     400
HOUSING               3000     250
BOOKS                  600      50
ENTERTAIN             1200     100
====================================
```

3. Use 1-2-3 to create a worksheet to compute a batting average and slugging average as illustrated below. The number of each type of hit and outs are entered as numbers. A formula is used to total the number of at bats. The batting average is computed by dividing the total number of hits by the total number of times at bat. The slugging average counts a home run as 4 hits, a triple as 3 hits, a

double as 2 hits, and a single as 1 hit in computing the batting average. You might wish to enhance this worksheet to include walks, different types of outs, and other batting occurrences. Save and print the completed worksheet.

```
BATTING AVERAGE COMPUTATION
===========================
RESULT             TIMES
===========================
SINGLE                12
DOUBLE                 4
TRIPLE                 2
HOME RUN               2
===========================
OUT                   41
===========================
TOTAL AT BATS         63
===========================
BATTING AVERAGE   0.327868
SLUGGING AVERAGE  0.557377
```

·21
Modifying a Worksheet

This chapter introduces the 1-2-3 features and commands that allow you to:

- retrieve a worksheet
- delete rows and/or columns from a worksheet
- insert additional rows and/or columns in a worksheet
- adjust column widths
- adjust the label-prefix character in a worksheet range
- fix the number of decimal places
- include % and $ symbols with numeric values
- erase portions or all of a worksheet

Overview

In Chapter 20 you learned to modify a worksheet by editing the contents of individual cells. If you have many changes to make, this can be a very tedious process. In this chapter you will learn some powerful methods for modifying many cells of a worksheet at the same time.

Specifically, in this tutorial you'll retrieve the worksheet you saved in Chapter 20 and modify it. After you have completed the

Figure 21.1
This is the finished worksheet that you will be creating in the tutorial presented in this chapter.

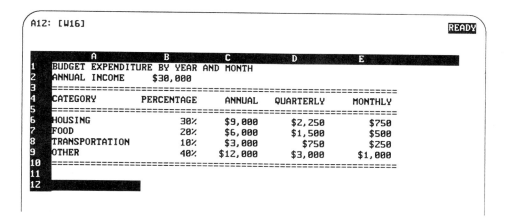

tutorial in this chapter, the worksheet will appear as in Fig. 21.1. Notice the modifications that will have taken place:

1. Previously blank columns are deleted.

2. The budget categories CLOTHING and ENTERTAINMENT are consolidated into a single category OTHER.

3. Column spacing is achieved by adjusting column widths.

4. An additional column, QUARTERLY, is added to the worksheet.

5. The column headings ANNUAL, QUARTERLY, and MONTHLY are aligned with the right edge of the cells.

6. The dollar figures for annual income and budget amounts in each category are formatted with dollar signs and commas.

7. The percentages are formatted with % signs.

The first step is to boot the operating system and load 1-2-3.

Retrieving a Worksheet

If you have properly loaded 1-2-3, you'll see an empty worksheet on the screen. Begin this tutorial by reading into memory the personal budget worksheet. Recall that this worksheet is stored in a disk file named BUDGET.

To ask 1-2-3 to read the worksheet from a disk file, use the menu system. Press

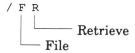

Figure 21.2

After choosing the menu options / F R, you are prompted to select the name of the file to retrieve. Use ⊡ or ⊡ to highlight the file name BUDGET, and press ⏎.

```
A1:                                                           FILES
Name of file to retrieve: B:\*.wk?
BUDGET.WK1          BUDGETA.WK1
```

to select primary menu option *File* and secondary menu option *Retrieve*. (Recall that you are encouraged to select menu options by highlighting the desired option and pressing ⏎, even though the tutorial instructs you to press the first letter of the desired options.) The control panel is shown in Fig. 21.2. Line 2 indicates that the file will be retrieved from a floppy disk in drive B:

```
Name of file to retrieve: B:\*.wk?
```

Line 3 of the control panel contains a list of all of the worksheet files (those with an extension beginning with the letters *wk*) in the given directory.

If the default drive and/or directory is not correct, press Esc to cancel the current operation. Then press / F D, type the correct drive and/or directory, and press ⏎. When 1-2-3 returns to READY mode, press / F R again.

At this point, 1-2-3 is in FILES mode and is waiting for you to select the name of the disk file to be retrieved. The first file name on line 3 is highlighted. To select a file name, use ⊡ or ⊡ to mark the file name desired and then press ⏎. In your case the desired file name is BUDGET. Highlight this file and press ⏎. After a brief delay, the worksheet stored in the disk file BUDGET is copied into memory and displayed on the screen (Fig. 21.3).

Figure 21.3

After retrieval of the worksheet stored in the disk file BUDGET, your 1-2-3 screen will look like this.

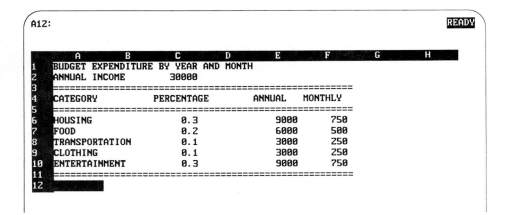

```
A12:                                                          READY

       A        B        C        D        E       F       G       H
1  BUDGET EXPENDITURE BY YEAR AND MONTH
2  ANNUAL INCOME        30000
3  ==============================================================
4  CATEGORY          PERCENTAGE        ANNUAL   MONTHLY
5  ==============================================================
6  HOUSING              0.3            9000      750
7  FOOD                 0.2            6000      500
8  TRANSPORTATION       0.1            3000      250
9  CLOTHING             0.1            3000      250
10 ENTERTAINMENT        0.3            9000      750
11 ==============================================================
12
```

■ *Keystroke*
Summary

Retrieve a file

Press: / F R

Press: ⊡ or ⊟ to select file name

Press: ⏎

■ *What Can*
Go Wrong?

1. You are using a floppy disk system. After choosing the menu option to retrieve a file, a brief delay occurs, and you receive the error message "Disk drive not ready" at the bottom of the screen.

Cause: 1-2-3 is trying to read the names of the worksheet files stored on the floppy disk in drive B, but no disk is there

Solution: Place the data disk you used to store the BUDGET worksheet in drive B. Press (Esc) to return to READY mode and start over.

2. The worksheet file BUDGET does not appear on line 3 of the control panel.

Cause: When 1-2-3 was initially set up on your hard disk system, a certain directory (the default directory) was established as the place where worksheet files are to be stored. These settings are indicated on line 2 of the control panel. Your BUDGET file is stored in a different directory. Or, on a floppy disk system, you have the wrong data disk in drive B.

Solution: In the first case, change the default directory, or if the directory name you wish is displayed on line 3 (directory names are followed by the \ character), use ⊡ or ⊟ to highlight that name and press ⏎. This will display the worksheet files in that directory on line 3. In the second case, place the correct data disk in drive B, press (Esc) until you return to READY mode, and start over. ■

Deleting Rows
and/or Columns

Now that you have retrieved the worksheet, look at it carefully. Notice that the cells in columns B and D contain no labels, values, or formulas other than the equals signs used to define worksheet boundaries in rows 3, 5, and 11. These columns were left blank intentionally to provide spacing in the table. Later in this chapter you will learn to adjust the width of individual columns, so you'll no longer need these extra columns for spacing. Delete them.

To delete column B, position the cell pointer in any row of column B and choose the *Worksheet* menu option by pressing

Figure 21.4

The *Worksheet* menu options are listed on line 2 of the control panel. All these options involve modifications to the entire worksheet. Use ⊟ or ⊟ to highlight each option, and read the description on line 3.

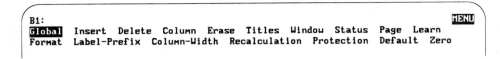

```
B1:                                                                    MENU
Global  Insert  Delete  Column  Erase  Titles  Window  Status  Page  Learn
Format  Label-Prefix  Column-Width  Recalculation  Protection  Default  Zero
```

Line 2 of the control panel (Fig. 21.4) lists the *Worksheet* menu options that provide choices for modifying the worksheet. You'll be using the first five options in this chapter (Fig. 21.5). Use ⊟ and ⊟ to highlight each of these options and compare the descriptions on line 3 of the control panel with the descriptions in Fig. 21.5.

To continue with the example, press

D
└──── Delete

The menu options will appear on line 2 of the control panel:

```
Column Row
```

One deletes columns; the other deletes rows. Press C. The prompt

```
Enter range of columns to delete: B1..B1
```

appears. At this point you are to define a range address that includes the columns to be deleted. Since you initially positioned the cell pointer in column B, 1-2-3 suggests a range address that includes the single column B (B1..B1). If you wanted to delete columns B through F, you would type a range address that included these columns, for

Figure 21.5

The *Worksheet* option in 1-2-3 provides options for modifying the entire worksheet. This chapter involves options in the first five groups.

Menu Choice	Provides Options for
Global	setting default format, label-prefix, column width, and other worksheet characteristics
Insert	inserting additional rows or columns
Delete	deleting rows or columns
Columns	setting the width and other characteristics of a column
Erase	erasing the worksheet

Figure 21.6

After deletion of
column B, the
contents of columns
C, D, E, and F move
one column to the left.

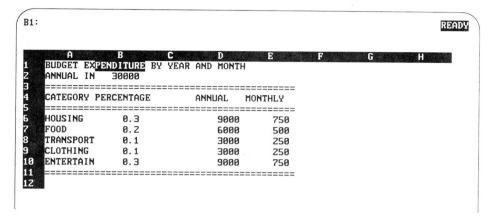

example, B1.F1 or B2.F5. In your case you wish to delete only column
B, so the suggested range address is fine. Do not type anything.

Press ⏎. The contents of all cells in column B are deleted, and the
rest of the worksheet moves over to fill in the free space (Fig. 21.6). The
contents of the cells in column C have moved to B, the contents of the
cells in column D have moved to C, and so on.

Note that some of the labels in column A have been truncated; for
example, see ANNUAL IN in cell A2. That's because column B no
longer contains empty cells. The entire label, ANNUAL INCOME, is
still stored in cell A2, but the column to the right is not empty.
Therefore the label is truncated to fit into the nine spaces available to
display the contents of cells in column A. You will learn to adjust the
column width later in this chapter.

Note also the formulas. Position the cell pointer over cell D6 (Fig.
21.7). Notice that the formula for the annual housing budget is

Figure 21.7

When columns are
deleted and the
following columns are
moved over, cells
containing formulas
are automatically
adjusted. The formula
in cell D6 was
originally in cell E6,
and the original
formula was +C2*C6.
Since the contents of
column C moved to
column B, the formula
was automatically
changed to +B2*B6.

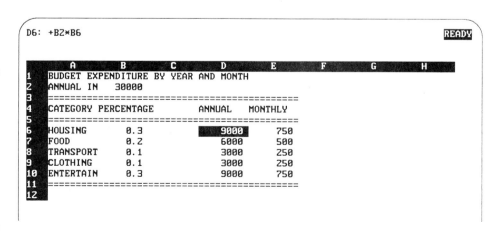

appropriately adjusted to +B2*B6. You originally entered the formula as +C2*C6 in Chapter 20, but since column B was deleted and column C moved over, the formula has been adjusted automatically by 1-2-3.

Follow the same procedure to delete column C. Position the cell pointer to any row in column C. Sequentially, press / W D C to choose the menu option to delete a column. You'll be prompted to enter a range address that includes the columns you wish to delete. The suggested range address will contain the single column, C. Press ⏎ to accept the suggested address. As before, the contents of the cells in columns D and E move one column to the left, and the formulas are adjusted automatically. Your worksheet now looks like Fig. 21.8.

Review Fig. 21.1 again. Note that the last two budget categories, CLOTHING and ENTERTAINMENT, are consolidated into a single category called OTHER. This is accomplished by deleting the CLOTH-ING row from the worksheet and then editing the category label and percentage number of the ENTERTAINMENT row.

First, delete row 9. The process is almost identical to deleting a column. Position the cell pointer to any column in row 9. Press

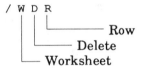

to choose the menu option to delete a row. You will be prompted as follows:

```
Enter range of rows to delete: A9..A9
```

Since you initially highlighted a cell in row 9, the suggested range address includes that single row. As with columns, you may type in a different range address that includes all the rows you wish to delete.

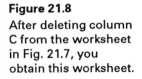

Figure 21.8
After deleting column C from the worksheet in Fig. 21.7, you obtain this worksheet.

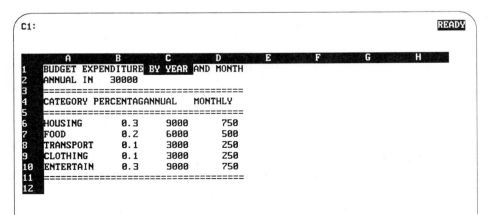

Figure 21.9

After deletion of row 9, the contents of row 10 are moved up to fill in row 9.

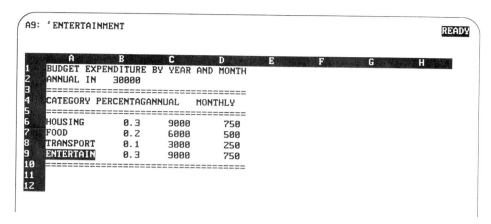

```
A9: 'ENTERTAINMENT                                                    READY

        A         B         C         D      E      F      G      H
1  BUDGET EXPENDITURE BY YEAR AND MONTH
2  ANNUAL IN    30000
3  =====================================
4  CATEGORY PERCENTAGANNUAL    MONTHLY
5  =====================================
6  HOUSING       0.3      9000      750
7  FOOD          0.2      6000      500
8  TRANSPORT     0.1      3000      250
9  ENTERTAIN     0.3      9000      750
10 =====================================
11
12
```

In your case you wish to delete only row 9, so press ⏎ to accept the suggested range address.

The worksheet now appears as in Fig. 21.9. The contents of the cells in rows below row 9 have moved up one row. As before, formulas are automatically adjusted as necessary.

To complete the consolidation of the last two budget categories in your worksheet, edit the category in cell A9 to contain the label, OTHER, and change the percentage in cell B9 to 0.4 (Fig. 21.10). Do this by positioning the cell pointer on the respective cells and either reentering the cell contents or pressing F2 and modifying the existing cell contents. If you've forgotten how to do this, review the section on modifying a worksheet cell in Chapter 20.

Figure 21.10

After editing the label in cell A9 and the number in cell B9, you obtain this worksheet.

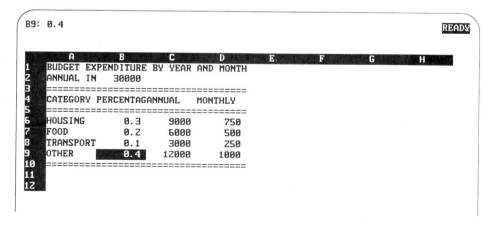

```
B9: 0.4                                                              READY

        A         B         C         D      E      F      G      H
1  BUDGET EXPENDITURE BY YEAR AND MONTH
2  ANNUAL IN    30000
3  =====================================
4  CATEGORY PERCENTAGANNUAL    MONTHLY
5  =====================================
6  HOUSING       0.3      9000      750
7  FOOD          0.2      6000      500
8  TRANSPORT     0.1      3000      250
9  OTHER         0.4     12000     1000
10 =====================================
11
12
```

▪ *Keystroke
Summary*

Delete rows or columns

Press: / W D (R or C)

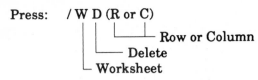

Type: *range address*

Press: ⏎

▪ *What Can
Go Wrong?*

1. You accidentally deleted the wrong columns or rows from your worksheet.

Cause: The range address that you specified contained the wrong columns or rows. Remember that when you are deleting columns (or rows), all columns (rows) in the specified range will be deleted.

Solution: If you have performed no other operations since your mistake, the simplest procedure is to use the *Undo* command, [Alt] and [F4]. Otherwise, you'll need to start over by retrieving the BUDGET file again. The original worksheet from disk will replace the modified worksheet, and you can retrace your steps. See the previous section to retrieve a worksheet. Incidentally, it is good practice to save your worksheet to disk periodically so that if something goes wrong, you can retrieve it. ▪

**Inserting Rows
and/or Columns**

In the last section you learned how to delete rows or columns from a worksheet. Similarly, 1-2-3 commands allow you to move in the opposite direction; that is, you can create additional space in a worksheet by inserting blank rows or columns. In the modified worksheet, illustrated in Fig. 21.1, an additional column containing the QUARTERLY budget amounts is inserted between the ANNUAL and MONTHLY columns. This is accomplished by inserting a blank column between the ANNUAL and MONTHLY columns and then entering labels, numbers, and formulas into the new column as appropriate.

To insert a blank column to the left of column D, position the cell pointer to any cell in column D. Choose the menu option

You'll then be given the menu options

```
Column Row
```

Press C to indicate that you wish to insert blank columns. You will be prompted as follows:

```
Enter column insert range: D1..D1
```

Enter a range address that contains the columns you wish to insert; any information that is already in these columns will be moved over as appropriate. The suggested address contains the single column D, since you positioned the cell pointer in this column when you chose this menu option. Press ↵ to accept this range address and to insert a single blank column (Fig. 21.11). Note that the contents of cells previously in column D are moved to column E, and a blank column is inserted. Any formulas affected by the change are automatically adjusted.

Now enter the appropriate labels and formulas into the cells of column D. This column contains quarterly budget expenditures and uses labels and formulas that are analogous to those you entered for the MONTHLY column in Chapter 20. Cells D3, D5, and D10 contain the label \= (recall that \ is a label-prefix character indicating that the following character, =, is to be repeated across the entire cell width) to provide a worksheet boundary. Cell D4 contains the column heading QUARTERLY. Cells D6 through D9 contain formulas to compute the quarterly budget available in each category. This is computed by taking the annual budget amount and dividing by 4. For example, the formula in cell D6 is +C6/4. Enter similar formulas in cells D7 through D9. After you have entered all the information in the new column, the worksheet will appear as in Fig. 21.12.

Inserting additional blank rows in the worksheet is almost identical to inserting columns. The tutorial example does not require any additional rows; but for practice, insert 3 additional rows between the budget categories FOOD and TRANSPORTATION and then delete them.

Figure 21.11
After a blank column is inserted in column D, the previous contents of column D are shifted to column E.

```
D1:                                                                    READY

        A         B         C         D         E         F         G         H
1   BUDGET EXPENDITURE BY YEAR AND MONTH
2   ANNUAL IN    30000
3   ============================                ========
4   CATEGORY PERCENTAGANNUAL                    MONTHLY
5   ============================                ========
6   HOUSING         0.3      9000                    750
7   FOOD            0.2      6000                    500
8   TRANSPORT       0.1      3000                    250
9   OTHER           0.4     12000                   1000
10  ============================                ========
11
12
```

Figure 21.12
Labels and formulas
are entered in the
cells of the newly
created column D to
obtain this worksheet.

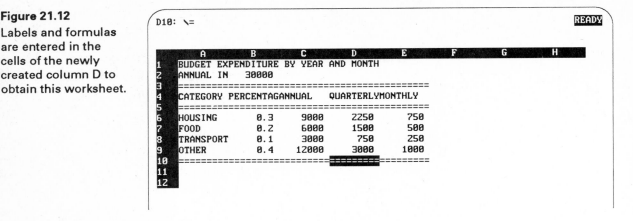

Position the cell pointer in cell A8 and choose the menu option,

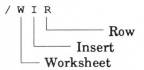

to insert additional blank rows above row 8. The prompt on line 2 reads:

```
Enter row insert range: A8..A8
```

Type

```
A8.A10
```

to insert 3 blank rows (rows 8, 9, and 10). Press ⏎. Three blank rows are inserted, and the last three rows of the worksheet are moved down.

Since this was just for practice, delete these three rows to return to the worksheet in Fig. 21.12. Position the cell pointer to cell A8. Press / W D R to choose the menu option to delete worksheet rows. Type the range address A8.A10 to specify that rows 8 to 10 are to be deleted, and press ⏎.

■ *Keystroke*
Summary

Insert rows or columns

Press: / W I (R or C)

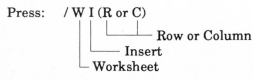

Type: *range address*

Press: ⏎

▪ *What Can Go Wrong?*

1. You accidentally inserted columns or rows in the wrong position of your worksheet.

Cause: The range address that you specified contained the wrong columns or rows. Remember that when you are inserting columns (or rows), blank columns (rows) will be inserted in each column (row) of the specified range.

Solution: Either use the *Undo* command or delete the newly inserted columns (rows) and start the procedure over. See the previous section to delete columns (rows) from a worksheet.

2. After you have entered a range address, the mode indicator flashes ERROR, and line 25 contains the message "Invalid cell or range address."

Cause: The range address you typed contains an erroneous character.

Solution: Press Esc to return to READY mode. Start the procedure over. Remember that a proper range address is composed of a cell address, one or two periods, and another cell address. Leave no blanks. This type of error can occur in any procedure requiring a range address. ▪

Adjusting Column Widths

Initially, the width of each column of a worksheet is set to nine spaces, but you can adjust the column width to allow appropriate spacing between columns. In your example worksheet (Fig. 21.12) the columns need to be widened to allow additional space for certain labels (for example, ANNUAL IN, PERCENTAG, and TRANSPORT). In this section you will learn to adjust the width of all columns or a single column.

Adjusting the Width of All Columns

When a worksheet is initially created, certain global worksheet characteristics are established, such as the default label-prefix character, the default number format (to be discussed later in this chapter), and the default column width. To change the global settings, press

A new menu will appear, and the worksheet will be replaced by a table containing the current global settings (Fig. 21.13); each option on this menu allows you to change one of the default settings of the worksheet. Use ⊡ to highlight each option on the menu, and read the description on line 3 to get a feel for the choices provided.

To change the global column width, press

Figure 21.13
After the menu options / W G are chosen, line 2 of the control panel provides menu options for setting default values for the worksheet, and the worksheet is replaced by a table of global settings. The option *Column-width* is highlighted. Choose this option to specify the number of spaces allocated to each column in the worksheet.

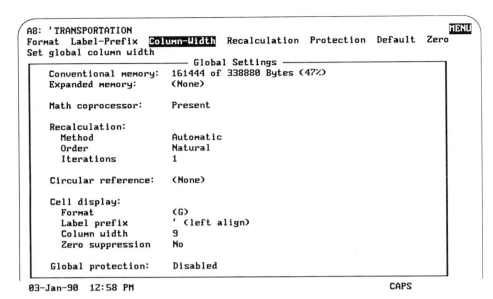

```
A8: 'TRANSPORTATION                                                      MENU
Format  Label-Prefix  Column-Width  Recalculation  Protection  Default  Zero
Set global column width
┌─────────────────── Global Settings ───────────────────┐
│                                                        │
│   Conventional memory:    161444 of 338880 Bytes (47%) │
│   Expanded memory:        (None)                       │
│                                                        │
│   Math coprocessor:       Present                      │
│                                                        │
│   Recalculation:                                       │
│     Method                Automatic                    │
│     Order                 Natural                      │
│     Iterations            1                            │
│                                                        │
│   Circular reference:     (None)                       │
│                                                        │
│   Cell display:                                        │
│     Format                (G)                          │
│     Label prefix          ' (left align)               │
│     Column width          9                            │
│     Zero suppression      No                           │
│                                                        │
│   Global protection:      Disabled                     │
│                                                        │
└────────────────────────────────────────────────────────┘
03-Jan-90  12:58 PM                                             CAPS
```

The worksheet will reappear, and you will be prompted (Fig. 21.14) as follows:

```
Enter global column width (1..240): 9
```

The default column width 9 is provided. At this point you could type the desired column width and press ⏎. However, don't. This is a good place to introduce POINT mode.

Note that the mode indicator says POINT. This is an indication that the desired input may be obtained by pointing with the cursor keys rather than typing the desired value. Press → once, and the column width increases to 10; the change is reflected on the screen. Press → again, and the column width increases another unit. Each time → is pressed, the column width increases by one unit, and the change is displayed on the screen. Pressing ← decreases the column width by one unit. Press → and ← several times so that you see how pointing works. Notice that as the column width decreases, more columns appear on the screen; as the column width increases, fewer columns appear on the screen.

Figure 21.14
Use → to increase the column width and ← to decrease it. Press ⏎ when you are satisfied with the setting.

```
A1: 'BUDGET EXPENDITURE BY YEAR AND MONTH                              POINT
Enter global column width (1..240): 9
```

Figure 21.15
The global column width is set to 12 spaces.

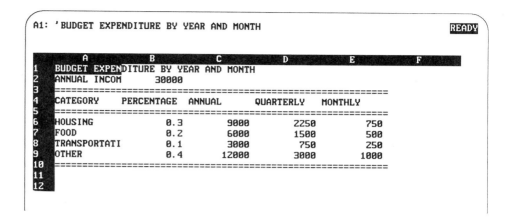

```
A1: 'BUDGET EXPENDITURE BY YEAR AND MONTH                              READY

        A           B           C           D           E           F
1   BUDGET EXPENDITURE BY YEAR AND MONTH
2   ANNUAL INCOM     30000
3   =================================================================
4   CATEGORY    PERCENTAGE  ANNUAL      QUARTERLY   MONTHLY
5   =================================================================
6   HOUSING          0.3        9000        2250         750
7   FOOD             0.2        6000        1500         500
8   TRANSPORTATI     0.1        3000         750         250
9   OTHER            0.4       12000        3000        1000
10  =================================================================
11
12
```

Use → or ← to select a column width of 12. Press ↵ to confirm your choice. Each column on your worksheet is now 12 spaces wide (Fig. 21.15). Notice that the labels ANNUAL INCOME and TRANSPORTATION are still truncated; clearly, 12 spaces are not enough for column A. You'll correct this in the next section.

■ *Keystroke Summary*

Adjust the width of all columns

Press: / W G C

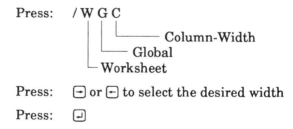

Column-Width
Global
Worksheet

Press: → or ← to select the desired width

Press: ↵

Adjusting the Width of a Single Column

The procedure described above is useful to change the default column width setting for all columns in the worksheet. However, it is frequently desirable to set each column individually to allow for variable-width columns.

To illustrate, set the width of column A to 16 spaces. Position the cell pointer in column A and press

/ W C

Column
Worksheet

Figure 21.16
The width of column A is set to 16 spaces.

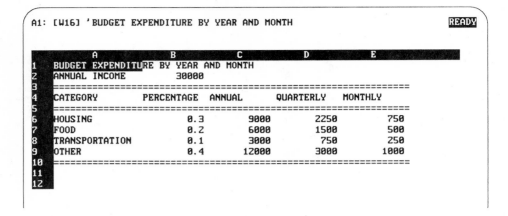

```
A1: [W16] 'BUDGET EXPENDITURE BY YEAR AND MONTH                    READY

          A              B         C          D          E
1  BUDGET EXPENDITURE BY YEAR AND MONTH
2  ANNUAL INCOME        30000
3  ====================================================================
4  CATEGORY         PERCENTAGE  ANNUAL     QUARTERLY  MONTHLY
5  ====================================================================
6  HOUSING              0.3      9000       2250        750
7  FOOD                 0.2      6000       1500        500
8  TRANSPORTATION       0.1      3000        750        250
9  OTHER                0.4     12000       3000       1000
10 ====================================================================
11
12
```

to access a menu of choices for setting parameters of the column containing the cell pointer:

```
Set-Width Reset-Width Hide Display Column-Range
```

Press S to set the column width. You will then be prompted as follows:

```
Enter column width (1..240): 12
```

This time the column width you choose applies only to this single column.

Press ⊟ four times until the column width equals 16, and then press ⏎ (Fig. 21.16). Notice line 1 of the control panel. In addition to the usual display of cell contents, line 1 contains the symbol [W16]. This indicates that the width of this column is set to 16 spaces.

Next, set the width of column B to ten spaces. Position the cell pointer on column B. Sequentially, press / W C S. Press ⊟ twice to set the column width to 10, press ⏎, and note the changes in the worksheet (Fig. 21.17).

Figure 21.17
The width of column B is set to 10 spaces.

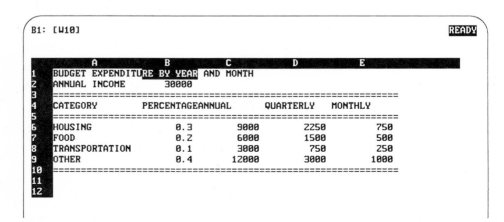

```
B1: [W10]                                                          READY

          A           B         C          D          E
1  BUDGET EXPENDITURE BY YEAR AND MONTH
2  ANNUAL INCOME     30000
3  ====================================================================
4  CATEGORY       PERCENTAGEANNUAL     QUARTERLY  MONTHLY
5  ====================================================================
6  HOUSING            0.3      9000       2250        750
7  FOOD               0.2      6000       1500        500
8  TRANSPORTATION     0.1      3000        750        250
9  OTHER              0.4     12000       3000       1000
10 ====================================================================
11
12
```

In summary, the menu option / W G C sets the column width of all columns in the worksheet, and the menu option / W C S *overrides* this setting for an individual column. 1-2-3 also provides a feature for overriding the setting for a group of columns (/ W C C).

▪ *Keystroke Summary*

Adjust the width of a single column

Press: / W C S

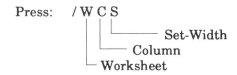

Press: ⊟ or ⊟ to select the desired width

Press: ⏎

▪ *What Can Go Wrong?*

1. You set the width of the wrong column to 10 or 16.

Cause: The cell pointer was positioned in the wrong column when you followed the procedure to set the column width.

Solution: Undo the last operation or reset the column width of the incorrect column to the default value. Position the cell pointer on this column and choose the following menu options:

Press: / W C R

Adjusting Label-Prefix Characters

Review the current version of your worksheet (Fig. 21.17). Notice that all the column heading labels are aligned with the left edge of their cells. Recall from Chapter 20 that when you entered these labels, they were automatically preceded by the default label-prefix character, ', which specifies this alignment. In most cases, left alignment is fine, but your worksheet would look better if the column headings ANNUAL, QUARTERLY, and MONTHLY were aligned with the right edge of the cell. This can be accomplished by editing each of these cells individually to replace the label-prefix character ' with " or by changing the label-prefix characters of an entire range of cells at once.

Position the cell pointer on cell C4 and choose the *Range* menu option:

Figure 21.18
After choosing the menu option / R, you obtain the menu options listed on line 2 of the control panel. All of these options involve modifications to a part (or range) of the worksheet. Use ⊡ or ⊟ to highlight each option and read the description on line 3.

```
C4: 'ANNUAL                                                    MENU
Format Label Erase Name Justify Prot Unprot Input Value Trans Search
Fixed Sci Currency , General +/- Percent Date Text Hidden Reset
```

The *Range* option provides a number of menu choices for modifying portions or ranges of the worksheet (Fig. 21.18). In this chapter you will be using the first three options (Fig. 21.19). Use ⊟ and ⊡ to highlight each of these options, and compare the descriptions on line 3 of the control panel with the descriptions in Fig. 21.19.

To continue with the example, press

```
L
└──── Label
```

to select the option for modifying the label-prefix characters. Line 2 of the control panel will display the following menu choices:

```
Left Right Center
```

Press R to select alignment with the right edge of the cell.

You will then be prompted to enter the range address of the labels to modify:

```
Enter range of labels: C4..C4
```

Type a range address that contains all the labels you wish to align with the right edge of the cell. If the range address includes cells with

Figure 21.19
The *Range* option in 1-2-3 provides options for modifying a specified range of the worksheet. This chapter involves options in the first three groups.

Menu Choice	Provides Options for
Format	determining the appearance or format of numbers in the worksheet
Label	modifying the label-prefix character of a range of worksheet cells
Erase	erasing the contents of a range of worksheet cells

numbers or formulas, they will not be affected because the label-prefix character does not apply to worksheet values; it applies only to labels. In your example, type

```
C4.E4
```

to modify the alignment of the last three column labels. Press ⏎, and watch the worksheet change (Fig. 21.20). Position the cell pointer over each of these column labels and notice that the prefix character displayed on line 1 of the control panel is " to indicate the right edge alignment of the label in that cell.

■ *Keystroke Summary*

Adjust the label-prefix character in a range

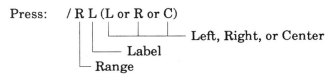

Press: / R L (L or R or C)

Left, Right, or Center

Label

Range

Type: *range address*

Press: ⏎

■ *What Can Go Wrong?*

1. You aligned labels other than the three column headings desired with the right edge of the cell.

Cause: You entered the wrong range address.

Solution: Use the procedures in this section to adjust the label-prefix character of the incorrect labels. After pressing / R L, choose option L to align the labels with the left edge of the cell. Carefully enter the desired range address. If you modified the label-prefix character of any cells containing repeating equal signs, you'll need to edit each of these cells individually.

Figure 21.20

The column labels ANNUAL, QUARTERLY, and MONTHLY are aligned with the right edge of the cell.

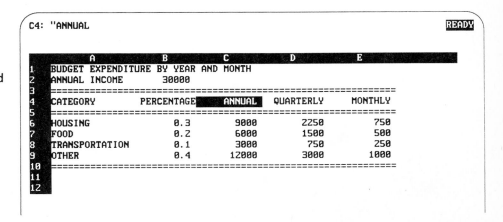

2. The three column headings are still aligned with the left edge of the cell, or they are centered in the cell.

Cause: You chose the wrong alignment option.

Solution: Start over again. After pressing / R L, choose option R to align the labels with the right edge of the cell. L aligns labels with the left edge and C aligns labels in the center. ■

Note: The *Undo* key combination (Alt *and* F4) may often be used to solve a problem identified in the "What Can Go Wrong?" box *if* the problem occurs as a result of the last operation. For the remaining Lotus tutorials, this option will not be suggested as a possible solution. Instead, the "What Can Go Wrong?" boxes will assume that you have tried *Undo* and are looking for a different solution.

Formatting Worksheet Values

1-2-3 provides several options for specifying how numeric values, including numbers and formulas, appear on the worksheet. Though 1-2-3 stores values with a precision of 15 decimal places, you may control the number of decimal places displayed and the formatting of these numeric values. In this section of the tutorial you will learn some of these **format** options and will modify the numeric values in the worksheet to display zero decimal places and to include dollar signs and percent signs where appropriate.

Format Options

1-2-3 provides many format options. The most common are *Fixed, Currency, Comma, General,* and *Percent.* All but the *General* option allow you to specify the number of decimal places displayed.

Numeric values are always aligned with the right edge of the worksheet cell. If the column width is not sufficient to display the

Figure 21.21
Examples are provided to illustrate how the format options *Fixed, Currency, Comma, Percent,* and *General* display various numeric values in a column width of ten spaces.

Internal Value	Format Option	Displayed Value
1234	Fixed, 2 decimal places	1234.00
1234.567	Currency, 0 decimal places	$1,235
1234.567	General	1234.567
1234567	Comma, 0 decimal places	1,234,567
123456789	Comma, 0 decimal places	**********
.1234	Percent, 1 decimal place	12.3%

numeric value (including an extra space for the sign) in the specified format, asterisks appear across the width of the cell. Some examples are provided in Fig. 21.21 to illustrate the various formatting options. In each case it is assumed that the column width is set to ten spaces. The *Fixed* format sets the number of decimal places, the *Currency* format adds dollar signs and commas, the *Comma* format just adds commas, and the *Percent* format multiplies the internal value by 100 and adds a percent sign. Normally, numeric values are displayed using the *General* format. This displays the value to as many decimal places as possible.

Formatting for numeric values may be specified for the entire worksheet by adjusting the default format setting, or it may be specified for a particular range of the worksheet. Each of these approaches is illustrated.

Formatting Values Throughout the Entire Worksheet

Consider the numeric values in the example worksheet (Fig. 21.20). Most of these numbers represent dollar figures, and nearest dollar accuracy is sufficient for budgeting purposes. Therefore it is reasonable to change these numbers to the *Currency* format and to display zero decimal places.

Choose the menu option that allows you to change the global format setting:

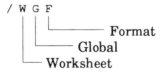

The worksheet is replace with the global settings table, and line 2 of the control panel lists the available format choices:

```
Fixed Sci Currency , General +/- Percent Date Text Hidden
```

Press C to select *Currency*. The prompt

```
Enter number of decimal places (0..15): 2
```

appears on line 2. Type

```
0
```

to replace the default value, 2. Press ⏎, and the worksheet changes (Fig. 21.22). Every numeric value in the worksheet is now preceded by a dollar sign, and commas are inserted in values where appropriate. Any future numeric values that are entered in the worksheet will also be displayed using *Currency* format.

Figure 21.22
The global format for numeric values is specified as *Currency* with zero decimal places.

```
A1: [W16] 'BUDGET EXPENDITURE BY YEAR AND MONTH                    READY

          A           B           C           D           E
1   BUDGET EXPENDITURE BY YEAR AND MONTH
2   ANNUAL INCOME      $30,000
3   ===================================================================
4   CATEGORY        PERCENTAGE      ANNUAL    QUARTERLY     MONTHLY
5   ===================================================================
6   HOUSING               $0      $9,000      $2,250        $750
7   FOOD                  $0      $6,000      $1,500        $500
8   TRANSPORTATION        $0      $3,000        $750        $250
9   OTHER                 $0     $12,000      $3,000      $1,000
10  ===================================================================
11
12
```

The only problem is that the *Currency* format is not appropriate for the percentages in column B. The *Percent* or *Fixed* format is more appropriate for these values.

■ *Keystroke Summary*

Adjust the format of all numeric values

Press: / W G F (F, C, P, or ,)

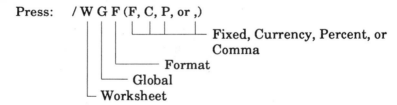

Fixed, Currency, Percent, or Comma

Format

Global

Worksheet

Type: *number of decimal places*

Press: ⏎

Formatting Values in a Given Range

Worksheets frequently require more than one display format for numeric values. When this is the case, the global worksheet format is set to the most common format as described in the previous section. Other formats for specific ranges of the worksheet are then set individually. To illustrate this idea, modify the display format for the budget category percentages to the *Percent* format.

Position the cell pointer to cell B6. Choose the menu option to define a display format for a given range:

/ R F

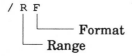

Format

Range

In response to the menu of format choices, press

P
└────── Percent

The prompt

```
Enter number of decimal places (0..15): 2
```

appears. Recall that the *Percent* format automatically multiplies the internally stored numeric value by 100 before displaying it. Thus it is not necessary to display any decimal places. Type

0

to replace the suggestion of two decimal places and press ⏎.
The next prompt,

```
Enter range to format: B6..B6
```

asks you to specify the range of cells that is to use the *Percent* format. Type

B6.B9

to overwrite the suggested range address of a single cell. (You want to change the format for cells B6 through B9.) Press ⏎. Note that the percentages are multiplied by 100 and a percent sign is displayed on the right (Fig. 21.23).

Notice the contents of cell B6 as displayed on line 1 of the control panel. The cell contains the numeric value .3, the special column width [W10] for 10 spaces wide, and the special format (P0) for *Percent* with 0 decimal places. The value .3 is displayed as 30% on the worksheet.

Figure 21.23
The range format for the numeric values representing budget category percentages are specified as *Percent* with zero decimal places. The notation (P0) for cell B6 confirms this range format specification.

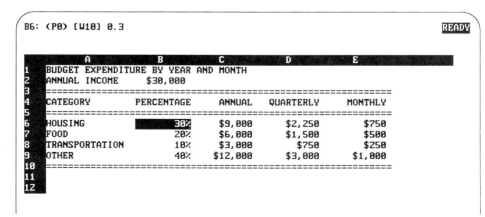

```
B6: (P0) [W10] 0.3                                                      READY

         A            B           C         D          E
1  BUDGET EXPENDITURE BY YEAR AND MONTH
2  ANNUAL INCOME     $30,000
3  ============================================================
4  CATEGORY       PERCENTAGE     ANNUAL    QUARTERLY    MONTHLY
5  ============================================================
6  HOUSING              30%      $9,000     $2,250        $750
7  FOOD                 20%      $6,000     $1,500        $500
8  TRANSPORTATION       10%      $3,000       $750        $250
9  OTHER                40%     $12,000     $3,000      $1,000
10 ============================================================
11
12
```

At this point you have successfully modified the worksheet created in Chapter 20 to appear as suggested in Fig. 21.1. However, the chapter tutorial is not complete. In the next section you will learn to modify the worksheet by erasing all or part of it. Save the worksheet on a disk. (If necessary, specify the drive and/or directory first.) That way if you make any mistakes erasing the worksheet, you'll be able to recover easily by retrieving it.

Press / F S to choose the menu option to save the worksheet and follow the procedures described in Chapter 20. Use a different file name, MODBUDGT, to indicate that this is a modified budget.

■ *Keystroke Summary*

Adjust the format of numeric values in a range

Press: / R F (F, C, P, or ,)

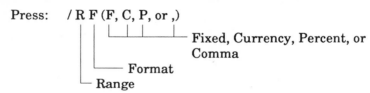

Type: *number of decimal places*

Press: ⏎

Type: *range address*

Press: ⏎

■ *What Can Go Wrong?*

1. The display format or number of decimal places is not correct.

Cause: You chose the wrong format option or typed the wrong number of decimal places.

Solution: Redo the procedure from the beginning. Carefully choose the format option and type the number of decimal places desired.

2. You changed the display format of the wrong group of cells.

Cause: You made a mistake in entering the range address.

Solution: Reset the display format of the incorrect group of cells to the default value. Choose the menu options as follows:

Press: / R F R

Type: Range address of incorrect cells

Press: ⏎ ■

Erasing
Worksheets

Erasing an Entire Worksheet

Sometimes you'll start a worksheet and simply want to throw away all that you've done and start over. 1-2-3 provides a handy menu feature for doing this. However, be extremely careful because once you have erased a worksheet from the screen, it's gone unless you have already saved it in a disk file.

If you haven't already done so, save the current worksheet in a disk file. Then erase the entire worksheet from the screen by choosing the *Erase* option from the *Worksheet* menu:

The following menu appears:

```
No Yes
```

Press Y for *Yes*, to erase the worksheet, or press N for *No*, to return to READY mode. Press Y. The contents, column width settings, label-prefixing, and numeric formatting of each cell in the worksheet is erased.

▪ *Keystroke*
Summary

Erase an entire worksheet

Press: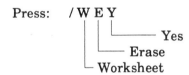

Erasing a Worksheet Range

More commonly, you'll want to erase only a portion of a worksheet. Earlier in this chapter, you learned to delete columns and rows from a worksheet. This feature allowed you to erase the contents of complete columns and rows and automatically moved succeeding columns and rows to fill in the vacant space. The *Range Erase* feature described in this section allows you to erase the contents of all cells in a range address (this may or may not be a complete column or row). This feature does not shift succeeding columns or rows; the erased cells are left blank.

To try this feature, retrieve the modified worksheet (/ F R), MODBUDGT, from disk. Position the cell pointer over cell B4. Choose the menu option to erase a range of the worksheet.

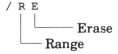

Figure 21.24

The contents of all cells in the range address B4..D7 are erased.

```
B6: (P0) [W10]                                               READY

           A          B          C          D          E
 1 BUDGET EXPENDITURE BY YEAR AND MONTH
 2 ANNUAL INCOME       $30,000
 3 ===================================================================
 4 CATEGORY                                              MONTHLY
 5 ==================                                ============
 6 HOUSING                                                    $0
 7 FOOD                                                       $0
 8 TRANSPORTATION       10%       $3,000      $750        $250
 9 OTHER                40%      $12,000    $3,000      $1,000
10 ===================================================================
11
12
```

You will be prompted to enter the range address you wish to erase:

        Enter range to erase: B4..B4

If you press ⏎, the contents of the highlighted cell, B4, will be erased. Instead, type

        B4.D7

to erase the contents of the cells in rows 4 to 7 and columns B to D. Press ⏎, and the range is erased (Fig. 21.24). This erases the contents and label-prefixing of each cell in the designated range. However, column width settings and display format settings remain intact. To see this, position the cell pointer to cell B6. Note that the contents are gone but the column width setting [W10] and display format (P0) are still associated with that cell.

Erasing worksheet ranges is a handy tool for modifying a worksheet, but extreme care must be taken. An error in entering a range address can cause major portions of a worksheet to be lost. A precaution taken by experienced 1-2-3 users is to periodically save the current worksheet in a disk file. Then you can recover from a major error by retrieving the most recently saved version of the worksheet and trying again.

■ *Keystroke Summary*

Erase a worksheet range

Press: / R E

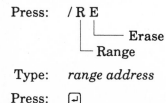

Type: *range address*

Press: ⏎

Exiting 1-2-3

This concludes the second 1-2-3 tutorial. To exit, press

There is no need to save the current worksheet, so type Y to confirm that you are ready to exit.

Summary

Function	Reference or Keystrokes	Page
Column width, set column	/ W C S, ⊟ or ⊟, ↵	343
Column width, set default	/ W G C, ⊟ or ⊟, ↵	341
Delete columns	/ W D C, range address, ↵	333
Delete rows	/ W D R, range address, ↵	336
Erase range	/ R E, range address, ↵	353
Erase worksheet	/ W E Y	353
Format menu options	Fixed, Currency, Percent, General, and Comma; Fig. 21.21	348
Format, set default	/ W G F, format option, decimal places, ↵	349
Format, set range	/ R F, format option, decimal places, ↵, range address, ↵	350
Insert columns	/ W I C, range address, ↵	338
Insert rows	/ W I R, range address, ↵	339
Label-prefix, set center	/ R L C, range address, ↵	346
Label-prefix, set left	/ R L L, range address, ↵	346
Label-prefix, set right	/ R L R, range address, ↵	345
Range menu options	Fig. 21.19	346
Retrieve file	/ F R, file name, ↵	331
Worksheet menu options	Fig. 21.4	334

Self-Test

1. Press _____ and then type or select the _____ to retrieve a file from disk.

2. Press _____ to delete the contents of selected rows.

3. Cell B8 contains the formula +A8/12. If row 7 is deleted from the worksheet, this formula is automatically converted to _____ and placed in cell B7.

4. Press _____ to insert blank columns into a spreadsheet.

5. When entering a column width using POINT mode, press _____ to increase the column width 1 unit and press _____ to decrease the column width 1 unit.

6. Press _____ to set the width of all columns in the worksheet.

7. Press _____ to align all labels in selected cells in the center of the cells.

8. Press _____ to set the display format of a selected range of numeric cells to *Fixed* format.

9. Press _____ to erase the current worksheet from memory.

10. Press _____ to erase the contents of the currently highlighted cell.

Exercises

1. Print the modified worksheet you created by following the tutorial in this chapter (Fig. 21.1) and submit it to your instructor.

2. Retrieve the college budget worksheet that you created in Chapter 20. Modify it so that it looks like the worksheet illustrated below. Delete any blank columns that you used for spacing. Set column A to 20 spaces and set all other columns to 12 spaces. Center the column headings ANNUAL, SEMESTER, and MONTH in their respective cells. Use formulas to compute the ANNUAL budget for the OTHER category and for all categories under SEMESTER and MONTH. Print a copy of the completed worksheet.

```
COLLEGE BUDGET
ANNUAL EXPENDITURE        $9,600.00
=============================================================
CATEGORY                  ANNUAL      SEMESTER      MONTH
=============================================================
TUITION                 $4,800.00    $2,400.00     $400.00
HOUSING                 $3,000.00    $1,500.00     $250.00
BOOKS                     $600.00      $300.00      $50.00
FRATERNITY                $300.00      $150.00      $25.00
CAR                       $300.00      $150.00      $25.00
OTHER                     $600.00      $300.00      $50.00
=============================================================
```

3. Retrieve the batting and slugging average worksheet that you created in Chapter 20. Modify it so that it looks like the worksheet illustrated below. Delete any extra columns that you used for spacing. Set column A to 20 spaces and set all other column widths

to 12 spaces. Align the column headings FIRST HALF, SECOND
HALF, and TOTAL with the right edge of their respective cells. Use
formulas to compute all TOTALS and AVERAGES. Print a copy of
the completed worksheet.

```
BATTING AVERAGE COMPUTATION
============================================================
RESULT               FIRST HALF SECOND HALF         TOTAL
============================================================
SINGLE                       8           4            12
DOUBLE                       2           2             4
TRIPLE                       2           0             2
HOME RUN                     1           1             2
OUT                         18          23            41
============================================================
TOTAL AT BATS               31          30            61
============================================================
BATTING AVERAGE          0.419       0.233         0.328
SLUGGING AVERAGE         0.710       0.400         0.557
```

·22

Some Worksheet Shortcuts

This chapter introduces the 1-2-3 features and commands that allow you to:

- use POINT mode to define range addresses
- use POINT mode to define cell addresses in formulas
- copy labels and numbers from one range address to another
- copy formulas from one range address to another
- move cell contents from one range address to another
- use 1-2-3 functions in cell formulas

Overview

In this chapter you will learn some handy shortcuts for specifying cell addresses and range addresses. Instead of typing a cell or range address, you can use the cursor keys to point to the desired address. This is easier and eliminates many mistakes.

You will also learn about the *Copy* and *Move* main menu options. These allow the contents of cells to be copied to other cells or to be moved to other cells. This saves time in creating worksheets. If a number of cells are to contain the same labels, numbers, or formulas, the labels, numbers, or formulas are entered once and "copied" to the other cells. Or, if part of the worksheet needs to be relocated, the cell contents are "moved" all at once to the new location.

Finally, you will learn to use some predefined functions in your formulas. Functions allow formulas to be simpler and perform more complex calculations.

Using Point Mode to Enter Addresses

Several times when you were prompted to enter a range address in Chapters 20 and 21, the mode indicator switched to POINT mode. This is to inform you that you can enter the range address by **pointing** to the desired range using the cursor control keys. Rather than pointing, you typed the range address, and the mode indicator changed to EDIT. Typing a range address is generally more difficult and subject to error, but it gave you valuable experience in dealing with range addresses. Now you are ready to learn the easy way— pointing!

Range Addresses

Begin the tutorial by retrieving (/ F R) the worksheet you saved at the end of Chapter 21 (Fig. 22.1). (If necessary, set the default drive and/ or directory first.) This worksheet is saved under the file name MODBUDGT. In this section you will learn about POINT mode by erasing parts of this worksheet. Specifically, you'll erase the boundary characters in row 3 and 5 and the formulas in range address C6..E9. Later, you'll restore this information using some shortcut methods.

Begin by erasing the boundary character labels in row 3 (range address A3..E3). Position the cell pointer on cell A3 and press

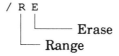

/ R E
       └──── Erase
   └──── Range

Figure 22.1
The tutorial begins with the MODBUDGT worksheet created in Chapter 21.

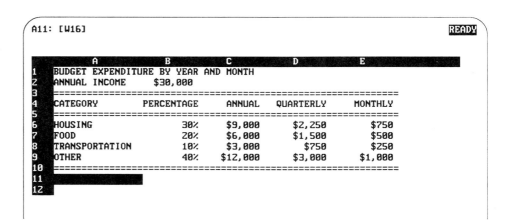

A11: [W16]   READY

	A	B	C	D	E
1	BUDGET EXPENDITURE BY YEAR AND MONTH				
2	ANNUAL INCOME	$30,000			
3	=============	=========	========	=========	========
4	CATEGORY	PERCENTAGE	ANNUAL	QUARTERLY	MONTHLY
5	=============	=========	========	=========	========
6	HOUSING	30%	$9,000	$2,250	$750
7	FOOD	20%	$6,000	$1,500	$500
8	TRANSPORTATION	10%	$3,000	$750	$250
9	OTHER	40%	$12,000	$3,000	$1,000
10	=============	=========	========	=========	========
11					
12					

Figure 22.2

After choosing the menu options / R E, you are prompted to point to the range address to be erased. Range address A3..A3 is automatically filled in and highlighted, since the cell pointer is on cell A3.

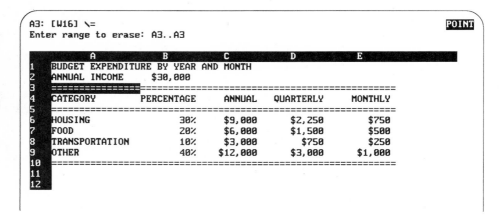

```
A3: [W16] \=
Enter range to erase: A3..A3                                    POINT

              A         B         C         D         E
1  BUDGET EXPENDITURE BY YEAR AND MONTH
2  ANNUAL INCOME      $30,000
3  ================
4  CATEGORY       PERCENTAGE     ANNUAL   QUARTERLY   MONTHLY
5  =============================================================
6  HOUSING               30%     $9,000     $2,250      $750
7  FOOD                  20%     $6,000     $1,500      $500
8  TRANSPORTATION        10%     $3,000       $750      $250
9  OTHER                 40%    $12,000     $3,000    $1,000
10 =============================================================
11
12
```

to choose the menu option to erase a range of the worksheet (Fig. 22.2). You are prompted to enter the range address to be erased. Since you positioned the cell pointer on A3, the range A3..A3 is automatically selected. The mode indicator is set to POINT.

In Chapter 21 you were instructed to type the range address to be erased; in this chapter you will use the cursor keys to point to it. Press ⊟. The range address changes to A3..B3, and the corresponding cells are highlighted. Press ⊟ three more times, and the range address A3..E3 will be highlighted and entered at the prompt (Fig. 22.3). Press ⏎ to accept the currently displayed range address, and the equals sign labels used to divide the table will be erased.

Notice that instead of typing the range address as in previous chapters, you are pointing to it. The cell highlighting gives you visual information that you are specifying the correct range. This reduces the chance of making a mistake in specifying a range address.

Figure 22.3

The worksheet looks like this after you press ⊟ four times to point to the range cells to be erased. Press ⏎, and the highlighted cells will be erased.

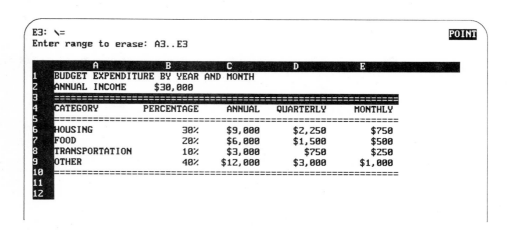

```
E3: \=
Enter range to erase: A3..E3                                    POINT

              A         B         C         D         E
1  BUDGET EXPENDITURE BY YEAR AND MONTH
2  ANNUAL INCOME      $30,000
3  =============================================================
4  CATEGORY       PERCENTAGE     ANNUAL   QUARTERLY   MONTHLY
5  =============================================================
6  HOUSING               30%     $9,000     $2,250      $750
7  FOOD                  20%     $6,000     $1,500      $500
8  TRANSPORTATION        10%     $3,000       $750      $250
9  OTHER                 40%    $12,000     $3,000    $1,000
10 =============================================================
11
12
```

Notice also that as you pointed to the range address, the first cell (A3) in the address was fixed. In many cases the cell highlighted by the cell pointer is automatically specified as a corner of the range. This initial corner is called an **anchor cell**. The cursor keys allow you to expand the range address from the anchor cell to the opposite corner. The automatic specification of the anchor cell is overcome by pressing (Esc) when you are prompted to point to the range address.

To illustrate the anchor cell concept, position the cell pointer on cell A1 and try to erase row 5 (range address A5..E5). Press / R E to select the range erase menu option. You'll be prompted to point to the range address starting with A1..A1. Press ⬇ to highlight the range in row 5. This is impossible because the range is automatically anchored with a corner in cell A1.

To free the anchor cell, press

(Esc)

Now press ⬇ four times to highlight cell A5. Notice that each time you press ⬇, the beginning cell of the range address (or anchor cell) changes. Press

. (period)

to fix the anchor cell as A5 (Fig. 22.4). Complete the erasure of row 5 by pressing ➡ four times to highlight the desired range. Press ⬅. Row 5 will be erased, and you will return to READY mode.

Generally, in using a command that asks you to point to a range address, it is easier to highlight a corner of the range address before you start. This becomes the anchor cell, and you only need to point to an opposite corner of the range address. But if you forget, simply press (Esc), and you may choose any cell as the anchor cell.

Figure 22.4

The cell pointer initially highlighted cell A1. This became the anchor cell of the range address. After you press (Esc), the anchor cell is released. A5 becomes the new anchor cell after you highlight it and press . (period).

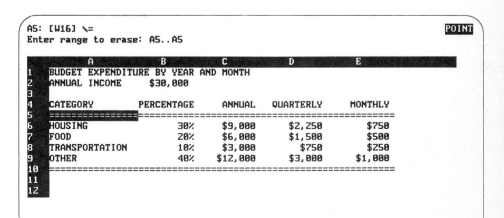

Figure 22.5
The cell pointer is
initially on cell E9.
You used ⊟ and ⊡
to highlight the range
address E9..C6. Press
⏎, and the
highlighted cells will
be erased.

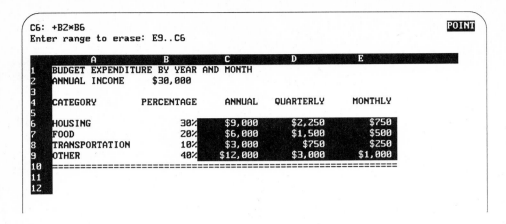

For additional practice and to prepare for the tutorial exercises
later in this chapter, erase the formulas in cells C6..E9. Point to this
range address in reverse order. Position the cell pointer on E9, the
lower right corner of the range. Press / R E to choose the *Range Erase*
menu option. E9 is the anchor cell. Press ⊟ twice and ⊡ three times
to specify the range address E9..C6 (Fig. 22.5). Press ⏎ to erase.

■ *Keystroke*
Summary

Point to a range address

Press: ⊟, ⊟, ⊡, or ⊡ to highlight a corner (or anchor) cell

Press: . (period)

Press: ⊟, ⊟, ⊡, or ⊡ to specify an opposite corner and
highlight the range of cells

Press: ⏎

Note: In some cases the cell containing the cell pointer is
automatically defined as the anchor cell, and you skip
Steps 1 and 2.

Cell Addresses

Pointing can also be used to reduce errors in typing cell addresses in
formulas. For example, the formula entered in cell C6 (before you
erased it) was +B2*B6. This formula can be entered by typing as you
did in Chapter 20 or by pointing first to cell B2 and then to cell B6.
Continue the tutorial by reentering this formula.

Position the cell pointer over cell C6. Type + to begin the formula,
and the mode indicator changes to VALUE. Instead of typing the cell
address, B2, press ⊟ once and press ⊡ four times to position the cell
pointer over B2 (Fig. 22.6). Notice that as soon as you press a cursor

Figure 22.6

After beginnning the formula for cell C6 with a plus sign, press ⊖ once and ⊤ four times to point to cell B2. Each time a new cell is highlighted, the cell address is inserted in the formula.

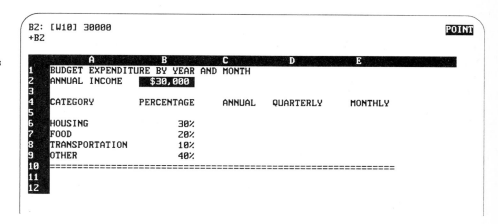

key, the mode indicator changes to POINT mode. Also notice that with each press of a cursor key, the address of the currently highlighted cell is inserted in the formula.

Once you have highlighted cell B2, continue the formula by typing an asterisk, the multiplication operator. The cell pointer returns to cell C6, and the mode indicator returns to VALUE (Fig. 22.7). The formula continues with another cell address. Press ⊖ once to highlight cell B6. The mode indicator returns to POINT mode, and the cell address B6 is inserted in your formula. Press ⏎ to complete the formula. The cell pointer returns to C6, the formula is entered in the cell, and the mode indicator changes to READY (Fig. 22.8).

When you are pointing to a cell address in a formula, there are two ways to complete the pointing process. One is to type a formula

Figure 22.7

After you type the multiplication operator (asterisk), the cell pointer returns to cell C6, the mode indicator returns to VALUE, and you may continue entering the formula.

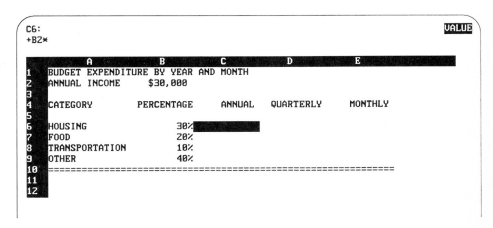

Figure 22.8
Continue the formula
for cell C6 by pointing
to cell B6 to insert this
cell address in the
formula. Pressing ⏎
completes the formula
and returns you to
READY mode as
illustrated.

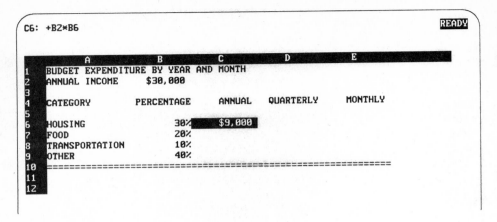

operator such as an arithmetic sign (+, −, *, or /) or a parenthesis; this
is appropriate when the formula is not complete and you wish to
continue. The other way to complete the pointing process is to press
⏎. This completes the formula and enters it in the worksheet cell.

For practice, enter the formula +C6/4 in cell D6. Position the cell
pointer over D6 and type +. Press ⊟ once to point to cell C6 (Fig. 22.9).
Type the division operator, /, to complete the pointing process.
Complete the formula by typing the divisor, 4, and pressing ⏎.
Use a similar procedure to enter the formula +C6/12 in cell E6 (Fig.
22.10).

Figure 22.9
After beginning the
formula for cell D6
with a plus sign,
press ⊟ once to point
to cell C6. This cell
address is entered in
the formula when you
continue by pressing
the division oper-
ator, /.

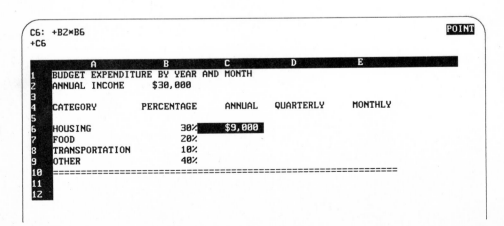

Figure 22.10
After you have reentered the formulas for ANNUAL, QUARTERLY, and MONTHLY HOUSING expense, the worksheet looks like this.

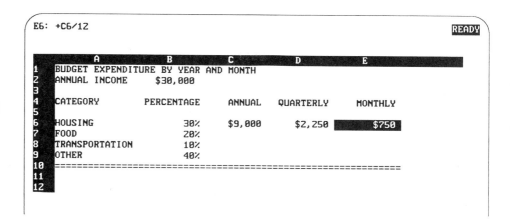

■ *Keystroke Summary*

Point to a cell address

Press: ⊖, ⊖, ⊙, or ⊙ to highlight the desired cell address

Press: ⏎ or a formula operator (for example: +, −,), (, *, or /) to place the cell address in the formula and return the cell pointer to the formula cell

---

■ *What Can Go Wrong?*

1. While typing a formula, you entered POINT mode and a cell address was inserted at the wrong place in the formula.

Cause: You pressed a cursor movement key while typing the formula.

Solution: Press Esc. This erases the address from the formula, returns the cell pointer to the formula cell, and returns the mode indicator to VALUE.

2. The formula is entered in the worksheet and you are returned to READY mode before the formula was complete.

Cause: You pressed ⏎ before the formula was complete. Remember that you may leave POINT mode by entering an arithmetic operator to continue the formula.

Solution: Position the cell pointer over the cell with the incomplete formula. Either reenter the formula from the beginning or press F2 to edit the formula. ■

Copying Data from One Part of the Worksheet to Another

One of the handiest features that 1-2-3 provides for quickly entering cell data is the *Copy* menu option. Press / and highlight the *Copy* option as illustrated in Fig. 22.11. This option allows you to **copy** the contents of a cell or range of cells to another location in the worksheet. This is a useful feature if you plan to enter repetitive information in

```
E6:  +C6/12                                                              MENU
Worksheet  Range  Copy  Move  File  Print  Graph  Data  System  Add-In  Quit
Copy a cell or range of cells
```

a worksheet. For example, in the tutorial worksheet, 15 cells contain the label \=. By using the *Copy* feature, this label is entered once and copied to the remaining cells. Also, similar formulas are used in the tutorial worksheet to calculate the ANNUAL, QUARTERLY, and MONTHLY expenditure in each category. These too can be entered once and copied to the corresponding cells in the remaining categories. Note also the *Move* menu option. This is similar to the *Copy* option and is discussed in the next section.

Copying Labels or Numbers

Press Esc to exit the menu system. Position the cell pointer on A3 and type the label

    \=

Press ↵ to restore the label in cell A3.

Copy this label to the remaining cells in row 3. Leave the cell pointer on A3 and press

    / C
      └── Copy

to select the *Copy* option from the menu. First, you'll be prompted to enter the range address to copy FROM (Fig. 22.12). Range address

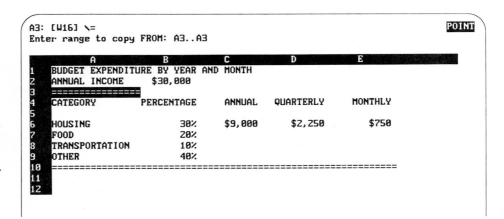

```
A3: [W16] \=                                                            POINT
Enter range to copy FROM: A3..A3

         A              B            C          D          E
 1  BUDGET EXPENDITURE BY YEAR AND MONTH
 2  ANNUAL INCOME        $30,000
 3  ================
 4  CATEGORY          PERCENTAGE    ANNUAL    QUARTERLY   MONTHLY
 5
 6  HOUSING               30%       $9,000     $2,250      $750
 7  FOOD                  20%
 8  TRANSPORTATION        10%
 9  OTHER                 40%
10  ==============================================================
11
12
```

Figure 22.13

Specify the range address B3..E3 to receive duplicate copies of the label contained in cell A3. It is necessary to specify an anchor cell, by positioning the cell pointer and typing a . (period), for the copy TO range.

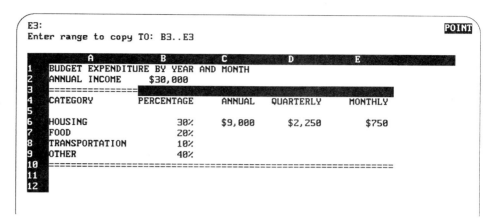

A3..A3 is automatically filled in, and A3 is fixed as the anchor cell. You're in POINT mode. Since you wish to copy only the label from this single cell, press ⏎ to accept the range address given.

Next, you'll be prompted to enter the range address to copy TO. You're in POINT mode, and there is no anchor cell fixed. Press → once to highlight cell B3. Press . (period) to fix B3 as the anchor cell, and press → three more times to highlight the range address B3..E3 (Fig. 22.13). Complete the copy operation by pressing ⏎. The label in the copy FROM range, A3..A3, is copied to all of the cells in the copy TO range, B3..E3.

There are a few considerations in using the copy feature. First, the copy FROM range does not have to contain the same number of cells as the copy TO range. In your example the copy FROM range contains one cell and the copy TO range contains four cells. Second, if the range addresses in the TO and FROM range contain the same number of cells, it is necessary to specify only the upper left corner of the TO range. This is illustrated below. Third, the range addresses may be typed rather than pointed to, though pointing seems easier and less prone to error.

For further practice, copy the labels in row 3 into row 5. Position the cell pointer on cell A3 and press / C to choose the *Copy* menu feature. In response to the prompt to enter the range to copy FROM, press → four times to point to the range A3..E3 (Fig. 22.14). Press ⏎, and the cell pointer returns to cell A3.

Next, enter the range to copy TO. Recall that the anchor cell is not fixed for the copy TO range. Press ↓ twice to point to cell A5 (the upper left corner of the copy TO range) as illustrated in Fig. 22.15. Since the copy FROM and copy TO range addresses contain the same number of cells, it is necessary to specify only the upper left corner of the copy TO range. Press ⏎ to complete the copy operation.

Figure 22.14
Specify the range
address A3..E3 to
copy the divider labels
in the cells of row 3 to
another range of the
worksheet.

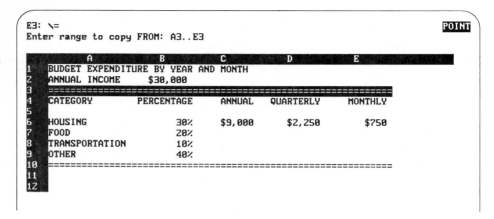

Copying Formulas

In copying labels and numbers an exact copy of the contents of cells in
the copy FROM range is made to the cells in the copy TO range. This
is not the case in copying formulas. The manner in which formulas are
copied depends on the way cell addresses in the formula are specified.
Cell addresses may be specified as **relative** or **absolute**. So far, all of
the formulas in the sample worksheet have been written using
relative cell addresses.

To understand the idea of a relative cell address, continue the
tutorial by copying the formulas in range D6..E6 to the range D7..E9.
Position the cell pointer on cell D6. Press / C to select the *Copy* menu
option. Press ⊡ once to select the copy FROM range D6..E6 and press
⏎. The cell pointer will return to cell D6. Now press ⊡ to position the
cell pointer on cell D7, and press . (period) to fix the anchor cell of the

Figure 22.15
Specify the upper left
corner of the range
address to receive a
copy of the divider
labels from row 3.
Press ⏎ to complete
the copy operation.

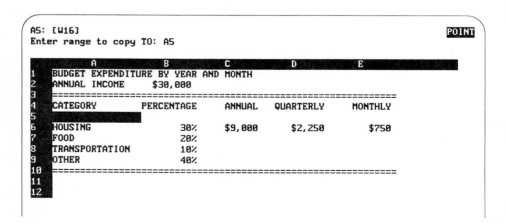

Figure 22.16

After you have copied the formulas in range address D6..E6 to D7..E9, the worksheet looks like this.

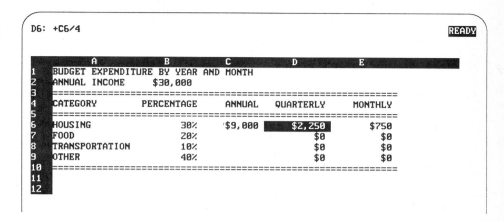

copy TO range. Press ⊟ once and ⬇ twice to select the copy TO range D7..E9. Press ⏎ to complete the copy operation (Fig. 22.16).

The formula in cell D6, +C6/4 is copied to cells D7, D8, and D9. Position the cell pointer on D7 (Fig. 22.17). Take a careful look at the copied formula, +C7/4. The cell address in the copied formula is adjusted so that it represents the same relative position to the cell being copied TO. That is, the formula in D6 specifies a relative cell location. It says to take the value in the cell one column to the left and divide it by 4. Therefore, when copied to cell D7, the formula is adjusted so that cell C7, which is one column to the left of D7, is divided by 4.

Likewise, the formulas in cells D8 and D9 are copied so that the cell one column to the left is divided by 4. Position the cell pointer on each of these cells and verify that each formula references the same relative cell location. All of these cells contain the value $0 because the cell one column to the left has no value at this time.

Figure 22.17

The formula in cell D6, +C6/4, involves a relative cell address. The formula takes the contents of the cell one column to the left and divides by 4. When copied to cell D7, the formula becomes +C7/4, since C7 is the cell one column to the left of D7.

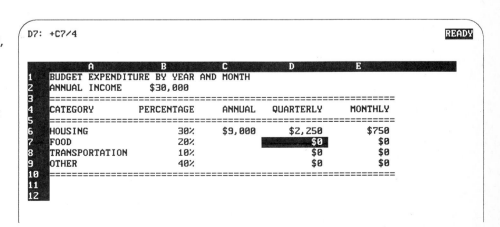

Similarly, the formula in cell E6, +C6/12, is copied to cells E7, E8, and E9 by adjusting the cell reference C6 so that it represents the same relative cell location to the cell being copied TO. That is, the value in E6 is computed by taking the value in the cell two columns to the left and dividing by 12. A similar formula appears in cells E7, E8, and E9. Position the cell pointer on each of these cells and verify that the formula contained in each represents the same relative calculation.

Position the cell pointer to cell C6. The formula is +B2*B6. In relative terms, the formula says to take the value in the cell one column to the left and four rows up and multiply it by the value in the cell one column to the left. If this formula is copied to cell C7 and adjusted to represent the same relative calculation, it becomes +B3*B7. This is not what is wanted, since cell B3 contains the label \=, rather than the annual income figure. Clearly, in some cases, copying the relative position of cells is useful, and in some cases it is not.

Ideally, to copy the formula +B2*B6 to cell C7, you want B2 to be copied exactly and B6 to be copied using the same relative position. This can be accomplished by declaring that B2 is an absolute cell address and that B6 is a relative cell address.

As you know, a cell address is composed of a column letter followed by a row number, for example, B2. This is treated as a relative cell address in copying a formula. If the column letter and the row number are each preceded by a $ sign, the cell address is treated as an absolute cell address in copying a formula. For example, $B$2 refers to cell location B2 but specifies that during a copy operation this cell address is to be treated as an absolute cell address and copied exactly.

Therefore to copy the formula in cell C6 to cells C7, C8, and C9 appropriately, the formula in cell C6 needs to be adjusted to read +$B$2*B6. That way, when the formula is copied, the cell address $B$2 is copied exactly, and the cell address B6 is adjusted to the correct relative position.

Edit the formula in cell C6. Position the cell pointer to cell C6 and press

F2

Press ⊟ so that the cursor is positioned anywhere under the cell address B2 in the formula. The additional $ signs can be typed, but 1-2-3 provides a function key to make a cell address absolute. This key can be used in EDIT mode as you are doing here or in POINT mode when you are pointing to a cell address. Press

F4

to convert the cell address B2 to $B$2 (Fig. 22.18). Press ⏎, and the revised formula is entered in cell C6.

Notice that converting this cell address from relative to absolute has no effect on the computation of the budgeted annual housing

Figure 22.18

Convert the cell address B2 to an absolute cell address $B$2 by editing the contents of C6. Move the edit cursor under cell B2 and press F4. The $ signs are inserted ahead of the column letter and row number.

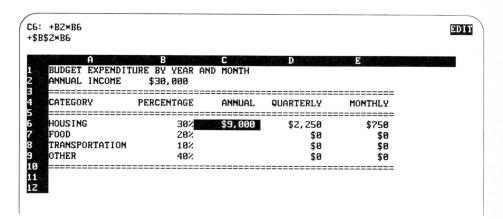

expenditure. The only reason you made the conversion is to use the *Copy* command to copy this formula to the other cells. However, the *Copy* command is so useful that you will want to design your formulas so that they may be easily and correctly copied.

Finally, you are ready to copy this formula to range address C7..C9. The cell pointer is positioned on cell C6. Press /C to choose the *Copy* menu option. Press ⏎ to accept the copy FROM range C6..C6. Press ↓ and . (period) to choose anchor cell C7 for the copy TO range. Press ↓ two times, and press ⏎ to complete the copy operation.

Now that the annual expenditure in each category is computed, the quarterly and monthly expenditures are filled in. Position the cell pointer on cell C7 (Fig. 22.19) and study the copied formula, +$B$2*B7. The absolute cell reference ($B$2) in cell C6 is copied exactly, and the

Figure 22.19

The formula in cell C6, +$B$2*B6, involves both an absolute cell address and a relative cell address. The formula takes the contents of absolute cell address B2 times the contents of the cell one column to the left. When copied to cell C7, the formula becomes +$B$2*B7. The absolute cell address is copied exactly, and the relative address is one column to the left of C7.

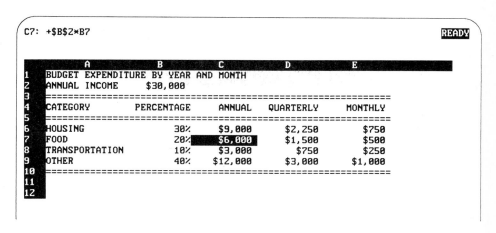

relative cell reference (B6) is adjusted to B7, the cell to the immediate left.

The *Copy* menu option is a 1-2-3 feature that is used over and over to create and modify worksheets quickly. The key to using this feature to copy formulas is to understand the appropriate use of the absolute and relative cell references.

■ Keystroke Summary

Copy cell contents

Press: / C
             └── Copy

Type or point: *range address to copy FROM*

Press: ↵

Type or point: *range address to copy TO*

Press: ↵

■ What Can Go Wrong?

1. You successfully pointed to the copy FROM range address, but when pointing to the copy TO range address, the cell pointer doesn't stay in one place so that you can highlight the correct range.

Cause: The copy FROM range address is automatically anchored using the cell address to which you pointed at the beginning of the copy operation. You must anchor the copy TO range address yourself.

Solution: Position the cell pointer at one corner of the copy TO range address. Press . (period) to fix this cell as an anchor. Now point to the desired range and press ↵.

2. You are editing the formula in cell C6 to make the reference to cell B2 an absolute address. The cell address is changed to B$2 or $B2 rather than $B$2 as expected.

Cause: You pressed F4 more than once. Each time F4 is pressed, the cell address changes among the forms: B2, $B$2, B$2, and $B2. The two unfamiliar forms are called mixed cell addresses.

Solution: With the EDIT cursor positioned under B2, continue to press F4 until the desired cell address is displayed. Press ↵.

3. After one of the copy operations, the worksheet is not as shown in the illustrations.

Cause: You incorrectly specified the copy FROM or copy TO range address. These range addresses should never overlap.

Solution: If there is not much damage, edit the contents of the incorrect cells by positioning the cell pointer and pressing F2. Otherwise, retrieve the file MODBUDGT and redo the tutorial. ■

Moving Data from One Part of the Worksheet to Another

Move is a main menu option to **move** the contents of cells from a given range to cells in another range. The cells in the move FROM range are erased after the contents are moved. This is almost identical to the *Copy* menu option, except that with the *Copy* option the cell contents of the FROM range are left as before rather than being erased. *Copy* is useful for duplicating cell labels, numbers, and formulas; *Move* is useful for rearranging the cells in a worksheet.

Position the cell pointer on cell C3. Press

/ M
└── Move

to choose the *Move* menu option. You will be prompted to enter the range of cells to move FROM. Press ⬇ seven times to highlight the range address C3..C10 (Fig. 22.20). Press ⏎ to accept the move FROM range.

Next, you'll be prompted to enter the move TO range. Press ➡ three times to specify F3 as the anchor cell of the move TO range (Fig. 22.21). As with the *Copy* command, it is enough to specify the upper

Figure 22.20

Specify the range address C3..C10 to move the contents of the cells in the ANNUAL column to another location on the worksheet.

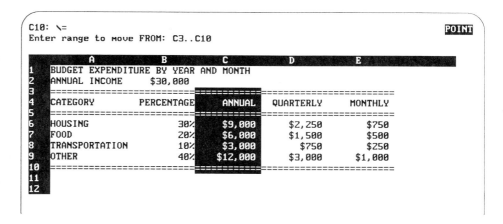

Figure 22.21

Specify the range address to receive the column of ANNUAL budget expenditures. It is enough to specify the upper left corner of the range.

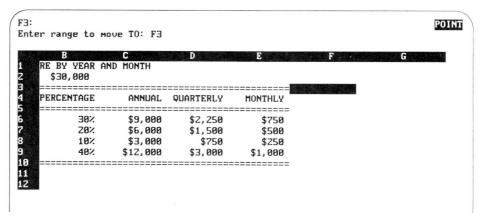

Figure 22.22
After the contents of the cells in the range C3..C10 are moved to column F of the worksheet, the cells in this range are erased.

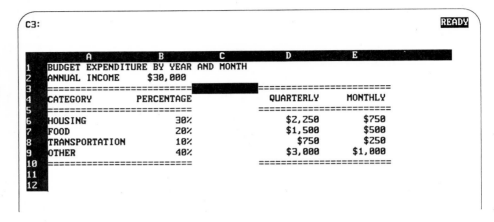

left corner of the TO range. Press ↵ to accept F3 as the upper left corner of the TO range.

The worksheet now appears as in Fig. 22.22. The contents of the move FROM range, C3..C10, are erased, and the labels, numbers, and formulas are moved to the move TO range, F3..F10. Move the cell pointer to column F and verify that the move has taken place.

Continue rearranging the columns by moving the MONTHLY column to column C. Position the cell pointer on cell E3. Press / M to select the *Move* menu option. Press ↓ seven times to highlight the move FROM range E3..E10, and press ↵. Press ← two times to highlight cell C3, the upper left corner of the move TO range, and press ↵. The contents of the cells in the MONTHLY column are moved to column C (Fig. 22.23).

The rearrangement can be completed by either moving the ANNUAL column (now in column F) to column E or deleting column

Figure 22.23
The cell contents of range address E3..E10 are moved to column C of the worksheet.

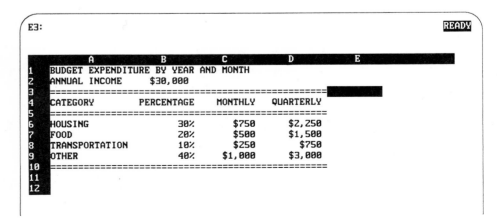

Figure 22.24
After you have deleted column E from the worksheet, Column F, containing the ANNUAL budget amount, moves over to fill in the vacant column. This completes the rearrangement of the worksheet columns.

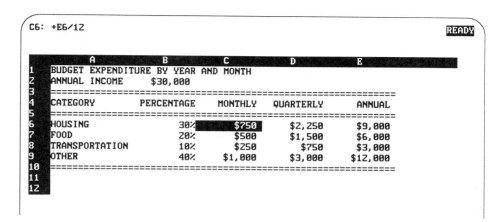

E. Use the latter approach, which you learned in Chapter 21. Position the cell pointer on any cell in column E and press / W D C to delete a column from the worksheet. Press ⏎ in response to the prompt to enter the range of columns to delete (Fig. 22.24).

The *Move* menu option is extremely useful in rearranging a worksheet. All formulas in the worksheet are automatically adjusted as appropriate. For example, notice the formulas in cells E6, D6, and C6, as given below:

```
E6:  +$B$2*B6
D6:  +E6/4
C6:  +E6/12
```

The formula in cell E6 is identical to the formula that used to be in cell C6, since the cells referenced are in the same location. The formulas in cells D6 and C6 are based on the ANNUAL budget expenditure and are updated to reflect the fact that the ANNUAL budget expenditure is now in column E.

■ *Keystroke Summary*

Move cell contents

Press: / M
                └── Move

Type or point: *range address to move FROM*

Press: ⏎

Type or point: *range address to move TO*

Press: ⏎

Functions

1-2-3 provides an extensive library of predefined procedures to perform certain calculations. These are called **functions** and are generally used in formulas. To illustrate the use of functions, you'll modify the tutorial worksheet to include a row of column totals in row 11.

Position the cell pointer on cell A11. Type the label

TOTAL

and press ⏎. Now position the cell pointer on cell C11 and consider entering a formula to total the monthly expenditures in each budget category. You could enter the formula +C6+C7+C8+C9. However, 1-2-3 provides a function called @SUM to simplify this formula.

All 1-2-3 functions begin with the @ sign and have a name that suggests the computation performed. @SUM is a function to sum the values in a list of cell range addresses. The form of the @SUM function listed in the 1-2-3 manual is

@SUM(*list*)

SUM is the name of the function, and *list* is the argument of the function; it is used in the 1-2-3 manual to refer to one or more range addresses. This function may be used in a cell formula. For example, the following formulas using @SUM are interpreted as follows:

Formula	Means
@SUM(C6..C9)	add the values in cells C6, C7, C8, and C9
@SUM(C6..C7,C8..C9)	same as above but the list contains two range addresses
@SUM(C6..C9)/2	same as above except the sum is divided by 2

Now enter the formula in cell C11. Type

@SUM(

and point to the range address. Press ⬆ five times to point to cell C6. Press . (period) to fix the anchor cell, and press ⬇ three times to highlight the range address C6..C9. Type

)

to complete the function, and press ⏎ to complete the formula (Fig. 22.25).

1-2-3 provides mathematical functions, logical functions, specialized cell functions, string functions, date and time functions, financial functions, and statistical functions. Some of the most commonly used functions are the statistical functions listed in Fig. 22.26. All of these

Figure 22.25
Use the built-in function @SUM(C6..C9) to add the MONTHLY budget expenditures.

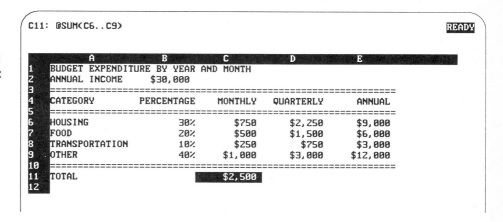

```
C11: @SUM(C6..C9)                                              READY

          A            B            C          D           E
1  BUDGET EXPENDITURE BY YEAR AND MONTH
2  ANNUAL INCOME       $30,000
3  =================================================================
4  CATEGORY          PERCENTAGE   MONTHLY    QUARTERLY    ANNUAL
5  =================================================================
6  HOUSING               30%        $750      $2,250      $9,000
7  FOOD                  20%        $500      $1,500      $6,000
8  TRANSPORTATION        10%        $250        $750      $3,000
9  OTHER                 40%      $1,000      $3,000     $12,000
10 =================================================================
11 TOTAL                          $2,500
12
```

functions require a list of range addresses as an argument and return a single computed value from the values in the cells of the listed ranges.

Some functions require more than one argument. For example, the function @PMT computes the periodic payment to pay back a sum of borrowed money. The form of the @PMT function listed in the 1-2-3 manual is

@PMT (*prin, int, term*)

This function requires three arguments: the initial amount of the loan (*prin*), the interest rate per period (*int*), and the number of payments required to pay back the loan (*term*). Each of these arguments is a single numeric value that may be entered directly or indirectly by referencing a cell containing the desired value.

Suppose the $30,000 annual income in the tutorial example is to be borrowed for 24 months at an interest rate of 0.015 per month. Use

Figure 22.26
These statistical functions are commonly used in 1-2-3 formulas. *Note: "List"* refers to a list of range addresses separated by commas.

Function	Calculates
@AVG(*list*)	the average value of all cells in the list
@COUNT(*list*)	the number of nonblank cells in the list
@MAX(*list*)	the largest value of all cells in the list
@MIN(*list*)	the smallest value of all cells in the list
@STD(*list*)	the standard deviation of the values of the cells in the list
@SUM(*list*)	the total value of all cells in the list
@VAR(*list*)	the variance of the values of the cells in the list

Figure 22.27
Use the built-in function @PMT(B2,.015,24) to calculate the monthly payment required to pay back a $30,000 loan (cell B2) at an interest rate of 0.015 per month, over a 24-month period.

```
E2:  @PMT(B2,0.015,24)                                          READY

            A          B          C          D          E
1     BUDGET EXPENDITURE BY YEAR AND MONTH
2     ANNUAL INCOME    $30,000              PAYMENT       $1,498
3     ===========================================================
4     CATEGORY        PERCENTAGE  MONTHLY   QUARTERLY     ANNUAL
5     ===========================================================
6     HOUSING            30%       $750      $2,250       $9,000
7     FOOD               20%       $500      $1,500       $6,000
8     TRANSPORTATION     10%       $250       $750        $3,000
9     OTHER              40%     $1,000      $3,000      $12,000
10    ===========================================================
11    TOTAL                       $2,500
12
```

the payment function to compute the monthly payment. Position the cell pointer on cell D2. Type

PAYMENT

and press ⏎ to enter a cell label. Now position the cell pointer on cell E2. Type

@PMT(B2,.015,24)

and press ⏎ (Fig. 22.27). The value of the first argument, the amount of the loan, is found in cell B2. The other two arguments, interest rate and number of payments, are entered directly. The resulting monthly payment is displayed in cell E2.

Formulas involving functions are copied to other cells just like any formula. For example, follow the usual procedure to copy the formula in cell C11, @SUM(C6..C9), to cells D11 and E11. Position the cell pointer on cell C11. Press / C to choose the Copy menu option. Press ⏎ to accept the copy FROM range address C11..C11. Press →, . (period), and → to highlight the copy TO range address D11..E11. Press ⏎.

Position the cell pointer to cell D11 (Fig. 22.28) and study the copied formula. Notice that the range address for the @SUM function, D6..D9, has the same relative position to cell D11, since both C6 and C9 in the formula copied FROM are relative cell addresses.

This concludes the third tutorial. Save the current worksheet as FINALBUD. (If necessary, set the default drive and/or directory first.) Then exit 1-2-3.

■ **What Can Go Wrong?**

1. You typed a function and pressed ⏎, and 1-2-3 beeped and put you in EDIT mode.

Cause: Something is wrong with the function: a misspelled name, an incorrect number of arguments, a blank space somewhere, or a missing parenthesis.

Solution: Use the EDIT mode keys to correct the function and press ⏎. ■

Figure 22.28
Copying formulas involving functions follows the same rules as copying any type of formulas. The formula in cell C11, @SUM(C6..C9), uses relative cell addresses. Thus when you copy it to D11 and E11, the cell addresses are adjusted to represent the same relative positions.

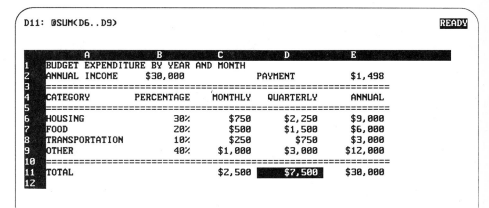

```
D11:  @SUM(D6..D9)                                              READY

           A           B           C           D           E
1    BUDGET EXPENDITURE BY YEAR AND MONTH
2    ANNUAL INCOME     $30,000             PAYMENT        $1,498
3    ==================================================================
4    CATEGORY          PERCENTAGE  MONTHLY   QUARTERLY     ANNUAL
5    ==================================================================
6    HOUSING                30%      $750      $2,250       $9,000
7    FOOD                   20%      $500      $1,500       $6,000
8    TRANSPORTATION         10%      $250        $750       $3,000
9    OTHER                  40%    $1,000      $3,000      $12,000
10   ==================================================================
11   TOTAL                          $2,500     $7,500      $30,000
12
```

Summary

Function	Reference or keystrokes	Page
Absolute cell address	F4	370
Copy cell contents	/ C, range address FROM, ↵, range address TO, ↵	366
Functions, built-in	—	376
Functions, statistical	Fig. 22.26	377
Move cell contents	/ M, range address FROM, ↵, range address TO, ↵	373
Point, complete	↵	364
Point, continue formula	Operator: + − * / ( )	364
Point, fix anchor cell	. (period)	361
Point, free anchor cell	Esc	361
Point, keys	←, →, ↑, ↓	360
Relative cell address	—	368

Self-Test

1. In pointing to a range address, the corner cell that remains fixed is called the _____ cell.

2. Press _____ to point to a cell 1 column to the right and press _____ to point to a cell 1 row up.

3. Press _____ to fix the anchor cell, and press _____ to free the anchor cell.

4. Many commands requiring a range address fix the location of the anchor cell at the position of the _____ when the command is activated.

5. When pointing to a cell address in a formula, press _____ to complete the formula and press _____ to continue the formula.

6. If the copy FROM range is A1..E1 and the copy TO range is specified as B3, the implied copy TO range is _____.

7. In EDIT mode, press _____ to convert the cell address above the cursor to an absolute cell address.

8. 1-2-3 functions begin with the _____ character.

9. The values contained in parentheses after the function name are called _____.

10. The formula _____ computes the sum of cells C3 through C9, inclusive.

Exercises

1. Print the worksheet you created by following the tutorial in this chapter (Fig. 22.28) and submit it to your instructor.

2. Retrieve the modified college budget worksheet that you created in Chapter 21. Erase part of the worksheet so that it looks like the one displayed below. Use POINT mode to define range and cell addresses.

```
COLLEGE BUDGET
ANNUAL EXPENDITURE      $9,600.00
================================================================
CATEGORY                ANNUAL     SEMESTER     MONTH

TUITION                $4,800.00
HOUSING                $3,000.00
BOOKS                    $600.00
FRATERNITY               $300.00
CAR                      $300.00
OTHER
```

Use the shortcuts described in this chapter to create and modify this worksheet so that it looks like the worksheet illustrated below. Enter cell formulas for SEMESTER and MONTH tuition. Enter a cell formula to compute the amount of money left over for OTHER expenses using the @SUM function. Complete the worksheet using the *Copy* command to duplicate cell information and using the *Move* command to rearrange the columns. Use the @SUM function to compute column totals. Print a copy of the completed worksheet.

```
COLLEGE BUDGET
ANNUAL EXPENDITURE      $9,600.00
=============================================================
CATEGORY                MONTH     SEMESTER     ANNUAL
=============================================================
TUITION                $400.00   $2,400.00   $4,800.00
HOUSING                $250.00   $1,500.00   $3,000.00
BOOKS                   $50.00     $300.00     $600.00
FRATERNITY              $25.00     $150.00     $300.00
CAR                     $25.00     $150.00     $300.00
OTHER                   $50.00     $300.00     $600.00
=============================================================
TOTALS                 $800.00   $4,800.00   $9,600.00
```

> 3. Retrieve the modified batting and slugging average worksheet that you created in Chapter 21. Erase part of the worksheet so that it looks like the one displayed below. Use POINT mode to define range and cell addresses.

```
BATTING AVERAGE COMPUTATION
=============================================================
RESULT              FIRST HALF SECOND HALF        TOTAL
=============================================================
SINGLE                   8          4
DOUBLE                   2          2
TRIPLE                   2          0
HOME RUN                 1          1
OUT                     18         23
=============================================================
TOTAL AT BATS
=============================================================
BATTING AVERAGE
SLUGGING AVERAGE
```

> Use the shortcuts described in this chapter to create and modify this worksheet so that it looks like the worksheet illustrated below. Use the @SUM function in all formulas computing totals. Enter a formula for TOTAL singles and copy it for each type of batting result. Enter a formula for TOTAL AT BATS, BATTING AVERAGE, SLUGGING AVERAGE, and OVER TEAM AVERAGE for the FIRST HALF. Copy these formulas all at once to the SECOND HALF and TOTAL columns. Format the cells in the new rows with the *Fixed* format with three decimal places.

```
BATTING AVERAGE COMPUTATION
============================================================
RESULT               FIRST HALF SECOND HALF        TOTAL
============================================================
SINGLE                    8           4             12
DOUBLE                    2           2              4
TRIPLE                    2           0              2
HOME RUN                  1           1              2
OUT                      18          23             41
============================================================
TOTAL AT BATS            31          30             61
============================================================
BATTING AVERAGE        0.419       0.233          0.328
SLUGGING AVERAGE       0.710       0.400          0.557
OVER TEAM AVERAGE      0.119      -0.067          0.028

TEAM AVERAGE           0.300
```

■23
Creating Worksheet Graphs

This chapter introduces the 1-2-3 features and commands that allow you to:

- create bar charts, line graphs, and pie charts based on worksheet data
- view these graphs on the screen
- add titles, axis labels, and legends to the graphs
- save a graph for printing
- learn additional graph features

Overview

The program name, 1-2-3, contains a double meaning. On one hand, the program is as easy to use as counting to 3. On the other hand, the program provides three major functions. The first three tutorials introduced the first and most important function, the use of 1-2-3 as an **electronic spreadsheet**. This chapter introduces the second function, the use of 1-2-3 as a **graphing** program. The third function, the use of 1-2-3 as a **data management** program, will not be covered in this book. *Graphing requires a computer system with graphics capability and 1-2-3 configured to use this capability.* Ask for help if you're not sure your system has this capability.

Figure 23.1
Create this worksheet
for the graphing
tutorial.

```
A10: [W24]                                                           READY

            A              B        ·C         D           E
 1  QUARTERLY REVENUE/COST PROJECTION:
 2                       QTR 1     QTR 2     QTR 3      QTR 4
 3  SALES (units)         100       200       150        80
 4
 5  REVENUES ($5/unit)   $500     $1,000     $750       $400
 6
 7  FIXED COSTS ($100/qtr)  $100     $100     $100       $100
 8  VARIABLE COSTS ($3/unit) $300    $600     $450       $240
 9  TOTAL COSTS          $400      $700      $550       $340
10
```

The graphing tutorial in this chapter is based on the worksheet
displayed in Fig. 23.1. This worksheet provides a quarterly projection
of revenues and costs based on a sales forecast (row 3). Revenues (row
5) are computed by multiplying the sales forecast by the selling price
($5 per unit). The costs include a fixed component ($100 per quarter)
and a variable component computed by multiplying the sales forecast
by the variable cost ($3 per unit). The total costs (row 9) are computed
by adding the fixed and variable components.

Begin the tutorial by creating this worksheet; refer to the fundamentals covered in Chapters 20–22. If you have difficulty, use the
steps outlined below. Keystrokes required to select appropriate menu
options are listed in parentheses.

1. Enter labels in the following cells:

   A1: QUARTERLY REVENUE/COST PROJECTION:

   A3: SALES (units)

   A5: REVENUES ($5/unit)

   A7: FIXED COSTS ($100/unit)

   A8: VARIABLE COSTS ($3/unit)

   A9: TOTAL COSTS

   B2: QTR 1

   C2: QTR 2

   D2: QTR 3

   E2: QTR 4

2. Enter numbers in the following cells:

    B3: 100

    C3: 200

    D3: 150

    E3: 80

    B7: 100

3. Enter formulas in the following cells:

    B5: 5*B3

    B8: 3*B3

    B9: +B7+B8

4. Copy the contents of cells B5..B9 to cells C5..E9 (/ C)

5. Set the global column width to 12 (/ W G C)

6. Set the column width of A to 24 (/ W C S)

7. Set the format of B5..E9 to *Currency* with 0 decimal places (/ R F)

8. Align the labels in B2..E2 with the right edge of the cell (/ R L R)

9. Save the worksheet, using the file name GRAPHEX (/ F S). If necessary, set the default drive and/or directory first.

Types of Graphs

A **graph** is a way of visually representing numeric information. For example, row 5 of the tutorial worksheet contains revenue values for each quarter of the upcoming year. These may be pictured as a **line graph**, a **bar graph**, or a **pie chart** (Fig. 23.2).

The line graph and the bar graph are graphs in which the horizontal axis (X-axis) contains a label to indicate the quarter represented and the vertical axis (Y-axis) contains a point or bar proportional to the numeric value represented. The pie chart provides a label (similar to the X-axis label) and a slice of pie proportional to the numeric value in each quarter. All of these graphs allow the viewer to visually observe the quarters with large or small revenues and the size of the differences.

Though 1-2-3 provides the ability to create other types of graphs, only these three types are discussed in the tutorial.

Figure 23.2
Three types of graphs
are used to represent
quarterly revenues.
(a) line graph, (b) pie
chart, (c) bar graph.

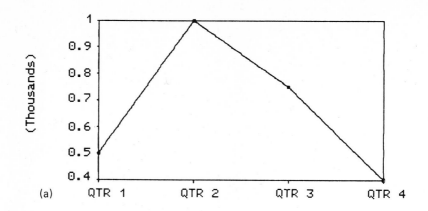

(a)

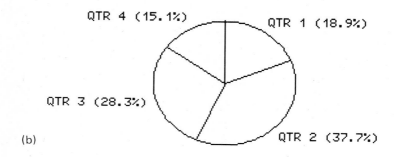

(b)

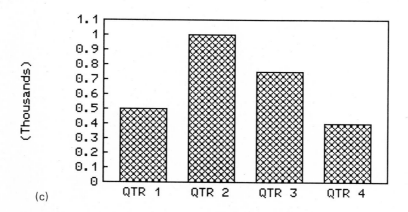

(c)

Creating Graphs

Creating graphs with 1-2-3 begins with the creation of a worksheet containing the data to be graphed; if you have not already done so, create the worksheet shown in Fig. 23.1. The next step is to select the primary menu option containing the graphing functions. With the cell pointer in any position, press

```
/ G
  └── Graph
```

Line 2 of the control panel lists the available graphing menu options, and the worksheet is replaced by a table listing the current graph settings (Fig. 23.3). This menu will be called the **Graph menu**.

The *Graph* menu is a "sticky" menu. When you select an option from this menu, you'll return to the menu rather than to READY mode as you did with previous menus. The only way to leave the *Graph* menu and return to READY mode is to select the menu option *Quit*. The *Undo* feature is not available until you return to READY mode.

Press ⊡ to highlight each of the menu options and read the descriptions on line 3. Compare these with the descriptions in Fig. 23.4 to get an idea of what graphing functions are available. Leave the *Graph* menu displayed as you continue the tutorial.

▪ *Keystroke Summary*

Access the *Graph* menu

```
Press:   / G
            └── Graph
Select:  one or more Graph menu options
Press:   Q
            └── Quit
```

Figure 23.3
Line 2 lists the graphing options available in 1-2-3 and the table displays the current graph settings. Select *Quit* to return to READY mode.

```
A10: [W24]                                                          MENU
Type X A B  C D E  F  Reset  View  Save  Options  Name  Group  Quit
Line  Bar  XY  Stack-Bar  Pie
                        ── Graph Settings ──
  Type: Line                   Titles: First
                                       Second
  X:                                   X axis
  A:                                   Y axis
  B:
  C:                                          Y scale:    X scale:
  D:                                   Scaling Automatic  Automatic
  E:                                   Lower
  F:                                   Upper
                                       Format  (G)        (G)
  Grid: None         Color: No         Indicator Yes      Yes

    Legend:              Format:   Data labels:        Skip: 1
  A                      Both
  B                      Both
  C                      Both
  D                      Both
  E                      Both
  F                      Both

05-Jan-90  01:09 PM                                      CAPS
```

Menu Choice	Provides Options for
Type	specifying the type of graph to draw
X	specifying the labels or values for the X-axis
A–F	specifying one to six sets of values to be represented on the Y-axis
Reset	clearing previously specified graph settings
View	viewing the currently specified graph
Save	saving the currently specified graph for later printing
Options	enhancing the appearance of a graph
Name	naming and saving multiple graph specifications as a part of the worksheet
Group	specifying the X values and all sets of data values (A–F) at once
Quit	returning to READY mode

Defining Values to Graph

The first step in creating a graph is to define a range address that contains a set of numeric values to be represented on the graph. The first value in the range is graphed in the first graph position, the second value in the second position, and so on. Up to six sets of values (named A, B, C, D, E, F) may be represented on a single line graph or bar graph (this is illustrated later). The pie chart may represent only one set of values.

To define data set A to be the quarterly revenue values, press

A
└───── A (Set A)

The worksheet returns to the screen, and you are prompted to define the range address containing the numeric values to be graphed:

```
Enter first data range: A10
```

Use POINT mode to define the range address containing the quarterly revenues; highlight cell B5 using the cursor keys, press . (period) to fix the anchor cell, and highlight the range address B5..E5 (Fig. 23.5). Press ⏎.

Figure 23.5

The quarterly revenue values in range address B5..E5 are the first set of values (set A) on the graph.

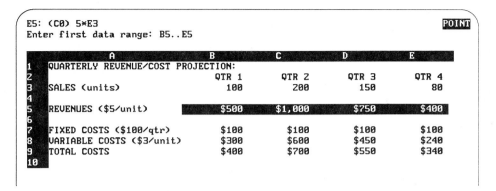

```
E5: (C0) 5*E3                                              POINT
Enter first data range: B5..E5
```

	A	B	C	D	E
1	QUARTERLY REVENUE/COST PROJECTION:				
2		QTR 1	QTR 2	QTR 3	QTR 4
3	SALES (units)	100	200	150	80
4					
5	REVENUES ($5/unit)	$500	$1,000	$750	$400
6					
7	FIXED COSTS ($100/qtr)	$100	$100	$100	$100
8	VARIABLE COSTS ($3/unit)	$300	$600	$450	$240
9	TOTAL COSTS	$400	$700	$550	$340
10					

The graph settings table indicates that data set A is contained in range address B5..E5 of the worksheet (the four numeric values 500, 1000, 750, and 400). These are used to position points on a line graph, to determine the height of bars on a bar graph, and to determine the angle width on a pie chart.

■ *Keystroke Summary*

Define values to graph

From the *Graph* menu (/ G):

Press: A or B or C or D or E or F   Six data sets

Type or point: *range address*

Press: ⏎

Defining Value Identifiers

The second step is to define a range address that contains a set of labels or numeric values that are used to identify the values on the graph. The first identifier is associated with the first value graphed, the second identifier with the second value, and so on. These identifiers appear on the X-axis of a line graph or bar graph and outside the wedges on a pie chart.

The column labels on the tutorial worksheet, QTR 1, QTR 2, QTR 3, and QTR 4, provide a convenient set of identifiers for the values to be graphed. To select these, press

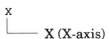

X   X (X-axis)

Figure 23.6
The column labels in range address B2..E2 are identifiers for the data values on the graph.

```
E2: "QTR 4                                                          POINT
Enter x-axis range: B2..E2

              A              B          C          D          E
1   QUARTERLY REVENUE/COST PROJECTION:
2                           QTR 1      QTR 2      QTR 3      QTR 4
3   SALES (units)            100        200        150         80
4
5   REVENUES ($5/unit)      $500     $1,000       $750       $400
6
7   FIXED COSTS ($100/qtr)  $100       $100       $100       $100
8   VARIABLE COSTS ($3/unit) $300      $600       $450       $240
9   TOTAL COSTS             $400       $700       $550       $340
10
```

The worksheet returns, and you are prompted as follows:

    Enter X axis range: A10

Use POINT mode to enter the range address B2..E2 (Fig. 23.6) and press ⏎.

You have now defined QTR 1 as the identifier for 500, QTR 2 as the identifier for 1000, and so on. The graph settings table indicates that the X labels are in range address B2..E2.

■ *Keystroke Summary*

Define value identifiers

From the *Graph* menu (/ G):

> Press: X
>   └─ X-axis or pie chart labels

> Type or
> point: *range address*

> Press: ⏎

Viewing the Graph

Once you have defined the values to graph and a set of identifiers, press

> V
> └──── View

to display the graph on the screen. The graph settings table disappears, and a line graph (Fig. 23.2a) fills the entire screen. 1-2-3 automatically defines a scale for the Y-axis and represents the revenues and associated identifiers on the graph. When you have finished inspecting the graph, press any key, and you're back to the *Graph* menu.

Your computer system must have graphics capability to display graphs on the screen. You may create and print graphs without this capability, but you will not be able to use the *View* feature.

■ *Keystroke Summary*

View a graph

From the *Graph* menu (/ G):

Press: V
           └── View

Press: *Any key*

Selecting the Graph Type

The numeric values in the data set may be represented by using several different types of graphs. The line graph obtained in the last section is the default type as indicated in the graph settings. Press

T
└──── Type

to select another type of graph. Line 2 of the control panel provides the following choices:

```
Line Bar XY Stack-Bar Pie
```

Press P to select a pie chart.

To see the new graph, press V. The quarterly revenues are now displayed as a pie chart (Fig. 23.2b). Press any key to return to the *Graph* menu.

Continue the tutorial by changing to a bar graph; press T B. Press V to view the bar graph on the screen (Fig. 23.2c). This is probably the most visually informative graph for this data set. Press a key to return to the *Graph* menu. The *View* feature allows you to look at several types of graphs and select the most informative.

You will be given the opportunity to explore the other graph types later in this chapter.

■ *Keystroke Summary*

Select a graph type

From the *Graph* menu (/ G):

Press: T (L or B or P)

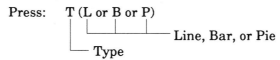

Defining Multiple Sets of Values to Graph

It was pointed out earlier that up to six sets of values may be represented on a single line graph or bar graph. This is illustrated below by graphing the quarterly total costs along with the quarterly revenues.

Data set A is defined as the quarterly revenues. Press

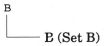

to define a set of numeric values for data set B. In response to the prompt

```
Enter second data range: A10
```

use POINT mode to select range address B9..E9 (Fig. 23.7). Press ⏎. Data set B now contains the four total cost values 400, 700, 550, and 340, corresponding to the X identifiers QTR 1, QTR 2, QTR 3, and QTR 4, respectively.

Press V to view the bar graph with two sets of data values (Fig. 23.8). The single bar in Fig. 23.2c is replaced with a pair of bars, one for each data set defined. Data set A (revenues) is the left bar, and data set B (total costs) is the right bar. This type of graph is useful to compare sets of numeric values. Press any key to return to the *Graph* menu.

Four additional data sets may be defined by selecting menu options C, D, E, and F.

Figure 23.7
The quarterly total costs in range address B9..E9 are the second set of values (set B) on the graph.

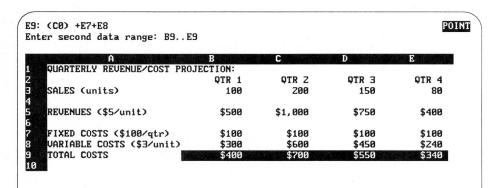

Figure 23.8
Quarterly revenues
(left bar) and quarterly
total costs (right bar)
are displayed side by
side on the same bar
graph.

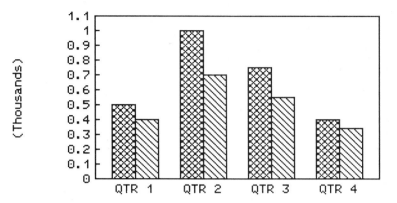

■ *What Can Go Wrong?*

1. You pressed V to view a graph, and the computer beeped and the screen went blank.

Cause: You have not defined a set of data values to graph.

Solution: Press any key to return to the *Graph* menu. Press A to define a set of data values to graph.

2. Your graph appears to have the wrong data values when compared to the illustrations.

Cause: You pointed to the wrong range address when defining the A or B data set. If the range address includes any labels, these are graphed as a numeric value of 0.

Solution: Press any key to return to the graphing menu options. Select menu option A or B as appropriate, and correct the range address. If the anchor cell is wrong, press [Esc] and define the complete range address. If the anchor cell is correct, use the cursor keys to highlight the appropriate range. Press [↵] and view the graph again.

3. You selected the XY graph type, and when you viewed the graph, all of the points are on the Y-axis.

Cause: The XY graph is similar to the line graph except that the values in the X range must be numeric and are positioned on the X-axis according to their numeric value. In the tutorial the X range contains labels. These labels are assigned the value 0, and thus all points on the graph are on the Y-axis.

Solution: Press any key to return to the graphing menu options. Select menu option T to change the *Type*. The XY graph is not appropriate for the X range specified. ■

Labeling Graphs

The graphs created in the previous section are useful for seeing relationships between numeric values, but they are not ready to show to anyone else. They need to be labeled so that the viewer will know what is represented. 1-2-3 provides a number of menu options for labeling and improving the appearance of graphs.

These menu options are accessed through the graphing menu choice called *Options*. Press

Line 2 of the control panel (Fig. 23.9) displays a list of these options. This is also a "sticky" menu and will be called the **Graph Options menu**. Press ⊡ to highlight each menu option and read the description on line 3 to familiarize yourself with some of the choices available. To return to the *Graph* menu, select the option *Quit*.

In this section of the tutorial you will label the previously created graph so that it appears as in Fig. 23.10.

■ *Keystroke Summary*

Access the *Graph Options* menu

From the *Graph* menu (/ G):

Press: O
              └── Options

Select: *one or more Graph Options choices*

Press: Q
              └── Quit

Figure 23.9
Line 2 of the control panel lists the menu choices in the *Graph Options* menu. These options are used to label and enhance the appearance of a graph.

```
A10: [W24]                                                              MENU
Legend  Format  Titles  Grid  Scale  Color  B&W  Data-Labels  Quit
Create legends for data ranges
```

Figure 23.10
The bar chart in Fig. 23.8 is finished by including a title, axis labels, and a legend.

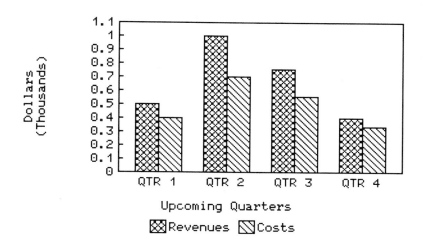

Titles and Axis Labels

Begin by placing a title at the top of the graph. From the *Graph Options* menu, press

```
T F
 |  └──────── First
 └────── Titles
```

to define the first (of possibly two) line of the title. In response to the prompt

```
Enter first line of graph title:
```

type

```
Quarterly Revenue/Cost Projection
```

Press ⏎ to return to the *Graph Options* menu.
Next, specify a label for the Y-axis. Press

```
T Y
 |  └──────── Y-axis
 └────── Titles
```

Answer the prompt

```
Enter Y axis title:
```

by typing

```
Dollars
```

Press ⏎ to complete this process.
Similarly, define the X-axis label by pressing

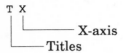

and typing

```
Upcoming Quarters
```

in response to the prompt. Press ⏎. All of the titles and labels specified
are listed in the graph settings table.

View the graph to confirm that the changes have taken place.
Press Q (for *Quit*) to return to the *Graph* menu. Press V to view the
graph. The graph now includes a one-line title, a Y-axis label, and an
X-axis label as in Fig. 23.10 (the legend at the bottom has not been
specified yet). Press any key to return to the *Graph* menu.

Define graph title and axis labels

■ *Keystroke*
Summary

From *Graph Options* menu (/ G O):

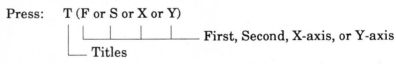

Type: *description*

Press: ⏎

Legends

Continue the tutorial by defining a **legend** to indicate the meaning of
each type of bar on the graph. Press O to return to the *Graph Options*
menu. Press

```
L
```
┗━━━ Legend

to specify a graph legend. Line 2 of the control panel displays

```
A B C D E F Range
```

so that you may choose a legend for one of the data sets. Press A to
specify a legend for the quarterly revenue data. In response to the
prompt

```
Enter legend for first data range:
```

type

    Revenues

Press ⏎, and the legend for data set A is defined.

    Follow a similar procedure to create a legend for data set B. Press L B and type

    Costs

in response to the prompt. Press ⏎. The specified legends are listed in the graph settings table.

    Now view the graph again. Press Q to return to the *Graph* menu followed by V to view the currently defined graph. The graph now includes the legend as in Fig. 23.10.

▪ *Keystroke Summary*

Define graph legend

From the *Graph Options* menu (/ G O):

Press: L (A or B or C or D or E or F)

                              — Six data sets
            — Legend

Type: *description*

Press: ⏎

▪ *What Can Go Wrong?*

1. You're looking for the *View* option to display your graph but can't seem to find it.

Cause: Remember that the *Graph* menu and *Graph Options* menu are "sticky" menus. When an option is selected from these menus, you're returned to the same menu. You are probably in the *Graph Options* menu.

Solution: Press Q (for *Quit*) to leave this "sticky" menu and return to the *Graph* menu, which contains *View*.

2. You have made some major mistakes in creating your graph and would like to cancel all settings and start over.

Cause: You made some incorrect menu selections.

Solution: Return to the main *Graph* menu. You may already be there, or you may need to press Q to leave the *Graph Options* menu.

Press: R G Q

to cancel all the graph settings. ▪

Saving Graphs

Once you have created and labeled a graph, you'll want to save it on a disk. Separate procedures are required to save a graph for screen viewing and for printing. If necessary, set the default drive and/or directory before you move on.

Saving a Graph for Screen Viewing

Saving a graph for screen viewing is simple. Whenever a worksheet is saved, all the settings for the current graph are automatically saved as part of the worksheet. Simply save the worksheet, using the procedures you learned in Chapter 20.

Press Q to exit the *Graph* menu and return to READY mode. Press / F S to resave the worksheet. On a hard disk system, Line 2 will display the prompt

```
Enter save file name: B:\GRAPHEX.wk1
```

indicating that you previously saved the worksheet on the diskette in drive B using the file name GRAPHEX. Press ⏎ to accept the file name, and press R to replace the previous version of GRAPHEX.

The settings for the graph in Fig. 23.10 are saved with the worksheet. You may later retrieve this worksheet and press / G V to view the graph.

Saving a Graph for Printing

Obtaining a printed copy of a graph is a two step process. First, the graph must be saved in a special disk file for printing. Then you must exit 1-2-3 and load another program, *PrintGraph*, to print the graph. *PrintGraph* reads the special disk file and prints the graph. The tutorial illustrates the procedure for saving a graph for printing, and Appendix C describes how to load and run *PrintGraph*.

Press / G to return to the *Graph* menu. Press

to select the menu option to save a graph for later printing. Respond to the prompt

```
Enter graph file name: B:\*.PIC
```

by typing

```
BARCHART
```

Press ⏎. The disk file BARCHART can now be accessed by the *PrintGraph* program to obtain a printed copy of the graph.

Note that the file BARCHART contains only information for printing the graph. BARCHART may not be retrieved or used by 1-2-3.

■ *Keystroke Summary*

Save a graph for printing

From the *Graph* menu (/ G):

Press: S
           └── Save

Type: *file name*

Press: ⏎

Other Graphing Features

There is not enough space to cover all of the graphing functions in detail in this tutorial. However, you are encouraged to explore some of the other graphing features on your own. You know how to use the menu system. Try some options that were not covered in the tutorial. Watch the control panel for information and prompts. If you have difficulty, press Esc to back out of a menu choice and start over. Also, use the 1-2-3 reference manual; consult the chapter that describes graph commands.

Some 1-2-3 graphing capabilities that you might wish to explore are listed below. Some of these are accessed from the *Graph* menu and others from the *Graph Options* menu. Try each one and view the graph to see what happens. The menu option name is included in parentheses.

From the *Graph* menu (/ G):

1. *Other graph types:* In addition to the graph types discussed in the tutorial, data may be represented by using a stacked bar graph and an XY plot. If you try an XY plot, change the X range to a set of numeric values. (*Type*)

2. *Specify shading on a pie chart:* Use data set B to specify the shading to be used in a pie chart. (B)

3. *Save multiple graphs with the worksheet:* To save more than one graph with the worksheet, the graphs must be assigned names. Named graphs may be declared current and deleted. (*Name*)

4. *Specify multiple data ranges at once:* If the X and A–F data ranges are in consecutive columns or rows, they may be specified at once using this feature. (*Group*)

From the *Graph Options* menu (/ G O):

1. *Specify the format of line and XY graphs:* Line and XY graphs may include lines only, points only, or lines and points. (*Format*)

2. *Include a grid on the graph:* All graph types except the pie chart may contain horizontal, vertical, or both types of grid lines. (*Grid*)

3. *Specify axis scaling:* The Y-axis and the X-axis (on an XY graph) are normally scaled automatically, but you can control the scaling manually if you wish. (*Scale*)

4. *Color or black and white:* If you have a color monitor, you may specify color for your graph. Otherwise, choose black and white. (*Color* and *B&W*)

5. *Label data points on the graph:* All graph types except the pie chart may include labels for individual points or bars on the graph. (*Label*)

Summary

Function	Reference or Keystrokes	Page
Graph, access menu	/ G	387
Graph, define axis labels	(/ G O) T, X or Y, label, ↵	395
Graph, define legend	(/ G O) L, A or B or C or D or E or F, legend, ↵	396
Graph, define title	(/ G O) T, F or S, title, ↵	395
Graph, define values	(/ G) A or B or C or D or E or F, range address, ↵	388
Graph, define X values	(/ G) X, range address, ↵	389
Graph, options menu	(/ G) O	394
Graph, select type	(/ G) T, L or B or P	391
Graph, view	(/ G) V	390
Print a graph	Appendix C	593
Save a graph to print	(/ G) S, file name, ↵	398
Save a graph to view	/ F S, file name, ↵	398
Sticky menu	—	387
Sticky menu exit	Q	387

Self-Test

1. 1-2-3 provides three major functions: _____, _____, and _____.

2. Press _____ to select the *Graph* menu, and press _____ to select the *Graph Options* menu.

3. The *Graph* menu and the *Graph Options* menu are called _____ menus because when a menu action is complete, you return to the menu rather than to READY mode.

4. A line graph and a bar graph may display up to _____ data sets, but a pie chart may display only _____ data set.

5. Press _____ from the *Graph* menu to define the numeric values for data set A.

6. Press _____ from the *Graph* menu to define the identifiers for the X-axis of a line graph.

7. Press _____ from the *Graph* menu to view the currently defined graph.

8. Press _____ from the *Graph* menu to change the graph type to a pie chart.

9. Press _____ from the *Graph Options* menu to enter a title at the top of the graph. Press _____ from the *Graph Options* menu to create a label for the X-axis of a bar graph. Press _____ from the *Graph Options* menu to define a legend for data set B.

10. Press _____ from the *Graph* menu to save a graph in the file name PLOT for later printing.

Exercises

1. Save a copy of the line graph, the bar graph, and the pie chart in Fig. 23.2 for printing. Print a copy of these graphs. Also save and print the graph in Fig. 23.10.

2. Use the graphing tutorial worksheet to create the following graph.

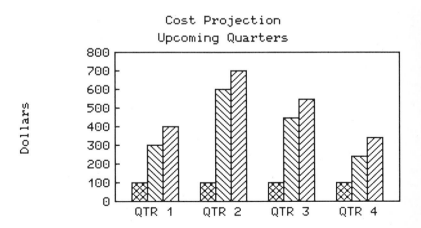

3. Use the MODBUDGET worksheet from the tutorial in Chapter 21 to create the following graph. The shading is optional. (To obtain shading, enter the values 1, 2, 3, and 4 in adjacent cells and define this range as data set B.)

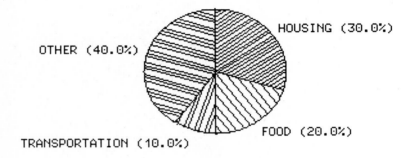

·24

Other Useful Features

This chapter introduces the 1-2-3 features and commands that allow you to:

- freeze column or row labels on the screen
- view separate portions of a worksheet on the screen
- create keystroke macros
- use 1-2-3 add-ins

Overview

This chapter completes the 1-2-3 tutorial by covering four particularly useful features. The first two are helpful in dealing with a worksheet that contains more rows and/or columns than will fit on a single screen. This is usually the case with most realistic applications. One feature (*Titles*) freezes certain rows and columns on the screen during scrolling. The other (*Windows*) allows two separate portions of the worksheet to appear on the screen simultaneously.

The third feature, *macros*, provides 1-2-3 users the ability to write programs to automate their work. Using macros is a relatively complicated subject requiring programming skills. The tutorial introduces the basic concepts involved using simple examples. To master this subject, the interested reader should read the 1-2-3 Reference Manual or other books that specifically address the topic of macros.

Figure 24.1
When you add QTR 5 through QTR 8 to the graphing tutorial worksheet, it no longer fits on the display screen.

```
I3: 110                                                                    READY

        D           E           F           G           H           I
1
2      QTR 3       QTR 4       QTR 5       QTR 6       QTR 7       QTR 8
3       150         80          120         190         100         110
4
5      $750        $400        $600        $950        $500        $550
6
7      $100        $100        $100        $100        $100        $100
8      $450        $240        $360        $570        $300        $330
9      $550        $340        $460        $670        $400        $430
```

Finally, you will be introduced to *add-ins*, programs that may be added to 1-2-3 to provide additional capabilities or features. 1-2-3 provides a menu option to access these features.

For this tutorial you will modify the graph worksheet to project eight quarters into the future (Fig. 24.1). Develop the worksheet as follows.

1. Retrieve the graph worksheet from disk under the file name GRAPHEX. (/ F R)

2. Copy the cell contents for quarters 1 to 4 (B2..E9) to columns F through I (F2..I9). (/ C)

3. Edit the new column headings to read: (F2)

   F2: "QTR 5

   G2: "QTR 6

   H2: "QTR 7

   I2: "QTR 8

4. Enter sales forecasts for the new quarters as follows:

   F3: 120

   G3: 190

   H3: 100

   I3: 110

5. Save the worksheet using the file name LARGEX. (/F S)

Freezing Row Labels and Column Headings

Look at the screen illustrated in Fig. 24.1. Data for quarters 3–8 are displayed, but without the row labels visible you don't know what the numbers represent. Using the *Titles* option on the *Worksheet* menu, you can freeze the labels in column A so that they do not scroll off the screen.

Figure 24.2

The row labels in column A are frozen on the display screen and will not scroll off if the cursor is moved to the right.

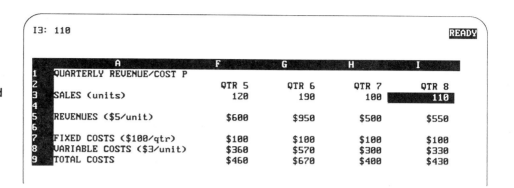

Position the cell pointer in column B (all columns to the left of the cell pointer will be frozen on the screen). Press

```
/ W T
    └──── Titles
  └── Worksheet
```

Line 2 of the control panel displays the options

```
Both Horizontal Vertical Clear
```

The *Horizontal* option freezes rows above the cell pointer on the screen; *Vertical* freezes columns to the left of the cell pointer; the *Both* option freezes both the rows above and columns to the left; and *Clear* cancels any previous settings. Press V to freeze column A.

Position the cell pointer in column I (Fig. 24.2). The screen now displays columns F through I, but column A remains frozen on the screen.

Column headings may also be frozen on the screen. Press PgDn and notice that everything scrolls off the screen. Press PgUp and position the cell pointer in row 3. Press / W T to choose the *Titles* option, and press H to freeze all rows above the cell pointer. Now press PgDn, and the first two rows remain on the screen (Fig. 24.3). Note that column A is no longer frozen. The *Both* option must be selected to freeze both columns and rows at the same time.

Figure 24.3

The column labels in rows 1 and 2 are frozen on the display screen and will not scroll off if the cursor is moved down.

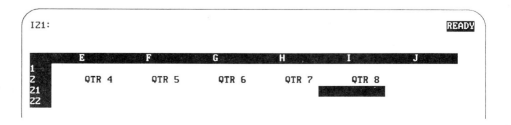

Figure 24.4

If the cell pointer is moved to a frozen row or column, duplicates of the frozen rows and columns are made for editing. The duplicates may be scrolled off the screen.

	A	B	C	D	E
	A1: [W24] 'QUARTERLY REVENUE/COST PROJECTION:				READY
1	QUARTERLY REVENUE/COST PROJECTION:				
2		QTR 1	QTR 2	QTR 3	QTR 4
1	QUARTERLY REVENUE/COST PROJECTION:				
2		QTR 1	QTR 2	QTR 3	QTR 4
3	SALES (units)	100	200	150	80
4					
5	REVENUES ($5/unit)	$500	$1,000	$750	$400
6					
7	FIXED COSTS ($100/qtr)	$100	$100	$100	$100
8	VARIABLE COSTS ($3/unit)	$300	$600	$450	$240
9	TOTAL COSTS	$400	$700	$550	$340

Press Home. Normally, this moves the cell pointer to cell A1. However, since row 1 and row 2 are fixed on the screen, the cell pointer moves to cell A3. The only way to position the cell pointer in a frozen cell is to press F5 and type the desired cell address as discussed in Chapter 20. Try it. Press F5, type A1 in response to the prompt, and press ↵ (Fig. 24.4). Row 1 and row 2 remain fixed on the screen, but a copy is made to allow the cell to be edited. To remove the duplicate rows, press PgDn to scroll them off the screen and PgUp to return to cell A3.

Complete this lesson by canceling the frozen rows. Press / W T to select the *Titles* option, and press C to clear the settings. Verify that the rows are no longer frozen by pressing PgDn to scroll them off the screen.

■ *Keystroke Summary*

Freeze rows and/or columns

Press: / W T (B or H or V or C)

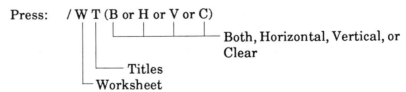

Both, Horizontal, Vertical, or Clear

Titles

Worksheet

Using Windows

1-2-3 provides the *Windows* option to view two separate portions of a large worksheet on the display screen. To illustrate, position the cell pointer in cell A11 and press

Window

Worksheet

Figure 24.5

The display screen is divided into two horizontal windows at row 11 (the position of the cell pointer), each showing part of the worksheet.

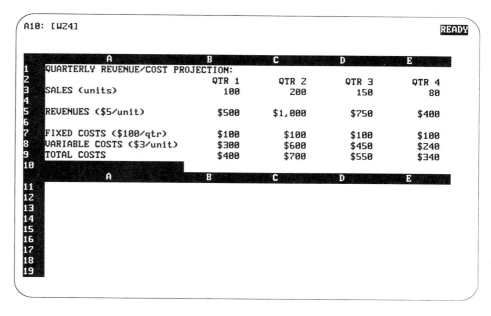

Line 2 of the control panel provides the options

```
Horizontal Vertical Sync Unsync Clear
```

The *Horizontal* option creates one window above the cell pointer and one below it; the *Vertical* option creates one window to the left of the cell pointer and one to the right. The other options will be explained shortly. Press H to create *Horizontal* windows (Fig. 24.5). The top window displays rows 1–10, and the bottom window displays rows 11–19.

Notice that the cell pointer is positioned in the top window. Press

F6

and the cell pointer is moved to the bottom window. F6 moves the cell pointer back and forth between windows.

With the cell pointer in the bottom window, press ↑ until both windows display the same cells. Position the cell pointer on cell B3 and type

150

to change the sales for quarter 1. Press ↵ and notice that the change is reflected in both windows (Fig. 24.6). The worksheet may be modified or edited from either window.

With the cell pointer still in the bottom window, press → until the cell pointer is in column I (Fig. 24.7). Notice that as the columns scroll left across the bottom window, they also scroll left across the top. This

Figure 24.6
Cell contents may be changed or worksheet options may be selected from either window and, if visible, will be reflected in the other window.

```
B3: 150                                                          READY

         A          ·         B          C          D •         E
 1 QUARTERLY REVENUE/COST PROJECTION:
 2                            QTR 1      QTR 2      QTR 3      QTR 4
 3 SALES (units)              150        200        150         80
 4
 5 REVENUES ($5/unit)        $750      $1,000       $750       $400
 6
 7 FIXED COSTS ($100/qtr)    $100       $100       $100       $100
 8 VARIABLE COSTS ($3/unit)  $450       $600       $450       $240
 9 TOTAL COSTS               $550       $700       $550       $340
10
         A                    B          C          D          E
 1 QUARTERLY REVENUE/COST PROJECTION:
 2                            QTR 1      QTR 2      QTR 3      QTR 4
 3 SALES (units)              150        200        150         80
 4
 5 REVENUES ($5/unit)        $750      $1,000       $750       $400
 6
 7 FIXED COSTS ($100/qtr)    $100       $100       $100       $100
 8 VARIABLE COSTS ($3/unit)  $450       $600       $450       $240
 9 TOTAL COSTS               $550       $700       $550       $340
06-Jan-90   12:14 PM      UNDO
```

is called synchronous scrolling. To change to independent (or unsynchronous) scrolling, press / W W to access the *Windows* option menu and press

```
U
└── Unsync
```

Figure 24.7
With the horizontal windows the columns may scroll synchronously across the screen.

```
I3: 110                                                         READY

         D          E          F          G          H          I
 1
 2      QTR 3      QTR 4      QTR 5      QTR 6      QTR 7      QTR 8
 3       150         80        120        190        100        110
 4
 5      $750       $400       $600       $950       $500       $550
 6
 7      $100       $100       $100       $100       $100       $100
 8      $450       $240       $360       $570       $300       $330
 9      $550       $340       $460       $670       $400       $430
10
         D          E          F          G          H          I
 1
 2      QTR 3      QTR 4      QTR 5      QTR 6      QTR 7      QTR 8
 3       150         80        120        190        100        110
 4
 5      $750       $400       $600       $950       $500       $550
 6
 7      $100       $100       $100       $100       $100       $100
 8      $450       $240       $360       $570       $300       $330
 9      $550       $340       $460       $670       $400       $430
06-Jan-90   12:18 PM      UNDO
```

Figure 24.8
By selecting the *Unsync* option the columns may scroll independently in each horizontal window.

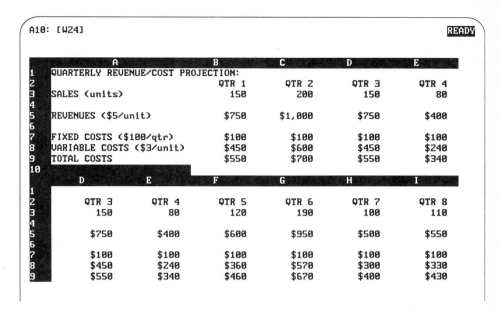

Now press [F6] to move the cell pointer back to the top window. Press
⊡ until the cell pointer is positioned in column A (Fig. 24.8). This time
the columns scroll right across the top window but remain fixed in the
bottom window; that is, they are not synchronized.

Complete this section by returning to a single screen. Press / W W
to access the *Windows* options and press

```
C
 └──── Clear
```

to remove the second window.

■ *Keystroke Summary*

Create a window

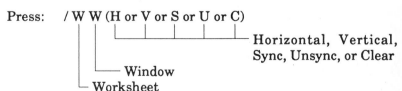

Introducing Macros

A **macro** is basically a set of instructions, like a computer program,
to perform a particular task. The instructions in a macro are made up
of keystrokes that perform 1-2-3 commands. The instructions are
stored in a blank area of the worksheet and executed by a single

keystroke combination. Macros are useful in several areas, saving keystrokes in commonly performed functions, eliminating the need to remember the keystrokes required to do certain tasks, and making 1-2-3 easier for the novice to use.

Creating and using macros is a three-step process:

1. Use a blank area of the worksheet to list the keystrokes required to perform the desired function.

2. Assign a name to the area of the worksheet containing the list of keystrokes (names consist of the backslash character (\) followed by a single letter of the alphabet (A–Z), for example \A).

3. Execute the macro by holding down [Alt] *and* pressing the letter of the macro name, for example, [Alt] *and* A.

To save the macro, simply save the worksheet as usual. Any macros defined in the worksheet are also saved.

The tutorial illustrates this process by creating, naming, and executing a macro to erase the contents of a highlighted cell.

Defining Macro Keystrokes

The first step in defining a macro is to recall or figure out the exact keystrokes required to perform the function. It's a good idea to step through the process and write *each* keystroke down as you press it. Begin the tutorial by erasing cell B3 and recording the keystrokes used. Position the cell pointer on cell B3 (don't count these keystrokes; you'll write the macro assuming that the cell pointer is already highlighting the cell to be erased). Four keystrokes are now required. Press these to verify:

■ / to access 1-2-3 menu system

■ R to select *Range* menu option

■ E to select *Erase* menu option

■ ⏎ to accept the range address consisting of the single highlighted cell

The sales estimate of 150 units is erased. Reenter the value 150 in cell B3 to restore the worksheet.

Now that the keystrokes for the macro are clear in your mind, they must be entered *as a label* in a blank worksheet cell. Position the cell pointer to cell B11 and type

'/RE˜

Press ⏎ (Fig. 24.9). The ' is a label-prefix character to indicate that the following keystrokes are to be entered as a label. Without this character, when you type /, the menu system will be activated and the

Figure 24.9
Cell B11 contains a label listing the keystrokes required to erase the highlighted cell of a worksheet. The ~ character is a special symbol used to represent ⏎.

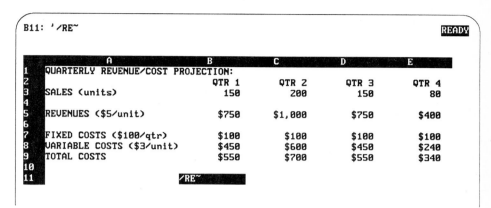

```
B11: '/RE~                                                      READY

              A              B           C           D           E
1  QUARTERLY REVENUE/COST PROJECTION:
2                          QTR 1       QTR 2       QTR 3       QTR 4
3  SALES (units)            150         200         150          80
4
5  REVENUES ($5/unit)      $750      $1,000        $750        $400
6
7  FIXED COSTS ($100/qtr)  $100        $100        $100        $100
8  VARIABLE COSTS ($3/unit)$450        $600        $450        $240
9  TOTAL COSTS             $550        $700        $550        $340
10
11                         /RE~
```

keystrokes will not be entered in the cell. The remaining characters represent the four keystrokes required to erase a cell. As usual, R and E may be uppercase or lowercase, since they represent menu selections. Tilde (~) is a special character used to represent the ⏎ key in a macro. (See Fig. 24.10 for ways to represent other special keys.) This special character is provided because pressing the ⏎ key normally marks the completion of a cell entry.

It is not necessary (and not advised for more complex macros) to enter all the keystrokes for a macro in a single cell. You may split the macro keystrokes between cells any way you like, but they must be entered in a single column of adjacent cells followed by a blank cell.

Figure 24.10
Use these symbols in macro definitions to represent the indicated key. Most of the symbols enclose a keyword in brackets. A complete list is contained in the 1-2-3 Reference Manual.

To Represent	Use the Symbol
⏎	~
→	{right}
↑	{up}
←	{left}
↓	{down}
Home	{home}
F5	{goto}
Pause for interaction	{?}

Figure 24.11
Macro keystrokes
must appear in
successive cells of the
same column but may
be subdivided as
desired between the
cells. Some
alternative ways to
enter the example
macro are illustrated
here. A blank cell is
required to mark the
end of the macro.

Row	Original	Alternative 1	Alternative 2
11	/RE˜	/R	/
12		/E˜	R
13			E
14			˜
15			

Fig. 24.11 contains alternative ways of representing the tutorial macro. All versions are acceptable.

■ Keystroke Summary

Define a macro

In adjacent cells of a single column:

Type: *label-prefix character* (')

Type: *macro keystrokes* (use Fig. 24.10 for special keys)

Press: ⏎

Naming a Macro

1-2-3 provides a menu function to assign a name to a range address. You have not used this in the tutorial; rather, range addresses have been defined by typing or pointing to obtain expressions such as A1..B12. By using the range-naming function, a name such as SALES or COSTS is assigned to a particular block of cells. Then, when prompted to enter a range address, you simply type the range name. This saves time if you refer frequently to the same range address. Assigning range names is also used to name macros.

To name the macro to erase a cell, press

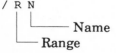

to access the range naming options

```
Create Delete Labels Reset Table
```

Press C to *Create* a range name, and you'll be prompted as follows:

```
Enter name:
```

For normal range names, you may enter any name up to 14 characters long, but for macros the name consists of two characters, backslash (\) and a single letter of the alphabet (\A, \B, ... \Z). Use the letter E to identify this macro as an erasing macro. Type

    \E

and press ⏎. Next, you'll be prompted to enter the range address associated with the given name:

    Enter range address: B11..B11

If you're not already there, POINT to the first cell containing the macro keystrokes, B11 (Fig. 24.12), and press ⏎. This assigns the name \E to the beginning cell of the tutorial macro. When you execute this macro, 1-2-3 will perform all of the keystrokes in cells B11, B12, and so on until a blank cell in column B is encountered.

▪ *Keystroke Summary*

Name a macro

Press: / R N C

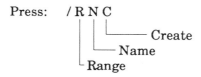

Create
Name
Range

Type: *macro name* (\letter)

Press: ⏎

Type or point: *range address*

Press: ⏎

Figure 24.12

The macro name \E is assigned to the beginning cell of the macro.

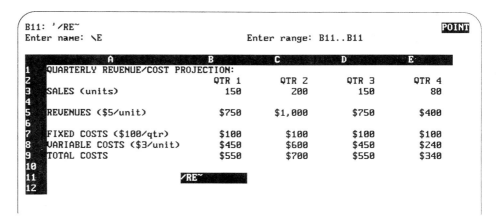

```
B11: '/RE~                                              POINT
Enter name: \E                    Enter range: B11..B11

             A              B         C         D         E
1   QUARTERLY REVENUE/COST PROJECTION:
2                        QTR 1     QTR 2     QTR 3     QTR 4
3   SALES (units)          150       200       150        80
4
5   REVENUES ($5/unit)    $750    $1,000      $750      $400
6
7   FIXED COSTS ($100/qtr) $100      $100      $100      $100
8   VARIABLE COSTS ($3/unit) $450    $600      $450      $240
9   TOTAL COSTS           $550      $700      $550      $340
10
11                      /RE~
12
```

Executing a Macro

To execute a macro, hold [Alt] down *and* press the letter of the macro name. To illustrate, erase the contents of cell B3 using the macro \E. Position the cell pointer over B3 and press

> [Alt] *and* E

The keystrokes specified in the macro named \E are executed, and the contents of cell B3 are erased. Now, reenter the value 150 in cell B3.

To clarify what is happening, execute this macro again, slowly, one keystroke at a time. 1-2-3 provides a *Step* mode to do this. Enable *Step* mode by pressing

> [Alt] *and* [F2]

An indicator, STEP, appears at the bottom of the screen. Position the cell pointer on cell B3 and activate the macro; press [Alt] *and* E. The keystrokes being executed are displayed in the lower left corner of the screen. Press

> space bar (or [↵] or any letter key)

and the first macro keystroke (/) is executed. Each time the space bar is pressed, another keystroke is executed. Trace through the remainder of this macro by pressing the space bar three more times and observe the effect of each keystroke.

When the macro is finished, turn off *Step* mode by pressing [Alt] *and* [F2]. *Step* mode is a handy feature for checking a macro. Reenter the erased value, 150, in cell B3.

Macros may be terminated before completion by pressing [Ctrl] *and* [Scroll Lock].

■ *Keystroke Summary*

Execute a macro

> Press: [Alt] *and* letter of macro name

Interactive Macros

The tutorial macro erases the contents of a single highlighted cell; no interaction is involved. This macro can be generalized by allowing the user to interact and specify a range of cells to erase. 1-2-3 provides the pause command

> {?}

to do this. Simply insert this command in the macro definition at a point where interaction is desired.

To illustrate, modify the tutorial macro to allow the user to specify the range of cells to erase. Position the cell pointer on cell B11 and press F2 to edit the macro definition. Insert the pause command between E and ~:

'/RE{?}~

Press ↵.

Test the revised macro by erasing the range address B3..E3. Press Alt *and* E to execute the macro. After executing the first three keystrokes, /RE, the macro pauses for interactive input. Respond by pointing to range address B3..E3 (Fig. 24.13). CMD on line 25 indicates that 1-2-3 is executing a macro. Press ↵ to mark the end of interactive input, and the remaining keystrokes of the macro will be executed. The desired range is erased.

In general, {?} may be positioned anywhere in a macro definition. When 1-2-3 encounters this command, it stops executing the macro until you respond and press ↵.

Before continuing, restore the erased values 150, 200, 150, and 80 in the worksheet.

Documenting a Macro

When worksheets contain complicated macros or several macros, it's a good idea to include names and descriptions of each macro as part of the worksheet. This serves as **documentation** for you or others who are using the worksheet.

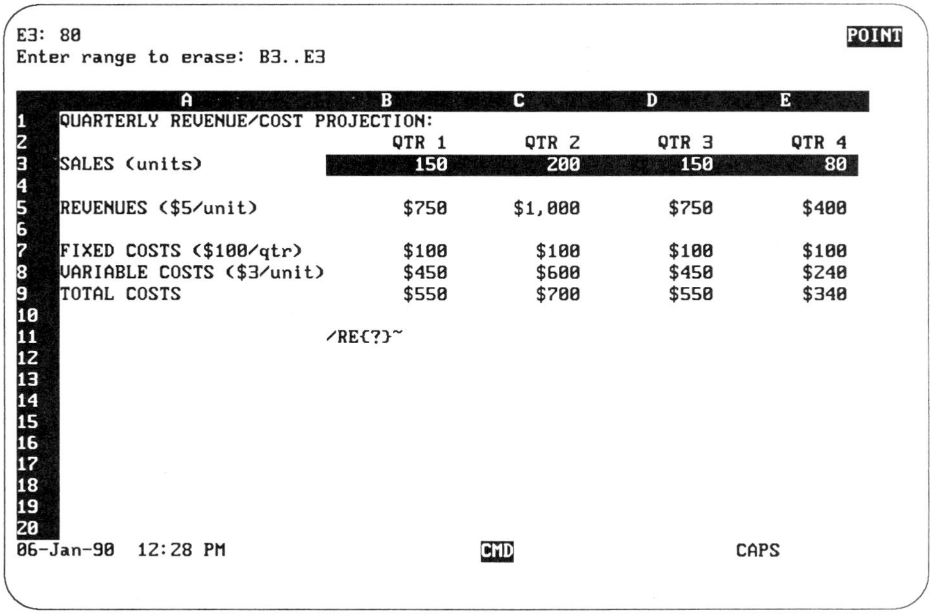

Figure 24.13

The macro pauses at {?} to allow you to point to the range address to erase. CMD on line 25 is an indicator that a macro is being executed.

```
E3: 80                                                              POINT
Enter range to erase: B3..E3

            A                   B           C           D           E
1  QUARTERLY REVENUE/COST PROJECTION:
2                              QTR 1       QTR 2       QTR 3       QTR 4
3  SALES (units)                150         200         150          80
4
5  REVENUES ($5/unit)          $750      $1,000        $750        $400
6
7  FIXED COSTS ($100/qtr)      $100        $100        $100        $100
8  VARIABLE COSTS ($3/unit)    $450        $600        $450        $240
9  TOTAL COSTS                 $550        $700        $550        $340
10
11                      /RE{?}~
12
13
14
15
16
17
18
19
20
06-Jan-90  12:28 PM                        CMD                  CAPS
```

Figure 24.14

Macros are commonly documented by placing the macro name in the column to the left of the beginning cell of the macro and a brief description of the macro keystrokes in the column to the right of each cell in the macro. Proper documentation of the tutorial macro is illustrated.

```
B11:  '/RE{?}~                                                    READY

                A            B          C          D          E
1   QUARTERLY REVENUE/COST PROJECTION:
2                            QTR 1      QTR 2      QTR 3      QTR 4
3   SALES (units)             150        200        150         80
4
5   REVENUES ($5/unit)       $750     $1,000       $750       $400
6
7   FIXED COSTS ($100/qtr)   $100       $100       $100       $100
8   VARIABLE COSTS ($3/unit) $450       $600       $450       $240
9   TOTAL COSTS              $550       $700       $550       $340
10
11  \E                   /RE{?}~      Erase cell range
```

Documenting is commonly done as shown in Fig. 24.14. The macro name is placed in the column to the left of the beginning cell of the macro, and a brief description is placed in the column to the right of each cell in the macro.

Document the tutorial macro. Position the cell pointer on cell A11 and type

    '\E

Press ⏎. Be sure to precede the macro name, \E, with the label-prefix character,', or the \ part of the macro name will be treated as a label-prefix and repeat the letter E across the cell. Move the cell pointer to cell C11 and type the description

    'Erase cell range

Press ⏎, and the macro is properly documented. The documentation in cells A11 and C11 is for your information; these labels are not part of the macro.

Macro Names

Beginning with Lotus 1-2-3 releases 2.2 and 3.0, macros may be assigned full-length names rather than the cryptic single-letter names described in this section. However, if a longer name is used, the macro must be executed by pressing [Alt] and [F3] and then selecting the macro name from a set of available range names. This requires additional keystrokes to execute the macro. It's up to you to decide whether the benefits are worth the cost.

Macro Examples

The only way to learn to use macros is to create and test them. Fig. 24.15 provides three examples for the tutorial worksheet. Continue the tutorial by doing each of these, one at a time. Enter the macro into the worksheet, name it, execute it, and verify that it works. Add the documentation in the adjacent cells if you wish.

Example 1

Example macro 1 freezes the labels in column A and rows 1 and 2 of the worksheet so that they will not scroll off the screen. Enter the macro definition in cells B14 and B15. In B14, type

    '{goto}B3~

The symbol {goto} represents F5, the function key to move the cell pointer to a particular address. B3 is the specified address, and ~ represents the ↵ key. In B15, type

    '/WTB

to select the *Worksheet* option to freeze *Titles*. B indicates that *Both* columns to the left of the cell pointer and rows above the cell pointer will be frozen.

Press / R N C to create a name for this macro. Type

    \T

for the macro name and specify

    B14..B14

as the range address containing the beginning cell.

Figure 24.15
For additional practice, add the three example macros to your worksheet. Enter the keystrokes, name the macro, execute it, and verify that it works properly.

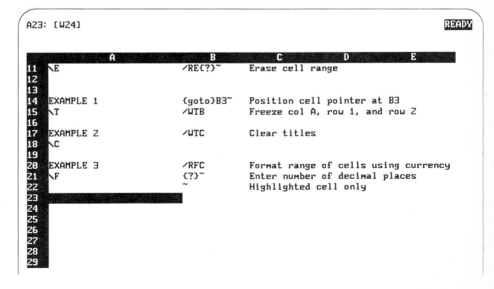

Press [Alt] *and* T to execute this macro. Make sure that it worked. Move the cell pointer to the right and down until columns and rows scroll off of the screen. Verify that column A and rows 1 and 2 remain in place.

Example 2

Example macro 2 unfreezes any rows or columns frozen on the screen. Enter this macro definition in cell B18:

    '/WTC

These keystrokes call the *Worksheet* menu option involving *Titles*. C selects the option to *Clear* all titles.

Name this macro by pressing / R N C and typing

    \C

as the macro name and

    B18..B18

as the macro address.

Execute this macro by pressing [Alt] *and* C. Test it as you did Example 1. Now column A and rows 1 and 2 will scroll off the screen.

Example 3

Example macro 3 formats a cell highlighted by the cell pointer to *Currency* format. The user interactively specifies the number of decimal places. Organize this macro definition in three cells. In cell B21, type

    '/RFC

to select the menu option to format a range of cells using the *Currency* format. In cell B22, type

    '{?}~

to allow the user to specify the number of decimal places during the macro execution. In cell B23, type

to accept the range address containing the highlighted cell.

Press / R N C to name this macro \F, and point to range address B21..B21 as the beginning cell.

To test this macro, position the cell pointer at any number on the worksheet. Press [Alt] *and* F. The macro will begin execution and pause for you to enter the number of decimal places. Type 2 and press [↵]. The macro will finish by formatting the cell to *Currency* with two decimal places. Execute this macro several times, each time specifying a different number of decimal places and observing the results.

■ *What Can Go Wrong?*

1. You are defining keystrokes in a worksheet cell that select a menu option. When you press these keys, the menu comes up rather than being entered in the cell as a label.

Cause: As soon as you press /, 1-2-3 goes into MENU mode.

Solution: Begin the cell entry with the label-prefix character ', so that it goes into LABEL mode first. This character is not one of the macro keystrokes.

2. You press ⟨Alt⟩ *and* a letter (A–Z), and the machine beeps without executing the macro.

Cause: 1-2-3 cannot find the named range.

Solution: Press / R N C as described above to assign an appropriate range name to the cells containing the macro definition.

3. The macro stops before completion. It is not at a point where user interaction is expected.

Cause: The macro definition is missing one or more keystrokes required to perform the given task or contains some incorrect keystrokes. A very common error is to omit a necessary ˜ (or ⟨⏎⟩).

Solution: Press ⟨Ctrl⟩ *and* ⟨ScrollLock⟩) to discontinue execution of the macro. Carefully check the keystrokes required and compare those with your macro definition. Look for a missing ⟨⏎⟩ key. If you still can't find your problem, execute the macro using *Step* mode and compare the keystrokes executed with what you expected. Once the missing or incorrect keystrokes are identified, press ⟨Ctrl⟩ *and* ⟨ScrollLock⟩ to terminate the macro, then highlight the cell with the error and press ⟨F2⟩ to edit the cell contents. ■

1-2-3 Add-Ins

Add-ins are programs written by Lotus and other software developers that provide 1-2-3 with additional capabilities, such as attaching notes to each cell entry, printing worksheets sideways across the page, creating three-dimensional graphs, solving linear programming problems, and adding special mathematical functions for use in cell formulas. Often, when using an add-in, a new menu listing the add-in's feature will appear on line 2 of the control panel. Features are selected from this menu in the same way that features are selected from the standard 1-2-3 menus. In effect, the add-in becomes part of 1-2-3.

Lotus provides two add-ins when you purchase 1-2-3, release 2.2. A *Macro Library Manager* allows macros to be stored in a library rather than associated with a specific spreadsheet. That, in turn, allows you to use the same macro in several worksheets without entering it in each one. The other add-in, called *Allways*, provides features for formatting and printing 1-2-3 worksheets, including variable type fonts and character sizes, variable row heights and column widths, horizontal and vertical lines, cell shading, and other graphing techniques. *Always* requires a hard disk.

The example illustrated below is intended for future reference; it is not part of the chapter tutorial. To use an add-in, it must first be loaded into memory. Press

```
/ A
  └── Add-In
```

to access the main menu *Add-In* option. Five options will appear on line 2 of the control panel.

```
Attach Detach Invoke Clear Quit
```

Attach loads an add-in program into memory; *Detach* removes it. *Invoke* is used to execute an add-in. *Clear* removes all add-ins from memory, and *Quit* returns to READY mode.

If you press A (for *Attach*), a prompt will be displayed:

```
Enter add-in to attach: A:\*.ADN
```

All add-in programs have the extension ADN. Respond by inserting the add-in disk, typing the add-in program's name, and pressing ⏎. For example, to load the *Macro Library Manager*, you might insert the disk containing that add-in into drive B, type

```
B:\MACROMGR.ADN
```

and press ⏎.

After the add-in is loaded into memory, line 2 of the control panel will list the following options:

```
No-Key 7 8 9 10
```

If you select *No-Key*, you will invoke the add-in from the *Add-In* menu by pressing

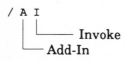

If you select a number, you will invoke the add-in by pressing Alt *and* the indicated function key; for example, if you select 7, you will invoke the add-in by pressing Alt *and* F7. After you indicate how you wish to invoke the add-in, press Q (for *Quit*) to return to READY mode. Later, when you invoke the add-in, the new program will display its own menu.

The ability to use add-ins is an important 1-2-3 feature. It allows users to obtain additional software capabilities without making 1-2-3 so big that it exceeds a personal computer's memory capacity. Add-in features can be loaded into memory when required and removed from memory when no longer needed.

Summary

Function	Reference (or keystrokes)	Page
Add-ins, invoke	/ A I	420
Add-ins, load	/ A A, file name, ⏎	420
Add-ins, remove	/ A D, file name, ⏎	420
Macros, define	—	410
Macros, document	—	415
Macros, execute	Alt and letter	414
Macros, interacting	—	414
Macros, name	/ R N C, \ letter, ⏎, range address, ⏎	412
Macros, special symbols	Fig. 24.10	411
Macros, step through	Alt *and* F2	414
Macros, stop	Ctrl *and* Scroll Lock	414
Titles, columns and rows	/ W T B	405
Titles, columns only	/ W T H	405
Titles, go to title cell	F5, cell address, ⏎	406
Titles, remove	/ W T C	406
Titles, rows only	/ W T V	405
Windows, change	F6	407
Windows, create side/side	/ W W V	406
Windows, create top/bottom	/ W W H	406
Windows, remove	/ W W C	409
Windows, synchronize	/ W W S	408
Windows, unsynchronize	/ W W U	408

Self-Test

1. After positioning the cell pointer appropriately, press _____ to freeze the rows above the cell pointer on the screen.

2. Press _____ to move the cell pointer to a cell that is frozen on the screen.

3. Press _____ to move the cell pointer to the other window.

4. With side-by-side windows, when the cell pointer is moved down, the rows scroll off the screen in unison. This is called _____ scrolling.

5. The symbol _____ is used in a macro definition to represent the ⏎ key, and the symbol _____ is used to represent the → key.

6. Press _____ before executing a macro so that the macro will pause after each keystroke until you press the _____.

7. The command _____ is used in a macro definition to suspend execution of the macro until the user responds and presses ⏎.

8. A macro definition may appear in several adjacent cells of a single _____. A _____ cell marks the end of the macro definition.

9. The name of the macro is assigned to the address of the _____ cell of the macro definition.

10. A 1-2-3 _____ is a software routine that provides a user with capabilities that are not available in the 1-2-3 program.

Exercises

1. Print copies of Figs. 24.2, 24.8, and 24.15.

2. Retrieve the tutorial worksheet used in this chapter and create the display illustrated below. Two windows have been created. The top window displays three example macros, and the bottom window displays projections for quarters 5 through 8. Notice that the columns are not synchronized and the bottom window has the row labels frozen on the screen. *Hint:* Rows and columns may be frozen independently in each window by using the Titles option while the

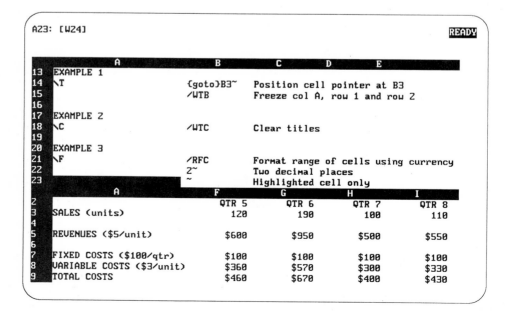

cell pointer is positioned in the desired window. Press ⊕ *and* PrtSc to obtain a copy of the display to submit to your instructor.

3. Start with a blank worksheet. Define, name, test, and document macros to perform the following functions.

   a. Create a macro named \W that creates side-by-side windows in which the left window contains columns A, B, and C.

   b. Create a macro named \C that centers the label in the highlighted cell.

   c. Create a macro named \I that increases the column width of the currently highlighted column by two spaces.

   d. Create a macro named \S that enters a sequence of numbers, 1, 2, 3,..., into an interactively specified range of cells.

   Print the area of the worksheet containing these documented macro definitions.

■ PART FIVE

dBASE III Plus

▪25

Data Management

This chapter:

- introduces essential database concepts
- previews *dBASE III Plus*

Data Management on a Computer

Every organization, be it large or small, requires information. Information is derived from data. Thus the organization collects data on its customers, its employees, its products, and a host of other things. Merely storing the data is not enough, of course; those facts must be retrieved and organized if their meaning is to be extracted. Storing, retrieving, and organizing data are the primary functions of a **database management system**. **dBASE III Plus** is a popular database management system that runs on IBM PC, PS/2, and compatible computers.

Database Concepts

A word processor supports writing text. Its function is obvious. The purpose of a spreadsheet program is clear to anyone with a knowledge of accounting. Database management is different; its utility is far from obvious. Thus it is useful to consider some basic database concepts before you begin learning dBASE III Plus.

Figure 25.1
In this example a supermarket checkout program reads a customer transaction, uses the data from that transaction to update inventory, and then outputs a receipt.

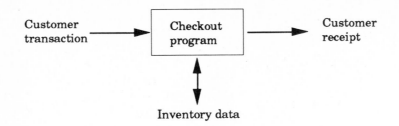

Some Key Terms

Figure 25.1 illustrates a supermarket checkout application. The program accepts a customer transaction, uses the data from that transaction to change the inventory level, and then prints the customer's receipt. Think of that application as you consider some basic data management terms.

The person, place, or thing about which data are stored is called an **entity**; the customer and the store's inventory are examples. An **attribute** is a single fact associated with an entity; for example, product description, price, and stock level are three inventory attributes. Each attribute occupies a **field**. A set of related attributes or fields is called a **record**; an inventory record might contain a product code, that product's description, its stock level, its price, and so on. Programs are generally written to read an input record, process the data, and write an output record. A **file** is a set of related records; for example, the inventory file contains one record for each product.

Traditional Files

A good program accepts *only* essential data, performs *only* the necessary functions, and generates *only* the required output. Programmers are trained to think in such straightforward, logical terms. Consequently, files and programs are typically designed together.

Consider, for example, two programs, one that prepares student grade reports and one that generates student bills. The grade report program has no need for financial data. Likewise, student grades are irrelevant to the billing program. Using the traditional approach to data management, separate files are created to support each program (Fig. 25.2). Separate files make logical sense, but they can lead to problems, too.

Figure 25.2
In the traditional approach to data management, separate files are created to support each application.

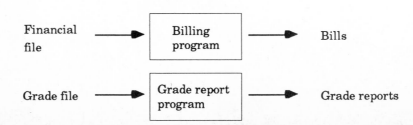

Figure 25.3

Both the financial and grade data files include student name and address. When the same data are independently stored in two or more places, you have data redundancy.

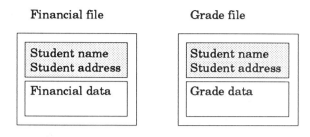

Data Redundancy

Although the files pictured in Fig. 25.2 are different, they do have some fields in common. For example, both programs need student names and mailing addresses, so student names and addresses will appear in *both* files (Fig. 25.3).

What happens if a student moves? If both the bursar and the registrar update their files at the same time, there is no problem. However, if one file is updated and the other is not, the computer will, at least for a time, hold two different values for the same attribute, one of which must be wrong. Redundant data are difficult to maintain. Simply put, **data redundancy** can lead to multiple, incompatible versions of the "truth," and that, in turn, compromises **data integrity**.

Data Dependency

If a program and its data are too tightly linked, changing the data might require changing the program. For example, imagine two programs that share a file (Fig. 25.4). Each record holds an individual's name, mailing address, and telephone number. Program A reads the file and prints mailing labels. Program B reads the file and prints a "telephone book" of names and phone numbers. What happens if you replace the five-digit zip code with the newer nine-digit zip code? Obviously, each record in the file will hold four additional characters; the data structure has changed. You might expect to modify program A; after all, it uses the zip code. But you might be surprised to discover that program B also needs modification simply because the zip code

Figure 25.4

In this example, programs A and B share a file but produce different outputs.

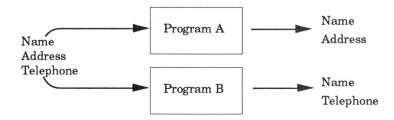

is part of its input record. The logic of a program that accesses a traditional file depends on the physical structure of the data, and this **data dependency** causes serious program maintenance problems.

The Database Approach

The solution to both problems is to create a centralized **database**. Rather than treating data as the "property" of an application, the database approach views data as an organizational resource to be shared by all programs. Since there is only one centralized copy of the data, redundancy is eliminated (or at least brought under control).

The fact that a database is used does not change the nature of the programs, however; they will still be written to process specific data. Thus a software routine called a **database management system** is placed between the application programs and the database (Fig. 25.5). Its function is to accept an application routine's request for data, access the database, extract and assemble the requested data, and pass them back to the application routine.

For example, program A might ask the database management system (DBMS) for an individual's name and address. In response, the DBMS will access the database, extract the name and address, and return these two fields to program A. Note that the program never sees the telephone number (which it doesn't need anyway). In a separate operation, program B might ask for an individual's name and telephone number. In response, the DBMS will access the database,

Figure 25.5
A database management system serves as a common interface between application programs and a central database.

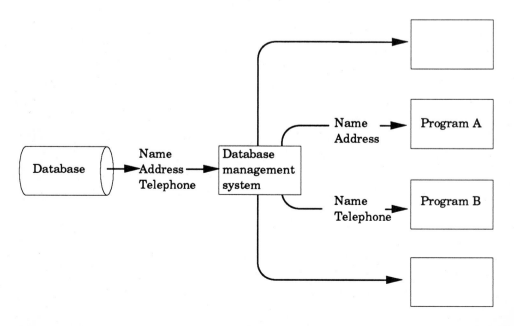

extract the name and the telephone number, and return these two fields to program B. Note that the program never sees the address.

A change in the zip code will require a change in program A, but because it never sees the zip code, program B will be unaffected. Similarly, a decision to add a long-distance access code to the telephone number will not affect program A. Placing a database management system between the database and the application routines promotes **data independence**.

Database Structure

A database consists of one or more files. For example, consider the billing and grade-reporting applications described earlier. Three entities can be identified: students, finances, and grades. If you need data about a student, chances are you need all the data about that student. If you need data about grades, chances are you need a complete set of grade data. It makes sense to create separate files for each entity (Fig. 25.6).

However, those entities are related. The billing program processes financial data for a given student; the grading program needs grade data for a given student. Rather than duplicating common data, a database management system allows the user to establish a relationship between two or more entities (Fig. 25.6). By following these **relationships** the database management system can assemble the

Figure 25.6

In a database a separate physical file might be created for each entity. Relationships can then be defined to link the files.

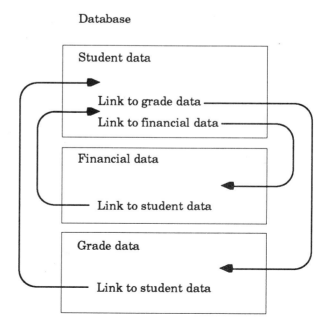

Database

Student data

Link to grade data

Link to financial data

Financial data

Link to student data

Grade data

Link to student data

data requested by an application program even if the requested fields are physically stored in different files.

dBASE III Plus

A database management system allows a user to create database files and define the relationships between them. Once the database is created, the user can then access the data through the database management system by embedding commands in an application program or, independently, by sending **queries** directly to the database management system.

dBASE III Plus incorporates all these features. In this book you will learn how to create database files and establish relationships between those files by defining indexes. You will also learn how to issue queries and generate reports. dBASE programming is a more advanced topic that is beyond the scope of these tutorials.

Conventions

Wherever possible, dBASE III Plus commands and features will appear in the tutorials much as they do on your screen. If necessary, references to specific commands will be italicized to distinguish them from the narrative. In a few cases, because of page width limitations, messages that are displayed on a single screen line will be spread over two lines in the text.

Depending on your system, the disk drive that holds your data could be almost anything. Rather than trying to show every possible permutation, the illustrations in this part of the book will assume that data are sent to drive B. Substitute your own disk drive where appropriate.

These tutorials do not pretend to cover every dBase III Plus feature; their intent is to help you get started. In Chapter 26 you'll learn how to create a database. Chapter 27 will show you how to maintain that database. In Chapter 28 you'll extract data from it; Chapter 29 introduces several advanced data manipulation features. Linking multiple databases is the topic of Chapter 30. When you finish, you'll be able to use the reference manual to learn additional features on your own.

Summary

No features were introduced in Chapter 25.

Self-Test

1. The person, place, or thing about which data are stored is called an
_____. An _____ is a single fact associated with that
person, place, or thing.

2. A record is a set of related _____. A _____ is a set of
related records.

3. Data _____ occurs when the same data are independently stored in two or more places. Data _____ occurs when the logic of a program is too tightly linked to its data structure.

4. With a central _____, data are treated as an organizational resource rather than as the property of a given application.

5. A _____ serves as the interface between application programs and a database.

Exercises

1. Explain the relationship between attributes and entities.

2. Relate the terms field, record, and file.

3. Briefly explain data redundancy. Why is it a problem?

4. Briefly explain data dependency. Why is it a problem?

5. Explain how the database approach can help to solve data redundancy and data dependency.

·26
Creating a Database

This chapter introduces the dBASE III Plus features and commands that allow you to:

- start dBASE III Plus
- quit dBASE III Plus
- use the dBASE III Plus assistant
- create a database
- add data to the database
- save your work to disk

Starting dBASE III Plus

This first tutorial shows you how to create a database, add data to it, and save your work. Don't just read it. You'll learn to use dBASE III Plus much more quickly if you actually sit down at a computer and follow along, step by step.

Necessary Equipment

You will need an IBM PC, PS/2, or compatible computer equipped with a keyboard, a screen, a printer (optional), and at least 256K bytes of memory.[1] It should have either two diskette drives or one diskette and a hard disk. If you have a two-diskette system, you'll also need a formatted data disk, a working copy of dBASE III Plus consisting of two disks labeled *System Disk #1* and *System Disk #2*, and a copy of PC-DOS (release 2.0 or higher) or MS-DOS (release 2.1 or higher).

The sample screens in this book will show the program disk in drive A and the data disk in drive B; if your system is different, mentally substitute your drives.

Loading dBASE III Plus on a Floppy Disk System

Skip this section if you are using a hard disk. Boot the operating system (see Chapter 6). Insert the dBASE III Plus System Disk #1 into drive A and your data disk into drive B, and close both drive doors. Type the program name, DBASE (using uppercase or lowercase letters). Your screen will resemble Fig. 26.1, with the last line reading

    A>DBASE

Then press ⏎. Drive A will activate, and after a brief delay the dBASE III Plus copyright screen will appear. The last line will read (on a single line)

    Press ⏎ to assent to the Licensing Agreement and begin dBASE
    III PLUS.

Press ⏎ (or simply wait several seconds), and a new message:

    Insert System Disk 2 and press ENTER, or press Ctrl–C to abort.

will appear. Remove the dBASE III Plus System Disk #1 from drive A, insert the dBASE III Plus System Disk #2, and close the drive door. Then press ⏎. The A drive will activate, and after a brief delay the dBASE assistant screen will appear.

---

[1] If you are using DOS 3.0 or higher, a minimum of 384K bytes of memory is required. Additional memory enhances dBASE III Plus performance.

Figure 26.1

To load dBASE III Plus on a two-disk system, insert the dBASE III Plus System Disk #1 into drive A, type DBASE, and press ⏎.

```
Current date is Tue  1-01-1980
Enter new date (mm-dd-yy): 6-1-89
Current time is 0:00:29:23
Enter new time: 10:15


The IBM Personal Computer DOS Version 3.30

A>DBASE
```

Loading dBASE III Plus on a Hard Disk System

Skip this section if you are using two diskettes.

Because a hard disk holds so much more than a floppy disk, it is generally divided into directories; see Chapter 11 for additional details. The first step in loading dBASE III Plus is to tell the operating system, DOS, the name of the directory that holds the program by issuing a change directory command. Boot the operating system (see Chapter 6). Following the C> prompt, type CD, a space, and then the directory name, DBASE; your last screen line should read

```
C>CD DBASE
```

(See "What Can Go Wrong?" immediately following this section if your directory name is not DBASE.) Then press ⏎. The hard disk will activate, and a new C> or C:\DBASE> prompt will appear on the screen.

Once you have identified the directory, tell DOS to load the program by typing its name, DBASE; your last screen line should read:

```
C>DBASE
```

or

```
C:\DBASE>DBASE
```

and your screen should resemble Fig. 26.2. Then press ⏎. The disk drive will activate, and the dBASE III Plus copyright screen will appear. The last line will read (on a single line)

```
Press ⏎ to assent to the Licensing Agreement and begin dBASE
III PLUS.
```

Press ⏎ to start dBASE III Plus.

Figure 26.2
Type two commands to load dBASE III Plus on a hard disk system. The CD DBASE command tells the operating system to change the default directory to DBASE. The second command, DBASE, tells the operating system to load the dBASE III Plus program.

```
Current date is Tue  1-01-1980
Enter new date (mm-dd-yy): 6-1-89
Current time is 0:00:29:23
Enter new time: 10:15


The IBM Personal Computer DOS Version 3.30


C>CD DBASE
C>DBASE
```

▪ *Keystroke Summary*

Load dBASE III Plus

Diskette:			**Hard Disk:**	
Insert:	System disk #1		Type:	**CD DBASE**
Type:	**DBASE**		Press:	⏎
Press:	⏎		Type:	**DBASE**
Press:	⏎		Press:	⏎
Remove:	System disk #1		Press:	⏎
Insert:	System disk #2			
Press:	⏎			

▪ *What Can Go Wrong?*

1. A screen message reads "Insufficient memory."

Cause: Your system does not have enough memory to run dBASE III Plus.

Solution: Consult the *Getting Started* booklet that came with your software for tips on using dBASE III Plus with limited memory. Consider adding memory to your system. If possible, move to another computer.

2. Following the CD DBASE command, an "Invalid directory" message indicates that the directory you named does not exist or could not be found.

Cause: Either you did not type the command properly, or, when dBASE III Plus was installed on the hard disk, the directory was given a name other than DBASE.

Solution: Retype the change directory command. If that doesn't work, type DIR following the C> prompt and press ⏎. Look through the directory list for a likely directory name, such as DBASE3, DB3, or DATABASE. If your system was installed from a student version of dBASE III Plus, look for DBSAMPLE. If you find no likely directory name, perhaps dBASE III Plus was never installed on the hard disk. If you find a likely directory name, retype the change directory command using that name instead of DBASE.

3. After you type the program name, DBASE, a "File not found" message appears.

Cause: You might have misspelled the program name. The disk in drive A might not contain dBASE III Plus. On a hard disk system the program might not be stored in the expected directory.

Solution: Make sure the dBASE III Plus disk is in drive A, retype DBASE, and press ⏎. On a hard disk system, type DIR following the C> prompt and press ⏎. If the dBASE III Plus software is in the expected directory, you will find a file named DBASE.EXE; if there is no such file, either you are in the wrong directory or the program is missing. Type CD, type a backslash (\), and press ⏎. Type DIR, press ⏎, and search the resulting directory list for a likely dBASE III Plus directory name. If you find one, type a new change directory command using the new directory name instead of DBASE. Then try loading the program again. If that doesn't work, get help. ▪

The dBASE III Plus Assistant Screen

There are two ways to interact with or instruct dBASE III Plus: through the **assistant** screen or by typing commands at the **dot (.) prompt**. The first tutorial will focus on the assistant. Dot prompt commands will be introduced in this chapter and Chapter 27 and used in Chapter 28.

The sample screens in this book show dBASE III Plus commands in uppercase letters. To avoid confusion, you should type uppercase letters too. Press CapsLock to activate the *caps lock* feature. With *caps lock* on, when you type an alphabetic key, you enter an uppercase letter. (Press ⇧ *and* the key to type lowercase.) Digits and punctuation marks are not affected; for example, you still must press ⇧ *and* the digit 4 to type a dollar sign. CapsLock acts as a toggle switch; press it once to turn *caps lock* on, and press it again to turn *caps lock* off.

The assistant screen (Fig. 26.3) normally appears when you start dBASE III Plus. However, if other people are using your system, the default may have been changed to the dot prompt. If so, your screen will resemble Fig. 26.4; look for a period just above the word *Command* in the lower left corner. So that you'll know how to respond if a dot prompt screen appears, the next section will show you how to exit to the dot prompt and then reenter the assistant.

Exiting to the Dot Prompt

If your screen resembles Fig. 26.3, press

Figure 26.3
The dBASE III Plus assistant screen.

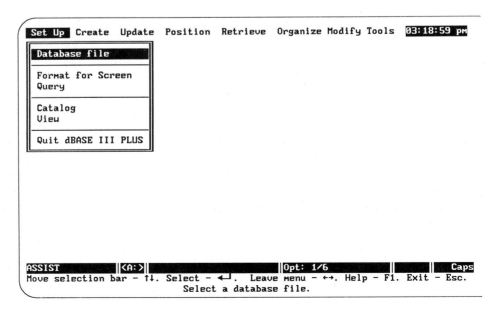

Figure 26.4
The dBASE III Plus dot
prompt screen.

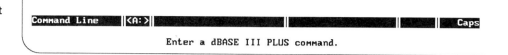

to exit to the dot prompt screen (Fig. 26.4). (If you already have a dot prompt, do nothing.) To return to the assistant screen, type

> ASSIST

at the dot prompt and press ⏎. Your screen will once again resemble Fig. 26.3.

∎ *Keystroke Summary*

Return to the assistant

    Type: **ASSIST**

    Press: ⏎

∎ *What Can Go Wrong?*

1. A message just above the dot prompt reads "*** Unrecognized command verb."

Cause: You misspelled the command.

Solution: Retype ASSIST and press ⏎.

2. The command name (ASSIST) appears in all lowercase letters.

Cause: The *caps lock* feature is off.

Solution: dBASE III Plus will accept commands typed in uppercase or lowercase, so don't worry about it. Press ⏎ to return to the assistant screen. Then press (CapsLock) once to activate caps lock for future commands. ∎

The Escape Key

It is relatively easy to issue a command accidentally through the assistant, and it's frustrating when you don't know how to recover. Fortunately, dBASE III Plus provides a simple solution: Just press (Esc).

    For example, when you first load the assistant, the *Set Up* menu appears on the screen with *Database file* highlighted. "Accidentally" press ⏎ to issue a *Database file* command. You should see a list of disk drives just to the right of the menu (Fig. 26.5). (The figure shows only drives A and B; your screen may show more.) Press (Esc). The list of drives will disappear, and you'll return to the original assistant screen (Fig. 26.3).

Figure 26.5

This screen will appear if you accidentally issue a *Database file* command from the *Set Up* menu.

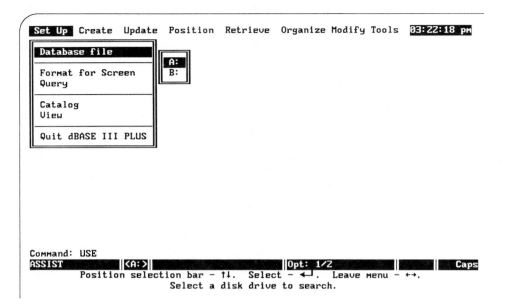

The escape key, (Esc), cancels your most recent action and, in effect, sends you back one screen. Keep pressing (Esc) until you reach the screen you want. Remember, however, that pressing (Esc) on the assistant screen sends you to the dot prompt. If that happens, type ASSIST and press (↵) to get back to the assistant.

The Assistant Screen

Look at the **menu bar** on the top line of the assistant screen (Fig. 26.3). It lists primary command groups; *Set Up* should be highlighted. Just below the menu bar, the **drop-down menu** lists the commands in the highlighted group; note that the first choice, *Database file*, is also highlighted. The screen's bottom line is called the **message line**; it should read

        Select a database file.

The highlighted menu choice allows you to select an existing database file.

The **navigation line** (just above the message line) summarizes the keys that move you through the menus. The **status bar** (Fig. 26.6) indicates that you are in assistant mode (ASSIST), that the default drive is A (C on a hard disk system), that the current menu choice (*Database file*) is the first of six possible choices (1/6 means 1 of 6), and that the *caps lock* feature is active (*Caps*). The **action line** is just above the status bar; it should be blank. Watch the changing contents of the bottom four screen lines as you work with the assistant.

Figure 26.6
The status bar.

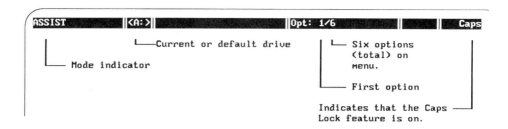

Press ⊟ or ⊡ to move the **selection bar** across the menu bar. For example, press ⊡, and the word *Create* will be highlighted (Fig. 26.7). Note that a new drop-down menu replaces the first one; it lists commands associated with creating a database. Now press ⊟. The selection bar will move back to *Set Up*, and your screen will once again resemble Fig. 26.3.

Menus can also be accessed or **opened** by typing the first letter of the group name. For example, type the letter *C* for *Create*. Your screen will once again resemble Fig. 26.7. Note that the message line now reads

```
Create a database file structure.
```

As the message suggests, the highlighted command allows you to create a database file structure.

Practice moving across the menu bar by pressing ⊡ several times. When you come to the end of the menu bar (*Tools*), pressing ⊡ again

Figure 26.7
The Create menu.

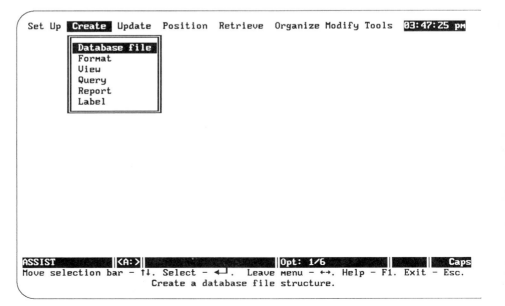

sends you back to *Set Up*. Next, move through the menu by pressing
⊟. Finally, practice opening a menu by typing the first letter of the
desired command: *C* for *Create*, *T* for *Tools*, and so on. You'll be using
the *Set Up* menu in the next section, so type *S* when you finish. Your
screen should once again resemble Fig. 26.3.

Quitting dBASE III Plus

To make a selection from an open menu, press the ⊡ and ⊡ keys to
highlight your choice and then press ⊡. For example, consider the last
choice on the *Set Up* menu,

      Quit dBASE III Plus

It closes all open database files and returns you to DOS.

If you haven't already opened the *Set Up* menu, type *S*. Press ⊡
to move the selection bar; note how the message line changes with
each command. Position the selection bar on *Quit dBASE III Plus*
(Fig. 26.8); the message line should read

      Finish this session of ASSIST and QUIT dBASE III PLUS.

Press ⊡ to execute the command, and you will return to DOS. Reload
dBASE III Plus; if you have forgotten how, refer back to the beginning
of this chapter. Also, briefly review the keys you pressed to move the
selection bar. ⊟ and ⊟ move it across the screen, from menu to menu.
⊡ and ⊡ move it up and down the screen, from line to line within a

Figure 26.8
To exit dBASE III Plus,
move the selection
bar to *Quit dBASE III
PLUS* on the *Set Up*
menu and press ⊡.

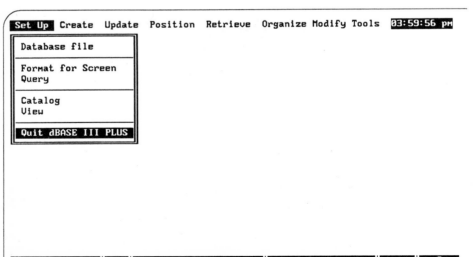

menu. If that seems obvious, then the designers of dBASE III Plus have achieved one of their objectives.

Incidentally, if you had changed your mind and decided not to quit, you could have pressed ⊡ or ⊡ to choose another menu or ⊡ or ⊡ to choose another command. A command is not executed until you press ⊡.

▪ *Keystroke Summary*

Exit dBASE III Plus

From the Assistant:		**From the Dot Prompt:**
Menu:	Set Up	Type: **QUIT**
Command:	Quit dBASE III Plus	Press: ⊡
Press:	⊡

Selecting a Data Drive

One of the first things you must do when you start dBASE III Plus is to tell it which disk drive to use as a data drive. Select the *Tools* menu by typing *T*. Since *Set drive* is the first menu selection, it is not necessary to move the selection bar; simply press ⊡ to issue the command. Note the submenu of available drives (Fig. 26.9). Note also that the action line, the fourth line from the bottom of the screen,

Figure 26.9
The *Set drive* command is on the *Tools* menu.

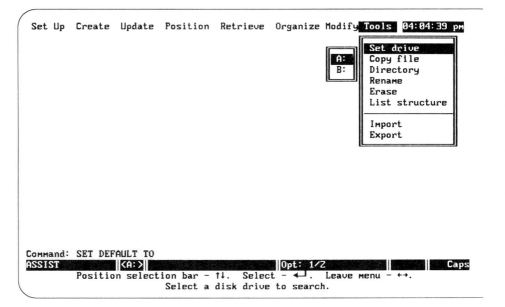

contains the message

```
Command: SET DEFAULT TO
```

The assistant accepts your menu choices and builds a command on the action line. As you become more familiar with dBASE III Plus, you will begin to type many of your own commands at the dot prompt rather than work through the assistant. The action line command matches the equivalent dot prompt command.

The length of the drives submenu can vary. A two-diskette system may list only A and B; a hard disk system may add C; a network system may list several drives. Your screen will identify the drives that are valid on your system. Note that the A drive is highlighted in Fig. 26.9.

If you are using a diskette-based system, press ⬆ or ⬇ until drive B is highlighted. If you have a hard disk system, you might want to use drive C or store your data on a diskette in drive A. After marking the desired drive, press ⏎. Note the status bar; the drive that you selected is now identified as the default drive.

▪ *Keystroke Summary*

Select data drive

From the Assistant:

Menu:	Tools
Command:	Set drive
Press:	⏎
Highlight:	drive letter
Press:	⏎

From the Dot Prompt:

Type:	**SET DEFAULT TO** *d:* (where *d* = drive)
Press:	⏎

▪ *What Can Go Wrong?*

1. You typed *S* to select *Set drive* from the *Tools* menu, but the *Set Up* menu dropped down.

Cause: Typing a letter opens a menu on the menu bar. Commands are selected from a menu by moving the selection bar to your choice and then pressing ⏎.

Solution: Open the *Tools* menu by typing *T.* Select *Set drive* by moving the selection bar and pressing ⏎.

2. The system does not respond when you type the drive letter.

Cause: Drive selections must be made by moving the selection bar to the drive choice and pressing ⏎.

Solution: Use the ⬆ or ⬇ key to move the selection bar to the proper drive letter and then press ⏎.

3. The selection bar skips over some choices.

Cause: Some choices are not available. For example, if you have not yet created a database, there are no data to manipulate, so data manipulation commands are meaningless. Choices that are not yet available appear dim.

Solution: At the appropriate time you'll be able to access these commands. ■

Creating the First Database File

Assume that you have recently started a small business named Campus Threads. You sell school sweaters, jackets, and other items of clothing to college students. Because your capital is limited, you maintain very little inventory; instead, you take orders, arrange to have the merchandise delivered, and then distribute it. You require a 50 percent deposit when the order is placed, the balance being due on delivery.

The business is going well, but you would like to expand. While going through the last few months' sales invoices, you notice several repeat customers. Perhaps sending monthly promotional mailings to all former customers might increase sales. In the following lesson you'll use dBASE III Plus to organize a database to support this application.

Planning a Database

The first step in defining a database is planning its structure. Start by listing the attributes that you'd like to store. For example, to prepare promotional mailings, you'll need each customer's first name, last name, dormitory, and room number. Also, it might be useful to keep track of the date on which a customer last placed an order and the amount he or she currently has on deposit.

Entering the Create Command

Given a list of attributes, the next step is to specify the database structure. From the assistant, open the *Create* menu. (Type *C*, or move the selection bar to highlight *Create*.) Your screen should resemble Fig. 26.7, with the first menu option

```
Database file
```

highlighted. Press ⏎ to select that first command. Now check the message line (Fig. 26.10); it should read

```
Select a disk drive to search.
```

Note also the action line. It reads

```
Command: CREATE
```

Figure 26.10

The first step in creating a database file is selecting a disk drive.

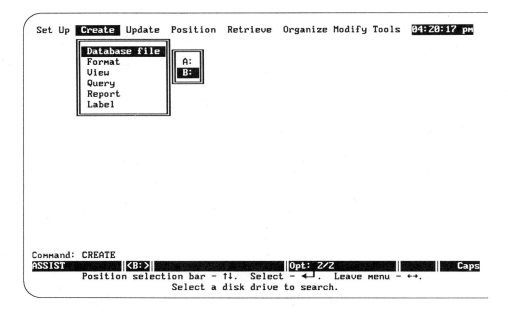

```
    Set Up  Create  Update  Position  Retrieve  Organize Modify Tools  04:20:17 pm
            ┌─────────────────┐
            │ Database file   │ ┌───┐
            │ Format          │ │ A:│
            │ View            │ │ B:│
            │ Query           │ └───┘
            │ Report          │
            │ Label           │
            └─────────────────┘




    Command: CREATE
    ASSIST        ║<B:>║                    ║Opt: 2/2║            ║ Caps
            Position selection bar - ↑↓.  Select - ◄┘.  Leave menu - ↔.
                        Select a disk drive to search.
```

A few more steps are needed to complete the command. Later, when you learn to use the dot prompt, you can type the command directly.

A submenu of drives is displayed to the right of the *Create* menu (Fig. 26.10). Earlier in the chapter, you identified the default drive; it should be highlighted. If the wrong drive is highlighted, press ⊺ or ⊥ to mark the correct one. Then press ◄┘.

The action line will change to

    Command: CREATE B:

(replace the B with your default drive), and a window reading

    Enter the name of the file:

will appear just below the drop-down menu. Database files are stored and retrieved by name, and it's up to you to provide a file name. You'll have to remember the file name when you want to retrieve the data, so choose a name that suggests the file's contents; for example, CUSTOMER is a good choice for a file that holds customer data. Type CUSTOMER; the window should read

    Enter the name of the file: CUSTOMER

Then press ◄┘. The disk drive will activate, and a new screen will appear (Fig. 26.11).

dBASE III Plus automatically adds the extension *dbf* to all database files. The name you assigned, CUSTOMER, plus the dBASE III Plus extension, *dbf*, make up the DOS file name CUSTOMER.dbf.

Figure 26.11
This dBASE III Plus table is used to define the database file structure.

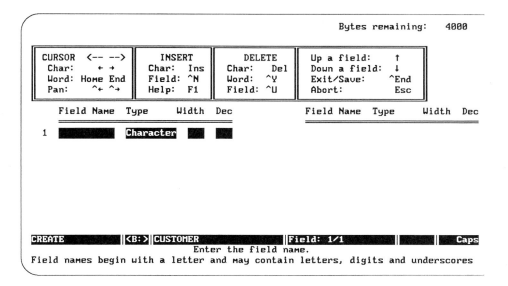

■ *Keystroke Summary*

Create a file

From the Assistant:		From the Dot Prompt:	
Menu:	Create	Type:	**CREATE** *d:\fileneme*
Command:	Database file		(*d* = drive)
Press:	↵	Press:	↵
Highlight:	drive letter		
Press:	↵		
Type:	*filename*		
Press:	↵		

■ *What Can Go Wrong?*

1. A message on the action line reads "B:CUSTOMER.dbf already exists, overwrite it? (Y/N).

Cause: There is a file named CUSTOMER stored on the disk. If you are sharing the computer or a data disk with other users, one of them might have created the file. If you overwrite it, you will destroy the old file.

Solution: If you know who created the old CUSTOMER file and have his or her permission to destroy it, type Y. Otherwise, type N. When the assistant screen reappears, repeat the CREATE command. This time choose a different file name; for example, you might type your initials followed by CUST. Remember your file name for future tutorials. ■

Defining the File Structure

The screen (Fig. 26.11) displays a table used to define the database file structure. At the top of the table is a help window; you can toggle it on or off by pressing F1. Try it. Press F1, and the help window will disappear. Press F1 again to get it back.

The help window summarizes the keys used to define the database structure. The caret symbol (^) represents the control key, Ctrl; it means that you should simultaneously press Ctrl *and* the companion key. For example, look to the right of the help window and find *Exit / Save:*. Next to it is the symbol *^End*. Later in the chapter, when you are ready to return to the assistant screen (*Note:* NOT NOW), you will hold Ctrl and tap End. Refer to the help window if you forget how to move from field to field or make a mistake in defining the database structure.

Just above the help window is a message that reads

```
Bytes remaining:  4000
```

The maximum allowable length of a record is 4000 bytes, each byte holding one character. You have not yet started defining the file's structure, so all 4000 bytes are still available.

Specifying a Field Name

A list of attributes is fine for describing a file's contents to a human being, but the computer needs more detail. The first step in defining a field is to name it. Field names can be up to ten characters long. You can use any combination of letters, digits, and underscore characters, but the first character must be a letter. Choose meaningful names; for example, FIRST_NAME is much better than X for a field containing a first name, although both are legal.

When you enter commands or field names, dBASE III Plus converts all letters to uppercase. That is not true for data, however. For now, to avoid confusion, make sure the *caps lock* feature is active and type everything in uppercase. To enter the first field's name, type

```
FIRST_NAME
```

in the highlighted space. (*Note:* The character between the T and the N is an underscore, not a dash.) If you make a mistake, press ← to erase it and then continue typing. When you enter the tenth character, the computer will beep and automatically advance to the column headed *Type*.

■ *What Can Go Wrong?*

1. The computer beeps, and it won't accept the character you typed.

Cause: You typed an illegal character; for example, you might have typed a dash instead of an underscore.

Solution: Read the message line; it states that "Field names begin with a letter and may contain letters, digits and underscores." Continue typing, but use legal characters.

2. A screen message reads "Press ENTER to confirm. Any other key to resume."

Cause: You pressed Ctrl *and* End. That key combination means "save the structure and exit."

Solution: Press the space bar to return to the file definition screen. ■

Specifying Field Type

Because different kinds of data are stored differently inside the computer, you must also specify the field type. **Character** fields hold such attributes as names, addresses, and telephone numbers. A **numeric** field contains numbers that will participate in arithmetic operations. **Date** fields hold calendar dates in a form that supports date arithmetic; for example, you might want to add 30 days to the current date to compute a due date. **Logical** fields hold yes/no or true/false values. A **memo** field can store up to 5000 characters of text and might be used to hold a memorandum or documentation.

There are two ways to indicate a field's type. Press the space bar, and the word *Numeric* will replace *Character*; press it again, and *Date* appears. Continue pressing the space bar until the correct choice is displayed and then press ⏎. An option is to type *C* for character, *N* for numeric, *D* for date, *L* for logical, or *M* for memo. A customer's first name is clearly a character field, so type *C*. The cursor will move to the column labeled *Width*.

■ *What Can Go Wrong?*

1. The computer beeps and the message line reads "Press any key to continue ..."

Cause: You typed the wrong character.

Solution: Read the navigation line; "Field type must be C, N, D, L, or M." Press the space bar and select a legal field type. ■

Specifying Field Width

The next step is to specify the field width. A character field can contain up to 254 characters. Numeric fields are accurate to as many as 15 digits and can hold no more than 19 characters. To determine a numeric field's width, count each digit. Count the decimal point, too, and if the number can be negative, include a position for the minus sign. For example, the number −123.45 is *seven* positions wide. Date fields are eight characters wide and consist of a two-digit month, a slash, a two-digit day, a slash, and a two-digit year. Logical fields occupy a single character.

A field should be just wide enough to hold its biggest possible value. That's tough to define for a name because tomorrow can always bring a new customer with an exceptionally long name. Fortunately, it's easy to change a dBASE III Plus file structure when the need arises. For now, 20 characters seems reasonable for first name, so type 20 and press ⏎.

Why press ⏎? When you entered the field name, FIRST_NAME, you typed the maximum allowable ten characters, so dBASE III Plus "knew" you were finished. But the field width can be anything between 1 and 254. Thus you must press ⏎ to let dBASE III Plus know when you have finished typing.

■ *What Can Go Wrong?*

1. The computer beeps. The navigation line reads "Illegal data length."

Cause: The value you typed exceeded the maximum allowable field width.

Solution: Press the space bar and try again. Character fields can be no more than 254 characters wide; numeric fields can hold no more than 19 characters. ■

Defining the Remaining Fields

Figure 26.12 shows the file structure after all six fields have been defined; use it as a guide and specify the remaining fields. Watch the

Figure 26.12
This screen shows the fields in the CUSTOMER database file structure.

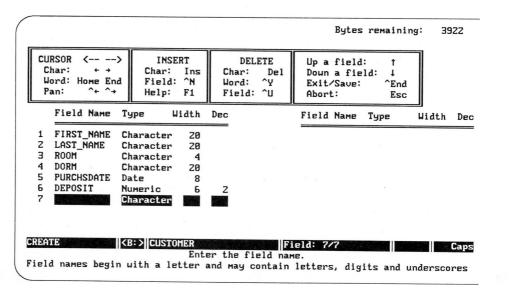

screen as you type; note how the message line guides you through the process. If you make a mistake, press ◄ to erase a character and then retype it. See "What Can Go Wrong?" following this section if you notice an error after you complete a field.

LAST_NAME is less than ten characters long, so you must press ◄┘ when you finish typing it. (How else would dBASE III Plus know you are finished?) Field 5, PURCHSDATE, has a ten-character name. When you type the tenth character, the computer will beep and automatically advance to the next column; do *not* press ◄┘ when you hear the computer beep. The width is automatically set to 8 for a date field; as soon as you define the type as *Date*, the cursor will advance to the next field.

DEPOSIT is numeric. You must indicate both the total field width and the number of digits to the right of the decimal point for a numeric field. (The number of decimal digits must be at least two less than the field width.) For example, DEPOSIT is six characters wide with two digits to the right of the decimal point; thus its biggest possible value is 999.99. (Yes, the decimal point counts.) Press ◄┘ after you type the number of decimal digits.

■ What Can Go Wrong?

1. You notice a typing error after you pressed ◄┘. For example, you notice that the field name is wrong as you are entering the field type.

Cause: You made a typing error.

Solution: Press ◄ to move the cursor to the incorrect entry. Press ◄ and/or [Del] to delete the entry (for example, delete the entire field name). Then retype it. When you finish, press ◄┘ one or more times until the cursor is back where you started, and continue defining the file structure.

2. After you press ◄┘, you notice a mistake in a prior field definition.

Cause: You made a typing error.

Solution: Press ↑ or ↓ to move the cursor to the target field. See the solution to problem 1 for suggestions on correcting the error.

3. You press ↑ to move back to the previous field to make a correction, but the computer beeps, and the message line says "Illegal data length".

Cause: You named the current field, but you didn't define its width.

Solution: Before you make corrections to a prior field, you must finish defining the current one. Enter the field width and then make the correction.

4. The computer beeps, and the navigation line reads "Illegal Decimal length".

Cause: Either you specified too many decimal digits or you typed the wrong field width.

Solution: Press the space bar. Check the field width; if it is wrong, press ◄ until the cursor moves back to field width, type the correct value, press ◄┘, and then type the number of decimal digits. If the field width is right, retype the number of decimal digits; remember that the value must be at least two less than the field width. Press ◄┘ when you finish. ■

452 ■ Creating a Database

Figure 26.13
The append screen is
used to add data to a
database.

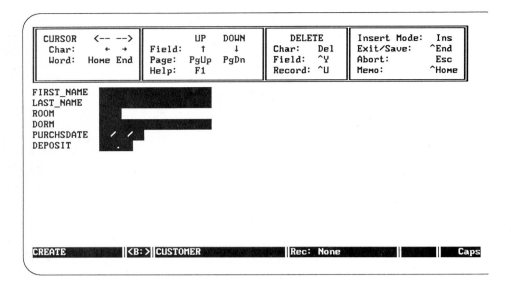

Exiting the Create Command

Read through the file structure (Fig. 26.12) and make sure all fields
are entered correctly. Fix any errors; see "What Can Go Wrong?" for
suggestions. When you finish, the cursor should mark field 7's empty
field name. Simultaneously, press Ctrl *and* End to save the database
file and exit the create command. A message

```
Press ENTER to confirm. Any other key to resume.
```

will ask you to confirm your decision; respond by pressing ↵. Pressing
any other key allows you to continue adding fields.

Next, you'll be asked whether you wish to

```
Input data records now? (Y/N)
```

Type Y, and the **append screen** will appear (Fig. 26.13); you'll use it
in the next section to add data to the database file. Typing N would
have saved the file structure to disk and returned you to the assistant
screen.

Entering Data into a Database

Figure 26.14 lists data for the first ten customers; enter them into the
database. Make sure the *caps lock* feature is active before you start.
Although commands can be entered in uppercase or lowercase, dBASE
III Plus is case sensitive with respect to data. Thus LISA and Lisa are
different. Although the rules for capitalizing names are fairly clear,
case can lead to confusion. Typing all letters uppercase will simplify
data retrieval in later chapters.

	First name	Last name	Room	Dormitory	Date	Deposit
Figure 26.14	LISA	KALO	108	EMERISON HALL	05/21/89	50.00
The first ten	PING	CHU	260	IRVIN HALL	03/13/89	20.00
CUSTOMER records.	FRODO	BAGGINS	105	BAG END HALL	05/04/89	
	ANN	AVERY	304	HAMILTON HALL	09/10/89	
	GARY	PINTA	13	TRINITY HALL	05/02/89	
	JASON	PLOETZ	1045	RAGGIN TOWER	05/19/89	50.00
	TAMMY	RAMBO	111	IRVIN HALL	12/18/88	
	RHONDA	PERUCCA	45	SWING HALL	05/18/89	25.00
	SUSAN	SMITHSON	65	ANN PASS HALL	04/30/89	
	ARAGORN	STRIDER	400	BRANDYWINE HALL	05/12/89	50.00

Type *LISA*. Then press ↵. Next, type *KALO* and press ↵. Follow the same procedure to enter Lisa's room number (108) and dormitory (EMERISON HALL).

The purchase date field is different. dBASE III Plus expects two-character months, days, and years, so add leading zeros where necessary; for example, type 05 instead of 5 for May. The slashes that separate the month, day, and year are inserted for you. Type 05, then 21, then 89. After you type the last character in the year, the computer will beep and advance to the next field. Date fields are, by definition, eight characters wide, and six digits plus two slashes fill the field. Thus dBASE III Plus automatically advances to the next field, saving you a keystroke.

A caution: Do not press ↵. If you press ↵ when the computer has already moved to the next field, that field will be left blank. *Do not press* ↵ *when you hear the computer beep.*

Enter the first customer's deposit next. Type 50.0 (Fig. 26.15). Then type the last zero to complete the field; once again the computer will beep and advance to the first field in the next record. *Do not press* ↵. Pressing ↵ when the cursor marks the first field of an empty record tells dBASE III Plus that you are ready to exit the append screen.

Integer values can be entered in an empty numeric field without typing the decimal point or the trailing zeros; for example, you could have typed 50 for the first customer's deposit and let dBASE III Plus take care of decimal alignment. However, unless you press ↵, the computer has no way of knowing you are finished typing the field.

Type the data for the remaining customers listed in Fig. 26.14. Several customers have no value in the deposit field; press ↵ to leave this field blank. As you type, note the status bar at the bottom of the

Figure 26.15

The first record just before the last digit is typed.

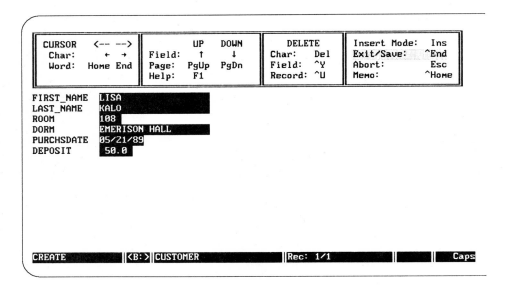

```
┌─────────────────┬─────────────────┬─────────────────┬────────────────────┐
│ CURSOR  <-- -->  │          UP  DOWN │    DELETE       │ Insert Mode:   Ins │
│  Char:    ←   →  │ Field:   ↑    ↓   │ Char:     Del   │ Exit/Save:    ^End │
│  Word:  Home End │ Page:  PgUp PgDn  │ Field:     ^Y   │ Abort:         Esc │
│                  │ Help:    F1       │ Record:    ^U   │ Memo:        ^Home │
└─────────────────┴─────────────────┴─────────────────┴────────────────────┘

FIRST_NAME   LISA
LAST_NAME    KALO
ROOM         108
DORM         EMERISON HALL
PURCHSDATE   05/21/89
DEPOSIT        50.0
```

```
CREATE        │<B:>│CUSTOMER              │Rec: 1/1                     Caps
```

screen. It reads

> Rec: EOF/n

EOF indicates you are at the "end of file," while *n* is the number of records already in the file.

If you make a typing error, press ⬅ to erase the last character and then retype it. The "What Can Go Wrong?" feature following this section suggests some error correction strategies. If you notice other errors, ignore them for now; you'll learn how to correct them in Chapter 27.

Unlike word processing or spreadsheet software, dBASE III Plus has no save command. Instead, it writes records to disk as they are typed. Be aware, however, that if you exit a database incorrectly (by just shutting off the computer or pulling the plug), files may be rendered useless. Consequently, a dBASE III Plus user risks not only current changes or additions, but the original database as well. *Always use the QUIT command* to exit dBASE III Plus.

Incidentally, an accidental power interruption can destroy a dBASE III Plus file, too. It is always wise to maintain a **backup** copy of important database files. See Chapter 10 for suggestions.

■ *What Can Go Wrong?*

1. When you try to enter leading zeros in a date field, the computer just beeps.

Cause: You might be typing the letter O instead of the digit zero.

Solution: Type zero (0).

2. The last name is in the same field as the first name.

Cause: You forgot to press ⏎ after typing the first name.

Solution: Press ↑ until you are in the first name field. Then press → or ← to position the cursor on the first letter of the last name. Press Del repeatedly until the last name is deleted. Press ⏎ to move to the last name field and then type the last name.

3. As you begin typing the dormitory name, the computer beeps. When you look at the screen, the first character or two of the dormitory name is in the room number field and the cursor is in the dormitory field.

Cause: You forgot to press ⏎ after you typed the room number. When additional characters filled the field, dBASE III Plus automatically moved to the next field.

Solution: Press ↑ until you are in the room number field. Press → to position the cursor on the alphabetic character and then press Del to delete it. Press ⏎ to move to the dormitory field and then type the dormitory name.

4. The dormitory name field is blank, and you are trying to type the name in the date field.

Cause: You typed a four-digit room number. The computer beeped and advanced to the dormitory name field, but you pressed ⏎ anyway.

Solution: Press ↑ to return to the dormitory name field. Type the dormitory name and then press ⏎.

5. The computer skipped over the deposit field.

Cause: After entering the last purchase date, you pressed ⏎. Because you filled the date field, the computer automatically advanced to the next field. When you pressed ⏎, you left that field blank.

Solution: Press PgUp until the record with the missing deposit appears. Press ⏎ until the cursor is in the deposit field and enter the correct amount; then press ⏎.

6. The computer beeps as you type a date, and the message line reads "Invalid date. (press SPACE)."

Cause: You typed illegal characters in the date field; only digits are legal. Perhaps you typed the slashes.

Solution: Press the space bar and try again.

7. After you press ⏎, the append screen is replaced by the assistant screen.

Cause: You probably pressed ⏎ when the cursor was marking the first field in an empty record. Perhaps you typed two digits after the decimal point and then pressed ⏎ after the cursor had automatically advanced to the first field in the next record. Pressing ⏎ while the cursor marks the first field of an empty record is one way to exit append.

Solution: The next exercise will show you how to issue an APPEND command to add records to an existing file. Add the missing records as part of that exercise. ▪

Exiting the APPEND Command

After you have entered the ten records, the cursor should be on a blank FIRST_NAME field, and the status line should read *EOF/10*. Note that record 11 is empty. With the cursor marking the first field of an empty record, press ⏎ to exit *Append*, save the file, and return to the assistant.

Pressing ⏎ while the cursor marks the first field of an empty record is the suggested way to exit *Append*, but there is another way. Check the help menu (Fig. 26.15) and find *Exit/Save:* in the fourth column. The entry *^End* means that you simultaneously press Ctrl and End to exit and save the file. Pressing Ctrl *and* End is used to exit from any record in the database file after you make changes. If you press Ctrl *and* End while the cursor marks an empty record, you will add that empty record to the database.

Appending More Records

The *Append* command is used to add records to a database file. Previously, you performed an append operation as part of the file creation process. This time, issue the command.

Move the selection bar to *Update* or type *U*. *Append* is the first choice on the update menu. If necessary, press ↑ or ↓ to highlight *Append*, and press ⏎. The append screen will appear. Check the status bar. Just to the right of the file name, CUSTOMER, the record pointer should read

    Rec: EOF/10

Figure 26.16 shows 15 more customer records. Enter them into your database. After you type the last one, the cursor will mark the

Figure 26.16

Use the *Append* command to add these 15 records to the database.

First name	Last name	Room	Dormitory	Date	Deposit
BILBO	BAGGINS	105	BAG END HALL	05/10/89	30.00
MARY	WORTH	43	SWING HALL	05/21/89	40.00
THORIN	OAKENSHIELD	113	ELROND HOUSE	04/30/89	90.00
MERRY	BRANDYBUCK	106	BAG END HALL	05/20/89	
PIPPIN	TOOK	106	BAG END HALL	09/17/88	
BELINDA	BAER	324	RAGGIN TOWER	05/21/89	20.00
KUNTA	KINTE	243	CHAD HALL	02/18/89	
MATA	HARI	119	RINELAND HALL	05/18/89	
JUAN	GOMEZ	1023	RAGGIN TOWER	09/17/88	
OPUS	BLOOM	13	SOUTH HALL	11/12/88	
MICHAEL	MOUSE	201	DISNEY HALL	10/18/88	
CLAYTON	COTTRELL	187	HAMILTON HALL	05/12/89	40.00
BRIAN	SMITH	894	RAGGIN TOWER	12/20/87	
DEEDRA	HOYT	308	IRVIN HALL	05/12/89	
BULLWINKLE	MOOSE	607	RAGGIN TOWER	09/10/88	

first field of an empty record (number 26), and the status line will read *EOF/25*. Press ↵ to exit *Append* and save the database file. The assistant screen will reappear. The file now contains 25 records, so the status line should read Rec: *25/25*.

Append records

From the Assistant:		From the Dot Prompt:	
Menu:	Update	Type:	**APPEND**
Command:	Append	Press:	↵
Press:	↵		

Exiting dBASE III Plus

This is a good time for you to take a break. *NEVER, NEVER* turn off the computer without first exiting dBASE III Plus. You could render your database files useless if you do.

The *Quit* command, selected from the *Set Up* menu, closes all dBASE III Plus files and then exits to DOS. Type *S*. Use the ↑ or ↓ key to move the selection bar to highlight

```
Quit dBASE III Plus
```

and then press ↵. A message near the top of the screen will read

```
*** END RUN  dBASE III PLUS
```

and the DOS prompt will appear just below it. Remove your data and (if appropriate) program disks.

Exit dBASE III Plus

From the Assistant:		From the Dot Prompt:	
Menu:	Set Up	Type:	**QUIT**
Command:	Quit dBASE III Plus	Press:	↵
Press:	↵		

Summary

Starting dBASE III Plus

Function	Page
Load dBASE III Plus from diskette	435
Load dBASE III Plus from hard disk	436

From the Assistant

Function	Menu	Command	Page
Append records	Update	Append	456
Create file	Create	Database file	445

Function	Menu	Command	Page
Exit dBASE III Plus	Set Up	Quit dBASE . . .	442
Select default drive	Tools	Set drive	443

From the Dot Prompt

Function	Command	Page
Append records	APPEND	456
Create file	CREATE	445
Exit dBASE III Plus	QUIT	442
Return to assistant	ASSIST	439
Select default drive	SET DEFAULT TO	443

Options and Functions

Option or Function	Format	Page
Cancel action	[Esc]	439
Exit to dot prompt	[Esc]	438

Self-Test

1. dBASE III Plus commands can be entered through the _____ screen or at the _____.

2. On the assistant screen the _____ lists primary command groups.

3. dBASE III Plus commands are listed below the menu bar in a _____.

4. You select a group of commands from the menu bar by moving the _____ or by typing the _____ of the group name.

5. The commands for creating a database file are accessed through the_____ menu.

6. A database file is stored and retrieved by its _____.

7. A person's name is an example of a _____ field.

8. _____ fields can participate in arithmetic operations.

9. Records are added to a database file through the _____ screen.

10. To exit the append screen, press _____ on an empty record or simultaneously press _____ on any record.

Exercises

1. Create a name and address file using these data. (If you prefer, substitute the names and addresses of your friends and relatives.)

First Name	Last Name	Street Address	City	St	Zip
John	Alexander	621 McGuffey	Columbus	OH	44236
Sharon	Anderson	206 Campus Dr	Hudson	OH	43606
Lisa	Benton	147 Hedden Ct	Wyoming	OH	43551
Susan	Billings	303 Boston Rd	Oxford	OH	45050
Chris	Bishop	152 Crest Dr	Randolph	NJ	07832
Karin	Clawson	101 Deer Run	Ashland	OH	44602
Steven	Climer	142 Winslow St	Rochester	NY	14352
Darlene	Cortez	720 Taylor Ave	Medina	OH	44365
Darrell	Culler	109 Lyon St	Oxford	OH	45050
Jeffery	Dennison	229 Main St	Westlake	MI	48235
Edward	Dorsey	200 High St	Loveland	OH	45024
Jay	Edwards	132 Elm St	Cincinnati	OH	45001
Rika	Fujii	618 Locust St	Berlin	WI	53740
Anjelika	Gonzalez	23 Tappan St	Fairfax	VA	22702
Lynn	Hahne	335 Scott Rd	Columbus	OH	44232
Mark	Hiestand	5 Walker Dr	Cleveland	OH	44120
Matthew	Krieger	Old Mill Rd	Oxford	OH	45050
Stacy	Lewis	190 Lime St	Tega Cay	SC	29735
Tina	Mam	616 Sundance	Lima	OH	45832
Tracy	Patten	161 Krebbs Ct	Monroe	OH	45002
Alex	Porter	26 Leda St	Dayton	OH	45454
Andrew	Reid	795 Linden Ave	Carmel	IN	46952
David	Scott	18 Walnut St	Chicago	IL	60624
Grant	Symmes	498 Joy Rd	Wawa	PA	19018
Deborah	Upham	202 Adams St	Oxford	OH	45050

2. Create a membership file for a campus organization called The Gold Key. Use the data from Exercise 1, or substitute names and addresses from your own organization.

3. Create an inventory file of a record collection. Use the following data, or use data from your own collection.

Title	Artist	Medium
Bach: Brandenberg	Boston Symphony	CD
Beethoven: Symphony #5	Philadelphia Phil.	CD
Grofe: Grand Canyon	Eugene Ormandy	tape
Mozart: Violin Concerto	New York Strings	LP
Vivaldi: Four Seasons	New York Phil.	tape
Born in the USA	Bruce Springsteen	tape
Song Remains the Same	Led Zeppelin	tape
Rumours	Fleetwood Mac	tape
The White Album	The Beatles	LP
Sergeant Pepper	The Beatles	LP
The Innocent Age	Dan Fogelberg	LP
Smiley Smile	The Beach Boys	tape
The Sheik of Araby	Kid Sheik	tape
Chariots of Fire	Vangelis	CD
Stranger in Town	Bob Seger	LP

·27

Maintaining a Database

This chapter introduces the dBASE III Plus features and commands that allow you to:

- retrieve (load) a database file
- view the contents of a database file
- examine and modify a database structure
- modify the contents of a database file
- locate records in a database
- delete selected records

The Second Tutorial

In Chapter 26 you created a database file. In this chapter you will learn how to load a previously created database file and edit it.

Boot DOS and load dBASE III Plus. If you saved your work on a floppy disk, insert the diskette in the appropriate drive and close the drive door. When the assistant screen appears, set the default drive by issuing a *Set drive* command from the *Tools* menu. Now you're ready to begin.

Loading a Database File from Disk

When you start dBASE III Plus, no database is active. The file you created in the first tutorial was saved to disk, but it must be loaded back into memory before you can use it. The *Database file* command, a choice on the *Set Up* menu, loads a database. To access it,

Type:	S
Highlight:	Database file
Press:	⏎

A list of drives will be displayed. Highlight the appropriate drive and press ⏎.

A submenu of the files on the selected drive will appear to the right of the *Set Up* menu (Fig. 27.1). A diskette-based system will probably list only the CUSTOMER file; a hard disk user might see numerous files. Move the selection bar to highlight CUSTOMER.dbf and press ⏎. (*dbf* is an extension added by dBASE III Plus.) Check the action line at the bottom of your screen; it should read

```
Command: USE B:CUSTOMER
```

A dialogue window reading

```
Is the file indexed? [Y/N]
```

will replace the list of database files. The CUSTOMER file is not indexed, so type *N*. (Indexing will be explained in Chapter 29.) The assistant screen will reappear (Fig. 27.2). Note that the status bar identifies CUSTOMER as the active file.

Figure 27.1

The database files stored on the disk in the indicated drive or under the indicated directory are listed to the right of the menu.

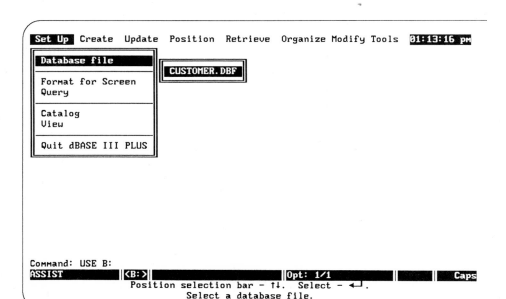

Figure 27.2
As this screen shows,
CUSTOMER is the
active file.

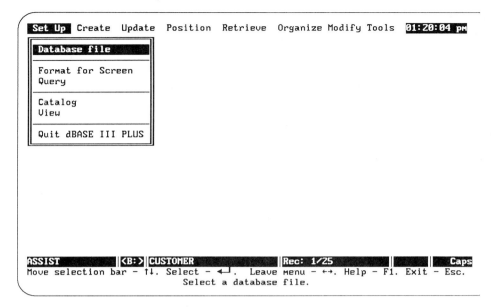

■ *Keystroke
Summary*

Load a database file

From the Assistant:	**From the Dot Prompt:**

From the Assistant:

Menu:	Set Up
Command:	Database file
Highlight:	drive letter
Press:	↵
Highlight:	filename
Press:	↵
Type:	**N** (unless indexed)

From the Dot Prompt:

Type:	**USE** *d:filename*
	(*d* = drive)
Press:	↵

■ *What Can
Go Wrong?*

1. The computer beeps and displays the message "No files of the requested type are present. Press any key to continue."

Cause: No files with *dbf* extensions were found on the indicated drive. There are at least five possible causes:

a. you inserted the wrong disk;

b. you indicated the wrong drive;

c. the file and the dBASE III Plus program are stored under different hard disk directories;

d. the file was never created;

e. the file was erased.

Solution: If you are using diskettes, verify that you have placed the proper disk in the computer and try again. If you are using a hard disk, determine the path name of the directory on which you saved the file; you might want to ask your instructor or another technical expert for help. Press ⌷Esc⌷ to go to the dot prompt screen and type the command

```
SET PATH TO c:pathname
```

where *c:pathname* is replaced by the appropriate path name. Press ⌷. Then return to the assistant and try again. If dBASE III Plus still can't find the file, go back to Chapter 26 and recreate it. ■

Opening and Closing Files

It might be useful to consider what happens when you load a database file from disk. Before the data can be processed, they must be copied into main memory. Because a disk can hold many files, the computer must find the file before it can read the data. Thus the first step in accessing a database file is to open it.

The key to the open process is the disk's **directory**. Like a table of contents, the directory lists, by name, every file on the disk and indicates the address where the file begins. Opening the file is a two-step process:

1. The user identifies the disk that holds the file. In response, software (in this case, dBASE III Plus and the operating system) reads the disk's directory. This function is performed when you specify a drive letter after selecting *Database file* from the *Set up* menu.

2. The user then indicates the file's name. In response, software searches the directory, finds the referenced file name, and determines where on disk that file is located. This function is performed when you select a file name as part of the *Database file* command.

Once the file is located, its records can be accessed.

Until a file is opened, the computer doesn't know where it is and so can't access it. An open file is accessible, but it is also vulnerable; valid changes and mistakes are *both* possible. Therefore when you finish working with a file, you normally **close** it. Open establishes a link between a program and a file. Close breaks that link. It is difficult to accidentally destroy the contents of an unopened file.

In dBASE III Plus the word *open* also refers to the process of activating a menu. For example, typing *S* opens the *Set Up* menu, while typing *T* opens the *Tools* menu. Opening a menu makes that menu accessible.

The Edit Command

Note the status bar. CUSTOMER is the **active** file. Thus dBASE III Plus will assume that any operations refer to CUSTOMER unless you specify otherwise.

Figure 27.3

The *Edit* command is found on the *Update* menu.

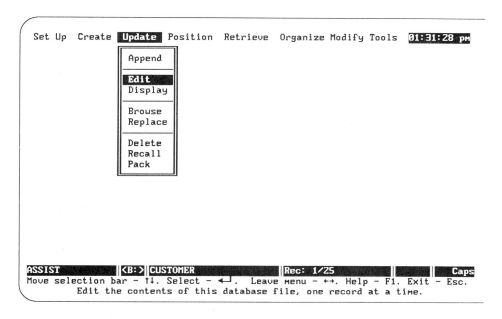

```
Set Up  Create  Update  Position  Retrieve  Organize Modify Tools  01:31:28 pm
                ┌──────────┐
                │  Append  │
                │┌────────┐│
                ││  Edit  ││
                │ Display │
                │          │
                │  Browse  │
                │  Replace │
                │          │
                │  Delete  │
                │  Recall  │
                │  Pack    │
                └──────────┘




ASSIST          ⟨B:⟩ CUSTOMER              Rec: 1/25                    Caps
Move selection bar - ↑↓. Select - ◄┘.  Leave menu - ←→. Help - F1. Exit - Esc.
          Edit the contents of this database file, one record at a time.
```

The database file is in memory, but how can you be sure it actually contains data? One way is to look at the records. Select the *Update* menu by moving the selection bar or typing *U*. Highlight *Edit* (Fig. 27.3) and press ⏎. The edit screen (Fig. 27.4) will replace the assistant screen; it displays a single database record. Check the status bar just to the right of the file name, CUSTOMER, and note the entry

```
Rec: 1/25
```

Figure 27.4

The *Edit* screen displays a single record. The pointer indicates that record's relative position in the database.

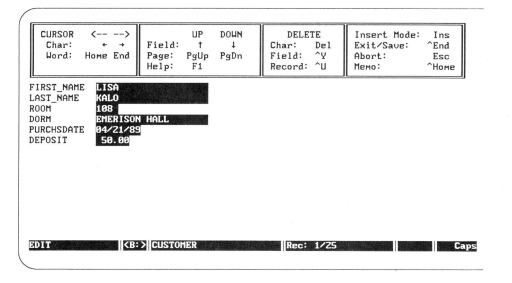

```
┌────────────────────┬──────────────────┬─────────────┬──────────────────┐
│ CURSOR   <-- -->   │        UP   DOWN │   DELETE    │ Insert Mode:  Ins│
│  Char:    ←   →    │ Field:  ↑    ↓   │ Char:   Del │ Exit/Save:   ^End│
│  Word:  Home End   │ Page:  PgUp PgDn │ Field:  ^Y  │ Abort:       Esc │
│                    │ Help:   F1       │ Record: ^U  │ Memo:       ^Home│
└────────────────────┴──────────────────┴─────────────┴──────────────────┘
FIRST_NAME  LISA
LAST_NAME   KALO
ROOM        108
DORM        EMERISON HALL
PURCHSDATE  04/21/89
DEPOSIT       50.00




EDIT            ⟨B:⟩ CUSTOMER              Rec: 1/25                    Caps
```

The first number, called the **pointer**, identifies the record currently being viewed as the first of 25 in the database file. Press `PgDn` to view record 2; note that a new record appears and that the status bar now reads *2 / 25*. Press `PgDn` to view a few more records; press `PgUp` to move the pointer back toward record 1. You can use the *Edit* command to verify a record's contents. Later in the chapter, you'll use an *Edit* command to modify the contents of a record.

Since no changes were made to the database, press `Esc` to return to the assistant screen.

■ *Keystroke Summary*

Edit a file

From the Assistant:		From the Dot Prompt:	
Menu:	Update	Type:	**EDIT**
Command:	Edit	Press:	`↵`
Press:	`↵`		

■ *What Can Go Wrong?*

1. You pressed `PgUp` or `PgDn` to move to a record and were returned to the assistant screen.

Cause: You probably pressed `PgUp` on the first record or `PgDn` on the last record. There are no records before the first one or after the last one. If you try to move to a nonexistent record, you will be returned to the assistant.

Solution: Select the *Edit* command from the *Update* menu to return to the edit screen. ■

Examining the Database Structure

You can examine a database file's structure with a *List Structure* command. From the assistant, type *T* to open the *Tools* menu. Move the selection bar to *List structure* and press `↵`. A dialogue window reading

```
Direct the output to the printer? [Y/N]
```

will appear. Type *N* to display the database structure on the screen (Fig. 27.5). You created the structure in Chapter 26, so it should be familiar.

■ *Keystroke Summary*

List database structure

From the Assistant:		From the Dot Prompt:	
Menu:	Tools	Type:	**DISPLAY STRUC-TURE**
Command:	List Structure		
Press:	`↵`	Press:	`↵`
Type:	**N** or **Y**		

Figure 27.5

The *List structure* command displays the database file's structure.

```
Set Up   Create   Update   Position   Retrieve   Organize Modify  Tools   01:36:34 pm




        Structure for database: B:CUSTOMER.dbf
        Number of data records:      25
        Date of last update   : 06/01/89
        Field  Field Name  Type       Width    Dec
           1   FIRST_NAME  Character     20
           2   LAST_NAME   Character     20
           3   ROOM        Character      4
           4   DORM        Character     20
           5   PURCHSDATE  Date           8
           6   DEPOSIT     Numeric        6        2
        ** Total **                     79
 ASSIST                   <B:> CUSTOMER                  Rec: 1/25            Caps
                  Press any key to continue work in ASSIST.
```

■ *What Can Go Wrong?*

1. The computer beeps, and the error message "Printer not ready" appears in the lower left corner of the screen.

Cause: You pressed the letter "Y", and the printer is not available, not on, or out of paper.

Solution: Correct the printer problem, press the space bar (or any other key) to return to the assistant, and try again. This time, type *N* when the system asks whether you want to direct the output to the printer. ■

Modifying the Database Structure

Briefly review the CUSTOMER file structure (Fig. 27.5). Space on disk is limited, so you don't want to make a field any wider than necessary. A check of the data should convince you that you can safely reduce the first name field to 12 characters. Also, consider the field names. Most of them clearly identify the contents of their field, but PURCHSDATE seems clumsy. It might make sense to change PURCHSDATE to LAST_SALE.

Finally, imagine that you want to add a new field to hold the customer's telephone number. A telephone number requires 12 characters (a three-digit area code, a slash, three digits, a dash, and four more digits). You could insert the new field almost anywhere, but put it between LAST_NAME and ROOM. Note the message line. It reads

```
Press any key to continue work in ASSIST.
```

Press the space bar (or any other key) to return to the assistant screen.

Figure 27.6

Issue a *Database file* command from the *Modify* menu to change a database file's structure. The equivalent dot prompt command is MODIFY STRUCTURE.

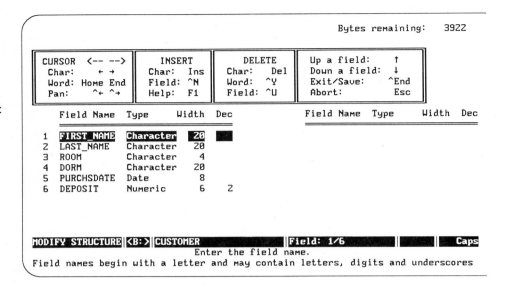

```
                                              Bytes remaining:    3922

 ┌──────────────┬──────────────┬──────────────┬──────────────────────┐
 │ CURSOR  <-- -->│   INSERT    │   DELETE    │ Up a field:      ↑   │
 │ Char:    ← →  │ Char:   Ins │ Char:   Del │ Down a field:    ↓   │
 │ Word: Home End│ Field:   ^N │ Word:    ^Y │ Exit/Save:     ^End  │
 │ Pan:    ^← ^→ │ Help:    F1 │ Field:   ^U │ Abort:          Esc  │
 └──────────────┴──────────────┴──────────────┴──────────────────────┘

     Field Name  Type    Width  Dec        Field Name  Type   Width  Dec

   1 FIRST_NAME  Character   20
   2 LAST_NAME   Character   20
   3 ROOM        Character    4
   4 DORM        Character   20
   5 PURCHSDATE  Date         8
   6 DEPOSIT     Numeric      6    2



 MODIFY STRUCTURE <B:> CUSTOMER                 Field: 1/6              Caps
                      Enter the field name.
 Field names begin with a letter and may contain letters, digits and underscores
```

The *List structure* command allows you to view a file structure, but you can't change anything. To modify the structure, select the *Database file* command from the *Modify* menu. A help menu is displayed near the top of the modify structure screen (Fig. 27.6); press F1 to toggle it on or off.

Modifying a database file's structure is somewhat risky. Existing data must be converted to the new format, and if you're not careful, some of the old data can be lost. Therefore each time you exit *Modify structure*, the database file is backed up. Recall that the old database had the extension *dbf*. The old file's extension is changed to *bak* and the new version of the database is then stored with extension *dbf*. Thus if you did happen to lose some data, you could recover the old database by loading the *bak* copy.

How can you avoid losing data? Rather than memorizing several rules, your best bet is to treat each modification as a separate operation. In other words, go to the modify structure screen, make a change, exit, check the data, and then issue a new command and make the next change.

Start by changing the first-name field's width. The cursor should mark FIRST_NAME; if it doesn't, move it there. Press ↵ twice to move to the field width column. Now type the new width, 12, and press ↵.

Press Ctrl *and* End to save the change and exit *Modify structure*. The message line will read

```
Database records will be APPENDED from backup fields of the
same name only!!
```

Since you haven't changed any field names, you have nothing to worry about. Check the navigation line; it reads

```
Press ENTER to confirm. Any other key to resume.
```

Press ⏎ to return to the assistant screen; the rapidly changing counter on the action line shows that the database records are being updated. Before you move on, issue an *Edit* command from the *Update* menu and check a few records to make sure no data have been lost. Press Esc to return to the assistant.

Change the date field's name next. Open the *Modify* menu, select the *Database file* command, and press ⏎. When the structure appears, press ⏬ to move to the PURCHSDATE field. Make sure the cursor marks the field name. Then type the new name, LAST_SALE, over the old one. Note that the last letter from the old name (an E) still appears; press Del to delete it. Then press ⏎. Your screen should resemble Fig. 27.7.

Press Ctrl *and* End to exit *Modify structure*. The navigation line will read

```
Should data be COPIED from backup for all fields? (Y/N)
```

Type Y and another message will appear:

```
Press ENTER to confirm. Any other key to resume.
```

Press ⏎, and after a brief delay you will return to the assistant. Once again, issue an *Edit* command (from the *Update* menu) and check a few records; press Esc when you're satisfied that no data have been lost.

Figure 27.7
This screen shows the changes in the file structure.

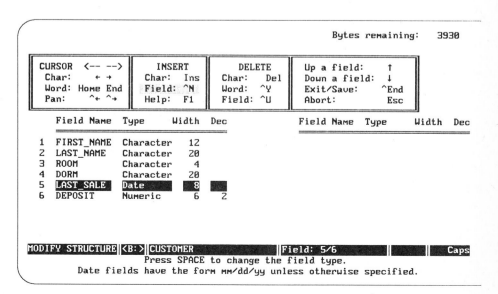

Figure 27.8
This screen shows the new field in place.

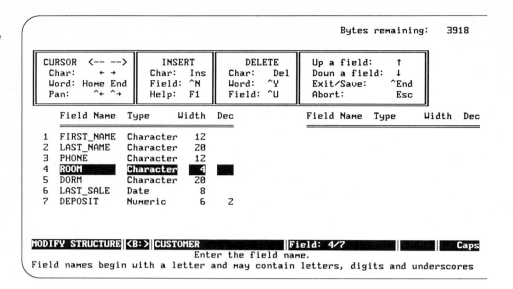

```
                                                    Bytes remaining:    3918

┌──────────────────┐┌──────────────────┐┌──────────────────┐┌────────────────────────┐
│ CURSOR  <-- -->  ││    INSERT        ││    DELETE        ││ Up a field:      ↑     │
│ Char:     ← →    ││ Char:    Ins     ││ Char:    Del     ││ Down a field:    ↓     │
│ Word: Home End   ││ Field:   ^N      ││ Word:    ^Y      ││ Exit/Save:       ^End  │
│ Pan:    ^← ^→    ││ Help:    F1      ││ Field:   ^U      ││ Abort:           Esc   │
└──────────────────┘└──────────────────┘└──────────────────┘└────────────────────────┘

    Field Name   Type     Width  Dec        Field Name   Type      Width  Dec

  1 FIRST_NAME   Character   12
  2 LAST_NAME    Character   20
  3 PHONE        Character   12
  4 ROOM         Character    4
  5 DORM         Character   20
  6 LAST_SALE    Date         8
  7 DEPOSIT      Numeric      6    2


 MODIFY STRUCTURE <B:> CUSTOMER                  Field: 4/7              Caps
                       Enter the field name.
 Field names begin with a letter and may contain letters, digits and underscores
```

The final change is to insert a field to hold the telephone number. Issue a *Database file* command from the *Modify* menu. As the help window indicates (Fig. 27.7), a new field can be inserted into a database file by pressing Ctrl *and* N. What the help window doesn't say is that the new field will be inserted just above the selection bar. Highlight the ROOM field and

Press: Ctrl *and* N

Space for the new field will be inserted just above the selection bar between LAST_NAME and ROOM.

Type the field name, PHONE, and press ↵. The telephone number is a character field, so type C. (Although it will store numbers, no arithmetic will be performed on them.) The field width is 12, so type 12 and press ↵. Your screen should resemble Fig. 27.8, with the selection bar marking ROOM. Correct any errors before you move on; see "What Can Go Wrong?" following this section. Press Ctrl *and* End to save the changes; respond to the confirmation message by pressing ↵. Once you're back to the assistant, use *Edit* (from the *Update* menu) to check a few records. Press Esc to exit *Edit*.

▪ *Keystroke Summary*

Modify database structure

From the Assistant:

Menu: Modify

Command: Database file

Press: ↵

From the Dot Prompt:

Type: **MODIFY STRUC-TURE**

Press: ↵

■ *What Can Go Wrong?*

1. You notice a typing error while modifying the file structure.

Cause: You made a typing error.

Solution: Press ⊤ or ⊥ to move the cursor to the incorrect field; press ⊖ or ⊖ to move the cursor to the error. If the field name, field width, or number of decimal positions is wrong, press Del several times to delete the entire field, retype it, and press ⏎. If the field type is wrong, type the first letter of the correct field type.

2. When you check the contents of the records after modifying the structure, you notice that data are missing from one or more fields for all the records.

Cause: You attempted more than one change on a single field, or you changed an old field name and inserted a new field during the same modify structure operation.

Solution: Reenter the data or exit to DOS and rename the backup (*.bak*) file using extension *.dbf*. (See Chapter 10.)

3. Part of the data in a field is missing, or the field contains a string of asterisks.

Cause: You reduced a field's width below the actual data width. Numeric fields display asterisks; character fields are truncated to the reduced width.

Solution: Increase the field width, reenter the data, or rename the backup file. (See 2 above.)

4. You lost your data while changing a field type.

Cause: If a character field containing nondigits is changed to numeric, the data will be lost.

Solution: Reenter the data or rename the backup file. (See 2 above.)

5. You inserted space for the new field in the wrong place. For example, you put it between FIRST_NAME and LAST_NAME.

Cause: Space is inserted above the cursor, not below it.

Solution: If you have not already pressed Ctrl *and* End to save your changes, press Esc to exit to the assistant and try again. If you have saved your changes, don't worry about it. You'll have a field out of order in future exercises, but as long as you remember what you did, it won't matter. ■

Locating a Record in the Database

Moving the Pointer with the *Goto* Command

Notice, on the status bar, the entry

    Rec: n/25

The second number indicates the total number of records in the database; you should have 25. The first number is the current record, or the pointer. If you issue an *Edit* command, this is the record that will be displayed.

Assume that you just called Opus Bloom and want to record his phone number before you forget it. His record is number 20. You can modify record 20 by making it the current record and then issuing an

Figure 27.9
Record 20 just before
the telephone number
is added.

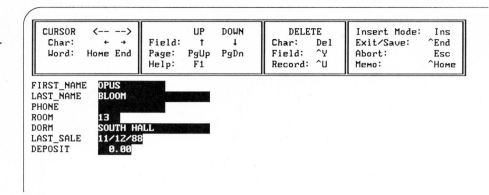

Edit command. Open the *Position* menu. Then highlight *Goto Record* and press ⏎. A submenu will appear to the right of the menu. RECORD sets the pointer to a specific record number; TOP sets the pointer to the first record in the file; BOTTOM sets it to the last record. Move the selection bar to RECORD and press ⏎. A dialogue window

    Enter a numeric value:

will appear. Type 20, press ⏎, and the status bar will indicate

    Rec: 20/25.

Record 20 is now the current record.

Use an *Edit* command to add Bloom's telephone number to his record. Open the *Update* menu, highlight *Edit*, press ⏎, and Opus Bloom's record will appear (Fig. 27.9). Press ⬇ to move the cursor to the phone number field and then type 513/782-9892. The computer will beep and advance to the room number field. Press Ctrl *and* End to save the updated record.

Before continuing with the next section, practice moving the pointer and viewing several records. Go to records 5, 10, 15, TOP, and BOTTOM and issue an *Edit* command to view each one. Press Esc to exit *Edit*.

■ *Keystroke Summary*

Move the pointer

From the Assistant:

Menu:	Position
Command:	Goto Record
Press:	⏎
Highlight:	RECORD
TYPE:	*record number*
Press:	⏎

From the Dot Pprompt:

Type:	**GOTO** *n*
	n = record number,
Press:	⏎

Moving the Pointer with the *Locate* Command

Imagine that you have Bilbo Baggins's telephone number written on your desk calendar but have no idea what his record number is. You do, however, know that the last name is BAGGINS, so you can use a *Locate* command to find his record.

Open the *Position* menu, highlight *Locate*, and press ⏎. A sub-menu will appear:

```
Execute the command
Specify scope
Construct a field list
Build a search condition
Build a scope condition
```

You are not yet ready to execute the command because you haven't told dBASE III Plus exactly what to do, but by building a **search condition** you can identify the record you want.

In general, a search condition consists of three parts: a field name, a **relational operator**, and a search value (Fig. 27.10). The key word FOR must be included; in fact, the search condition is often called a FOR condition. The field name, as you probably guessed, is the name you assigned to the target field when you created the database. The allowable conditions are shown near the bottom of Fig. 27.10. The search value will be compared to the specified field. For example, in this case you want dBASE III Plus to find a record in which "LAST_NAME is equal to BAGGINS."

Figure 27.10

The components of a search condition.

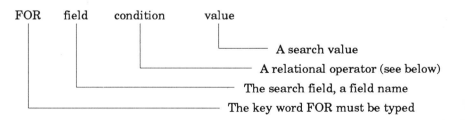

Relational Operator	Meaning
=	equal to
<	less than
>	greater than
<=	less than or equal to
>=	greater than or equal to
<>	not equal to

Figure 27.11
The initial search field
is LAST_NAME.

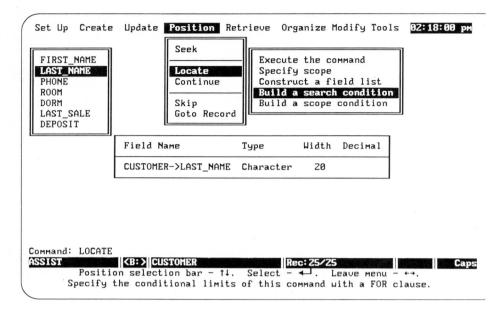

```
    Set Up  Create  Update  Position  Retrieve  Organize Modify Tools   02:18:00 pm

   ┌─────────────────┐  ┌──────────────┐  ┌────────────────────────────┐
   │ FIRST_NAME      │  │ Seek         │  │ Execute the command        │
   │ LAST_NAME       │  │              │  │ Specify scope              │
   │ PHONE           │  │ Locate       │  │ Construct a field list     │
   │ ROOM            │  │ Continue     │  │ Build a search condition   │
   │ DORM            │  │              │  │ Build a scope condition    │
   │ LAST_SALE       │  │ Skip         │  └────────────────────────────┘
   │ DEPOSIT         │  │ Goto Record  │
   └─────────────────┘  └──────────────┘

            ┌────────────────────────────────────────────────────────┐
            │ Field Name            Type        Width  Decimal        │
            │                                                          │
            │ CUSTOMER->LAST_NAME   Character    20                    │
            └────────────────────────────────────────────────────────┘




    Command: LOCATE
   ASSIST            <B:> CUSTOMER            Rec: 25/25               Caps
          Position selection bar - ↑↓.  Select - ◄┘.  Leave menu - ←→.
          Specify the conditional limits of this command with a FOR clause.
```

Move the selection bar to highlight

```
Build a search condition
```

and press ◄┘. A field list will appear to the left of the menu, with a
description of the highlighted field below the menu. The last name
field is your target, so highlight LAST_NAME (Fig. 27.11). Press ◄┘ to
select the last name field. Check the action line; it should read

```
Command: LOCATE FOR LAST_NAME
```

A table of relational operators will appear next. You want the last
name to be *equal to* BAGGINS, so highlight

```
= Equal To
```

(the first entry) and press ◄┘. The action line will change to

```
Command: LOCATE FOR LAST_NAME = `
```

and a new window will appear:

```
Enter a character string (without quotes):
```

Type BAGGINS (in all uppercase letters) and press ◄┘. (dBASE III
Plus would recognize *Baggins* as a different name.) Note the action
line; it reads

```
Command: LOCATE FOR LAST_NAME = `BAGGINS'
```

Read the command; it should make sense.

A new submenu will appear. Highlight

```
No more conditions
```

and press ⏎. The command is now complete. Move the selection bar to

```
Execute the command
```

and press ⏎. A message at the bottom left of your screen reports that the current record is 3. The navigation line tells you to:

```
Press any key to continue work in ASSIST.
```

The space bar is a good choice. When the assistant screen appears, note the status bar; it should point to record *3/25*. Open the *Update* menu and highlight *Edit*. Then press ⏎, and Frodo's record will appear on your screen. Unfortunately, you wanted Bilbo's record.

Press Esc to return to the assistant. Reopen the *Position* menu. This time mark *Continue* and note the message at the bottom of the screen:

```
Search for next record meeting the LOCATE condition.
```

Press ⏎ and the pointer will advance to record 11. Press the space bar to return to the assistant, open the *Update* menu, select *Edit*, press ⏎, and Bilbo's record will appear (Fig. 27.12). Press ⏄ to move to the telephone number field and then type his phone number: 513/782–9001. Press Ctrl *and* End to save the data and return to the assistant.

Use the *Locate* command to make another change to the file. Assume that Ping Chu gives you a $30 deposit for a new purchase and you want to add it to his previous $20 deposit. Issue the *Locate* command from the *Position* menu. Then build a search condition. Since there is only one CHU, search by LAST_NAME to find his record. When you execute the command, you should discover that CHU's record is number 2.

Figure 27.12

After the pointer is set, you can view the target record by issuing an *Edit* command.

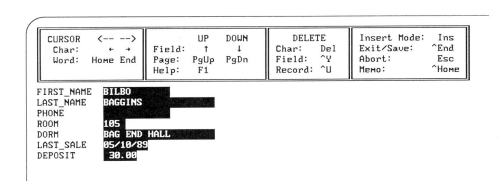

Return to the assistant and issue an *Edit* command to view CHU's record. The LAST_SALE and DEPOSIT fields must be changed. Start with the date. Press ⬇ to move the cursor to LAST_SALE and type today's date. (No date is suggested; check the calendar.)

The computer will beep and move the cursor to the deposit field. Type 50 followed by a decimal point, and then press ↵. Because DEPOSIT is the record's last field, the cursor will advance to the first field in record 3. Press Ctrl *and* End to save the change and exit the edit screen.

■ *Keystroke Summary*

Locate a record

From the Assistant:

Menu:	Position
Command:	Locate
Press:	↵
Highlight:	Build a search condition

Repeat the next seven steps until there are no more conditions

Highlight:	field name
Press:	↵
Highlight:	relational operator
Press:	↵
Type:	*search value*
Press:	↵
Highlight:	Combine with ...
Highlight:	No more conditions
Press:	↵
Highlight:	Execute the command
Press:	↵

From the Dot Prompt:

Type:	**LOCATE FOR** *search-condition*
Press:	↵

▪ *What Can Go Wrong?*

1. You entered 50 in the deposit field, but the value reads 500.00.

Cause: You forgot to type the decimal point. When you type the decimal point, the value is automatically aligned. If you don't type the decimal point, dBASE III Plus assumes that you want to correct a digit or two. Consequently, the 5 and the 0 replaced the space and the 2 in the original field value, leaving 0.00 unchanged.

Solution: Return to the field and type 50 followed by a decimal point. Then press ⏎.

2. A message indicates that the target record could not be found.

Cause: Either the record is not in the database file or you made an error in selecting the search field, selecting the condition, or typing the search value.

Solution: Try again. If you entered the data using all uppercase letters, make sure your search values are typed uppercase. If necessary, issue an *Edit* command, search through the database to find the desired record, note the precise spelling of the contents of the search field, exit from edit, and try to locate the record again. ▪

Entering Data in a Record with the *Replace* Command

Because all your customers live on campus, all their telephone numbers begin with 513/782–. Computers are supposed to save work. There must be a way to enter these first eight characters without typing them for every single customer.

The solution is to use the *Replace* command. Open the *Update* menu, select *Replace*, and press ⏎ (Fig. 27.13). Note the field list to the

Figure 27.13

Use a *Replace* command to enter repetitive data.

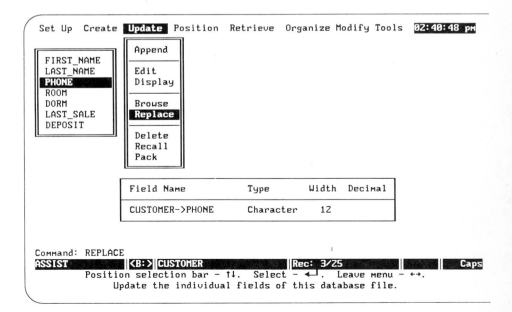

left of the menu. You want to replace telephone numbers, so highlight PHONE and press ⏎.

A dialogue window will appear:

```
Enter a character string (without quotes):
```

Enter the constant portion of the phone number, 513/782–, followed by XXXX. When you type the last X, the computer will beep, the window will disappear, and you will be returned to the list of fields. The string of X's holds space until the actual data can be added; it has no other significance. Note the action line; it reads

```
Command: REPLACE PHONE WITH '513/782–XXXX'
```

You could specify more fields at this time, but only the telephone number is to be changed.

Press ⊡ to exit the field list, and a new submenu will appear. (Pressing ⊡ to exit a menu might seem strange, but the next menu is to the right, so you're moving across the screen.) Because you want to change several records, it is necessary to identify the records that are to be changed. Highlight

```
Specify scope
```

and press ⏎. A new window will appear, and the message line will read

```
Process the default number of records. Default for this
operation is NEXT 1.
```

Unless you specify otherwise, the *Replace* command will change only a single record. To update *all* the records, highlight

```
ALL
```

in the window. The message line will change to

```
Process all records.
```

Press ⏎. The action line will read:

```
Command: REPLACE PHONE WITH '513/782–XXXX' ALL
```

Can you explain the purpose of everything in this command?

To execute the command, highlight

```
Execute the command
```

and press ⏎. After a brief delay the action line should read:

```
25 records replaced
```

As the message line suggests, press the space bar to return to the assistant.

Use an *Edit* command to verify that the telephone number field was updated for several customers. The two telephone numbers that you entered earlier were replaced, too, but that's a small price to pay for the many keystrokes you will save. Press Esc to return to the assistant.

▪ *Keystroke*
Summary

Replace a field

From the Assistant:

Menu:	Update
Command:	Replace
Press:	⏎
Highlight:	*field name*
Press:	⏎
Type:	*value*
Press:	⏎
Press:	→
Highlight:	Specify scope
Press:	⏎
Highlight:	ALL
Press:	⏎
Highlight:	Execute the command
Press:	⏎

From the Dot Prompt:

Type:	**REPLACE** *field* **WITH** *value* **ALL**
Press:	⏎

▪ *What Can*
Go Wrong?

1. You made a typing error while entering the REPLACE command.

Cause: Typing errors happen.

Solution: Press Esc twice (or until the assistant screen reappears) and start over. ▪

**Full-screen
Editing with the
Browse
Command**

The *Replace* command was used in the previous section to enter common characters. You could use *Edit* to enter the four unique digits for each customer's telephone number, but consider instead the *Browse* command.

Browse is a powerful and potentially dangerous command. It displays multiple records on the screen in a tabular format and gives

Figure 27.14
The *Browse* screen
displays data in
tabular form.

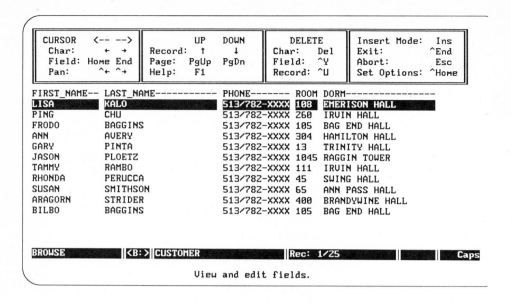

```
┌─────────────────────┬───────────────────┬───────────────────┬──────────────────────┐
│ CURSOR   <-- -->     │        UP   DOWN  │      DELETE       │ Insert Mode:   Ins   │
│  Char:    ←    →     │ Record:  ↑    ↓   │  Char:    Del     │ Exit:         ^End   │
│  Field: Home End     │ Page:  PgUp PgDn  │  Field:   ^Y      │ Abort:         Esc   │
│  Pan:     ^← ^→      │ Help:    F1       │  Record:  ^U      │ Set Options:  ^Home  │
└─────────────────────┴───────────────────┴───────────────────┴──────────────────────┘
```

```
FIRST_NAME-- LAST_NAME----------  PHONE------- ROOM DORM---------------
LISA         KALO                 513/782-XXXX 108  EMERISON HALL
PING         CHU                  513/782-XXXX 260  IRVIN HALL
FRODO        BAGGINS              513/782-XXXX 105  BAG END HALL
ANN          AVERY                513/782-XXXX 304  HAMILTON HALL
GARY         PINTA                513/782-XXXX 13   TRINITY HALL
JASON        PLOETZ               513/782-XXXX 1045 RAGGIN TOWER
TAMMY        RAMBO                513/782-XXXX 111  IRVIN HALL
RHONDA       PERUCCA              513/782-XXXX 45   SWING HALL
SUSAN        SMITHSON             513/782-XXXX 65   ANN PASS HALL
ARAGORN      STRIDER              513/782-XXXX 400  BRANDYWINE HALL
BILBO        BAGGINS              513/782-XXXX 105  BAG END HALL
```

```
BROWSE          <B:> CUSTOMER              Rec: 1/25            Caps
```

View and edit fields.

the user full-screen editing capability. Thus you can move the cursor
to any record or field on the screen and make changes. Unfortunately,
stray keystrokes can introduce errors into your data.

Editing a Record in the *Browse* Screen

The *Browse* command is accessed through the *Update* menu. To
ensure that you begin browsing the file at its first record, issue a *Goto
Record* command (from the *Position* menu) and set the pointer to TOP.
(The status bar will indicate *Rec: 1/25*.) Then type *U*, select *Browse*,
and press ⏎. The records in your database file will appear in tabular
form (Fig. 27.14); press F1 to toggle the help screen on or off. Note that
the current record (number 1) is highlighted. Had you started *Browse*
with a different current record, that record would have appeared at
the top of the screen. Records preceding it would be in memory, but you
would have to press ↑ to see them.

Figure 27.15 summarizes the keys that control the cursor on the
browse screen. Press → and ← to move from character to character
within a field. Press Home to move a field to the left or End to move a
field to the right. ⏎ moves the cursor to the next field. Press ↑ or ↓
to move from record to record. If the entire database won't fit on a
single screen, press PgDn or PgUp to scroll through it one screen at a
time.

Most screens display an 80-character line. If the record width
exceeds 80 characters, press Ctrl *and* → to *pan* one field to the right.
To pan back to the left, press Ctrl *and* ←. For example, the LAST_SALE
and DEPOSIT fields cannot be seen in Fig. 27.14. Press Ctrl *and* →.

Figure 27.15

Use these keys to control the cursor on the *Browse* screen.

Key	Action
←	one character to the left
→	one character to the right
Home	one field to the left
End	one field to the right
↵	next field (to the right)
↑	next lower numbered record
↓	next higher numbered record
Ctrl *and* ←	pans to the left
Ctrl *and* →	pans to the right
PgUp	prior screen
PgDn	next screen

FIRST_NAME will disappear, and the last two fields will pan in from the right. Press Ctrl *and* ← to get FIRST_NAME back.

Move the cursor to the first record's (KALO's) PHONE field. Press → to move the cursor to the first X and type 4321, the last four digits of the phone number. The computer will beep, and the cursor will advance to the ROOM field. Press ↓ and then → to move the cursor to the first X in the next customer's phone number. Then type 3376.

You could continue to enter phone numbers in this manner, but every time the cursor moves to the ROOM field, you risk an accidental keystroke that could change someone's room number. There is a safer way.

▪ *Keystroke Summary*

Enter *Browse*

From the Assistant:

Menu:	Update
Command:	Browse
Press:	↵

From the Dot Prompt:

Type:	**BROWSE**
Press:	↵

The *Freeze* Option

Note the

```
Set Options: ^Home
```

choice at the bottom right of the help window. (Press F1 if the help window is not visible.) Simultaneously press Ctrl *and* Home. A menu will appear at the top of your screen:

```
Bottom      Top      Lock      Record No.      Freeze
```

Press ⊡ to move the cursor from option to option and note the explanations on the message line. *Bottom*, *Top*, and *Record No.* move the pointer. *Lock* is used when the record is too wide to fit on the screen; it locks one or more fields on the left of the screen so that they don't scroll out of sight as you pan to the right. *Freeze* is used to limit editing to a selected field. The *Freeze* option reduces the risk of making an error and also eliminates the need to move the cursor to the field being edited.

Type *T* to select *Top*, and the highlight bar will move to the first record in the file (Lisa Kalo's). Press Ctrl *and* Home to open the menu again. Then type *F* to select *Freeze*. A dialogue window

```
Enter field name to freeze:
```

will appear just below the word *Freeze*. Enter the name of the field to be frozen (the one you plan to edit). Type PHONE; the box should read

```
Enter field name to freeze: PHONE
```

Then press ⏎.

The telephone number field will be highlighted on the current record. Try moving the cursor to another field. You can't. Press ⏎, and the cursor will move to the same field in the next record. Press ⊡ or ⊡ to move the pointer from record to record; note that it will always stay in the same field. Within the field, ⊡ and ⊡ move the cursor from character to character.

■ *Keystroke Summary*

The Freeze option

From the Assistant:		From the Dot Prompt:	
Menu	Update	Type:	**BROWSE FREEZE** *field*
Command:	Browse		
Press:	⏎	Press:	⏎
Press:	Ctrl *and* Home		
Type:	**F**		
Type:	*field name*		
Press:	⏎		

Editing a Record with the *Freeze* Option

Figure 27.16 shows a list of customer telephone numbers; use it as a guide to update your database file. The first two numbers were already entered, so press ⊡ or ⊡ to move the pointer to the third record (Frodo's). Move the cursor to the first X and type his number, 3333. The computer will beep and advance to the next record. Con-

Figure 27.16

Use the *Freeze* option when you enter these telephone numbers.

LAST_NAME	PHONE	LAST_NAME	PHONE
KALO	513/782-4321	BRANDYBUCK	513/782-4455
CHU	513/782-3376	TOOK	513/782-5670
BAGGINS	513/782-3333	BAER	513/782-0074
AVERY	513/782-2212	KINTE	513/782-1007
PINTA	513/782-4564	HARI	513/782-8904
PLOETZ	513/782-5654	GOMEZ	513/782-4668
RAMBO	513/782-6776	BLOOM	513/782-9892
PERUCCA	513/782-3421	MOUSE	513/782-9780
SMITHSON	513/782-5546	COTTRELL	513/782-6752
STRIDER	513/782-5511	SMITH	513/782-8901
BAGGINS	513/782-9001	HOYT	513/782-8341
WORTH	513/782-7871	MOOSE	513/782-5634
OAKENSHIELD	513/782-5430		

tinue entering the remaining phone numbers. Note as you reach the bottom of the screen that the next record scrolls into sight.

After you enter the last phone number (Fig. 27.17), the navigation line will read

```
Add new records? (Y/N)
```

Figure 27.17

The *Browse* screen just after the last telephone number has been added.

```
┌──────────────────┬──────────────────┬──────────────────┬──────────────────┐
│ CURSOR   <-- -->  │        UP   DOWN  │     DELETE        │ Insert Mode:  Ins │
│ Char:     ←   →   │ Record:  ↑    ↓   │ Char:     Del     │ Exit:        ^End │
│ Field: Home End   │ Page:  PgUp  PgDn │ Field:    ^Y      │ Abort:        Esc │
│ Pan:     ^← ^→    │ Help:   F1        │ Record:   ^U      │ Set Options: ^Home│
└──────────────────┴──────────────────┴──────────────────┴──────────────────┘
FIRST_NAME-- LAST_NAME----------- PHONE------- ROOM DORM---------------
PIPPIN       TOOK                 513/782-5670 106  BAG END HALL
BELINDA      BAER                 513/782-0074 324  RAGGIN TOWER
KUNTA        KINTE                513/782-1007 243  CHAD HALL
MATA         HARI                 513/782-8904 119  RINELAND HALL
JUAN         GOMEZ                513/782-4668 1023 RAGGIN TOWER
OPUS         BLOOM                513/782-9892 13   SOUTH HALL
MICHAEL      MOUSE                513/782-9780 201  DISNEY HALL
CLAYTON      COTTRELL             513/782-6752 187  HAMILTON HALL
BRIAN        SMITH                513/782-8901 894  RAGGIN TOWER
DEEDRA       HOYT                 513/782-8341 308  IRVIN HALL
BULWINKLE    MOOSE                513/782-5634 607  RAGGIN TOWER



BROWSE        |<B:>|CUSTOMER              |Rec: 25/25     |          | Caps
              ===> Add new records? (Y/N)
                   View and edit fields.
```

Like *Append*, the *Browse* command can be used to add records to the file. However, with the *Freeze* option active, you would be permitted only to enter values for the "frozen" field. Type *N* and then press Ctrl *and* End to save your changes and exit the browse screen.

The *Fields* Option

Another *Browse* option allows you to display selected portions of a database. For example, imagine that you want to update the deposit field to reflect new purchases. All you need is the customer's name, the deposit amount, and the last sale date; the telephone number, room number, and dormitory are irrelevant to this task. Unfortunately, the three required fields do not even appear on the same browse screen because the record's width exceeds 80 characters. The *Fields* option allows you to select the fields to be displayed.

The Fields option is available only from the dot prompt. Exit the assistant by pressing Esc. At the dot prompt, type

```
BROWSE FIELDS DEPOSIT, LAST_SALE, LAST_NAME, FIRST_NAME
```

The field names that follow the key word FIELDS will be displayed in the listed order; note that they are separated by commas. You could freeze one of the listed fields by adding the key word FREEZE and the field name, but ignore that option for now. Press ↵ to issue the command. Press Ctrl *and* Home and type *T* to select TOP. The cursor will move to the first record in the file. The help window hides a few records; press F1 to toggle it off. Your display will resemble Fig. 27.18.

Figure 27.18
The *Fields* option allows you to view selected fields.

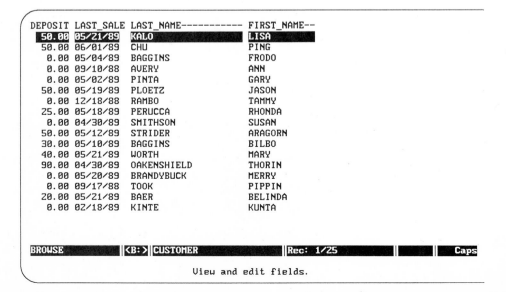

Assume that Rambo and Baer have given you $50 deposits. Press ⬇ to move the cursor to Rambo's record. Type 50 followed by a decimal point in her deposit field and press ⏎. Next, type today's date; the computer will beep and advance to the next field. Press ⬇ to move the cursor to Baer's record; then press [Home] twice to move to her DE-POSIT field. She has already paid $20. The additional deposit brings her total to $70, so type 70 followed by a decimal point and press ⏎. Then type today's date. When you finish, press [Ctrl] *and* [End] to save the changes and return to the dot prompt.

■ *Keystroke Summary*

Fields option

From the Dot Prompt:

    Type: **BROWSE FIELDS** *field–1, field–2, ...*

    Press: ⏎

■ *What Can Go Wrong?*

1. A message, "*** Unrecognized command verb," and the command you entered appear at the bottom left of the screen. A question mark above the command indicates an error. The message line reads: "Do you want some help? (Y/N)."

Cause: The command name was misspelled.

Solution: Type N. Then retype the command using the proper spelling.

2. A message, "Syntax error," and the command you entered appear at the bottom left of the screen. A question mark above the command indicates an error. The message line reads: "Do you want some help? (Y/N)."

Cause: The command name is correct, but something else is wrong. For example, trying to freeze an unlisted field is a syntax error. The question mark will identify the error.

Solution: Type N. Correct the error and reissue the command.

3. A message, "Variable not found," and the command you entered appear at the bottom left of the screen. A question mark above the command indicates an error. The message line reads: "Do you want some help? (Y/N)."

Cause: The specified field was not in the database, or the name was misspelled.

Solution: Type N. Correct the error; if necessary, issue a *Display structure* command to verify the field name. Then reissue the command using the correct spelling.

4. A message, "Unrecognized phrase/keyword in command" appears on the screen.

Cause: Although the command name itself is correct, something is wrong with one of the other key words. Perhaps you misspelled or forgot to type FIELDS.

Solution: Correct the error and reissue the command. ■

Deleting Records

Database maintenance involves adding, updating, and deleting data. You used an *Append* command to add records. *Edit*, *Browse*, *Goto*, and *Locate* are all used to update data. But why would you want to delete a record? The answer, if you think about it, is obvious. Students graduate and leave school for other reasons, and there is little point to maintaining data on people who are no longer potential customers.

Deleting records in dBASE III Plus is a two-stage process. First you mark records for deletion. Later, you issue a *Pack* command from the *Update* menu. When a database is packed, deleted records are removed, and the remaining records are physically shifted to fill in the newly freed space on disk. That can take a great deal of time, especially on a large database, so many organizations issue the *Pack* command only as part of their regular backup procedures.

One way to delete a record is to point to it (using a *Goto* command) and then issue a *Delete* command from the *Update* menu. More often, however, you will delete records from an *Edit* or a *Browse* screen. Return to the assistant by typing the command ASSIST and pressing ⏎. Issue a *Browse* command from the *Update* menu, and move the cursor to record 5 (Gary Pinta's). Press F1 to toggle on the help window and look under DELETE (the third column). The symbol ^U to the right of *Record:* indicates that you can press Ctrl and U to delete a record. Try it. Note the abbreviation *Del* near the right side of the status bar (Fig. 27.19). It indicates that the record is marked for deletion.

Press ↓ to move the cursor to record 6. Your disk drive should activate; dBASE III Plus saves *Browse* screen changes as soon as you

Figure 27.19

Press Ctrl and U (on a *Browse* or *Edit* screen) to mark a record for deletion.

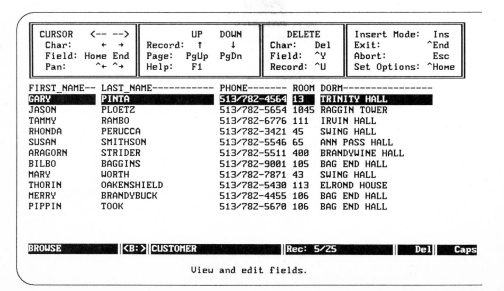

move to a new record. Note that *Del* disappears from the status bar; record 6 is *not* marked for deletion. Press ⬆ to move back to record 5, and *Del* will reappear.

Gary Pinta's record is still there. It is merely marked for deletion; it won't be physically deleted until you issue a *Pack* command. What if you change your mind? Make sure the cursor highlights the record you want to *undelete* and press Ctrl *and* U again. That key combination acts as a toggle switch. Try it; highlight record 5, press Ctrl *and* U, and *Del* will disappear. An option (from the assistant screen) is to point to the record and issue a *Recall* command from the *Update* menu.

"Deleted" records remain available until a *Pack* command is issued. When you browse or edit a file, the deleted records will be displayed. If you generate a mailing list from the database file, the deleted records will be included. If you do *not* want to see the deleted records, issue a SET DELETED ON command from the dot prompt.

Because this database is so small, it won't be necessary to issue a *Pack* command in this tutorial. Press Ctrl *and* End to save any changes you may have made and return to the assistant. (*Note:* If you press Esc, Gary Pinta's record may still be marked as deleted. Changes are saved only if you move to a new record or press Ctrl *and* End.)

Exiting dBASE III Plus

This ends the second tutorial. Press Esc to exit to the dot prompt. To exit dBASE III Plus from the dot prompt, type *QUIT* and press ⏎. This will close all databases and return you to the operating system.

Summary

From the Assistant

Function	Menu	Command	Page
Browse database	Update	Browse	479
Delete record*	Update	Delete	486
Edit file	Update	Edit	465
Exit dBASE III Plus	Set Up	Quit dBASE ...	487
Go to record	Position	Goto Record	472
List database structure	Tools	List structure	466
Load database file	Set Up	Database file	462
Locate next record	Position	Continue	475
Locate record	Position	Locate	473
Modify database structure	Modify	Database file	468
Remove deleted records	Update	Pack	486
Replace field	Update	Replace	477
Undelete record	Update	Recall	487

* Press Ctrl *and* U to delete the highlighted record on an edit or a browse screen.

From the Dot Prompt

Function	Command	Page
Browse database	BROWSE	479
Delete record*	DELETE	486
Edit file	EDIT	465
Exit dBASE III Plus	QUIT	487
Go to record	GOTO	472
List database structure	DISPLAY STRUCTURE	466
Load database file	USE	462
Locate next record	CONTINUE	475
Locate record	LOCATE FOR	474
Modify database structure	MODIFY STRUCTURE	468
Remove deleted records	PACK	486
Replace field	REPLACE	477
Undelete record	RECALL	487

*   Press Ctrl *and* U to delete the highlighted record on an edit or a browse screen.

Options and Functions

Option or Function	Format	Page
Define fields	command FIELDS options	484
Freeze field	command FREEZE field	481

Self-Test

1. Issue a _____ command to load a database file into memory.

2. Issue an _____ command to view or update the records on a database file one by one.

3. The _____ indicates the number of the current record.

4. Issue a _____ command to examine a database file's structure. Issue a _____ command to modify a database file's structure.

5. Each time you exit *Modify structure*, a _____ copy of the file is created.

6. Issue a _____ command to set the pointer to a specific record when you know the record number. The _____ command can be used to search a database file by content.

7. Use a _____ command to enter a constant value in several different records.

8. The _____ command supports full-screen editing.

9. Use the _____command's _____ option to limit editing to a single field. Use the _____option to view selected fields from a database file.

10. Deleted records are physically removed from a database file by a _____ command.

Exercises

1. Add a birth date and a telephone number to each of the records you created in Exercise 1 of Chapter 26. Use the following data, or substitute data for your relatives and friends.

Last Name	Telephone	Birth Date
Alexander	315/553-1291	04/02/70
Anderson	596/488-0406	05/11/72
Benton	803/426-5862	11/13/70
Billings	513/523-8182	02/26/73
Bishop	233/780-6399	02/25/70
Clawson	139/785-1766	03/16/72
Climer	505/649-5655	04/07/71
Cortez	851/560-2157	01/14/72
Culler	513/523-5736	12/20/71
Dennison	108/406-8813	01/22/73
Dorsey	306/337-3464	11/04/72
Edwards	412/297-3269	06/08/70
Fujii	510/472-0251	04/14/71
Gonzalez	424/284-2845	08/16/71
Hahne	315/720-0657	02/18/70
Hiestand	202/557-3451	10/01/72
Krieger	513/523-3028	04/26/70
Lewis	501/289-0564	10/12/71
Mam	450/608-0098	11/07/72
Patten	405/435-6380	01/21/71

Last Name	Telephone	Birth Date
Porter	480/639-2043	04/22/70
Reid	306/204-2424	10/19/70
Scott	301/582-7469	03/09/71
Symmes	331/116-3674	08/11/71
Upham	513/523-4897	08/02/72

2. Add each member's telephone number, membership date, and dues paid to the membership file you created in Exercise 2 of Chapter 26. Use the following data, or substitute data from your own organization.

Last Name	Telephone	Date	Paid
Alexander	315/553-1291	04/02/70	25
Anderson	596/488-0406	05/11/72	25
Benton	803/426-5862	11/13/70	20
Billings	513/523-8182	02/26/73	
Bishop	233/780-6399	02/25/70	
Clawson	139/785-1766	03/16/72	25
Climer	505/649-5655	04/07/71	
Cortez	851/560-2157	01/14/72	25
Culler	513/523-5736	12/20/71	25
Dennison	108/406-8813	01/22/73	
Dorsey	306/337-3464	11/04/72	
Edwards	412/297-3269	06/08/70	
Fujii	510/472-0251	04/14/71	25
Gonzalez	424/284-2845	08/16/71	10
Hahne	315/720-0657	02/18/70	25
Hiestand	202/557-3451	10/01/72	25
Krieger	513/523-3028	04/26/70	
Lewis	501/289-0564	10/12/71	25
Mam	450/608-0098	11/07/72	
Patten	405/435-6380	01/21/71	

Last Name	Telephone	Date	Paid
Porter	480/639-2043	04/22/70	25
Reid	306/204-2424	10/19/70	25
Scott	301/582-7469	03/09/71	25
Symmes	331/116-3674	08/11/71	
Upham	513/523-4897	08/02/72	25

3. Add the purchase date and purchase price to each record in the inventory file you created in Exercise 3 of Chapter 26. Use the following data or substitute your own data.

Title	Date	Cost
Bach: Brandenberg	02/18/87	22.50
Beethoven: Symphony #5	04/09/87	14.95
Grofe: Grand Canyon	10/30/89	32.50
Mozart: Violin Concerto	07/14/88	12.95
Vivaldi: Four Seasons	07/14/88	12.95
Born in the USA	06/21/87	10.95
Song Remains the Same	08/02/89	9.95
Rumours	07/15/89	6.95
The White Album	05/09/86	10.95
Sergeant Pepper	04/04/79	12.95
The Innocent Age	12/23/86	13.95
Smiley Smile	04/02/80	7.95
The Sheik of Araby	02/21/85	5.95
Chariots of Fire	05/30/86	10.95
Stranger in Town	09/10/87	8.95

·28

Extracting Information from a Database

This chapter introduces the dBASE III Plus features and commands that allow you to:

- enter commands from the dot prompt
- set the dBASE III Plus operating environment
- clear the screen
- access help screens
- recall and edit previously issued commands
- display, list, and print selected records and fields

Working from the Dot Prompt

In Chapters 26 and 27 you learned how to create and maintain a database. In this chapter you will learn how to *use* the database by selectively extracting and organizing data.

Up to this point you have worked through the assistant. Now that you know the basics, you will probably find it much easier to issue commands at the dot prompt. Boot DOS and load dBASE III Plus. When the assistant screen appears, press Esc to exit to the dot prompt.

When you created the database file in Chapter 26, all the data were typed uppercase. Press CapsLock to activate *caps lock*; the abbreviation *Caps* will appear near the right of the status bar. With *caps lock* on, you won't have to worry about case when you type search conditions later in the chapter.

Figure 28.1
The structure of a
dBASE III Plus
command.

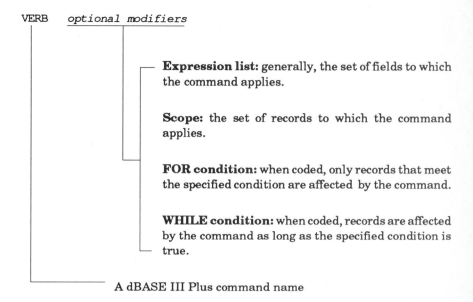

VERB   *optional modifiers*

Expression list: generally, the set of fields to which the command applies.

Scope: the set of records to which the command applies.

FOR condition: when coded, only records that meet the specified condition are affected by the command.

WHILE condition: when coded, records are affected by the command as long as the specified condition is true.

A dBASE III Plus command name

Command Syntax

From the dot prompt you can direct dBASE III Plus by entering querylike commands (Fig. 28.1). Each one begins with a command name, a **verb** such as APPEND, EDIT, or BROWSE. The verb indicates the action to be taken. To save time, you can type only the first four characters of the command name, but complete names will be shown throughout this book. The optional modifiers serve to limit or modify the action, thus allowing you to access the data selectively.

The fields to be affected by the command are listed in an **expression list**. Normally, the list consists of field names; later, you'll learn how to use variables, constants, functions, and operators to manipulate the contents of those fields.

A command's **scope** identifies the set of records to which it applies. For example, a DISPLAY or LIST command might be used to display the current record, the next ten records, or all the records in the database. A **FOR condition** limits the command to those records for which the specified condition is true; a **WHILE condition** means the command will continue to affect records as long as the condition is true.

Setting the Default Drive

The first step in accessing data is to open the file. If your data are stored on diskette, insert your data disk into drive B and shut the drive door. To specify a data drive, type the command

```
SET DEFAULT TO B
```

(Substitute the appropriate drive letter.) Then press ⏎. The status bar will change to reflect the new default drive.

Note that the status bar reads B:, not B. Technically, B: is the proper DOS form for specifying a drive, but you can type it either way. For example, type

```
SET DEFAULT TO B:
```

(Substitute your drive letter if appropriate.) Then press ⏎. The status bar will not change because the default drive has not been changed, but the fact that no error message was displayed indicates that dBASE III Plus accepted the command.

The SET DEFAULT TO command is one of a series of SET commands that control the dBASE III Plus operating environment. Other SET commands allow the user to specify screen colors, turn the bell on and off, reprogram the function keys, and set numerous other parameters.

■ *Keystroke Summary*

Set default drive

Type: **SET DEFAULT TO** *n*

Press: ⏎

Loading the Database

To load the CUSTOMER database, type the command

```
USE CUSTOMER
```

and press ⏎. The disk drive will activate, and after a brief delay a new dot prompt will appear (Fig. 28.2). Check the status bar; it should identify CUSTOMER as the active database. By setting the drive and identifying the file, you defined the path to that file. Thus dBASE III Plus was able to open the file and can now access its data.

■ *Keystroke Summary*

Load a database file

Type: **USE** *filename*

Press: ⏎

Figure 28.2
The screen after the first few commands have been issued. Note that the status bar lists the default drive and the active database file.

```
. SET DEFAULT TO B
. SET DEFAULT TO B:
. USE CUSTOMER
.
```

| Command Line | | |B:>||CUSTOMER | |Rec: 1/25 | | | |Caps|

Enter a dBASE III PLUS command.

The CLEAR Command

Commands are entered on the action line just above the status bar. When you enter a new command, the old one scrolls toward the top of the screen. Thus you can always see your last several commands.

Generally, viewing recent commands is useful, but as you will discover, other data are retained on the screen, too. If your screen becomes cluttered, you can clear it by typing

    CLEAR

and pressing ⏎. Try it. The old commands will disappear.

▪ *Keystroke Summary*

Clear the screen

    Type: **CLEAR**

    Press: ⏎

The Memory Buffer

Clearing the screen does not erase all traces of prior commands, however. dBASE III Plus retains the last 20 commands in a memory buffer called HISTORY. To view them, type

    DISPLAY HISTORY

and press ⏎. After the first command scrolls into sight, a message

    Press any key to continue ...

will appear on the screen; dBASE III Plus is pausing to give you time to read the screen. Press the space bar, and the rest of the commands will be displayed.

Look carefully at the last command. The verb is DISPLAY; HISTORY is a modifier. More precisely, HISTORY is part of the expression list. In this case it identifies a buffer rather than a field name.

Once you learn dBASE III Plus and begin using it regularly, you will often find yourself issuing a series of similar commands. Rather than independently typing each one, you can recall the prior command from HISTORY, modify it, and reissue it.

To recall a command, simply press ⬆. Try it. Your most recent command (DISPLAY HISTORY) will appear on the action line. Press ⬆ again, and the next most recent command (CLEAR) will appear. Continue pressing ⬆ until you reach your very first command. Then press ⬆ again. The computer will beep, indicating that you have reached the end of the history buffer. Press ⬇ to move back through the commands one by one until you reach the dot prompt. Press ⬇ again, and the computer will beep; you can't view commands you have not yet typed.

When a command is on the action line, you can move the cursor, insert characters, and delete characters to modify it. Once the command is correct, pressing ⏎ with the cursor located anywhere on that command tells dBASE III Plus to execute it. For example, press ↑ twice (or until the CLEAR command appears on the action line). Then press ⏎. The screen will clear, exactly as if you had entered a new CLEAR command.

Try another experiment. Type the command

```
DISLAY HISTORY
```

intentionally misspelling the command name. Then press ⏎. An error message will indicate that dBASE III Plus could not recognize the command verb; the message line will ask whether you need help. Respond by typing N for no. Press ↑, and the incorrect DISPLAY command will appear at the dot prompt. Move the cursor to the letter L and then press Ins; the abbreviation *Ins* will appear on the status bar. Type P, and the letter P will be inserted just to the left of the cursor. The command will now read

```
DISPLAY HISTORY
```

Press Ins to exit insert mode. Then press ⏎ to execute the command. After dBASE III Plus pauses, press the space bar to view the remaining commands; the cursor will return to the dot prompt.

The Help Screens

The dBASE III Plus **help screens** can be very useful when you forget a command's syntax. Type HELP at the dot prompt or press function key F1 to access them. Try it. Type

```
HELP
```

press ⏎, and the *Help Main Menu* will appear (Fig. 28.3). It lists six choices. Eventually, you should explore each of them, but for now, type 6 to select *Commands and Functions*.

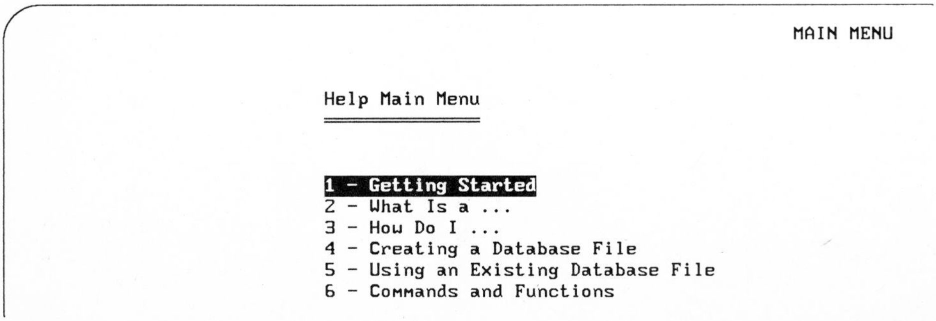

Figure 28.3
The *Help Main Menu*. To access it, type HELP and press ⏎ or press function key F1.

```
                                                    MAIN MENU

        Help Main Menu
        ══════════════

        1 - Getting Started
        2 - What Is a ...
        3 - How Do I ...
        4 - Creating a Database File
        5 - Using an Existing Database File
        6 - Commands and Functions
```

Figure 28.4

If you select option 6, *Commands and Functions*, from the *Help Main Menu*, this menu appears.

```
                                                        COMMANDS/FUNCTIONS

        dBASE III PLUS Commands and Functions


        ┌─────────────────────────────────┐
        │ 1 - Commands (Starter Set)      │
          2 - Commands (Advanced Set)
          3 - Functions
          4 - SET TO Commands
          5 - SET ON/OFF Commands
```

Another menu will appear (Fig. 28.4). Type 1 to select the *Starter Set*. (You can select from the menu by moving the cursor to mark your choice and pressing ⏎ *or* by typing the number of your choice.) The next screen will display a rather lengthy list of commands (Fig. 28.5). To choose one, type the command name or its number and then press ⏎. For example, you used the BROWSE command in the last chapter. Type BROWSE (or the number 4) and press ⏎. The next screen (Fig. 28.6) will explain the BROWSE command.

Press Esc to exit the help screen and return to the dot prompt. Pressing Esc on *any* help screen will return you to the dot prompt.

If you know a command's name, you can bypass the menus and go directly to its help screen. For example, type

```
HELP EDIT
```

Figure 28.5

This list of commands appears when you select the *Starter Set*. To obtain more information on a given command, type its name or its number and press ⏎.

```
                                                             STARTER

              dBASE III PLUS Commands --- Starter Set


   1 - ?           12 - DELETE FILE    23 - LABEL      34 - REPORT
   2 - APPEND      13 - DIR            24 - LIST       35 - SCREEN
   3 - AVERAGE     14 - DISPLAY        25 - LOCATE     36 - SEEK
   4 - BROWSE      15 - DO             26 - MODIFY     37 - SET
   5 - CHANGE      16 - EDIT           27 - PACK       38 - SKIP
   6 - CLEAR       17 - ERASE          28 - QUERY      39 - SORT
   7 - CONTINUE    18 - EXPORT         29 - QUIT       40 - STORE
   8 - COPY        19 - FIND           30 - RECALL     41 - SUM
   9 - COUNT       20 - GO/GOTO        31 - RELEASE    42 - TOTAL
  10 - CREATE      21 - IMPORT         32 - RENAME     43 - TYPE
  11 - DELETE      22 - INDEX          33 - REPLACE    44 - USE


HELP        |<B:>|CUSTOMER            |Rec: 1/25        |      |Caps
      Enter the name of a menu option. Finish with ⏎. Previous menu - F10.
             ENTER > ▬▬▬▬▬▬▬▬▬▬
```

Figure 28.6

This help screen explains the BROWSE command. To exit to the dot prompt, press Esc.

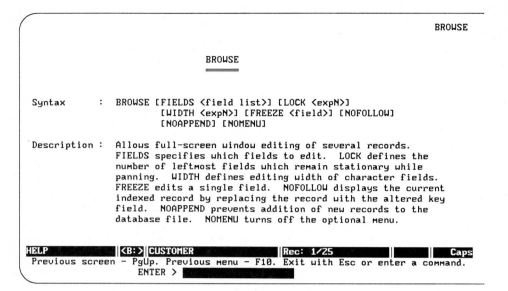

and press ↵. A description of the EDIT command will appear on the screen. After you read it, press Esc to go back to the dot prompt.

When you make a syntax or spelling error while typing a command, the message line may read

    Do you want some help? (Y/N)

Assuming that the command name is spelled properly, typing Y will display the help screen for that command. However, if the command's name is spelled incorrectly, a Y response will send you to the *Help Main Menu*.

■ *Keystroke Summary*

HELP

Type: **HELP** *command*

Press: ↵

Retrieving Records from a Database

The APPEND, BROWSE and EDIT commands that you used in Chapters 26 and 27 allow you to view the contents of a database, but they were never meant for routine queries because they allow data to be changed. Database integrity is crucial. Modifications to the data must be carefully controlled. Thus most users are not permitted to add or change data. The DISPLAY and LIST commands allow you to access but not to change the data. From the assistant, both are accessed through the *Retrieve* menu.

The DISPLAY Command

Earlier in the chapter, you displayed the contents of the history buffer. The modifier HISTORY is known to dBASE III Plus, so the contents of the memory buffer were displayed. If you type just the command name with no modifiers, the current record will be displayed. Try it. Type

    DISPLAY

and press ⏎. The screen will look a bit cluttered (Fig. 28.7), but a careful review should convince you that all the fields are there. Check the status bar; unless you moved the pointer, it should indicate *Rec: 1/25*. Record 1, LISA KALO's, should be on your screen. By default, DISPLAY gives you the current record.

The reason the output looks so bad is because most screens can display only 80 characters, and the CUSTOMER records exceed 80 characters in width. Since you did not modify the DISPLAY command, dBASE III Plus assumed, reasonably, that you wanted to see the entire record. Thus the field names and then the field values were each wrapped to a second line.

■ *Keystroke Summary*

Display the current record

    Type: **DISPLAY**

    Press: ⏎

■ *What Can Go Wrong?*

1. The message "*** Unrecognized command verb" appears at the bottom of the screen. The command is above the message, and a question mark sits above and to the right of the command.

Cause: You misspelled the dBASE III Plus command name.

Solution: Type N. Press ⬆ to recall the command. Correct the spelling and then press ⏎ to reissue the command. ■

Figure 28.7
By default a DISPLAY command displays the current record.

```
. DISPLAY
Record#  FIRST_NAME   LAST_NAME           PHONE         ROOM DORM
   LAST_SALE DEPOSIT
        1  LISA        KALO               513/782-4321  108  EMERISON HALL
   05/21/89    50.00
.
```

| Command Line | ‹B:› | CUSTOMER · | | Rec: 1/25 | | | Caps |

Enter a dBASE III PLUS command.

Setting the Pointer

Unless you specify otherwise, the DISPLAY command always retrieves the current record. To select a specific record, you can use a GOTO command to move the pointer. For example, to view record 10, type

    GOTO 10

and press ⏎. Check the status bar; it should indicate record *10/25*. Now type

    DISPLAY

Press ⏎, and record 10 will appear.

■ *Keystroke Summary*

Set the pointer

 Type: **GOTO** *n*

 Press: ⏎

The LIST Command

Unlike DISPLAY, the LIST command's default is to show all the records in the database file. Type

    LIST

and press ⏎. The very first record, LISA KALO's, will appear. Next, the second record will scroll up from the bottom, seemingly pushing the first record toward the top of the screen. (Watch closely because the screen changes quickly.) Eventually, the first several records will scroll out of sight; when the operation stops, your screen should resemble Fig. 28.8. Note that the pointer reads *EOF/25*, indicating that you have reached the end of the file.

By default, DISPLAY retrieves the current record, while LIST retrieves the *entire* file. The fact that the pointer was set to 10 before the LIST command was issued is irrelevant. Given no modifiers, the LIST command starts at the top of the database and scrolls through all the records.

Issue another DISPLAY command by typing DISPLAY and pressing ⏎. Note that only the field names appear. Check the pointer; it reads *EOF/25*. Since the pointer has passed the last record, there is no current record to display.

Note that your screen shows both data and commands. Clear it by typing a CLEAR command and pressing ⏎. Then type DISPLAY HISTORY and press ⏎. A list of your most recent commands will appear. Note that the data are *not* retained in the history buffer; only the commands are kept.

Issue another CLEAR command before you move on.

Figure 28.8
By default a LIST command displays all the records in the database file.

```
09/17/88      0.00
    16  BELINDA        BAER              513/782-0074 324  RAGGIN TOWER
06/01/89     70.00
    17  KUNTA          KINTE             513/782-1007 243  CHAD HALL
02/18/89      0.00
    18  MATA           HARI              513/782-8904 119  RINELAND HALL
05/18/89     70.00
    19  JUAN           GOMEZ             513/782-4668 1023 RAGGIN TOWER
09/17/88      0.00
    20  OPUS           BLOOM             513/782-9892 13   SOUTH HALL
11/12/88      0.00
    21  MICHAEL        MOUSE             513/782-9780 201  DISNEY HALL
10/18/88      0.00
    22  CLAYTON        COTTRELL          513/782-6752 187  HAMILTON HALL
05/12/89     40.00
    23  BRIAN          SMITH             513/782-8901 894  RAGGIN TOWER
12/20/87      0.00
    24  DEEDRA         HOYT              513/782-8341 308  IRVIN HALL
05/12/89      0.00
    25  BULLWINKLE     MOOSE             513/782-5634 607  RAGGIN TOWER
09/10/88      0.00
.
Command Line    |<B:>||CUSTOMER                  |Rec: EOF/25       |     ||    | Caps
                   Enter a dBASE III PLUS command.
```

■ *Keystroke Summary*

List all records

Type: **LIST**

Press: ↵

Modifying Commands

The FIELDS Option

One way to improve the appearance of the output generated by DISPLAY or LIST is to select the fields to be displayed. The FIELDS option allows you to specify a set of fields and to determine their order. You first encountered the FIELDS option in Chapter 27, where you used it with a BROWSE command. It consists of the key word FIELDS followed by a list of field names separated by commas.

For example, type the command

```
LIST FIELDS DORM, ROOM, LAST_NAME, PHONE
```

and press ↵. The spaces separating the fields are optional, but they do make the command easier to read. (The key word FIELDS is also optional on a LIST or DISPLAY command.) Your screen should resemble Fig. 28.9. The number to the left of each record is a record number assigned by dBASE III Plus.

■ *Keystroke Summary*

FIELDS option

Type: *command* **FIELDS** *list*

Press: ↵

Figure 28.9

The FIELDS option allows you to select the fields to be displayed.

```
      5   TRINITY HALL      13    PINTA          513/782-4564
      6   RAGGIN TOWER     1045   PLOETZ         513/782-5654
      7   IRVIN HALL        111   RAMBO          513/782-6776
      8   SWING HALL         45   PERUCCA        513/782-3421
      9   ANN PASS HALL      65   SMITHSON       513/782-5546
     10   BRANDYWINE HALL   400   STRIDER        513/782-5511
     11   BAG END HALL      105   BAGGINS        513/782-9001
     12   SWING HALL         43   WORTH          513/782-7871
     13   ELROND HOUSE      113   OAKENSHIELD    513/782-5430
     14   BAG END HALL      106   BRANDYBUCK     513/782-4455
     15   BAG END HALL      106   TOOK           513/782-5670
     16   RAGGIN TOWER      324   BAER           513/782-0074
     17   CHAD HALL         243   KINTE          513/782-1007
     18   RINELAND HALL     119   HARI           513/782-8904
     19   RAGGIN TOWER     1023   GOMEZ          513/782-4668
     20   SOUTH HALL         13   BLOOM          513/782-9892
     21   DISNEY HALL       201   MOUSE          513/782-9780
     22   HAMILTON HALL     187   COTTRELL       513/782-6752
     23   RAGGIN TOWER      894   SMITH          513/782-8901
     24   IRVIN HALL        308   HOYT           513/782-8341
     25   RAGGIN TOWER      607   MOOSE          513/782-5634
.
Command Line    ‖<B:>‖CUSTOMER              ‖Rec: EOF/25  ‖        ‖ Caps

           Enter a dBASE III PLUS command.
```

■ *What Can Go Wrong?*

1. The message "Variable not found" appears on the screen. The command is above the message with a question mark to the right of a field name.

Cause: You probably misspelled the field name indicated by the question mark.

Solution: Correct the field name and reissue the command. If you can't remember the proper spelling, issue a DISPLAY STRUCTURE command, find the desired field name, note it, and then correct the DISPLAY or LIST command.

2. An asterisk appears to the left of one or more records.

Cause: The asterisk indicates that the record is marked for deletion. Perhaps you pressed (Esc) to exit from a browse or edit screen after undeleting a record. When you exit by pressing (Esc), any changes to the current record are lost.

Solution: Because you will not issue a PACK command in these tutorials, you can ignore the asterisk. To undelete the record, type RECALL RECORD n, where n is the record's number, and press (⏎). ■

Setting Fields

A SET FIELDS TO command defines the fields for subsequent commands. It is particularly useful when you must issue a series of commands that refer to the same fields. For example, type

```
SET FIELDS TO DORM, ROOM, LAST_NAME, PHONE
```

Figure 28.10

A SET FIELDS TO command defines the list of fields to be displayed by subsequent commands.

```
     9  SMITHSON           513/782-5546 65    ANN PASS HALL
    10  STRIDER            513/782-5511 400   BRANDYWINE HALL
    11  BAGGINS            513/782-9001 105   BAG END HALL
    12  WORTH              513/782-7871 43    SWING HALL
    13  OAKENSHIELD        513/782-5430 113   ELROND HOUSE
    14  BRANDYBUCK         513/782-4455 106   BAG END HALL
    15  TOOK               513/782-5670 106   BAG END HALL
    16  BAER               513/782-0074 324   RAGGIN TOWER
    17  KINTE              513/782-1007 243   CHAD HALL
    18  HARI               513/782-8904 119   RINELAND HALL
    19  GOMEZ              513/782-4668 1023  RAGGIN TOWER
    20  BLOOM              513/782-9892 13    SOUTH HALL
    21  MOUSE              513/782-9780 201   DISNEY HALL
    22  COTTRELL           513/782-6752 187   HAMILTON HALL
    23  SMITH              513/782-8901 894   RAGGIN TOWER
    24  HOYT               513/782-8341 308   IRVIN HALL
    25  MOOSE              513/782-5634 607   RAGGIN TOWER
.  GOTO 15
.  DISPLAY
Record#  LAST_NAME          PHONE        ROOM  DORM
    15   TOOK              513/782-5670 106   BAG END HALL
.
```

`Command Line` `<B:>CUSTOMER` `Rec: 15/25` `Caps`

Enter a dBASE III PLUS command.

and press ↵. Then type

    LIST

and press ↵. The last several lines of your screen can be seen near the top of Fig. 28.10. Note that the field order does not match the sequence specified in the SET FIELDS TO command. A FIELDS option on a command controls the order of the fields. However, when you issue a SET FIELDS TO command, the fields will be displayed in the order in which they are physically stored in the database file.

Point to record 15 by typing

    GOTO 15

and pressing ↵. Then type

    DISPLAY

and press ↵. Your screen should resemble Fig. 28.10.

Earlier, when you issued a DISPLAY command with no modifiers, all the fields were displayed. Now, only the fields listed in the SET FIELDS command are displayed, in spite of the intervening LIST and GOTO commands. Once you set fields, they stay set. As an experiment, type EDIT and press ↵; once again, only the four selected fields will be displayed. Press Esc to return to the dot prompt. Then type BROWSE and press ↵. Once again you should see only the selected fields. Press Esc to return to the dot prompt.

To add fields, issue another SET FIELDS TO command and list only the new field names. For example, type

```
SET FIELDS TO FIRST_NAME
```

and press ⏎. Then issue a DISPLAY command and note that the first name has been added to the four previously specified fields. If you want to change to a *different* list of fields, first reestablish the default (*all* fields) by issuing a SET FIELDS TO command with *no* field names. Then specify the new list in a *second* SET FIELDS TO command.

When fields have been set, only the active fields can be displayed. For example, type the command

```
DISPLAY FIELDS LAST_NAME, LAST_SALE
```

and press ⏎. An error message will appear because LAST_SALE is not one of the active fields. dBASE III Plus will offer to help; respond by typing N. To temporarily deactivate the fields, type

```
SET FIELDS OFF
```

and press ⏎. Press ⬆ twice to recall the most recent DISPLAY command, press ⏎, and the current record's last name and last sale date will appear.

Because the next exercise will assume fields off, leave them off. For future reference, typing SET FIELDS ON and pressing ⏎ reactivates the list of fields. SET FIELDS [ON/OFF] allows you to turn fields on or off.

■ *Keystroke Summary*

Set fields

Type: **SET FIELDS TO** *field-1,field-2, . . . field-n*

Press: ⏎

Type: **SET FIELDS [ON/OFF]**

Press: ⏎

The Scope Clauses

By default a LIST command gives you every record in the file, while a DISPLAY command gives you only one. What if you want some intermediate number of records? You can control the number of records displayed by adding a SCOPE clause to the command. Four possible scopes can be defined. ALL means every record in the file. NEXT, followed by a number, specifies that number of records starting with the current record; for example, if the current record is 15, NEXT 1 accesses only record 15, while NEXT 3 accesses records 15,

Figure 28.11

Defining SCOPE allows you to control the records that are displayed.

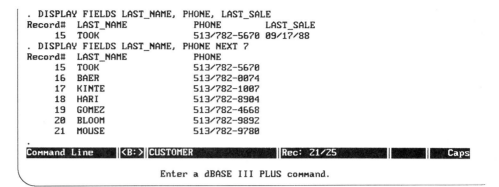

```
. DISPLAY FIELDS LAST_NAME, PHONE, LAST_SALE
Record#   LAST_NAME           PHONE        LAST_SALE
      15  TOOK                513/782-5670 09/17/88
. DISPLAY FIELDS LAST_NAME, PHONE NEXT 7
Record#   LAST_NAME           PHONE
      15  TOOK                513/782-5670
      16  BAER                513/782-0074
      17  KINTE               513/782-1007
      18  HARI                513/782-8904
      19  GOMEZ               513/782-4668
      20  BLOOM               513/782-9892
      21  MOUSE               513/782-9780
.
Command Line    ||<B:>||CUSTOMER            ||Rec: 21/25   ||      ||  Caps
```

Enter a dBASE III PLUS command.

16, and 17. RECORD followed by a number refers to the record with the indicated number; for example, RECORD 10 accesses the tenth record in the file. Finally, REST gives you everything from the current record to the end of the file. If you ask for more than a full screen of data, a DISPLAY command pauses when the screen is full and asks you to "press any key to continue." A LIST command, on the other hand, scrolls the records across the screen without pausing.

The status bar should point to record 15; if it doesn't, issue a GOTO command to move it there. Then type

    DISPLAY FIELDS LAST_NAME, PHONE NEXT 7

and press ⏎. Your screen will resemble Fig. 28.11; note that the status bar points to record *21/25*. Press ⬆, and the DISPLAY command will reappear on the action line. Press ⏎ to issue it again. Mr. Mouse's record will appear, followed by the next *four* records, for a total of five. You asked for *seven*. What happened? Look at the status bar; it points to *EOF/25*. You reached the end of the file, so there are no more records to display.

Try one more experiment before you move on to the next section. Type the command

    LIST RECORD 10 FIELDS LAST_NAME, PHONE

and press ⏎. As you might expect, the contents of record 10 will appear on the screen. Note, however, the relative position of the scope modifier in the last two commands. In the DISPLAY command, it followed the list of fields; in this command, it *precedes* the list. dBASE III Plus does not rely on position to determine the meaning of modifiers; they can be coded in any order. The only restriction is that you must complete one option before starting another; for example, you *cannot* type several fields, insert a scope clause, and then type more fields.

■ *Keystroke*
Summary

Scope

Type: *command* $\begin{bmatrix} \textbf{ALL} \\ \textbf{NEXT } n \\ \textbf{RECORD } n \\ \textbf{REST} \end{bmatrix}$ *options*

Press: ⏎

■ *What Can*
Go Wrong?

1. You issued a command with a SCOPE clause, but only the field headings were displayed.

Cause: The pointer was at the end of the file (EOF).

Solution: Issue a GOTO command to position the pointer at the first record to be displayed. Then issue the command with the SCOPE clause.

2. A message reads "Variable not found." The command appears above the message with a question mark to the right of SCOPE.

Cause: You probably typed a comma after the last field name and then typed the scope clause. When dBASE III Plus sees a comma, it looks for a field name.

Solution: Correct the command by deleting the comma between the last field name and the scope clause. Then reissue the command. ■

**Condition
Clauses**

Imagine that you need a list of customers with active deposits. Perhaps the easiest way to obtain it is to code a DISPLAY command with a FOR condition.

You need a list of records for which the deposit is greater than zero. In dBASE III Plus terms, that condition is

```
FOR DEPOSIT > 0
```

Clear the screen. Then type the command

```
DISPLAY FIELDS LAST_NAME, DEPOSIT FOR DEPOSIT > 0 ALL
```

and press ⏎. The output will resemble Fig. 28.12. Technically, the scope ALL was not necessary because the FOR condition changes the default scope to ALL, but specifying the correct scope never hurts.

The field referenced in the FOR condition need not be included in the list of fields. For example, type the command

```
LIST ALL FIELDS LAST_NAME, ROOM, DORM FOR DEPOSIT > 0
```

and press ⏎. Your screen will list the last names, rooms, and dorms of the same customers you saw in Fig. 28.12.

Figure 28.12
A list of all customers who have deposits greater than zero.

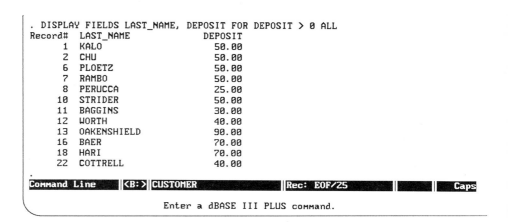

```
. DISPLAY FIELDS LAST_NAME, DEPOSIT FOR DEPOSIT > 0 ALL
Record#   LAST_NAME                 DEPOSIT
      1   KALO                        50.00
      2   CHU                         50.00
      6   PLOETZ                      50.00
      7   RAMBO                       50.00
      8   PERUCCA                     25.00
     10   STRIDER                     50.00
     11   BAGGINS                     30.00
     12   WORTH                       40.00
     13   OAKENSHIELD                 90.00
     16   BAER                        70.00
     18   HARI                        70.00
     22   COTTRELL                    40.00
.
```
| Command Line | \<B:\> | CUSTOMER | | Rec: EOF/25 | | | Caps |

Enter a dBASE III PLUS command.

Note that the scope, ALL, *follows* the list of fields in the first LIST command and *precedes* the fields in this one. Modifiers can be coded in any order.

DEPOSIT is a numeric field, so it was compared with a number, the constant 0. A FOR condition can also compare two character items, such as a character field and a character constant. Character constants must be enclosed in single or double quotation marks. For example, to find the record for someone named Smith, you might code

```
FOR LAST_NAME = 'SMITH'
```

Because numbers and character strings are stored differently inside the computer, it is illegal to mix numbers and characters in the same FOR condition.

Date fields are stored inside the computer in numeric form. Unfortunately, the slash characters that separate the day from the month and the month from the year imply division in a numeric field and so will be misinterpreted by dBASE III Plus. Fortunately, you can code a date in character form and then convert it to a numeric date by using a **CTOD** (Character TO Date) **function**. For example, to list the customers who last purchased from CAMPUS THREADS before January 1, 1989, type

```
LIST ALL FIELDS LAST_NAME, LAST_SALE

FOR LAST_SALE < CTOD('01/01/89')
```

and press ⏎. Your screen will resemble Fig. 28.13. The date, 01/01/89, is a character constant and must be enclosed in quotation marks. The character string is the function's **argument** and must be enclosed in parentheses. The CTOD function is a dBASE III Plus subroutine that converts the character constant into internal date (numeric) form.

Figure 28.13

You can also select records on the basis of a date field.

```
         1   KALO             108   EMERISON HALL
         2   CHU              260   IRUIN HALL
         6   PLOETZ          1045   RAGGIN TOWER
         7   RAMBO            111   IRUIN HALL
         8   PERUCCA           45   SWING HALL
        10   STRIDER          400   BRANDYWINE HALL
        11   BAGGINS          105   BAG END HALL
        12   WORTH             43   SWING HALL
        13   OAKENSHIELD      113   ELROND HOUSE
        16   BAER             324   RAGGIN TOWER
        18   HARI             119   RINELAND HALL
        22   COTTRELL         187   HAMILTON HALL
. LIST ALL FIELDS LAST_NAME, LAST_SALE FOR LAST_SALE < CTOD ('01/01/89')
Record#   LAST_NAME          LAST_SALE
         4   AVERY            09/10/88
        15   TOOK             09/17/88
        19   GOMEZ            09/17/88
        20   BLOOM            11/12/88
        21   MOUSE            10/18/88
        23   SMITH            12/20/87
        25   MOOSE            09/10/88
.
┌──────────────┬───┬──────────┬───────────┬──────────┬──────┐
│ Command Line │<B:>│ CUSTOMER │  Rec: EOF/25 │      │ Caps │
└──────────────┴───┴──────────┴───────────┴──────────┴──────┘
              Enter a dBASE III PLUS command.
```

CTOD is just one of many dBASE III Plus functions. Its converse, DTOC (Date TO Character), converts a date to a character string. Other functions trim leading or trailing spaces from field entries, return the system date, and perform numerous other tasks; they will be introduced as needed.

■ *Keystroke Summary*

FOR condition

Type: *command options* **FOR** *condition*

Press: ⏎

■ *What Can Go Wrong?*

1. A message reads "Unterminated string." The command and a question mark appear above the message.

Cause: Either you did not type a closing quotation mark or you typed a single quotation mark on one end of the string and a double quotation mark on the other.

Solution: Press ⬆ until the command appears on the action line. Correct the error and then press ⏎ to reissue the command. ■

The SET EXACT Command

Clear the screen, type the command

```
DISPLAY FIELDS LAST_NAME FOR LAST_NAME = 'S'
```

Figure 28.14

Character conditions do not require an exact match.

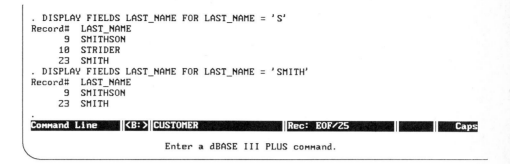

```
. DISPLAY FIELDS LAST_NAME FOR LAST_NAME = 'S'
Record#  LAST_NAME
       9  SMITHSON
      10  STRIDER
      23  SMITH
. DISPLAY FIELDS LAST_NAME FOR LAST_NAME = 'SMITH'
Record#  LAST_NAME
       9  SMITHSON
      23  SMITH
.
Command Line    <B:> CUSTOMER                Rec: EOF/25              Caps
         Enter a dBASE III PLUS command.
```

and press ⏎. Three names will appear (Fig. 28.14, near the top); a quick review of the file's contents should convince you that the DISPLAY command has selected everyone whose last name begins with S. Now type the command

```
DISPLAY FIELDS LAST_NAME FOR LAST_NAME = 'SMITH'
```

and press ⏎. Strider will drop from the list, but both SMITHSON and SMITH will be included (Fig. 28.14). By default, dBASE III Plus will find all records that meet the indicated search condition. Note, however, that if you define only the first several characters in a field, only those characters are checked. That's a useful feature. For example, it can help you find an individual's record when you have forgotten the exact spelling of his or her name. But it can also cause problems.

For example, imagine that you need SMITH's record. Type

```
LOCATE FOR LAST_NAME = 'SMITH'
```

and press ⏎. In response, dBASE III Plus will search through the database, stop on the first record that meets the condition, and set the pointer to that record. Now type

```
DISPLAY
```

and press ⏎. Which record will you see? The answer depends on the records' relative positions. If SMITH just happens to precede SMITH-SON in the database file, you'll see SMITH's record. In this case, however, SMITHSON came first, so you see SMITHSON's record. In other words, because dBASE III Plus does not look for an *exact* match, the outcome can be unpredictable.

One way to tell dBASE III Plus to look for an exact match is to type every character in the field. For example, the LAST_NAME field is 20 characters long. Because SMITH is only five characters long, to find an exact match, you would have to check for SMITH followed by 15 blanks.

Fortunately, there is an easier way. Type the command

    SET EXACT ON

and press ⏎. With exact on, dBASE III Plus will accept *only* an exact match. Then, rather than typing the trailing blanks on the search constant, use a dBASE III Plus function to trim the trailing blanks from the contents of the database field. For example, type the command

    LOCATE FOR TRIM(LAST_NAME) = 'SMITH'

and press ⏎. The TRIM function strips trailing blanks from the last name before the comparison is performed. SMITHSON is an eight-character field (after trimming) and so cannot exactly match SMITH. However, SMITH will match SMITH, so dBASE III Plus will find the right record. Type

    DISPLAY

press ⏎, and SMITH's record will appear.

You won't need an exact match very often, so you will normally want to set the exact option off. Type the command

    SET EXACT OFF

and press ⏎. If you don't, you could encounter problems in the next section.

■ *Keystroke Summary*

Set exact

Type: **SET EXACT [ON/OFF]**

Press: ⏎

■ *What Can Go Wrong?*

1. A message reads "Variable not found." The command appears above the message with a question mark to the right of your search condition.

Cause: You probably forgot to enclose the search field in quotation marks.

Solution: Press ⊺ to recall the command. Move the cursor to the first character in the search field, press ⟨Ins⟩, type a quotation mark, and press ⟨Ins⟩ again. Move the cursor to the end of the search field and type the closing quotation mark. Then press ⏎ to reissue the command. ■

Compound Conditions

What if several customers have the same last name? To locate a specific customer, you might have to code a **compound condition** by typing a **logical operator** to link two conditions. The logical operators are summarized in Fig. 28.15. Note that periods precede and follow each logical operator.

Figure 28.15
The dBASE III Plus
logical operators.

Compound Condition:	Is True If:
A .OR. B	either A or B is true
A .AND. B	both A and B are true
.NOT. (A)	A is not true

For example, imagine that you have just received a shipment from your supplier, but the label is damaged. You know that the order goes to someone in Irvin Hall, but you don't know who. To find the right person, you might obtain a list of customers who have made a deposit *and* who live in Irvin Hall. The search condition is

```
FOR DEPOSIT > 0 .AND. DORM = 'IRVIN HALL'
```

Clear the screen and type the command

```
LIST FIELDS LAST_NAME, ROOM, DEPOSIT, PHONE
FOR DEPOSIT > 0 .AND. DORM = 'IRVIN HALL'
```

That command is more than 80 characters long; note how the line scrolls to the left as you type. (The maximum length of a command is 254 characters.) Press ⏎. Your screen will list two customers (Fig. 28.16). A single phone call should be all you need to verify the order.

▪ *What Can Go Wrong?*

1. You issue a LIST command that contains a condition, but only field titles appear.

Cause: You probably forgot to enter the SET EXACT OFF command at the end of the previous section.

Solution: Type SET EXACT OFF and press ⏎. Then reissue the LIST command. ▪

Printing the Output

A screen display is not always acceptable; sometimes you need a printed **hard copy**. As you will discover, dBASE III Plus supports sophisticated report generation. For now, however, you can obtain a printed copy of output generated by a LIST or DISPLAY command by adding a TO PRINT option.

Figure 28.16
Compound conditions allow you to select records on the basis of the contents of two different fields.

```
. LIST FIELDS LAST_NAME, ROOM, DEPOSIT, PHONE FOR DEPOSIT > 0 .AND. DORM = 'IRVI
N HALL'
Record#    LAST_NAME              ROOM DEPOSIT PHONE
      2    CHU                     260   50.00 513/782-3376
      7    RAMBO                   111   50.00 513/782-6776
.
```

```
Command Line      |<B:>|CUSTOMER              |Rec: EOF/25      |         |  Caps
                      Enter a dBASE III PLUS command.
```

For example, try generating a printed copy of the entire database. Turn the printer on. (Obviously, you can't do this exercise if your computer doesn't have a printer.) Then type the command

```
LIST TO PRINT
```

and press ⏎. You should have little trouble recognizing the printed output.

You can, of course, combine TO PRINT with other options. For example, type the command

```
LIST ALL FIELDS LAST_NAME, FIRST_NAME, PHONE TO PRINT
```

and press ⏎. The printed list should show each customer's last name, first name, and telephone number.

To advance the paper to the top of the next page, type the command

```
EJECT
```

at the dot prompt and press ⏎. Consider using EJECT commands after each print operation so that each set of output data starts on a separate page. That makes it easier to physically separate the reports.

■ *Keystroke Summary*

To print

Type: *command modifiers* **TO PRINT**

Press: ⏎

■ *What Can Go Wrong?*

1. The printer won't print.

Cause: Unfortunately, the list of possible causes is almost endless, but there are some common problems that you can correct.

Solution: Make sure the printer is on. If you are working in a computer lab, two computers often share a single printer. Look for a little box (usually called a T-switch) between the computer and the printer and make sure the switch is set to your printer. Check to see that the printer has paper and a ribbon and that neither the paper nor the ribbon is jammed. Check the cables to make sure the printer is physically connected to the computer. ■

Exiting dBASE III Plus

That ends the third tutorial. To exit dBASE III Plus, type QUIT and press ⏎.

■ *Keystroke Summary*

Exit dBASE III Plus

Type: **QUIT**

Press: ⏎

Summary

From the Assistant

Function	Menu	Command	Page
Display record(s)	Retrieve	Display	499
Display record(s)	Update	Display	499
Exit dBASE III Plus	Set Up	Quit dBASE . . .	512
Go to selected record	Position	Goto Record	500
List records	Retrieve	List	500
Load database file	Set Up	Database file	494
Point to a record	Position	Goto Record	500
Select default drive	Tools	Set drive	493
Undelete a record	Update	Recall	502

From the Dot Prompt

Function	Command	Page
Clear screen	CLEAR	495
Display commands	DISPLAY HISTORY	495
Display record(s)	DISPLAY	499
Exit dBASE III Plus	QUIT	512
Go to selected record	GOTO	500
List records	LIST	500
Load database file	USE	494
Request help	HELP	496
Select default drive	SET DEFAULT TO	493
Set fields	SET FIELDS TO	502
Set fields	SET FIELDS [ON/OFF]	504
Skip to top of page	EJECT	512
Specify exact conditions	SET EXACT [ON/OFF]	508
Undelete record	RECALL RECORD	502

Options and Functions

Option or Function	Format	Page
Character to date	CTOD('mm/dd/yy')	507
Date to character	DTOC(date)	508
Define fields	command FIELDS list	501
Define scope	command *scope* options	504

Option or Function	Format	Page
Exit to dot prompt	Esc	492
FOR condition	command FOR condition	506
Print output	TO PRINT	511
Trim trailing blanks	TRIM(string)	510

Self-Test

1. A command's _____ identifies the set of records to which it applies. A dBASE III Plus _____ allows you to select records on the basis of the contents of selected fields.

2. The fields to be accessed or manipulated by a command are defined in an _____.

3. The dBASE III Plus _____ command allows you to control or specify the dBASE III Plus physical environment.

4. Type a _____ command to load or open the active file.

5. Type a _____ command to clear the screen.

6. Type _____ or press function key _____ to access the dBASE III Plus help screens.

7. A _____ option defines the fields to be displayed by the current command. A _____ command defines the fields to be displayed by a series of commands.

8. Type the scope _____ to display the current record plus the next six. Type the scope _____ to display the entire file.

9. Type the condition _____ to obtain a list of all the customers who have a deposit equal to $50.

10. The _____ option sends output to the printer.

Exercises

1. Print a list of the names and addresses of all the people on your name and address file (Exercises 1 of Chapters 26 and 27) who were born before 1972.

2. Print a list of the names of all the people on your membership file (Exercises 2 of Chapters 26 and 27) who have not yet paid their dues. Print a separate list of those who have paid less than $25.00

3. Print a list of all the items in the inventory file (Exercises 3 of Chapters 26 and 27) that are worth more than $10 and that were purchased before 1988.

■29

Manipulating a Database

This chapter introduces the dBASE III Plus features and commands that allow you to:

- index a database
- quickly find selected records
- use a WHILE condition to limit a command
- set filters
- build queries
- prepare mailing labels

Rearranging Database Order

Records are generally added to a database as events occur, but chronological order is often less than ideal when you want to *access* the data. For example, if you need data on a particular customer, it might be better to arrange the records in alphabetic order by last name. On the other hand, dormitory order might make the most sense if you are planning a delivery route. The dBASE III Plus INDEX command can be used to control the order in which a database's records are stored and/or displayed. Boot the operating system and load dBASE III Plus. When the assistant screen appears, press Esc to exit to the dot prompt. Then press Caps Lock to activate *caps lock*. Enter a SET DEFAULT TO command to identify the default drive and a USE command to select CUSTOMER as the active database. Now you're ready to begin.

Indexing

A database **index** is a table that relates the values stored in a key field to the associated record numbers. For example, Fig. 29.1 shows the database indexed by LAST_NAME. The index can be used to quickly find a specific record. For example, imagine that you want AVERY's record. Visually search the index in Fig. 29.1 and find AVERY. The second index column indicates that AVERY's record is number 4. Access record 4, and you have her data.

The INDEX command

You will almost certainly want to access the data by customer name, so index the database on LAST_NAME and then on FIRST_NAME.

The structure of an INDEX command is shown in Fig. 29.2. The **key expression** indicates the field name or names that will form the index. The command builds an **index file** and stores it under the file name you specify; dBASE III Plus adds the extension *ndx*. Although file names are largely a matter of personal taste, it helps to choose a meaningful name derived in some way from the database file name and the index field or fields. For example, CUSTNAME is a good choice for a CUSTOMER file indexed on LAST_NAME and FIRST_NAME.

When an index file is active, the records appear in ascending order of the key expression. Character, date, or numeric fields can be used. The key expression may be a single field, a combination of fields, or even the difference between two fields. When the key expression contains more than one field, list the most important field first.

In other commands, when you wanted to identify multiple fields, you typed a list of field names separated by commas. A key expression is different because, technically, it is a *single* field formed by

Figure 29.1

An index is a table that links the values stored in a key field or fields with associated database records.

The index			The database file	
Last name	Record	Record	Last name	First name
		1	KALO	LISA ...
		2	CHU	PING ...
AVERY	4	3	BAGGINS	FRODO ...
BAER	16	4	AVERY	ANN ...
BAGGINS	11	5	PINTA	GARY ...
BAGGINS	3	6	PLOETZ	JASON ...
BLOOM	20	7	RAMBO	TAMMY ...
BRANDYBUCK	14	8	PERUCCA	RHONDA ...
CHU	2	9	SMITHSON	SUSAN ...
COTTRELL	22	10	STRIDER	ARAGON ..
GOMEZ	19			

Figure 29.2
When you index a database, you create a separate file to hold the index. The general form of an INDEX command is shown below the flow diagram.

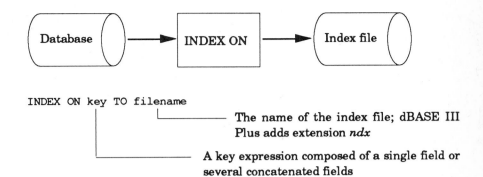

```
INDEX ON key TO filename
```

The name of the index file; dBASE III Plus adds extension *ndx*

A key expression composed of a single field or several concatenated fields

combining the listed fields. Therefore instead of using commas to separate fields, you use plus signs; the + symbol means *and* when you **concatenate** character fields. For example, to index on both LAST_NAME and FIRST_NAME, code the expression

```
LAST_NAME + FIRST_NAME
```

(The blank spaces are optional, but they make the expression easier to read.)

Clear the screen. Then type

```
INDEX ON LAST_NAME + FIRST_NAME TO CUSTNAME
```

and press ↵. After a brief delay a message

```
100% indexed    25 Records indexed
```

will appear near the bottom of the screen, indicating that the operation is complete. Check the pointer on the status bar; it should read *4/25*. (If you originally entered your data in a different order or skipped one or more records, your pointer might not be 4. If that's the case, don't worry.) If the records were listed in alphabetical order, the fourth record in the database would appear first.

To view the current record, type the command

```
DISPLAY FIELDS LAST_NAME, FIRST_NAME, PHONE
```

and press ↵. Ann Avery's record, number 4, should appear on your screen. Next type

```
LIST NEXT 10 FIELDS LAST_NAME, FIRST_NAME, PHONE
```

and press ↵. Your screen will resemble Fig. 29.3, with the last names in alphabetic order. Note that Bilbo Baggins comes before Frodo Baggins. First name was the secondary index; thus when the last names for two or more records are the same, those records are sorted by first name. The record numbers indicate the original database order.

Figure 29.3
The active index controls the order in which the records are accessed.

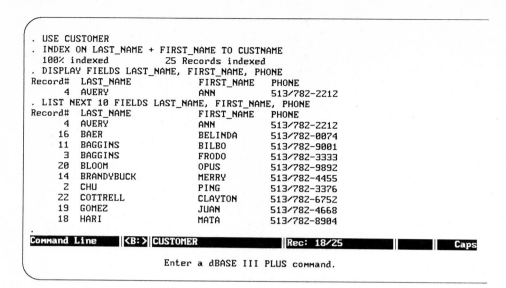

```
. USE CUSTOMER
. INDEX ON LAST_NAME + FIRST_NAME TO CUSTNAME
  100% indexed            25 Records indexed
. DISPLAY FIELDS LAST_NAME, FIRST_NAME, PHONE
Record#  LAST_NAME           FIRST_NAME   PHONE
      4  AVERY               ANN          513/782-2212
. LIST NEXT 10 FIELDS LAST_NAME, FIRST_NAME, PHONE
Record#  LAST_NAME           FIRST_NAME   PHONE
      4  AVERY               ANN          513/782-2212
     16  BAER                BELINDA      513/782-0074
     11  BAGGINS             BILBO        513/782-9001
      3  BAGGINS             FRODO        513/782-3333
     20  BLOOM               OPUS         513/782-9892
     14  BRANDYBUCK          MERRY        513/782-4455
      2  CHU                 PING         513/782-3376
     22  COTTRELL            CLAYTON      513/782-6752
     19  GOMEZ               JUAN         513/782-4668
     18  HARI                MATA         513/782-8904
.
```

| Command Line | \<B:\> CUSTOMER | Rec: 18/25 | Caps |

Enter a dBASE III PLUS command.

▪ *Keystroke Summary*

Index database file

Type: **INDEX ON** *key* **TO** *filename*

Press: ⏎

▪ *What Can Go Wrong?*

1. The error message "Unrecognized phrase/keyword in command" appears on the screen after you issue the INDEX command. A question mark appears above FIRST_NAME.

Cause: You probably typed a comma instead of a plus sign to separate the fields in the key expression.

Solution: Type a plus sign over the comma and reissue the command. ▪

Creating a Second Index

A list of customers grouped by dormitory will also prove useful, so index CUSTOMER by DORM. Type the command

    INDEX ON DORM TO CUSTDORM

and press ⏎. Then type

    LIST FIELDS LAST_NAME, DORM

and press ⏎. Note that the data appear in dormitory order (Fig. 29.4).

Figure 29.4

When the database is indexed by DORM, the data are listed in dormitory order.

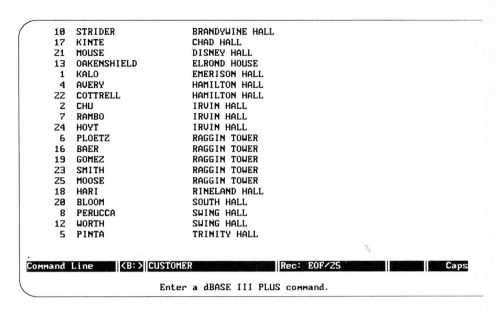

```
     10   STRIDER            BRANDYWINE HALL
     17   KINTE              CHAD HALL
     21   MOUSE              DISNEY HALL
     13   OAKENSHIELD        ELROND HOUSE
      1   KALO               EMERISON HALL
      4   AVERY              HAMILTON HALL
     22   COTTRELL           HAMILTON HALL
      2   CHU                IRVIN HALL
      7   RAMBO              IRVIN HALL
     24   HOYT               IRVIN HALL
      6   PLOETZ             RAGGIN TOWER
     16   BAER               RAGGIN TOWER
     19   GOMEZ              RAGGIN TOWER
     23   SMITH              RAGGIN TOWER
     25   MOOSE              RAGGIN TOWER
     18   HARI               RINELAND HALL
     20   BLOOM              SOUTH HALL
      8   PERUCCA            SWING HALL
     12   WORTH              SWING HALL
      5   PINTA              TRINITY HALL
```

```
 Command Line    ||<B:>||CUSTOMER          ||Rec: EOF/25   ||      || Caps
```
Enter a dBASE III PLUS command.

Opening Index Files

So far you have created two indexes, CUSTNAME and CUSTDORM. The INDEX command that created CUSTDORM performed two transparent functions, closing CUSTNAME and opening CUSTDORM. That presents a potential problem if you append records to the database or change the value of a key field because only *open* indexes are automatically updated by dBASE III Plus. If an index is used temporarily and then discarded, that's not a problem; but if you have indexes that are used frequently, it is important that they *all* be open when you update the database.

There are two ways to identify the indexes to be updated with the database. One method is to include them in a USE command, such as

```
USE filename INDEX key-1, key-2, ...
```

An alternative is to issue a SET INDEX TO command before you begin updating the data; for example,

```
USE filename
SET INDEX TO key-1, key-2, ...
```

In either case the first index listed is the **active index**.

To illustrate what happens when you do not open your indexes, clear the screen, type

```
SET INDEX TO
```

Figure 29.5
Append a record to
the end of the
database.

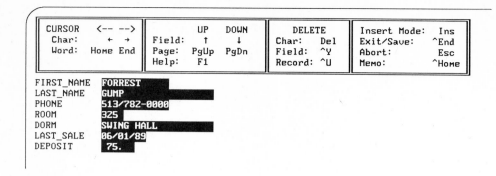

```
┌─ CURSOR    <-- -->  ┬           UP   DOWN ┬──  DELETE       ┬─ Insert Mode:  Ins ─┐
│  Char:     ←    →   │ Field:    ↑     ↓   │ Char:    Del    │  Exit/Save:    ^End │
│  Word:   Home  End  │ Page:   PgUp  PgDn  │ Field:   ^Y     │  Abort:        Esc  │
│                     │ Help:     F1        │ Record:  ^U     │  Memo:       ^Home  │
└─────────────────────┴─────────────────────┴─────────────────┴─────────────────────┘

  FIRST_NAME   FORREST
  LAST_NAME    GUMP
  PHONE        513/782-0000
  ROOM         325
  DORM         SWING HALL
  LAST_SALE    06/01/89
  DEPOSIT         75.
```

(with no list of indexes) and press ⏎. A SET INDEX TO command with no parameters closes all indexes. Now type

    APPEND

press ⏎, and append a new record to the database. Figure 29.5 shows the almost completed append screen; use it as a guide and type the new record. (*Note:* Substitute the current date for the last sale date in Fig. 29.5.) After you type the deposit amount (75.) and press ⏎, the cursor will advance to the first field in the next (empty) record. Press ⏎ to save the new record and return to the dot prompt. The pointer should indicate record *26/26*; if it doesn't, GOTO record 26. Then type a DISPLAY command to prove to yourself that the record is there.

Clear the screen again. Then type the two commands

    SET INDEX TO CUSTNAME, CUSTDORM
    LIST FIELDS LAST_NAME, FIRST_NAME

pressing ⏎ after each command. The output can be seen in Fig. 29.6. Forrest Gump's record should be between Gomez's and Hari's, but it isn't there. Gump's record is in the database but not in the index.

Figure 29.6
If an index is not
open, it will not be
updated when you
modify the database.

```
  20   BLOOM          OPUS
  14   BRANDYBUCK     MERRY
   2   CHU            PING
  22   COTTRELL       CLAYTON
  19   GOMEZ          JUAN
  18   HARI           MATA
  24   HOYT           DEEDRA
   1   KALO           LISA
  17   KINTE          KUNTA
  25   MOOSE          BULLWINKLE
  21   MOUSE          MICHAEL
```

■ *Keystroke Summary*

Open index file

Type: **SET INDEX TO** *keys*

Press: ↵

■ *What Can Go Wrong?*

1. After you issue the SET INDEX command, an error message reads "File does not exist." A question mark precedes one of the index names.

Cause: You probably misspelled the index name.

Solution: Correct the spelling and reissue the command. ■

The REINDEX Command

Fortunately, it's easy to add the missing index references by issuing a REINDEX command. Try it. Type

    REINDEX

and press ↵. A series of messages will tell you that dBASE III Plus is rebuilding the indexes. When the dot prompt reappears, reissue the command

    LIST FIELDS LAST_NAME, FIRST_NAME

and press ↵. This time, Gump's name will appear (Fig. 29.7).

■ *Keystroke Summary*

Reindex database file

Type: **REINDEX**

Press: ↵

The FIND Command

In an earlier chapter you used a LOCATE command to move the pointer to a record with a specified attribute. For example,

    LOCATE LAST_NAME = 'BAGGINS'

Figure 29.7
The REINDEX command updates the index.

```
14  BRANDYBUCK      MERRY
 2  CHU             PING
22  COTTRELL        CLAYTON
19  GOMEZ           JUAN
26  GUMP            FORREST
18  HARI            MATA
24  HOYT            DEEDRA
 1  KALO            LISA
17  KINTE           KUNTA
25  MOOSE           BULLWINKLE
21  MOUSE           MICHAEL
```

tells dBASE III Plus to search the database and set the pointer to the first record with the last name BAGGINS.

The basic problem with the LOCATE command is speed, particularly on a large database. It works by checking each record sequentially until it finds a match. Imagine using that strategy to look up a number in a telephone book. The idea of starting with A and reading, line by line, until you reach the desired name is absurd. The FIND command, in contrast, applies an efficient search technique to the active index and thus can find the target record very quickly.

Clear the screen. Then type the command

```
FIND BAGGINS
```

and press ↵. The pointer will change. To verify that dBASE III Plus has found the right record, type

```
DISPLAY FIELDS LAST_NAME, FIRST_NAME
```

and press ↵. Bilbo's record will appear (Fig. 29.8).

You might have noticed a difference in the LOCATE and FIND command syntax. Compare them:

```
LOCATE LAST_NAME = 'BAGGINS'
FIND BAGGINS
```

The LOCATE command needs a complete search condition, while FIND requires only the target character string. Also, BAGGINS is enclosed in quotation marks in the LOCATE command but not in the FIND command. Why?

FIND searches the active index, CUSTNAME. When CUSTNAME was defined, the last name and then the first name were specified. Since the field or fields that form the index are known, there is no need to "remind" dBASE III Plus about the identity of the field to be searched. The type of the index is also known. The purpose of the quotation marks in the LOCATE command is to identify a character string, but since CUSTNAME is, by definition, character, adding quotation marks to the FIND command's search string would be redundant. Finally, FIND always searches for an *equal* condition, so there is no need to specify the condition.

Figure 29.8
A FIND command can be used to quickly search an indexed database for a specific record.

```
. FIND BAGGINS
. DISPLAY FIELDS LAST_NAME, FIRST_NAME
Record#  LAST_NAME          FIRST_NAME
    11   BAGGINS            BILBO
.
```

| Command Line | <B:> CUSTOMER | Rec: 11/26 | Caps |

```
       Enter a dBASE III PLUS command.
```

■ *Keystroke Summary*

Find record

> Type: **FIND** *string*
>
> Press: ⏎

■ *What Can Go Wrong?*

1. After you issue a FIND command, the message "No find" appears just above the dot prompt.

Cause: No record containing the search string was found. You might have mistyped the string, perhaps using lowercase instead of uppercase. The record you want might have been deleted, or the record might be hidden by a filter (to be discussed later in the chapter). Finally, the wrong index (or no index) might be active.

Solution: If you know that the target record exists, check the spelling or the case (Baggins is *not* the same as BAGGINS), correct the search string, and reissue the command. If that doesn't work, activate potentially deleted records by typing SET DELETED OFF and pressing ⏎. Then cancel any active filters by typing SET FILTER TO and pressing ⏎. Finally, reissue the FIND command. If that doesn't work, make sure the correct index is active by issuing a SET INDEX TO *index* command, and then reissue the FIND command. ■

Searching on More Than One Field

As you may recall, there are two customers named Baggins. The active index, CUSTNAME, lists LAST_NAME as the primary index and FIRST_NAME as the secondary index; that's why Bilbo's record was displayed. What if you wanted Frodo's record? Because CUSTNAME indexes the database by both last and first name, you should be able to find the record that meets both conditions. Clear the screen, type the command

```
FIND BAGGINS + FRODO
```

and press ⏎. A message

```
No find.
```

will appear just above the dot prompt. Try

```
FIND BAGGINS, FRODO
```

and then

```
FIND BAGGINSFRODO
```

They also won't work (see the error messages near the top of Fig. 29.9).

The problem is the trailing spaces in the last name field; if you were to type 13 spaces between BAGGINS and FRODO, you would find the proper record. A better solution is to remove the trailing

Figure 29.9
To facilitate finding records indexed by two key character fields, trim the trailing spaces from the first field before concatenating the second field to it.

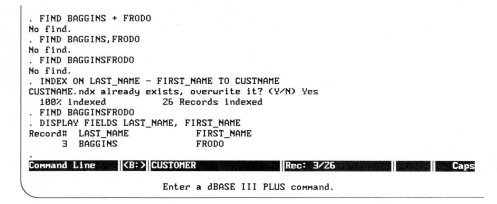

```
. FIND BAGGINS + FRODO
No find.
. FIND BAGGINS,FRODO
No find.
. FIND BAGGINSFRODO
No find.
. INDEX ON LAST_NAME - FIRST_NAME TO CUSTNAME
CUSTNAME.ndx already exists, overwrite it? (Y/N) Yes
   100% indexed          26 Records indexed
. FIND BAGGINSFRODO
. DISPLAY FIELDS LAST_NAME, FIRST_NAME
Record#  LAST_NAME          FIRST_NAME
      3  BAGGINS            FRODO
.
```

| Command Line | ‹B:› CUSTOMER | Rec: 3/26 | | Caps |

Enter a dBASE III PLUS command.

spaces from the last name field when the index is created. You can do that by enclosing the last name field in a TRIM function or by using a minus sign to concatenate LAST_NAME and FIRST_NAME.

For example, type the command

    INDEX ON LAST_NAME - FIRST_NAME TO CUSTNAME

The minus sign between LAST_NAME and FIRST_NAME means to trim trailing blanks from the last name field before concatenating the first name to it. Press ⏎. A message

    CUSTNAME.ndx already exists, overwrite it? (Y/N)

will appear. Type Y for yes, and the new version of the index will replace the old one. Now type the command

    FIND BAGGINSFRODO

and press ⏎. Then type

    DISPLAY FIELDS LAST_NAME, FIRST_NAME

and press ⏎. The target record will appear (Fig. 29.9).

Try one more experiment before you move on. Type

    FIND BAGGINSB

and press ⏎. Then type

    DISPLAY FIELDS LAST_NAME, FIRST_NAME

and press ⏎ again. Bilbo's record will appear. The first letter of his first name, B, is enough to distinguish it from Frodo.

WHILE Conditions

Assume that you have just received a catalog from a new supplier. Included among the items is a line of sports clothing embossed with a decal that looks just like the Raggin Tower intramural team's mascot, and you suspect that your Raggin Tower customers will be excited. To plan your sales call, you need a list of their names, room numbers, telephone numbers, and active deposits.

You want to access the file in dormitory order, so make CUST-DORM the active index by typing the command

```
SET INDEX TO TO CUSTDORM, CUSTNAME
```

and pressing ⏎. To move the pointer to the first Raggin Tower customer, type

```
FIND RAGGIN
```

and press ⏎. Next type, on a single line,

```
LIST FIELDS LAST_NAME, ROOM, DORM, PHONE, DEPOSIT
WHILE DORM = 'RAGGIN'
```

and press ⏎. The output is shown in Fig. 29.10. The WHILE condition means that the command will be repeated as long as the condition is true; in other words, the specified fields will be listed as long as the dormitory is Raggin Tower.

■ *Keystroke Summary*

WHILE condition

Type: *command* **WHILE** *condition*

Press: ⏎

Maintaining an Indexed Database

With the new catalog and the customer list in hand, you call on your five Raggin Tower customers. As you expected, they love the new line and decide to order matching warmup suits, giving you new deposits of 25 dollars each. When you return to your room, your first task is to update the database to reflect the new purchases. You could use EDIT or BROWSE commands as you did in Chapter 27; but given the nature of these transactions, there is an easier way.

Figure 29.10
A WHILE condition causes the command to be repeated as long as the specified condition is true. WHILE conditions are normally used on indexed or sorted database files.

```
. INDEX ON DORM TO CUSTDORM
  100% indexed        26 Records indexed
. FIND RAGGIN
. LIST FIELDS LAST_NAME, ROOM, DORM, PHONE, DEPOSIT WHILE DORM = 'RAGGIN'
Record#  LAST_NAME        ROOM DORM           PHONE         DEPOSIT
     6   PLOETZ          1045 RAGGIN TOWER    513/782-5654    50.00
    16   BAER             324 RAGGIN TOWER    513/782-0074    70.00
    19   GOMEZ           1023 RAGGIN TOWER    513/782-4668     0.00
    23   SMITH            894 RAGGIN TOWER    513/782-8901     0.00
    25   MOOSE            607 RAGGIN TOWER    513/782-5634     0.00
.
Command Line   |<B:>|CUSTOMER        ||Rec: 18/26   ||      || Caps
              Enter a dBASE III PLUS command.
```

Clear the screen. To make sure you have the right database active and all indexes open, type

```
USE CUSTOMER INDEX CUSTDORM, CUSTNAME
```

and press ⏎. (Even if the file and the indexes had been properly set, repeating the USE command wouldn't hurt anything.) CUSTOMER is now the active file, and CUSTDORM is the active index.

Position the pointer on the first Raggin Tower record by typing

```
FIND RAGGIN
```

and pressing ⏎. Then type the command

```
REPLACE DEPOSIT WITH DEPOSIT + 25 WHILE DORM = 'RAGGIN'
```

and press ⏎ again. A message will indicate that five records were replaced.

Take a closer look at the REPLACE command. Note that the key word FIELDS does *not* precede the name of the field to be replaced. Because REPLACE works with one field at a time, FIELDS is not necessary, and, if coded, it will be marked as an error.

Note also the WITH clause. Had you coded

```
DEPOSIT WITH 25
```

the value 25 would have been stored in each record. For customers who previously had a zero deposit, that would be fine, but Ploetz, to cite one example, had 50 dollars on deposit before this transaction. The clause

```
DEPOSIT WITH DEPOSIT + 25
```

tells dBASE III Plus to get the old value of DEPOSIT, add 25 to it, and then store the answer in DEPOSIT. When a plus sign links two character fields, it means to concatenate; when a plus sign links two numeric fields, it means to add.

One more change remains. The five customers in Raggin Tower have just placed an order, so you must update their last sale fields. To set the pointer to the first Raggin Tower record, type

```
FIND RAGGIN
```

and press ⏎. Then type the command

```
REPLACE LAST_SALE WITH DATE() WHILE DORM = 'RAGGIN'
```

and press ⏎ again. The DATE function returns the current system date. (You set the date when you booted the system.) A message will indicate that five records were replaced. To verify that the database has been updated, type

```
FIND RAGGIN
```

Figure 29.11
The REPLACE command can be used to modify the contents of a database.

```
. FIND RAGGIN
. REPLACE DEPOSIT WITH DEPOSIT + 25 WHILE DORM = 'RAGGIN'
      5 records replaced
. FIND RAGGIN
. REPLACE LAST_SALE WITH DATE() WHILE DORM = 'RAGGIN'
      5 records replaced
. FIND RAGGIN
. LIST LAST_NAME, ROOM, DORM, DEPOSIT, LAST_SALE WHILE DORM = 'RAGGIN'
Record#  LAST_NAME          ROOM DORM              DEPOSIT LAST_SALE
      6  PLOETZ             1045 RAGGIN TOWER        75.00 06/01/89
     16  BAER                324 RAGGIN TOWER        95.00 06/01/89
     19  GOMEZ              1023 RAGGIN TOWER        25.00 06/01/89
     23  SMITH               894 RAGGIN TOWER        25.00 06/01/89
     25  MOOSE               607 RAGGIN TOWER        25.00 06/01/89
.
```

| Command Line | ‹B:›|CUSTOMER | Rec: 18/26 | | Caps |

Enter a dBASE III PLUS command.

press ⏎, and then type (on a single line)

```
LIST LAST_NAME, ROOM, DORM, DEPOSIT, LAST_SALE
WHILE DORM = 'RAGGIN'
```

Press ⏎ again. Your screen will resemble Fig. 29.11

■ *Keystroke Summary*

Replace field

Type: **REPLACE** *field* **WITH** *expression options*

Press: ⏎

■ *What Can Go Wrong?*

1. A message indicates that no records were replaced.

Cause: You might have used an ALL scope. ALL implies "start with the first record." You might have used the wrong case; Raggin is not the same as RAGGIN. Perhaps you forgot to move the pointer to the first record referenced by the WHILE condition.

Solution: FIND the first Raggin Tower record, correct any typing errors, and reissue the REPLACE command.

2. No records are listed following a LIST command with a WHILE option.

Cause: You might have forgotten to reset the pointer to the first record in the group.

Solution: FIND the first record in the group and then reissue the LIST command.

3. A "Variable not found." message appears after you issue a REPLACE command.

Cause: Either you misspelled the field name or you typed the key word FIELDS before the field name.

Solution: Correct your spelling or delete FIELDS. Then reissue the command. ■

Filters and Queries

Defining Filters

Imagine that you need a list of the customers with active deposits. One option is to attach a FOR clause to a LIST command. An alternative is to define a **filter**. Like a FOR clause, a filter limits dBASE III Plus to processing only those records that meet a specified condition. A FOR clause affects a single command. A filter, on the other hand, screens the records processed by subsequent commands. Additionally, filters are the basis for creating queries. Setting a filter does for records what setting fields does for fields.

A filter is defined in a SET FILTER TO command. Clear the screen. You want to list the customers who have a positive (greater than zero) deposit, so type the command

```
SET FILTER TO DEPOSIT > 0
```

and press ↵. To verify that the filter works, type

```
LIST FIELDS LAST_NAME, DEPOSIT
```

and press ↵. Your screen will resemble Fig. 29.12.

The filter condition does not take effect until the pointer is moved. A LIST command automatically moves the pointer to the top of the file, but if you had issued a BROWSE command after a filter condition had been invoked, the screen probably would have displayed some records that did not meet the filter condition. If you issue a command and the filter doesn't seem to work, you might try a GOTO, LOCATE, or FIND command before reissuing the original command.

Figure 29.12
A filter screens the records processed by subsequent commands.

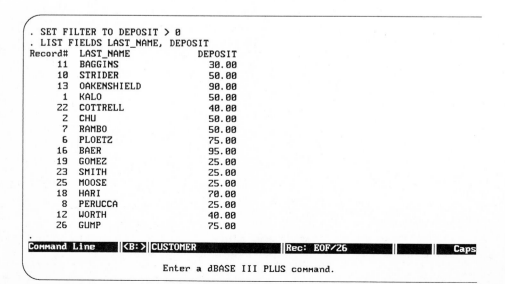

```
. SET FILTER TO DEPOSIT > 0
. LIST FIELDS LAST_NAME, DEPOSIT
Record#   LAST_NAME              DEPOSIT
    11    BAGGINS                  30.00
    10    STRIDER                  50.00
    13    OAKENSHIELD              90.00
     1    KALO                     50.00
    22    COTTRELL                 40.00
     2    CHU                      50.00
     7    RAMBO                    50.00
     6    PLOETZ                   75.00
    16    BAER                     95.00
    19    GOMEZ                    25.00
    23    SMITH                    25.00
    25    MOOSE                    25.00
    18    HARI                     70.00
     8    PERUCCA                  25.00
    12    WORTH                    40.00
    26    GUMP                     75.00
.
```

| Command Line | <B:> | CUSTOMER | Rec: EOF/26 | Caps |

Enter a dBASE III PLUS command.

Define filter

    Type: **SET FILTER TO** *condition*

    Press: ⏎

Defining Queries

It is always possible to define filters as you need them, but you'll often find yourself using the same complex condition again and again, and retyping the same SET FILTER TO command every time you access dBASE III Plus can be a bother. A frequently used filter can be saved as a **query file** and invoked with a SET FILTER command.

For example, you will probably want to identify your active customers. They might be defined by either of two tests. Clearly, those who have made deposits and are waiting for delivery are active. Additionally, you might want to include all those customers who have made a purchase within the last 90 days. Therefore you want to create a filter to identify customers who have an active deposit *or* who have made a purchase within the last 90 days.

The first step in creating a query is to type a CREATE QUERY command (Fig. 29.13). The command allows you to define a filter and then store it in a query file. In this case, CUSTACT seems a good name for a query that searches the CUSTOMER database to find recently active customers, so type

```
CREATE QUERY CUSTACT
```

and press ⏎. A **query creation screen** will appear (Fig. 29.14); it guides you through the process of creating a query much as the assistant screen guides you through creating commands.

As you begin, the *Set Filter* choice is highlighted on the menu bar. A second bar marks menu choice *Field Name*. Press ⏎ to select the first field name. A list of fields will appear to the right of the first

Figure 29.13
A CREATE QUERY command defines a query and stores it on a query file. The general form of the command is shown below the flow diagram.

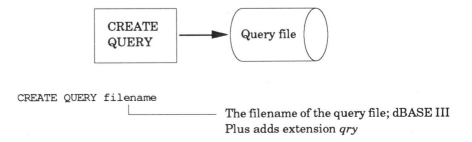

```
CREATE QUERY filename
```
The filename of the query file; dBASE III Plus adds extension *qry*

Figure 29.14
The query creation
screen.

```
┌─────────────────────────────────────────────────────────────────────────┐
│  Set Filter           Nest          Display           Exit  11:26:58 am   │
│  ┌──────────────────────────────────────────────────────┐                │
│  │ Field Name                                             │                │
│  │ Operator                                               │                │
│  │ Constant/Expression                                    │                │
│  │ Connect                                                │                │
│  │ ─────────────────────────────────────                 │                │
│  │ Line Number          1                                 │                │
│  └──────────────────────────────────────────────────────┘                │
│                                                                           │
│  ┌───────┬─────────┬───────────────┬─────────────────────┬────────────┐  │
│  │ Line  │ Field   │ Operator      │ Constant/Expression │ Connect    │  │
│  ├───────┼─────────┼───────────────┼─────────────────────┼────────────┤  │
│  │  1    │         │               │                     │            │  │
│  │  2    │         │               │                     │            │  │
│  │  3    │         │               │                     │            │  │
│  │  4    │         │               │                     │            │  │
│  │  5    │         │               │                     │            │  │
│  │  6    │         │               │                     │            │  │
│  │  7    │         │               │                     │            │  │
│  └───────┴─────────┴───────────────┴─────────────────────┴────────────┘  │
│  CREATE QUERY    <B:> CUSTACT.QRY              Opt: 1/2            Caps    │
│         Position selection bar - ↑↓.   Select - ⏎.   Leave menu - ←→.     │
│               Select a field name for the filter condition.               │
└─────────────────────────────────────────────────────────────────────────┘
```

menu. Highlight

    DEPOSIT

and press ⏎. The word DEPOSIT will appear under the header *Field*
on the bottom section of your screen, and the highlight bar will move
to *Operator*.

Press ⏎ to indicate that you wish to specify an operator. A list of
operators will appear to the right of the menu; highlight

    > more than

and press ⏎. The specified condition will appear on the bottom section
of the screen, and the highlight bar will move to *Constant / Expression*.
Press ⏎ to indicate that you wish to make an entry. Then type 0 (zero)
and press ⏎ again. Note that the first line in the window (Fig. 29.15)
resembles the condition you might type in a SET FILTER TO command.

The highlight bar now marks *Connect*. If only one condition were
to be coded, you would be finished, but the 90-day condition must still
be added. Because the second filter will be connected to the first one,
press ⏎. A submenu of logical operators will appear. Highlight

    Combine with .or.

and press ⏎.

Figure 29.15

The query creation screen after the first condition has been entered.

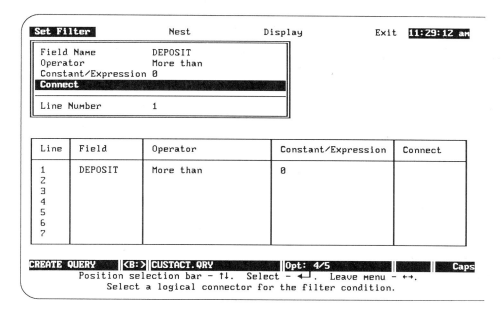

```
┌─────────────────────────────────────────────────────────────────────────┐
│ Set Filter            Nest           Display            Exit  11:29:12 am │
│ ┌───────────────────────────────────────────────────────────┐           │
│ │ Field Name           DEPOSIT                                │           │
│ │ Operator             More than                              │           │
│ │ Constant/Expression  0                                      │           │
│ │ Connect                                                     │           │
│ │                                                             │           │
│ │ Line Number          1                                      │           │
│ └───────────────────────────────────────────────────────────┘           │
│                                                                           │
│  ┌──────┬──────────┬───────────┬──────────────────────┬─────────┐        │
│  │ Line │ Field    │ Operator  │ Constant/Expression  │ Connect │        │
│  ├──────┼──────────┼───────────┼──────────────────────┼─────────┤        │
│  │  1   │ DEPOSIT  │ More than │ 0                    │         │        │
│  │  2   │          │           │                      │         │        │
│  │  3   │          │           │                      │         │        │
│  │  4   │          │           │                      │         │        │
│  │  5   │          │           │                      │         │        │
│  │  6   │          │           │                      │         │        │
│  │  7   │          │           │                      │         │        │
│  └──────┴──────────┴───────────┴──────────────────────┴─────────┘        │
│                                                                           │
│ CREATE QUERY      <B:> CUSTACT.QRY          Opt: 4/5              Caps    │
│      Position selection bar - ↑↓.   Select - ↵.  Leave menu - ←→.        │
│          Select a logical connector for the filter condition.            │
└─────────────────────────────────────────────────────────────────────────┘
```

The highlight bar will move to *Field Name*; press ↵, highlight

LAST_SALE

and press ↵ again. The highlight bar will move to *Operator*; press ↵, select

>= More than or equal

and press ↵. The highlight bar will move to *Constant/Expression*. Press ↵ again. Then type the condition

DATE() - 90

and press ↵. The DATE function returns the current date; subtracting 90 from it defines a date 90 days in the past. Figure 29.16 shows the second filter in row 2.

That completes the query. Press →, and the highlight bar at the top of the screen will move to *Nest*. Press → again to highlight *Display*. This choice allows you to preview the filter. Press ↵ to view the first record that passes the filter; press PgDn to view additional records. (PgUp backs up a record.) If the output is wrong, move the highlight bar back to *Set Filter*, make any necessary corrections, and then use the display option to check your work again. When you are satisfied, press → to highlight *Exit*, select option *Save*, and press ↵. The query file will be saved under the name you specified (CUSTACT), and you'll be returned to the dot prompt.

Figure 29.16
The query condition
screen with the
second filter in place.

```
┌────────────────────────────────────────────────────────────────────┐
│ █Set Filter█         Nest          Display         Exit  █11:30:56 am█│
│  ┌──────────────────────────────────────────────────┐                │
│  │ Field Name          LAST_SALE                      │               │
│  │ Operator            More than or equal             │               │
│  │ Constant/Expression DATE() - 90                    │               │
│  │ █Connect█                                          │               │
│  │                                                    │               │
│  │ Line Number         2                              │               │
│  └──────────────────────────────────────────────────┘                │
│                                                                       │
│  ┌──────┬────────────┬──────────────────┬───────────────────┬────────┐│
│  │ Line │ Field      │ Operator         │ Constant/Expression│ Connect││
│  ├──────┼────────────┼──────────────────┼───────────────────┼────────┤│
│  │  1   │ DEPOSIT    │ More than        │ 0                 │ .OR.   ││
│  │  2   │ LAST_SALE  │ More than or equal│ DATE() - 90      │        ││
│  │  3   │            │                  │                   │        ││
│  │  4   │            │                  │                   │        ││
│  │  5   │            │                  │                   │        ││
│  │  6   │            │                  │                   │        ││
│  │  7   │            │                  │                   │        ││
│  └──────┴────────────┴──────────────────┴───────────────────┴────────┘│
│                                                                       │
│ █CREATE QUERY█   █<B:>█CUSTACT.QRY█        █Opt: 4/5█          █Caps█  │
│         Position selection bar - ↑↓.  Select - ↵.  Leave menu - ↔.    │
│              Select a logical connector for the filter condition.     │
└────────────────────────────────────────────────────────────────────┘
```

■ *Keystroke
Summary*

Create query

Type: **CREATE QUERY** *filename*

Press: ↵

■ *What Can Go Wrong?*

1. With the query definition screen visible and the highlight bar marking *Constant/Expression*, dBASE III Plus seems to ignore the characters you type.

Cause: You probably started typing a constant or an expression before pressing ↵.

Solution: When working on the query creation screen, you must select an action before you do it. With the highlight bar on *Constant/Expression*, press ↵. A triangle will appear just to the left of the cursor; now you can type the constant or the expression. Press ↵ again when you finish typing.

2. dBASE III Plus ignores what you type, and the highlight bar at the top of the screen marks *Nest*, *Display*, or *Exit* instead of *Set Filter*.

Cause: You started typing before pressing ↵, and you typed the letter N, the letter D, or the letter E. On the assistant screen you selected a menu by typing the first character of the menu name; the same rule allows you to navigate the query creation screen.

Solution: Type *S* to move the highlight bar back to *Set Filter*. Then highlight *Constant/Expression*, press ↵, and type the constant or the expression.

3. dBASE III Plus rejects your constant/expression value.

Cause: The value is probably the wrong type. A character field must be compared with characters; a numeric field must be compared with numbers, and so on. Either you mistyped the expression or you selected the wrong field name.

Solution: Check the constant/expression. One common error is forgetting to enclose a character constant in quotation marks. If you selected the wrong field (for example, LAST_NAME instead of LAST_SALE), recovery is a bit more tricky. Complete the condition, coding a constant or expression to match the field name's type. Then move the cursor to *Exit*, abandon the operation, and start over. ▪

Invoking Queries

To invoke the query from the dot prompt, type the command

    SET FILTER TO FILE CUSTACT

and press ⏎. Then type

    LIST FIELDS FIRST_NAME, LAST_NAME, LAST_SALE, DEPOSIT

and press ⏎ again. The resulting list (Fig. 29.17) will show only those records that pass the filter. As this book was written, the date when you would complete the tutorial was unknown. Because most of the records in your file are probably more than 90 days old, your screen might not show every record in Fig. 29.17.

Figure 29.17

This screen shows the records selected by the query named CUSTACT.

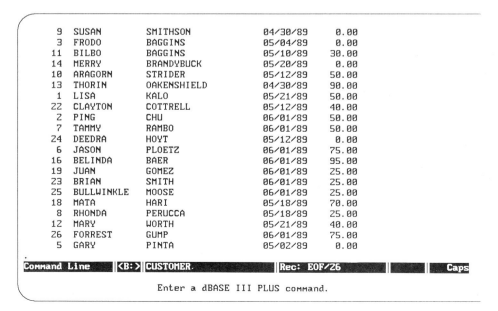

```
    9  SUSAN       SMITHSON      04/30/89    0.00
    3  FRODO       BAGGINS       05/04/89    0.00
   11  BILBO       BAGGINS       05/10/89   30.00
   14  MERRY       BRANDYBUCK    05/20/89    0.00
   10  ARAGORN     STRIDER       05/12/89   50.00
   13  THORIN      OAKENSHIELD   04/30/89   90.00
    1  LISA        KALO          05/21/89   50.00
   22  CLAYTON     COTTRELL      05/12/89   40.00
    2  PING        CHU           06/01/89   50.00
    7  TAMMY       RAMBO         06/01/89   50.00
   24  DEEDRA      HOYT          05/12/89    0.00
    6  JASON       PLOETZ        06/01/89   75.00
   16  BELINDA     BAER          06/01/89   95.00
   19  JUAN        GOMEZ         06/01/89   25.00
   23  BRIAN       SMITH         06/01/89   25.00
   25  BULLWINKLE  MOOSE         06/01/89   25.00
   18  MATA        HARI          05/18/89   70.00
    8  RHONDA      PERUCCA       05/18/89   25.00
   12  MARY        WORTH         05/21/89   40.00
   26  FORREST     GUMP          06/01/89   75.00
    5  GARY        PINTA         05/02/89    0.00

Command Line    <B:> CUSTOMER.              Rec: EOF/26              Caps
                Enter a dBASE III PLUS command.
```

The current filter will remain in effect until you cancel it. To cancel a filter, issue a SET FILTER TO command with no parameters. Because the next section will use the entire database, type

```
SET FILTER TO
```

and press ⏎.

Invoke query

Type: **SET FILTER TO FILE** *filename*

Press: ⏎

■ *What Can Go Wrong?*

1. You typed a SET FILTER TO command and referenced a query file, but an error message indicated "Variable not found."

Cause: You probably did not type the key word FILE just before the query file name.

Solution: Press ⬆ to recall the command, insert the word FILE between TO and the file name, and reissue the command.

2. No records passed the filter, or *all* records passed the filter.

Cause: You might have neglected to set the system date when you booted DOS.

Solution: Recreate or modify the query. This time, type the condition

```
CTOD('06/01/89') - 90
```

Then reissue the SET FILTER TO and LIST commands. ■

Printing Mailing Labels

The Label Definition Screen

Generating **mailing labels** is one of the most commonly used features of dBASE III Plus. A business concern can save money on mass mailing postage by sorting the mail into zip code order. Campus addresses do not have zip codes, but sorting by dormitory will facilitate delivery, so the file should be indexed by dormitory. The first step is to specify the database file and the index to be used by typing

```
USE CUSTOMER INDEX CUSTDORM
```

and pressing ⏎.

The general form of a CREATE LABEL command is shown in Fig. 29.18. The command reads the active file and creates a new file that defines the address label format. You must provide a name for that file; dBASE III Plus will automatically add the extension *lbl*. Type the command

```
CREATE LABEL CUSTOMER
```

Figure 29.18
The CREATE LABELS command creates a new file to hold the mailing label format. The general form of the command is shown below the diagram.

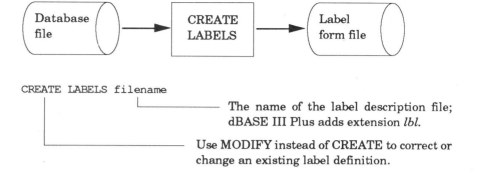

The extension *lbl* distinguishes the label file from the original database file, CUSTOMER, which, as you may recall, has the extension *dbf*. Press ↵, and the **label definition screen** will appear (Fig. 29.19).

The first menu choice, *Options*, allows you to define the label format; if necessary, type the letter O to highlight it. The highlight bar should mark *Predefined size:*; if it doesn't, press ↑ to move it there. A standard label is 3 1/2 inches wide by 15/16 inches high, and you can buy sheets that are one, two, three, or even more labels wide. The highlighted line defines a standard, one-label-wide form. Press ↵ to change the predefined format to two labels wide. Press ↵ again to change to three; there are five predefined label formats. Keep pressing ↵ until the initial "3 1/2 x 15/16 by 1" form reappears.

Figure 29.19
The label definition screen.

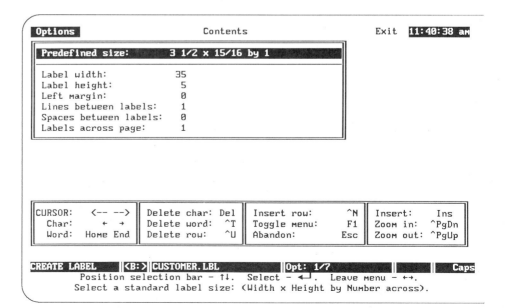

Listed below the label size are the label width, label height, and several other parameters. Single-width labels are 35 characters wide, and up to five lines can be printed on each label. The left margin is set to 0. One line will be skipped between labels, and since only one label is printed across the page, there is no horizontal space separating adjacent labels.

If you are using standard labels, there is no reason to change the parameters, but they are easy to change. The ⬇ key moves the highlight bar to the selected parameter. Pressing ⏎ indicates your desire to change that parameter; just type the correct value and press ⏎ again. For now, however, make no changes; one-wide is fine for illustrating how labels are printed.

■ *What Can Go Wrong?*

1. You pressed ⬇ to move the selection bar to an option.

Cause: You saw a reference to a key, and you pressed it.

Solution: Assuming that you changed nothing, press ⬆ to get back to the *Predefined size* line. If the cursor won't move, check the message line; it should tell you how to escape. If you pressed ⏎ to select an option, press ⏎ again to accept the value and then press ⬆. If you changed an option, select that option and change the value to agree with Fig. 29.19. Then press ⏎ and ⬆. ■

Defining the Label Contents

Press → to leave the options menu and move to the *Contents* menu. The screen will show a dummy label with one numbered line for each of the five label lines. The highlight bar should mark the first line. Press ⏎, and a triangle will appear at the beginning of the line. The first line should contain the customer's first name and last name, so type FIRST_NAME, a comma, and LAST_NAME, and then press ⏎. (*Note:* Because you typed a comma to separate the fields, dBASE III Plus will trim spaces from the end of the first name field.) If you forget a field name, press F10 to get a list of field names; use ⬆ or ⬇ to highlight the desired field and press ⏎ to select it. Press ⏎ again to indicate that you are finished editing the line.

Press ⬇ to move to the second line, press ⏎, type the field names ROOM and DORM, and press ⏎ again. Your screen should resemble Fig. 29.20. Note that you must press ⏎ before you can define a line.

■ *What Can Go Wrong?*

1. dBASE III Plus ignores what you type. As you type the first line, the *Contents* menu may disappear.

Cause: You probably forgot to press ⏎ to select an option before starting to type.

Solution: Open the *Contents* menu, select an option, press ⏎, and *then* start typing. ■

Figure 29.20
Define the general
format of the labels
on the file contents
screen.

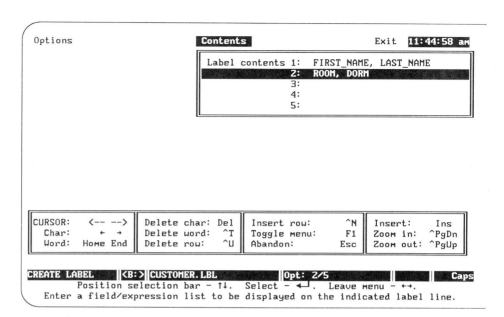

Exiting the Label Definition Screen

When you are satisfied with the label's contents, press ⊡ to move to the *Exit* menu. Highlight *Save* and press ⏎. You'll notice a slight delay as dBASE III Plus creates the label file. Unfortunately, the label screen does not have a display command, so you can't preview the results.

▪ *Keystroke Summary*

Create mailing labels

Type: **CREATE LABEL** *filename*

Press: ⏎

▪ *What Can Go Wrong?*

1. When you type a field name and press ⏎, the computer beeps and will not accept it.

Cause: You probably misspelled the field name or typed the name of a field that is not in the active database.

Solution: Correct the spelling and then press ⏎ again. If you do not know the proper spelling, press [Ctrl] *and* U to delete the line. Then press [F10] to get a list of valid fields and select a name from the list. ▪

Generating the Labels

To display the labels on the screen, type the command

```
LABEL FORM CUSTOMER
```

Figure 29.21
This screen shows the finished address labels as they will appear on your screen.

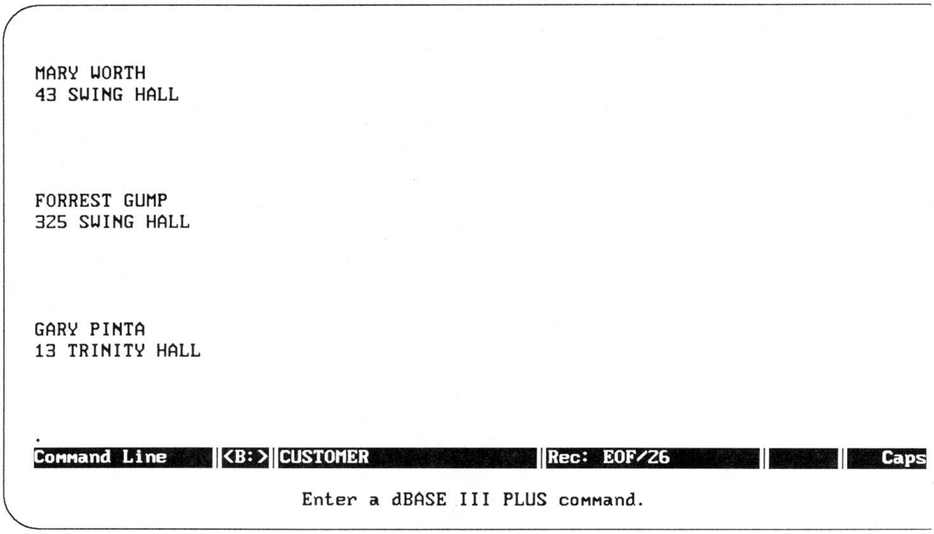

```
MARY WORTH
43 SWING HALL




FORREST GUMP
325 SWING HALL




GARY PINTA
13 TRINITY HALL



.
Command Line    |<B:>||CUSTOMER           |Rec: EOF/26              |   Caps
            Enter a dBASE III PLUS command.
```

and press ⏎. Note that the second word is FORM, *not* FROM; inverting the O and the R is a common typing mistake. Remember that you are *not* creating the labels *from* the specified file. Instead you are indicating the *form* to be used to create labels. Most of the labels will scroll out of sight; when the operation stops, your screen should resemble Fig. 29.21. Note that the labels are in dormitory order reading down the page.

If the labels are correct, print them. (Because address label sheets are relatively expensive, simulate them by printing a set of labels on regular printer paper.) Press ⬆ to recall the last command from the buffer. Then press End three times to move to the end of the command and add a TO PRINT clause. Press ⏎ to issue the command. Then issue an EJECT command to advance to the end of the last page.

When you load real address labels, you will normally want the score that separates the pages just above the print mechanism, but the proper position varies from printer to printer. You might have to experiment a bit.

For future reference, note that you must load the associated database and indexes *before* issuing a LABEL FORM command. When you define labels, you create a label *form*, not an independent label file.

■ *Keystroke Summary*

Generate mailing labels

Type: **LABEL FORM** *filename* [**TO PRINT**]

Press: ⏎

■ *What Can Go Wrong?*

1. After you enter the LABEL FORM command, a message reads "Syntax error in contents expression."

Cause: You made an error entering the fields. For example, you might have forgotten to separate the field names with a comma.

Solution: Type the command MODIFY LABEL CUSTOMER and press ⏎. Press ⊟ to highlight *Contents* and then identify and correct the problem. When you finish, press ⊟ to highlight *Exit* and save your label file again. Print the labels to the screen, check them, and, if necessary, modify the label format again. ■

Exiting dBASE III Plus

That completes the tutorial. At the dot prompt, type QUIT and exit dBASE III Plus.

Summary

From the Assistant

Function	Menu	Command	Page
Create mailing labels	Create	Label	534
Create query file	Create	Query	529
Generate mailing labels	Retrieve	Label	537
Index database file	Organize	Index	516
Modify query file	Modify	Query	
Open index file	Set Up	Database file	519
Replace field	Update	Replace	526

From the Dot Prompt

Function	Command	Page
Create mailing labels	CREATE LABEL	534
Create query file	CREATE QUERY	529
Define filter	SET FILTER TO	528
Find record	FIND	522
Generate mailing labels	LABEL FORM	537
Index database file	INDEX ON	516
Invoke query	SET FILTER TO	533
Modify mailing labels	MODIFY LABEL	
Modify query file	MODIFY QUERY	
Open index file	SET INDEX TO	519
Reindex database file	REINDEX	521
Replace field	REPLACE	526

Options and Functions

Option or Function	Format	Page
Extract system date	DATE()	531
Specify index	command INDEX index	519
WHILE condition	command WHILE condition	524

Self-Test

1. To create an index from two or more fields, use a _____ to separate the field names. This operation is called _____.

2. Issue an _____ command to create an index.

3. A _____ command with no parameters closes all indexes.

4. Use a _____ command to add missing records to an index.

5. A _____ command searches a file sequentially. A _____ command can search an indexed file much more quickly.

6. If a _____ condition is coded, dBASE III Plus repeats the command as long as the condition is true.

7. A _____ command can be used to make the same change to several database records.

8. A _____ clause limits the records processed by a single command. A _____ limits the records processed by subsequent commands.

9. Frequently used filters can be defined and saved to a _____ file.

10. Issue a _____ command to create a file of address labels. Issue a _____ command to print a set of address labels.

Exercises

1. Index the name and address file (prior chapters, Exercise 1) by zip code. Then print a set of name and address labels sorted by zip code. (*Note:* Simulate the labels on plain printer paper.)

2. Index the membership file (prior chapters, Exercise 2) by last name. Print a list of all the people in the group whose last names begin with S.

3. Index the inventory file (prior chapters, Exercise 3) by item value. Print a list of the ten most expensive items in inventory.

∎30

Using Multiple
Database Files

This chapter discusses several basic database design principles and then introduces the dBASE III Plus features and commands that allow you to:

- copy data from one database file to another
- delete fields from a database file
- select multiple work areas
- load multiple database files
- display the status of work areas and the operating environment
- relate records from multiple databases
- create a view file
- create a report form

Designing a Database

If you were running Campus Threads, you would probably want to know more about your current sales than the value of each customer's deposit. In addition to the deposit amount, you would almost certainly record for each order a description of the merchandise, the name of the supplier, the amount due on delivery, and other data such as the expected arrival date.

If you were to add the supplier, a product description, the amount due, and the expected arrival date to the existing CUSTOMER database, the result would be considerably more data stored for each customer. Several customers have *no* deposit. Their deposit fields are empty, and the new fields would also be empty in their records. Unused fields represent wasted space. Although modern computers have a great deal of secondary storage, the amount is still limited, and well-designed databases do not waste space. The solution is to create *two* related database files.

Although a detailed introduction to database theory is beyond the scope of this book, there are some simple guidelines you can use to decide how best to structure those files. One is to group attributes by the entity they describe. An *entity* is the person, activity, or thing about which data are stored. In this example there are two: customers and orders. Data elements associated with a customer should be stored in one file; data elements associated with a sales order should be stored in the other (Fig. 30.1).

Relating the Files

Although it makes sense to separate attributes by entity, the two files are still related. (It is, after all, customers who place orders.) Thus you need some way to relate the records. Typically, files are related by placing a common field in each.

LAST_NAME is one possibility. Unfortunately, the last name is not unique; for example, there are two people named Baggins in CUSTOMER. You might add the first name, but as the database grows, you will eventually encounter two John Smiths (or some other common set of names). The customer's room number and dormitory might be added to last name and first name to create a truly unique identifier, but if you are going to duplicate all the fields to link the files, why bother creating two files? The solution is to define a customer identification code to link CUSTOMER to the new sales order file.

Figure 30.1

In a multiple-file database, attributes should be grouped with the entity they describe.

CUSTOMER

Last name
First name
Room
Dormitory
Telephone number
Date of last order

ORDER

Deposit
Supplier
Order date
Expected delivery date
Product description

Creating a Second Database File

Boot DOS and load dBASE III Plus. Press [Caps Lock] to activate the *caps lock* feature and press [Esc] to exit to the dot prompt. Then set the default drive and issue a USE command to make CUSTOMER the active database.

Adding a Customer Identification Code

The objective is to create a separate database file to hold customer orders. The two files will be linked by a common field, a customer identification code, so start by defining the code. Adding the record number assigned by dBASE III Plus to the first two characters of a customer's last name yields a simple but effective code. The letters facilitate finding a record when you know the customer's last name. The record number makes the code unique.

The first step is to add the identification code to the CUSTOMER database. Start by changing the file's structure. Type the command

```
MODIFY STRUCTURE
```

and press ↵. With the highlight bar marking the first field, FIRST_NAME, press [Ctrl] *and* N to insert space for the customer identification code at the beginning of the structure. Figure 30.2 shows the attributes for CUSTID; use it as a guide and define the field. After you type the field width and press ↵, the selection bar will move to FIRST_NAME. Press [Ctrl] *and* [End] to save the new structure. Respond to the confirmation message by pressing ↵.

Figure 30.2
Add the customer identification code, CUSTID, to the CUSTOMER database.

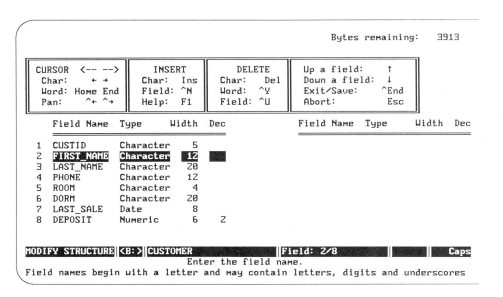

Next, consider the identification code. Each customer's code should begin with the first two letters of his or her last name. You can use a substring function to get them:

```
SUBSTR (LAST_NAME, 1, 2)
```

SUBSTR returns a *portion* of a string. The first argument, LAST_NAME, is the name of a character field. The next two arguments indicate that the substring starts with the string's first character (1) and is two characters long. Thus the function returns the first two characters of the last name.

The next step is to concatenate the dBASE III Plus record number to the LAST_NAME substring. The RECNO() function returns the record number. Unfortunately, it is numeric, and you can't concatenate numbers and characters. The function

```
STR (RECNO(), 3)
```

converts the number to a three-character string. It doesn't solve the whole problem, however, because the STR function replaces leading, nonsignificant zeros with blank spaces. Thus the third customer's (Frodo Baggins') code would consist of the letters BA followed by two spaces and the digit 3 (BA 3). Visually, that's not very clear; including the leading zeros (BA003) is a much better choice.

One solution is to add 1000 to the record number. For example, the function

```
STR (RECNO()+1000, 4)
```

adds 1000 to the record number and then generates a four-character string. You can use a RIGHT function to extract the rightmost three characters from that string. For example,

```
RIGHT (STR (RECNO()+1000, 4), 3)
```

returns the rightmost three digits.

Because the identification code is derived from existing data, you can use the REPLACE command to quickly generate the values. On one line, type

```
REPLACE  ALL  CUSTID  WITH  SUBSTR(LAST_NAME,1,2)  +
RIGHT(STR(RECNO()+1000,4),3)
```

and press ⏎. (*Note:* Do not code the key word FIELDS in a REPLACE command.) To verify the REPLACE operation, type

```
LIST ALL FIELDS CUSTID, LAST_NAME, FIRST_NAME
```

and press ⏎ (Fig. 30.3).

Figure 30.3
The CUSTOMER database with the customer identification code added.

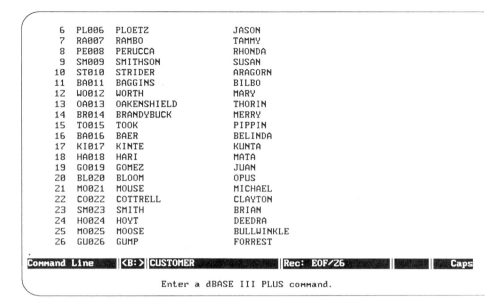

```
    6   PL006   PLOETZ          JASON
    7   RA007   RAMBO           TAMMY
    8   PE008   PERUCCA         RHONDA
    9   SM009   SMITHSON        SUSAN
   10   ST010   STRIDER         ARAGORN
   11   BA011   BAGGINS         BILBO
   12   WO012   WORTH           MARY
   13   OA013   OAKENSHIELD     THORIN
   14   BR014   BRANDYBUCK      MERRY
   15   TO015   TOOK            PIPPIN
   16   BA016   BAER            BELINDA
   17   KI017   KINTE           KUNTA
   18   HA018   HARI            MATA
   19   GO019   GOMEZ           JUAN
   20   BL020   BLOOM           OPUS
   21   MO021   MOUSE           MICHAEL
   22   CO022   COTTRELL        CLAYTON
   23   SM023   SMITH           BRIAN
   24   HO024   HOYT            DEEDRA
   25   MO025   MOOSE           BULLWINKLE
   26   GU026   GUMP            FORREST
```

Command Line   <B:> CUSTOMER   Rec: EOF/26   Caps

Enter a dBASE III PLUS command.

■ *What Can Go Wrong?*

1. A "Variable not found" message appears after you issue the REPLACE command.

Cause: Either you misspelled the field name or you preceded the field name with the key word FIELDS, which is illegal on a REPLACE command.

Solution: Correct your spelling or delete FIELDS. Then reissue the command.

2. You made a typing error on the REPLACE command.

Cause: Typing errors are common on such lengthy commands.

Solution: Press ⬆ to recall the command, correct the error, and then press ⏎ to reissue the command. ■

Creating the Sales Order File

Now that you have the customer identification number to relate the files, you are ready to create the second file. Because it holds customer orders, call it ORDER. You could use a CREATE command to define the new file's fields, but then you would have to enter the identification codes and deposit amounts one by one. It's much easier to copy the existing data to the new file. The general form of a COPY command is shown in Fig. 30.4.

The new ORDER file should contain the CUSTID and DEPOSIT for all customers with a positive deposit. Type the command

```
COPY TO ORDER FIELDS CUSTID, DEPOSIT FOR DEPOSIT > 0
```

Figure 30.4
The COPY command.

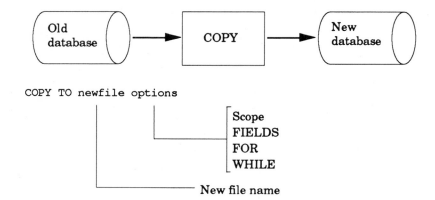

COPY TO newfile options

```
                                    ┌ Scope
                             ┌──────┤ FIELDS
                             │      │ FOR
                             │      └ WHILE
                             │
                             └───────────── New file name
```

and press ⏎. Since no file named ORDER exists, dBASE III Plus will create the file and assign space to hold the specified fields. The FOR clause ensures that only records with positive deposits will be copied to the new file. To verify the COPY operation, issue a USE command identifying ORDER as the active database, and then issue a LIST command with no options. Your screen should resemble Fig. 30.5.

In the real world you might now issue a MODIFY STRUCTURE command to add such fields as the supplier, the order date, the expected delivery date, and a description of the product ordered. Then you could use a BROWSE command to add the data for each of those fields. However, a simple ORDER file containing only the customer

Figure 30.5
A list of the records in the new ORDER database.

```
. COPY TO ORDER FIELDS CUSTID, DEPOSIT FOR DEPOSIT > 0
      16 records copied
. USE ORDER
. LIST
Record#   CUSTID DEPOSIT
       1   KA001    50.00
       2   CH002    50.00
       3   PL006    75.00
       4   RA007    50.00
       5   PE008    25.00
       6   ST010    50.00
       7   BA011    30.00
       8   WO012    40.00
       9   OA013    90.00
      10   BA016    95.00
      11   HA018    70.00
      12   GO019    25.00
      13   CO022    40.00
      14   SM023    25.00
      15   MO025    25.00
      16   GU026    75.00
.
```

```
Command Line    |<B:>|ORDER                    |Rec: EOF/16    |    |    |Caps
```

Enter a dBASE III PLUS command.

identification code and the deposit amount is enough to support this tutorial.

Copy a file selectively

Type: **COPY TO** *newfile* **FIELDS** *list options*

Press: ⏎

Deleting a Field

Issue a USE command to make CUSTOMER the active database. Because the value for deposit has been moved to ORDER, you no longer need the DEPOSIT field in CUSTOMER. To delete the field, type

```
MODIFY STRUCTURE
```

and press ⏎. Highlight DEPOSIT and press Ctrl *and* U. The DEPOSIT field will disappear. Press Ctrl *and* End to save the modified structure. Press ⏎ to confirm the operation, and after a brief delay you will return to the dot prompt. To verify that the deposit field has been deleted, issue a DISPLAY command for the current record. No deposit field will appear.

Working with Multiple Databases

dBASE III Plus can concurrently access as many as ten database files. Each file is loaded by a USE command into a work area known as a **select area**. The ten work areas can be referenced by number (1 through 10), by letter (A through J), or by the **alias** of the file loaded in the work area. An alias is an alternative name for the file; it is useful when the database file name is nondescriptive. If no alias is specified, the file name is used as the alias.

In previous tutorials you did not worry about work areas because you were dealing with only one database file. By default the current select area is 1. Issue the command

```
USE CUSTOMER INDEX CUSTNAME, CUSTDORM
```

Press ⏎, and the designated database and specified indexes will be loaded into work area 1 or A.

To load a database into a work area other than select area 1, you must first select a different work area. Type the command

```
SELECT 2
```

and press ⏎. Note that no active database is identified on the status bar because no file has been loaded into select area 2. Type the command

```
USE ORDER
```

and press ⏎. The new file, ORDER, will be loaded into work area 2. Its name should appear on the status bar.

All the files placed in use are *open*, but only one file can be *active* or selected at any time. To identify the active file, issue a SELECT command. For example, type

SELECT 1

and press ⏎. CUSTOMER will replace ORDER on the status bar. (Alternatively, you could have selected A or CUSTOMER.) Now type

SELECT ORDER

and press ⏎. ORDER will become the active database file. (You could have selected 2 or B.)

For future reference, to close the database file in a given work area, select the work area and then issue a USE command with no file name. Of course, loading a different database into a given select area closes the previous database. The CLOSE ALL command closes the files in all work areas.

■ *Keystroke Summary*

Select work area

Type: **SELECT** *n*

Press: ⏎

Indexing the New File

ORDER should be the active file. (If not, select it.) Index ORDER on CUSTID by typing

INDEX ON CUSTID TO ORDID

and pressing ⏎. (Note that the name, ORDID, suggests that database file ORDER is indexed on CUSTID.) The new index file will be stored under file name ORDID.ndx. Type LIST and press ⏎ to check the results of the index operation (Fig. 30.6).

The DISPLAY STATUS Command

With multiple database files and multiple indexes it is easy to lose track of exactly what is open. To find out, type

DISPLAY STATUS

and press ⏎. Your screen will resemble Fig. 30.7. For each work area you will see the name of the database, its alias, and associated open index files.

Note the message "Currently Selected Database:" just above select area 2, the *active* work area. Note also that the current work

Figure 30.6

This list shows the ORDER file in customer identification code sequence.

```
. SELECT ORDER
. INDEX ON CUSTID TO ORDID
  100% indexed              16 Records indexed
. LIST
Record#   CUSTID DEPOSIT
      7   BA011    30.00
     10   BA016    95.00
      2   CH002    50.00
     13   CO022    40.00
     12   GO019    25.00
     16   GU026    75.00
     11   HA018    70.00
      1   KA001    50.00
     15   MO025    25.00
      9   OA013    90.00
      5   PE008    25.00
      3   PL006    75.00
      4   RA007    50.00
     14   SM023    25.00
      6   ST010    50.00
      8   WO012    40.00
.
Command Line    <B:> ORDER              Rec: EOF/16          Caps
```

Enter a dBASE III PLUS command.

area is identified in a line near the bottom of the screen. For each work area the controlling index is indicated by the word "Master" at the beginning of the line that identifies the index file and shows the index key.

Figure 30.7

The status screen.

```
      4   RA007    50.00
     14   SM023    25.00
      6   ST010    50.00
      8   WO012    40.00

. DISPLAY STATUS

Select area:  1, Database in Use: B:customer.dbf    Alias: CUSTOMER
     Master index file:  B:custname.ndx  Key: LAST_NAME - FIRST_NAME
             Index file:  B:custdorm.ndx  Key: DORM

Currently Selected Database:
Select area:  2, Database in Use: B:order.dbf    Alias: ORDER
     Master index file:  B:ordid.ndx  Key: CUSTID

File search path:
Default disk drive: B:
Print destination:  PRN:
Margin =      0
Current work area =    2

Press any key to continue...
Command Line    <B:> ORDER              Rec: EOF/16          Caps
```

Enter a dBASE III PLUS command.

Press any key (the space bar is a good choice) to see the second status screen. It shows the status of various SET options and the meanings associated with the function keys. The cursor will return to the dot prompt.

■ *Keystroke Summary*

Display status of environment

Type: **DISPLAY STATUS**

Press: ⏎

Relating Multiple Databases

You now have two database files. The records in those databases should be related by customer identification code. You can formally define that relationship to dBASE III Plus by issuing a SET RELATION command (Fig. 30.8).

Each database must be loaded into its own work area. One, in this case CUSTOMER, is the **parent** database. The other, ORDER, is the **child**. The child must be indexed on the common field, CUSTID; the parent's indexes do not affect the command. Select the work area that contains the parent database by typing

```
SELECT CUSTOMER
```

and pressing ⏎. Now type the command

```
SET RELATION TO CUSTID INTO ORDER
```

CUSTID is the name of the key field; it must be common to both databases. ORDER is the name of the child database. (Technically, it is the *alias* of the child database, but since no alias was specified, the database name is assumed.) Press ⏎ to issue the command.

Figure 30.8
The SET RELATION command.

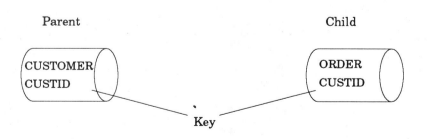

Figure 30.9
Following a SET
RELATION command,
the status screen will
show the relationship.

```
. SELECT CUSTOMER
. SET RELATION TO CUSTID INTO ORDER
. DISPLAY STATUS

Currently Selected Database:
Select area:  1, Database in Use: B:customer.dbf   Alias: CUSTOMER
     Master index file:  B:custname.ndx  Key: LAST_NAME - FIRST_NAME
            Index file:  B:custdorm.ndx  Key: DORM
       Related into: ORDER
       Relation: CUSTID

Select area:  2, Database in Use: B:order.dbf   Alias: ORDER
     Master index file:  B:ordid.ndx  Key: CUSTID

File search path:
Default disk drive: B:
Print destination:  PRN:
Margin =     0
Current work area =    1

Press any key to continue...
Command Line    ||<B:>||CUSTOMER              ||Rec: 4/26       ||        || Caps

          Enter a dBASE III PLUS command.
```

Issue a DISPLAY STATUS command to verify the relationship.
As the status screen shows (Fig. 30.9), the database in select area 1
(CUSTOMER) is related to ORDER through CUSTID. Press Esc to
skip the second status screen and return directly to the dot prompt; a
message will indicate that the display status operation was interrupted.

■ *Keystroke*
Summary

Setting a relation

Type: **SET RELATION TO** *key* **INTO** *child*

Press: ⏎

■ *What Can*
Go Wrong?

1. After you enter the SET RELATION command, the message "alias not
found" appears on the screen.

Cause: You probably misspelled the file name. Remember, the SET RELA-
TION command uses the alias, not the file name; that's why the message
refers to the alias.

Solution: Issue a DISPLAY STATUS command and check the spelling of
the alias name. It should match the file name; if not, use the alias instead of
the file name. Reenter the SET RELATION command with the correct *alias.*

2. An error message reads "database is not indexed."

Cause: Either you forgot to open the index file on the child database or the specified key field does not exist in the child.

Solution: Make sure you have specified the correct key field and that you have not misspelled the field name. If the error is not obvious, issue a DISPLAY STATUS command and verify that the child index is open. If it isn't, select the work area containing the child database, issue a SET INDEX command, select the parent work area, and then reissue the SET RELATION command.

3. An error message reads "cyclic relation."

Cause: Either you are in the work area containing the child database or you typed the parent database name after the key word INTO. In effect, you are telling dBASE III Plus to establish a relationship between the child and the child or between the parent and the parent.

Solution: Select the work area containing the parent and reissue the SET RELATION command. Be sure the *child* database name follows INTO.

4. An error message reads "variable not found."

Cause: The key field does not exist in the parent.

Solution: Reissue the SET RELATION command using a field common to both databases. ▪

Initiating a Search

Assume that you just received from the supplier a partial order for Mata Hari. After delivering the merchandise and collecting the balance due, you want to reduce her deposit by $30 so that the remaining amount reflects the undelivered portion of the order. Her name is recorded in the CUSTOMER database. Check the status bar. If the active file is *not* CUSTOMER, select CUSTOMER.

You want to search CUSTOMER for the name MATA HARI, so you want CUSTNAME to be the master index. Since the index files are all open, you can select the master index by typing a SET ORDER command. For example, type the command

```
SET ORDER TO 2
```

and press ⏎. A message will identify the master index. If the message reads

```
Master index: B:CUSTNAME.ndx
```

fine; that's what you want. If CUSTDORM is identified as the master index, type the command

```
SET ORDER TO 1
```

and press ⏎.

■ *Keystroke Summary*

Select master index

Type: SET ORDER TO *n*

Press: ⏎

Limiting Fields with Multiple Databases

To record the change in the deposit amount, you will need only a limited subset of fields. Make sure CUSTOMER is the active database and type on one line the command

```
SET FIELDS TO FIRST_NAME, LAST_NAME, CUSTID,
ORDER->DEPOSIT
```

The first three field names are in the current database, but DEPOSIT is located in a *different* database, ORDER, and so its name must be qualified. The minus sign followed by a greater than symbol (–>) separating ORDER from DEPOSIT indicates that DEPOSIT is in ORDER and not in the current database; read the qualified name as ORDER *contains* DEPOSIT. Press ⏎ to issue the SET FIELDS command.

To verify both the SET RELATION and SET FIELDS commands, type LIST and press ⏎. Your screen will resemble Fig. 30.10. Note that data are displayed for all the customers. The deposit field is blank for those who have no active order, while those who have active orders

Figure 30.10
A list of selected fields from the related databases.

```
   14  BR014  MERRY       BRANDYBUCK
    2  CH002  PING        CHU              50.00
   22  CO022  CLAYTON     COTTRELL         40.00
   19  GO019  JUAN        GOMEZ            25.00
   26  GU026  FORREST     GUMP             75.00
   18  HA018  MATA        HARI             70.00
   24  HO024  DEEDRA      HOYT
    1  KA001  LISA        KALO             50.00
   17  KI017  KUNTA       KINTE
   25  MO025  BULLWINKLE  MOOSE            25.00
   21  MO021  MICHAEL     MOUSE
   13  OA013  THORIN      OAKENSHIELD      90.00
    8  PE008  RHONDA      PERUCCA          25.00
    5  PI005  GARY        PINTA
    6  PL006  JASON       PLOETZ           75.00
    7  RA007  TAMMY       RAMBO            50.00
   23  SM023  BRIAN       SMITH            25.00
    9  SM009  SUSAN       SMITHSON
   10  ST010  ARAGORN     STRIDER          50.00
   15  TO015  PIPPIN      TOOK
   12  WO012  MARY        WORTH            40.00
```

| Command Line | <B:> CUSTOMER | Rec: EOF/26 | Caps |

Enter a dBASE III PLUS command.

Figure 30.11
Mata Hari's record.

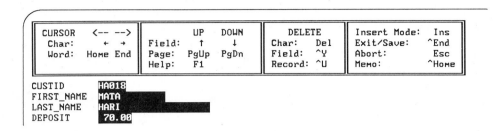

```
┌─────────────────────────────────────────────────────────────────────────┐
│ CURSOR    <-- -->  ║        UP   DOWN ║   DELETE      ║ Insert Mode:  Ins  │
│   Char:     ←  →   ║ Field:   ↑    ↓  ║ Char:   Del   ║ Exit/Save:   ^End  │
│   Word:  Home End  ║ Page:  PgUp PgDn ║ Field:  ^Y    ║ Abort:        Esc  │
│                    ║ Help:   F1       ║ Record: ^U    ║ Memo:       ^Home  │
│                                                                           │
│ CUSTID      HA018                                                         │
│ FIRST_NAME  MATA                                                          │
│ LAST_NAME   HARI                                                          │
│ DEPOSIT     70.00                                                         │
└───────────────────────────────────────────────────────────────────────── │
```

show their deposit amount. The first and last names are stored in CUSTOMER, while the deposit amount is stored in ORDER. Clearly, dBASE III Plus has extracted selected data from *both* files.

Editing Records on Multiple Databases

Find Mata Hari's record by typing the command

    FIND HARI

and pressing ⏎. The pointer will stop at record 18. Type EDIT and press ⏎ to display her record (Fig. 30.11). Note that data from *both* database files are displayed.

Press Esc to return to the dot prompt. Then type

    SELECT ORDER

and press ⏎. Type another EDIT command and press ⏎. Ms. Hari's deposit amount will appear on the screen. Setting the pointer in the parent database sets it to the related record in the child database.

Mata's first and last names are not displayed because they are stored in CUSTOMER; the relation links the child to the parent, not vice versa. In fact, only the deposit amount will appear because CUSTID was not included in the list when you SET FIELDS. You *did* type CUSTID, but CUSTOMER was the active file, so dBASE III Plus assumed that you meant CUSTID in CUSTOMER, *not* CUSTID in ORDER. Had you added ORDER–>CUSTID to the list, the customer identification code would have been displayed.

You might feel uncomfortable about changing a deposit amount when no customer identification is visible on the screen. (If not, you should.) To add CUSTID to the fields list, press Esc to return to the dot prompt. Then type

    SET FIELDS TO CUSTID

and press ⏎. Because ORDER is now the active database, CUSTID in ORDER will be added to the list. Note that you could have typed ORDER–>CUSTID, but because ORDER is active, the qualifier is redundant.

Figure 30.12

Moving the pointer in
the child database
does not affect the
pointer in the parent
database.

```
. SELECT CUSTOMER
. DISPLAY
Record#  CUSTID FIRST_NAME   LAST_NAME            CUSTID DEPOSIT
    18   HA018  MATA         HARI                 KA001   50.00
.
```

Command Line |<B:>||CUSTOMER |Rec: 18/26 | | Caps

Enter a dBASE III PLUS command.

Issue another EDIT command. This time both CUSTID and
DEPOSIT will be displayed. Mata's old deposit amount was $70, and
you want to reduce it by $30, so move the cursor to the deposit field,
type 40 and a decimal point, and press ⏎. The next record in the
ORDER database (KA001) will appear. Press Ctrl *and* End to save the
change and return to the dot prompt.

Issue another SELECT command for CUSTOMER. Then DIS-
PLAY the current record (Fig. 30.12). Note that the name is still
MATA HARI, but the deposit amount and the second CUSTID belong
to another customer. KA001 is KALO's identification code, and $50.00
is KALO's deposit; KALO's record *follows* HARI's in the ORDER
database. When you changed the deposit amount, you moved the
pointer in the child database. Moving the pointer in the child database
does *not* move the pointer in the parent database.

Adding New Orders

Assume that you have just received a $40 deposit from Frodo Baggins
and wish to record it. Make sure CUSTOMER is the active database.
Then type the command

    FIND BAGGINSFRODO

and press ⏎. The pointer should indicate record 3. Issue a DISPLAY
command to verify that the current record is, indeed, Frodo's. Note
that the CUSTID header is displayed twice because both
CUSTOMER–>CUSTID and ORDER–>CUSTID are active fields.
The second CUSTID field and the DEPOSIT field are both empty
because Frodo has no deposit.

The EDIT command cannot be used to add a record to the related
database. You want to add a new order, so type the command

    SELECT ORDER

and press ⏎. Note the pointer; it should indicate EOF because dBASE
III Plus searched the entire ORDER database before concluding that
there was no record for BA003. To append a new order, type

    APPEND

and press ⏎. Type BA003 as the customer identification code; the computer will beep and advance to the DEPOSIT field. Type 40 followed by a decimal point and then press ⏎. A new blank record will appear; press ⏎ to save Frodo's order and return to the dot prompt. SELECT CUSTOMER again and then issue a DISPLAY command. The new deposit amount will appear on your screen.

Using a View File

In real world applications it is not unusual for a dBASE III Plus user to access the same database files and indexes day after day. With multiple database files and their related indexes open and several SET options active, repeating the same commands can be tedious. The solution is to create a **view file** by issuing a CREATE VIEW command (Fig. 30.13). A view file records each work area's open database and index files and any established relations. If any filters or format files were invoked, they would also be noted. Subsequent use of the view file automatically restores the environment captured when the view file was created.

One way to create a view file is to capture the existing environment. Type the command

```
CREATE VIEW CUSTOMER FROM ENVIRONMENT
```

and press ⏎. The view file will be saved under file name CUSTOMER.vue.

Type the command

```
CLOSE ALL
```

and press ⏎. Then type

```
DISPLAY STATUS
```

Figure 30.13
The CREATE VIEW command.

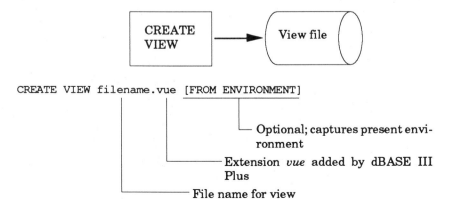

```
CREATE VIEW filename.vue [FROM ENVIRONMENT]
```

└─ Optional; captures present environment

└─ Extension *vue* added by dBASE III Plus

└─ File name for view

and press ⏎. The status screen will show only five summary lines because no files are open. Press Esc to return to the dot prompt. Then type the command

    SET VIEW TO CUSTOMER

and press ⏎. Issue another DISPLAY STATUS command and note that the environment has been restored. Press Esc to return to the dot prompt.

The Create View Screen

You can also create a view through the view screen. For example, imagine that you frequently need a list of customers' last names, first names, rooms, dormitories, and deposit amounts grouped by dormitory. DORMVIEW might be a good name for this view. Type the command

    CREATE VIEW DORMVIEW

and press ⏎. A create view screen will appear (Fig. 30.14). The menu's first choice, *Set Up*, should be highlighted, and a list of all the databases on the default drive should appear below the menu. A triangle to the left of a database name indicates that the file has been selected; since both CUSTOMER and ORDER are loaded in memory, they should automatically be marked.

Figure 30.14
The create view
screen.

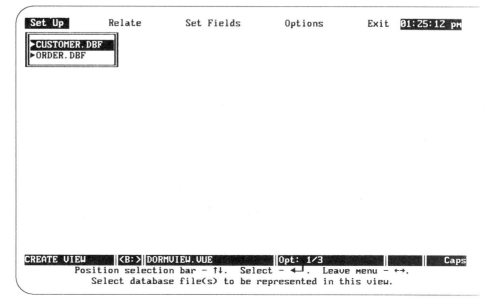

Highlight CUSTOMER and press ⏎. The triangle will disappear, indicating that CUSTOMER has been deselected. Press ⏎ again to select CUSTOMER. The triangle will reappear, and a list of index files will be displayed. To select an index, highlight it and press ⏎; the first index selected is the master index. Select CUSTDORM by highlighting it and pressing ⏎. In this view there is no need to open the other indexes, so press ◄ or ► to return to the list of files.

Highlight ORDER and press ⏎. Then press ⏎ again to select it. Once again the available index files will appear; highlight ORDID, press ⏎, and then press ►. The list of index files will disappear.

Press ► again to move to the second menu bar choice, *Relate*. The selected database files will appear on your screen, and the message line will read

```
Select the database that will initiate the relation.
```

(In other words, select the parent.) Highlight CUSTOMER and press ⏎. The message line will change to

```
Select the database file that will accept the relation.
```

(In other words, select the child.) The remaining databases (in this case, only ORDER) will be listed as possible children. Highlight ORDER and press ⏎. The message line will change to

```
The master index key expression is CUSTID.
```

Enter the key field by typing CUSTID and pressing ⏎. Note the relation chain at the bottom of your screen:

```
Relation chain: CUSTOMER.DBF->ORDER.DBF
```

It indicates that CUSTOMER has a link to ORDER.

Press ► twice to leave the list of child databases and move to the *Set Fields* menu. Highlight CUSTOMER and press ⏎. All the customer fields will appear; the triangles indicate that all are preselected. Deselect PHONE by highlighting the field and pressing ⏎; then deselect LAST_SALE. Press ►. Then select the ORDER database and deselect its CUSTID field. Press ► when you finish.

Pressing ► a second time opens the *Options* menu; you can use it to invoke a filter or a format file, but they are not needed in this view. Press ► again to move to the *Exit* menu. Choose *Save* and press ⏎. The new view will be saved, and you will return to the dot prompt. You will use DORMVIEW when you design a report form in the next section.

Once a view has been created, you can open it by typing SET VIEW TO followed by the view name. To close a view, type a CLOSE DATABASES command.

■ *Keystroke Summary*

Create a view file

Type: **CREATE VIEW** *filename* [**FROM ENVIRON-MENT**]

Press: ⏎

■ *Keystroke Summary*

Set a view

Type: **SET VIEW TO** *filename*

Press: ⏎

Creating a Report Form

You could, of course, issue a LIST command to get a list of customer orders grouped and totaled by dormitory, but the CREATE REPORT command (Fig. 30.15) allows you to quickly prepare sophisticated reports complete with page and column headings, subtotals, and totals. To access the create report screen, type

```
CREATE REPORT BYDORM
```

BYDORM is the name of the file that will hold the newly created report form; dBASE III Plus will automatically assign the extension *frm*. Press ⏎ to issue the command; your screen will resemble Fig. 30.16.

Start with the *Options* menu. The first choice is *Page title*; press ⏎ to select it. A triangle will appear to the right of *Page title*, and the cursor will move to a window. In it you can type a page title of up to four half-lines; whatever you type will be centered at the top of each report page. Enter the three-line title shown in Fig. 30.17; press ⏎ at the end of each line. Exit the page title window by pressing Ctrl *and* End.

The other options control the physical layout of a printed page. The defaults are fine for most reports on standard 8 1/2 by 11 paper; there is no need to change them for this exercise.

Figure 30.15
The CREATE REPORT command.

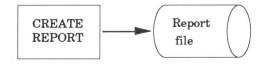

```
CREATE REPORT filename.frm
```
———— Extension *frm* added by dBASE III Plus
———— File name for report form

Figure 30.16
The create report screen.

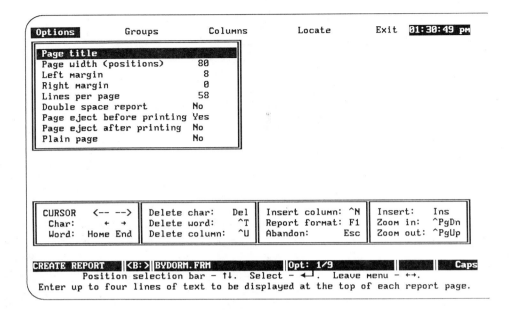

```
  Options          Groups          Columns          Locate          Exit   01:30:49 pm
 ┌──────────────────────────────────────┐
 │ Page title                           │
 │ Page width (positions)        80     │
 │ Left margin                    8     │
 │ Right margin                   0     │
 │ Lines per page                58     │
 │ Double space report           No     │
 │ Page eject before printing    Yes    │
 │ Page eject after printing     No     │
 │ Plain page                    No     │
 └──────────────────────────────────────┘



 ┌─────────────────────┬───────────────────────┬──────────────────────────┬────────────────────────┐
 │ CURSOR   <-- -->    │ Delete char:    Del   │ Insert column:   ^N      │ Insert:      Ins       │
 │ Char:      ←  →     │ Delete word:    ^T    │ Report format:   F1      │ Zoom in:   ^PgDn       │
 │ Word:   Home End    │ Delete column:  ^U    │ Abandon:        Esc      │ Zoom out:  ^PgUp       │
 └─────────────────────┴───────────────────────┴──────────────────────────┴────────────────────────┘

CREATE REPORT    <B:> BYDORM.FRM               Opt: 1/9                              Caps
          Position selection bar - ↑↓.  Select - ↵.  Leave menu - ←→.
   Enter up to four lines of text to be displayed at the top of each report page.
```

Printing Subtotals

Unless you specify otherwise, end-of-report totals are printed for all numeric fields. Additionally, dBASE III Plus can generate up to two levels of subtotals. The database must be sorted or indexed by the expressions or fields on which you wish to subtotal; for example, to generate subtotals by dormitory, the CUSTOMER database must be indexed by dormitory. The view you just created, DORMVIEW, made CUSTDORM the controlling index, so you have already met that test.

Press → to move to the second menu, *Groups* (Fig. 30.18). Select the first choice, *Group on expression*, by pressing ↵. A triangle will indicate that the choice has been selected; the cursor will follow the triangle. In this case you want subtotals generated each time the value of DORM changes, so type DORM and press ↵.

Press ↓ to highlight the second menu item, *Group heading*; then press ↵ to select it. Type DORMITORY and press ↵. When the report

Figure 30.17
The page title for your report.

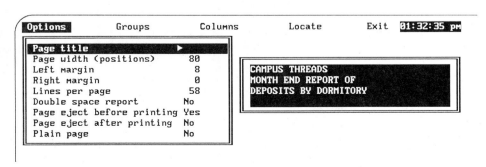

```
  Options          Groups          Columns          Locate          Exit   01:32:35 pm
 ┌──────────────────────────────────────┐
 │ Page title                      ►    │   ┌──────────────────────────────┐
 │ Page width (positions)        80     │   │ CAMPUS THREADS               │
 │ Left margin                    8     │   │ MONTH END REPORT OF          │
 │ Right margin                   0     │   │ DEPOSITS BY DORMITORY        │
 │ Lines per page                58     │   └──────────────────────────────┘
 │ Double space report           No     │
 │ Page eject before printing    Yes    │
 │ Page eject after printing     No     │
 │ Plain page                    No     │
 └──────────────────────────────────────┘
```

Figure 30.18
The *Groups* menu allows you to specify the field or fields on which summary totals are to be generated.

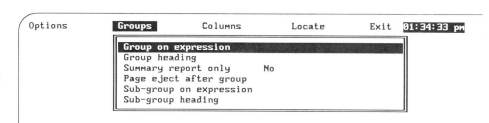

is printed, the heading DORMITORY followed by the dorm name will be printed on the line preceding the first customer from that dormitory.

Other items on this menu allow you to limit your output to summary totals, eject to a new page for each dormitory, and define subgroups, but there is no need to change them. Move to the *Columns* menu by pressing ⊡.

Specifying Columns

The *Columns* menu allows you to specify the fields to be included in the report. Select FIRST_NAME, LAST_NAME, ROOM, DORM, and DEPOSIT.

Highlight the first menu choice, *Contents*, and press ⊡. A triangle indicates that the choice is selected. Press F10 to get a list of fields; your screen will resemble Fig. 30.19. Highlight FIRST_NAME and press ⊡; the entry

```
CUSTOMER->FIRST_NAME
```

Figure 30.19
The *Columns* menu with available fields displayed.

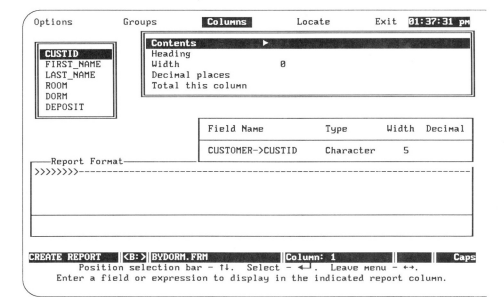

will appear to the right of *Contents.* Press ⏎ to accept the first field. Then press ⬇ to highlight *Heading* and press ⏎ to select it. A triangle will appear, and the cursor will move to a window. Type FIRST NAME on the first line; then press Ctrl *and* End to exit the window. Note that the report format is displayed near the bottom of the screen; the X's under the column header represent the field width. No other parameters are required for this first field.

To define the second field, press PgDn. Press ⏎ to select *Contents.* This time, *type* the next field name, LAST_NAME, and press ⏎. (If you have forgotten the field name, press F10 to get a list of fields, select the one you want, and press ⏎ twice.) Press ⬇ to highlight *Heading* and ⏎ to select it. Type the column header LAST NAME; then press Ctrl *and* End to exit the window.

Press ⬇ to move to the next field. Repeat the process for ROOM, DORM, and DEPOSIT; don't forget to press ⏎ to select *Contents* or *Heading* before you begin to type. When you finish, your screen should resemble Fig. 30.20. If you make a mistake, you can go back and edit any column by pressing PgUp. An option is to highlight *Locate* on the menu bar. A list of the columns will be displayed. Highlight the column you want to edit and press ⏎. Then make your corrections.

When you are satisfied, select *Exit,* highlight *Save,* and press ⏎. You will return to the dot prompt.

Figure 30.20

The completed report format.

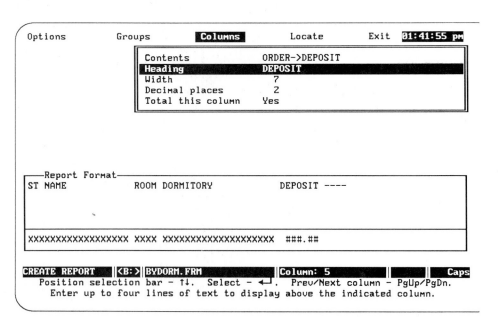

■ *Keystroke Summary*

Create a report

Type: **CREATE REPORT** *filename*

Press: ⏎

Executing the Report Form

Before you can print a report, you must load the proper database and index files. This is where a view file proves useful. Type the command

```
SET VIEW TO DORMVIEW
```

and press ⏎. All the appropriate files and indexes will be loaded and opened, saving you the trouble of remembering each one. Now type the command

```
REPORT FORM BYDORM FOR ORDER->DEPOSIT > 0
```

and press ⏎. dBASE III Plus will respond by displaying the report; the last few lines can be seen in Fig. 30.21. If you want a printed report, add a TO PRINT option, issue the REPORT FORM command, and then issue an EJECT command to get the last page.

■ *Keystroke Summary*

Generate a report

Type: **REPORT FORM** *filename options* [**TO PRINT**]

Press: ⏎

Figure 30.21
This screen shows the last several lines of the report.

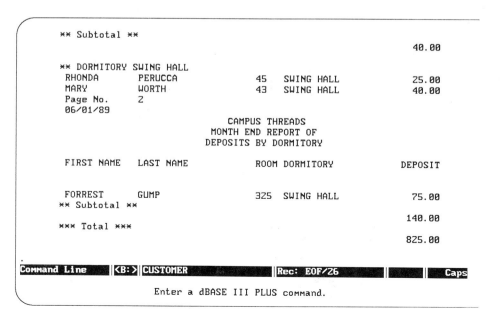

```
** Subtotal **
                                                              40.00

** DORMITORY SWING HALL
RHONDA          PERUCCA            45    SWING HALL       25.00
MARY            WORTH              43    SWING HALL       40.00
Page No.        2
06/01/89
                                  CAMPUS THREADS
                               MONTH END REPORT OF
                               DEPOSITS BY DORMITORY

FIRST NAME     LAST NAME            ROOM DORMITORY           DEPOSIT


FORREST        GUMP                 325   SWING HALL          75.00
** Subtotal **
                                                            140.00
*** Total ***
                                                            825.00
```

Command Line |<B:>|CUSTOMER |Rec: EOF/26| | Caps

Enter a dBASE III PLUS command.

Exiting dBASE III Plus

That completes the final tutorial. Exit dBASE III Plus and return to DOS.

If you have carefully worked through all the tutorials, you should have a solid understanding of dBASE III Plus basics. The secret to becoming an expert is to use your newly acquired skill and build on it. Good luck!

Summary

From the Assistant

Function	Menu	Command	Page
Copy file selectively	Organize	Copy	545
Create report	Create	Report	559
Create view file	Create	View	556
Generate report	Retrieve	Report	563
Modify database structure	Modify	Database file	543
Modify report	Modify	Report	
Modify view	Modify	View	
Replace contents of field	Update	Replace	544
Select view	Set Up	View	557

From the Dot Prompt

Function	Command	Page
Close databases	CLOSE ALL	556
Copy file selectively	COPY TO	545
Create report	CREATE REPORT	559
Create view file	CREATE VIEW	556
Display status	DISPLAY STATUS	548
Generate report	REPORT FORM	563
Modify database structure	MODIFY STRUCTURE	543
Modify report	MODIFY REPORT	
Modify view	MODIFY VIEW	
Replace contents of field	REPLACE	544
Select index	SET ORDER TO	552
Select view	SET VIEW TO	557
Select work area	SELECT	547
Set relation	SET RELATION TO	550

Options and Functions

Option or Function	Format	Page
Convert number to string	STR(expr,length)	544
Extract rightmost characters	RIGHT(expr, length)	544
Extract substring	SUBSTR(expr,start,length)	544
Get record number	RECNO()	544

Self-Test

1. Good database design suggests that you group attributes by _____.

2. Typically, database files are related by placing a _____ in each.

3. A _____ function returns a selected portion of a string. A _____ function returns the rightmost characters.

4. Use a _____ command to selectively copy data from one file to another.

5. dBASE III Plus can concurrently access as many as _____ database files. Each file is loaded into its own _____.

6. Issue a _____ command to determine which files and indexes are open.

7. Issue a _____ command to define a relation between two database files.

8. Issue a _____ command to change the master index from one open index file to another.

9. Create a _____ file to capture a dBASE III Plus operating environment.

10. Issue a _____ command to define a report format. Issue a _____ command to generate a report.

Exercises

1. Create a view file to support printing address labels from the name and address file (prior chapters, Exercise 1). Then print the address labels.

2. Create a separate file to keep track of the dues status of the people in your organization and link it to the membership file (prior chapters, Exercise 2). Include the amount due, the due date, and the amount paid.

3. Create a report format to print the contents of your inventory file (prior chapters, Exercise 3).

■ PART SIX

Networks

·31
Data Communication and Networks

This chapter introduces key data communication concepts, including:

- networks
- signals and communication media
- protocols
- network control
- data communication software

Networks

Historically, computers were so expensive that most large organizations did all their data processing on a single, centralized machine. While quite efficient for such tasks as generating payroll and accounting reports, the centralized approach could not effectively provide a quick response to a unique, local problem. Centralized data processing is inconvenient because the people who need information do not necessarily work in the computer center.

During the 1970s, many organizations began to support remote access by linking **terminals** to their mainframes. A terminal is an input/output device that consists of a keyboard, a display screen, and (sometimes) a printer. Terminals allow remote users to access a computer and perform such tasks as data entry, data retrieval, and report generation. A terminal operates under the control of the central computer, responding to commands issued by that central computer.

Given today's low-cost computers, almost anyone who wants one can have one, but multiple stand-alone machines are difficult to maintain and support. The solution is often to link them. Two or more computers linked by communication lines form a **network** (Fig. 31.1). The computers that comprise the network can share data, hardware resources, and software and, because they are still *computers*, can be used to independently solve local problems.

Many networks support a central database. Users working through remote computers can access the database via the network. With this central source of data it is easy to provide up-to-date information to all users.

Resource sharing is another advantage. For example, a laser printer produces higher-quality output than a dot matrix printer, but at a significantly higher cost. Attaching a laser printer to each user's microcomputer is much too expensive for most organizations. But with a network, users can generate draft-quality output on their own inexpensive dot matrix printers and send finished documents over the network to a shared laser printer.

In many organizations, software sharing was the most important reason for implementing a network. Popular commercial packages, such as dBASE III Plus, WordPerfect 5.0, and Lotus 1-2-3, are sold

Figure 31.1
A network consists of two or more computers linked by communication lines.

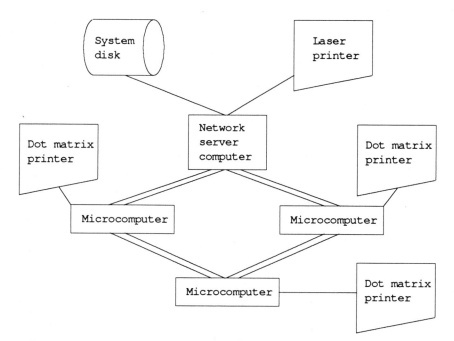

under a license agreement that, essentially, limits use to one machine per copy. Consequently, the organization faced the almost impossible task of stocking, distributing, maintaining, and accounting for dozens, sometimes even hundreds, of individual program disks.

Given a network, a single copy of each program can be stored on the central database. Then, on demand, the program can be downloaded to a user's computer. With only one copy, software maintenance is greatly simplified. Because all access is through the central computer, appropriate accounting records are easily maintained. Recognizing the value of this approach, most software development firms offer special network versions of their programs.

Network Configurations

Figure 31.1 shows a typical microcomputer network configuration. One computer, the **network server**, controls the network. It houses the central database and other shared resources. The user computers are linked to the network server by wires; often, a single loop runs from the server through each user computer, and then back to the server. *All* communication is routed through the network server.

One alternative is to link the network's computers to form a hierarchy (Fig. 31.2). For example, in a supermarket checkout system, several checkout station microcomputers are linked to the store's minicomputer, and the store minis, in turn, are linked to a central mainframe at supermarket headquarters. A *ring* network (Fig. 31.3)

Figure 31.2
A hierarchical network.

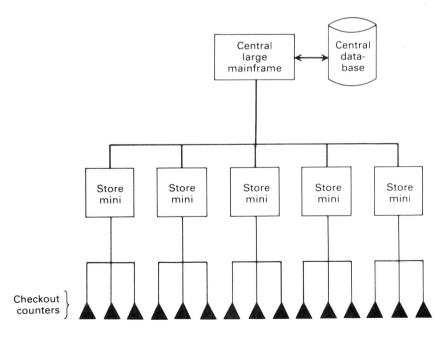

Figure 31.3
A ring network.

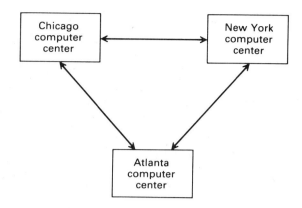

allows an organization's divisions and offices to exchange information. Less obvious is the backup provided by such a network; if one computer fails, its work can be switched to the others.

On a **local area network**, all the computers are in a limited area, typically within a single building or on a single campus. Often, dedicated wires are used, but some local area networks use existing internal telephone wires to carry both voice and data. A **wide area network** is composed of computers that are more widely separated. In most cases, at least some data are transmitted over public or leased telephone lines or by other communication services.

Local area networks generally link microcomputers, with one microcomputer or a minicomputer acting as the network server. A **workstation** is a powerful microcomputer, often equipped with advanced graphics features. Workstations are usually linked to a dedicated minicomputer or a mainframe and support such tasks as engineering design.

Signals

Data communication implies transmitting data over a distance. When a signal is transmitted over a distance, several things happen. First, the signal loses intensity or "dies down" because of the resis-

Figure 31.4
An electronic signal moving over a wire tends to lose intensity or die down because of the wire's resistance. Eventually, noise overwhelms the signal, and no data can be transmitted.

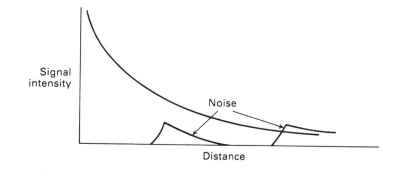

Figure 31.5

Often, data are carried in the context of a carrier signal such as this sine wave.

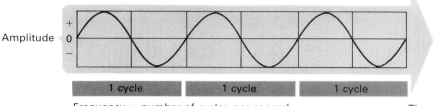

Frequency = number of cycles per second   Time

tance of the wire (Fig. 31.4); this problem is called **signal degradation**. At the same time it picks up interference or **noise**; the static in the background of a distant radio station is a good example. The signal grows weaker and weaker as it moves away from its source, and the noise becomes more intense until eventually the signal is overwhelmed. If data are to be sent over a distance, the noise must be filtered and the signal boosted occasionally.

Modulation and Demodulation

Data are often transmitted in the context of a **carrier signal** such as the sine wave pictured in Fig. 31.5. One complete "S-on-its-side" pattern is called a cycle. The height of the wave is its amplitude; the number of cycles per second is its frequency. Because the carrier signal's frequency and amplitude are known, equipment can be designed to filter and boost it.

A data signal is merged with the carrier signal in a process called **modulation** (Fig. 31.6); the sum of the carrier and data signals is what is transmitted over the line. At the other end of the line the carrier signal is subtracted (or filtered) from the signal (**demodulation**) leaving the data. These functions are performed by a **modem** (modulator/demodulator). Normally, there is one modem at each end of a communication line.

Radio works on essentially the same principle. The radio station transmits a constant carrier signal at an assigned frequency (say, 102.7) and adds music and voice (data) to it. To tune that station, you set the radio dial to the station's frequency. Your receiver then filters out the carrier signal, leaving the data. If you set the dial to a different

Figure 31.6

A data signal is merged with a carrier signal in a process called modulation. At the other end of the line the carrier signal is subtracted, leaving the data.

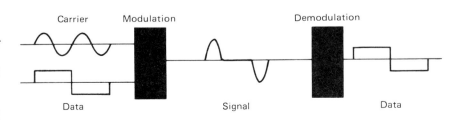

frequency, a different carrier signal is filtered, leaving different data. The carrier signal allows you to tune your radio to your favorite station.

Data are often transmitted using a binary code such as ASCII (the American Standard Code for Information Interchange). The transmission speed, or **baud** rate, is a function of the signal's frequency. Typically, one bit is transmitted during each cycle, so a 2400-baud line has a carrier frequency of 2400 cycles per second and can transmit 2400 bits per second.

Analog and Digital Transmission

A **local** terminal or peripheral device is linked directly to a computer. Because the electronic signals must travel such a short distance, amplification and filtering are not necessary. Local data transmission is limited to a few hundred feet, however. With a **remote** device, amplification and filtering *are* necessary because of signal degradation and noise.

The data are discrete electrical pulses. The wave is a continuous analog representing the data. Analogs are used every day. The height of a column of mercury in a thermometer isn't the actual temperature; it represents temperature. The position of a needle on your automobile's control panel isn't speed but represents speed. A continuous wave passing over a communication line isn't the data, but it is analogous to the data.

Historically, communication lines worked strictly with the analog signal, amplifying it in much the same way a cassette player amplifies sound. The problem with such **analog** data transmission is quality. Just as turning up the volume on your tape deck amplifies the hiss as well as the music, amplifying an analog signal boosts the noise along with the data. The result is often poor data quality. With modern **digital** data transmission the signal is read by a digital repeater, reconstructed, and then retransmitted in almost precisely its original form. The result is much less noise and thus higher quality. Incidentally, on some dedicated digital lines, data are transmitted without a carrier signal.

Communication Systems

Communication Media

The telephone network is the best-known data communication medium. A typical voice-grade line is rated at roughly 2400 baud. High-speed, wide-band channels can transmit at rates approaching 1 million baud, and several baud rates between these two extremes are available. Early telephone lines were analog, and most local lines still are. However, as new lines are installed, most are digital. One interesting new digital technology transmits data with light waves through fiber optic cables.

Microwave data transmission is an alternative to telephone lines. Unfortunately, microwave transmission is restricted to a "line of

Figure 31.7
Microwave data
transmission is
limited to a "line of
sight." Long-distance
microwave
transmission requires
relay stations or
satellites.

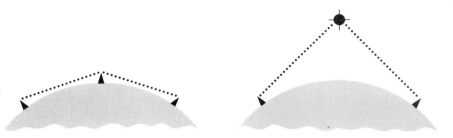

sight." The earth, as we all know, is round; it curves. This curvature limits the range of microwaves, making expensive relay stations or communication satellites necessary (Fig. 31.7).

Considerable time could be spent discussing various communication media, but that would be needlessly confusing. Instead, the general term **line** can be used to describe any data communication medium.

Protocols

Data are transmitted from a sender to a receiver following a precise set of rules called a **protocol**. For two devices to communicate, they must both follow the same rules.

You use a primitive protocol when you answer the telephone. When the phone rings, you pick up the receiver and say "hello." The caller responds with something like "Hello, this is X; may I speak to Y, please." If the desired party is not present or a wrong number has been dialed, the call quickly ends. Otherwise, communication begins. Transmission ends when both parties say "goodbye" and hang up.

Electronic devices do much the same thing when data are transmitted. First, an electronic pulse indicates that a signal is coming. Next, the sender and receiver must electronically synchronize their signals and identify each other. Data are then transmitted using a common code and baud rate. Often, the message is checked for accuracy, and, if necessary, the receiver requests retransmission. Finally, the message is acknowledged, and the transmission ends.

Network Management

A network may include numerous terminals, computers, and communication lines. Each terminal or computer may support an independent user accessing an independent program. Data intended for user A are useless to user B, so data must be routed to specific computers or terminals. Also, with multiple users active, it is inevitable that two or more will try to transmit data at the same time. Consequently, it is essential that access to the network be managed.

One way to manage the network is through a process called **polling**. Start with a user computer. As data are typed, they are stored in the user computer's memory. Eventually, the user issues a command to send the data to the central database, thus marking his or her computer "ready."

Inside the central computer the operating system has a table listing every active user computer. Referring to this table, the operating system sends a polling signal to the first user computer (Fig. 31.8a), in effect asking whether it is ready to transmit data. Assume that the user is still typing. Seeing that the computer is not ready, the operating system issues another polling signal, this time to your computer. Your computer is ready (Fig. 31.8b), so the data are transferred across the network (Fig. 31.8c).

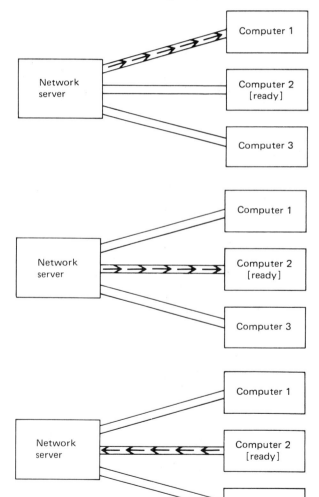

Figure 31.8a
A polling signal is sent to the first computer.

Figure 31.8b
Because the first computer is not ready, a polling signal is sent to the second computer.

Figure 31.8c
Because the second computer is ready, it transmits its data to the network server.

Figure 31.9
On a large computer system, network control is sometimes assigned to a front-end device.

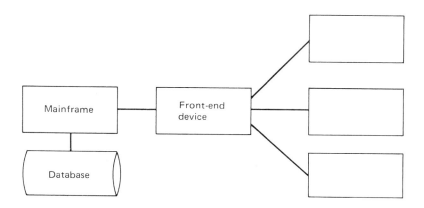

Polling is not the only way to manage a network. In a **token passing** network an electronic signal called a token is continuously passed from computer to computer. Only the computer that holds the token is allowed to transmit data; all others must wait their turn.

With **collision detection**, on the other hand, the individual computers or terminals are allowed to transmit data whenever they want. Sophisticated electronic equipment then monitors the line, "listening" for the noise that is generated when two or more messages "collide." If a collision is detected, the affected computers retransmit in turn.

Data Communication Software

A computer can do nothing without a program to provide control. Software is needed to check protocols, manage the network, and perform other essential tasks. A microcomputer network is controlled by a **network operating system** that is usually found on the network server. Often, each user computer contains a communication program that *emulates* a terminal. The emulation software is sometimes stored in read-only memory (ROM) on a data communication board inside each user computer. Mainframe computers often assign responsibility for controlling the network to a program called **data communication monitor**. Sometimes, the necessary tasks are performed by a program on a separate microcomputer or minicomputer called a **front-end device** (Fig. 31.9).

Summary

A network is a group of computers linked by communication lines. Networks allow users to share data, hardware, and software. On many microcomputer networks, one computer, the network server, houses a central database and other shared resources. The computers that form a local area network are generally quite close to each other. The computers in a wide area network can be widely separated.

When data are transmitted over a distance, amplification and filtering are necessary because the signal tends to degrade and to pick up noise. Often, data are transmitted in the context of a carrier signal. Adding data to the carrier signal is called modulation; extracting the data is called demodulation; these tasks are performed by a modem. With analog data transmission the entire signal, including noise, is amplified. With digital data transmission the signal is reconstructed and then retransmitted. Perhaps the best known data communication medium is the telephone network. Microwave is an alternative.

If two electronic devices are to communicate, they must follow a consistent protocol. Because conflicts are possible, access to the network must be managed by using a technique such as polling, token passing, or collision detection. Software is needed to perform these tasks. On a microcomputer network the network operating system is usually found on the network server, often with terminal emulation software on the user computers. A mainframe computer may use a data communication monitor or a front-end device.

Key Words

analog	modulation
baud	network
carrier signal	network operating system
collision detection	network server
data communication	noise
data communication monitor	polling
demodulation	protocol
digital	remote
front-end device	signal degradation
line	terminal
local	token passing
local area network	wide area network
modem	workstation

Self-Test

1. Several computers linked by communication lines form a _____.

2. On a microcomputer network the central computer that controls the network is called the _____.

3. When electronic signals are transmitted over a distance, they tend to _____ and pick up _____.

4. Data are normally transmitted in the context of a _____ to simplify boosting and filtering.

5. The process of adding data to a carrier signal is called _____. The process of extracting the data is called _____. These tasks are performed by a _____.

6. The basic measure of data communication speed is the _____ rate.

7. With _____ data transmission, noise is amplified along with the data. With _____ data transmission the signal is reconstructed and retransmitted.

8. If two electronic devices are to communicate successfully, they must both follow the same _____.

9. With _____, a central computer asks each user computer, in turn, if it is ready to transmit data. With _____, only the computer holding a special electronic signal is allowed to transmit data.

10. On a microcomputer network a software routine called the _____ is often stored on the network server.

Exercises

1. What is a network?

2. What advantages are derived from using a network?

3. Why is it necessary to filter and boost the signal when transmitting data over a distance?

4. What is a carrier signal? Why are carrier signals used?

5. Briefly explain modulation and demodulation.

6. Distinguish between analog and digital data transmission.

7. What is a protocol? Why are protocols necessary?

8. Briefly explain polling.

9. Briefly explain collision detection and token passing.

10. Why is network software necessary?

Appendixes

▪A

DOS Quick Reference

For a more complete DOS reference see *PD-DOS & MS-DOS: A Ready Reference Manual* by Craig A. Wood (Addison-Wesley, 1988) or your DOS reference manual.

Special DOS Control Keys

Control Key	Description of Action
Ctrl *and* Alt *and* Del	Instructs DOS to start a warm system boot (restart or reset DOS).
Ctrl *and* Pause Ctrl *and* C	Instructs DOS to cancel whatever the system or a program is doing and return you to command level.
Ctrl *and* NumLock	Instructs DOS to suspend (halt) whatever the system is doing until you press another key.
Ctrl *and* PrtSc Ctrl *and* P	Acts as a printer echo switch. Pressing Ctrl *and* PrtSc (Ctrl *and* P) the first time instructs DOS to turn the printer echo mode on. That is, DOS starts printing every line at the same time as it is being displayed on the screen. Pressing Ctrl *and* PrtSc (Ctrl *and* P) a second time instructs DOS to turn the printer echo mode off.

Control Key	Description of Action
⌜Ctrl⌝ *and* S ⌜Pause⌝	Instructs DOS to suspend output to the display unit (screen).
⌜Ctrl⌝ *and* Z ⌜F6⌝	⌜Ctrl⌝ *and* Z generates an end-of-file marker. This can also be accomplished by pressing the ⌜F6⌝ function key.
⌜↑⌝ *and* ⌜Prt Sc⌝	Instructs DOS to copy the information that is currently displayed on the screen to the printer.

Note: When you type the characters for a DOS command, they are stored in a temporary storage area called the **command line buffer** or **keyboard buffer**. DOS always displays the contents of the command line (keyboard) buffer. The system processes the command line buffer after you press the ⌜↵⌝ key. Pressing the ⌜↵⌝ key initiates three tasks.

1. The contents of the command line buffer are sent to COMMAND.COM for interpretation and execution.

2. The command line buffer is copied into another temporary storage area called the **template**.

3. The command line buffer is cleared.

The last DOS command you entered is usually saved in the template, but not all commands are saved in the template.

DOS Editing and Function Keys

Editing Key	Editing Key Description
⌜F1⌝ ⌜→⌝	Copies the next character from the template to the command line buffer.
⌜F2⌝ *c*	Copies all characters up to (not including) the specified character *c* from the template to the command line buffer.
⌜F3⌝	Copies all remaining characters in the template to the command line buffer.
⌜F4⌝ *c*	Skips over (does not copy) the characters in the template up to (not including) the specified character *c*.
⌜F5⌝	Copies the command line buffer to the template and clears the command line buffer.

Editing Key	Editing Key Description
⟵ Backspace	Erases (deletes) the previous character from the command line buffer without changing the template.
Esc	Clears the command line buffer without changing the template.
Ins	Puts DOS in insert mode. This allows you to enter characters from the keyboard without changing the current reference position in the template.
Del	Skips over (does not copy) a character in the template.
Num Lock	Activates the numeric key pad mode or activates the arrow key/special function key mode. It is used to toggle between these two modes.

DOS Commands

Command	Internal/ External	Description of Function	Page
CHDIR or CD	Internal	Change/display current directory	144
CHKDSK	External	Display disk and memory status	94
CLS	Internal	Clear the screen	63
COMP	External	Compare two sets of files	134
COPY	Internal	Copy one or more files	106
DATE	Internal	Display or set the current date	61
DEL or ERASE	Internal	Delete filespec from directory	114
DIR	Internal	Display directory entries	84
DISKCOMP	External	Compare contents of two disks	134
DISKCOPY	External	Copy entire contents of a disk	
ERASE or DEL	Internal	Delete filespec from directory	114
FORMAT	External	Prepare disk for use	72
LABEL	External	Assign or change volume label	99

Command	Internal/ External	Description of Function	Page
MKDIR or MD	Internal	Create a directory	140
MORE	External	Display data screen by screen	93
PATH	Internal	Set DOS search directory	151
PROMPT	Internal	Set new DOS prompt	148
RENAME or REN	Internal	Rename a file or files	121
RMDIR or RD	Internal	Delete a directory	154
SORT	External	Sort contents of text file	92
SYS	External	Transfer system files to disk	77
TIME	Internal	Display or set current time	62
TREE	External	Display directory structure	151
VER	Internal	Display DOS version number	64
VOL	Internal	Display volume label	98
XCOPY	External	Selectively copy files	132

·B
WordPerfect Quick Reference

Topic or Feature	Command or Reference	Option	Page
Block copy	Ctrl *and* F4	1	202
Block delete	Alt *and* F4	Del	203
Block, mark	Alt *and* F4	—	197
Block move	Ctrl *and* F4	1	198
Boldface text	F6	—	246
Box, clip art	Alt *and* F9	1	280
Cancel command	F1	—	176
Center line	⇧ *and* F6	—	245
Change print size/appearance	Ctrl *and* F8	1 or 2	275
Clear screen	F7	—	213
Clip art	Alt *and* F9	1	280
Columns, define	Alt *and* F7	4	262
Copy block	Ctrl *and* F4	1	202
Copy file	F5	8	
Cursor control	Fig. 13.7	—	179
Date, insert	⇧ *and* F5	1	219
Delete block	Alt *and* F4	Del	203
Delete text	Fig. 13.9	—	182

Topic or Feature	Command or Reference	Option	Page
Delete to end of line	Ctrl *and* End	—	182
Delete to end of page	Ctrl *and* PgDn	—	182
Double-space text	⇧ *and* F8	1	242
Draw line	Alt *and* F9	5	277
End column	Ctrl *and* ↵	—	264
Exit WordPerfect	F7	—	173
Flush right	Alt *and* F6	—	218
Footnote, create	Ctrl *and* F7	1	247
Footnote, edit	Ctrl *and* F7	1	248
Format menu	⇧ *and* F8	—	192
Go to	Fig. 13.8	—	181
Hard page	Ctrl *and* ↵	—	265
Headers and footers	⇧ *and* F8	2	240
HELP feature	F3	—	208
Hidden codes, reveal	Alt *and* F3	—	200
Indent block	F4	—	195
Indent from left and right	⇧ *and* F4	—	201
Justify text	⇧ *and* F8	1	245
Line format menu	⇧ *and* F8	1	193
List files screen, exit	F5	0	215
List files screen, go to	F5	—	214
Load WordPerfect (diskette)	—	—	169
Load WordPerfect (hard disk)	—	—	170
Macro, define	Ctrl *and* F10	—	251
Macro, execute	Alt *and* F10	—	253
Mark block	Alt *and* F4	—	197
Mark column	Alt *and* F4	—	259
Merge code, insert	⇧ *and* F9	—	230
Merge, start	Ctrl *and* F9	—	231
Move block	Ctrl *and* F4	1	198
Move marked column	Ctrl *and* F4	2	259
Page format menu	⇧ *and* F8	2	238
Page numbering	⇧ *and* F8	2	241
Paper size, select	⇧ *and* F8	2	237
Parallel columns, define	Alt *and* F7	4	262

Topic or Feature	Command or Reference	Option	Page
Print document	⬆ *and* F7	1	183
Print options	⬆ *and* F7	6	253
Print quality	⬆ *and* F7	T or G	253
Printer control screen	⬆ *and* F7	4	253
Replace document on disk	F10	—	178
Replace (search and)	Alt *and* F2	—	221
Retrieve document, list files	F5	1	189
Retrieve document, work	⬆ *and* F10	—	189
Reveal hidden codes	Alt *and* F3	—	200
Save document	F10	—	176
Search and replace	Alt *and* F2	—	221
Secondary file field, end	F9	—	227
Secondary file record, end	⬆ *and* F9	E	228
Spacing, line	⬆ *and* F8	1	242
Spell check document	Ctrl *and* F2	3	205
Switch screens	⬆ *and* F3	—	223
Tab stops, set	⬆ *and* F8	1	192
Undelete text	F1	1	204
Underline text	F8	—	246

·C

1-2-3 Quick Reference

Function	Reference or Keystrokes	Page
Absolute cell address	F4	370
Add-ins, invoke	/ A I	420
Add-ins, load	/ A A, file name, ↵	420
Add-ins, remove	/ A D, file name, ↵	420
Cell entry, formula	Formula, ↵	310
Cell entry, label	Label, ↵	303
Cell entry, number	Number, ↵	305
Cell pointer, move cursor	Fig. 20.3	300
Cell pointer, move direct	F5, cell address, ↵	302
Column width, set column	/ W C S, → or ←, ↵	343
Column width, set default	/ W G C, → or ←, ↵	341
Copy cell contents	/ C, range address FROM, ↵, range address TO, ↵	366
Delete columns	/ W D C, range address, ↵	333
Delete rows	/ W D R, range address, ↵	336
Drive/directory, set	/ F D, directory, ↵	317
Edit cell contents	F2, Fig. 20.22	319
Erase range	/ R E, range address, ↵	353
Erase worksheet	/ W E Y	353

Function	Reference or Keystrokes	Page
Macros, step through	Alt *and* F2	414
Macros, stop	Ctrl *and* Scroll Lock	414
Menu, access	/	312
Menu, back out	Esc	316
Menu, select method 1	→ or ←, ↵	313
Menu, select method 2	First letter of menu option	315
Move cell contents	/ M, range address FROM, ↵, range address TO, ↵	373
Point, complete	↵	364
Point, continue formula	Operator: + - * / ( )	364
Point, fix anchor cell	. (period)	361
Point, free anchor cell	Esc	361
Point, keys	←, →, ↑, ↓	360
Print a graph	This appendix, following table	593
Print a worksheet	/ P P R, range address, ↵, G, Q	324
Range, definition	—	323
Range menu options	Fig. 21.19	346
Relative cell address	—	368
Retrieve file	/ F R, file name, ↵	331
Save a graph to print	(/ G) S, file name, ↵	398
Save a graph to view	/ F S, file name, ↵	398
Save a worksheet	/ F S, file name, ↵	317
Sticky menu	—	387
Sticky menu exit	Q	387
Titles, columns and rows	/ W T B	405
Titles, columns only	/ W T H	405
Titles, go to title cell	F5, cell address, ↵	406
Titles, remove	/ W T C	406
Titles, rows only	/ W T V	405
Windows, change	F6	407
Windows, create side/side	/ W W V	406
Windows, create top/bottom	/ W W H	406
Windows, remove	/ W W C	409
Windows, synchronize	/ W W S	408
Windows, unsynchronize	/ W W U	408
Worksheet menu options	Fig. 21.4	334

Printing Graphs

1. Boot DOS if necessary.

2. Place the PrintGraph Disk backup in drive A and the data disk containing the graph to be printed in drive B.

3. Type the command

   PGRAPH

   and press ⏎.

4. Press

   Use ⬇ to highlight the file containing the graph you wish to print and press the space bar. Press ⏎.

5. Press

   to begin printing.

6. Press

   to exit the PrintGraph program.

·D

dBASE III Plus Quick Reference

Starting dBASE III Plus

From the Assistant

Function	Menu	Command	Page
Edit file	Update	Edit	465
Exit dBASE III Plus	Set Up	Quit dBASE ...	442
Generate mailing labels	Retrieve	Label	537
Generate report	Retrieve	Report	563
Go to record	Position	Goto Record	472
Index database file	Organize	Index	516
Label file, create	Create	Label	534
Label file, modify	Modify	Label	
Label file, select	Retrieve	Label	537
List database structure	Tools	List structure	466
List records	Retrieve	List	500
Load (use) database file	Set Up	Database file	462
Locate next record	Position	Continue	475
Locate record	Position	Locate	473
Mailing labels, create	Create	Label	534
Mailing labels, generate	Retrieve	Label	537
Modify database structure	Modify	Database file	468
Modify label file	Modify	Label	
Modify query file	Modify	Query	
Modify report	Modify	Report	
Modify view file	Modify	View	
Open index file	Set Up	Database file	519
Query file, create	Create	Query	529
Query file, modify	Modify	Query	
Query file, select	Set Up	Query	533
Remove deleted records	Update	Pack	486
Replace field	Update	Replace	477
Report, create	Create	Report	559
Report, generate	Retrieve	Report	563
Report, modify	Modify	Report	
Select drive	Tools	Set drive	443
Select label file	Retrieve	Label	537
Select query file	Set Up	Query	533
Select view file	Set Up	View	557
Undelete record	Update	Recall	487
Use (load) database file	Set Up	Database file	462

Function	Menu	Command	Page
View file, create	Create	View	556
View file, modify	Modify	View	
View file, select	Set Up	View	557

From the Dot Prompt

Function	Command	Page
Append records	APPEND	456
Assistant, return to	ASSIST	439
Browse database	BROWSE	479
Clear screen	CLEAR	495
Close databases	CLOSE ALL	556
Copy file selectively	COPY TO	545
Create database file	CREATE	445
Create mailing labels	CREATE LABEL	534
Create query file	CREATE QUERY	529
Create report	CREATE REPORT	559
Create view file	CREATE VIEW	556
Define filter	SET FILTER TO	528
Delete record	DELETE	486
Display commands	DISPLAY HISTORY	495
Display record(s)	DISPLAY	499
Display status	DISPLAY STATUS	548
Display structure	DISPLAY STRUCTURE	466
Drive, select	SET DEFAULT TO	493
Edit file	EDIT	465
Exact conditions, specify	SET EXACT [ON/OFF]	508
Exit dBASE III Plus	QUIT	487
Filter, define	SET FILTER TO	528
Find record	FIND	522
Generate mailing labels	LABEL FORM	537
Generate report	REPORT FORM	563
Go to record	GOTO	500
Help, request	HELP	496
Index database file	INDEX ON	516
Index file, open	SET INDEX TO	519
Index, select	SET ORDER TO	552

Function	Command	Page
Set fields	SET FIELDS [ON/OFF]	504
Set relation	SET RELATION TO	550
Skip to top of page	EJECT	512
Specify exact conditions	SET EXACT [ON/OFF]	508
Undelete record	RECALL RECORD	502
Use (load) database file	USE	494
View file, create	CREATE VIEW	556
View file, modify	MODIFY VIEW	
View file, select	SET VIEW TO	557
Work area, select	SELECT	547

Options and Functions

Option or Function	Format	Page
Cancel action	[Esc]	439
Character to date	CTOD ('mm/dd/yy')	507
Convert number to string	STR(expr,length)	544
Date (system), extract	DATE()	531
Date to character	DTOC(date)	508
Define fields	command FIELDS list	484
Define scope	command *scope* options	504
Exit to dot prompt	[Esc]	438
Extract rightmost characters	RIGHT(expr, length)	544
Extract substring	SUBSTR(expr,start,length)	544
Extract system date	DATE()	531
FOR condition	command FOR condition	506
Freeze field	command FREEZE field	481
Get record number	RECNO()	544
Index, specify	command INDEX index	519
Number to character string	STR(number,length)	544
Print output	TO PRINT	511
Record number, get	RECNO()	544
Rightmost characters, extract	RIGHT(expr, length)	544
Specify index	command INDEX index	519
Substring, extract	SUBSTR(expr,start,length)	544
Trim trailing blanks	TRIM (string)	510
WHILE condition	command WHILE condition	524

·E

Answers to Chapter Self-Tests

Chapter 1

1. data
2. information
3. data
   information
4. input
5. output
6. stored program
7. memory
8. processor
9. hardware
10. software

Chapter 2

1. byte
   word
2. address
3. instruction control unit
   arithmetic and logic unit

4. keyboard
   display screen
5. volatile
6. tracks
   sector
7. address
8. directory
9. interfaces
10. network

Chapter 3

1. assembler
   compiler
2. interpreter
3. nonprocedural language
4. word processing
5. desktop publishing
6. Visicalc
   Lotus 1-2-3

7. Database management
8. commands
   menu
9. end user
   support, or system
10. operating system

Chapter 4

No self- test

Chapter 5

1. PC-DOS
   MS-DOS
2. command processor
3. input/output control
   system
4. COMMAND.COM
   IBMBIO.COM
   IBMDOS.COM
   system files
5. boot
6. internal
   external
7. batch
8. default
9. eight
   three
10. COM
    EXE

Chapter 6

1. booting
   turning on computer
   Ctrl *and* Alt *and* Del
2. COMMAND.COM
   IBMBIO.COM
   IBMDOS.COM

3. date
   time
4. DATE
   TIME
5. B:
6. CLS
7. VER
8. ↑ *and* PrtSc
9. Ctrl *and* PrtSc
10. remove disks
    turn computer off

Chapter 7

1. formatted
   FORMAT
2. tracks
   sectors
3. addresses
   bad or defective
4. root directory
   file allocation table
   boot record
5. erases or destroys
6. COMMAND.COM
   IBMBIO.COM
   IBMDOS.COM
7. /S
8. /V
9. FORMAT /S/V
10. SYS

Chapter 8

1. DIR
2. Ctrl *and* S
   /P
3. /W
4. DIR T*
   DIR *.WK

5. >
6. |
7. SORT
    MORE
8. CHKDSK
9. VOL
10. LABEL

Chapter 9

1. COPY
2. COPY MYFILE
    MYFILE.BAK
3. COPY MYFILE.WPF B:
4. COPY A:*.* B:
5. DEL or ERASE
6. DEL B:*.WKS
7. RENAME
8. text
9. CON
10. TYPE

Chapter 10

1. DISKCOPY
2. COPY
3. XCOPY
4. XCOPY
5. COMP

Chapter 11

1. root
    Subdirectories
2. current
3. path
4. root
    delimiter
5. MD or MKDIR
6. CD or CHDIR
7. PROMPT

8. TREE
9. PATH
10. RD or RMDIR

Chapter 12

1. word wrap
2. revising
3. function key
4. template
5. default

Chapter 13

1. mm-dd-yy
    hh.mm
2. status line
3. word wrap
4. F10
5. file name
6. a. →
    b. ↑
    c. Ctrl *and* →
    d. ← or Home *then* ↑
    e. Home *then* ←
    f. Home, *then* Home, *then* ↓
    g. End, or Home *and* →
    h. ← *then* ←
7. insert
    typeover
8. ⇧ *and* F7
9. F7
10. F1

Chapter 14

1. file name
2. ⇧ *and* F10
3. F5
4. ⇧ *and* F8
5. F4

⬆ *and* F4
↵
6. Alt *and* F4
   Ctrl *and* F4
7. buffer
8. hidden codes
9. move
   copy
10. Ctrl *and* F2

Chapter 15

1. boilerplate
2. template
3. mail merge
4. 0
   1
5. F7
   N
6. 2
7. primary
8. secondary
9. field
   record
10. Ctrl *and* F9

Chapter 16

1. page format
2. line format
3. Headers
   footers
4. right-justified
5. ⬆ *and* F6
6. F6
7. F8
8. Footnotes
   endnotes

9. Ctrl *and* F7
10. Ctrl *and* F10
    Alt *and* F10

Chapter 17

1. rows
   columns
2. tabs
3. maximum
4. Ctrl *and* End
5. Alt *and* F7
6. newspaper
7. parallel
8. Ctrl *and* ↵
9. block protect
10. page

Chapter 18

1. appearance
2. laser printer
3. text
   graphics
4. PRINTER.TST
5. Ctrl *and* F8
6. Size
   Appearance
7. Alt *and* F9
8. Fonts/Graphics
9. box
10. Paragraph

Chapter 19

1. Visicalc
2. rows
   columns
3. calculation accuracy
   recompute

4. Lotus 1-2-3
5. menu

Chapter 20

1. A1
   E3
2. label
   number
   formula
3. label-prefix character
4. +A1+A2
5. /
   F
6. / F S
7. [F2]
8. [Esc]
   [↵]
9. / P P R
   G
10. / Q Y

Chapter 21

1. / F R
   file name
2. / W D R
3. +A7/12
4. / W I C
5. [→]
   [←]
6. / W G C
7. / R L C
8. / R F F
9. / W E Y
10. / R E [↵]

Chapter 22

1. anchor
2. [→]
   [↑]
3. . (period)
   [Esc]
4. cell pointer
5. [↵]
   an arithmetic operator
6. B3..F3
7. [F4]
8. @
9. arguments
10. @SUM(C3.C9)

Chapter 23

1. spreadsheets
   graphing
   data management
2. / G
   O or / G O
3. sticky
4. 6
   1
5. A
6. X
7. V
8. T P
9. T F
   T X
   L B
10. S, PLOT, [↵]

Chapter 24

1. / W T H
2. [F5]

3. F6
4. synchronous
5. ~
    {right}
6. Alt *and* F2
    space bar
7. {?}
8. column
    blank
9. first
10. add-in

Chapter 25

1. entity
    attribute
2. fields
    file
3. redundancy
    dependency
4. database
5. database management system

Chapter 26

1. assistant
    dot prompt
2. menu bar
3. drop-down menu
4. selection or highlight bar
    first letter
5. Create
6. file name
7. character
8. Numeric
9. append
10. ↵
    Ctrl *and* End

Chapter 27

1. Use, or Database file
2. Edit
3. pointer
4. List structure
    Database file, or
    Modify structure
5. backup
6. Goto
    Locate
7. Replace
8. Browse
9. Browse
    Freeze
    Fields
10. Pack

Chapter 28

1. scope
    condition
2. expression list
3. SET command
4. USE
5. CLEAR
6. HELP
    F1
7. FIELDS
    SET FIELDS
8. NEXT 7
    ALL
9. DEPOSIT = 50
10. TO PRINT

Chapter 29

1. plus (or minus) sign
    concatenation
2. INDEX ON

3. SET INDEX
4. REINDEX
5. LOCATE
   FIND
6. WHILE
7. REPLACE
8. FOR
   filter
9. query
10. CREATE LABEL
    LABEL FORM

Chapter 30

1. entity
2. common field
3. SUBSTR
   RIGHT
4. COPY
5. ten
   select (work) area
6. DISPLAY STATUS
7. SET RELATION

8. SET ORDER
9. view
10. CREATE REPORT
    REPORT FORM

Chapter 31

1. network
2. network server
3. die down, or degrade
   noise
4. carrier signal
5. modulation
   demodulation
   modem
6. baud
7. analog
   digital
8. protocol
9. polling
   token passing
10. network operating system

·F

WordPerfect 5.1

WordPerfect 5.1 was released as this book went to press. The new version represents a minor change from release 5.0, and, except for a few details, the procedures described in the tutorials will work with either version. This appendix highlights some key differences and indicates how they affect the tutorials.

System Requirements

One significant change from release 5.0 is that WordPerfect 5.1 requires either a hard disk or two 720K diskette drives; you *cannot* run the new version on an IBM PC/XT/AT with dual 360K diskette drives. Otherwise, the system requirements are comparable. If you are using a hard disk, standard installation procedures call for a WordPerfect 5.1 directory named WP51, so substitute WP51 for WP50 in the tutorials.

Pull-Down Menus

Perhaps the most dramatic change is the addition of pull-down menus to WordPerfect 5.1. The function key commands still work exactly as they did before, but users now have the option of using a point-and-select interface.

To access the menu system from the work screen, press [Alt] *and =* (an equals sign). A menu bar will appear on the top line:

    File Edit Search Layout Mark Tools Font Graphics Help

Each entry on the menu bar represents a group of related commands. To select a primary menu item, type the first letter of the command's name (O for fOnt), or highlight the name (using the arrow keys or a mouse) and press ↵. A secondary menu of associated commands will then drop down. Use the ⬆ or ⬇ keys to select a command from the drop-down menu and press ⏎ to execute it. Press Esc, or F1, or the space bar to back up one menu. Press exit (F7) to return to the work screen.

The following table relates selected primary and secondary menu selections to the equivalent function key commands:

Menu bar	Pull-down menu command	Function key command
File	Retrieve	⬆ *and* F10
	Save	F10
	List Files	F5
Edit	Move	Ctrl *and* F4
	Copy	Ctrl *and* F4
	Delete	Ctrl *and* F4
	Undelete	F1
	Block	Alt *and* F4
	Switch Document	⬆ *and* F3
	Reveal Codes	Alt *and* F3
Search	Forward	F2
	Backward	⬆ *and* F2
	Replace	Alt *and* F2
Layout	Line	⬆ *and* F8
	Page	⬆ *and* F8
	Document	⬆ *and* F8
	Columns	Alt *and* F7
	Tables	Alt *and* F7
	Footnote	Ctrl *and* F7
	Justify	⬆ *and* F8
Tools	Spell	Ctrl *and* F2
	Macro	Alt *and* F10
	Date Text	⬆ *and* F5
	Merge Codes	⬆ *and* F9
	Merge	Ctrl *and* F9
Font	Appearance	Ctrl *and* F8
	Small	Ctrl *and* F8
	Extra Large	Ctrl *and* F8
Graphics	Figure	Alt *and* F9
	Line	Alt *and* F9
Help	Help	F3

Note that some menu selections are equivalent to a function key command *and* a selection from a menu.

Tab Stops and Line Positions

WordPerfect 5.0 sets tab stops relative to the edges of the (imaginary) sheet of paper simulated on the work screen. WordPerfect allows you to define the tab stops relative to the margins you define. Tab stops are set in Chapters 13 and 17. Subtract 1 from each 5.0 tab setting to get the equivalent 5.1 setting.

You may notice that the line positions in release 5.1 do not always match the equivalent positions in release 5.0; for example, what was line 1.16 becomes line 1.17 in the new release. WordPerfect 5.1 uses a different rounding rule.

Command Menus

Several menus are slightly different in release 5.1. For example, the print menu contains a new option, *U - Multiple Copies Generated by WordPerfect*, but the other options remain as they were. A second example can be seen on the page number menu, where release 5.0 option 6, *New Page Number*, has disappeared. (It moves to a sub-menu.) If you see slight differences between the menu on your screen and the illustration in the text, don't panic. If you read the new menu carefully, its meaning should be obvious.

Tables

One very significant change is the improved table-handling facilities in WordPerfect 5.1. However, the tutorials in Chapter 17 can still be done as illustrated in the text. Subtract 1 from the tab settings to get equivalent tabs. (If the last table entry goes beyond the right margin, try subtracting 1.2 or even 1.3 to be safe.) When you turn to the parallel columns example, pressing [Alt] *and* [F7] gives you a different menu:

```
1 Columns; 2 Tables; 3 Math: 0
```

Select 1 for the columns feature. Subsequent menus will differ a bit from 5.0, but you should have little difficulty understanding them.

Consider redoing the tabular table using the new table feature. Type the titles at the top of the screen, skip a line, and then press [Alt] *and* [F7]. When the menu appears, select 2 for *Tables*. Subsequent prompts will ask you to indicate the number of columns and then the number of rows; respond by typing the appropriate number and pressing [↵]. For example, the table pictured in Fig. 17.3 shows five columns and six rows (including the headers). Respond to *Number of Columns:* by typing 5 and pressing [↵]. Respond to *Number of Rows:* by typing 6 and pressing [↵]. After a brief delay, a spreadsheet-like grid with the indicated number of rows and columns will appear on your screen (Fig. F.1).

At this point, you have two options. If WordPerfect's default table is acceptable, press [F7] to return to the work screen and begin typing data in the table's cells. If you want to edit the table to vary column widths or make other changes, refer to the menu at the bottom of the

Figure F.1
WordPerfect 5.1's new table feature allows you to define and work with a spreadsheet-like grid.

```
                        THE BETAGOSA HILLBILLIES
                          Correspondence Record


  ┌──────────┬──────────┬──────────┬──────────┬──────────┐
  │██████████│          │          │          │          │
  ├──────────┼──────────┼──────────┼──────────┼──────────┤
  │          │          │          │          │          │
  ├──────────┼──────────┼──────────┼──────────┼──────────┤
  │          │          │          │          │          │
  ├──────────┼──────────┼──────────┼──────────┼──────────┤
  │          │          │          │          │          │
  ├──────────┼──────────┼──────────┼──────────┼──────────┤
  │          │          │          │          │          │
  ├──────────┼──────────┼──────────┼──────────┼──────────┤
  │          │          │          │          │          │
  └──────────┴──────────┴──────────┴──────────┴──────────┘




Table Edit:   Press Exit when done          Cell A1 Doc 1 Pg 1 Ln 1.64" Pos 1.12"

Ctrl-Arrows Column Widths; Ins Insert; Del Delete; Move Move/Copy;
1 Size; 2 Format; 3 Lines; 4 Header; 5 Math; 6 Options; 7 Join; 8 Split: 0
```

screen. For example, select option 2, *Format,* and a new menu will appear. Select option 2, *Column,* from that menu and then option 1, *Width,* from the next menu to set the first column's width. Type the desired width in inches (for example, 2.0) and press ⏎. Then press → to move the cursor to the second column and follow a similar procedure to set its width. When you finish editing the table, press F7 to return to the work screen. Figure F.2 shows how the correspondence table might look if you use the new table feature and set the column widths.

Figure F.2
This table was created using the new table feature.

```
                        THE BETAGOSA HILLBILLIES
                          Correspondence Record


  ┌──────────────┬──────────┬───────┬──────────┬──────────┐
  │SENT TO       │FILENAME  │DATE   │RESPONSE  │REACTION  │
  ├──────────────┼──────────┼───────┼──────────┼──────────┤
  │Charlie Angel │CBS       │3/1/89 │          │          │
  ├──────────────┼──────────┼───────┼──────────┼──────────┤
  │James Beam    │SOURMASH  │3/1/89 │          │          │
  ├──────────────┼──────────┼───────┼──────────┼──────────┤
  │Rive Gauche   │ORIGINAL  │3/1/89 │          │          │
  ├──────────────┼──────────┼───────┼──────────┼──────────┤
  │Forrest Gump  │ABC       │3/1/89 │          │          │
  ├──────────────┼──────────┼───────┼──────────┼──────────┤
  │Juan Valdez   │NBC       │3/1/89 │          │          │
  └──────────────┴──────────┴───────┴──────────┴──────────┘




  B:\TABLE                                   Doc 1 Pg 1 Ln 1.33" Pos 1"
```

For future reference, you can perform spreadsheet-like mathematical operations on the numeric data in a table. You can also import into a WordPerfect document spreadsheets created using Lotus 1-2-3, PlanPerfect, and similar programs.

Index